The
Psychology
of Human
Development

LELAND H. STOTT The
Psychology
of Human
Development

HOLT,   *New York Chicago San Francisco*
  RINEHART   *Atlanta Dallas Montreal*
AND WINSTON, INC.   *Toronto London Sydney*

Library of Congress Cataloging in Publication Data

Stott, Leland, Hyrum, 1897-
 The psychology of human development
 1. Child study. 2. Developmental psychology.
3. Developmental psychobiology. I. Title. [DNLM:
1. Psychology. BF701 S888p 1974]
BF721.S827   155   73-14664

ISBN: 0-03-089236-8

Printed in the United States of America

3 4 5 6 7   038   9 8 7 6 5 4 3 2 1

Acknowledgments

The author is indebted to the following for the photographs in this text:

Chapter 1, John B. Watson, photographed by Nicholas Murray, N.Y. Wolfgang Köhler, courtesy of Clark University Press. Reprinted from Garrett, H. E., *Great experiments in psychology*. New York: The Century Co., 1930.
Chapter 2, photographed by Ahmed Essa.
Chapter 3, photographed by Burt Pritzker.
Chapters 4 through 14, 16, and Figures 5.6 and 8.5, courtesy of The Merrill-Palmer Institute, photographed by Donna S. Harris.
Chapter 15, courtesy of Niles Township Community High School, East Division, Skokie, Illinois.
Figure 2.1, "Madonna with the Long Neck" by Francesco Parmigianino, courtesy of Alinari Art Reference Bureau.

For permission to reprint excerpts from copyrighted materials, the author is indebted to the following:

Addison-Wesley, Reading, Mass. Allport, G. W., *The nature of prejudice,* 1954.
Columbia University Press, New York. McGraw, M. B., *The neuromuscular maturation of the human infant,* 1943, p. 5. By permission of the publisher.
Grune & Stratton, New York. Ausubel, David P., *Theory and problems of child development,* 1958.
International Universities Press, New York. Piaget, J., *The origins of intelligence in children,* 1952.
J. B. Lippincott Company. Duvall, Evelyn M., *Family development.* Reprinted by permission of the publisher. Copyright © 1967.
W. W. Norton & Co., New York. Erikson, E., *Identity—youth and crisis,* 1968; Sullivan, H. S., *The interpersonal theory of psychiatry,* 1953.
Prentice-Hall, Inc., Englewood Cliffs, N.J. Jersild, Arthur T., *Child psychology,* 5th ed., © 1960, p. 261. By permission of the publisher, and *Child Development Monographs,* Jersild, A. T., and F. B. Holmes, "Children's fears," 1935, No. 20.

Stanford University Press, Stanford, Calif. Greulich & Pyle, *Radiographic atlas of skeletal development of the hand and wrist*, 1959.

University of Minnesota Press, Minneapolis. Harris, J. A., et al., *The measurement of man*, 1930.

American Psychologist. Bayley, Nancy, "On the growth of intelligence," pp. 811, 815. Copyright 1955 by the American Psychological Association; Bruner, J. S., "The course of cognitive growth," 19: 1-15. Copyright 1964 by the American Psychological Association. Reprinted by permission.

Child Development. White, B. L., P. Castle, and R. Held, "Observations on the development of visually-directed reaching," 1964, 35: 349-364; Bayley, Nancy, "Individual patterns of development," 1956, 27: 45-74; Bridges, Katharine M. Banham, "Emotional development in early infancy," 1932, 3: 324-341.

Journal of Abnormal Social Psychology. Schaefer, E. S., "A circumplex model for maternal behavior," 59: 226-235. Copyright 1959 by the American Psychological Association. Reprinted by permission.

Journal of the American Medical Association. Wetzel, N. C., "Physical fitness in terms of physique: development and basal metabolism," 1941, 116: 1187-1195.

Journal of Pediatrics. Jackson, R. L., and H. G. Kelly, "Growth charts for use in pediatric practice," 1945, 27: 213-229.

Journal of Teacher Education. Ausubel, D. P., "Cognitive structure and the facilitation of meaningful verbal learning," 1963, no. 14, 217-221.

Merrill-Palmer Quarterly, 71 East Ferry Avenue, Detroit, Mich. 48202. Stott, L. H., "The persisting effects of early family experiences upon personality development," Spring 1957.

Fels Composite Sheet, Lester W. Sontag, M.D./Fels Research Institute, and Dr. Earle Reynolds.

Iowa Child Welfare Research Station, University of Iowa, Iowa City.

Foreword

The American Association for the Advancement of Science proposes to assess the meaning and significance of science for men and to search out important interrelationships among its components that enhance this significance and meaning. Similarly great teachers seek to assess the meaning and significance of their subject matter and in some measure to reveal the place of that subject in the broader frame of human knowledge. Students continually seek such meaning from their teachers and textbooks. Not all can respond. As human knowledge grows more complex and interrelated, the request grows more urgent and the answers more difficult to state.

Once in a great while a textbook does this task exceptionally well for the beginning student. Such is the case with *The Psychology of Human Development*. It delineates and outlines the field of human development, provides a solid foundation of concepts for the student who wishes to push on to more specialized and detailed knowledge, yet establishes a broad base for the student who wants a general understanding with perspective on significant relationships among contributory disciplines. The emphasis, of course, is on psychology as the discipline most concerned with behavior and experience of the individual.

This text presents the aim and task of science, and particularly science as applied to man, not just to his abstract behavior. It gives an appreciation of development in relation to significant concepts of human biology, human ecology, and behavior genetics. It recognizes the strong contemporary move toward naturalistic studies and the study of behavior *in situ,* and shows how these trends are reaffirmations of man's historic and primary questions about himself. The qualitative orientation of much of the newer social science, remarked in the writings of Rogers, Keniston, Coles, Lifton, and others, is reflected in Stott's individualistic approach. He balances eclecticism by a steady emphasis on rigor, precision, and data. Psychology's traditional concern with stimuli and environmental input is amply represented. Structural theory finds its place as well as incremental learning theory.

But this book is not merely an assemblage of viewpoints. It develops its own point of view which incorporates these various, sometimes disparate, approaches. Its viewpoint responds warmly to students' and scientists' concern for humanism, which asks that we regard individuals as unique, not merely as items in data distributions yielding an abstract average. Stott is concerned with growth potential and with human welfare, and he continually brings the students back to the specific case. What is his theme? The human being, an organism interacting with its environment, perpetually participates in its own becoming.

DALE B. HARRIS

Preface

In recent years there has developed a great surge of interest in the beginnings of human behavior. This has resulted in new research findings about the nature of infancy and very early childhood. As a consequence *developmental* psychology has become an active and growing division of the general field of psychology. The research of developmental psychologists has added to the body of knowledge about human development and is proving most useful in explaining little understood specifics of behavior. Developmental psychologists, however, quite consistently neglect the relationship of behavior to the development of the structure which behaves. For the beginning student in education, counseling, human ecology, and nursing, as well as psychology, who needs an understanding of the growing, changing, human being in all facets of his development, the broadly based, integrated view presented in *The Psychology of Human Development* will hopefully be welcomed. In my view, a truly developmental approach requires that the student be presented with information from the wide variety of sources that reflect the interdisciplinary character of human development. In this study I have attempted to do that.

This book, then, is about human development with a primary and major interest in the functional aspects—psychological development. In a sense it represents a revision of its predecessor, *Child Development,* but it is much more than a revision. Its scope has been expanded. The organization of the subject matter has been changed. The findings of an unusually productive period of research have been incorporated. New chapters have been written. In certain important respects emphases have been modified to reflect some interesting shifts that are occurring in disciplinary interests and domain boundaries.

Our basic theoretical position concerning human nature and development is (1) that the individual human being, the person, is an integrated functioning organism, constantly changing both structurally and functionally from the beginning to the end of individual existence; (2) that changes in size and organization of that physical being, and the associated changes in its functioning, can best be regarded *as different aspects of the same basic process* of change. This is human development.

In the organization and presentation of developmental material a choice is usually made between two general approaches. One may deal with the various topics and facets of development separately, tracing each through the individual life span, or one may adopt the age-stage approach. The major portion of this book follows the former approach, dealing with each aspect separately but stressing always their interrelatedness. The last three chapters, however, present a recap and a review in which the integrated nature of development is especially emphasized. The various aspects of change are traced together through the successive age periods and developmental levels of the complete life span. More importantly, these chapters focus upon the impact of family living, especially its interaction patterns and intergenerational relationships, upon the personal growth of all its members.

Many individuals have contributed to the viewpoints and the thinking which characterize this volume, as well as to its actual production. To these I owe a debt of gratitude.

First I wish particularly to acknowledge with much appreciation the very special assistance of Edward Hoppe. His help, particularly in assembling and organizing the material of the first few chapters, was invaluable. Chapters 1 and 3 were organized and largely written in first draft by him. His editorial assistance throughout I acknowledge with appreciation.

I am especially grateful for the hospitality and support of the Merrill-Palmer Institute. I thank the administration—President William Rioux and Vice-President William McKee—for allowing me office space and free access to all the facilities of the Institute. The library staff has been especially helpful. I owe a special debt to Helene Barnes, the Institute librarian, for her expert assistance and the time she has freely given me in my library research. I want also to thank Donna Harris, Institute photographer, for granting the use and helping in the selection of suitable pictures from her files.

I am indebted to the many authors to which I have referred and often freely quoted, and for the permissions granted by their publishers.

Again I acknowledge with much appreciation the professional support and encouragement of Professor Dale B. Harris and others who read the manuscript and offered valuable criticisms and suggestions. I am also indebted to our two "subjects," twins Paul and Sally, for permission to make special use of their record files to illustrate individual development in its various aspects.

And finally to my wife, Rena, I am profoundly grateful for her patience, her help, and her encouragement throughout the period of my concentration on this text.

Detroit, Michigan   LELAND H. STOTT
January 1974

Contents

Chapter 14   From Dependency toward Autonomy 335

Chapter 15   Moving into Adulthood—Adolescence 362

Chapter 16   Maturity and Intergenerational Influences 388

CHAPTER 1

JOHN B. WATSON WOLFGANG KÖHLER

A Historical Introduction

Human development is a broad field with many facets involving the collaboration of a number of scientific disciplines. The total functioning individual develops. His physical body with its elaborate system of organs and parts grows and matures. His intellect, his coordinated, overt acts and skills, his emotionality, his patterns of interaction with others—functions of bodily structure—also change with time as they are exercised and practiced. In general terms the many aspects of total development can be grouped into two main categories: structural, or physical development, and functional, or psychological development. Stated in another way, the unified development of a living being is made manifest in his changing physical body, and in the functioning of that body and its parts as they change with time.

This text is concerned with both of these categories of phenomena. Since psychological phenomena as they change are functions of the physical organism, we must be concerned with those underlying physical changes. Our primary purpose, however, is to examine especially and with some detail the functional category of change phenomena—psychological development.

Developmental psychology is the most recently articulated area of interest in the general field of psychology. It is concerned more specifically with *developmental change* in the various kinds of human functioning with which general psychology has always been concerned. As a background for the study of this special division of psychology we shall now examine briefly some of the important events in the history of general psychological thinking.

A Universal Interest of Mankind

Perhaps what most differentiates man from all other living forms is his self-consciousness—his awareness of himself in relation to his surroundings and of the fact that he is acting with respect to what he sees around him. Man presumably has always been curious about his own conscious processes, his awareness and his ability to think about events in his past experience, and he has always felt a need to understand them. As man began to seek understanding, to speculate, and to theorize, philosophy was born. The most general of the disciplines, philosophy consisted of the techniques of seeking wisdom, and of the wisdom man had sought and gained. Originally, then, philosophy was the rational explanation of anything—the general principles in terms of which all observed facts could be explained. Modern philosophy, of course, is a general overriding discipline whose function is to organize and integrate the findings of the various sciences and to make sense of them in relation to the problems of living.

The Roots of Psychology

Psychology, one of the newest of the sciences, has its roots in philosophy, and only rather recently has it been divorced from that discipline. It is important, therefore, to note some of the early philosophical thinking concerning the nature of man and his functioning. Early Greek philosophy is relevant here. To the Greek thinkers of the sixth century B.C., man appeared to be a peculiar combination and modification of certain universal principles. He was seen primarily as matter, and as such as part of the material world. He exhibits modes of behavior which are often initiated from within. Above all, he shares with other animate beings the peculiar quality of being alive. Equally important is his *awareness* of being alive.

Much of pre-Socratic philosophy sought to determine what man might be composed of. The popular notion that human nature consisted of the four elements (earth, air, fire, and water) provided a starting point. The pre-Socratics were mainly "physical" or "physiological" philosophers, basing their findings upon natural observations. The importance of this period of speculation cannot be overestimated because it set the stage for much of the thinking that was to follow.

With the Sophists and Socrates a new era in the history of the origins of psychology began. Criticism of unbridled speculation and the arrogant assertions of knowledge and truth ushered in the rudiments of the scientific tradition. Men had now to answer to the questions of "How do you know?" and "What do you mean?" Knowledge must be founded upon reason and must withstand inquiry. Philosophy began to distinguish itself from the mythology of the time. It will be recalled that Socrates was accused of contaminating the youth of his day with his thinking and methodology. He had made many enemies by questioning and criticizing the conventional religious and moral standards of his time and was tried for being subversive of democracy because he believed that government should be in the hands of trained experts. Perhaps the birth trauma of the scientific method was best typified by Socrates' classic reply to his accusers:

> Men of Athens, I honor you and love you; but I shall obey truth rather than you, and while I have life and strength I shall never cease from the practice and teaching of philosophy. . . . I shall never alter my ways, not even if I have to die many times. [Plato, *Apologia*]

Plato (428–348 B.C.) was one of the greatest of the Greek philosophers for two main reasons: his psychological descriptions were revived again and again by later writers, and his more general assumptions about the method of obtaining knowledge rather than mere opinion exercised a profound influence on many later theorists.

Plato carried on the epistemological tradition of Socrates, but with the additional qualification that knowledge proper could come only to those who used the instrument of reason. Plato, therefore, is attributed as the starting point of the rationalist tradition. Man, in Plato's view, does not need to learn from experience because the seeds of all knowledge (ideas) exist in his mind at birth. The modern student may find this doctrine of recollection somewhat strange, but many of Plato's speculations concerning the nature of motivation, cognition, and emotion have survived into modern psychology. One of the most important of these is the doctrine of association, which states that a human being associates two or more things or events in memory because they previously occurred together in his experience. Our common belief in mind and matter duality has its origin in Plato's view of man as a union of dual essences, a body and a soul.

Of importance to the present book is that Plato was one of the earliest philosophers to recognize that children differ in their abilities, and that training for a particular type of service should take these differences into account. In postulating the criteria for the formation of the ideal state (the *Republic*), Plato outlined an elaborate system for the breeding, education, and control of children to mold them into a structured society in which all men would be educated by the state to their optimal capacities.

Aristotle, a pupil of Plato's, is often extolled as the founder of the scientific method. Few people would dispute that from a scientific point of view Aristotle's work goes a great deal beyond that of Plato. The notion that science is a systemized body of knowledge, classified and categorized, developed largely from Aristotle's monumental work of classifying the totality of existing knowledge in his time. Man's life, according to Aristotle, was the result of a union of several "functions." Among these was a vegetative function, which described the physiological functioning of the body. There were also animal functions and rational functions. To man alone was attributed the rational function, but all animal life was seen as manifesting a union of the vegetative and animal functions. Aristotle's account of these functions provides us with the first genuine treatise on psychology. Thus modern psychology began with an attempt to synthesize these opposing views and then developed by a gradual abandonment of Platonism and an elaboration of the Aristotelian position and the scientific method.

This synthesis is best seen in the work of René Descartes (1596–1650), who was responsible for the influential theory that mind and body are completely separate entities. These entities, though independent of each other, are in constant interaction. Descartes integrated Aristotle's concept of the body as a physical system whose motions are reflexive responses to external stimuli and Plato's concept of man as differing from the animals in possessing a mind that has no substance but serves as the repository for ideas. Descartes perceived the mind and body as interacting, with the body receiving direction from the mind and the mind receiving impressions (images or ideas) from the actions of the body. This concept of *dualism* is so pervasive that many students are unable to grasp alternative theories.

Descartes is also an important figure in the history of the study of emotion and in the history of *nativism*. Nativism is that school of thought which believes that human perception, in structure and content, is innate rather than acquired. By virtue of his reliance on ancient theories. Descartes belongs with the last phase of the medieval tradition.

At the close of the seventeenth century John Locke (1632–1714) wrote his famous *Essay*. Locke was not an academic person, and he disliked the fetters of academic curricula. He was educated in medicine at Oxford and practiced that profession somewhat informally all his life. In his *Essay* Locke asserted that a child is born with his mind a *tabula rasa*, a blank slate. He refuted the doctrine of innate ideas because he said no such ideas were found in the minds of children or savages. Experience, sensation, and association mold the child into what he will become. Locke viewed man as a rational being, capable of controlling himself:

> The great principle and foundation of all virtue and worth is placed in this, that a man is able to deny himself his own desires, cross his own inclinations, and purely follow what reason directs as best, though the appetite lean the other way. [p. 28 in Adamson, 1922]

Jean Jacques Rousseau (1712–1778), writing in the latter half of the eighteenth century in *Emile*, spoke of the child as a "noble savage." He believed the child was endowed with an intuitive knowledge of right and wrong, and if left to his own designs would grow up virtuous and productive. But society in general, and the family in particular, contaminate the child with the evil tendencies he later manifests. Therefore, the child must be free and unstifled in his exploration of the world. Rousseau postulated that the child responds actively to the world around him:

> I am showing him [Emile] the path to knowledge, not indeed difficult, but without limit, slowly measured, long, or rather endless and tedious to follow. . . . Obliged to learn by his own efforts, he employs his own reason, not that of another. Most of our mistakes arise less within ourselves than from others; so that if he is not to be ruled by opinion, he must receive nothing upon authority. Such continued exercise must invigorate the mind as labor and fatigue strengthen the body. [p. 155]

Obviously, the views of Locke and Rousseau are in sharp contrast. Locke believed that the child is shaped by his experience and education and that he must be taught to be successful. Rewards and punishments are to be used to discipline the child and mold him into a good, productive member of society. Rousseau, on the other hand, felt that the less interference from the parents, the better. A permissive attitude should be adopted to let the child develop his innate virtues.

Psychology Emerges as a Science

Science rests on the assumption that theories of nature can be put to the test of experiment or observation rather than be defended solely in terms of rational argumentation. The scientific revolution began in Europe in the late Renaissance. The works of Galileo and Newton paved the way for giant steps forward in scientific thinking and methodology.

Gustav Fechner (1801–1887), in the middle of the nineteenth century, published his *Elements of Psychophysics*, which investigated problems in sensation and perception. Fechner was looking for a general law to relate all mental phenomena to the physical events that caused them. His methods of psychophysics represent the first special methods for the experimental study of psychology.

It is Wilhelm Wundt (1832–1920) whom we credit with launching experimental psychology as a separate scientific discipline. Wundt, founder of the structuralist[1] school of psychological thought, inaugurated experimental psychology at the University of Leipzig in 1879. Building on the earlier work of Fechner, he established the method of introspection as the observational means of collecting psychological data. Many of Wundt's students were to play a prominent role in the advancement of psychology as a science.

An important landmark in the history of psychology was the work of Hermann Ebbinghaus (1850–1909) on memory. His account of his study of his own memory in 1885 provided the beginning of a nonphysiological laboratory approach to the study of the so-called higher mental processes.

Charles Darwin (1809–1882) was responsible for the first important study of human psychological development. He was a dedicated student of emotional expression in men and animals. His theory of *natural selection* and *organic evolution* precipitated so much controversy that many of his astute observations of interest to psychologists were ignored.

Methods of measuring psychological differences in intelligence and personality are rooted almost entirely in the work of Sir Francis Galton (1822–1911), a scientist and cousin of Darwin. Galton was interested in the improvement of the human race and believed that personality and intelligence are inherited from one's progenitors. He was therefore first concerned with genetics and was a modern formulator of the controversy between the relative influences of heredity and environment.

Galton clearly saw that his first step in a scientific study of human differences would be to make objective measurements of human intellectual capacities. In so doing he invented one of the most important tools in the statistical treatment of data, the *correlation coefficient*. This coefficient enables the study of the degree of relation between different capacities or entities.

The beginning of learning theory in experimental psychology came with the investigations of Ivan P. Pavlov (1849–1936) concerning the *conditioned reflex*. Pavlov's view of learning is often contrasted with *instrumental learning* as described by Edward L. Thorndike (1874–1949). Thus current investigators postulate at least two different processes interacting in the

---

[1] See pages 8 and 9 of this chapter for a discussion of structuralism in comparison with the concurrent point of view called functionalism.

learning situation: classical conditioning and operant conditioning. These milestones are treated more fully in the chapter on learning (Chapter 10).

Psychology in America

The importance of Wilhelm Wundt's laboratory in Leipzig and his establishment of psychology as a scientific discipline was cited earlier. Among his students were a number of men who later became prominent in the development of American psychology, a brand of thinking quite different from its European counterpart. James McKeen Cattell (1860–1944), famous in the development of quantitative methods in psychology, in many ways epitomizes the American spirit. According to a famous story circulated in psychological circles, Cattell went to Germany for his doctoral work and presented himself to Wundt, informing him that he needed an assistant and nominating himself (Cattell) as that assistant. He had the further temerity to dictate his own research problem—an exploration of the psychology of individual differences.

Cattell, however, soon became interested in problems and approaches that were not strictly in line with the Wundtian school. He was basically obedient to Wundt in his study of cognitive reaction times, but became especially interested in individual differences in reaction time which could be observed without the control of introspection. Wundt's brand of psychology specified introspection as the only valid means of gathering data; yet Cattell found himself intrigued with a variety of techniques of statistical analysis of data that were to make immense contributions to the advancement of psychology, but that removed him from the good graces of the Wundtian school. Cattell is perhaps best known for his psychological laboratory at Columbia University and his work on reaction time and the areas of testing and statistical analysis. It is interesting to note that of the influential American students of Wundt, all came to represent different schools of psychological thinking.

Edward B. Titchener (1867–1927) was an Englishman by birth and more than any other man represented the structuralist school in America. He is said to have "out-Wundted Wundt" in his insistence on the methods and content of structuralism. Titchener regarded consciousness as the *raison d'être* of psychology. The objective of psychology was the elaboration of consciousness into its elements—sensations, images, and feelings.

Granville Stanley Hall (1846–1924), the third of Wundt's famous American students, is of particular importance in connection with the beginnings of child psychology. He was interested in investigating the contents of children's minds in the structuralist tradition, but is perhaps better known for sponsoring Freud's first tour of the United States. Hall, more than any other man, ushered in the beginning of systematic work in child psychology in the United States.

Among the other prominent figures in the development of the American *functionalist* point of view were men such as William James, James R. Angell, John Dewey, and Harvey Carr. Though James is regarded as the ideological father of functionalism, Dewey was the founder of a specific functionalist school of thought at the University of Chicago.

Psychology from the functional point of view, of course, was concerned with problems of the *how* of consciousness (with causes, capabilities, and capacities) as opposed to the structuralist preoccupation with the *what* of consciousness (the elements of which consciousness is composed).

Structuralism and Functionalism

As stated earlier, the objective of the "new experimental psychology," as conceived by Wundt, was to analyze consciousness into its elements. The approach was introspective because consciousness was the subject matter. It was analytical and elementistic because its concern was with the elements of consciousness—sensations, sensory images, feelings. It was also associationistic because, as it was reasoned, it was through the associations and combinations of these elements that perception and "meaning" came.

It was William James who proposed the terms "structural" and "functional" to differentiate between the two opposing points of view. Titchener characterized structural psychology as the "psychology of the *is*," which he believed should be cultivated, developed, and better understood "in order to know enough to deal properly with the *is for*" (Boring, 1950, p. 555).

The University of Chicago, during the late 1800s, became the locus for the development of functional psychology, with Dewey, Carr, and Angell among the leaders of this movement. Angell, who came to Chicago directly from the influence of James at Harvard, gave perhaps the clearest expositions of the functional point of view in his address to the American Psychological Association as its president in 1906. He characterized functional psychology as the "psychology of the fundamental utilities of consciousness," as the "psychology of mental operations in contrast to the psychology of mental elements." The mind, he said, "is primarily engaged in mediating between the environment and the needs of the organism."

We have already mentioned that Cattell, Wundt's first laboratory assistant, had been influenced in the direction of the functionalist point of view. He established graduate study in psychology at Columbia University, which was free from the introspective controls of the German school. Thorndike and Robert S. Woodworth were his associates in this atmosphere of freedom. Thorndike, a student of James, was interested in "animal intelligence." One of his most important contributions was in the area of educational psychology. Woodworth, motivated in part by his reaction against Titchener, wrote his *Dynamic Psychology* in which he urged an understanding of cause and effect in human thought and action.

Behaviorism in American Psychology

Behaviorism, in a sense, grew out of functionalism. John B. Watson, a student of Angell, at first accepted functionalism along with its view of the role of consciousness. His swing to "mindless" behaviorism took place at Johns Hopkins University. He was disenchanted with introspective methods and reinforcement theory, and his reaction was to announce a new school of psychology. According to Watson, if psychology was to survive as a science, it had to purge itself of its "unscientific methods" and recognize that its only rightful province was observable behavior. According to the behaviorist, all that is important is that an organism behaves. It is stimulated, it responds, and a knowledge of stimulation enables prediction of response. From this point of view it does not matter what happens in the conscious or subconscious mind. Consciousness was regarded by the behaviorists as of no importance to psychology. The only goal of psychology, they believed, should be the prediction and control of behavior.

Unfortunately, many of Watsons conclusions were hastily drawn, and he created more questions than he attempted to answer. But from his theoretical position has come unquestionably significant experimentation, and perhaps most important, an emphasis on laboratory technique and scientific methodology. He adapted the conditioned reflex of Pavlov, the Russian physiologist, as a substitute for the mentalistic concept of association. Behavior became the object of a psychology of stimulus and response.

Behaviorism seemed to fit quite well into the American temperament at the time. It came rather quickly to characterize in general American psychology. The preoccupation became that of making psychology a true science —a discipline patterned, in its methodology, after physics and chemistry.

The German Influence

As behaviorism became the American protest against the German tradition and the study of consciousness generally, a comparable protest was developing simultaneously in Germany. Gestalt psychology was the German reaction against the Wundtian tradition. The term *Gestalt* was not an especially apt name for this movement in psychology. It is directly translated as "form" or "shape," terms which do not carry the true meaning of the gestalt point of view. Perhaps its most concise characterization is that it is concerned with *wholes* in consciousness rather than with elements into which consciousness is analyzed. Wholes (*Gestalten*) are taken as the phenomena for psychological study. The whole, it is insisted, is more than the sum of its parts. A melody, for example, is perceived as a melodic form or whole, not as a string of notes. Situations generally are perceived in their entirety with the constituent parts interrelated into a perceived, integrated whole. The nature of the perceptual process is a central concern of the Gestalt psychologist.

The Gestalt orientation came to the United States with the published works of Kurt Koffka and Wolfgang Kohler during the 1920s. Max Wertheimer, an older man, was the originator of the movement, and the work of Koffka and Kohler served to promote Wertheimer's preeminence.

Another German psychologist with the Gestalt orientation, Kurt Lewin (1890–1947), came to the United States in 1932. He was especially interested in problems of motivation. In the years to follow he developed his *field theory* of human behavior. Lewin's insights and originality and his remarkable leadership ability made him a strong influence in American psychology.

These two rather dramatically opposed points of view, objective behaviorism and the Gestalt "mentalism," continue to dominate and characterize the two main camps in American psychology. There are, of course, a wide variety of theoretical positions within each camp. Out of these have come many theories concerning the nature of human learning. Learning, of course, is of vital interest to the developmental psychologist as a process of change.

The Contributions of Sigmund Freud

No overview of the historical antecedents of modern psychology, however brief, could be complete without some mention of the work of Sigmund Freud. Our discussion thus far has traced scientific and philosophical roots of psychology. Freud is a departure from this framework, for his contributions stem from the field of medicine. Originally trained as a physician in Vienna, Freud became intensely interested in the treatment of *hysteria*, a condition in which a patient manifests physical symptoms, but without any apparent organic basis or cause.

Influenced by the pioneer work of Janet, Charcot, and Itard, Freud observed that the symptoms of hysteria could often be alleviated temporarily through suggestion while the patient was in a hypnotic trance. He began his investigation into the nature of hysteria in collaboration with Josef Breuer, also a Viennese physician.

Freud was led to the conclusion, through experience with numerous clinical cases of hysteria, that the hysteric's symptoms were the result of willful forces being exerted by the hysteric, but below his level of conscious awareness. Further, the patient's past history would reveal that during childhood development conflict, shame, and guilt resulting from infantile sexuality were repressed or banished from consciousness.

These findings eventually led Freud to assert his theoretical concept of psychoanalysis. For Freud psychoanalysis had a three-part function: (1) it was a theoretical explanation of the structure of personality and of psychosexual development; (2) it encompassed a method of treatment of the neurotic; and (3) it was a means of collecting scientific data that could not be gathered any other way.

Since Freud was a physician by training, he felt that all mental illness had an organic basis. He recognized, however, that science had not developed to the point of being able to reckon with the problems posed by neuroses. He therefore asserted his psychoanalytic theory as a hypothetical construct to serve as a basis for understanding and treatment until such time as science had gained the capability of understanding the physiology and biochemistry of mental illness.

Freud's work has been vitally influential in a variety of fields, and many of his followers have built upon the foundation he laid. The field of child development is pervaded by Freudian concepts and thinking. The work of Freud has been criticized by many people for numerous reasons, but the fact remains that he was, and is, one of the main forces in American psychology today. We will examine his work and the work of some of his "followers" in some detail in later chapters.

Appropriate Subject Matter of Psychology

Science as Method

There are obviously many disciplines that are referred to as sciences. But the very fact that different disciplines exist—doing different things to different kinds of subject matter—indicates that the *content* of science is different for every discipline. Perhaps the label science as applied to a particular discipline is a misnomer. It would be more accurate to describe a particular discipline as *scientific* to the degree that it is characterized by a common method of approach or set of procedural rules. For example, biology is called the science of living things. But it would be more accurate to say that biology is the *scientific study* of living things. Similarly, some people think of psychology as the science of human and animal behavior, yet it is more accurate to think of psychology as the *scientific study* of human and animal behavior.

If, then, the concept of science is not to be defined by content, we might properly ask, "What is science?" In tracing the history of psychology earlier in this chapter, we saw that psychology evolved as a procedure or method or set of rules used to gather, treat, and classify data about the subject matter with which the discipline is concerned.

Observable Behavior versus Cognitive Processes

The question of the appropriate nature of the subject matter of psychology, however, has long been, and still is, a source of radical disagreement among psychologists. As we have noted, two basically different general schools of thinking prevail, and within each a wide variety of specific theoretical positions have been taken. These two opposed viewpoints have been described as the *objective, behavioristic, mechanistic,* and the *cognitive, experiential (mentalistic)*. The nature of the subject matter—the specific phenomena to be investigated—as well as the techniques of investigation seen as appropriate to a *science* of psychology are radically different from these two viewpoints.

From the "objective" point of view, for example, the focus is always upon publicly observable responses (behavior) and the stimuli that elicit them. "Consciousness is regarded as a 'mentalistic' concept that is both highly resistive to scientific inquiry and not too pertinent to the real purposes of psychology as a science" (Ausubel, 1965, p. 4). Furthermore, in a "scientific" (strictly objective) study all variables and all findings are described in "operational" terms, that is, as objectively measured *quantities* resulting from outwardly observable and clearly describable "operations." The behavioral scientist, for example, would *not* define hunger as "a gnawing feeling in my stomach that tells me I need something to eat." He is forced, by adherence to his set of scientific rules, to define hunger as so many hours of deprivation from food, as a quantity measurable by an instrument, a clock. His descriptions are *operational*; that is, they are made in terms of the operation performed to arrive at the quantity that is specified to arrive at a state of being. When hunger is defined operationally as, say, 24 hours of food deprivation, then anyone interested in repeating the study of hunger is able to duplicate it and thus to verify it. The fact that hunger and its alleviation are human conscious experiences vitally related to human welfare and behavior is regarded as irrelevant to the study of hunger as such.

The opposing cognitive viewpoint is clearly described by Ausubel (1965):

> Exponents of the cognitive viewpoint, on the other hand, take precisely the opposite theoretical stance. Using perception as their model they regard differentiated and clearly articulated conscious experiences (for example, knowing, meaning, understanding) as providing the most significant data for a science of psychology. Instead of focusing mechanistically on stimulus-response connections and their organismic mediators, they endeavor to discover psychological principles of organization and functioning governing these differentiated states of consciousness and the underlying cognitive processes (for example, meaningful learning, abstraction, generalization) from which they arise. [p. 4]

The "mentalistic" psychologist is interested primarily in conscious *experience*, in "what goes on inside"—knowing, understanding, thinking, imagining, feeling, and meaningfully coping with the environment. In many instances, and for certain purposes, he is also concerned with unconscious mental processes and motivation. In any event, of course, experience, or mental processes, conscious or unconscious, cannot be observed directly by another. But the sensitive clinician and the imaginative and ingenious investigators have developed ways and means of gathering meaningful data and formulating significant principles with regard to these inner experiences and how they relate to individual functioning in life situations. The methods and procedures of the "cognitive" psychologist, as in the case of the behaviorally oriented psychologist, are scientific to the degree to which his findings can be replicated and verified.

Purposes of Psychology

We have suggested that any science should be defined in terms of the techniques and procedures used in the investigation of the particular set of phenomena with which it is concerned. It is also clear that the *purposes* of those procedures, in any case, are the eventual prediction and control of those phenomena.

Prediction in science means that if the findings of a study are accurate, then by reproducing the same conditions we may expect the same results.

Control, as a goal of science, is simply the use of description and prediction to manipulate phenomena to our own purposes. An example of control in science would be the application of the findings of one experiment as the basis of other experiments. If we were studying hunger in children, we would notice a change in the amount of activity corresponding to the amount of hunger manifested, or the number of hours of food deprivation.

It is vital to look at behavior in its setting of place and in time. If we were to read a current study of women smoking, for example, we might not be impressed with the results. But if this study took place at the turn of the century, before it was socially acceptable for women to smoke, then the study would have much greater importance. The identification of place and time is critical to psychological studies, simply because social values vary from place to place and over time.

The Fields of Psychology

The broad discipline of psychology is composed of a number of specialties. Though all of these specialties share a somewhat common subject, namely, individual behavior and experience, we recognize that they vary both in scope and in intent.

The broad specialty of experimental psychology, as its name implies, is one of the main research arms of psychology. It regards itself as staunchly scientific and is normally hyperdefensive toward any suggestion to the contrary. It rigorously enforces the use of scientific methodology in general and the experimental method in particular.

But there are specialties in psychology that place far greater stress on the application of knowledge than on research. This is not to imply that other specialties are not contributors to the body of scientific knowledge in psychology—quite to the contrary. But the clinical psychologist, for example, when engaged in his practice, is more of an artist—in the sense of the physician being an artist—than a scientist. The industrial psychologist is applying psychology to the field of human productivity. The educational psychologist is trying to enhance the learning situation so that the time spent in education will be more rewarding.

Developmental Psychology

The field of developmental psychology, which has emerged as a branch of psychology only very recently, is usually seen as having three main roots. Child psychology, of course, is one of its main contributors. As a matter of fact the distinction between child psychology and developmental psychology is not clearly seen. It is perhaps only one of relative emphasis. The older field of child psychology has always been concerned with the various forms of human behavior as they appear in childhood at various age levels. Present-day developmental psychologists are more interested in origins of human functioning and in tracing developmental change in these functions through the complete individual life span.

A second main contributor to developmental psychology has been the medical specialty of pediatrics, drawing on the field of physical anthropology. Pediatricians have made significant contributions to the understanding of development in children, both healthful and pathological.

Much of the early research in psychological aspects of child development was done from the sponsorship of home economics. The women of this broad, interdisciplinary field regarded "family life" and relationships, particularly parent–child relations, as one of their important areas of concern. These interpersonal relationships are basically psychological in nature, and psychologists in the field of home economics made important contributions.

One of the strengths of developmental psychology as a field is that it is interdisciplinary in nature. It relies heavily upon the skills of the anthropologist, the sociologist, the home economist, and the practicing pediatrist, as well as the purer scientific disciplines of biology, physiology, neurology, and biochemistry. The various types of physical therapists from the field of special education are also important contributors.

All of these disciplines, and several others, are vital to arriving at an understanding of what takes place between conception and death. None is preeminent. Thus a textbook in developmental psychology is much different from a textbook of general psychology or child psychology. It is not restricted to the single discipline of psychology, but rather presents the findings of the team approach.

At the same time, however, the developmentalist is first and foremost a psychologist. He is attempting to explain development from the standpoint of a psychologist. But he should not feel contaminated when he borrows from other fields!

Since developmental psychology has emerged as an independent entity in just the last few years, it is only natural for it to be an infant discipline. It may be considered in much the same position as physics in the Renaissance or as chemistry just after the Middle Ages. It is the new frontier of psychology and is very deficient in theory.

Summary

In this chapter we traced briefly the origin and history of psychology as a science. We saw its roots in the need on the part of man to understand his "inner life" and his relation to external reality. This need led to the development of certain systems of thinking—the discipline of philosophy. Early theorizing about the mind and about human behavior was "philosophical" rather than scientific in nature. Thus psychology grew out of philosophy.

It was not until the beginning of the nineteenth century, however, that psychology as a science emerged, first in Europe. Students of the mind began to test their theories by means of experimentation and controlled observation rather than solely by rational argument.

These beginnings of a scientific approach soon spread to America. Models of scientific procedure were developed and the necessary initial assumptions were identified. In these early investigations introspection was the main method of data collection. "Mental states" and mental "functions" were the phenomena for study.

With the discovery of the conditioned reflex by the Russian physiologist Pavlov, American psychologists felt the need for more objective methods of investigation and the need to study outwardly observable and measurable behavior. Thus the question of the legitimate *content* of psychology became an issue. In the general drive to model psychology after the physical sciences, the main trend in American psychology was away from a concern with mental phenomena in the direction of directly observing *behavior*. The tendency was to regard things mental as of no importance to scientific psychology because they are not subject to objective observation.

The impact of the so-called Gestalt movement in Germany, early in the twentieth century, was soon felt in America. This signaled the beginning of the renewal of interest in "mentalistic" processes. The emphasis of the Gestalt movement upon the importance of perception (the primary *cognitive* process) led to the development of the so-called cognitive-field point of view. Many theoretical positions within the two main "schools" of psychology— the *objective behavioristic* and the *cognitive* (*mentalistic*) points of view— were developed.

Psychology has branched out and has become concerned with many areas of human activity and functioning. A number of different "fields" of psychology were mentioned. The field with which we are concerned in this book is *developmental psychology*.

CHAPTER 2

Human Development— An Overview

In the previous chapter we traced the origins and history of psychology as an academic discipline in order to provide a background for a better understanding of its youngest, and one of its most active branches, developmental psychology. At the beginning of that discussion we indicated briefly how developmental psychology relates to a broader field of human concern, the field of ontological human development. It was pointed out that the subject matter of developmental psychology has primarily to do with the functional, or psychological, aspect of the broad field of human development. It was also suggested that from the present point of view, if a student is really to understand the development of a function, he must also look at the bodily structures which perform that function.

The intent of the present chapter is to trace briefly the history, and to present some of the basic concepts and concerns, of total human development as an academic field. We shall note that although psychological research has been one of its major sources of data and knowledge, the field of human development arose quite independently and apart from academic psychology. It is also interesting to note that developmental psychology is, in a rather real sense, an outgrowth—a sort of specialization—from the broad interdisciplinary field of human development.

Child Development

Interest and research activity regarding individual human development from the beginning has been largely confined to the so-called "developmental period"—birth to adulthood. "Child development" thus gradually became a separate academic subject matter field during the first half of the present century. Private foundations were established which made funds available for graduate fellowships and research activity "related to children." A number of institutes and research centers in which longitudinal research programs were initiated were established in colleges and state universities throughout the country.

In these centers different special emphases came to characterize their programs depending upon which particular discipline took the lead in each case. Thus there developed, for instance, the "physical growth" emphasis along with the field of physical anthropology. In other instances "healthy" development became the central interest stemming from the medical speciality of pediatrics. There was also a growing sense of need for parental guidance which gave rise to the amorphous fields of "family life" and parent education. A somewhat more inclusive point of view in child development arose in answer to this need. This was "child development" as viewed by women in the field of home economics. The "whole child," physical and psychological, was the emphasis here.

Sociologists also began research and teaching about the family and its relationships. Problems of general education stimulated educational research.

These various special emphases, all concerned with the child and his welfare, constituted the emerging multidisciplinary field of child development.

To foster the growing field, the National Research Council established a special committee on child development. The activities of this committee soon gave rise to the organization of the *Society for Research in Child Development*. This, of course, gave scientific status to child development as an autonomous academic discipline. The student of child development, as has already been noted, is primarily interested in phenomena of change in the individual human child—in his structure as well as in his functioning.

The Nature of Childhood

We must begin our study of human development at the beginning of individual life. We are first of all interested in the nature of the infant and young child.

Curiously, it is not easy for an adult to understand and to perceive directly the condition of childhood and what it means to be a child. It would seem natural that a parent, wishing to understand his children, would find great insight in reviewing his own experiences in growing up. And with a little effort we can usually recall vividly many of the problems that beset us in childhood and that loomed as crises to us then. Nevertheless, as we left our childhood behind us the nature of the transition from child to adult has very largely eluded us.. Time, experience, and distance blurred our recollection of what it was like to grow up. Social pressures were exerted for us to "put away childish things" and to "act our age." Throughout the process each of us has retained his sense of identity, his sense of being the same person all along without being aware of his changing personality. In reality, however, we have passed through various phases of development of an ongoing and irreversible nature which have taken us from infancy to adulthood. Each phase had its hurdles and tasks. Each hurdle had to be surmounted for us to prepare for the next.

As adults we look upon the world of childhood as strangers. Perhaps we look with wonder, or perhaps with awe, but certainly we look with little, if any, basis for understanding. In the words of one discerning student of childhood.

It is only in the minds of adults that childhood is a paradise, a time of innocence and serene joy. The memory of the Golden Age is a delusion for, ironically, none of us remembers this time at all. At best we carry with us a few dusty memories, a handful of blurred and distorted pictures which often cannot tell us why they should be remembered. This first period of childhood, roughly the first five years of life, is submerged like a buried city, and when we come back to these times with our children we are strangers and we cannot find our way. [Fraiberg, 1959, p. ix]

Historical Concepts of Childhood and Development

Philosophers and students of human nature have pondered the problems of childhood and of the nature of the transition from child to adult through the ages. Children are, in fact, human beings. The resemblances of the child to the parental adult are often too striking to escape notice. To what, then, can we attribute the nature of childhood? What happens to change the infant into a child, an adolescent, an adult and then finally brings him to advanced age and death? This metamorphosis takes place so gradually and imperceptibly that its nature escapes detection. How can one help but wonder at a process that bridges the enormous gap between childhood and adulthood and that at the same time preserves the sense of identity, of being the same person?

Various philosophical positions regarding the nature of human development have been asserted through history, and each in its time dominated the thinking concerning what children are and how they develop. Each view has involved the question of the relative importance of inherited make-up versus the influence of the environment. In earlier times only one of these factors was usually emphasized. Philosophical speculation tended toward either biological determinism or environmental (situational) determinism.

Biological Determinism

During the first few centuries in the Christian world the idea developed that mortal man is by nature evil. Being "born in sin" he cannot be other than sinful. Thus it was believed that the most important task of the individual was to redeem himself from his sinful state. To do this he must overcome his evil appetites. From this point of view the child, having been born in sin and not having lived long enough to have overcome his mortal impurities, became an object of particular attention. According to this Augustinian view, the child possessed, by his very nature, all of the weaknesses and evil tendencies of mortal men.

Preformationism

If the infant, being very small, possesses all of the traits and characteristics of mortality, he must possess them in miniature. The theory thus developed that the newborn infant was to be regarded as a miniature adult. Indeed, even at the moment of conception the individual was thought of as beginning his existence completely formed in miniature.

Development, from this medieval point of view, was purely quantitative in nature, merely a process of increase in physical size and in magnitude of traits and perverse tendencies that are present from the beginning. This preformationistic concept of human development is reflected in the art of

Figure 2.1   Francesco Parmigianino (1503–1540). Madonna with the Long Neck. (Photo: Alinari-Art Reference Bureau)

that age (Fig. 2.1). Phillippe Aries (1962), a French student of the history of family life, has described that period of medieval art as follows:

> Medieval art until about the twelfth century did not know childhood and did not attempt to portray it. It is hard to believe that this neglect was due to incompetence or incapacity; it seems more probable that there was no place for childhood in the medieval world. An Autonian miniature of the twelfth century provides us with a striking example of the deformation which an artist at that time would inflict on children's bodies. The subject is the scene in the Gospels in which Jesus asks that little children be allowed to come to him. The Latin text is clear; parvouli. Yet the miniaturist has grouped around Jesus what are obviously eight men, without any of the characteristics of childhood. They have simply been depicted on a smaller scale. In a French miniature of the late eleventh century the three children

brought to life by St. Nicholas are also reduced to a smaller scale than the adults, without any other differences in expression or feature. A painter would not even hesitate to give the naked body of a child, in the few cases when it was exposed, the musculature of an adult. [p. 33]

Since in the medieval view of childhood children were not qualitatively different from adults, they were forced to behave according to adult standards and in terms of the acceptable behavior patterns of that era. The literature of the Middle Ages contains many anecdotal records of extremely severe and cruel beatings of children by "righteous" parents who interpreted every slight infraction of rules and every failure to assimilate arbitrary parent-imposed standards as an act of perversity from which the child must be purged.

No understanding of the nature of immaturity, or of the need for immature expression, existed. Hence, there was little sympathy for or toleration of behavior natural to and appropriate for children. The idea that children "should be seen and not heard" is a fairly common contemporary remnant of this conception of child nature. The concepts of innate ideas, prenatal mentation, and racial instincts are, in reality, preformationist concepts.

Predeterminism

In chapter 1 we reviewed the part played by J. J. Rousseau in shaping psychological thinking during the latter half of the eighteenth century. According to his "noble savage" conception of the nature of children, they are not already preformed in detail at birth. On the contrary, the child is naturally endowed with an order and a design—a sort of blueprint for optimum, healthy development. He inherits a moral sense. The efforts of society to control or to supervise his development only interfere with, rather than facilitate, his optimal development (Kessen, 1965). Rousseau saw children as basically and innately "good." The function of the environment, therefore, was to protect rather than to purge. Parents and teachers were charged with the responsibility of allowing and encouraging natural tendencies and inclinations to develop without interference.

Rousseau's theories have influenced much of the thinking of later students of human development. His writings, for example, suggested the essential elements of the doctrine of recapitulation which was promulgated by Granville Stanley Hall (1905) a hundred years later. According to this doctrine, individual development parallels that of the species through the various stages of its evolution. Because of Hall's prestige and the clarity and completeness with which he elaborated his view, it became widely accepted. As developmental data accumulated, however, and as relations between the biological and the cultural aspects of development were more carefully examined, Hall's system of parallelisms no longer constituted an acceptable theory of ontological development.

Environmental Determinism

In the history of speculation about human development there have also been theories advanced in which the environment was emphasized as the all-important factor. In contrast to the theories of biological determinism, the child was regarded as highly pliable and modifiable. The child enters life as a *tabula rasa*, a blank slate, upon which environmental experience etches personality characteristics. This view as we noted in Chapter 1, was asserted by John Locke (1634–1714). He emphasized the importance of intelligent discipline and rational thinking in rearing children.

Jean de Lamarck, a French zoologist and evolutionist of the early nineteenth century, promulgated an influential theory in which environment was of extreme importance. He believed that new traits and characteristics, both physical and mental, acquired through environmental influence could genetically be transmitted to offspring. Thus, according to Lamarck, the environment was the critical factor in phylogenetic as well as ontogenetic development.

The environmental philosophy has dominated much of the recent thinking and practice in the education and upbringing of children. Ausubel (1958) has stated:

> The humanistic movement in philosophy and education has consistently championed the environmentalist position that, given proper conditions of nurturance, man's developmental potentialities are virtually unlimited in scope or direction. Implicit in this optimistic appraisal is (a) the belief that "human nature" is essentially amorphous and can be molded to whatever specifications man chooses to adopt as most compatible with his self-chosen destiny, and (b) unbounded confidence in the possibility of attaining this objective through appropriate educational procedures. [p. 38]

Extreme behaviorism, under the leadership of J. B. Watson (1928), was strongly environmentalistic, stressing in more psychological terms the *tabula rasa* emphasis and rejecting the idea of inherent developmental designs and predispositions.

Currently, the child developmentalists strongly emphasize the importance of stimulation in early infancy. There is a suggestion that infant learning capacity is much greater than has previously been recognized, and that under appropriate conditions of stimulation, and by means of simple experimental procedures, this inherent learning capacity can be mobilized at an earlier age.

The Assumption of Organism–Environment Interaction

The essential roles of both endogenous and environmental factors in individual development are, of course, generally recognized today.

Organism-environment interaction, it is assumed, underlies all developmental change. Even in such "biological" processes as cell proliferation and differentiation in the growth of the embryo, the essential role of the environment is recognized by biologists. The pattern of pressures, stresses, and pulls of gravity is different for differing portions of the rapidly forming organism. This sort of environmental influence in interaction with genetic determinants is presumed to bring about the differentiation of cell groups to form specialized tissues, organs, and parts of the body.

Functional development likewise results from a continuous interaction between the child's endogenous capacities and his environment. His inherent temperamental nature immediately present at birth is thus a predisposing factor. As time goes on his individual nature, as it is continually modified through development, continues in interaction with environmental influences to affect further development.

The Nature of Development

Child development as a scientific field has contributed significantly to our understanding of children and, in a general way, to our knowledge of how they develop. But there is still much that is not yet well understood. Human development is a broad and complicated field, which, for its adequate exploration, must be entered separately by a number of scientific disciplines. Each has its kit of tools, concepts, and approaches, and each views the phenomena to be studied from its own particular point of view.

Development, as we noted above, means *change* through the process of living through time. The phenomena for study, common to all the various scientific approaches, are *change* phenomena. But developmental processes in the living human being are not open to easy observation. The physical anthropologist, from his level of observation, can see and measure change that the processes of development have brought about. He can measure and record the various physical attributes and dimensions of the body periodically, each set of observations separated from the preceding one by a specific interval of time. Then by comparing his observations he can describe precisely in quantitative terms the changes that have taken place. But he has not really observed development as such. The same is true for the physiologist, the psychologist, the sociologist, and so on. Each can observe the direction and measure the magnitude of change that has taken place in a given interval of time and at a particular stage of human development, but the actual process of development cannot be seen.

Undoubtedly, the nearest approach to the actual observation of the fundamental process of biological development is being made by the biochemist in collaboration with the geneticist. Their techniques converge upon the very beginnings of individual life and the elemental life processes.

In our present study of individual development we shall have to content ourselves with observations and measurements made at a number of grosser levels of observation (for example, those of the physical anthropologist, the developmental psychologist, the psychoanalyst, and the specialist in education) at different levels of development. Our present knowledge of child development is based essentially upon data obtained at these levels of observation.

We have already stressed the continuity and the "process" nature of development and the fact that only the products, or outcomes, of the processes of development can be observed. We can note that the change has taken place because things are different from time to time. The child is larger now than he was a month ago. But developmental change can be noted not only in the child's physical being (the structure) but also in what the child is able to do (the functioning of that structure).

For our purposes the term "development" is given a very broad meaning. Throughout this text the term is used to include *all change* associated with time in both the structure and the functioning of the living organism.

Structural Development

In an organism as complex as the human being, the various aspects and manifestations of development are numerous, interrelated, interdependent, and difficult (if not impossible) to differentiate clearly. It has proved useful, however, in a discussion of physical development to differentiate two aspects of what is fundamentally the same process of change, namely, *growth* and *maturation*—measurable *quantitative* change and change in *kind* or quality, *qualitative* change.

Growth

First of all, growth involves obvious changes in size of bodily dimensions. During infancy and childhood the body steadily becomes larger, taller, and heavier. The rate of growth in the various parts of the body, however, is not the same in either an absolute or a relative sense. Growth, therefore, necessarily involves changes in body parts as well as in overall stature and weight. All of these changes are *quantitative* in nature. They are readily measurable in terms of standardized quantitative units.

Maturation

As the body grows it is also maturing. This maturing aspect of change is not directly measurable in quantitative terms. New and qualitatively different features become incorporated in the inner structural organization of a body part—features that are discrete and discontinuous. This aspect of developmental change is called *maturation*.[1]

For example, changes in the structure of the brain during childhood are largely maturational in nature. These changes apparently do not consist of cell proliferation; they are characterized not by the addition of dimensional increments, but rather by a subtle rearrangement and organization of interconnections between neurons already present, thus making ready for functioning at progressively higher levels.

M. J. Baer (1973) clearly differentiates these two aspects of change in his discussion of bone development:

> by development we mean all of the normal predictable changes that occur in the body. To understand the nature of these changes in the skeleton we must examine the mechanisms through which the bones grow in size, and the sequence of qualitative changes through which the skeleton matures. . . . The orderly sequence of qualitative change is the very heart of every maturational system. [p. 58]

Inseparability of Growth and Maturation

It must be emphasized that these two aspects of development are aspects of the same phenomenon. In an overall sense, growth, or quantitative change, also has qualitative aspects. One can, to be sure, measure quantitatively the lengths of all the segments of the body and describe them in those terms, but in total pattern the change cannot be adequately described except in qualitative terms. The body of the 6-year-old, for example, is not only larger but also different in general appearance, in proportion, and in quality than it was when the child was six months old.

Likewise, when the development of a structure such as the skelton is assessed in qualitative terms and referred to as maturation, growth is also involved. As we shall see later, the very process of bone maturation produces quantitative change, or change in the overall size of the organism. Growth and maturation are different aspects of physical development, but they are not separable in any real sense. Some physical developmental phenomena can be measured with quantitative measuring scales. These changes we call growth. Others cannot adequately be measured in quantitative terms. Qualitative changes involving new features, new parts, new relations, and new qualities are called maturational changes rather than growth. Growth and

---

[1] In its actual usage the term "maturation" has a variety of meanings. Among the common definitions as listed in *A Comprehensive Dictionary of Psychological and Psychoanalytical Terms* (English and English, 1958) is the following: "All development is conceived of as having a maturational aspect. In this meaning maturation is neither a change nor a process of change, but an abstracted *aspect* of change.

maturation are different aspects of the complex process of physical development. They are the concern of Chapter 4.

An excellent example of physical development begins 9 months before birth. The union of the female and the male reproductive cells create a new organism with a unique growth potential and developmental design. That single-cell organism becomes immediately active in preparation for the first cell division. During the first month of its individual existence, this tiny organism has already grown to some 10,000 times its original size. It has grown and it has also matured.

> The total journey from a speck of watery material to a seven pound, nineteen-inch-long human being takes 267 days and is a marvel of refinement. One change prepares the way for the next, and the plan, for all its subtlety, is marked by an incredible accuracy, both in running true to form and in staying on schedule. [Thomas and Blevin, in Baller, 1962, p. 166]

In the very beginning the process is largely one of growth. The growth process is well underway several days before the tiny bit of protoplasm finds its way down one of the fallopian tubes to the uterus, a distance of only about two inches. But by the time of the 16-cell stage (even at this early stage differentiation is under way), a qualitative change is taking place. An outer layer of cells, flatter in form, begins to envelop the inner mass of roundish cells.

During the first week of conception this tiny ball of cells floats freely and passively in the uterine fluid. At about that time, however, it contacts the wall of the uterus, whereupon a rather dramatic change takes place in its behavior. It becomes "aggressively" active, and within a short time it has completely imbedded itself in the wall of the uterus. It has also sent out tiny processes called villi that have intermingled with the blood-rich tissue of the uterine wall and which by osmosis are beginning to absorb the oxygen, carbohydrates, proteins, and minerals necessary for survival and further growth. The new organism has now become a true parasite.

With the establishment of a source of oxygen and a food supply, the growth-maturation process continues at a rapid pace. Cell layers are further differentiated. One end of the embryo becomes established as the head. At the beginning of the third month it is still little more than an inch in length, but already body parts and organs have differentiated. The tiny organism is now entering a critical period of its existence. Qualitative changes are now of vital importance. The organs and vital body parts are rapidly forming and so are especially vulnerable to the influence of any noxious chemical substances that may be present in the mother's blood. These substances can be absorbed along with the nutrients and oxygen. The various malformations to which the human organism is subject are thus brought about during this *organogenetic* period, a period of vital qualitative change (maturation) as well as of rapid growth.

Now the baby-to-be is called the fetus. It has its own independent nervous system and circulatory system. The fetal blood supply and the maternal blood stream simply exchange materials within that remarkable organ, which, in a sense, is shared by mother and fetus—the placenta.

During the remaining months of the prenatal period growth is rapid and qualitative changes continue to take place. Although there is some muscle contraction, along with much organic functioning, the period is primarily one of physical development in which the relation between its two aspects, growth and maturation, is clearly evident. Prenatal development is discussed in much greater detail in Chapter 3.

Functional Development

The functional manifestations of development are, of course, the special subject matter of developmental psychology. Functioning generally begins when the structure is developmentally *ready* to function. Muscle tissue begins exercising its contractile function early in the prenatal period, and as the various organs and specialized tissues are formed they begin the activity for which they are specialized. This initial exercise, furthermore, brings about change in the function itself, which we call *learning.*

A large portion of this book is concerned with learning in this broad sense. The development of patterns of overt activity consists of processes of motor learning. The child, for example, does not walk instinctively. He must learn to walk in spite of the fact that as a human being it is "natural" for him to walk. He learns to walk by perfecting an intricate coordination of sensory, nervous, and muscular functioning. This is accomplished through exercise and practice.

The same is true of the effective use of the hands in reaching, grasping, and manipulation. It is upon these two complex basic patterns of motor functioning—bipedal locomotion and reaching-prehension-manipulation— that the myriad specialized overt behavior patterns are superimposed. One learns in the course of a lifetime an almost endless variety of skills involving the agility of the feet and the intricate coordinations of eye and hand.

The development of the so-called higher functions is likewise a matter of learning. Even intelligence, which is basically one's overall effectiveness in total functioning, is achieved through learning. One is effective in meeting the problems of life to the extent to which one has been able to acquire through exercise the necessary abilities and skills.

Among the facilities necessary for general effectiveness in life as a human being are, of course, vocal speech and the related communicative skills. It is presumed that man is unique among living forms in his ability to deliberately, and with intent, convey to and receive from others meanings and information by means of sounds and other symbols. Equally unique is his ability to represent and to mentally manipulate objects and situations not actually present. This tremendously important thinking function is largely a product of learning and experience.

The quality and richness of one's affective life (his emotions) are very dependent upon learning from experience in interpersonal relations. As we shall see, according to considerable evidence, our ability to receive from, as well as to give to, another genuine love depends largely upon the amount and the quality of interactive experience we have had with a nurturing person during the critical period of babyhood.

Finally, the quality of uniqueness and identity—the individuality of our total functioning, that pervasive quality we call personality—we gain from learning. We learn to be kindly or timid or hostile or empathetic or cowardly or cruel as we grow from babyhood and interact with others and experience the world around us. Functional development is the main concern of this book. It is treated specifically in Chapter 5.

General Approaches to the Study of Human Development

The Cross-sectional Approach

Research in human development has centered around two main kinds of study. The *cross-sectional* method is the most economical in time and cost. The investigator specifies a particular trait that he wishes to study and a sample of subjects for this trait and records his findings. Next, he might sample a different age group for the same trait to see if it has changed. This type of investigation, which relies heavily on sampling techniques and statistics, will produce "norms" to which individual subjects might be compared. As will become clear in chapters to follow, a norm is a standard of reference, usually an average measurement or score for a particular age group.

Suppose, for example, a researcher wished to investigate sleep as a function of age. He might select 100 infants from each age group at 6-month intervals from the age of 6 months to 36 months. In conducting this cross-sectional study he might see a typical pattern emerge. As age increased, the amount of sleep might decrease. In that case he would conclude that the normal child needs less sleep as he gets older. It should be pointed out here that the word "normal" does not denote an individual, but a statistically derived profile to which an individual is compared.

Longitudinal Study and Its Importance

A second type of investigation, and the one emphasized in this text, is the longitudinal approach. In this type of study the investigator samples some specific subjects and then closely follows the development of some trait or facet of development in specific subjects for a prolonged period of time. This type of research is time consuming and more expensive than the cross-sectional approach, but reveals individual patterns of development much more clearly than does the cross-sectional study. An added complication is that often the subjects will move, and continued access to them is made difficult. But the added persistence pays dividends. Most of the really significant developmental theories resulted from longitudinal investigations. The work of Piaget is a case in point. His monumental epigenetic theory of cognitive development began with his longitudinal study of his own children.

There is now a trend developing toward a third type of investigation, the abbreviated longitudinal study. In this type the researcher follows several groups of subjects for shorter periods of time, each group representing a short age period. This "compromise" technique may well utilize the best features of both types of studies and permit the divestiture of their disadvantages. It costs less in time and money on one hand, but retains a touch of individuality on the other.

The intensive study of the changing characteristics—physical and psychological—of an individual child is an extremely valuable approach to an understanding and appreciation of the principles of human development. In such a study we are able to see growth in its true perspective and in relation to some of the conditioning factors. Certain meaningful relations between one phase of development or one set of circumstances and the next, relations which are difficult to discern in other types of studies, may clearly come to light in the longitudinal view.

Longitudinal orientation is personalistic rather than statistical or normative. Records and direct observations assemble numerous facts regarding the course of a child's developmental changes and associated behavior trends, interests, and abilities. These facts, examined and interpreted in terms of their interrelations, render quantitative measurements and qualitative data meaningfully. To be sure, these data should be examined against the background of previously established standards and norms for purposes of appraising developmental status and progress.

But primarily we must see the child as a totally and uniquely integrated personality, a being who is constantly changing (developing) according to his own individual pattern. We must also discern, whenever possible, the relation between the facts of the individual child's development and his behavior, feelings, private meanings, and social adjustments. G. W. Allport (1942) has stressed the importance of the individual study approach:

> Not until we are prepared to dwell upon the unique patterning of personality, and to concede that lawfulness need not be synonymous with frequency of occurrence in a population, and to admit that prediction, understanding and control are scientific goals attainable in the handling of one case and of one case alone—not until then are we in a position to assess the full value of personal documents. [p. 64]

Acquaintance with particulars is the beginning of all knowledge—scientific or otherwise. In psychology the font and origin of our curiosity in, and knowledge of, human nature lies in our acquaintance with concrete individuals. To know them in their natural complexity is an essential first step . . . psychology needs to concern itself with life as it is lived, with significant total-processes of the sort revealed in consecutive and complete life documents. . . . If each personality harbors laws peculiar to itself; if the course of causation is personal instead of universal, then only the intensive ideographic study of a case will discover such laws. [pp. 56–57]

The Assessment of Functional Change

The study of development always involves measurement, or some other appraisal procedure. In some instances measurement constitutes a rather involved problem. As we have already noted, physical development presents two aspects, or orders, of change—changes in amount and changes in kind or quality. The same is true of the functional aspect of development. In some instances status or progress in learning can be appraised quantitatively in terms of standard units. The child at age six, for example, can run faster, jump farther, and use more words than he could when he was three years old. These are quantitative changes.

But here again, there are changes in quality and kind also involved in the child's increase in running speed and in the size of his vocabulary. Likewise, there are measurable changes in amount involved in the smoothness and grace of his walk at age six as compared with his tottering, insecure amble at nine months. Magnitude changes in functioning can be distinguished from changes in quality and character of functioning, but again, the two aspects of development are inseparable.

We have no words that are consistently used to designate these two different aspects of behavioral change comparable to the terms "growth" and "maturation" with reference to physical development. In certain instances, however, common usage has made the term "growth" seem appropriate with reference to functional change. Very often, for example, increase in intelligence is referred to as mental growth. Further, no distinction is usually drawn between changes in amount and changes in kind in mental development.

The Concept of Stages

As we have already indicated, when development appears as change in kind, that is, when the change consists of a series of qualitatively different events, features, or stages, it is not then amenable to measurement by any standard scale of units. Other means must be devised for the appraisal of this sort of development. In this connection the concept of stages becomes useful. Changes in kind usually follow one after another in a fixed sequence. When such an invariable sequence of events or stages is observed, that sequence can be made the basis for the assessment of an individual's status with reference to that particular line of development.

The term "stage," however, has little, if any, scientific or explanatory value. We often hear people say of a bratty child, "He's just passing through a negative stage." In this type of context the term has no meaning. Stage theory to the developmental psychologist is not so simple. We speak of stages in development when some *striking change* in behavior has occurred, or some task has been achieved which rapidly and significantly alters the total functional effectiveness of the organism.

A number of "developmental sequences" have been established and are commonly used in the assessment of development. The use of certain of these sequences is a main topic in Chapter 4, which deals with growth and maturation.

Functional changes frequently are not open to direct observation, and for that reason relatively few attempts have been made to appraise functional development in terms of sequential stages. The area of gross physical activity—the so-called motor functions—of course, is an exception. Bodily acts and changes in the quality of their execution can be observed and recorded. Such functions as the use of the hands in reaching, grasping, and manipulation and the locomotor functions have been studied, and useful developmental sequences have been established. Chapter 7 deals with these functions in some detail.

Other areas of functional development, which perhaps involve to a greater extent the so-called higher mental processes, such as the acquisition of speech and other social skills, are subject to study and appraisal in their quantitative aspects, as well as in terms of developmental sequences. These matters are examined in chapters 10 and 11.

Psychological activity, an emotional experience in another person, for example, obviously cannot be observed directly. Consequently, it is not amenable to quantitative appraisal. The objective outcomes and behavioral manifestations of those hidden processes, however, often can be observed. These outward aspects often change in kind and quality with development in general. The problem of measurement thus becomes one of noting these observable changes and, when possible, ordering them into their natural and invariable sequences as they occur in individual development.

An outstanding example of this approach is Piaget's (1952, 1960) analysis of the development of intelligence. Piaget states that the course of development of mentality involves four main periods, each in turn being a further development of the one preceding it, yet each being characterized by features that are new. This view of mental development is perhaps most clearly seen in the first period (sensorimotor), which Piaget sees as consisting of six stages. The whole period is regarded as one of *continuous* change in the sense that each stage is characterized by new features, which *grow out* of the previous stages, and the stages emerge as an invariable sequence. This particular developmental sequence is discussed in Chapter 8.

Individuality in Developmental Pattern

In the longitudinal study of development, the fact that every individual is different from every other in overall pattern of development becomes strikingly clear. We shall mention here two important respects in which individuals differ. First, children vary widely in general "developmental pace." That is, some children develop in general faster than others. This is particularly evident in their physical growth and maturation. Since growth in stature is a manifestation of the development of the skeleton, the processes of skeletal development are of interest in this connection (Bagley, 1943).

The Significance of the Development of Bodily Structure in Relation to Psychological Development

The relation between the general rate of physical growth and psychological development and adjustment has been the subject of a number of studies. Such relations become especially significant during the early stages of adolescence. Of necessity, the child revises his self-concept, and often also his feelings about himself, as his childish body makes its transition to the proportions and contours of the adult form. During this period he is acutely aware of his body and is very sensitive to any deviations it may take from the usual and the expected. Hence, being a "fast grower" or a "slow grower" can be of importance in the personal and emotional adjustments during this period. The results of one study of slow-growing as compared to fast-growing adolescent boys indicates that the former "are more likely to have negative feelings and rebellious attitudes, feelings of inadequacy, strong feelings of being rejected and dominated, prolonged dependency needs, and rebellious attitudes towards parents" (Mussen and Jones, 1957, p. 255).

A comparable study of adolescent girls suggested that the rate of physical maturity tends to be a factor affecting their adjustments to a lesser degree, but in the same direction as with boys (Jones and Mussen, 1958).

Intraindividual variation in developmental level is a second aspect of development in which children differ rather widely. Indeed, it is another aspect of individuality. One child, for example, may be slow in walking but may learn to talk months earlier than average; another child might achieve these functions in the reverse order. Whenever status measurements are made on a series of changing attributes, the developmental profile is always irregular and the pattern of irregularity is different for every individual. Likewise, when developmental progress for each of these various traits is plotted over time (chronological age), the resulting growth curve differs to a greater or lesser degree from each of the others. Again, the degree of developmental discordance varies from individual to individual. The research literature suggests a negative relation between developmental discordance, or degree of irregularity in the developmental profile, and psychological adjustment as appraised by means of Rorschach and other personality data (Millard, 1957; More, 1953; Olson, 1937).

Summary

The nature of childhood and development is difficult for the adult to understand. He has been conditioned to "grow up" and to avoid the child's perspective. This problem of perceiving childhood is as old as philosophical speculation. The controversy between biological determinism and environmental determinism developed in the early centuries of the Christian era. Biological determinism holds that hereditary endowment is responsible for the totality of development, while environmental determinism holds that environmental stimulation is responsible for molding the child. This "nature-nurture" controversy has never been completely settled. The current accepted viewpoint is that heredity sets certain biological limits to ultimate achievement, but that all development comes about through the interaction of the organism with its environment. The actual relative weight of these influences is still unresolved.

Development, in its broad sense, means change. By living through time, certain changes occur. Changes in quantity, such as height and weight, are referred to as *growth*. Changes in biological quality which affect performance are products of maturation. Growth and maturation are inseparable and are but different aspects of the same process. Functional development, (development of the ability to *do*), is dependent on structural development and is a function of learning in the broad sense of the term.

Assessment of developmental change depends upon empirical measurement of growth of the structure, or maturation as expressed as more efficient performance of some task.

Development occurs in *sequences* of phases or stages. As an example of stage theory Piaget's epigenetic theory of cognitive development was briefly outlined.

It is known that each child passes through each stage before he reaches the next, but it is also known that a wide range of individuality exists at any and all stages. An "average" or "normal" child is usually a statistical figment.

The intensive longitudinal study of changing characteristics of an individual child permits examination of development in its most revealing perspective. The cross-sectional approach produces statistical norms that are very useful as diagnostic tools if not abused. The ideographic techniques are individual-oriented, while the nomothetic techniques are of statistical derivation. Both techniques are essential to an overall understanding of development.

CHAPTER 3

Genetics
and Reproduction

To begin to grasp the significance of development, it is necessary to consider the beginnings of life. The mature man is often thought of as an individual, but we know that individuality is really the integration of many dynamic systems and forces. Physical, mental, social, and emotional factors all exert an integrated influence that molds man as he passes through time and experience.

It is vital to our understanding to realize that all of the factors that eventually integrate into adult individuality stem from a single source. Life for the individual begins with the union of a sperm and an ovum in the female reproductive system, and from this union of two cells all else follows. It is only when we bear in mind that man, in all his splendor and complexity, develops from such a seemingly simple and fundamental fertilized cell that the concept of development takes on its true meaning.

What is present in that fertilized cell that gives it such miraculous abilities? What influences, or stimuli, are brought to bear to foster its proliferation? How much and what kind of growth, maturation, and learning occur before birth? What processes can be identified in the prenatal developmental sequences? There are literally hundreds of intriguing qustions that arise from the realization that all our hopes, all our dreams, all our lives stem from this single incident.

To begin a study of the individual we must study his origins. To study his origins we must study his parents. The act of sexual intercourse, from which under certain circumstances, conception occurs, results in the ejaculation of spermatozoa from the male reproductive system into the vagina of the female reproductive system. But even this most fundamental cause-and-effect relation of conception is not known to many societies existing today. Further, this reproductive act of sexual intercourse is not the beginning of the reproductive process, but simply one of the links in a long chain of events from which an individual is given the chance to live. Much has happened *before* the act of sexual intercourse that is of infinite importance to the human being that later develops. It is our purpose now to consider some of the links in this long chain of events that culminates in the emergence of an individual, for it is from these that a legitimate concept of development must come.

The Male Reproductive System

The male reproductive system consists of (1) a pair of testes suspended in a scrotum; (2) numerous vasa efferentia in each testicle, which lead into a single convoluted collecting tubule per testicle; (3) the pair of vasa deferentia, or sperm ducts, which lead from the collecting tubules to the pair of seminal vesicles just behind the bladder; (4) the small prostate gland which surrounds the urethra and the ejaculatory ducts;

(5) the ejaculatory ducts, leading from the seminal vesicles to the single tubular urethra; (6) the pair of small Cowper's glands posterior to the urethra and connected to it by a pair of small ducts; and (7) the urethra itself, which leads from the ejaculatory ducts through the penis to the outside.

Each of the testes contains many seminiferous tubules which produce sperm (spermatozoa) by a proliferation of the cells that line the tubules. The number of sperm cells discharged at one time may normally vary from 50 million to 500 million. The sperm are suspended in a small amount of nourishing and lubricating fluid secreted primarily by the prostate gland, called semen.

The sperm produced by the seminiferous tubules pass through the vasa efferentia into the convoluted tubule, called the epididymis. From the vasa efferentia through the epididymis, the sperm pass through the vasa deferentia, in which they are mixed with fluids from both the seminal vesicles and the prostate glands. The sperm collect in the ejaculatory duct, to be discharged through the urethra to the outside during the ejaculation that climaxes sexual intercourse. This entire process is closely associated with and regulated by the endocrine system. Hormones from the pituitary and the adrenal glands are vital to the function of the reproductive system.

The sperm cell itself is a tiny tadpole-shaped cell with the nucleus in the "head" and a relatively long tail. It contains 23 chromosomes, which is *half* the normal human number. In the normal human cell there are 23 *pairs* of chromosomes, or 46 chromosomes in all. It is this "peculiar" characteristic of mature reproductive cells—having only half of the normal number of chromosomes—which gives them the ability to unite in conception and begin a new and eventually independent life.

The Female Reproductive System

The human female reproductive system consists of (1) the pair of ovaries in the lower abdominal cavity; (2) the pair of fallopian tubes (oviducts) which lead from the area of the ovary to the uterus; (3) the pouchlike uterus in which the embryo develops; and (4) the vagina, which connects the uterus to the outside.

The walls of the uterus contain smooth muscles that contract vigorously during childbirth. The inner lining of the uterus, called the endometrium, is a heavy mucous vascular lining to which the fertilized ovum may adhere.

The fallopian tubes, about three inches long, extend from the upper lateral uterine walls to "wrap around" the ovaries. The fallopian tubes are not physically connected to the ovaries, but the funnel-shaped end of the fallopian tube (called the *infundibulum* or the *ostium*) catches the ovum as it "drops" from a ruptured follicle (sac) in the ovary in which it ripened.

With the onset of sexual maturity (puberty) the female begins to ovulate, or produce mature ova from the graafian follicles. At birth the female has all of the oogonia (primitive ova) that she will have in her life—a total of about 450,000. The average female ovulates once every 28 days for a period of about 35 years.

Before going further, we will digress to discuss briefly the two basic processes of cell division: *mitosis* and *meiosis*. Certain levels of maturity must have been reached before reproduction is possible. The processes of mitosis and meiosis are essential to that development.

Mitosis

Mitosis is the normal process of cell division that is constantly in progress in all living things, both animal and vegetable. It is the process by which a cell divides into two cells, both of which will be exact duplicates of the original cell. Biologists have divided mitosis into five distinct stages. The resting stage, called *interphase*, is not really a stage of mitosis, but is simply the state of the cell when no division is in progress. The other four stages (*prophase, metaphase, anaphase,* and *telophase*) are each characterized by a specific activity that is vital to the process of cell division.

As Figure 3.1 shows, during interphase the cell nucleus contains pairs of chromosomes that appear long and are tightly twisted together. It is estimated that if the chromosomes from a single cell were completely uncoiled and joined end to end, they would measure approximately *five feet*! They are often so thin and drawn out during this stage that they are not visible without special treatment—even under the highest magnification.

Note also in the figure that just outside the nucleus is a small body called the *centrosome*. It is the division of the centrosome into two parts that signals the beginning of cell division called *prophase*. We should note that while the interphase is a stage of rest between cell divisions, it is not really a stage of rest in the absolute sense. The cell is at the height of metabolic activity during interphase, manufacturing the substances of which living tissue is made.

Prophase

Prophase begins as the centrosome splits and the two resulting *centrioles* begin to move apart. During the latter part of this stage the paired chromosomes appear quite distinct from each other except at the point where they are joined. Note also that as the centrioles are moving apart, lines are visible between them. These lines, called *astral rays*, radiate out from each centriole. Also, as the centrioles move apart, the nuclear membrane begins to dissolve.

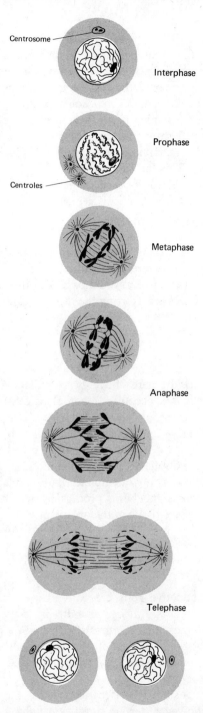

Figure 3.1   Mitosis, the process of cell division, the basic process by which new cells are continually being produced to replace tissue in the organism.

Metaphase

The metaphase stage of mitosis begins when the centrioles have moved to the opposite sides of the cell and the chromosomes are lined up on an equatorial plate in the center of the cell. Note that fibers are seen to join the centriole to the point where the chromosomes are fastened in pairs. A fiber is seen to go from each fastening point to *both* centrioles. These fibers, called *spindle fibers*, developed from the astral rays mentioned in prophase.

In the last part of metaphase the fastening points of the chromosome pairs begin to separate. This fastening point, called the *centromere*, duplicates into two centromeres—one for each of the spindle fibers.

Anaphase

The anaphase stage begins as the chromosomes are pulled into two distinct groups. The centromeres are pulled to the centrioles, and the remainder of the chromosome is dragged along. It is this phenomenon that suggests that the spindle fibers are exerting the mechanical force that separates the chromosomes in mitosis.

Telophase

In telophase the centromeres have been pulled all of the way to the centriole, and the centriole becomes a complete centrosome again. A new nuclear membrane forms around each of the new sets of chromosomes, and a *cleavage furrow* develops and constricts the cell into two distinct daughter cells. Each now has its own nucleus containing a full complement of chromosomes and is an exact duplicate of the original cell.

The process of mitosis is now complete. It takes place in an average time of about one hour and is the basic process by which cells are being continually produced to replace tissue in the organism.

Meiosis

The reproductive cells are formed by a companion process of cell division called *meiosis*. Meiosis results in cells containing half the usual number of chromosomes. It consists of *two divisions* of the nucleus accompanied by only *one division* of the chromosomes. Each of the two divisions in meiosis has the same stages described above: prophase, metaphase, anaphase, and telophase.

The process of meiosis in the two sexes is for the most part essentially the same. There are, however, certain significant differences—spermatogenesis—meiosis in the case of the male, and oogenesis in the case of the female.

Spermatogenesis

The process by which sperm cells are generated in the male reproductive system is called spermatogenesis. As mentioned earlier, the testes contain thousands of cylindrical seminiferous tubules. These tubules are lined with a layer of germinal epithelium cells, so called because they germinate the *spermatogonia*, each having its full count of 46 chromosomes. These are the "raw material" from which the sperm cells are eventually formed.

After sexual maturity is reached some of the spermatogonia continue to divide by mitosis to maintain a constant supply. Other spermatogonia undergo the two meiotic divisions necessary to form the sperm cells.

Spermatogenesis begins as the spermatogonia increase in size to form primary *spermatocytes* (See Figure 3.2.) These undergo a second division to form cells of equal size, called *secondary spermatocytes*. These secondary spermatocytes, of course, have half the number of chromosomes as the primary spermatocytes. The secondary spermatocytes undergo the second meiotic division to produce four oval *spermatids*. It is the spermatid which undergoes further maturation (without cell division) to become a mature spermatozoa (sperm cell).

Oogenesis

The process of oogenesis in the female, illustrated in Figure 3.3, is analogous to spermatogenesis in the male. The ovaries contain a layer of germinal epithelium cells, each of which divides by mitosis to produce the oogonia. As the female reaches sexual maturity, under the stimulating influence of hormones, an oogonium enlarges to form a primary oocyte, which contains yolk to serve as a food supply in case the egg is fertilized, and also contains the full number of 46 chromosomes.

The primary oocyte, upon completion of its growth phase, divides by the first meiotic cell division. This cell division results in two cells of unequal size. One of the cells is the secondary oocyte which has received the yolk and most of the cytoplasm and which will continue to develop.

The other, much smaller cell is known as the first polar body. Both the secondary oocyte and the polar body, of course, have half the original number of chromosomes. Both of these cells then undergo a second division. In the case of the secondary oocyte the result is an *ootid* (immature ovum) and a second polar body. The division of the first polar body "results in two equal sized polar bodies, provided the division is complete, which is not always the case" (Stern, 1960, p. 73). In any case, the polar bodies, being nonfunctional, disintegrate and disappear. The ootid, like the spermatids, will undergo further maturation without cell division and become a

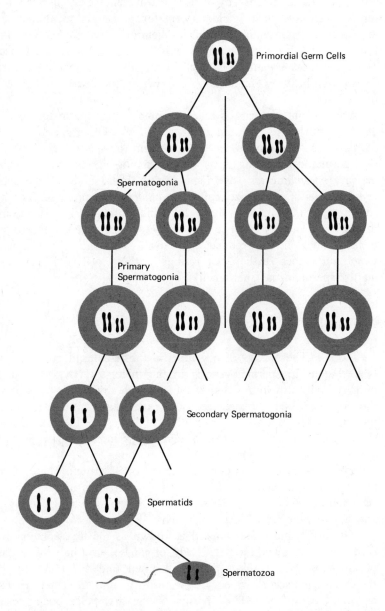

Figure 3.2   Spermatogenesis, a process of meiosis, in which mature male reproductive cells are produced. Note that 16 mature sperm cells result from a single primordial germ cell.

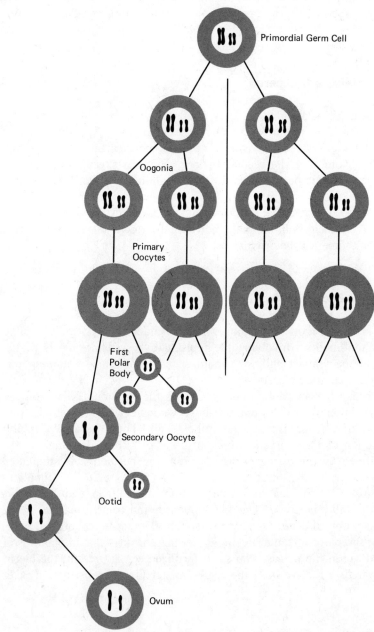

Figure 3.3   Oogenesis, the process of meiosis in which mature female reproductive cells (ova) are produced. In oogenesis only four ova can result from a single primordial germ cell.

mature ovum. Note that while in spermatogenesis a single spermatogonia produces four spermatids, in oogenesis a single oogonia produces only a single ootid.

Mitosis and Meiosis Compared

Meiosis is seen to be very similar to mitosis, except that anaphase I in meiosis is dissimilar to anaphase in mitosis. The difference is simply that in the first cell division of meiosis no replication of chromosomes occurs. Note that the second meiotic division is essentially one of mitosis—except that it occurs with a cell containing only half the original number.

It should also be noted that mitosis results in two cells that are duplicates of the original. In meiosis in the male, however, four cells result, each having half the chromosomes of the original.

The Role of the Endocrine System

The secretion of hormones by the endocrine system is vital to all phases and functions involving the reproductive system. This is particularly true in the female, and we should spend some time examining this hormonal influence more closely.

In the female the anterior pituitary secretes the hormone FSH (follicle-stimulating hormone), which controls the development of the follicles and the secretion of estrogens from the follicle cell. These estrogens inhibit further secretion of FSH and thus prevent other ova from ripening. As the FSH is inhibited by the estrogens, LH (leutinizing hormone) is stimulated to be secreted from the pituitary. As the LH is secreted, it stimulates ovulation, in which the mature ovum ruptures its follicle and begins its journey in the fallopian tube. The LH influences the transformation of the empty follicle into the *corpus luteum*, which then secretes progesterone. Progesterone prepares the uterine lining for pregnancy—the implanting of the fertilized egg in the uterus. Thus, if a fertilized egg is present, the uterus will be prepared to receive it. If the egg is not fertilized, menstruation takes place.

Menstruation

If fertilization does not take place, the corpus luteum continues to secrete progesterone, which will then inhibit further secretion of LH from the pituitary. This decrease in LH permits the corpus luteum to disintegrate, thereby inhibiting further secretion of progesterone. Without the influence of progesterone the uterine lining begins to break up, and the resulting blood and tissue are passed through the vagina as the menstrual flow. This takes place about two weeks after ovulation and marks the beginning of a new cycle of preparation for pregnancy.

The menstrual cycle is divided into three phases. The first phase, the menstrual phase, lasts from the first day to the fourth day of the cycle. Here, menstruation occurs when the expectation of implantation of the fertilized ovum is not fulfilled. The second phase, proliferation, extends from the fifth day to about the fourteenth day, during which time an ovum develops and ovulation occurs. The third phase, secretory, is the secretion of progesterone and the resulting preparation of the uterine lining for implantation of the fertilized ovum.

Hereditary Transmission

Having examined how conception occurs, we are confronted with the question of what forces are at play that will influence the individual from conception to the grave. We mentioned the nature-nurture controversy in an earlier chapter, and we have noted that heredity sets the maximum limits in which development occurs. How does this come about?

We've just seen that the sperm and the ovum both have a haploid number, or half, of the chromosomes found in other cells. When the head of a sperm penetrates the cell membrane of the ovum, the head of the sperm disintegrates and deposits its chromosomes inside the ovum. At the same time, the nucleus of the ovum ruptures and releases its 23 chromosomes.

The 23 chromosomes from the father represent the total heritage from the father that the child will have. The 23 chromosomes from the mother similarly represent her genetic contribution. Thus, all of the child's ultimate limitations are set by the combination of these 46 chromosomes.

Genes

The 46 chromosomes are each composed of *genes*. A gene is composed of a chemical enzyme called deoxyribonucleic acid, abbreviated DNA. DNA is the molecule of heredity, and there are about 100,000 DNA molecules (genes) per cell. Each chromosome is composed of an average of about 20,000 genes. While a thorough examination of genetics and protein synthesis is beyond the scope of this text, some of the basics should be indicated.

It has been established that DNA is the molecule of heredity and that a gene controls protein synthesis, or the formation of the substance of which living cells consist. The DNA molecule is a large molecule consisting of a five-carbon sugar *deoxyribose*, a phosphate group, and a nitrogenous ring compound. The phosphorylated nitrogenous compound is called a *nucleotide,* hence the name deoxyribonucleic acid (DNA), or an acid made of the sugar deoxyribose and the nucleotide.

There are two kinds of nucleotides. Those having a single ring are known as pyrimidines, and those having a double ring structure are known as purines. In man, there are two purines (adenine and guanine) and three pyrimidines (cytosine, thymine, and uracil). DNA is composed of a double chain of sugar and phosphate, and the two chains of the molecule are held together by combinations of *four* of the nucleotides: adenine, guanine, cytosine, and thymine. It is the *sequence* of these nucleotides that is responsible for all of the hereditary characteristics in man. When you consider that there are 100,000 genes per cell, and that each is composed of a double chain of numerous nucleotides, the number of possible combinations of the four nucleotides is astronomical. This accounts for the great variation in the human species. As we will see later, it also tells us why identical twins look alike.

DNA has two functions: (1) the formation of more DNA and (2) the formation of messenger RNA (ribonucleic acid). RNA is chemically very similar to DNA. The only differences are that the sugar in RNA is ribose instead of deoxyribose, and it replaces one of the nucleotides found in DNA, thymine, with uracil (the fifth nucleotide).

You may recall from basic biology courses that protein synthesis takes place in the ribosomes of the cell. RNA is at work at the ribosomes performing the function of protein synthesis. When messenger RNA is produced from DNA, the messenger RNA is transferred from the nucleus of the cell to the ribosomes in the cytoplasm. The messenger RNA is a blueprint for the protein that will be formed by the other RNA at the ribosomes. Thus DNA forms messenger RNA, which in turn dictates to the RNA at the ribosomes what kind of protein is to be made.

The sequence of nucleotides of DNA is responsible for the production of 20 different amino acids that are needed to make all of the proteins found in the body. This sequence of nucleotides is able to *code* the "information" needed to manufacture the different proteins from amino acids. It has been found that the genetic code consists of groups of three nucleotides. These groups, or triplets, in turn, form 20 different *coded* combinations of DNA to form the 20 amino acids. For instance, the amino acid tryptophan (known to be the precursor of serotonin, a hormone critical to the nervous system) is coded by a uracil and two guanines. This RNA triplet permits only the manufacture of tryptophan. No other combination of UGG (uracil, guanine, guanine) exists except for the production of tryptophan. Therefore, in a long RNA molecule, during protein synthesis, whenever in that molecule the sequence of UGG is found, the amino acid tryptophan will be coded into the protein structure. This is true of all of the other amino acids manufactured by the body into proteins.

What this means to us is that the father is passing half of his DNA coding to the child, and the mother is doing the same. We can see that certain features in the child may well therefore "resemble" the parents because the same coding is being used. We also see that since the child has received coding from both parents, his own coding will be a synthesis of the two and thus quite different from either. He could actually more closely resemble an ancestor than either parent.

Can Two Children Be Alike?

We can see from the above that children in the same family ordinarily will be different, simply because they have differences in the "coding" procedures through which heredity is transmitted. The next question is, "Is it possible for two children to be identical?" We know that this will not happen except in the case of identical twins, who have developed from the same fertilized ovum, and only later split into two individuals with the same hereditary endowment.

To further complicate the procedure, when the chromosomes line up for the first cell division in spermatogenesis and oogenesis, they exchange genetic material. This "jumbling" of genetic material is called *crossing over*. If crossing over did *not* occur, it is estimated that there could be about 64 trillion different kinds of children. This number far exceeds by many factors the number of people on the earth today. But since we know that crossing over *does* occur, we have no way of knowing how astronomical the actual number of possibilities is. For all intents and purposes, it may be considered infinite.

Sex Determination

Both the sperm and the ovum contain the haploid number of chromosomes. All of the female chromosomes are X chromosomes—so called because they are long and large and when joined together form an X-shaped pair of chromosomes. If, when the chromosomes from the sperm and ovum join together, all of the chromosomes have this appearance, the child will be a girl (Fig. 3.4).

In the male child, it will be seen that one of the pairs of chromosomes does not have this X appearance. One of the "legs" of the X will be missing. The result is a Y chromosome, which determines the male sex. Therefore, if an X from the mother unites with an X from the father, the result will be a girl. If an X from the mother unites with a Y from the father, the result will be a boy.

Dominant and Recessive Genes

Gregor Mendel, an Austrian monk, in 1857 experimented with two strains of peas. From his experiments were formed what are known as the Mendelian laws of genetics. He found that genes are passed down from

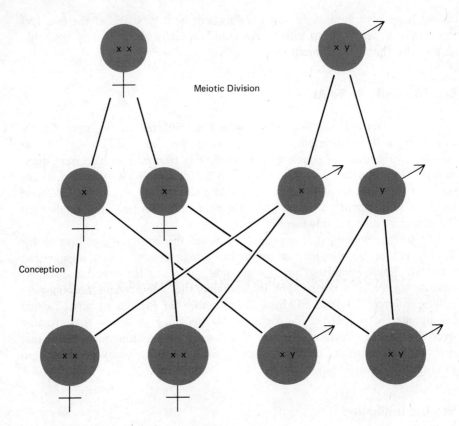

Figure 3.4   Genetic determination of sex.

one generation to the next and remain unaltered unless a mutation occurs. Further, he found that genes are always paired together. When two paired genes are found to be different in the effect they produce, one gene will dominate the other. The gene responsible for the dominant condition is termed a *dominant* gene, and the gene which is dominated is termed a *recessive* gene.

A number of human features are determined by dominant or recessive genes: eye color, baldness, hair color, blood type, to name a few. Let us say that brown eyes are dominant over blue eyes. This means that the gene for brown eyes is dominant over the gene for blue eyes. There are three possible gene combinations in the child: he might receive two dominant genes (one from each parent), in which case he will have brown eyes; he might receive one dominant and one recessive gene (a dominant from one parent and a recessive from the other), in which case he will have brown eyes; or he may receive two recessive genes (one from each parent), in which case he will have blue eyes.

Heredity as a Factor of Influence in Development

We know that all human characteristics are the result of genetic influence as it interacts with conditions within and surrounding the organism. We do *not* know the extent of that influence. There are a number of reasons why the extent of genetic influence is an elusive question. First, some characteristics are more susceptible to genetic influence than others. Second, genetic influence can vary with maturity. Some traits will not appear until adulthood or late in life, while others may appear in childhood and disappear later. Third, the strength of environmental influences also varies from trait to trait and from time to time. Hence, no trait can in reality be attributed entirely to either heredity or environment. Fourth, traits vary widely in nature and complexity. In spite of these limitations, we may tentatively assert a few conclusions:

1. Heredity as a factor exerts a direct influence upon anatomical features and physiological functioning. Consequently, it may be a strong predisposing influence in relation to many physical weaknesses and diseases.

2. The role of heredity in relation to functional traits and processes, such as temperamental tendencies and traits of intellect, is, of course, much less direct. These qualities are functions of the physical organism. It is pretty clear that heredity sets the bounds of intellectual potentiality, but beyond that the extent of direct hereditary influence upon intellectual functioning is not now known.

3. The question of the extent to which mental illness is an inherited phenomenon is nearing some kind of an answer, but cannot yet be stated conclusively. It appears that *differences* in the tendency or predisposition to mental illness may indeed be inherited, but will still need an environmental stimulus to activate it.

As to psychological traits in general, we might say that the genetic make-up of a person determines his preferred response to environmental stimulation because of the close relation between psychological and physiological functioning. Some psychological traits show definite relations to hereditary influence; others are more elusive.

The heredity-environment relation in connection with different aspects of development is further dealt with in other chapters.

Prenatal Development

We have seen how conception occurs as the sperm cell penetrates the membrane of the ovum and deposits its chromosomes there. The time when this can occur is physiologically limited. If intercourse occurs before ovulation has occurred, or after the progesterone level has dropped and diminished the capacity of the uterine wall to maintain the fertilized egg, pregnancy does not occur. Assuming that the timing is "right," fertilization will normally occur four to six hours after the sperm has been deposited. Conception itself occurs in the fallopian tube. The sperm must travel through the cervix, up the uterus, into the fallopian tube to encounter the ovum. This process is still under investigation and is not understood. It is, however, easy to see why so many sperm are needed, since the odds are slim that a single sperm will complete such an arduous journey successfully. Yet a single sperm cell is responsible for fertilization, and the others will be eventually expelled as waste material.

Once conception has occurred the fertilized ovum is referred to as the *zygote*. The first cell division of the zygote takes place 24 to 36 hours after conception and marks the first developmental task after conception. At this time the chromosomes have been organized into a meaningful pattern to generate a complete organism—barring a debilitating mutation of the gene structure which could interfere with the developmental process.

Prenatal development is usually divided into three basic periods. The period of the zygote begins at conception and lasts until the zygote has passed down the fallopian tube and has implanted itself in the uterine wall. The period of the zygote typically lasts about two weeks. The second period, that of the *embryo*, begins with implantation in the uterine wall and lasts until the eighth week when most of the differentiation of the organism is complete. The final period of the *fetus* lasts from the eighth week until the birth process some 40 weeks after conception.

Morphogenesis in the Zygote

Figure 3.5 illustrates the various stages of development during the periods of the zygote and the embryo. The first cell division occurs to 4 to 6 hours after conception. The second cell division occurs at a right angle to the first, and produces a total of four *blastomeres*. As cell division continues by mitosis a few more times, the mass of blastomeres increases. At this time, after several cell divisions but before any differentiation has occurred, the tiny mass is termed the *morula*.

Shortly after the morula is formed the first process of differentiation occurs. The cells begin to form a sphere with a hollow center filled with fluids. The entire morula is now termed the *blastula*.

The blastula stage consists of (1) an outer, transparent, jellylike capsule; (2) a dark, pigmented "animal hemisphere," composed of smaller, more numerous cells; and (3) a light-colored unpigmented "vegetal hemisphere" which is composed of larger and fewer cells. The vegetal cells contain yolk or food that is supplied to the animal cells of the upper hemisphere. The active growth at this point occurs in the "animal" side.

The outer layer of the blastula begins to grow hairlike tendrils called *villi* with which the blastula will eventually implant itself into the uterine wall.

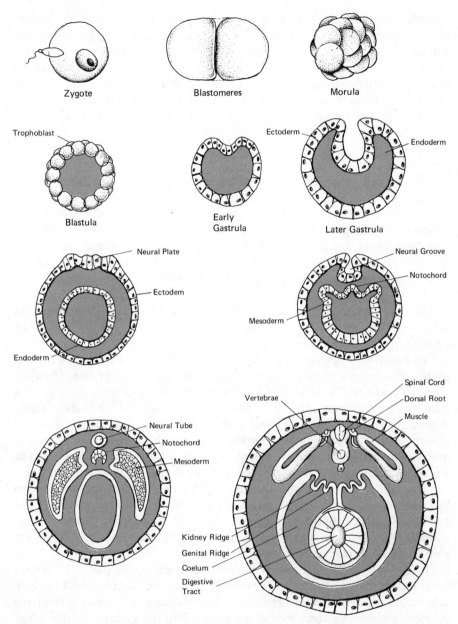

Zygote

Blastomeres

Morula

Trophoblast

Blastula

Early Gastrula

Ectoderm

Endoderm

Later Gastrula

Neural Plate

Ectodem

Endoderm

Neural Groove

Notochord

Mesoderm

Neural Tube

Notochord

Mesoderm

Kidney Ridge

Genital Ridge

Coelum

Digestive Tract

Vertebrae

Spinal Cord

Dorsal Root

Muscle

Figure 3.5   Development during the periods of the zygote and the embryo.

The last phase of activity in the zygote period is the *gastrula* stage. The blastula undergoes a dramatic change from a simple hollow sphere as the animal cells continue to grow much faster than the vegetal cells of the lower hemisphere. The pigmented animal cells grow and begin to overlap the vegetal cells. A fold is formed in the unpigmented vegetal cells, which will eventually close on itself as the growth of the animal cells forces the vegetal cells together. This process serves to enclose the vegetal cells within the animal cells. The animal cells on the outside become the *ectoderm*, while the inner vegetal cells become the *endoderm*. The point of the fold which closes in on itself will leave exposed to the outside a small *"yolk plug."* The central cavity thus formed is the "primitive gut," the beginning of the gastrointestinal system, hence the name gastrula (Rugh and Shettles, 1971).

The Period of the Embryo

The *neurula* stage follows the gastrula stage and is characterized by the formation of a neural groove, which in turn closes in on itself to form the neural tube, destined to become the nervous system. This development occurs opposite the yolk plug area, which is now implanted in the uterine wall. The villi have burrowed into the blood-rich mucous lining of the uterus, and the yolk plug area, which was the exposed area of what is now the endoderm, has formed the *amnionic cavity* and the yolk sac. The yolk plug itself will, with the surrounding ectoderm, form the *umbilical cord*. The villi, which have imbedded the embryo into the uterine wall, will form the *placenta*—that amazing membrane that separates the embryo from its mother.

Three growths appear in the endoderm on the side opposite the amnionic cavity. These are growing simultaneously with the neural groove described above. These three growths become the *mesoderm*—so named because it is between the ectoderm and the endoderm. The middle of these three mesodermic growths will in time envelop the neural tube and develop into the *skeletal system*. The two mesodermic folds on either side will grow and individuate into the *muscular system* and some of the internal organs. The endoderm remains as a tube and becomes the *digestive tract*.

We should note from the foregoing that the only contact that the embryo has with the mother is across the placental barrier. The entire system of the embryo is distinct and separate from the mother's system, except for the nourishing chemicals—enzymes, hormones, and carbohydrates—that are able to diffuse through the placenta.

By the end of the first month the embryo is about one half a centimeter long. The primitive heart begins beating by the end of the third week. During this month all of the basic life-support systems have individuated from the ectoderm, endoderm, and mesoderm layers. But the embryo at this point still has no arms or legs or definitive features.

When the period of the embryo is reaching its conclusion at the end of the second month, the embryo is quite recognizable as human. The face, mouth, eyes, arms, legs, and so on, have begun to take on defined forms, and the sex organs have begun to form. It is interesting to note that for the first four months of life the sex organs are the same for both sexes. It is only later, under genetically programed hormonal stimulation, that the sex organs develop the characteristics that distinguish the sexes.

This period of the embryo is characterized by the rapid development of the nervous system and may be designated as a very *critical* period. Mechanical or chemical interference with the developmental sequences that are occurring may have serious and permanent effects on the embryo (Rugh and Shettles, 1971).

The Period of the Fetus

The third and final period of prenatal development is the fetal period. It is distinguished by quantitative growth. As the fetal period begins between the eighth and ninth week after conception, the fetus may begin to respond to the most basic kinds of stimulation. If subjected to tactile stimulation, the fetus can arch the trunk or extend the head. These are the beginnings of the motor functions which will follow with continued growth and maturation.

The head is seen to be disproportionately large, though the fetus is definitely recognizable as human. By the end of the third month the fetus is about 10 centimeters long and weighs about three to four ounces. By the end of the third month the sex is distinguishable, eyelids and fingernails have begun to form, and muscles are becoming well developed.

By the end of the fourth month the mother is able to feel the movement of the fetus. Various basic movements are being practiced for the time when they will be essential to survival. Hair is beginning to grow, and the hands are capable of grasping. The fetus is about 18 centimeters long.

As the fifth month ends the fetus has grown to almost 25 centimeters and weighs about 9 ounces. The hair and nails and skin are assuming adult form, and such processes as the sweat glands are developing (Stern, 1960; Humphrey, 1968).

The fetal age of twenty-eight weeks is an important one. The fetus is passing through the stage of development in which, if necessary, it could survive in the external environment. This age of viability occurs toward the end of the seventh month, and though the remaining two months of interuterine development are desirable, the fetus has a good chance of surviving if prematurely born.

Prenatal Influences

We have thus far described a straightforward process of development in which everything is orderly. It is true that prenatal development is much the same for most children, but this is not to say that the mother's life-style or physical condition has no effect on the fetus.

The interuterine environment is often thought of as a stable and constant one which is optimal for the development of the fetus. Usually this is a well-founded assumption—insofar as the mother enhances the environment by exercising common sense. There are many variations in the interuterine environment that are caused by the mother's emotional as well as physical state. The mother's diet and age may also exert influences of varying strength.

Maternal Age

Evidence shows that the optimal age for the mother is between twenty-three and twenty-nine years. The infant mortality rate rises on either side of this interval, and the incidence of mental retardation rises sharply when mothers are under twenty or over thirty-five. Evidence shows that the difficulties arise from the inadequate development of the reproductive system in the younger women and the decline in functional ability of the reproductive system of the older women. Difficulty in labor and Caesarean sections follow the same pattern of increase when correlated with maternal age.

Maternal Diet

Diet is very important during pregnancy. Reliable studies have shown that women with properly nutritional diets have much easier times in labor, have much improved health during pregnancy, and have much lower incidence of prematurity, stillbirth, and miscarriage than do mothers whose diet is deficient in basic nutritional requirements. Severe malnutrition is known to be an etiological factor of mental retardation in children whose mothers have severely deficient diets. This is particularly true as the myelin covering of the nerve fibers is developing during the seventh month of pregnancy. A deficient diet can affect the myelin coating, which in turn causes severe malfunction or dysfunction of the nervous system.

Maternal Diseases

Maternal diseases can be significant influences in certain critical times in pregnancy. German measles contracted during the first 16 weeks of pregnancy can cause great damage to the fetus. Cases of deafness, visual handicaps, mental retardation, and heart trouble have all been traced to rubella (German measles).

The incidence of fetal infection from a mother is rare. The placenta is apparently an effective barrier to most infective agents. Syphilitic infection is a notable exception, however. Syphilis is extremely hazardous to children and causes symptoms ranging from weakness through deformity to miscarriage and death.

Mothers with diabetes mellitus often give birth to children with circulatory and respiratory abnormalities. Toxic conditions can also have far-reaching effects, often resulting in mental retardation, convulsive disorders, and miscarriage.

Drugs

Mothers who take drugs must do so knowing that often the drug will have some effect on the fetus. The problem often is not that pregnant women take drugs, but that women who take drugs get pregnant. Mothers who smoke or consume alcoholic beverages must do so at the risk of affecting the fetus.

The question often arises as to the feasibility of taking drugs or anesthetics during delivery. It is safe to assume that whatever sedates the mother will also sedate the baby. This means that the baby must overcome the effects of the sedative, which was strong enough to sedate the mother! Certain drugs may so overload the blood stream that permanent brain damage results in the baby.

Maternal Emotional States

We have seen that there is no connection directly between the maternal nervous system and that of the fetus. Nevertheless, the mother's emotional state has a direct bearing on the reactions and development of the fetus. The emotional state is directly linked to the autonomic nervous system. In the general state of arousal that accompanies emotion, the endocrine system, particularly the adrenal glands, secretes various hormones into the blood stream. Prolonged emotional reactions can thus raise blood levels of certain hormones to "abnormal" levels. These can, in turn, induce changes in the fetal system as these hormones cross the placental barrier.

Research has shown that fetal activity increases several hundred percent when the mother is undergoing emotional stress (Sontag, 1941). Furthermore, prolonged emotional stress, as in time of war, can have enduring consequences on the fetus. Anxiety and tension during pregnancy may also increase the difficulty of labor and delivery. We may conclusively state that the emotional state of the mother is capable of affecting the fetus adversely and of handicapping the newborn infant in his adaptation to the extrauterine environment. We must also admit that the long-term consequences of prolonged emotional stress are difficult to evaluate because it is difficult to differentiate between prenatal and early postnatal influences.

The attitude of the mother to her pregnancy is also directly linked to the activity and development of the fetus in much the same manner as her emotional state, for the simple reason that emotion accompanies attitude. Women who have poor attitudes toward their role of impending motherhood, or who are under tension from husbands who do not want children, may well be expected to have a more difficult time than mothers who are happy and satisfied by their pregnancy. The mother's attitude toward her pregnancy is also a good predictor of her later attitude toward the child. It is a definite conclusion supported by a great deal of evidence that the psychological state of the mother may have enduring consequences, for good or for bad, on the future psychological integrity of the child.

The Paranatal Process—Birth

Birth is traumatic for the neonate. He undergoes a radical change in environment and changes from his status as a parasite to an independent organism. The mechanics of the birth process subject the baby to a variety of stresses and strains. There are two basic factors of concern during delivery. First, mechanical pressure is exerted on the baby's head and body during the delivery process, and a lack of oxygen that can result from obstruction of the umbilical cord can affect the baby's ability to breathe as he passes through the distended cervix. Anoxia, or lack of oxygen, in the neonate will affect the brain stem, on which the most vital functions of the body are dependent for control. The second main danger is the possibility of hemorrhage. A loss of blood also can cause anoxia with the resultant problems. Cerebral palsy is a general term denoting the motor defects associated with damage to the brain cells, possibly as a result of anoxia. Even when motor defects are not evident after birth, and there is no direct observation of symptoms following birth trauma involving anoxia, evidence shows that there may be specific differences in intellectual development for the first two or three years of life. By age seven or eight, such differences are less clearly discernible. In short, severe anoxia may kill the neonate, and mild anoxia can cause a wide range of damage from mild dysfunction to profound retardation and a host of nervous disorders related to motor functioning.

Summary

This chapter is concerned with the technicalities of biological heredity and the process of reproduction. The reproductive organs, male and female, were briefly described and the processes of conception and prenatal development were explained.

The human organism is composed of millions of living cells, each containing in its nucleus 23 pairs (46 in all) of the minute structures called *chromosomes*. Each chromosome is composed of *genes*, which are actual carriers of heredity. A gene is essentially a chemical enzyme—a dioxyribonucleic molecule (DNA). Each chromosome carries approximately 20,000 genes, and since each cell of the body has within its nucleus 46 chromosomes, its gene content is nearly one million genes.

Conception, of course, consists of the union of the two reproductive cells —the spermatozoon from the male parent and the female ovum within the genital system of the female. The development of the new individual begins with this union and continues through the process of cell division and proliferation known as *mitosis.* In every mitotic cell division each chromosome splits lengthwise into two identical parts, one going to each of the two new cells. Thus every cell of the body contains the full set of 23 pairs of chromosomes. This means that the original sperm cell and the ovum each must have possessed at the time of union only one member of each pair of chromosomes in order that the fertilized ovum have only its complete set of 23 pairs. This of course, insures that the genetic inheritance of the new being-in-process will come equally from the two parents.

This is made possible through a prior maturational process. The cells which, early in the life of the individual are set aside and destined to become *reproductive* cells, must undergo a special kind of cell division called *meiosis.* In this process the individual chromosomes do not split, but the *pairs* of chromosomes separate in a random fashion, thus giving each sperm cell and ovum different genetic content, but with half the number of chromosomes.

Each gene, minute as it is, presumably performs extremely important and fantastically precise functions in the development of the individual. Within the confines of the cell's nucleus in each case genes bring about the synthesis of proteins, the building material of living tissue, making possible the proliferation of new body cells. They also set the ultimate limits, and in interaction with environmental influences, guide the course and outcome of the development of all the organs and parts of the body.

The approximately nine months of prenatal development begin immediately with conception. Three main periods have been identified: the periods of the *ovum* or *zygote,* the *embryo,* and the *fetus.* The zygote is a minute, free-floating ball of rapidly multiplying, undifferentiated cells which finally arrange themselves in a bipolar fashion. The embryo-forming cells remain at one pole, with the placenta-forming cells at the other. A portion of this development takes place in one of the fallopian tubes before the zygote reaches the uterus.

At about the end of the first week the mass of cells attaches itself to the wall of the uterus. This begins a two-month period of qualitative change, the period of the embryo. Out of the cell layers already laid down, all of the organs and features of the new body are formed. By the end of the third week the tiny heart begins to beat. At two months the embryo is recognizable as that of a human being. This period is an extremely critical one during which disturbances—mostly chemical in nature, and for most of which the mother is responsible—can cause serious malformations in the rapidly changing new organism.

The third period, the period of the fetus, is largely one of quantitative growth. The detailed modeling of the body continues, however, and the fetus becomes very active and sensitive to many external stimuli. The fetus becomes viable at about seven months of prenatal development.

CHAPTER 4

Physical Development— Growth and Maturation

In Chapter 2 the term "development" was defined in its broad sense as change—any and all change in a living organism with the passage of time. This broad definition includes changes that are ongoing, and generally irreversible, changes in both the physical organism and in its functions which come about in the processes of living and functioning.

Developmental psychology, by definition, has as its particular domain *behavioral* change, that is, the development of *psychological* functioning. It is concerned especially with cognitive development, with developmental change in emotionality, with verbal behavior as it relates to the thinking function, and with how these things change with age.

We should remind ourselves, as we become preoccupied with the various modes and patterns of functioning which we call behavior, that there is always a *behaver*—a real, flesh and blood, physical being who is growing and maturing and learning to function at progressively more effective levels! We must remember that without some consideration of the nature of this behaver, and how he develops, our view of behavioral development will lack a real foundation.

Developmental psychology, then, should also be concerned with developmental changes in the physical structure which performs and behaves and functions—the physical child. As we have already suggested, physical development and psychological (functional) development might well be regarded as two manifestations of the same underlying process of change that constitutes organic living.

In this chapter we are concerned particularly with the physical aspects of development at the *gross* level, and we will observe that this development is very complex. Some changes will be observable, some will be hidden. It will be recalled further (Chapter 2) that some kinds of change are measurable in terms of *amount* of change from time to time, while many of the most significant changes are in *quality* and cannot be measured directly in quantitative units.

We shall use the term "growth" to refer to change in amount (quantitative change) and the term "maturation" to refer to change in kind (qualitative change).

Growth

One of the most striking things about children is the rapidity with which they grow. Striking as it is, this aspect of development is so obvious that we tend to take it for granted. This continuous change in dimensions, though obvious and commonplace, is not as simple as it may seem. Together with other aspects of developmental change, it may have tremendously important implications in the life of the developing individual. An assessment of the child's growth status in its various dimensions, thus depicting his individuality as a physical being, can make his behavior more comprehensible and meaningful. By comparing the various aspects of his growth status with what is typical and expected in a child of his age, valuable information for his guidance can be gained. Is the child developing at a satisfactory rate? In which aspects is he at the expected level and in which is he ahead or behind schedule?

In individual studies the significance of intraindividual variation is also best realized. No two "developmental profiles" are alike in total pattern. Each has its own peculiarities. In such studies the whole concept of what is "normal" is reexamined, and much of the concern about differing from the *average* is lessened. Individual studies foster a heightened respect for the uniqueness of each individual child (Olson and Hughes, 1942; Olson, 1951, 1952).

It is, of course, only in terms of a series of status measurements or assessments over a period of time that an individual's developmental *progress* can be plotted. Development is obviously continuous, and in a strict sense one is never exactly the same from one moment to the next. Life itself is a dynamic process of change. In our efforts to understand what is happening continuously, we attempt to look intensively at a particular "stage" of development as though the process of change were brought to a halt to permit our inspection. It is as if one were to examine a single frame from a motion picture. By examining a series of such stills we may deduce certain facts about the processes that have gone on between them. It is also important to study the course of individual development in its different aspects throughout the complete developmental cycle, noting that each individual is different from every other in total pattern of developmental change. This implies that we must begin by examining the beginnings of individual existence.

Chapter 3 described the amazing developmental change that takes place before the child is born into the external world. It was noted that the human being begins its existence with the union of two minute reproductive cells, the ovum of the mother and the spermatozoon, or sperm cell, of the father. Each of these original "germinal" cells contains in its nucleus all of the hereditary determinants coming from its donor. Biological heredity is thus determined in each new individual at his conception.

But from the moment of conception the conditions surrounding this minute "organism" are of crucial importance to its development. Through the interaction of these two sets of factors, heredity and environment, change in magnitude begins. Thus the organism changes from a minute bit of protoplasm to a complex functioning individual, perhaps 19 or 20 inches long and weighing about 7 pounds at birth. This change, the increase in size and weight before birth, will continue throughout the so-called developmental period, but also throughout the total life of the individual to some degree.

Not only does the organism as a whole get taller and heavier, but the various parts and segments change in their relative dimensions. With growth every linear dimension of the body increases. The child gets taller, his head and trunk lengthen, his shoulders get broader, his arms and legs get longer, and each of these dimensions changes at its own individual rate and during different periods of time. This continuous, yet variable, change in body proportions is an interesting and significant feature of growth. W. M. Krogman (1948) has suggested an easy rule of thumb which suggests the general pattern of proportional change between birth and adulthood. Accordingly, the head portion increases in length by two times, the trunk segment by three times, the arms by four times, and the legs by five times (Krogman, 1955, 1956). Figure 4.1 dramatically shows these changes in proportion.

The significance of growth can not be overstated. But there is another equally significant manifestation of change which will become clearer as we examine the nature of development in its various stages.

Patterns of Growth in Discrete Body Tissues

Although human development in general is a well-coordinated and integrated system of processes, the various tissues and organs of the body do not all follow the same developmental time schedule. This fact was clearly noted in our discussion of prenatal development in Chapter 3. The general course of growth for different types of body tissues was studied many years ago (Scammon, in Harris, 1930). Figure 4.2 shows curves based upon this early research which represent in general these diverse courses of growth. These curves are plotted in each case in terms of the percentage of average adult status at age 20 years which children attain at the various ages.

Curve C in the figure represents the generalized course of body growth as a whole. It has the shape of a normal body-growth curve. It shows the typical rapid but gradually decreasing rate during the first four or five years of life, followed by a more nearly constant rate during the so-called latency

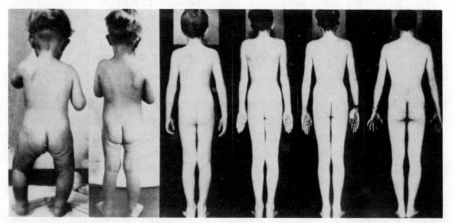

Figure 4.1   Changes in body proportions with growth, shown with photographs of the same boy at six ages, all adjusted to the same height. From Bayley (1956), p. 48, by permission.

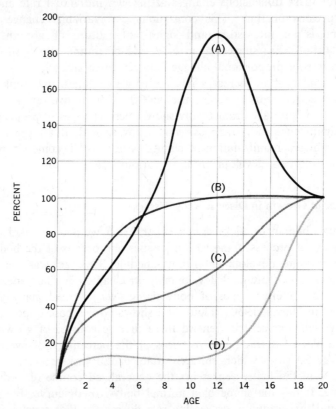

Figure 4.2   Growth curves of different parts and types of body tissues. (A) Lymph-oid type: thymus, lymph nodes, intestinal lymphoid masses. (B) Neural type: brain tissue, dura, spinal cord, certain dimensions of the head. (C) General type: body as a whole, external dimensions (except head), respiratory and digestive organs, musculature as a whole, skeleton as a whole. (D) Genital type: testes, ovary, epididymus, uterine tube, pros-tate, urethra, seminal vesicles. Adapted from Harris (1930), p. 193, by permission. Copyright 1930 by the University of Minnesota.

period (6–11 years). With the onset of puberal changes the rate of growth begins to increase. This positively accelerated phase of the curve represents what is usually referred to as the puberal growth spurt. In later adolescence, around age 15, another negatively accelerated phase, or decreasing rate, of growth begins, culminating in a leveling off at adulthood.

Curves A, B, and D of Figure 4.2 contrast rather sharply with the curve of general body growth (C). Curve A represents the growth changes in the lymphoid tissue of such a structure as the thymus gland or the tonsils or the intestinal lymph tissue. The figure clearly shows that this type of tissue, taken as a whole, reaches nearly twice its adult mass at the time of the adolescent growth spurt and then rather promptly decreases to the normal adult level.

The nervous tissue of the brain (B), on the other hand, increases in amount at a much more rapid rate during early childhood than does the body in general. The development of the brain is discussed in more detail in a later section of this chapter. Curve D represents the growth of the reproductive organs, internal and external. Early growth of these organs is very slow, and during the period of childhood there is little, if any, increase. During the puberal period, however, growth is very rapid. This rather wide diversity in relative rate and timing of growth in different body tissues and organ systems may be seen as an important aspect of the overall coordination and regularity of biological development.

Dimensions of Growth

At the naive level of analysis of overall physical growth, each successive assessment of status differs only quantitatively from the one preceding it, and the change is expressed simply as the addition of more of the same quantitative units of measurement of overall weight and height. Students of physical growth, however, are much more analytical in their studies (Krogman, 1956). The fact that total weight and total height increase with time is only a sample of the many dimensional changes that take place in the developing human organism. As mentioned earlier, the relative length and weight of the different portions of the body change markedly. Krogman has also directed his attention to the structures that constitute or determine total height and total weight (pp. 25–30). Wide individual variations are found in the measurements of the various component structures as they relate to different body types.

Much that was earlier assumed to be true about the course and the complexity of structural development based on cross-sectional studies has proved to be of limited value in the understanding of individual development. It is a mistake now to assume that we have a completely adequate knowledge of human growth, which on the surface appears to be a simple matter of quantitative change. Much is yet to be learned about the complex beneath-the-surface processes involved in what appear to be simple changes in dimensionality.

Some extremely important relations between the physical and other aspects of development have been observed and appraised. There are many possible connections between variations in structural development and psychological functioning yet to be investigated.

Growth, as defined herein, is increase in size (note, however, that when the complete lifespan of the individual is to be considered, growth defined as change may involve *decrease* as well as increase in size). But size, of course, is not a simple dimension. Along with the overall vertical dimension (height or stature), the width or the horizontal circumferences of the different body segments, as well as their various lengths, obviously would be involved in a complete assessment of body size. In practice, however, the two overall indexes of size most commonly used are total height and total body weight.

These two dimensions in relation to each other tell us much about *body type,* and they permit an appraisal of the individual child's growth status in terms of general expectations.

Growth in Height

Growth is commonly represented graphically in two ways. One of these is the simple growth curve in which height is plotted against age. The other way is to plot the amount of *gain* or increase in height from age to age.

In Figure 4.3 the course of growth in height is shown in terms of total

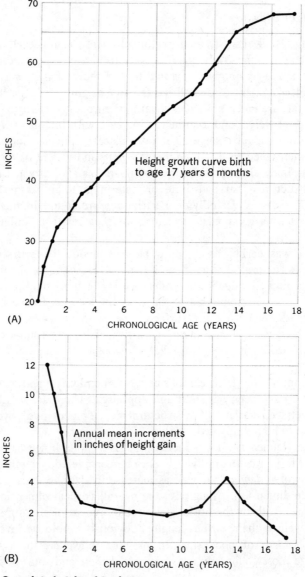

Figure 4.3   Growth in height of Paul 695.

height (A) and in terms of successive increments of gain (B). These curves are typical and correspond closely in form to other published height-growth curves (Stolz and Stolz, 1951; Tanner, 1961). Normally, as stated earlier, there are two periods of rapid growth. The first comes during infancy (roughly the first two years of life) after the baby has made his initial adjustment to extrauterine life. Growth accelerates to a rapid pace. The second period of acceleration corresponds roughly with the early teen years (ages 10–15).

Sex Differences

The course of growth in height in girls is quite similar in general pattern to that in boys. There are, however, some interesting sex differences in *timing* of the various phases of growth, particularly of the adolescent growth spurt (Fig. 4.4). During early childhood the average height of boys is somewhat greater than that of girls. Girls, however, tend to catch up with the boys and, for a short time before the beginning of the growth spurt, become slightly taller on the average than boys. Girls also tend to reach their spurt of growth at ages 10 to 12 years—approximately 2 years earlier than boys. They also begin leveling off and reach their terminal height at an average age of about 16 years. Boys generally continue to grow for another 2 years, reaching an average terminal height of 5 feet 9 inches. Girls, on the average, reach a

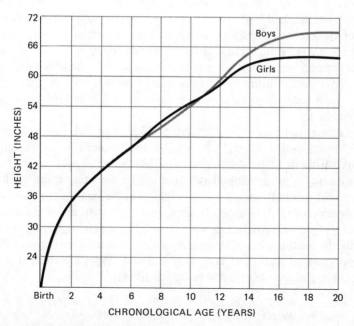

Figure 4.4 Average growth curves (height) of boys and of girls, drawn from the Iowa growth data, Tables A.1 and A.2 in the Appendix. (Jackson and Kelly, 1945)

terminal height some five inches shorter than boys (Meredith, 1935; Jackson and Kelly, 1945).

However, these averages were obtained some three or four decades ago. They were also based entirely upon measurement of American youth. There is some indication of a secular change since then in average height of young American adults. This change is generally attributed largely to better nutrition. *Potentiality* for tallness in the human individual is, of course, genetically determined, but that ultimate potentiality can be reached only "under the shaping influence of stimuli from the environment" (Dubos, 1968, p. 84; Falkner, 1966, pp. 24, 25). It is probably true that Americans generally are currently enjoying more nutritionally adequate food intake and better health care than were common during the period when most of the physical growth data were accumulated. Perhaps such a change has furnished the "shaping influence" in the environment toward a closer approach, on the average, to the genetically imposed growth potentiality.

The factors underlying the changes in *rate* of growth, and the sex differences in rate and timing, are not well understood in their details. It is quite clear, however, that increases in secretions of the endocrine glands, and changes in pattern and balance of endocrine functioning, play an exceedingly important role, particularly at the time of the dramatic growth changes at adolescence (Falkner, 1966).

Body-Growth in Weight

Weight is a very useful comparative index of body size and body type. Much has been learned also about human growth from group and population studies of weight measurements, along with measurements of stature. In the longitudinal study of individual children in relation to their individual environments, weight becomes an especially significant measurement variable because of its susceptibility to the influence of such factors as physical health and nutritional adequacy, as well as emotional and other factors of psychological well-being.

As a single indicator of the course of biological development, however, weight is not as useful as height because of the former's instability and wide variability. Growth in height is nonreversible because progress in height is based primarily upon developmental changes in the bony framework of the body. A child normally never loses height, but he can and often does lose weight for short periods of time. Progress in weight gain alone as an indicator of growth progress clearly has its limitations, but when weight measurements are plotted in combination with height measurements, a very useful index of growth progress, as well as of body size and body type, is provided. (See the Wetzel grid technique,[1] Figure A.4 in Appendix A.)

[1] Norman C. Wetzel, a pediatrician, in 1941 developed his "grid," a device for depicting graphically changes in an individual child's body size and shape in terms of the relation between height and weight throughout the "developmental period."

Use of Growth Norms

Crude measurements of body size by themselves have no meaning. It is only when such measurements are seen in relation to standards of reference that they become meaningful. The standard, or reference point, in the case of a quantitative measurement is usually some index of central tendency, such as the arithmetic mean or the median for the population of which the child is a member (Appendix A). A measure of variation within the population is also essential for the adequate appraisal of an individual child.

A number of earlier, well-known studies of physical growth have provided sets of norms, that is, average measurements and indexes of variation, based on the particular sample of children used in each case (Baldwin, 1921; Jackson and Kelly, 1945; Krogman, 1948, 1957; Meredith, 1935, 1948). Since children involved in these studies were representative of different sections of the United States of different eras or periods of time, and of different segments of the population, their respective normative values vary somewhat in magnitude. It is important, therefore, to note the source of any set of norms and to use discretion in using them to interpret a particular child's measurements.

For our purpose, in the lack of currently collected data, we have derived a set of average weights and heights, with measures of variation, from the Iowa growth data (Jackson and Kelly, 1945). These Iowa norms (see Tables A.1 and A.2 in Appendix A) are based upon the study of some 1500 boys and 1500 girls, mostly from the higher economic and education levels of the population. It was believed that these data set a standard of growth that most nearly approached the optimum.

In order to see clearly how such standards give meaning to individual measurements, the student should compare the measurements shown in Table 4.1 with the Iowa standards in Appendix A (Table A.1). Note, for example, that when Paul[2] was 6 and a half years old he was 46.2 inches tall and weighed 52.8 pounds. The Iowa group of 6 and a half year-olds, with which Paul can reasonably be compared, averaged 46.8 inches tall, and their median weight was 48.0 pounds. Paul's measurements thus begin to take on meaning. Such comparisons tell us that he was very close to the average, or "expected," height, but was a bit heavier than the average of the group.

Plotting the Course of Growth

There are a number of methods along with appropriate graphing devices that have been developed for the longitudinal study of individual growth from recorded measurements. Some of these are discussed in some detail and illustrated in Appendix A. Behind each technique is its rationale. Each has its advantages and disadvantages.

---

[2] The developmental records of a pair of twins, Paul and Sally (695) are occasionally used for illustrative purposes throughout this text. The number 695 is the family file number in a research series.

TABLE 4.1   Growth Data (Height and Weight Measurements) of Paul 695 from Birth to Age 17 years 8 months

Age	Weight (pounds)	Height (inches)
Birth	8.3	20.0
3 days	7.8	20.0
15 days	8.3	20.5
0-2	11.3	22.5
0-3	12.4	23.4
0-6	16.5	25.8
0-8	21.7	27.1
0-9	21.3	27.8
1-1	25.0	30.1
1-6	28.3	32.3
2-1	31.8	34.1
2-7	33.1	35.9
3-1	36.5	37.8
3-7	37.0	38.8
4-6	40.6	41.2
5-7	43.3	43.5
6-6	52.8	46.2
7-6	57.3	49.0
8-6	64.8	51.3
9-3	68.4	52.5
10-3	74.9	54.6
11-3	88.0	57.1
11-9	91.7	58.1
12-3	102.5	59.4
12-9	113.3	61.4
13-3	119.3	63.6
13-9	132.3	64.9
14-2	130.6	66.0
16-2	147.0	67.7
17-8	147.7	67.9

The simplest and most obvious way of depicting growth progress is to plot raw weights and stature measurements against chronological age. Figure 4.3A is an example of this method of plotting. These growth curves show how rates of growth change from time to time during the developmental period. They show the general course of growth with its fluctuations and irregularities.

Another frequently used method of plotting growth is in terms of "developmental ages." The concept of developmental age was introduced in Chapter 2. In plotting a child's growth, his height and weight measurements are compared with *average* measurements which have been established for the various age levels. The *age* of the group of children whose *average height* corresponds to the height of the particular child under study is taken as the child's "height" age regardless of his chronological age. Likewise, his "weight" age is the *average weight* of a particular age group with which he corresponds. An advantage of this method is that height and weight—and any other quantitative measurement for which norms have been established—can be plotted together and are directly comparable. Figure 4.5 shows Paul's growth record in terms of growth ages.

Individual Growth Patterns

It is interesting to examine in some detail the growth records of our subjects, Paul and Sally. These records reveal the relative stability and regularity of growth in stature as compared with growth in weight. The sex differences in growth pattern referred to earlier are also clearly seen.

Weight, as we have noted, is more readily influenced by environmental conditions and by variations in nutritional adequacy and health than height. Although Paul was a somewhat smaller baby than average during his first six months, and continued to be shorter than average, at eight months he was considerably heavier than average. From that point on, with some fluctuations in relative weight, he continued to be a bit heavy for his height. By contrast, Sally at birth was more than an inch shorter and nearly three pounds lighter —smaller and of a more slender build than her brother. Paul retained his larger size, especially during their first two years. As early as age two months,

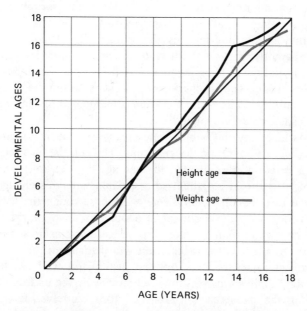

Figure 4.5 Growth of Paul, birth to 17 years, plotted in terms of age equivalents (developmental ages).

however, Sally had attained a physique, or body type, very similar to that of her brother.

Both of these children continued to grow very consistently according to expectations. Although their growth curves showed some decline in *rate* of growth during their pre-school years, a consistent relation between height and weight continued (see the Wetzel grid record, Figure A.4 in Appendix A).

In connection with this slight decline in growth status, which was largely a change in relative weight, it is interesting to look for changes in conditions of living—in feeding regime, in kind and level of daily activity, in health hazards—changes in the general developmental milieu that come naturally with increasing age. In such an examination of these children's records certain relations between what was inherent in their nature and what the environment contributed to the course of their development are clearly suggested.

Factors Related to Growth Progress

In the first place, both Paul and Sally were breast-fed "on demand" during their first eight months. This early period coincides with Paul's most rapid gain in both height and weight (Fig. 4.6). Day-to-day records were kept on the frequency of feeding and the times at which each child was fed. Study of these records reveals that some regularity of feeding pattern began to appear in both babies as early as the beginning of their third month when they were usually demanding four feedings a day, with some uniformity as to times of feeding. A month later a pattern of three feedings a day began to predominate, and by the age of four months this pattern had become quite well established. Apparently the twins thrived on this regime and in general gained weight in relation to their lengths. The fluctuations and the changing relation between height and weight can best be seen in the Wetzel grid records of these children. The Wetzel grid and the method of plotting growth are explained in some detail in Appendix A.

At eight months of age the babies were weaned to cup feeding, and day-to-day behavior charts were no longer kept. During the ensuing month, apparently as a result of this change in feeding, they actually lost weight while continuing to grow in length. Also associated with this change toward slimness was the fact that the twins were working through the early stages of their upright locomotor development at about this time. As the shift was made to bottle, cup, and spoon feeding, unusual care was exercised jointly by the conscientious mother and a pediatrician who had taken the twin infants as a special project to insure their optimal health and welfare. The "self-regulation" feeding regime was continued, although by the end of the period of breast feeding the babies had established for themselves fairly regular three-meal feeding schedules.

Normally as a child enters the so-called preschool period certain changes

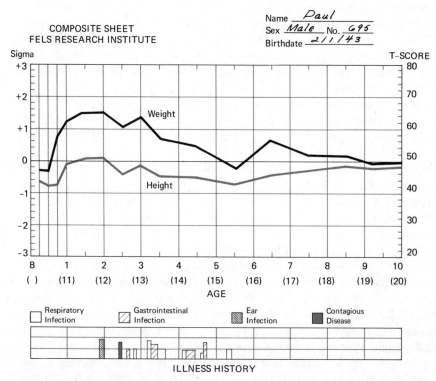

COMPOSITE SHEET
FELS RESEARCH INSTITUTE

Name _Paul_
Sex _Male_ No. _695_
Birthdate _2/1/43_

Figure 4.6   Height and weight standard scores for Paul 695 on the Fels Composite Sheet (used by permission).

are underway which may tend to alter his rate of growth. These conditioning factors may affect some children relatively more than others and thus bring about a change in a particular child's growth status relative to his age group.

Because of these rather radical changes in pattern of energy expenditure with the greatly increased energy requirements of activity and learning, "the preschool period, contrary to much prevailing practice, is still a period for continuation of a substantial form of closely sustained child health supervision" (Stuart and Prugh, 1960, p. 116).

Illness in Relation to Growth

Along with these changes in functioning and in the nurturing demands made upon the environment come a significant broadening of the child's "world" and its associated hazards to health and well-being. He is no longer confined to the protecting boundaries of his home and play yard. He ventures forth much more frequently into the larger neighborhood. He enters nursery school or a neighborhood play group, thus coming in contact with more people and increasing the chances for infection and contagion. Consequently, the preschool period generally is one in which certain communicable diseases become somewhat common. In summarizing the findings of the Harvard studies of child health and development regarding the relative frequency of various kinds of illnesses at different age levels, Stuart and Prugh (1960) stated that "these [communicable] diseases occurred more frequently from 0 to 6 years; they increased rapidly between 2 and 6 years, remaining high during the school-age period, then rapidly declined" (p. 30).

Associated with the chronological scale, the Fels composite sheet (Fig. 4.6) provides a means and a system for coding and recording the illness history of a child. This record can be seen in association with the record of changes in the child's growth status. Figure 4.6 presents an approximate record of Paul 695. The most frequent types of illnesses were respiratory infection and gastrointestinal infection. The approximate age at which the illness episode occurred is indicated by the location of the symbol on the chronological age line. The severity of the illness, as estimated from the written record, is indicated by the height of the illness symbol.

It will be noted that the age period, roughly the preschool period, during which Paul was most frequently ill is also the period during which there was a decline in his growth status. It should be emphasized once more at this point that these status curves, plotted in standard deviation units, even though the trend is downward, do *not* represent a general decrease in height and weight. Paul was growing normally all the while. At only one point did he lose slightly in weight only. (He weighed 0.4 pounds lighter at age 9 months than at 8 months.) These curves, instead, show a decline in Paul's *relative* position—his growth status in relation to the total Fels sample of boys.

Maturation

Thus far we have been concerned with the quantitative aspect of structural development—with changes that are directly measurable. As was suggested in Chapter 2, some of the most significant physical changes with age in relation to psychological functioning is change in *kind* or *quality* —that is, changes which cannot be measured directly in quantitative units. We shall now consider briefly some of these qualitative manifestations of development, what we term *biological maturation.*

During childhood we grow; that is we increase in dimensions, or less literally, we put on weight. But we also grow up. And when childhood is over and we are grown up we begin to grow older, and ultimately we grow old. This business of growing up, growing older, growing old is quite different from growing; it implies progressive maturity, not increase in dimensions. Maturity is not experience; it is that upon which experience imprints itself and without which experience does not register. . . . Progressive maturity is something we all share, no matter what our size, no matter what our experience.

There is, in the concept of progressive maturity, another implication not found in growth or in experience, namely inevitability. If John has not grown so tall as his brothers or has not learned the calculus, he is not therefore handicapped for life. But suppose he should not grow up! He may be a little young for his age or a little old for his years, but the possibility of a major or permanent modification in the growing up process is well-nigh unthinkable. [Todd, 1937, p. 11]

This growing-up aspect of development is what we call *maturation*. It is indeed "something which we all share," an aspect in which "there is no implication of dimensions or of training." Along with measurable increases in size of a particular body structure, such as the child's hand, examination reveals that certain new and different structural features, changes in kind or quality, also become evident.[3] Generally, however, qualitative changes are not readily accessible to direct observation.

Sequences of intrinsic change take place in the various organs and parts of the body. New tissues and new specific structural features emerge, differentiate, and specialize in form and function in an orderly manner. Maturational changes, along with growth, prepare the different organs and organ systems, and the total organism, to begin to function in new and specific ways and at progressively higher levels.

The qualitative aspect of development is clearly evident from the beginning. Not only does the tiny organism begin to grow very rapidly, but it also soon changes in its shape and contours as various areas and portions differentiate and accommodate to one another. The location or position that each cell group occupies in embryological development seems to play a part in guiding the direction and nature of specialization. Details of this early phase are given in Chapter 3.

Maturation is a lifelong process. The inner body structure and organization of tissues and parts continue to change throughout life. In the skeletal framework of the body, for example, qualitative change is constantly underway. At birth, even though the skeleton is in an early formative stage, some 21 separate "bones" are already present and identifiable in the hand and wrist. By the time the child is 10 years of age, 29 new bones have formed in the child's hand and wrist, making a total of 50 separate, identifiable bony

---

[3] It should be mentioned here that as body structures (organs, muscles, nervous tissues, and so on) begin to perform their indigenous functions, the effects of that exercise of function (learning in the broad sense) becomes a factor in development. As is emphasized throughout this text, development is conceived of as a *unitary* process of change resulting from the *interaction* of the organism "as is" and the environmental influences brought to bear. Growth, maturation, and learning, therefore, should not be regarded as separate developmental processes but rather as different facets of the same not-well-understood intrinsic process of change incidental to living.

structures. Ten years later certain of the bones that were apparent at age 10 are no longer present as separate entities; they have fused with each other and thus have lost their individual identity. The total number of individual bones in the region now is 29 (see Fig. 4.7). And all the while, throughout life, gradual changes are also taking place in the shape, the contours, and the inner structure of each of these bones as they accommodate to each other and fuse together. Fusion of separate bones in the skull, for example, along with other subtle changes in overall shape and contour, continue into old age. Such changes are changes in quality or kind, rather than in amount, changes that no calibrated measuring device could adequately portray in quantitative terms.

It is evident also that the maturation and growth of certain discrete systems of the body become highly related and interdependent. The most striking evidence for this fact has come from the study of cases of pathological development such as precocious puberty and hypergonadism (Greulich and Pyle, 1959, pp. 2–10). As such cases clearly show, there is a close correspondence between the maturational status of the reproductive and the skeletal systems. The development of the primary and secondary sexual characteristics is controlled by the gonadal and other related endocrine secretions. Likewise, growth of the skeleton, skeletal muscles, and other bodily features is controlled by the same system. The development of the skeleton, therefore, reflects the maturational and functional status of the reproductive system and

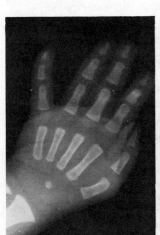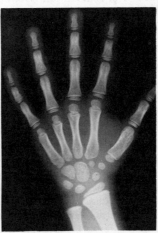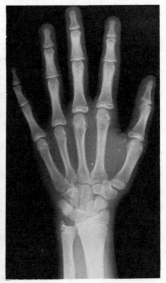

Figure 4.7   X-ray photographs showing stages in the development of the bones of Sally 695's hand and wrist at (left) age 3 months, (center) age 4 years 6 months, and (right) age 11 years 9 months.

is regarded as a reliable index of the body's general level of development. More will be said of this relation later.

Appraising Development from Qualitative Data

In Chapter 2 the concept of the age equivalent was introduced. By converting raw-measurement values into age equivalents, developmental status in quite different and disparate aspects of development (height, motor achievement, intelligence, and so forth) are made directly comparable. In the case of growth phenomena for which the data are in the form of quantitative measurements, an age equivalent is simply the average measurement value, or average "score," of a specific age group of children. The age-level average to which an individual score corresponds is the age equivalent of that individual score. The age equivalent of a given child's measured growth status or achievement (height, weight, and so forth) is also his developmental age in that particular aspect of his growth at that particular point in time.

In dealing with the qualitative aspects of development, however, the problem is somewhat more complicated. As noted in Chapter 2, in order to assess the maturational status of the child at any point in time, or to trace his development through time, qualitative information must somehow be expressed in quantitative terms.

It is obviously impossible to gain direct access to most of the maturational effects in the growing child, for they are internal and thus hidden from direct observation. The various stages of maturation in the embryo, and later in such structures as the brain, of course, have been studied and charted through the gross and microscopic examination of nonliving tissue. In that way the reality of maturational change in those parts has been established. Maturation in certain bodily structures has also been inferred on the basis of change in functional level. In most of the body systems, however, developmental status cannot be evaluated directly in the growing child with present techniques.

Developmental Sequences

Expressing qualitative "events" in quantitative terms requires preliminary observational research. First, the *order of occurrence* of the discrete changes in the structure under consideration must be noted. Generally, in maturational development such changes (stages) occur in a fixed sequence. Developmental change generally consists in an invariable series of stages, each in turn "growing out of" the previous one in order. The identification of such a developmental sequence is the first step in the quantification of maturational change. The next step is to observe in a large number of individual cases the age at which each stage occurs. Individual ages of occurrence, in most instances, vary over a considerable range. Individuality thus expresses itself. In a developmental process, as a rule, the *sequence*—the order of occurrence of events or of the appearance of stages—is fixed and invariable. But the *timing*—the specific ages at which they occur—is a matter of individual variation. From the distribution of individual ages at which a particular stage appears, an *average* age, and a measure of variation for that stage, are obtained. These average ages—age equivalents, in each instance, of a developmental stage—can be ordered in a developmental-age scale. Thus, each qualitative event, or stage in the series, acquires a quantitative value in terms of age units.

There is no implication in this concept of stages that development is discontinuous. Rather "striking changes" in functioning do occur. Developmental achievements often manifest themselves rather suddenly. But they are, in reality, "sudden" *only* in their manifestation and in the immediate advantage they give to the individual in terms of higher-level functioning. They simply mark the culmination of what, in a particular instance, might have been a long period of gradual, continuous development. They constitute in each case the "nodal stage" in a "developmental sequence." A developmental sequence is simply a sequence in time of a series of such culminations. The year-old child, for example, has traversed such a developmental sequence in the process of his learning to walk. During the past months he has more or less "suddenly," in each instance, achieved a series of "nodal" points. First he became able to turn over from his back to his stomach. Then he was able, in sequence, to get up on his hands and knees, to rise to a standing position, to take an independent step, and so on. "Suddenly" he began to walk. The assumption, from our point of view, is that the *developmental process* underlying this series of "stages," hidden and not understood, is continuous and unbroken. Perhaps this concept of stages will become clearer when some of the stage theories are examined later. Stages are convenient in developmental theory and are therefore used extensively.

Maturity Indicators in Skeletal Maturation

As "age equivalents" of the stages in a developmental sequence are established, a stage may then be taken as a "maturity indicator," that is, an indicator of achieved status in a particular aspect of development. The study of maturation in the development of the skeletal system is the prototype of maturational research.

In the intensive examination of many series of X-ray films of wrist and ankle bones of children, it is possible to identify series of qualitatively different stages of development. These stages (events) are fixed in order of appearance and are universal in occurrence. The time intervals between these various discontinuous and qualitatively different stages, however, are highly variable from individual to individual. Since the order of their appearance is invariable, each stage in turn can be taken as an indicator of a bone-developmental stage which is more advanced than the one preceding. These stages are therefore called *maturity indicators* (M. J. Baer, 1973).

In recent years the concept of the maturity indicator has been broadened to include any clearly defined stages of development, either of a function or of a structure or body part. In 1947, for a series of discussions on the attributes of maturity indicators at Western Reserve University Medical School, Dr. Idell Pyle described maturity indicators as

> features of a body part, secretory products of the cells of a part, or specialized forms of behavior which appear in a fixed or universal order to mark the progress of a child toward young maturity, or the progress of an adult toward senescence. They are strictly ontogenetic in nature, *i.e.*, they appear in human beings around the world in an order which is universal but at a speed which is characteristic of the child or adult in question.

A maturity indicator, then, is an identifiable point or stage in the development of a structure or function which occupies a fixed position in a series. Series of maturity indicators were first established in the maturation of the skeletal system. The average chronological age at which each feature (indicator) made its appearance was noted. Thus a series of maturity indicators for use in tracing skeletal maturation was established.

Sally's progress in bone development, observed as the successive achievement of stages of a series, is thus plotted (Figure 4.8) in terms of the average

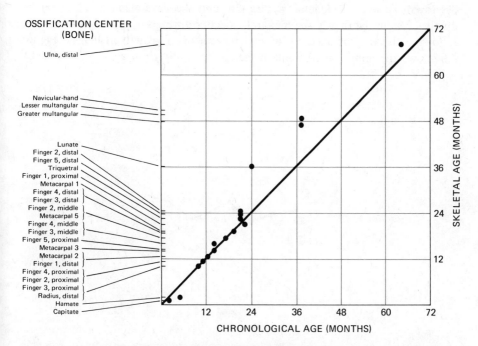

Figure 4.8   Early skeletal development (first six years) of Sally 695 in terms of ages of onset of ossification in centers of the hand and wrist. Age equivalents from Greulich and Pyle, 1959, p. 17.

ages of girls in general when they reach those various stages (maturity indi-cators). Since these stages appear as discrete and qualitatively different, the points in the "curve" in each case are not connected with a line, as was done in the case of height and weight in Figure 4.5, where the curves represent continuous *increase* in amount.

Significance of Skeletal Maturation in Relation to Other Aspects of Development

The maturation of the skeleton, more than any other single fact of development, can be taken as an index of the body's development in general. The relation between skeletal development and the maturation of the repro-ductive system has already been mentioned. The girl described by Greulich and Pyle who suffered precocious puberty had her first menstruation when she was only 7 months old (1959, pp. 2–9). Other signs of sexual maturity began to appear in very early childhood. When she was only 5 years of age her skeletal age was 12 years 11 months. Along with this extreme precocity in sexual and skeletal maturation there was also acceleration of growth in stature. Growth, however, ceased very early in life, due to the early maturing of the long bones of the skeleton.

In normal girls also there is a clearly established relation between rhythm of growth in stature, skeletal maturation, and the development of the repro-ductive system. Normally the menarche occurs during the period immediately following the year of maximal annual increment of growth in height. Figure 4.9 shows the annual increments in height for Sally from ages 2 years to 13

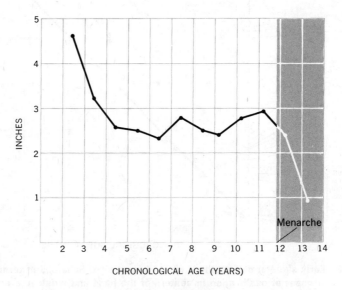

Figure 4.9 Annual increments in height of Sally 695.

years. The period of her most consistent and rapid increase in rate of growth in stature was around 9½ to 11 years of age. Her first menstruation occurred at age 11 years 10 months.

Figure 4.10 is a plotting of Sally's height and skeletal maturation in terms of developmental ages. It will be noted that this girl's height-age curve was considerably below the standard of reference throughout the whole period covered by the graph. The prepuberal growth spurt is clearly in evidence here, as it is in Figure 4.9. The period of most rapid growth was between ages 11 years 3 months and 11 years 9 months.

Although shorter than average in stature, Sally was somewhat advanced in her skeletal development. At the time her menarche occurred (11 years 10 months) her assessed skeletal age (average of the skeletal-age assessments of all the bones of the hand and wrist) was 13 years 4 months. The X-ray film taken at age 11 years 3 months matches quite well the female standard (number 21), which is the standard for skeletal age 13 in Greulich and Pyle's (1959) *Atlas*. This film shows the beginning epiphysial-diaphysial fusion in the distal phalanges of the fingers. Another film, taken 6 months later at age 11 years 9 months (see Figure 4.7), shows that in the meantime fusion at those centers had been completed. This film matches the standard photo (number 22) in the *Atlas* that indicates a skeletal age of 13 years 6

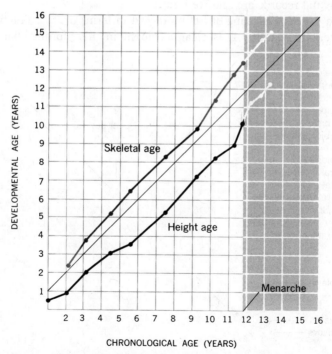

Figure 4.10 Skeletal maturation and growth in height of Sally 695 shown in relation to the time of menarche.

months. According to Greulich and Pyle, this standard "illustrates the stage of skeletal development usually attained by girls at about the time of the menarche" (p. 168). Sally's menarche occurred at age 11 years 10 months, about 1 month after the latter of the two X-ray pictures was taken.

Dental Development

Dentition, as a process of development, is also manifested in a series of stages that are essentially qualitative in nature, some of which may be observed directly. For example, a child's teeth erupt above the gum in a fairly definite ordinal sequence. This sequence may be regarded as a series of maturity indicators.

The validity of an appraisal of status of dentition at any particular point in the child's life depends directly upon the accuracy with which the eruption dates are known. Owing to the relatively wide variation in age at which the various teeth appear, the age equivalents may be taken to represent only a crude developmental scale.

In order to trace dental development, examinations must be made at frequent intervals beginning in early infancy. These appraisals, furthermore, must be carefully made by an experienced observer. They must be more than a casual glance in the child's mouth. Unfortunately, good dental-developmental records are relatively rare.

Figure 4.11 is a plotting of Sally's record in terms of the available data in developmental-age units. It is clearly evident in this plotting that from the

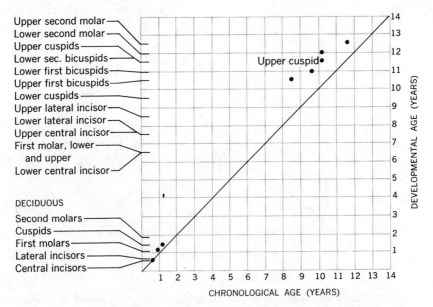

Figure 4.11   The development of dentition in Sally 695 from available records.

beginning of her second year Sally continued to be somewhat advanced in dentition.

Growth and Maturation of the Nervous System

The processes of development in the nervous system are even more remarkable in their complexity and precision than are those in other organs and systems of the body. Munn (1955) wrote of this developmental marvel:

> How is this intricate architecture of the nervous system laid down? How do the billions of embryonic nerve fibers reach their appropriate destinations in muscles, glands, receptors and central nervous nuclei and projections? They do this with precise developmental timing, in a manner characteristic of the species, and independent of activity. Indeed, until they find their destinations, no activity of the parts of the organism to which they go can normally occur. [p. 161]

Much of the growth in brain size occurs prenatally. In terms of weight, at birth the brain has already attained about 25 percent of its adult value. At 6 months of age it has grown to 50 percent, and by the time the child is 10 years of age his brain has gained 95 percent of its ultimate weight (Tanner, 1961).

Like physical development in general, different parts of the brain grow at different rates and reach their maximum rates of change at different times. The midbrain and the spinal cord are the most advanced-functioning parts throughout the period of growth, with the cerebrum third.

But as we have seen, growth in amount is only one aspect of development. The 10-year-old brain, although it has attained 95 percent of its ultimate weight, is far from being a mature brain. Conel (1939, 1941, 1947, 1951, 1955, 1959) has contributed greatly to our present knowledge about the early development of the human brain, particularly the cerebral cortex (Tanner, 1961).

The Embryonic Stages

In the processes of cell differentiation and the modeling of the embryo, the nervous system develops from the ectodermal layer of cells. The first stage in this development is the thickening of a strip, or plate, of cells on the dorsal (top) side of the embryo. Soon from this plate a tubular structure develops. The entire adult central nervous system is formed from this neural tube. Chapter 3 discusses this development in more detail.

Conel's findings concerning the prenatal development of the cerebral cortex are summarized by Tanner (1961) as follows:

At about eight weeks of age (postmenstrual) the cortex begins to assume its typical structure of six somewhat indeterminate layers of nerve cells, the grey matter, on the outside of the cortex, with a layer of nerve fibers, the white matter, on the inside. All the nerve cells present in the adult are formed within the following two or three months, or so it is thought at present. Probably no new nerve cells appear after about six lunar months, though cells of the supporting tissue, the neuroglia, may perhaps differentiate for somewhat longer. [p. 77]

The nerve cells themselves undergo continuous change as well. At first they consist for the most part of nuclei with very little cytoplasm and with only a few small processes. As they develop they grow in size, and dendrites, axons, and smaller processes appear. Myelin sheaths form on many of the axons, particularly the larger ones. Some of the smaller axons get very little or no insulating myelin.

Conel was able to formulate nine maturity indicators of the cerebrum. Presumably these maturational changes take place in a fixed and orderly sequence, but since they are not open to direct observation in the growing individual there is no direct way of assessing the developmental status of the brain. Detailed information about brain maturation after age 2 years is practically nonexistent.

Morphological Development

As we have noted (Chapter 3), one of the earliest and most fundamental processes of cell specialization and organization in the embryonic development of the human organism is the formation of the three layers, *ectoderm, endoderm*, and *mesoderm*. This basic process of specialization and its further differential elaboration in the development of the three groups of structures and organs involved, according to the theory of Sheldon (1940), gives rise to another kind of overall qualitative difference among individuals. Presumably, as a result of the relative predominance of one or another of these three sources of tissue origin, one or another of the corresponding structural tissue groups may tend to "dominate in the body economy" and to result in a tendency toward a particular morphological type.

Since the civilization of ancient Greece, students of mankind have worked to devise systems for classifying people in terms of morphological differences. This interest generally arises from the common belief that behavior is related in important ways to physical make-up.

The earliest well-known theoretical system of morphological classification was that of Hippocrates. He identified two basic physique types—the short and thick and the long and thin—and suggested that each type was especially prone to certain diseases. Associated also with these physique types, according to Hippocrates, were temperamental types, each of which was determined by the relative predominance of a particular "humor" (fluid) within the body—a suggestion not greatly different from the present-day conception of the role of the endocrine secretions in the affective life of the individual. A number of scholars after Hippocrates proposed modifications of his classification scheme; others suggested systems of their own. Among the better known of these other classification schemes were the formulations of Kretschmer (1925), Rostan (1824), and Viola (1909).

Somatotypes

Perhaps the best-known modern student of morphology is W. H. Sheldon (1940, 1954), whose work was based on the fundamental belief that function is always and ever related to structure. In his search for criteria for the classification of human physiques, Sheldon studied three primary aspects of bodily constitution, selected because they appeared "to behave in bodily morphology as though each were a component of structure—something which enters in different amounts into the making of a body" (1940, p. 4). These three components of structure were briefly described by Sheldon as follows:

> *Endomorphy* means relative predominance of soft roundness throughout the various regions of the body. When endomorphy is dominant the digestive viscera are massive and tend relatively to dominate the body economy. The digestive viscera are derived principally from the endodermal embryonic layer.
> *Mesomorphy* means relative predominance of muscle, bone, and connective tissue. The mesomorphic physique is normally heavy, hard and rectangular in outline. Bone and muscle are prominent and the skin is made thick by a heavy underlying connective tissue. The entire bodily economy is dominated, relatively, by tissues derived from the mesodermal embryonic layer.
> *Ectomorphy* means relative predominance of linearity and fragility. In proportion to his mass, the ectomorph has the greatest surface area and hence relatively the greatest sensory exposure to the outside world. Relative to his mass he also has the largest brain and central nervous system. In a sense therefore, his bodily economy is relatively dominated by tissues derived from the ectodermal embryonic layer. [pp. 5–6]

The particular patterning of these three morphological components in an individual determines his "somatotype." All individuals, it is assumed, possess each component to some degree. Using the method devised by Sheldon, one can appraise an individual's somatotype from a study of nude photographs taken in three specially posed positions: front, side, and back. A recently devised refinement of Sheldon's original procedure involves the use of objective measurements taken on the photographs. Each of the three components is rated on a scale from 1 (minimum) to 7 (maximum). Thus, a rating of 7-1-1 would represent the component ratings of an extreme endomorph, ratings of 1-7-1 would describe the extreme mesomorph, and 1-1-7, the extreme ectomorph. A person with the somatotype ratings of 4-4-4 would possess a moderate, or average, amount of all three components.

Stability of the Somatotype

One important question in relation to individual morphology is its relative stability with age. Dupertuis, a co-author of Sheldon's, wrote as follows:

> One of the tenets of the philosophy behind somatotyping is that the basic component combination of an individual remains constant throughout life. It is only recently however, that there have been objective techniques to demonstrate this thesis. [Personal correspondence with present author]

Sheldon's (1940) own research indicated rather significant relations between morphological types and corresponding temperamental types. Walker (1962, 1963) studied this sort of relation at the early-childhood level. He obtained somatotyping photographs on a group of nursery school children and, using Sheldon's procedures, was able to rate each child in terms of the three body components. It is interesting to note that Walker also found important relations between physique and certain behavior characteristics in the nursery school children. These relations, furthermore, showed "considerable similarity to those described by Sheldon of college-age men" (1962, p. 79).

Other developmental studies (H. E. Jones, 1943; M. C. Jones, 1957; M. C. Jones and Bayley, 1950) leave no room for doubt that physique and other physical attributes are important in relation to other aspects of individual development. The relation of these findings to personality development is discussed in greater detail in Chapter 13.

A Somatotype Appraisal

Through the cooperation of C. W. Dupertuis, a collaborator of Sheldon, we have a professional somatotype appraisal of our subject Paul 695 based on photographs taken when he was age 16 years. These photographs are shown in Figure 4.12.

To the layman these pictures are likely to suggest a perfectly healthy, normal, and vigorous young man. He is likely to be a bit surprised upon reading the expert appraisal:

> This boy [Paul] possesses one of the most displastic physiques in the entire series. He is predominantly mesomorphic above the waist and predominantly endomorphic below the waist. At the same time he shows a very high gynic (feminine) aspect of the physique from the waist down. This boy could do most athletics, but would probably be quite frustrated in competition with more mesomorphic boys. He might do very well, however, in swimming. [From personal communication]

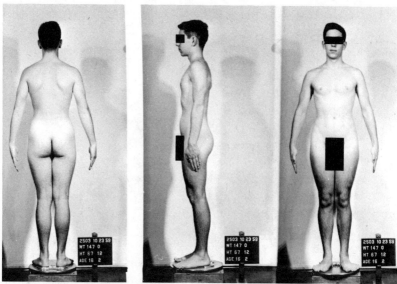

Figure 4.12   Photographs of Paul 695 in the posed positions for somatotyping. Used by permission.

Summary

In this chapter the concern has been with human development as it manifests itself in the physical organism. We have for the most part dealt with the postnatal periods of development. We have examined the facts, principles, and relations of growth and maturation very largely in terms of actual data from the developmental records of two living individuals who were studied from birth to adulthood. We concerned ourselves first with those aspects of body change that are dimensional—that appear as continuous quantitative increments—that are open to observation and measurement. Second, we examined those aspects of change that are serial rather than continuous—that consist in the orderly emergence of new qualities or stages in sequence—that are not amenable to direct measurement.

Now as we begin to look at the functional aspect of development—the changes in behavior in the functioning human being—from birth through life, we shall again, wherever possible, observe the principles of developmental psychology in the actual records of this same pair of fraternal twins: Paul 695 and Sally 695.

CHAPTER 5

Functional Development— Learning

Learning Is Development

In our discussions thus far it has been clearly evident that there is, in reality, no clear separation between the processes of change (development) in the physical organism and those which refer specifically to the *functioning* of physical structures. This is to say, again, what has been emphasized earlier, that growth, maturation, and learning are in reality but three aspects of overall total change in the individual associated with his living through time. In this chapter we shall concern ourselves primarily with developmental changes in behavior—with that aspect of total development which we call *learning*.

The term "behavior" is used here in a broad sense to include all activity, that is, all functioning of the whole person, vital,[1] overt motor, intellectual, emotional, and social. Learning is the primary aspect of development in all of these.

For example, even though the level of a person's ultimate potentiality for intellectual development, as we shall see, is genetically determined and is therefore basically related to the maturation of physical structures, his specific *mental abilities* within the limits of that inherent potentiality are *acquired* (learned). He learns them as he copes with and gains control over, or accommodates himself to situations of everyday life. For example, a child's ability to "pass" a particular test of intelligence, or the abilities necessary for him to function effectively upon entering public school, presumably have or have not been acquired by him in his preschool experiences. The actual abilities to perform at any level of effectiveness in everyday life are products of learning.

Likewise, the child's original temperamental predispositions, constitutionally based as they are, also undergo change through learning. A very bright and active preschool child, for example, in one sort of home situation, with a particular set of parents, might become an effective and responsible social leader. This same child, had he been born into a very different family environment, could become a domineering, hostile, and emotionally disturbed person. The direction and extent of learning is a matter of great importance in relation to an individual's emotional adjustment and his total personality development. General adequacy of functioning in life is very largely a matter of learning in this broad sense.

Just as maturation refers to development as seen in body structure, so learning in a broad sense is developmental change in functionability that comes from functioning itself. Function is simply the *doing* of something. It is behavior. It may be very simple, as in the case of a reflex act, or it may be very complex. It may be outwardly observable, as with motor behavior, or it may be implicit and hidden from direct view, as with mental behavior.

[1] The term "vital" we shall use to refer to those activities which are essential to the life and well-being of the individual (Chapter 6).

Obviously, the very processes of living are processes of change. Living itself constitutes a continuous progression of changes in the way the individual (and his behavior) interact with his environment. These are changes in functional facility due to the exercise of function itself. This is learning.

Activity in all its forms is presumed to involve to some degree the functioning of three complex body systems: the sensory system, the nervous system, and the response system. This functioning, it is presumed, results in modifications of the physical structures as well as in their functioning. Functioning apparently leaves something in the nature of "traces" in the physical structure involved. Physiological psychologists are hard at work trying to learn the nature of these traces. Some researchers are intensively studying what happens chemically at the synapses with the passage of nervous impulses through them as learning takes place (Deutsch and Deutsch, 1966). Others are concentrating on hypothetical changes in the molecular activity within the nerve cells involved as changes in function take place (Rucker and Halstead, 1967). In any event, as functional patterns are repeated and as new related acts are performed, portions of the already present traces apparently become strengthened and new traces are left. Complex systems of interconnected traces thus become established.

This means that the child's behavioral possibilities become augmented. His readiness for progressively higher-level functioning results not only from his continuing biological development (maturation) but also from the actual functioning of the physical structures involved. This, of course, suggests the great importance of the kinds and amounts of stimulation and opportunity to function that the environment provides.

Obviously, there are various specific ways in which functional patterns become changed with experience. There may be an increase in the strength or the precision of an overt behavior pattern itself. The golfer, for example, learns to combine an appropriate measure of strength with the accuracy of his stroke for each situation in which he finds himself. Or the change may be a matter of replacing a customary (natural) response with a different, more appropriate, and more effective one. It may also be a matter of becoming responsive to new and different stimuli in the situation. As we have seen, temperamental predispositions may be modified, strengthened, or directed into different behavioral channels. Attitudes, values, and interests change through experience and through the interest of others.

Modification and augmentation of the more implicit "inner" forms of activity also come about through exercise and experience. These functional changes constitute cognitive development. Here, as in other sorts of functional development, structural "traces" also presumably take place, particularly in the brain. The psychological counterpart of this change in physical structure is developmental change in the "cognitive structure." In terms of cognitive theory, new learnings—new knowledge and new patterns of mental activity—are acquired only as they become incorporated or assimilated into this hierarchically organized cognitive system. In short, we learn new things in terms of what we already know. We will return to this topic later in this chapter.

What the child has already learned and *how well* he has learned to perform in relation to life's requirements and the expectations of his environment constitute his level of "ability." Ability means functional effectiveness. As is shown in Chapters 8 and 9, ability, in the sense of one's repertoire of available learned reactions to the environment and the tasks it presents, is what the usual tests of so-called intelligence purport to sample and thus measure directly. This repertoire of acquired responses, of course, depends upon one's capacity to acquire progressively more adequate behavior patterns. It also depends upon the richness of the environment in terms of stimulation and opportunity to learn.

Factors Affecting Learning

Since the child is constantly doing something, he is constantly learning something. The conditions about him, the events that happen to him or about him, the attitudes and behaviors of others toward him, and many other aspects of his daily milieu all conspire to determine what he learns. But subjective, or "inner," factors also play a vital role as conditions of learning.

Many of the factors within the individual which affect learning are discussed in other connections. Mental capacity, for instance, is described in Chapter 9 as a fundamental condition of learning. The child's capacity to acquire new levels of functioning controls his learning at any particular point in his development. In other words, an individual must be ready to learn. This readiness level, as we noted above, results largely from both the biological maturation of the physical structure and the functioning of that structure.

Previous Learning

As mentioned earlier, a fundamental factor that determines not only what but how well or how rapidly the child learns in a given situation is "what he already knows." In the words of Gagné (1965):

> The child who is learning to tie his shoelaces does not begin this learning "from scratch"; he already knows how to hold the laces, how to loop one over the other, how to tighten a loop and so on. The child who learns to call the mailman "Mr. Wells" also does not begin without some prior capabilities: he already knows how to imitate the words "Mister" and "Wells," among other things. The theme is the same with more complex learning. The student who learns to multiply natural numbers has already acquired many capabilities, including adding and counting and recognizing numerals and drawing them with a pencil. The student who is learning how to write clear

descriptive paragraphs already knows how to write sentences and to choose words. [p. 21]

The parent or the teacher who is concerned with providing a child with optimal conditions for further learning must obviously use as his guide the child's already acquired capabilities. The child can learn only what he is "ready" (able) to learn in terms of his level of maturation *and* what he already knows or has learned to do. He is not "ready" to learn trigonometry if he has not yet mastered the operations of simple arithmetic.

Motivation

The problem of motivation is an extremely complex and involved subject, far too complicated for adequate treatment here. Our purpose therefore is simply to touch upon a few broad aspects of motivation that seem particularly pertinent to the matter of increasing individual functional effectiveness.

In connection with the discussion of the relation between the learner's present capabilities and new learnings, the factors of *interest* and *challenge* are of crucial importance. Clearly, there must be a "felt need," a desire on the child's part, to learn the new material or to acquire a new level of ability. If the new learning task does not have a basis for its achievement in the child's present capabilities, he will be perplexed, frustrated, and discouraged rather than motivated with a desire to achieve the new learning. On the other hand, new material must be new enough to be challenging, not boring.

Relevance

A somewhat related motivational factor is personal relevance. If the material to be learned, or the tasks to be engaged in, are to have value in promoting personal effectiveness, they must have real relevance to and be consistent with the child's cognitive-emotional structure, including his self-image. Lecky (1951) discussed the principle of self-consistency as follows:

> According to self-consistency, the mind is a unit, an organized system of ideas. All of the ideas which belong to the system must seem to be consistent with one another. The center or nucleus of the mind is the individual's idea or conception of himself. If a new idea seems to be consistent with the ideas already present in the system, and particularly with the individual's conception of himself, it is accepted and assimilated easily. If it seems to be inconsistent, however, it meets with resistance and is likely to be rejected. This resistance is a natural phenomenon, it is essential for the maintenance of individuality. [p. 246]

The nature of the child's "mind," in the sense in which it was used in the above quotation, of course, varies greatly among children. It is true that preadolescent boys generally have a strong need to regard themselves and to be regarded by others as "manly." Sex typing, by the time children reach the age of 8 or 9 years, has been very effective in establishing an image of manliness in the minds of boys, as well as a general idealized cultural stereotype of the attractive female in the minds of girls. But self-images vary widely from one subculture to another, from one occupational group to another, and from one social class to another. A boy in a lower-class family whose father, and perhaps other adult males who play prominent roles in his life, are engaged in work requiring physical strength, courage, and skill—for example, in the operation of heavy machines—gets a very different view of what is manly than does a boy in a middle or upper-class home whose father is engaged in a high-prestige profession or business. Likewise, what a girl develops as her image of the appropriate or desirable feminine role is determined very largely by the models she lives with and associates with but modified in various ways by what she sees on television or the motion picture screen or what she reads.

With such wide differences in experiential background, what is self-consistent for one child in the way of subject matter to be learned or school activities and interest might be anything but self-consistent for another. What is regarded as "sissyish" by one boy might be quite consistent with another boy's conception of manliness.

Also, in our rapidly changing society, the whole picture of sex typing is probably changing. Such factors as the women's liberation movement and the more common entrance of women into occupations and activities formerly regarded as men's will tend to break up sex-role stereotypes and to make for less clearly defined sex models for children to follow. Some signs of confusion of sex-role images seem even now to be in evidence.

Motivation to learn, of course, is often stimulated by external conditions. Interest, for example, a subjective factor so vital to school learning, often depends to a large extent upon the nature of the material to be learned, the objects to be examined and manipulated, and other physical facilities and surroundings provided by the school. Certainly the little boy's concept of manliness has its origin in the models of manhood about him and the portrayals of manly acts he is exposed to through the mass media. Our present purpose is to center attention more directly and specifically upon the external, or environmental, conditions of learning.

Environmental Stimulation

Our basic assumption has been that all development comes about through the interaction of organism and environment. Activity in response to environmental stimulation is an outcome of such interaction. Since changes in the level of one's functioning result directly from functioning, and since functioning (activity) is basically a matter of responding to the stimuli, internal and external, that impinge upon one's sense receptors, the vital importance of stimulation—its quality and appropriateness as well as its adequacy—becomes clearly apparent.

Only in recent years has the importance of stimulation to development in general become an area of special concern and active research by psychologists. The earlier assumption was that the development of mentality, during infancy and early childhood, particularly, along with the development of the organism in general, was purely a matter of maturation. This assumption was especially apparent in the prevailing theories of mental development during the first quarter of the present century. It is pointed out in Chapter 8 that intelligence had been generally thought of as a single, general ability factor that was fixed by heredity and impervious to environmental influences.

As is explained in Chapter 8, the first real challenge to this point of view came during the 1930s with the publication of the research findings of the Iowa Child Welfare Research Station concerning the influence of nursery school attendance upon children's tested IQ's. The main implication of these studies was the importance of the factor of variable environmental stimulation in mental development. The controversy among students of intelligence provoked by the Iowa findings finally led to the only tenable position regarding the factors of mental development, namely, the interaction point of view. Mental development, in the sense of the acquisition of new functional capabilities, results from the interaction between organism and environment. Thus, optimal learning, from the beginning, requires optimal stimulation (Hunt, 1961, p. 263).

In the recent past a great deal of research activity has been concerned with the importance of environmental stimulation upon learning achievement in infancy, particularly. In this exciting area much is being discovered about the capacity of the infant to learn that was unheard of a few years ago.

Early Institution Environment

Studies made during the early 1940s of the development of children who were cared for as infants in orphanages and other institutions provided what appeared to be substantial evidence of the importance of access to and full contact with the "culture" from the beginning of extra-uterine life. These studies (Bowlby, 1940; Goldfarb, 1943, 1944, 1945; Spitz, 1945; Spitz and Wolf, 1946; Brodbeck and Irwin, 1946) generally revealed a seriously retarding effect of the institution environment upon psychological development. Spitz (1945), for example, found that the measured developmental quotients (DQ's) of an orphanage group dropped from 130–140 at 2 months of age to an average of 76 after 4 months in the institution, while a control group of home-reared infants with the same range of initial DQ's maintained the level through the 4-month period.

Spitz's studies, along with the other contemporary investigations of the effects of institution care, have been severely criticized on various counts, including the lack of rigorous control of variables (Casler, 1961; Orlansky, 1949; Pinneau, 1955). Pinneau, for example, noted specifically that Spitz's data did not support the conclusions and interpretations he placed upon them.

Dennis and Najarian (1957) conducted a study in Lebanon which in certain respects was comparable to the Spitz (1945) study. These experimenters concluded that their data with respect to behavioral development in the institution environment showed no effect during the first 2 months of life, but there was marked retardation during the age period of 3–12 months.

The newborn infant has very limited—if existing—visual ability to perceive objects and persons *as such*. He also almost completely lacks responsiveness to social stimuli. These observations are pertinent in relation to the Spitz study as well as to that of Dennis and Najarian. On the basis of such observations it seems reasonable to conclude that with normal infant handling and adequate physical care, and with the usual tactual and kinesthetic stimulation that babies receive, special kinds of stimuli from the external environment are relatively unimportant to functional development during the early days of life.

But developmental change in infancy is very rapid. As the baby's sensorimotor and perceptual abilities emerge and develop, and as his affiliative need arises, the external environment—particularly its social aspects—becomes increasingly important to his continued cognitive and affective development. Dennis concluded that the relatively unstimulating environment of the foundling home, or the *Creche* of Lebanon, provided no opportunity for the infants to learn to perform the tasks or react effectively to the situations presented to them in the developmental test. Hence, their poor showing and low DQ's during infancy beyond age 3 months.

Adequate and appropriate stimulation is essential to optimal development from the very beginning. Many of the more recent observers of infant behavior have stressed the importance to the newborn, especially, of the stimulation he gets from maternal handling and holding, particularly from close skin-to-skin contact (Brody, 1956; Escalona, 1953; Frank, 1957; Montagu, 1953; Wolff, 1959). Mirsky (in Escalona, 1953), for example, wrote: "In the earliest stages, an infant's security is a matter of skin contact and of the kinesthetic sensations of being held and supported" (p. 29). Frank (1957) views the "tactile-cutaneous processes" as an extremely important communication facility, particularly for the young infant. "The skin is the outer boundary, the envelope which contains the human organism and provides its earliest and most elemental mode of communication" (p. 211). Frank further stated:

> babies and children especially require these [tactual] contacts to recover from acute disturbances. Prolonged deprivation of such tactual contacts and soothings may establish in the baby persistent emotional or affective responses to the world, since his initial biological reactions to threat have not been allayed and hence may become chronic. [p. 220]

In discussions of the importance of tactile and kinesthetic stimulation during infancy little mention is made of their specific relations to learning or cognitive development. However, the theoretical question remains of whether or to what extent stimulation during childhood is a factor affecting the maturation of the bodily structure underlying functional capacity or whether the factor is merely a matter of the relative abundance of learning opportunities, as Dennis prefers to believe. The bulk of the evidence suggests that under conditions of extreme stimulus deprivation some irreversible retardation in development may result, but there is no doubt that, in a general sense, stimulation is a prime condition for learning as well as for other aspects of development.

There has also been some discussion in the psychological literature as to whether extensive intellectual stimulation during the early years of childhood might have deleterious effects, such as frustration resulting in negative attitudes, learning inhibitions, and overall psychosocial maladjustment. Fowler (1962a) summarized the literature concerned with this question. He found much expression of opinion on the matter but little research evidence. On the basis of available evidence and in terms of his own experience in teaching a 2-year-old to read, however, Fowler (1962b) came to the conclusion that the risk is minimal and that there is "promise of considerable success with other young children, given further refinement of techniques and method."

Cultural "Techniques" and Cognitive Development

In a provocative article published in the *American Psychologist* (1964, *19*, 1–15) Bruner discusses another important aspect of outside influence, the culture, as an important interacting factor in cognitive development. He states:

> the development of human intellectual functioning from infancy to such perfection as it may reach is shaped by a series of technological advances in the use of the mind. Growth depends upon the mastery of techniques and cannot be understood without reference to such mastery. These techniques are not, in the main, inventions of the individuals who are "growing up," they are rather skills transmitted with varying efficiency and success by the culture—language being a prime example. [p. 1]

Bruner goes on to point out that "techniques" such as language provide growing individuals with effective means of representing in a meaningful way "the recurrent features of the complex environments in which they live." Thinking, the major process of cognitive development (learning), is a process of selectively representing objects and events not immediately present to the senses and then examining them, categorizing them, recombining them, and otherwise manipulating them, and thus coming to know and better understand them. Thus the "culture" encompasses the exciting features of a changing, stimulating environment and at the same time provides the growing individual with the "techniques" for constructing models of the various features of the environment. "Cognitive growth, then, is in a major way from the outside in, as well as from the inside out" (p. 1).

Bruner then, taking his cue from an article by Washburn and Howell (1960), suggests the probable effects of such processes of individual development upon the evolutionary development of cognitive ability in mankind. He stated that "the principal change in man over a long period of years—perhaps 500,000—has been allopathic rather than autopathic. That is to say, he has linked himself with new external implementation systems"—systems that amplify human motor capacities (tools), that amplify sensory capacities (instruments of magnification, for example), and amplifiers of human capacity to think methodically and logically (language systems, theory, explanation).

> Any implement system to be effective, must produce an appropriate internal counterpart, an appropriate skill necessary for organizing sensorimotor acts, for organizing percepts, and for organizing our implement systems. These internal skills, represented genetically as capacities, are slowly selected in evolution. In the deepest sense, then, man can be described as a species that has become specialized by the use of technological implements. His selection and survival have depended upon a morphology and a set of capacities that could be linked with the allopathic devices that have made his later evolution possible. We move, perceive, and think in a fashion that depends upon techniques rather than upon wired-in arrangements in our nervous systems. [Bruner, 1964, Pp. 1–2]

The Nature of the Learning Processes

"Not only has man wanted to learn, but often his curiosity has impelled him to try to learn *how* he learns" (Bigge, 1964, p. 3). To learn the "how" of learning is a difficult and involved problem. Human functioning is multifaceted, and since learning is functional change resulting from functioning, there are, in a sense, as many kinds of learning as there are kinds of activities in which human beings engage. Nevertheless, because of man's curiosity about the fundamental nature of learning, certain individuals through the ages have speculated and experimented and thus developed explanatory ideas. During the past three hundred years many of these speculations have been formulated into theoretical proposals designed to account for at least some of the facts of learning. Because of the extreme complexity of the problem, however, these theories generally leave much yet to be explained.

The various currently held learning theories can be grouped very roughly into two main categories, each representing a fundamentally different point of view in psychology. One is the so-called objective, or behavioristic, point of view; the other is the relativistic, mentalistic, or cognitive point of view.

From the first point of view, the phenomena to be observed and measured are behavior patterns, functions of the organism in response to stimuli of external or internal origin. This basic concept, the *stimulus-response relationship*, is symbolized by the simple formula S→R. From the mentalistic point of view, the basic phenomena of psychology are of quite a different order. They are conscious experiences, or responses to stimuli, rather than objectively observable acts. Ausubel (Anderson and Ausubel, 1965) draws a sharp contrast between these two viewpoints:

> Like the behavioristic position from which it was derived, the neobehavioristic view focuses on publicly observable responses and their environmental instigators and reinforcers as the proper objects of investigation in psychology. Consciousness is regarded as a "mentalistic" concept that is both highly resistive to scientific inquiry and not very pertinent to the real purposes of psychology as a science; it is considered an epiphenomenon that is important neither in its own right nor as a determinant of behavior. Furthermore, say the neobehaviorists, it cannot be reliably (objectively) observed and is so extremely idiosyncratic as to render virtually impossible the kinds of categorization necessary for making scientific generalizations.
>
> Exponents of the cognitive viewpoint, on the other hand, take precisely the opposite theoretical stance. Using perception as their model they regard differentiated and clearly articulated conscious experience (for example, knowing, meaning, understanding) as providing the most significant data for a science of psychology. [pp. 3–4]

It should be emphasized that we are here comparing two very general *classes* of approaches and points of view about learning and that within each of these classes are different specific conceptions of the nature of the learning process. Hence the specific terms used by different theorists here roughly classed together are, only in a very broad sense, equivalent in meaning. Terms such as "behavioristic," "neobehavioristic," "objective," "associationistic," and "stimulus-response" characterize in a very general way a number of different specific points of view, but they have in common, however, a more empirical, mechanistic, and absolutistic way of viewing human behavior. On the other hand, the second group tends to be more pragmatic and relativistic, being labeled by terms such as "mentalistic," "cognitive," and "Gestalt field," which are not univocal but are used by different students of learning with different shades of meaning. The term "mentalistic," for example, is more frequently used by adherents of the so-called objective school in referring to the contrasting theoretical position, whereas the term "cognitive" is most frequently used by the adherents of the position themselves in referring to their own viewpoint.

As a general rule, neither the neobehaviorists nor the cognitive psychologists are particularly concerned with the structure-function relationship, which is an integrating concept throughout this book. The adherents of the objective school are intent, rather, upon establishing cause-and-effect relations between objective happenings as symbolized by the S→R formula, whereas the cognitive people are concerned with the structure of consciousness and with the activities and manipulations within the cognitive field itself that constitute meaning and "coming to know."

Each in his own way, however, both the neobehaviorist and the mentalist, of necessity, deal with the individual-environment relation. As Bigge (1964) points out:

> The term *interaction* is commonly used in describing the person-environment process through which reality is perceived. Both families of psychology use the term but define it in sharply different ways. Whereas S→R association theorists mean the *alternating reaction* of organism, then of environment, Gestalt-field psychologists always imply that the interaction of a person and his environment are *simultaneous* and *mutual*—both mutually participate at the same time. [pp. 74–75]

The objectivist is much more specific and atomistic in his references to the environment. He speaks of stimuli, and his objective is to identify direct connections between specific stimuli, or forms of energy, and discrete reactions. However, the present tendency is somewhat more often to use "stimulus situation" and "moral behavior," thus recognizing the complexity of the behavior-interaction process (Bigge, 1964, p. 60).

The cognitive-field psychologist, on the other hand, is more likely to see the environment in less specific and more relativistic terms. The cognitive field varies from moment to moment. It includes every aspect of the momentary situation—even the behaving individual himself—which, at the moment, plays a part in influencing behavior. The individual, from this point of view, is not seen simply as one end of an acting and reacting bipolar system (S→R relationship) but rather as an integral aspect of the cognitive field.

Earlier Objective Theories

The problem in connection with learning theory is that of conceptualizing the essential nature of the changes—that is, the variations, the complications, the elaborations that take place in the functioning person— largely as a consequence of his own activity. We shall first examine some of the more prominent theories of the objective school of thought.

"Trial and Error" Learning

E. L. Thorndike, one of the earliest American learning theorists, began publishing his work on learning (the associative processes) in animals in 1898. In Thorndike's thinking, learning is a matter of substituting effective or satisfying responses to stimulating situations for responses that do not produce satisfying results. For example, a hungry animal in a new situation will perform many ineffective acts in response to the total stimulating situation. Eventually it will, by chance, hit upon the act that will make food available to it. According to Thorndike's theory, the "bond" between the response that brought relief from hunger and the stimulus is strengthened. Learning has taken place. A "connection" is established between the situation and the response. The effective response from that time on, in that and similar situations, will tend to be substituted for the ineffective ones. This is trial-and-error learning, and Thorndike believed it to be the basic process in all learning (see Fig. 5.1).

It will be noted in Figure 5.1 that two sorts of stimuli are involved in trial-and-error learning: the internal stimulus (the hunger) and the stimuli, mainly visual, which arise from the various objective features of the situation and to which the animal has been responding differentially. The former, the internal stimulus of hunger, is referred to as the *drive*, the motivating factor that keeps the animal active until he chances to make the response that is instrumental in bringing satisfaction. Motivation brings about activity, which consists of random "seeking" responses to the various aspects of the situation and which is necessary if learning is to take place. Learning thus consists of forming connections (bonds) between specific stimuli and specific responses.

Thorndike's Laws of Learning

As an elaboration of his theory and based upon his observations and experimentation, Thorndike (1912) formulated his well-known laws of learning. Among his primary laws are the following:

1. The law of exercise. "Other things being equal, exercise strengthens the bond between stimulus and response" (p. 95). By the same principle, the lack of exercise of a connection tends to weaken it. This law, of course,

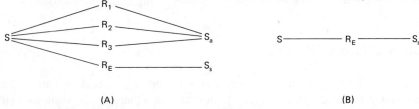

(A)   (B)

Figure 5.1   "Trial and error" learning
   A. A hungry cat is placed in a cage, but within sight and smell of food (S)—a strange situation for the cat. Being highly motivated it responds to the situation in a random manner—claws at the bars (R_1), tries to squeeze between the bars (R_2), bites at the confining walls (R_3). The result is a continuing "annoying state of affairs" (S_a).
   In its random biting behavior the cat chances to bite at the wooden latch of the door of the cage (R_E). The door opens and the cat gets to the food, thus bringing about a "satisfying state of affairs" (S_s).
   B. With additional trials, random behavior is eliminated. Only the successful response, R_E, remains. A bond is thus formed between the situation, S, and biting the latch (R_E). The cat has learned a means of escape. (after Thorndike, 1924)

is universally taken for granted and is implicit in all efforts of rote memorization.

2. The law of effect. Again, in Thorndike's words, when a "modifiable" connection is being made "between an S and an R and being accompanied or followed by a satisfying state of affairs man responds, other things being equal, by an increase in the strength of that connection. To a connection similar, save that an *annoying* state of affairs goes with or follows it, man responds, other things being equal, by a decrease in the strength of the connection" (p. 172). This law has special significance in connection with current theoretical developments discussed later in this chapter.

3. The law of readiness. This law is concerned with the physiological functioning of the nervous system and its conductive units. Thorndike assumed that when an S→R connection is formed, a conduction unit, consisting of a specific set of neurons and their synapses, is established. These conduction units vary in degree of readiness to function according to the particular situation: *"for a conduction unit ready to conduct, to do so is satisfying, and for it not to do so is annoying"* (p. 127).

Thorndike and his followers in theory regarded this conceptualized process of establishing S→R bonds through the stamping-in effects of "drive reduction" and the stamping-out effects of unsatisfying or painful responses as the prototype of all learning.

The Conditioned Response

From the work of Pavlov (1927), the famous Russian physiologist, came the concept of the conditioned reflex. A conditioned reflex is a unit of behavior which can be elicited by a previously inadequate (neutral) stimulus. The learning process in which this substitute stimulus becomes "connected" to the response is called conditioning. This process is as follows: the neutral stimulus is paired with an adequate stimulus—one that already has the capacity to elicit a particular response. In a series of joint occurrences of these two stimuli (the originally inadequate one slightly preceding in time the adequate one), the inadequate stimulus becomes functionally connected with (conditioned to) the response. The learning, in this case, is the acquisition of a substitute stimulus rather than a substitute response, as in Thorndike's formulation. Conditioned-response learning is diagramed in Figure 5.2.

Many experiments in conditioning have been conducted with both human and animal subjects, thus establishing it as an important learning process. Attempts have been made to expand the concept to explain all learning. Conditioned-response theory quite soon became a rival to the trial-and-error, or connectionist, point of view that Thorndike developed.

Modifications and Extensions of Basic Concepts

Clearly, both trial-and-error learning and conditioning are importantly involved in functional change. Neither theory by itself, however, has

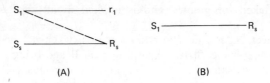

(A)   (B)

Figure 5.2   The conditioned response
   A. S$_s$ (nipple in infant's mouth) is the adequate stimulus to sucking and saliva secretion (R$_s$). S$_1$ (sight of the bottle), in the beginning, is a neutral stimulus to the feeding responses, eliciting perhaps only passive viewing behavior. S$_1$ always precedes slightly in time S$_s$ (nipple in mouth). The two stimuli soon become associated in the infant's food-taking experience.
   B. S$_1$ becomes a "conditioned" (adequate) stimulus to sucking, saliva flow, etc. (R$_s$).

been found adequate to account for all forms of learning. Each of them specifies conditions essential to certain forms of learning, but neither accounted for or explained the basic nature of the learning process. The quest continued, therefore, for more adequate theoretical models.

All of the so-called associationistic, or connectionistic, theories and viewpoints that have been developed since the time of Thorndike and of Pavlov have taken as their starting point the concept of the stimulus-response relationship. They differ mainly with respect to the specific aspect of the process that is regarded as crucial in establishing the connection between the stimulus and the response. Some theorists have found it necessary to postulate certain conditions, or intervening variables, within the S→R sequence to account for the fixation of the bond; others have seen no such need.

Behaviorism

John B. Watson, "the behaviorist" (1928), regarded Pavlov's simple formulation of the conditioned reflex as a sufficient basis for explaining all learning. He simply generalized and expanded the concept by adopting Thorndike's law of associative shifting, which states that it is possible to *"get any response of which a learner is capable associated with any situation to which he is sensitive"* (Thorndike, 1913, p. 15).

Contiguous Conditioning

Edwin R. Guthrie (1952) is strictly an S→R learning theorist, but he views the S→R situation in quite a different way than do other students of conditioning. In his thinking, the objective, measurable stimulus and the outcome—the conditioned response or act that follows—are not the crucial elements in the associative, or learning, process. Rather, the elemental movements that *constitute* the response in the usual sense and the stimuli produced by or inherent in those movements become connected by association. This simultaneous contiguity between movement and movement-produced stimuli in a single occurrence, according to Guthrie, results in a conditioned response. Guthrie's one law of learning is: "A combination of stimuli which has *accompanied* a movement will on its recurrence tend to be followed by that movement" (1952, p. 23). In an earlier paper Guthrie also stated that "a stimulus pattern gains its full associative strength on the occasion of its first pairing with a response" (1942, p. 30). He thus saw no need for such concepts as reinforcement or drive reduction to explain learning.

The Biological Adaptation Theory

One of the most influential theorists, particularly during the 1930s, was Clark L. Hull. More than any of his predecessors, Hull worked consistently toward a completely comprehensive formulation of the learning process. His theory is basically S→R conditioning. In contrast to Guthrie's principle of simultaneous contiguity, Hull assigned great importance to what happens during the brief interval between stimulus and response. He spelled out in considerable detail these happenings and the integrating elements involved, as he envisaged them, as "intervening variables," and he postulated a series of laws that defined the roles of these variables in the learning process.

Hull's (1943) formulation, however, is characterized particularly by his concept of reinforcement. He viewed a drive arising from a state of organic need as an indication that the conditions of survival for the organism are not being adequately met. When such a need, with its drive stimuli, develops, the organism becomes active, and when a particular act alleviates the need, that act tends to be stamped in as a biological adaptation of the organism. Thus, Hull theorized that all learning, whether of the conditioned-response order or the Thorndikian trial-and-error habit formation, might be explained in terms of a process of reinforcement from biological adaptation.

Operant Conditioning, the Currently Prevailing Objective Theory

Under the leadership of B. F. Skinner, a vigorous movement is currently underway among "objective" psychologists in the experimental study of learning. The underlying theory in this work is known as operant conditioning (Skinner, 1938, 1953, 1957, 1958, 1959; Staats, 1957, 1961, 1964; Staats and Staats, 1959, 1962). Reinforcement is also fundamental to this point of view. The unique feature of the operant conditioning theory, however, is that reinforcement comes not between the stimulus and response and *not* simultaneously with the response, as in the case of Guthrie's theory of contiguity, but *following* the response. Staats and Staats (1963) state this concept of reinforcement as follows:

> When certain stimuli closely follow a certain behavior they increase the probability of that behavior occurring again in the future. Stimuli that serve

this function are called positive reinforcers, S^{R+}. Other stimuli increase the probability of behavior occurring again when their *removal* closely follows that behavior. These stimuli are called negative reinforcers, S^{R-}. [pp. 47–48; italics added]

This type of conditioning is called operant because in order for the learner to get a reward he must *do* something. It is his act that is rewarded (reinforced). In classical conditioning, by contrast, the learner remains relatively passive.

The Concept of Reinforcement

The idea of the reinforcement following the response was first enunciated and studied by Thorndike (the law of effect, 1913). This idea has been elaborated and refined, however, by Skinner and his collaborators. The concept of the "feedback" is used to explain the operation of the reinforcer.

A common example of operant learning is seen in the behavior of a young infant who awakens hungry from his nap. The condition of hunger motivates much overt activity. He kicks, squirms, thrashes about with his arms, sucks his fist (which finds its way into his mouth), and begins to cry lustily. As a result of his crying he is immediately fed. Crying, then, is the successful (instrumental) response bringing relief from hunger, which relief is a satisfying stimulus closely following the crying response. Crying when hungry is thus reinforced, and the probabilities of the infant's crying when hungry thereafter are increased. He has learned a *habit*. Figure 5.3 is a schematic representation of the operant-conditioning process.

The reinforcing stimulus in the foregoing example was *intrinsic* in the situation. The natural outcome of drive reduction was the satisfaction of hunger. This was the primary reinforcer. There are, of course, other sorts of reinforcers, both positive and negative. In experimental work in learning, the experimenter can arbitrarily introduce various rewards for a correct

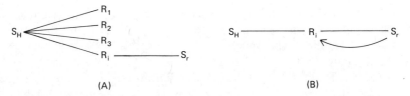

(A)   (B)

Figure 5.3 Operant conditioning.
　　　A. S_H represents the stressful condition of hunger in the infant. He becomes restless, awakens, kicks, thrashes about, vocalizes, makes suckling movements, etc. (R_1, R_2, R_3, etc.) He then makes his discomfort known through lusty crying (R_i). Crying is the instrumental response which brings relief and satisfaction (S_r). He is taken up, comforted, fed.
　　　B. The satisfaction, S_r, immediately following crying thus becomes a strong "reinforcer" for crying to bring relief from discomfort.

response. Punishments which can be avoided only by the correct response are also in the nature of primary reinforcers because the rewards are made direct consequences of the instrumental act. By their nature rewards are either pleasant and satisfying or unpleasant. An electric shock, for example, is naturally painful to the animal; a piece of candy or a colorful trinket is immediately pleasant to the child.

Secondary Reinforcement

Other stimuli which are associated in time and are contiguous with the performance of the correct (instrumental) response and its primary reinforcement may quickly become conditioned (secondary) reinforcers. Such acquired reinforcers have become very important in learning theory as intervening variables. There are, of course, inherent in any learning situation extraneous stimuli that are potential conditioned reinforcers. Noises connected with the training box in animal experimentation may quickly acquire reinforcing value with respect to the instrumental response and thus become crucial factors in the acquisition and "shaping" of behavior. Skinner (1959) found that conditioned reinforcers were important facilitating factors in the establishment of new behavior patterns in pigeons.

In the course of a child's experience, as he interacts with his parents and others, he acquires many conditioned reinforcers that are of extreme importance in shaping his social behavior and his personal development. The sight of his mother and the sounds she makes are paired with natural reinforcers to the responses he is learning. As a young infant he clings to his mother as part of the total pattern of nursing behavior which is instrumental to his experience of satisfaction and comfort (primary reinforcer). As he nurses he gazes into his mother's face and hears her voice. He also experiences olfactory, tactile, and kinesthetic stimulation, all of which become part and parcel of his experience of comfort and satisfaction. They thus become conditioned reinforcers to his clinging "attachment" to his mother. During the first 12 to 15 months of the child's life this attachment to his mother is an important factor in his emotional development.

Research in Operant Conditioning

Operant conditioning concepts and procedures lend themselves readily to precise mechanical regulation. Through early experimentation, largely with animal subjects, the basic principles of operant conditioning as formulated by Skinner in 1938, and others, have been established. As a consequence much interest has been generated in this approach to the study of learning. Recent work has more frequently involved human subjects. Many neobehavioristically inclined students of psychology have been attracted by the apparent ease with which the experimental variables and procedures involved in operant work can be placed under rigid mechanical control.

Currently the operant-conditioning approach is being used in the experimental modification of behavior in a wide variety of human subjects. It is particularly adaptable to learning experiments with infants and young children because with them stimulus controls and procedures other than those built into the experimental apparatus are very difficult to impose. Hence, a greatly increased interest in the learning capabilities of infants and very young children has recently developed (Bijou, 1957; Brackbill, 1958; Rheingold, Gewirtz, and Ross, 1959; Simmons and Lipsitt, 1961; J. S. Watson, 1966, 1967; Kagan, 1963, 1964, 1972).

Exceptional children are also being studied by use of operant-learning techniques. Some of these studies have been concerned with the experimental evaluation of variations in stimulus controls (Bijou and Orlando, 1965; Ellis, Barnett, and Pryer, 1960). D. M. Baer (1962a, 1962b) and others have applied these approaches to the treatment of child problems such as thumb-sucking.

In general, wide interest has developed in the operant-conditioning point of view, particularly in its potential application to practical problems. Skinner (1938, 1953, 1957, 1958, 1959) has led out in demonstrating as well as proposing practical applications of his procedures. He believes that "programmed" instruction, with reinforcements spaced properly to make them contingent upon the desired behavior in the schoolroom setting, could result in greatly increased effectiveness in teaching.

D. M. Baer (1962b) and Bijou and Baer (1963) particularly have applied operant principles to problems of social learning and the modification of social behavior patterns in children. They have developed both laboratory (experimental) techniques and field-experimental methods of behavior modification through the control of stimulus consequences. Baer (1962b), by means of a mechanized, talking puppet, demonstrated the use of attention and approval as social reinforcers. He also found wide individual differences in the effectiveness of these two classes of social stimuli as reinforcers.

Bijou and Baer (1963) even more strongly emphasized the importance of individuality among children at the preschool level and the different kinds of social reinforcements which have, in the children's past, operated in the development of their social behavior patterns and problems. These authors point out that through the careful and continuous observation of a child with a particular behavior problem it is possible to note the various stimulus situations in which the objectionable behavior occurs, and particularly its *stimulus consequence* in each instance. Then by controlling and modifying the consequences (reinforcements) of the behavior, the behavior itself is controlled and modified. The most effective consequences which reinforced these undesirable patterns, they found, were the reactions of others, such as their attention, their approval or disapproval, their support and affection. Bijou and Baer briefly describe an example:

> This program has been applied to a case in which the child crawled rather than walked almost all of every morning. It was observed that the teachers

responded to crawling with a great deal of attention and support, with a view toward improving the child's "security." When this was stopped, and the reinforcement shifted to the child's "upright" behavior, the crawling weakened greatly within a few days and was largely replaced by upright behaviors of standing, walking, running, etc. Reversal of the contingencies to the old pattern reversed this outcome; reinstatement of the new contingencies again produced the new, desirable pattern. The result generalized well to the child's home environment, where the parents used similar contingencies (demonstrated for them in the nursery school) to maintain the upright behavior. [1963, pp. 227–228]

Bijou and Baer also found that other behavior problems such as excessive crying, overdependence, aggression, and inattention could be successfully treated through this method of social reinforcement control.

A lively interest is also developing in verbal behavior as an area of operant-learning research (Rheingold, Gewirtz, and Ross, 1959; Skinner, 1957; Staats, 1961; Staats and Staats, 1959, 1962). This research area gives promise of considerable practical significance.

Neobehaviorism and the Problem of Meaning

One of the most intriguing problems connected with human learning is the problem of meaning. That one thing comes to mean or represent another in human experience is a matter of common knowledge and observation. This process of signification is involved in functional modification at all levels. Even in the simplest forms of learning such as the conditioned reflex, one stimulus, or sign, comes to mean, represent, or become a substitute for another. In perceptual learning, which is more fully dealt with in a later section, the mere smell of an orange, for example, becomes a sign which represents the complete pattern of sense experiences that have become associated with the object (orange). The smell—or the sight or the feel—of the object alone becomes sufficient as a basis for the act of categorization. The object is immediately placed in the category orange.

In other aspects of human learning, however, the signification process is not so readily understood or so easily described. In the psychology of language, for example, the phenomenon of meaning involves learned reactions more complex than any we have so far discussed. In our study of these more complex learning processes the concept of mediation (the role of intervening variables) becomes especially important.

As we have seen, the problem of mediation has long been a central one in learning theory. Hull (1943), in the elaboration of his point of view, postulated a set of laws in which he defined the intervening variables essential to learning. In the more recent operant-conditioning formulations, secondary reinforcement and the concept of feedback are regarded as important mediating factors.

On the basis of a great deal of animal experimentation, the *fact* of a mediating process in learning is rather generally accepted. As to the nature of this process—the mechanism itself—there is considerable disagreement. Mowrer (1960a, 1960b), Staats and Staats (1959), and others hold that meaning and representational reactions constitute the mediating factor. Skinner and others of his school, on the other hand, rather generally reject the concept of meaning, or understanding, insisting that mediation involves nothing more than vocal or subvocal responses of an associative nature, and that ultimately what is involved is simple shaping of behavior through the mediation of conditioned reinforcers.

The Nature and Role of Punishment

The explanation of the role of punishment, or negative reinforcement, in learning in terms of a mediating process has been particularly difficult. Thorndike in his original formulation stated the matter simply and in terms of human experience: "When a modifiable connection between a situation and a response . . . is made and is accompanied or followed by an annoying state of affairs, its [the connection's] strength is decreased" (1913, p. 4).

In his discussion of the punishment aspect of Thorndike's original theory, Mowrer (1960a) wrote as follows:

> For at least two decades now, it has been clear that the "negative" half of the law (Law of Effect), in its more molecular aspects, was miscast. . . .
> Whatever learning may be in its "forward," position phase, it became increasingly clear that unlearning, or "*punishment*," *is not* a simple matter of obliterating, stamping out stimulus-response "bonds." But a more declarative approach to the negative side of learning could not occur until at least certain forms of that type of learning known as conditioning were taken into account. [pp. 23–24]

As Mowrer pointed out, Thorndike himself came seriously to question the punishment side of his theory. He came to the conclusion, after a long series of learning experiments, that punishment itself was *not* instrumental in eliminating wrong responses. This reversal of his position, in the face of much accumulated evidence that punishment was indeed an effective factor in learning, clearly suggested a need for a more adequate account of the operation of mediating variables in "negative" learning. Most writers in discussing the role of punishment in learning have little to say regarding the mediation process involved. Conditioned aversive stimuli—negative reinforcers—however, are mentioned in explanations of the effects of punishment. Staats and Staats (1963), for example, explain that the stimuli produced by the punished act "acquire negative reinforcing properties, that is, elicit conditioned aversive, or *anxiety* responses" (p. 98, italics added). In effect, the punished act produces its own negative conditioned reinforcers (anxiety). Thus, "stopping the response, or responding in another manner is strengthened" (p. 98).

The rather common spanking-the-hand training procedure used by parents with their toddler-age children exemplifies the indirect effects of punishment. The child reaches for a breakable object on the shelf. As he reaches, the parent says "No, no" and then spanks the reaching hand. The natural response to the pain from the spanking is the fear-withdrawal reaction. The proprioceptive stimuli produced by the act of reaching *and* the "No, no"—both of which slightly precede the pain—immediately become conditioned stimuli to the fear naturally elicited by the pain stimulus. On future occasions, as soon as the child begins to reach for the forbidden object or hears the command "No, no," he becomes afraid or anxious and inhibits the act which gives rise to the fear. "This notion of punishment is obviously and importantly different from Thorndike's conception of bond erasure; and it is now generally conceded that punishment achieves its inhibitory effect, not by the direct stamping out of S—R bonds, but by the intermediation of fear" (Mowrer, 1960a, p. 25). Figure 5.4 is a representation of this view of the role of punishment in learning.

Response-produced Stimuli and the Feedback

The inadequacy of earlier learning theory in explaining the "how" of reinforcement effects generally has been pointed out by Mowrer. In rather close agreement with the view of Staats and Staats mentioned above, Mowrer (1960a) postulated an intermediary emotional variable in the learning process which constitutes a modification of the concept of secondary reinforcement, and which, he feels, more adequately deals with this problem. In Mowrer's thinking, the effective conditioned reinforcers are the *response-produced stimuli*—proprioceptive, tactile, and other—that are inherent in the instrumental response itself. As we saw in the case of punishment, these stimuli, since they occur *with* the act, precede the reward—the satisfying (or dissatisfying) state of affairs which that instrumental act brings about. Through the repeated pairing of these response-produced stimuli with the reward, the former become conditioned to the affective component of the outcome. In the case of positive reinforcement, the emotional component is hope; in the case of negative reinforcement it is fear. Mowrer's contention is that these emotions of hope and fear, which become connected through the process of conditioning to response-produced stimuli, or stimuli inherent in the response itself, are the effective conditioned reinforcers. In effect, the response itself acquires the function of signaling, through hope or fear, its own outcome. Figure 5.5 is designed to represent the establishment and operation of secondary reinforcement in terms of Mowrer's theory. An important point which Mowrer emphasizes is that only the involuntary, autonomically controlled reflexive responses involved in emotion, such as changes in heartbeat rate, constriction of the blood vessels, endocrine secretions, and so forth, rather than voluntary acts, are subject to conditioning in the classical sense.

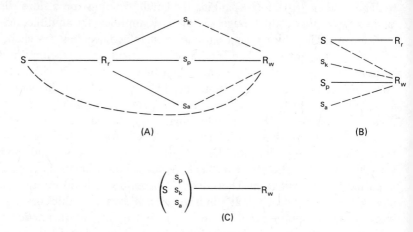

Figure 5.4 Avoidance learning.
    A. The toddler finds himself within reach of an attractive object, a vase on a shelf (S). R_r is his natural response of reaching and grasping the vase. S_K represents the accompanying kinesthetic and tactual stimuli from reaching. S_a is the auditory stimulus, "No! No!," and S_p is the pain from the slap on the hand—all "response produced" stimuli. Pain (S_p), of course, is especially significant biologically and thus elicits the fear-withdrawal-avoidance response, R_W, which is immediately associated with the total situation, S.
    B. The learning process involved is one of classical conditioning as illustrated. The situation (S), (along with S_K, S_a, etc.) becomes a conditioned stimulus to fear-avoidance (R_W).
    C. The "response produced" stimuli become aspects of the total situation which is one to be avoided. "No! No!" now signals the avoidance response, R_W.

To further illustrate Mowrer's formulation in terms of functional development in children we shall reillustrate the infant in the process of acquiring an emotional attachment to his mother. As the infant nurses at his mother's breast he clings to her as part of the total pattern of nursing behavior. This pattern of behavior (R_i in Figure 5.5) is accompanied by and gives rise to a great deal of sensory stimulation, much of which is response-produced. The infant's muscles involved in clinging, grasping, and so forth, and in sucking and other motor components of the total pattern, produce proprioceptive stimuli (s, s, s). These stimuli begin slightly in advance of the pleasure-producing reward, gratification (S_r). "It is assumed that a part of the total response, R_r, which is produced by S_r, will become conditioned to the stimuli (s, s, s), inherently connected with R_i" (Mowrer 1960b, p. 14). This component of R_r Mowrer calls hope (r_h). The connection between the response-produced stimuli (s, s, s) and the positive *emotion*, hope, thus becomes established. These stimuli come to mean, or signal, hope. The baby's clinging-

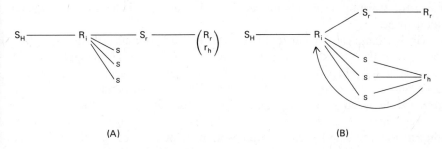

(A)   (B)

Figure 5.5   Secondary reinforcement from response-produced stimuli.

   **A. The hungry infant (S$_H$) begins nursing at his mother's breast (R$_i$),
   R$_i$ is a complex pattern including clinging, grasping behavior. Hence there
   are many response-produced stimuli (sss). These precede slightly
   the reward (S$_r$). S$_r$, in turn, elicits the "total response" (satisfaction,
   comfort), R$_r$, of which r$_h$, the affective reaction of "hope," is hypothesized
   as a component.**

   **B. In association with S$_r$, stimuli sss become functionally connected with
   r$_h$, "the conditionable component of R$_r$." These stimuli can now "signal"
   hope and thus become secondary (conditioned) reinforcers to the nursing, clinging pattern, R$_i$, which produces them. (adapted from Mowrer
   1960b, p. 14)**

nursing activity has its built-in reinforcers. The stimuli that are inherently a
part of the response pattern itself quickly become conditioned stimuli that
elicit the same positive, hopeful reaction that gratification (S$_r$) originally
elicited. These conditioned, response-produced stimuli are the effective secondary reinforcers.

The Mentalistic or Cognitive Viewpoint

         During the first quarter of the present century, the thinking of
American psychologists about learning was predominantly associationistic
(behavioristic) in character. As we have seen, a number of competing theoretical positions were developed, but they were all primarily concerned with
the problem of explaining the nature of the process by which stimuli become
connected with responses. In 1924 Kurt Koffka's book *Growth of the Mind*
was published in English and was introduced to American psychologists. A
year later Kohler's book *Mentality of Apes* appeared. These two books introduced into the United States for the first time a view of learning that was in
direct contrast to the theories current at the time.

   From this "new" point of view learning, that is, change in functional
adequacy, occurs as a result of *insight*—seeing into the total complex and
integrated situation—on the part of the learner rather than as the result of
his going "through the laborious processes of stamping out incorrect responses
and stamping in correct ones" (Hilgard, 1956, p. 222). The principle of

insightful learning was demonstrated in the learning behavior of Kohler's chimpanzees.

Good examples of what looks like "insightful" animal learning are often observed in the "tricks" of the common grey squirrel as he manages to gain access to food which has been specially arranged for birds, and presumed to be out of the squirrel's reach. The birdfeeder is suspended from a wire stretched between two trees. The squirrel, "seeing" the relations between the tree, the wire, and the feeder, climbs the tree, manages to walk on, or cling to the wire, and perhaps after a number of failures, finally makes his way to the vicinity of the feeder. He then scrambles to the baffle above the food container, and eventually to the food. He presumably has gotten insight into the total gestalt and has learned a way to obtain food.

Kohler's and Koffka's attacks were specifically leveled at Thorndike's view of learning. As Hilgard pointed out, the idea of insight was not a new idea. "It was a return to a conception laymen had never abandoned" (p. 224). The influence of this "Gestalt" viewpoint in psychology was a timely and useful one.

A central concept in the Gestalt point of view concerns the essential nature of the situation in which the individual acts and learns. Insightful perception in relation to the total situation was an area of great emphasis. We shall return to the topic of perception in a later section.

The "Cognitive Field"

The name of Kurt Lewin is inseparably connected with the "field" theory of learning in the United States. Lewin was a German and a member of the Gestalt group. His thinking concerning learning, therefore, grew out of the Gestalt tradition. His theoretical position is usually referred to as the field-theoretical position.

A basic feature of field theory is its relativistic emphasis, as contrasted with the absolutistic and mechanistic view of behavior and its changes held by the objectivists. "The basic principle of relativism is that nothing is perceivable or conceivable as a thing-in-itself. Rather, everything is perceived or conceived in relation to other things" (Bigge, 1964, p. 176). Learning is regarded as a process by which the learner gains insights into a situation in terms of the relations among its various aspects and component parts. Lewin conceptualized the psychological field as a space in which the individual moves or lives psychologically. It is one's "life space" at the moment and it can include anything in one's life which one has anything to do with— people, objects, ideas, memories. The life space is influenced and conditioned by what is ordinarily referred to as the environment—physical, social, and so on—but life space and environment are not identical. Life space can change independently of environment. It is conceived, in a sense, to account for the psychological situation from moment to moment (Hilgard, 1956).

Cognitive Structure

The life space is structured in varying degrees. An unstructured region in that structure represents an unresolved problem situation or a lack of understanding. As learning progresses, the total space becomes more and more structured in the sense of being more highly differentiated, and paths connect the various subregions. This means, simply, that increased learning enables us to see facts more clearly in their interrelations. Facility in problem-solving increases as structuring progresses. One learns only in relation to his cognitive structure. New facts are related to and integrated with already understood and interrelated facts; they are integrated into the cognitive structure.

As activities are repeated, they are learned. The cognitive structure is thus changed. The need-tension system is also changed as goals are attained. The relative attractiveness (valence) of goals and values also change with attainment.

Individual Cognitive Structure and Meaning

The difficulty of dealing with the problem of meaning in behavioristic terms was previously noted. Since the concept of meaning is basically mentalistic in nature, it presents no special problem for the cognitive-field theorist. In his discussion of the concept Ausubel explained the acquisition of meaning:

> According to the cognitive structure view, meaning is an idiosyncratic phenomenological product of a meaningful learning process in which the potential meaning inherent in symbols and sets of symbols become converted into differentiated cognitive content within a given individual. Potential meaning thus becomes converted into phenomenological meaning when a particular individual, employing a meaningful learning set, incorporates a *potentially* meaningful sign or proposition within his cognitive structure.
>
> New meanings are therefore acquired when potentially meaningful symbols, concepts and propositions are related to and incorporated within the cognitive structure on a nonarbitrary, substantive basis. [Anderson and Ausubel, 1965, pp. 67–68]

Ausubel further clarifies this concept in another article:

> The human nervous system as a data processing and storing mechanism is regarded as so constructed that new ideas and information can be meaningfully learned and retained only to the extent that appropriately relevant and typically more inclusive concepts or propositions are already available to serve a subsuming role or provide ideational anchorage. [Anderson and Ausubel, 1965, p. 8]

Accordingly, as a new item is discovered or a new idea is introduced in the experience of an individual, its meaning comes to him as it is "seen" by him in relation to his already meaningfully organized body of knowledge. Learning (cognition, coming to know) is indeed the proliferation of meaning. New systems of information, new ideas, new ways of relating to the outside world, thus become meaningful, or are learned, as the learner "subsumes" them into his "cognitive structure."

Reception Learning

Ausubel (1963) has been concerned with the kind of learning that generally takes place in the school room, namely, *reception learning*— the progressive acquisition and retention of new subject matter—and particularly with the problem of how such learning can be facilitated. His research in this area has been based

> on the premise that the existing cognitive structure, that is, an individual's organization, stability, and clarity of knowledge in a particular subject-matter field at any given time, is the principle factor influencing learning and retention of new material. If existing cognitive structure is clear, stable, and suitably organized, it facilitates the learning and retention of new subject matter. If it is unstable, ambiguous, disorganized, or chaotically organized, it inhibits learning and retention. Hence it is largely by strengthening relevant aspects of cognitive structure that new learning and retention can be facilitated. When we deliberately attempt to influence cognitive structure so as to maximize meaningful learning and retention, we come to the heart of the educative process. [p. 217]

But, as he points out, reception learning is not simply a passive receiving of what is poured in:

> simply because in reception (expository) learning the content of what is to be learned is *presented* rather than discovered, we cannot assume that it is a purely passive phenomenon. It is still necessary for the learner to *relate* the new material to relevant established ideas in his own cognitive structure to apprehend in what ways it is similar to, and different from, related concepts and propositions; to translate it into a *personal* frame of reference consonant with his idiosyncratic experience and vocabulary; and often to formulate what is for him a completely new idea requiring much reorganization of existing knowledge. [1965, p. 9]

The concern of the cognitive-field theorists, then, primarily is with what transpires psychologically. Cognitive-field theory has real relevance and significance, therefore, in relation to the problem of understanding the nature

Figure 5.6   Reception learning.

of developmental change in mental functioning. Functional adequacy generally is very largely a result of learning. One's level of functional effectiveness is raised as one gradually subsumes new facts, new ideas, and new abilities to the stable, organized elements of one's cognitive structure.

Perceptual Learning

The function of perceiving—the process of coming to know of conditions external to as well as within the organism by means of the sense organs—is the primary cognitive (mental) process. It is important at the outset to point out that perceptual knowledge is a highly personal matter; there is considerable variation in perceived reality among individuals and from time to time in the same individual (Berlyne, 1957). Many studies have shown that perceiving is influenced to a remarkable degree by motivational factors, personal experiences, and the overall psychological organization (personality) of the perceiver (Henle, 1955; Prentice, 1961; Witkin, Lewis, Hartzman, Meissner, and Wabner, 1954).

Individual variation in perception is not surprising, however, with the realization that perceptual ability, like human abilities generally, is not innate but is developed through living experience. The newborn infant possesses a full complement of sense organs which for the most part are ready to function, but there is no real evidence for actual perception on the part of the neonate.[1] Ausubel (1958) draws the distinction between preperceptual behavior and perception:

> Since all perceptual and cognitive phenomena deal by definition with the *contents of processes of awareness*, they cannot always be inferred from overt behavior. Behavior, for example, frequently reflects the organism's capacity for experiencing differentially the differential properties of stimuli. Nevertheless, since all differential psychological experience preceding or accompanying behavior does *not* necessarily involve a content or process of awareness, we cannot always consider it perceptual or cognitive in nature. Several examples may help to elucidate this distinction.
>
> We have previously shown that a young infant will follow a patch of color moving across a multi-colored background, will cease crying when he hears his mother's footsteps, and will respond differentially to various verbal commands. Conditioning experiments during infancy also show that the child is able to "discriminate" between different sizes, colors, and shapes of objects and between pitches of sound. Does this constitute evidence of genuine perception, memory, discrimination, and understanding of representational symbols?
>
> . . . it is reasonable to suppose that much of the sensory experience impinging on the infant is too diffuse, disorganized, and uninterpretable to constitute the raw material of perception and cognition, despite evidence of differential response to stimulation. Clear and meaningful contents of awareness presupposes some minimal interpretation of incoming sensory data in the light of an existing ideational framework. In the first few months of life not only is the experiential basis for this framework lacking, but the necessary neuroanatomic and neurophysiologic substrate for cortical functioning is also absent. [pp. 544–545]

Not only must the "neuroanatomic and neurophysiologic substrate" necessary for perceptual functioning be developed in the infant through further maturation, but he must also gradually develop his *percepts* through learning from sensory experience.

Recent research in infancy has made important contributions to our understanding of infant capabilities (Bower, 1966, 1970; Charlesworth, 1966, 1968; Horowitz, 1968; Lipsitt, 1966; J. S. Watson, 1966, Kagan, 1972). The evidence suggests that by the end of the first 4 to 6 months certain aspects of visual perception are demonstrable in infants. Eleanor Gibson (1963), for example, found that 6-month-old babies could not be prevailed upon to crawl across an area covered with heavy glass arranged so as to give the illusion of a drop off to a dangerous depth. The infants apparently perceived the drop-off, or "cliff," effect, which meant danger to them. How this learning

---

[1] The question of neonatal perception, of course, revolves around the meaning with which the term is used. In this text, the meaning is as follows: Perception "is the awareness, or the process of becoming aware, of extraorganic objects or relations or qualities by means of sensory processes and under the influence of set and of prior experience" (English and English, 1958, p. 387).

takes place, is again a matter of theory. Some students of perception place emphasis upon the stimulus input rather than upon the S→R relationship. From this point of view the structuring or categorizing of information furnished by the senses is the essential aspect of the perceiving function. Bruner (1957) describes the process as follows:

> Perception involves an act of categorization. Put in terms of antecedent and subsequent conditions from which we make our inferences, we stimulate an organism with some appropriate input and he responds by referring the input to some class of things or events. "That is an orange," he states. . . . On the basis of certain defining or critical attributes in the input which are usually called cues, although they should be called clues, there is a selective placing of the input in one category or identity rather than another. The category need not be elaborate: "a sound," "a touch," "a pain," are examples of categorized inputs. [p. 225]
>
> A second feature of perception, beyond its seemingly categorical and referential nature is that it can be described as varyingly veridical [true to reality]. This is what has classically been called the "representative function" of perception: what is perceived is somehow a representation of the external world. [p. 228]

Imitation, Observational Learning

Generally, the term "perceptual learning" refers to the categorizing process as described by Bruner (1957). We come to know the outside world and its complexities through our senses, and we categorize and organize that knowledge and subsume it into our ever-changing cognitive structure. But our knowing and categorizing are not limited to objects and situations. Often involved in these situations are other individuals and their acts and performances, and we not only *categorize* these observed performances in a cognitive sense, but in many instances we are also able, upon observing them, to reproduce those performances ourselves. This is also perceptual learning— learning in which we acquire new performance patterns by observing them in other individuals. Bandura (1962) describes this process as *response learning*

> in which subjects combine fractional responses into relatively complex novel patterns solely by observing the performances of social models often without any opportunity to perform the model's behavior in the exposure setting, and without any reinforcers delivered immediately either to the models or to the observers. Here, clearly, social cues constitute an indispensable aspect of the learning process. [pp. 216–217]

Bandura also pointed out that in present-day theorizing about observational learning the many commonly observed instances of the direct and immediate taking on of "novel" performances simply by seeing them being performed by others are generally ignored.

Operant Conditioning in Relation to Observational Learning

The accounts of learning from models, however, are usually limited to descriptions of changes in overt behavior such as the learning and perfection of motor skills. In such instances, of course, the principles of operant conditioning are particularly applicable (Bijou and Baer, 1961; Skinner, 1953). Skinner's principle of *shaping* through successive approximations is assumed to be the underlying process in the acquisition of all novel performances. Accordingly, this process always involves the positive reinforcement of any element or aspect of the desired new pattern which the learner chances to approximate, while all other components of his behavior are left unrewarded. As practice continues, the standards of closeness of the approximations to the model performance which are required for reward are gradually raised until, through successive trials, the perfected pattern is achieved. Skinner's (1953) generalized description of the shaping process is as follows:

> Operant conditioning shapes behavior as a sculptor shapes a lump of clay. Although at points the sculpture seems to have produced an entirely novel object, we can always follow the process back to the original undifferentiated lump, and we can make the successive stages by which we return to this condition as small as we wish. At no point does anything emerge which is very different from what preceded it. The final product seems to have a special unity or integrity of design, but we cannot find a point at which this suddenly appears. In the same sense, an operant is not something which appears full blown in the behavior of the organism. It is the result of a continuous shaping process. [p. 91]

This is clearly the process by which skilled performances are acquired and perfected. The model performance is carefully observed, and continued efforts are made to approximate that model, with each partial success receiving its reinforcement. Performance learning is often rewarded directly by the one who is setting the model, but the sense of achievement is also a rewarding consequence. Skill learning is facilitated by differential reinforcement. This, of course, is learning by observation (imitation).

But, as Bandura insists, there are many instances in common experience of direct and immediate learning through imitation which do not involve the principle of successive approximations. "It is doubtful . . . if many of the responses that almost all members of our society exhibit would ever be acquired if social training proceeded solely by the method of successive approximations" (Bandura and Walters, 1963, p. 3). Young children readily pick up simple acts which they observe in adults. In their play they often go through rather elaborate performances in imitation of the daily routine activities of their parents.

In such direct acquisition of response patterns through imitation—"solely by observing the performance"—there is no implication of an instinctive ability independent of previous learning. The imitator in these instances, through much previous practice and experience in diverse areas of motor activity, has become proficient in a great many *fractional* responses which he is capable of combining and structuring into any of a variety of possible performance patterns. The novel aspect of the imitated performance is the *patterning* of fractional responses. It should also be pointed out that these immediately imitated performances are not usually, if ever, exact copies in every respect and detail of the observed performances. They may, in fact, be very inaccurate copies.

Nevertheless, the reality of direct learning of overt performance patterns through the observation of models has been clearly demonstrated (Bandura, 1962; Bandura, Ross, and Ross, 1961; Bandura and Walters, 1963), and this should be taken into account in any adequate theory of social learning. But it is equally true, as we have seen, that generally in the learning and the perfection of motor skills there is much shaping of behavior through continued practice resulting in successive approximations with reinforcements. It is quite obvious that the skills of the concert violinist or the expert typist, for example, could never be acquired solely by the observation of models, no matter how expert and precise these models may be.

The influence of models is a very important factor in many areas of functional development, and particularly in social learning and personality development.

Summary

Our primary objective throughout this book is to understand as clearly as possible the nature of the processes of development in the human individual. Our interest in learning theory, therefore, stems from this developmental orientation. Learning is a process of developmental change, and the term subsumes all aspects and degrees of change in the functioning of the individual that are not the result of biological developmental processes, that is, those which come about through exercise, activity, and experience (functioning).

The infant is born with a certain repertory of reflexes that are simple, ready-to-function responses to specific stimulations. No learning is necessary for the baby's performance of stimulus-response sequences, although the muscles involved undoubtedly have been strengthened through exercise prior to birth.

From the initial moment on, a complicated learning process is underway, a process too complex and involved to be explained in terms of any single simple formula. In the first place, each separate movement in each reflex produces its indigenous stimulation, thus meeting Guthrie's (1952) simultaneous-contiguity requirement for strengthening the S→R connection. The reflex patterns themselves through exercise become strengthened and "shaped" (Ferster and Skinner, 1957) for more effectiveness. Out of many random responses in the total pattern certain ones are selected (Thorndike's trial and error) and receive primary reinforcement. New stimuli, both extraneous and response-produced, become associated, through "classical" conditioning, with gratification and thus become secondary reinforcers.

When semisolid and solid foods are introduced to the child, he must learn through trial and error, and shaping, the way to manage food in his mouth. Food likes and dislikes are acquired through various processes of association. Throughout the developmental period the child learns to eat and to like many foods. He acquires skill in the use of tableware, and through verbal association and practice he learns the many niceties of social behavior at the dinner table. All of these learnings require not just one but a number of theoretical formulations to account for them adequately.

What is true of early functional development is even more obviously true of the acquisition of the "higher" forms of functioning. If one could trace the course of development in detail of the many motor, intellectual, and social skills that make for adequate and effectual personal functioning in our complex society, one would undoubtedly find all of the theories of learning exemplified.

CHAPTER 6

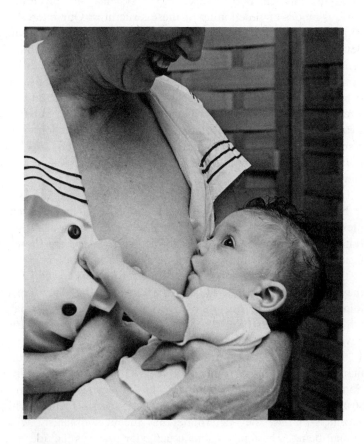

The Vital Functions

Functional Development

Our focus now shifts from the growth and maturation of structure—the physical body and its organ systems—to the development of the various modes of functioning of these structures. Our interest is the behavior of the whole individual, in his integrated individual functioning and how it develops. We again note that in reality we are but shifting to a different aspect of the same phenomenon. Living tissue begins to function as it is formed, and in the manner for which it is fitted, by nature. This exercise of function contributes to the change of the structure—to an increase in its adequacy and strength. Thus we see that structure permits function, but function develops structure. Learning, or developmental change in functioning is, of course, a result of exercise of the function. Growth, maturation, and learning, all may thus be regarded as but different aspects of the same process of developmental change in the living organism.

The functional aspect of development, like the structural, involves change in both quantity and quality. The human being is characterized by great complexity and endless variation of functions. Three general categories of human functioning, however, may be identified. First there are those general bodily functions which obviously are not confined to human beings, but are common to the higher forms of animal life. We refer to them as *vital functions* because they are essential to individual life and well-being. They are basically physiological in nature, but they involve rather complex behavioral patterns which vary widely with the specific nature of the organism, its level of development, and its environmental conditions.

A second category of functional patterns includes those that characterize mankind and set him apart from all other life forms. These *phylogenetic* functions develop in conjunction with the biological maturation of the human structure. These are determined by genetic agents (genes) which are species specific—that is, they determine that the new organism will be that of a human being. These phylogenetic behavior patterns include such functions as verbal speech, bipedal locomotion, and symbolic thinking.

Another category of functions are those that are *ontogenetic*[1] in nature. They develop through sustained individual exercise and practice. These are the special learned skills and abilities, both motor and cognitive, that are superimposed upon the basic universal human functions.

We should again remember that functional development is the behavioral aspect of individual structural development. In all instances the genetic factor designs the general character of that progressive change and sets

---

[1] The two terms *phylogeny* and *ontogeny* refer, respectively, to the developmental history of a particular species or group and to the development of a particular member of the species. A *phylogenetic trait* is one common to and characteristic of a particular species, while an *ontogenetic trait* or achievement is one *not* common to or generally characteristic of the species, but is differentially developed by the individual from his own potentiality and effort.

the sequence and the limits within which functional development takes place. The environmental factor, in interaction with genetic endowment, determines the direction, rate, and magnitude of functionability.

The General Nature of Vital Functions

In this chapter we examine certain of the most basic human functions; we say they are most basic because they are what the organism does to maintain life and health. Of the many vital functions, we shall here limit our discussion to the following three:

1. The ingestion of food
2. The elimination of waste
3. Activity, sleep, and rest

These three are given special consideration for several reasons. They are the means of satisfying fundamental biological needs which regularly and persistently intrude themselves into the affairs of the moment. Because of this intrusiveness there is much personal and social concern with the regulation of these functions. The problems of child care and socialization which give parents most concern have to do with the regulation and modification of these vital functions. Also because of their intrusiveness and their persistent demands for attention, these functions bear an important relation to the so-called higher behavioral and cognitive functions and their development.

The Eating Function

The acquisition of the ability to take and to manage foods of different qualities and consistencies and to deal with eating situations of increasing complexity is a developmental task of childhood. Eating is a vital function of the total organism and is essential to the satisfaction of a biological need. The specific nature of the need itself changes with age, as do the physiological patterns and the overt behavioral patterns of the eating function.

The Development of Nutriture

Birth is without doubt the most severe crisis generally encountered by the individual in his life from conception to death. In prenatal existence the food supply to the developing organism is constant and comes without effort. This food is elemental in nature, consisting of such essentials as calcium, phosphorus, and iron, and enters the blood stream of the fetus directly. At birth the way in which the infant gets his food suddenly becomes quite different: he must now take food into his own digestive system. For the first time his lungs become filled with air. The prenatal detour route of the blood for oxygen, from the fetal heart to the placenta and back to the heart, suddenly is closed and the life route for oxygen to the baby's lungs becomes functional. The necessary process of oxidation of tissue-building materials is, in turn, caused by the presence of food in the stomach. The infant's food supply must enter his mouth.

Thus, the event of birth marks the beginning of the development of the independent food-taking function. During these first few days (the neonatal period) the transition must be made from fetal existence to that of an independent organism. The whole digestive system, which thus far has not functioned, is immature and capable only of managing food in a highly simplified form. Thus in this first stage in the "development of nutriture" the infant is dependent upon a food substance from his mother, *colostrium*. This substance is especially adapted to the newborn's needs and his ability to utilize it.

Development resumes immediately, however, and continues at a rapid rate. The infant soon reaches a second developmental stage, that of *liquid feeding*. The products of the maternal body no longer sufficiently supply his need for nutrients. He must now utilize foods from other sources, a stage that marks a real achievement in nutritive development. The supplementary foods at this stage, however, must be in liquid form. Orange juice and other fluids furnish the infant's expanded needs for vitamins and minerals.

At this point in his development the baby is very inept at taking in liquids by any means other than sucking. His tongue tends to push from his mouth any material that may be introduced by cup or spoon. He must be carefully helped to achieve a measure of competence in sucking into his system sufficient amounts of supplementary foods during the *third* developmental stage.

The introduction of *semisolid foods*, such as cereals and pureed vegetables and fruits, marks a *fourth stage* in the development of the food-taking function. By this time the baby's ability to manage food in his mouth without spitting it out is improving. However, he is still unable to handle anything but soft and uniformly consistent foods free from chunks.

The *fifth developmental stage* that has been tentatively identified is characterized by the baby's ability to tolerate *chopped foods*. This transitional period begins with the infant's inability to deal with foods that are not at least partially liquified and ends with the more mature stage in which he can, by himself, masticate and prepare solid foods for digestion. In this period the food still must be partially broken down from the solid state, because the child has an inadequate complement of teeth and has not yet learned to use them to chew. This fifth stage has been called the "premature" stage in the development of the nutriture. The ability to manage solid foods marks a *sixth stage*.

Rand, Sweeny, and Vincent (1953) summarize the situation with respect to this aspect of functional development:

> These six stages of maturation of the nutriture, it is believed, can be detected by observing the concurrent maturational changes of oral activities which are related to the ingestion of food. The *rooting* and *sucking reflexes*, present *at birth*, are the infant's mechanism for finding and taking fluids into the mouth. Some time later, a *biting reflex and salivation* appear. The infant bites and begins drooling. This behavior is an indicator for introducing pureed food. The next oral indicator includes two kinds of behavior which appear close together, namely, *the ability to swallow small lumps and destructive biting.* Now the infant can manage chopped foods. The final oral indicator is *chewing*, by which the infant is able to reduce food to a consistency which can be swallowed. This requires at least the first molars. By this time the child can eat solid, non-simplified adult foods. With this concept one can apply these and any other nutritive indicators to a better understanding of the reasons underlying individual differences which are not explained by age alone. It seems quite possible that a child can be five years old chronologically and yet immature nutritionally. [p. 177]

The development of the eating function, then, is a matter of maturation and learning. The nutriture, which is the changing capacity of the organism to ingest and to utilize foods of various qualitative characteristics, is tied in its development to the maturation of the bodily structures involved. But beyond the sucking and swallowing reflexes and the physiological processes of digestion, which are functional at birth, the child must *learn* to eat. He must learn to take liquids from the spoon and the cup. He must learn to manage semiliquids and lumps and later solid foods. All through the course of development, from the level of simple sucking and swallowing to the ability to tolerate, then relish, the great variety of tastes, smells, and textures of adult foods and to manipulate the socially prescribed implements of eating in a manner acceptable to society, *learning* is an essential aspect of development.

Oral Pleasure

The rooting, sucking, and swallowing reflexes are built-in mechanisms for getting the life-maintaining fluid foods into the stomach of the newborn infant. In recent decades *psychoanalytic theory* has invested this process of food ingestion with far greater significance than the mere satisfaction of nutritional needs. Much is made of the importance of oral gratification to psychological development.

The psychoanalytic theory of "stages" in psychosexual development, briefly stated, is that through the basic metabolic and other processes in the organism certain tensions are built up. For example, as the supply of nutrients in the body become depleted, tension increases to a point of sheer discomfort. This discomfort is experienced as hunger. The taking of food gives gratification or release from tension. The continual seeking for release from tension and for gratification of all sorts requires energy. Freud called this energy *libido*, or libidinal energy.

In psychoanalytic theory the mouth is regarded as an erogenous zone—a tissue area that gives sensuous pleasure. Observers of infant behavior refer to the passionate quality of the child's thumbsucking and to the persistent continuation of sucking long after his hunger has been satisfied. In times of stress or fatigue, particularly, the child seems to find great relief and gratification in oral activity. The mother naturally senses the comfort and pleasure her baby derives from sucking, and she is usually inclined to facilitate his indulgence and to take empathic delight in the sounds he makes and the playfulness of his oral behavior.

During early infancy, then, the taking of food through nursing at the breast, and the comfort derived from this process, are seen as the totality of the infant's waking life. Release from tension and gratification come from it. With gratification comes pleasure. When tension has mounted feelings of frustration are experienced and anxiety and a sense of insecurity arise.[2]

Specialists in child care, however, long ignored the pleasure aspect of the sucking activity. Their theorizing was confined to the food-taking function of the activity. Thumbsucking was regarded simply as a bad habit that was to be prevented or overcome, not only because of its unhygienic dangers but also because of its possible deleterious effects upon the child's dentition. Parents also tend to become concerned when their children continue to suck their fingers to an age well beyond the period of babyhood. The tendency generally was to disregard the obviously pleasurable quality of oral activity in children and its possible influences upon their emotional and personal development.

The question as to the origin of the pleasure drive in oral activity is one of considerable theoretical importance. According to Freudian theory, oral pleasure is "instinctual" in nature. Another feasible explanation is based on the theory that the pleasure drive to oral activity is an early conditioned (learned) affective response. Since the mouth is "a utilitarian organ subordinate to the hunger drive," the gratification of the hunger drive has primacy, and, with repetition, the pleasure of relief from hunger becomes associated with the oral reflex of sucking. This connection in the infant's

---

[2] One early student of neonatal life (Ribble, 1943) believed that probably a greater source of comfort during early food taking derives from other sense modalities such as skin sensitivity—the close, warm skin-to-skin contact with the mother—than from food ingestion as such. This view more recently has received support from the research of Harlow (1958), Harlow and Zimmerman (1959), Harlow and Harlow (1966), and others. The issue is further discussed in connection with the development of emotionality (Chapter 12).

experience between sucking and pleasure gets repeated reinforcement. The mouth thus becomes "a pleasure organ coordinate with other zones of libidinal satisfaction" (Munroe, 1955, p. 198).

Regardless of the origin of the pleasure aspect of sucking, eating is an important area of human experience. From early infancy oral pleasure joins forces with the hunger drive to insure adequate food intake. The alleviation of hunger through oral activity thus constitutes a main source of gratification and pleasure for the infant. The first stage in the development of the eating function, therefore, is also the first stage in affective development: the *oral stage*.

Furthermore, since nursing is the infant's primary pleasurable contact with the world outside himself, the experience is of great importance to his cognitive development as well. The infant naturally begins to "perceive" at the point of his greatest interest. It is through the various sense modalities that are centered in the oral region that the infant comes to be aware of and to know the world immediately around him. He sees an object; his hand comes in contact with it and he feels its shape and texture; he brings it to his mouth where he tastes it; he smells it. He gradually becomes aware of the differences between his sensory experiences of his own hands and toes and those of objects that are not a part of himself. Oral pleasure is thus an important factor in cognitive development.

Throughout the course of maturation of the nutriture, the pleasures of eating continue to spread from sheer orality and the pleasures of tactile and proprioceptive stimulation to those that are gustatory and olfactory in nature. Social stimuli of various sorts also combine with the rest. Sounds, colors, textures, tastes, aromas, and total Gestalts become pleasurably or unpleasurably associated with eating. Food likes and dislikes are established. The eating situation becomes an important aspect of social living.

Appraising the Developmental Status in Food Taking

Table 6.1 presents a summary of a tentative sequence of stages in the development of the eating function in children arrived at jointly by Dr. Charles G. Jennings and Mary E. Sweeny.[3] The stages appear to meet fairly well the requirements of a series of indicators of developmental progress. The table also suggests tentative age equivalents. These mean ages represent summarizations of clinical observations without benefit of actual records and should, therefore, be regarded as tentative until measures of variability can be established through systematic observation and recording.

To use this sequence of indicators for appraising a child's status in this area of functional development it is necessary either to have access to records

[3] Dr. Jennings was consultant in pediatrics, and Mary Sweeny was for many years assistant director and head of the Physical Growth Department, Merrill-Palmer Institute.

TABLE 6.1   Tentative Progress Indicators of the Development of the Ability to Manage Increasingly Complex Foods and Feeding Situations

Stage	Behavior	Age Expected To Begin
1. Highly specialized food—colostrum, mother's milk	Sucking and swallowing	Birth–1 day
2. Liquid feeding	Sucking and swallowing supplementary liquids by spoon	4 weeks
3. Augmented liquid feeding	Able to swallow pureed foods as easily as milk	13 weeks
4. Infant solids	Capable of reducing lumps by chewing	35 weeks
5. Solids by feeding	Capable of chewing and swallowing table food	14 months
6. Self-feeding	Can feed self with spoon or fork, prefers fingers	24 months
7. Young mature eating	Can serve and feed self	36 months

of diet and descriptions of eating behavior for the particular time in the child's life or to make firsthand observations of eating behavior and inquiries regarding the child's diet and patterns of food intake. Such data may then be referred to the sequences in Table 6.1 and an appropriate age equivalent of the child's level of eating development may be found.

Plotting Developmental Progress

The process of ingesting food, then, is highly complex and involves the whole organism. The process of ingestion changes radically with the maturation of the nutriture, as well as through learning and socialization. In its learned aspects, at least, this function may be regarded as a developmental task, the achievement of which, in its expected adult form, may be marked by identifiable stages.

Figure 6.1 represents the course of Sally's development in the eating function.

A factor that may have had some bearing on Sally's eating behavior and its development is that she was fed and otherwise cared for as an infant under the self-regulation regime. Under the guidance of the pediatrician in charge, a "behavior-day-chart" (so named by Gesell) was kept by the mother. This chart furnished a detailed record of Sally's food intake day by day as well as the exact time of day or night when each feeding occurred during the first eight months of her life. This chart shows that by age sixteen weeks the infant had established for herself a fairly regular three-feeding schedule which corresponded reasonably well with the usual morning-midday-evening eating pattern of our culture. The early stages of the development of Sally's eating function are clearly shown in her behavior-day record.

As in previous plotting of qualitative change, the developmental stages

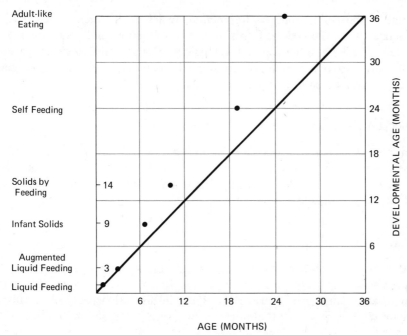

Figure 6.1   The development of the eating function (Sally).

are indicated in Figure 6.1 on the developmental age scale (vertical axis) in each case at a point representing the mean, or expected, age of its appearance. The approximate actual age at which Sally achieved each stage is plotted against the expected age.

At about 1 month of age Sally began to receive supplementary liquids such as cod liver oil and orange juice. At three months of age, as expected, she was getting cereal and pureed vegetables and fruits (augmented liquid stage). From that point on, this child's developmental progress in eating was somewhat advanced. At ten months of age she was eating solid foods, a stage which on the average is not reached until approximately age fourteen months. At age nineteen months Sally was able to feed herself with a spoon like a two-year-old child. When she was two years of age she was almost a full year advanced in the development of her eating behavior, according to the record.

Some Important Factors in the Development of the Food-Taking Function

Although, as we have seen, there are certain more or less biologically based stages of eating development through which children generally pass, there are, nevertheless, certain widely varying factors, some inherent in the child, some environmental, which in interaction may affect the course of development of this particular function and, perhaps more importantly, the total personal development of the child. Some of these factors begin to operate almost from birth and affect the direction and quality of developmental change.

Temperamental Nature

Perhaps the most basic factor is the congenital temperamental nature of the child.[4] The baby with a quiet, contented nature is likely from the beginning to respond differently to early food-taking experiences than the more reactive, restless, or irritable baby.

Early Feeding Experience

A second basic factor, which can be very important in interaction with the baby's nature, is the manner in which food is presented to him, and under what conditions. I. D. Harris (1959), in discussing peculiar reactions of eight- and nine-year-old children who were "not so well adjusted," speculated that these reactions

> could be indicative of a certain type of experience during the early dependency of the child, a period in which the mode of relating to the mother (the first human object) is predominantly by means of oral experience. The mother can be the source of nutriment and pleasure for the infant as he feeds, but she can also be the source of pain, tension, and frustrations. [p. 25]

Thus, the early eating experiences of the infant are potentially very important in establishing attitudes and emotional reactions to the whole food-taking situation and in determining the direction and nature of the development which the eating function takes. It is important, therefore, that babies be fed under conditions which provide affection and security.

> In the development of hunger and feeding behavior, both of which are basic to physical survival, there grow up many conditioned feelings and emotions (closely associated with the feeding situation) which affect the vigor of the hunger drive, the willingness to try new foods, the rejection of certain once-accepted foods, and many things related to food and hunger which do not appear on the surface. As the child grows and widens his social contacts the emotional satisfactions from food or frustrations in the feeding area become extended to objects and relationships which are not always apparent to the observer. Food, generally and specifically, acquires different meanings to different people and to the same person at

[4] This factor receives much fuller attention in Chapter 9.

different times. Thus human relationships play a profound role in maintaining a sound hunger drive and thereby influence food habits. [Breckenridge and Vincent, 1965, p. 123]

Many children's appetites and their general enjoyment of eating are affected by the degree of freedom they are granted or the extent to which they are pressured into eating certain foods and certain amounts. The practice of resorting to spoon feeding the child in order to make sure that he gets the proper amounts of the proper foods long after he is capable of feeding himself makes of the eating function a passive, if not unpleasant, process rather than an active and enjoyable one. The development of this important function in the young child is thus hampered or facilitated by the attitudes and behavior of those who care for him.

The Eliminative Functions

The processes of living and of bodily upkeep require a constant movement of materials through the body. The eating function, including the intake of fluids, brings into the body the supply of nutritive materials. The metabolic processes within the gastrointestinal system subject these materials to complex chemical transformations in which the energy and tissue-building elements are extracted and made ready for assimilation. The remaining useless or injurious end-products must be eliminated from the body.

The processes of separating these waste products from the digestive tract and other tissues of the body and collecting them in readiness for elimination is the work of the organs of excretion—the intestinal tract and the kidneys. The main organs of elimination are the colon, the bladder, the lungs, and the skin.

The Bowel Function and Its Control

The elimination of bodily waste products obviously is necessary for health and well-being. Undigested materials, wastes from the digestive process, bacteria of the digestive tract, and waste salts are eliminated as fecal matter. The amount of fecal elimination, of course, depends upon the nature and amount of food–fluid intake. Liberal amounts of vegetables and fruits provide roughage and increase the amount of fecal elimination.

The peristaltic action of the digestive tract keeps up the movement of materials through the digestive tract. The speed of the peristaltic movements is influenced mainly by the nature of the diet and occasionally by the individual's emotions.

There is no hard and fast rule as to when or how frequently elimination should take place. Ordinarily it occurs once a day at a regular time, but there is much variation in children. "Regularity in a child's pattern of elimination is more important than conformity of his pattern to that of others" (Breck-enridge and Vincent, 1965, p. 129).

The eliminative functions in early infancy are purely passive and reflexive in nature. Voluntary control must await the development of the nervous and muscular structures involved. Studies indicate that it is not until near age eighteen months, on the average, that structural readiness is attained for the achievement of voluntary control of the sphincter. By this time the child walks easily and is aware of and can become interested in the control of his eliminative functions. He also has some language facility to signal his situa-tion and is inclined to imitate those around him. Some time is required, however, for the achievement of perfect control. There are wide individual differences in age at which readiness for eliminative learning is reached and in the length of time required for perfect control. Too frequently parents do not recognize or understand the time factor and exert undue pressure on their child, sometimes with unfortunate results.

The Anal Stage

The second stage in emotional (psychosexual) development, according to psychoanalytic theory, is the *anal stage*. This period corresponds roughly to the second year of the child's life, the period when training for sphincter control is underway. The onset of this period, of course, does not mean the cessation of the activities and satisfactions of the oral period, which tend to continue through life. It means, rather, that in order to conform to social demands, the child must now be attentive to new activities. By this time the child is able to move about and explore his world. His interests in the world around him are expanding, and at the same time new demands are made upon him. For example, society's attitudes toward cleanliness require him to control his bowel and bladder functions.

Since the eliminative functions pertain to and directly involve his own body and its feelings, they are "closer" to him than are any other activities in the sense that they involve tension, release from tension, frustration, and gratification. The attitudes and feelings of those about the child have much to do with the kinds of feelings, reactions, and adjustments he is able to make during this period of concentration upon eliminative activities and the anal area.

The Development of Bladder Control

Urethral sphincter control and its achievement often is a problem for both the child and his parents. The wide variation in the time of readiness for learning is part of the problem. Children who are not yet ready develop-mentally for training are sometimes subjected to pressure or punishment. Often, too, the child, in his efforts to maintain his sense of power, resists all regulations from the outside. Munroe (1955), writing in psychoanalytic terms, clearly portrayed the parent-child interaction problem in relation to the child's personal development:

> Techniques of toilet training and, above all, the mother, are, therefore, of great moment in personality development. The child must give up his narcissistic omnipotence. If he can identify happily with the mother and accept her requirements as his own, the emerging pride in his personal mastery of instinctual impulses can be constructively directed toward socially acceptable regulation. His own sense of achievement is enhanced by parental praise. On the other hand, if he is forced to give up his self-determination out of fear, whether of direct chastisement or severe loss of love, his inner determination tends to develop in opposition to the outside world. The upshot may be anxious effort at compliance, not from shared interest in regulation but from fear of authority. Or there may be defiance instead. Or, most common of all, a mixture of the two. [p. 197]

As a general rule, the bladder eliminative function develops gradually. Sometimes the developmental curve is quite irregular, indicating very erratic performance. This irregularity is probably due more to adult interference than to anything inherent in the process of development.

Tracing Development in Bladder Control

No maturity indicators have been established for evaluating status and tracing progress in the development of the function of bladder control. Table 6.2, however, presents the mean number of "dry nights" achieved by a

TABLE 6.2   Average Dry Nights per Month for Boys and Girls at Different Chronological Ages

Chronological Age Range (Months)	Average Dry Nights per Month	
	Boys (N=49)	Girls (N=43)
26–28	18.2	23.2
29–31	21.0	23.5
32–34	20.6	25.7
35–37	23.9	27.8
38–40	26.5	28.6
41–43	27.5	28.9
44–46	28.5	29.2
47–49	29.2	29.3
50–52	28.6	29.9
53–55	29.1	29.6
56–58	28.4	30.0
59–61	30.0	30.0

group of children, 49 boys and 43 girls, within successive 30-day periods, during the age span of 26 to 61 months. These children were among the subjects of a longitudinal investigation conducted at Merrill-Palmer Institute. The values are highly tentative, since the data were recorded by parents and records were not in every instance complete. The numbers of cases were small and the variability within the groups was wide.

Each *chronological* age for which an "average performance" (mean number of dry nights) was obtained for these children may be taken as the *age equivalent* for that particular level of performance. A tentative developmental-age scale for bladder control is thus derived (Table 6.3). Although these values are tentative, they may be used for an approximate assessment of a child's status in the development of this function. As an example of the use of this scale, whenever a boy is able to achieve 27 dry nights during a 30-day period, according to this scale, he has a "bladder-control age" of 40 months regardless of his actual age. His performance is like the *average* performance of 40-month-old boys.

Figure 6.2 depicts the course of Sally's achievement of urethral sphincter control in terms of the number of dry nights per month at different ages. The point on the chronological-age scale marked by a dot, in each case, is the midpoint of the 30-night period. The upper curve in the figure represents the average course of achievement of the 43 girls described in Table 6.3.

The striking feature of the figure is the wide difference between Sally's

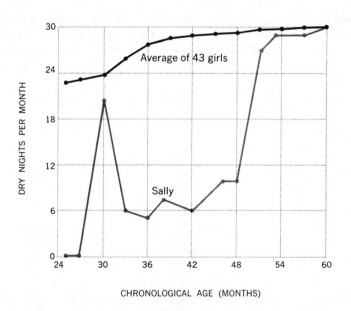

Figure 6.2   The development of overnight bladder control in Sally 695 as compared to the average of a tested group of 43 girls.

TABLE 6.3   Tentative Age Equivalents for Boys and Girls of Mean Number of Dry Nights per Month

Dry Nights per Month	Age Equivalent (Months)	
	Boys (N=49)	Girls (N=43)
18	26	21
19	28	23
20	30	24.5
21	32	26
22	34	27
23	35	28.5
24	36	30
25	37	31.5
26	38	33
27	40	35
28	44	37
29	50	42
30	66	60

curve of bladder-control achievement and the average curve for the group of girls. Sally was almost four years old before she showed any consistent trend to remain dry through the night.

It will be recalled that Sally was reared on the self-regulation regime. The regulation of her eliminative processes as well as her feeding schedule were largely self-initiated rather than imposed upon her from without. According to the record, no "training" of any sort had been initiated at age eighteen months. At age twenty-seven months, although she still wet her bed nightly, Sally had gained good daytime control. Although she was "taken" periodically and was encouraged to indicate her need, no pressure was ever used, and the only reward she received for her successful self-regulation were the words "good girl." Sally's record illustrates dramatically the wide individual variation that must be expected in the achievement of voluntary sphincter control; ultimately, when success is achieved, it may occur rapidly.

In this chapter we have been considering the developmental elaboration of certain specific functions of the living organism that are essential to life and to growth and maturation. These functions, to be sure, are activities. The function of eating, as it develops in the life of the individual, becomes much more than the simple original reflex function of ingesting food. It becomes a complex of learned activities organized into cultural patterns adaptable to the various social situations of modern living in which the partaking of food and drink are involved. The simple eliminative reflexes, likewise, evolve, through the processes of learning, into culturally acceptable activity patterns.

We shall now use the term "activity" in a more generic sense, not with specific reference to patterns associated with a particular organ system but rather with reference to activity as a generalized function of the individual in healthy development.

Activity, Rest, and Sleep

The importance of optimum activity for the developing child is better appreciated when considered in relation to the current emphasis upon the vital role of stimulation in healthy development. Actually, it is the activity resulting from stimulation rather than stimulation itself that is so essential to the realization of inherent potentiality. Activity associated with rest, furthermore, is an important consideration in connection with the care and nurture of growing children.

> Both activity and rest are important because of their relation to nutrition and growth. Muscular activity is important in that it improves circulation and respiration, stimulates appetite, aids digestion, improves muscle tone, thereby fostering good posture and normal elimination, lessens tensions, and increases endurance, strength, and accuracy. The amount and kind of activity satisfactory for a child depends upon his bodily strengths and weaknesses, his general physical health, and his stage of development. [Breckenridge and Vincent, 1965, p. 129]

Balance between Rest and Activity

At any age a proper balance between activity and rest is essential to the individual's well-being. Children in their eagerness for life and experience are inclined to work their bodies constantly during their waking hours. Their need for long hours of rest, in the form of sleep, in comparison with adult need is obvious. Complete rest means complete inactivity and relaxation of the body. Since healthy children while awake are rarely if ever completely inactive, their rest comes largely from change in type of activity. Their relatively short span of interest and their inability, generally, to pursue a given task or maintain a particular line of activity for long are factors of advantage in their bodily economy, for their change of activity relaxes them.

The Problem of the Hyperactive Child

There is, however, no hard and fast line between "healthy" (normal) and pathological levels of activity, lengths of attention span, and tendency to flit from one activity or interest to another. As always, it is a matter of degree on a continuum. In most instances such pathological activity levels are associated with other behavioral irregularities, for example, as subnormal or retarded cognitive functioning. Professional treatment is indicated for children thus afflicted. They are incapable of responding positively to the ordinary school-room programs of regulating rest and activity.

Problems of hyperactivity are most frequently diagnosed as due to brain injury. Clinicians have devised various means for detecting brain damage in overactive children. Some of these are relatively simple, requiring little time to administer. The Bender-Gestalt test is one such device which has proved useful (Bender, 1947). On the other hand, some rather elaborate sets of criteria are used in diagnosis. For example, Strauss (Strauss and Kephart, 1955) has proposed four criteria for detecting the presence of minimal brain damage:

> (1) a history of trauma or inflammatory processes before, during or slightly after birth; (2) slight neurological signs; (3) the existence of immediate family with normal intelligence; (4) the presence of psychological disturbance in perception and conceptual thinking. . . . [p. 173]

The lack of understanding on the part of parents and others who must deal with hyperactive children, presumably with brain injury, appears to be an extremely important contributing factor. This difficulty of understanding is described by Strauss and Kephart (1955):

> we cannot appreciate the problem of the *brain*-injured fully because we cannot fully experience it. We cannot reproduce in ourselves unpatterned behavior and therefore we cannot empathize with the individual who has few patterns. Because our patterns group and regroup themselves constantly and are always in a state of flux, meeting new demands of new situations, we find it impossible to imagine the plight of the individual in whom it is not so. We cannot see what he sees, we cannot feel what he feels, and we cannot follow the processes which bring him to a certain result. To us, his performance seems only bizarre. [p. 214]

There is, however, a danger in assuming such a wide difference between the brain-injured child and the non-brain-injured. In the words of Jane W. Kessler (1966):

> If one thinks this child is so different that it is impossible to empathize with him, then one does not provide the ordinary preparations, explanations and reassurances. Children with known organic brain disease have the same developmental crises as those without. They are even more susceptible to trauma and need more understanding and support. [p. 174]

Granting that it is extremely difficult to "understand" the pathologically overactive and disrupting child, he nevertheless deserves to be treated with respect, and in dealing with him every effort should be made in the way of "explanations and reassurances." Empathy is not completely dependent upon diagnostic understanding. It is a quality to which even the severely disturbed are likely eventually to respond.

Normal Children Also Need Understanding

Emphathetic understanding is also an essential factor in dealing effectively with the problem of achieving an optimal balance between activity and rest among the less disturbed, more "normal" children in the ordinary school situation.

In the primary grades much can be done to maintain such a balance through proper scheduling and management of the sequence of activities. Reading and other sedentary activities or rhythms, including relaxation, can be interspersed with vigorous activity such as dancing or group games. Relative proportions of time that should be spent in different kinds of activities and in activity relaxation, of course, change with age and level development. Furthermore, individuals within the "normal" range, as suggested earlier, differ in their need for activity and rest, as in other aspects of behavior and development. The child who has been temporarily ill, or the naturally less strong and less vigorous child, needs more rest and less strenuous muscular activity.

In this connection a factor which is sometimes overlooked or ignored in elementary school, particularly in the area of physical education, is the fact that children by that time in their lives are individuals with different interests, abilities, and strengths, that they vary widely in inclination, interest, or ability to perform without embarrassment the kinds of activities in which they are expected to participate and the competitive games they are pressured into. These differences among children have, of course, come about because of differing patterns of inherent predispositions and widely contrasting family backgrounds and the ways in which these factors combine and interact (Chapter 14). For some children, because of their particular patterns of individuality, the "gym class" is a veritable nightmare. They do not fit the popular American stereotype of the budding athlete or the "little league" baseball player. The experiences they have in "physical education" under the domination of a well meaning but nonunderstanding instructor can make the difference between a generally happy school experience and one of embarrassment and discouragement. To be placed publicly in a situation of being unable to compete at an acceptable level with his peers is a traumatic experience for the ordinary school-age child. Again, empathetic understanding is called for in dealing with children.

Sleep

Rest and recuperation are most complete in the condition of sleep, the natural response to fatigue. Physiologically, there is in sleep a sharp drop in body temperature and a general depression of organ activity. Blood circulation slows down. Breathing becomes more regular and its tempo is considerably reduced. Because of this general physiological slowdown, less energy is actively expended and more of it is available for growth and maturation.

Psychologically, there is in sleep a diminution or cessation of conscious activity. Munroe (1955) describes the condition as follows:

> The conscious mind is *relatively* inactive, mainly because it is released from its reality-testing functions and from immediate responsibility for the execution of its decisions. The *motorium* is almost entirely excluded from participation in the psychic life, the *seniorium* drastically limited. Thus the inward intellective and affective processes continuously operative have relatively free play without the usual corrective controls of immediate physical and social contacts. [p. 49]

Considerable learning as well as maturation are involved in the development of appropriate sleep-wakefulness patterns in children. In the neonate the pattern is subcortically controlled. Infant fatigue leads to diminution of activity and to sleep. Infant physiological needs bring about an increase in bodily activity and wakefulness. But as the cerebral cortex develops and as the experiences of living accumulate, the child's pattern begins to adapt itself to the daily periods of darkness and relative quiet followed by the light and noise of daytime. He thus gradually adjusts his schedule of sleep and wakefulness to conform to the activity timetable of society. In the words of Breckenridge and Vincent (1965):

> The process of establishing this rhythm, which is easy for some and difficult for others, will depend upon circumstances and the personality of the child. The general requirement, however, is the maintenance of regularity in the timing of the day's activities, including eating, bathing, playing, etc., initiated by the infant's physiologic clock and later tempered by reasonable adaptation of the child to his family situation and the society in which he lives. [p. 130]

This process of adaptation—of learning to regulate one's sleep and wakefulness to the social pattern—with wide individual variations, extends through the period of childhood. As Gesell and his associates point out, even during the elementary school period, bedtime is still a time when the child demands close association and confidential interaction with his parents. Such experiences apparently help the child to "release into sleep." He has not yet completely achieved for himself the ready means of going to sleep at the appropriate time, of staying asleep, and of awakening again according to the schedule of the family. Later, during the period when the child is striving to establish his sense of independence, his resistance to going to sleep is more likely to be a manifestation of his general resistance to external authority.

The amount of sleep a child needs decreases generally with age. Children of the same age have been known to vary widely in the amount of sleep they need. Such factors as health, temperament, emotional make-up, rate of growth, and the general tempo of daily activities have much to do with sleep needs.

Growth in the effectiveness of those patterns of activity that are vital to individual life and well-being are but one facet of functional development. These functions are basically physiological in nature, and therefore, in their early stages especially, they parallel the development of the organs involved. The baby, at first, for example, cannot manage coarse or solid foods because of the immaturity of his organs of ingestion and digestion. As development continues, however, more and more does the total person become involved. The specific patterns of behavior utilized in food taking, of course, might vary greatly in relation to the child's developmental milieu—the culture in which he grows, his parents and others who exercise control over him. But the biological needs that are served and the basic nature of the functions as such are basically the same even though the specific behaviors through which they are carried out are in general extremely varied. These patterns, in any case, are learned as the child cooperates with those who care for him and upon whom the nature of his learning depends. As we have also seen, the attitudes, the feelings, the methods used, and the degree of understanding which characterize those who care for and assist the child during the period of his complete dependency, as well as in later stages, may have profound effects upon his total personal and social development.

Summary

In this chapter we shifted our attention from developmental change in the organism itself (structural change) to developmental change in the *functioning* of the organism. Organismic functioning is clearly a broad and inclusive topic. In fact, it relates closely to the field of psychology, since human behavior is the functioning of the human individual.

We focused upon certain of the *vital* functions—vital in the sense that they are functions essential to the life, health, and optimal development of the individual. These were the food-taking activities, the eliminative functions, and the more general function of maintaining an appropriate balance of activity, rest, and sleep. It was noted that these functions largely involve the whole organism and that they, being vital, are intrusive and insistently demanding of attention. Consequently, the cognitive and emotional life and functioning of the child are involved in their development, and there is much parental and social concern with their regulation.

Since there are specific action patterns involved in carrying out these functions the child must learn, the behavior and the personal qualities of those in whose care and under whose guidance the learning takes place can profoundly affect the child's personal and social development.

CHAPTER 7

Motor
Development

From the moment of birth, and throughout life, the individual is enveloped by, and must cope with, a complex and constantly changing external world—his "environment." Obviously, his most immediate and direct mode of coping with his world of stimulation is by overt body activity. *Motor functioning*, then, is the first and primary mode of responding to the external environment.

The Pervasiveness of Motor Functioning

The totality of the young infant's behavior, insofar as it can be observed and studied directly, is motor in nature, and quite obviously it continues throughout life to be a basic and essential element in most, if not all, human behavior. The vital functions, certain of which were discussed in their broader implications in the preceding chapter, are essentially motor in nature, and their development in the sense of increase in effectiveness and facility is largely motor development—maturation and learning.

As the infant develops, his mental functioning cannot be distinguished as anything separable from his motor behavior, if indeed it is anything different. Tests designed to appraise infant mentality are purely tests of neuromuscular functioning. They can be nothing more. Intelligence during infancy, or at any other level, for that matter, can be evaluated objectively only in terms of what the individual *can do*.

The Swiss psychologist Jean Piaget, in tracing the development of mentality in children, refers to the first eighteen to twenty-four months of life as the "sensorimotor period."[1] During this period the child's activity becomes progressively more complicated, more controlled, and deliberate. Such behavior, of course, can be regarded in its purely motor aspect, but it can also be regarded in its mental, or cognitive, aspect. It seems safe to assume, however, that in all instances of cognition the functioning of physical structure is involved to some degree. Kagan (1971) presents his "concept of schema" as a "representation of an event" on the part of the very young infant which "need not involve an action component" (p. 7). It is postulated as the cognition of an event which is purely "mental." Even here, however, it can be assumed that there is something in the way of an "action component." The process of seeing is not purely passive. Seeing an object or event involves the use of certain postural muscles, muscles of the eye in focusing and accommodation and so on.

The baby's reaching for and grasping an object held before him involves cognitive awareness. Such acts obviously are directed visually and with awareness and intent. The level of the infant's mental development, however, can be judged objectively only in terms of the *outcome*—the quality—of his motor performance.

[1] A review of Piaget's account of mental development is given in Chapter 8.

Infant emotionality, likewise, can be judged only on the basis of overt behavior, and the developmental changes that occur in these areas of functioning can be inferred and traced only on the basis of what the child does.

The primary developmental tasks of the early months and years of a child's life are to gain control of his body and its parts. With the gradual achievement of bodily control comes control of the external environment, which means the ability to move and orient the body with reference to objects and conditions about the individual. Bodily control also makes possible the manipulation of objects—moving them about, experiencing them. The child thus *perceives*. He comes to know the nature of things outside himself. As control of his body is achieved, as he gains manipulative ability, he also gains a sense of adequacy and emotional control.

In later childhood and in adolescence smoothness in bodily control and strength and skill in sports and games have far-reaching influences upon the young person's social and emotional development.

Harold Jones (1946, 1949), in studies of adolescent development, found that boys who were outstanding in strength tended also to be early maturing, taller, heavier, and of mesomorphic build. These same boys were, as a group, also high in popularity and social prestige and were rated as "well adjusted." By contrast, "the ten boys low in strength showed a pronounced tendency toward an asthenic physique, late maturing, poor health, social difficulties and lack of status, feelings of inferiority, and personal maladjustment in other areas" (1946, p. 297). Jones pointed out that relations such as those between strength and motor ability, and reputational and psychological variables were especially striking when extremes were compared. His earlier statistical analyses (1944) of a group of 78 boys portrayed the same relation between physical ability and popularity-social esteem.

In the waning years of life also, motor facility—habits of physical activity and manipulative skills acquired in early life—have much to do with mobility, vitality, and sense of personal adequacy (Cavan, Burgess, Havighurst, and Goldhammer, 1949; Lansing, 1952).

Prenatal Development

As we noted in Chapter 3, complicated modeling of the nervous system is already underway when the embryo is yet only a fraction of an inch in length. Cell differentiation occurs very early in prenatal development. In the stage of the embryo the brain has already begun to take shape; the eye structures are already emerging from already differentiated brain and muscle tissues; the skeletal musculature is being "invaded" by minute fibers from developing nerve cells, and very early these various specialized structures begin to function in an elemental way.

The very first muscular contractions, presumably stimulated from within the tissue itself, are probably so slight as to be microscopic in extent. But this is exercise, and soon muscle tonus and contractility come under sensory and nervous control. Muscles thus begin, almost from the beginning of their existence as such, to "practice" their contractile function. Growth and maturation of structure become interwoven with the development of function through exercise.

Ordinarily, learning is thought of as something that begins during childhood, and of course it is with postnatal learning that we shall be mainly concerned in connection with motor functioning. But for a fuller appreciation of the marvels of human development it is important to examine its origins.

Prenatal Organism–Environment Interaction

It goes without saying that structure must precede the appearance of function (behavior). Sense organs and effector structures must first take form, and the basic elements of the neural mechanism must establish connections between receptors and effectors before there can be any response to stimulation. The nervous system is among the first of the body tissues to begin to differentiate. In fact, its basic structure is already established before the sensory and motor organs are structured. This qualitative kind of development continues long after the receptors and effectors are fully functional. Progressively more intricate interconnections are established, thus providing the basis for the development of more coordinated organismic functioning.

One of the developmental mysteries not yet adequately explained is how these interconnections between receptors and effectors are made—how "the billions of embryonic nerve fibers reach their appropriate destinations in muscles, glands, receptors, and central nervous nuclei and projections" (Munn, 1955, p. 161). The important fact is that these connections *are* made, thus completing and readying the complex structures involved before motor activity in the usual sense can take place.

It is well known that the genes play a dominant role in not only determining but actually regulating structural development. Bits of new facts as to the exact nature and function of genes are steadily coming forth from the biochemical and genetics laboratories, but the picture, as yet, is incomplete.

From the very beginning of organismic development environmental factors play their part. From the outset organism and environment are in interaction. In the first place, the environment must be appropriate and suitable for development or none will take place. Intercellular conditions presumably are important aspects of the early environment. Even after the first division of the fertilized ovum, each new cell, in its position in relation to and its contact with the other, is part of the other's environment. As further divisions occur and as the mass of cells grows, the cells in different positions in the mass become subject to different patterns of intercellular contacts, pressures, and other influences. The regulating action of the genes in interaction with differing environmental influences causes differentiation in form and inner structure of the cells. By the end of a brief 8-week period, these structures and their interconnections have reached a stage of development where elementary functioning is possible.

Origins of Motor Behavior

Studies of embryos and fetuses delivered by Caesarian section have shown that by the end of the eighth week of intrauterine life the human embryo is capable of responding by muscular contraction to tactual stimuli. Histological studies also have shown that by that time reflex pathways between certain muscles and the fifth cranial nerve are already established. The only area responsive to light tactual stimulation at this early stage, however, is the face. These early movements have been described as "mass movements" of the trunk, arms, and legs. By the end of the third month the sensitive areas have become more extensive; tactual stimuli applied to the hands and feet bring responses that are somewhat more specific and more frequent.

During the fourth month, in addition to mass responses, a number of clear-cut reflexes can be elicited. These reflexes, according to the careful observations of Hooker (1962), "are not all in the final form they will assume, but, with the addition of a number not yet present, they lay the framework for gradual development into the reflexes of postnatal life" (p. 73). It is quite evident, then, that the neuromuscular basis for the motor behavior characteristic of the newborn is not solely a product of maturation. Much "learning" through exercise has already taken place. In a specific way certain neuromuscular functions essential to postnatal life, such as sucking and even breathing, have actually been practiced *in utero*.

Motor Activity of the Newborn

Even though he is born with a complete lack of voluntary, consciously directed motor ability, the infant comes equipped with muscle groups that are, of themselves, strong and capable of functioning. He also possesses at birth a rather complete set of sense organs along with their essential neural connections that are structurally ready to function. This readiness is largely a product of maturation, but exercise also contributes to their ability to function. Many, perhaps all, of the muscles of the newborn infant's body have been exercised a great deal prior to birth. With this level of structural readiness and having been suddenly thrust at birth into an environment with a greatly increased range and intensity of stimulation, it is no wonder that the neonate presents a picture of mass muscular activity.

As we shall see, this congenital random activity is of real significance in relation to subsequent motor development, for it is out of the unorganized "mass" of elemental movements that the great variety of voluntary, precisely coordinated behavior patterns of later childhood and adulthood gradually are structured. As we have already noted, this congenital behavior, present at birth, has a developmental history extending back to within 2 or 3 months after the time of conception. During this time individual muscles, responding to indigenous and other sorts of stimulation, have been exercising their contractile function.

Gesell and Amatruda (1941) have described the neonatal stage of development and the general character of the neonate's behavior:

> Much of the behavior of the neonate (from birth to 4 weeks) is suggestive of earlier fetal stages. The neonate is not fully prepared for the demands of postnatal life. Hence his physiological ineptitudes. His respiration may be irregular, his temperature regulation unsteady. Peristalsis and swallowing are under precarious directional control. He startles, sneezes, or cries on slight provocation. His thresholds are low and inconstant. [p. 32]

Undifferentiated Mass Activity

The newborn infant, of course, is completely incapable of voluntarily coordinated motor responses, yet when awake, he is the picture of muscular activity. He is active all over—kicking, wiggling, thrashing about with arms and legs—but he has no coordination or specificity of movement. This "amorphous mass of activity," because of its rapidity and nonspecificity, is difficult to observe and describe analytically. Almost any stimulus will release it, but it is largely the result of organic excitants, and, due to the immaturity of the nervous system, there is complete absence of cortical inhibition. Abrupt and intense noxious stimuli tend to produce an increase in mass activity, while mild and soothing external stimuli tend to reduce it. The important point regarding this generalized, nonreflex activity of the newborn is that the development of voluntary, coordinated motor activity common to later levels of functioning is largely an outgrowth of it.

Reflexes

In contrast to the amorphous mass activity, the newborn's reflexes are individuated and highly coordinated and specific responses. They are regulated by the spinal and subcortical nervous centers which are largely intact and functional at birth.

Of the numerous reflexes that have been observed in neonatal behavior, certain of them are vital to survival; others have protective significance. Of the former group, sucking and breathing have already been mentioned. In classifying and describing these responses, researchers have categorized them in terms of the parts of the body which produce them (Dennis, 1934). The following is a partial representative list:

1. Eyelid responses: opening and closing the eyes. Adequate stimuli for these responses, particularly for closing the eyes are numerous—blasts of air, bright light, touching the face near the eye.
2. Pupilary responses: the size of the pupil changes in response to varia-

tions in the intensity of light to which the eyes are exposed. It has also been found that strong cutaneous stimuli also may cause widening of the pupils of the neonate's eyes.

3. Ocular reflexes: pursuit movements, coordinated compensatory eye movements. When the head is jerked quickly around, the eyes move in a compensatory direction. This has been observed in infants as early as the second day of life.

4. Facial and mouthing responses: opening and closing the mouth, sucking, grimacing, yawning, pushing objects from the mouth, frowning, smiling, and so on.

5. Throat responses: crying, cooing, sobbing, sneezing, coughing, gagging, swallowing, and so on.

6. Head movements.

7. Hand and arm reflexes: closing hand, arm flexion, and so on.

8. Trunk reactions: arching the back, twisting.

9. Genital organ reflexes: cremasterec reflex (raising the testes), penis erection.

10. Foot and leg reflexes: the knee jerk and the Achilles tendon reflexes have been observed in some infants. Flexion and extension of the legs, kicking, fanning the toes in response to stroking the sole.

Numerous coordinated responses of many body parts, reflex in nature, have also been observed in very young infants. Among these are lifting the head and rear quarters, stretching, creeping, shivering and trembling, supporting body weight by grasp, and the startle response.

Processes of Differentiation and Integration

The last category of congenital coordinate response, involving as it does many body parts and, in many instances, the total infant organism, appears to constitute a class of behavior that in one respect is like mass activity in that the whole organism is involved yet different in that it is coordinated. At the same time, this behavior is like the specific reflex in that it is coordinated and not random; and it is unlike the simple reflex in that it is complex and widespread.

The question naturally arose among the authoritative observers as to the developmental origin of these patterns. Are they differentiations, "individuations," from fetal mass activity, or are they integrations, or coordinations, of specific reflexes that come about during fetal development? The investigators became divided on this question. Irwin (1930) took the position that since mass activity is the predominant type of prenatal behavior, coordinated patterns—simple and complex—are individuations from the matrix of primitive mass activity. Dennis (1932) and Gilmer (1933), on the other hand, maintained that the observed complex coordinated patterns are prenatal integrations of simple response units.

The truth of the matter seems to be that both differentiation and integration are involved in motor development. Some adaptive responses are differentiations from undifferentiated activity, and some are integrations of simple, specific reflexes. Both of these processes, furthermore, continue throughout the developmental period. Piaget's (1952) epigenetic account of mental development emphasizes the integrative aspect of the process. He described each stage of development during the sensorimotor period as growing out of the preceding stage through a continuing process of coordination. Piaget characterized his second stage, the stage of *primary circular reactions*, for example, as the progressive coordination and assimilation of congenital schemata to form motor habits and perceptions. His concept of assimilation and accommodation in development implies both coordination of specifics and differentiation. During infancy motor development can be seen as a combination of these two developmental processes. In the neonate reflex activity has already reached the stage of almost complete individuation. We have already noted the many discrete reflexes that comprise the neonate's behavioral repertoire. As development continues, these reflexes become integrated and coordinated into effective patterns of behavior. At the same time, individuation of the nonreflex mass activity is underway. These differentiated patterns will eventually come under cortical (voluntary) control, and, as learning continues, these patterns become functionally interconnected and coordinated.

Motor Development During Infancy

The brief neonatal period is the time when the infant recovers from the effects of the sudden and radical environmental change he had to survive at birth. As these adjustments are made, development gets underway at an accelerated rate. Maturation and the exercise of neuromuscular structures, as we have already noted, give rise to more and more highly individuated and coordinated functional patterns. Although he continues to be profoundly dependent, the human infant nevertheless makes rapid progress in the development of a number of motor functions.

There are two rather complex functional areas that may be regarded as special motor "developmental tasks" of infancy. They are developmental tasks in the sense that they must be achieved by the infant if he is to live autonomously and to function as a normal human being. These are *manipulability*—the ability to reach with the hand, grasp, and manipulate objects in the external environment—and *upright locomotion*. First, let us consider the development of reaching-prehensile ability.

The Reaching-Prehensile Pattern

The prehensile function is a voluntary motor pattern quite distinct from the grasp reflex. The grasp reflex is present in the unborn fetus and is quite strong in infants during the first month or so of life. The only connection between the grasp reflex and prehension is that some of the same muscles are involved in both, and, in a sense, the muscular exercise from the grasp reflex prepares (strengthens) the structures involved in prehensile behavior. In the much more complex reaching-prehensile pattern, visual stimuli, as well as tactual and kinesthetic ones, are involved. Prehensile behavior is a permanent motor function, and it soon comes under voluntary control.

As the prehensile function develops, eye-hand coordination becomes essential. Visually guided reaching, the portion of the total pattern preliminary to actually grasping the object, becomes possible through the maturation —and exercise—of the visual mechanism for space perception as well as the neuromuscular structures involved in reaching.

One of the most thorough earlier students of the reaching-prehensile function in infants was Myrtle McGraw (1943). Her insight into the nature of the prehensile pattern and of the physical structures involved is revealed in the following excerpt:

> From inception this function calls for the coordination of visual and motor mechanisms. Object vision reflects functioning of the striate area. As stated earlier there is sound reason to doubt that the newborn infant is capable of object vision. The optic nerve tracts and pathways are not myelinated at the time of birth, and Conel has pointed out that the motor area in the precentral gyrus is more advanced than is the striate area in the occipital lobe. Even during the first month of postnatal life there is not much gain in structural development of the striate area as indicated by any of the criteria for evaluating such development. Both structurally and functionally it is reasonable to assume that *object* vision is not a part of the neonate's behavior repertoire. Since from the onset reaching-prehensile behavior requires the collaboration of visual and motor mechanisms, the criteria used in appraising the development of this function were formulated in terms of this relationship. [p. 94]

With such criteria in mind, McGraw, in her study of the complete reaching-prehensile pattern, identified six phases in its development.

Infant Vision

At the time McGraw made her observations, it was generally believed by students of infant vision, from the evidence at hand, that the very young infant does not yet possess the power of accommodation and convergence of the eyes, that he is unable to focus clear retinal images of objects at varying distances. Hence "object vision" would not be possible for him, even though he may appear to fixate an object held in his lines of vision. More recent studies (Fantz, Ardy, and Udelf, 1962; Gorman, Cogan, and Gellis, 1957), however,

> give behavioral evidence that the neonatal infant in spite of being hyperopic, can focus sharply enough at a very short distance to resolve a near-threshold

pattern, thus implying considerable power of accommodation. This is in agreement with anatomical and ophthalmological information (Mann, 1950; Peiper, 1949) suggesting that the optical system of the eye is functional at birth. [Fantz, et al., 1962, p. 911]

In a later investigation Fantz (1963) studied the visual responses of 18 neonates ranging in age from 10 hours to 5 days. These younger babies also exhibited a visual-discrimination ability in the sense that they showed a "preference" for simple, black-and-white-striped patterns over plain-colored surfaces. Fantz, however, seems to have been a bit overenthusiastic about the cognitive abilities of infants when he interpreted this simple sensory "preference" to indicate "an innate ability to perceive form" (p. 296).

Actually, the evidence regarding infant visual perceptual ability and its development is contradictory. Nash (1970) summarized the available evidence as follows:

Vision is relatively undeveloped at birth, and it is not until this time that the visual cortex of the occipital lobe begins to differentiate. Also it is not until about sixteen weeks after birth that the macula and fovia are structurally differentiated. About this time, or a little before, the visual fibers complete their myelinization. The development of the macula continues and the ability to fixate accurately and hence to see details is correlated with this development. [p. 2]

According to ophthalmologists, the fusion of the visual images from the two eyes is not achieved until about age 6 years (Walsh 1957). This is said to be due to the immaturity of the central mechanisms involved. The original authority for this statement, however, is not given. The implication here is that up to the end of the preschool years children "see double." Observation of the behavior of young children does not suggest any significant degree of such disability. On the contrary, there is some early reported evidence of stereoscopic vision in children as young as 2 years (Johnson and Beck, 1941).

Recent research previously referred to (Fantz, 1963, 1964, 1965) indicates that fixation is possible quite early in infancy. An experiment by Bower (1970) gave evidence also that infants do integrate their two eyes' views (binocular fusion).

In any event, with such widely differing findings in this area of infant development, there is no firm basis for attributing visual perceptual ability to very young infants. Granting that the infant, even at birth, possesses power of accommodation and that he is capable of a level of visual acuity sufficient to react differentially to patterns in his visual field, he may still be completely incapable of object vision, or perception in the sense of awareness of the properties of objects and situations. There is no clear evidence that the neonate possesses this level of cognitive ability. Object vision in this sense, of course, is an essential prerequisite to the deliberate reaching-prehensile pattern with which we are here concerned.

The Early Development of Reaching

Gesell and Amatruda (1941) in their study of the development of prehension emphasized the importance of another motor pattern, the *congenital postural reflexes*, as follows:

> Prehension emerges out of posture. It involves a focalization of posture and a coordination of eyes and hands. The tonic neck reflex (t-n-r) attitude which is one of the most conspicuous behavior patterns throughout the first 12 post-natal weeks almost literally paves the way for prehension. During much of his waking life the 4-week-old infant lies in this attitude which resembles a fencing stance—his head rotated to one side, the other tonically fixed at the shoulder. This attitude promotes and channelizes visual fixation on his extended hand. By gradual stages it leads to hand inspection, to active approach upon an object, and to manipulation of the object. [pp. 32–33]

The tonic neck reflex was also regarded as an important factor in the development of the reaching response by White, Castle, and Held (1964). This study was concerned with the stages in reaching behavior that appear during the first 6 months of life. The subjects of the study were 34 infants born and reared in an institution. All were physically normal and had acceptable medical histories. A uniform pretest and testing procedure was followed. Each infant was observed daily in an especially arranged crib, the surroundings remaining constant. First, a 10-minute observation (pretest) of spontaneous activity was made, followed by a 10-minute standardized test session. A stimulus object was especially selected to elicit attention and reaching behavior. With this procedure, these investigators "found that under our test conditions infants exhibit a relatively orderly developmental sequence which culminates in visually-directed reaching" at the end of the first 5 months of life. On the basis of frequency analysis of their data, the investigators described spontaneous behaviors exhibited during the 10-minute pretest and characteristic test responses for each half-month interval throughout the 5-month period.

During the first 2 months especially, the tonic neck reflex characterized the infants' pretest behavior. This appeared to be significant in that the infants tended to fixate and to regard the extended hand in this reflex position. This was also regarded by Gesell and Amatruda (1941) as a significant stage in the development of reaching.

As to the question of fixation and accommodation during the early period (1½ to 2 months), according to White *et al.* (1964):

> Retinoscopic studies indicate that infants have not yet developed flexible accommodative capacities at this age: their focal distance when attending to stimuli between 6 and 16 inches appears to be fixed at about 9 inches. Visual stimuli closer than 7 inches are rarely fixated. [p. 354]

In the series of brief descriptions at half-month intervals, there was evidence of a gradual development of fixation and an emergence of hand movements in the direction of the object that gradually became more positively directed. Figure 7.1 shows the sequence of stages in the development of reaching as observed in these infants.

Reaching-Prehension-Manipulation

As was stated earlier, our interest is in the individual's development of the capacity to manipulate creatively with his hands the material aspects of his world. McGraw carefully observed that as the child acquires this ability he passes through six developmental phases (McGraw, 1941; see Fig. 7.2).

The earliest of these phases (Phase A) is particularly characteristic of the neonatal period and it extends roughly through the first 4 to 8 weeks of the baby's life. It is marked particularly by a lack of visual perceptual awareness of objects as such. During this period, of course, the infant will close his fingers over an object when it is brought in contact with the palm of his hand (the grasp reflex); but there is, in such grasping, no connection between seeing the object and the neuromuscular movements induced.

According to McGraw's observations at about the end of the second month, there is a noticeable change in the infant's visual behavior. He begins

CHRONOLOGY OF RESPONSES

RESPONSE	OBSERVED IN[a]	N[a]	MEDIAN AND RANGE OF DATES OF FIRST OCCURRENCE
Swipes at object	13	13	(2:5)
Unilateral hand raising	15	15	(2:17)
Both hands raised	16	18	(2:21)
Alternating glances (hand and object)	18	19	(2:27)
Hands to midline and clasp	15	15	(3:3)
One hand raised with alternating glances, other hand to midline clutching dress	11	19	(3:8)
Torso oriented toward object	15	18	(3:15)
Hands to midline and clasp and oriented toward object	14	19	(4:3)
Piaget-type reach	12	18	(4:10)
Top level reach	14	14	(4:24)

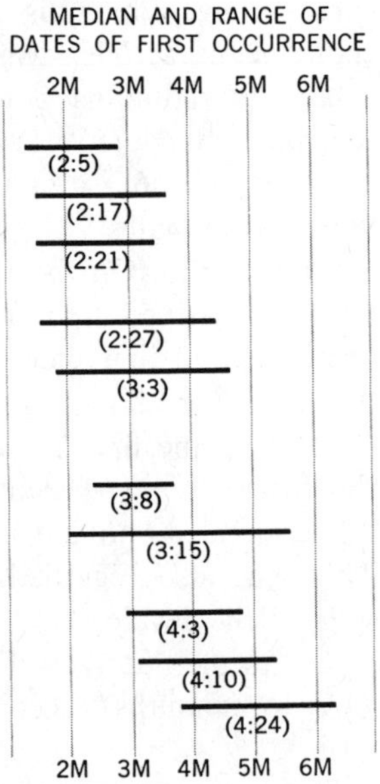

[a] The columns "Observed In" and "N" indicate that some of the responses were not shown by all the infants.

Figure 7.1 The chronology of 10 response patterns related to the development of reaching, seen most consistently in a group of 34 infants during their first six months of life. From White et al. (1964), p. 357, by permission.

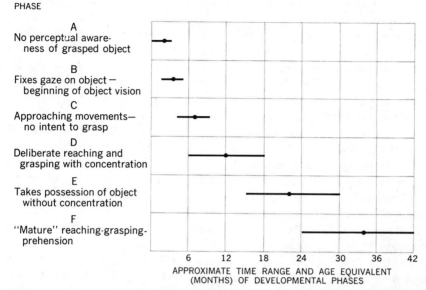

PHASE

A
No perceptual aware-
    ness of grasped object

B
Fixes gaze on object —
    beginning of object vision

C
Approaching movements—
    no intent to grasp

D
Deliberate reaching and
    grasping with concentration

E
Takes possession of object
    without concentration

F
"Mature" reaching-grasping-
    prehension

6   12   18   24   30   36   42
APPROXIMATE TIME RANGE AND AGE EQUIVALENT
(MONTHS) OF DEVELOPMENTAL PHASES

Figure 7.2   The chronology of phases (McGraw) in the development of the reaching-grasping-manipulative response pattern.

unmistakably to give attention to objects held within his near visual range. He now clearly fixes his gaze on an object. McGraw regarded this stage as the beginning of object vision. More recent work, as we have already indicated, has shown quite clearly that infants almost from birth can fixate patterns. Such "pattern vision," however, becomes progressively more acute during the first 6 months (Fantz, 1962). Also, according to these findings, there is a rather marked increase in pattern-vision acuity at about the end of the second month, which corresponds roughly with the period when McGraw discerned the onset of object vision. This is the beginning of McGraw's Phase B. The infant can, without doubt, fixate and regard the object, but there is no distinct neuromuscular movement in the direction of the visual stimulus. However, McGraw did observe changes in neuromuscular activity which characterized this onset phase of object vision. At its very beginning, diffuse movements were observed to abate as the child intently regarded the object. Later on, but before the inception of any distinct muscular movement in the direction of the object, the sight of the object would usually excite disorganized activity.

It was during the interval covered by McGraw's Phase B that White *et al.* (1964) differentiated their complete sequence of stages in the development of the infant reaching pattern. This behavior and its changes were described by McGraw simply as random and diffuse activity stimulated by the sight of the object but not directed specifically toward it. McGraw was looking for evidence of a functional connection between the sight of the object and specific arm movements in its direction as the indicator of the onset of a new phase.

Evidence of a new phase (Phase C) was not noted in McGraw's observations until the babies were around 7 months of age. She observed in this phase certain behavioral qualities that indicated a functional connection between the visual and the neuromuscular mechanisms involved in reaching-prehension. As the object is brought within the infant's near field of vision, approach movements of the arms and hands are evoked as he gazes at it. However, even at this stage there are no indications of any real intent on the child's part to take possession of or to manipulate the object. There is as yet no total, coordinated prehensile pattern. As the baby's hand comes in contact with the object, prehension as a motor pattern is still largely undifferentiated. There is visually directed reaching, but no actual grasping or manipulation of the object.

Phase D is identified by evidence "that the child's behavior has taken on a voluntary or deliberate quality, that it has lost the compulsive quality which characterizes Phase C. It is evident that the child must give undivided attention to the performance" (McGraw, 1943, p. 97). The whole performance of reaching, grasping, and manipulating the object is given sustained attention. There is a deliberate quality about the movements involved.

With further practice and experience in grasping objects in varying sizes and shapes the infant reaches Phase E. Now he need no longer give undivided attention to the actual reaching-grasping sequence. With one glance he may now sufficiently appraise the situation to make possible the completion of the act of taking possession of the object while glancing at other aspects of the situation. The whole performance is more precise and efficient.

In the final, "mature" Phase F, "both the visual and the neuromuscular aspects of the performance "have been reduced to the minimum essentials required by the circumstances" (McGraw, 1943, pp. 98–99). The total operation is smooth and efficient. These phases are summarized in Figure 7.2, which represents McGraw's sequence in its time relations.

It should be pointed out that in her full account of this developmental sequence McGraw stressed the fact of continuity. Each phase, even though characterized by new and different qualities and features, is actually in a period of constant gradual change, merging gradually into the next phase in order. Development, in both its structural and functional aspects, is continuous and unbroken, even though qualitatively different stages or phases following each other in definite sequences may be identified.

As recent research by a number of investigators has shown, however, the *rate* at which a child achieves the various phases and stages in such sequences is very largely dependent upon the amount and appropriateness of stimulation which the environment affords. Early stimulation is an exceedingly important factor in all aspects of development (Levine, 1960, 1962, 1967; Fantz and Nevis, 1967; Rheingold, 1961).

The Assessment of Status and Progress in Prehensile Development

As is true of other areas of development, change that eventuates in the perfected pattern of reaching-prehension is both quantitative and qualitative in nature. For example, when true visual "following" with effective convergence and accommodation of the eyes is established, these features continue to change in the direction of *more* precision. Eye-hand coordinations become speedier, more efficient. Such changes are quantitative in nature. Some of them at least are subject to standardized measurement, perhaps in units of time and of objective efficiency.

However, when the achievement of a total developmental task, for example, prehensile ability, is to be assessed, and when progress toward its perfection is to be traced, it becomes necessary also to look at development qualitatively. It becomes more than a matter of measuring the amount of increase in speed or efficiency of part functions. As is true in the case of maturation, qualitatively different stages must be identified and ordered in a *time sequence.* A particular child's developmental status at a particular time, and his progress from time to time, can then be appraised in terms of the *average ages* at which children in general reach those various stages in the sequence. Functional development, like maturation, can thus be appraised and expressed as age equivalents, or developmental ages.

The series of phases described by McGraw and briefly outlined above is a developmental sequence covering the development of the complete reaching-grasping-manipulation pattern. The results of McGraw's study show the age period in which each of the six developmental phases is representative of the greatest number of children. The midpoint of this age period (the mode) in each case is a measure of central tendency. Figure 7.3 was constructed as a form for tracing progress in terms of this sequence.

The appraisal of a child's developmental status in this function in terms of McGraw's criteria would, of course, require careful testing and observation, following the procedure used in her study (1941).

As was stated earlier, no such procedure was followed in the study of our subjects, Paul and Sally. The Gesell Developmental schedules, however, were administered to them periodically. A number of items in these schedules involve eye-hand coordinated reaching, grasping, and manipulation of test materials. Each of these test items Gesell assigned to a particular age level in the schedules.

In order to equate Sally's manipulative behavior on the Gesell schedules roughly with McGraw's phases in prehensile development, the age equivalents of Sally's various performances on the relevant items of the Gesell schedules are plotted in Figure 7.3. The dots on Sally's prehension-age curve in each case represent the age level of her performance at the time the schedule was administered. The point at which her curve crosses each of the McGraw-phase developmental-age lines may be taken as an approximation

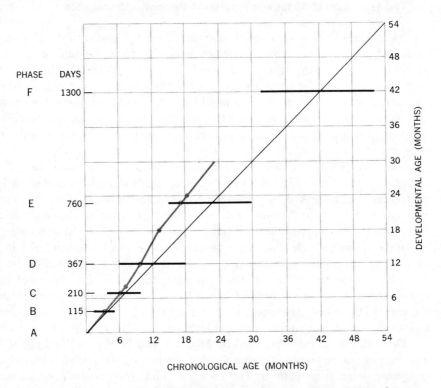

Figure 7.3 **The course of Sally's prehensile development estimated from her performances on the relevant items of the Gesell Developmental Schedules.
The dots in this curve show the developmental-age level of the child's performance at the three chronological ages indicated on the horizontal scale
(7 months, 13 months, and 18 months). Horizontal lines are drawn at the
mean age levels of McGraw's sequence of phases of prehensile development. The length of the line in each case represents roughly the age
range during which that phase generally prevails.**

of Sally's status with respect to McGraw's criteria of reaching-prehension at
the chronological age indicated. For example, the Gesell schedules were
administered to Sally when she was 7 months old and again when she was
13 months old. The average performance levels (Gesell standards) that she
achieved were 8 months and 18 months, respectively. The line connecting
those two points in the graph crosses the age-equivalent line for Phase D
(McGraw) at a point corresponding to chronological age 9½ months. Thus
Sally at 9½ months of age, had an estimated prehension age of 367 days, or
approximately 12 months, according to McGraw's criteria.

Locomotor Development

Another developmental task of the young child is the achievement of the ability to walk upright. This type of locomotor functioning

facilitates visual exploration and completely frees the hands for manual exploration and manipulation, both of which are very important in the total psychological development of the individual.

More attention has been given by parents to the achievement of erect walking in children than to any other motor activity. Learning to walk is regarded as an important milestone in the baby's development. For the child, it is a big step toward independence.

The roots of locomotor ability, in a sense, are found in the prenatal period. As we have seen, the individual muscles of the trunk and limbs, those involved in bipedal locomotion, are exercised in a random, nonspecific way even prior to birth. But the real developmental task—the individuation of specific neuromuscular units for specific functions and the coordination of these many units into the complex, voluntary acts of balancing in the upright position, bending, turning, stooping, and taking progressive steps—is a major accomplishment of the first 12 to 15 months of postnatal life.

Many investigators, working in their respective fields of embryology, developmental anatomy, neurology, and behavior, have contributed to the understanding of this area of functional development. A number of observational studies of the activity sequence itself have been made in which stages (phases) in achievement have been identified and described.

Quadrupedal Locomotion

Various modes of infant locomotion develop in many children as intermediate means of reaching their objectives. Crawling and creeping have been analyzed by a number of careful observers with the purpose of identifying phases in the developmental sequence. Ames (1937), for example, described 14 stages in the development of "prone progression." Her results were based on an analysis of motion pictures of this activity in 20 infants. She was able to note the time of onset of each stage and to establish a median age at which it appeared. These stages ranged from one in which the infant characteristically brought one knee and thigh forward in complete ineffectiveness (median age 28 weeks) to rather efficient quadrupedal progression, or creeping on hands and feet, the final stage (median age 49 weeks).

A few years later McGraw (1943) published her observations of the same function in 82 infants. She identified nine phases. McGraw's first phase occurs some 100 days earlier than the first stage described by Ames. McGraw's observations (see Fig. 7.4) began with the responses of the young infant placed in the prone position; both arms and legs are flexed and his face rests on the floor in complete helplessness. This phase usually subsides by about age 14 weeks and is replaced by the second phase in which the baby can hold his head off the floor for a period of time instead of simply bobbing his head up and down. This phase, McGraw felt, suggests the beginning of cortical control over posture and movement. The final phase of the sequence begins at about 29 weeks of age and is marked by the child's ability to creep on all fours in a rather smooth, integrated fashion. According to McGraw,

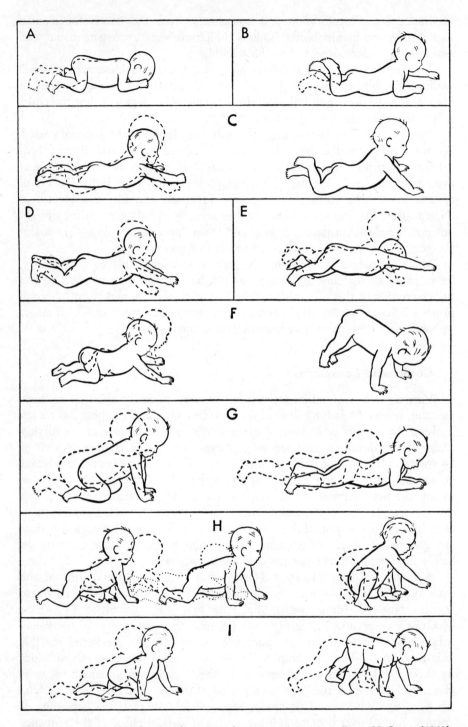

Figure 7.4   Phases in the development of prone progression. From McGraw (1943), p. 51, by permission.

this series of developmental phases reflects development of control over the skeletal muscles by the cerebral cortex.

There is, of course, a lack of correspondence in the sequences described in these two studies. Other observers have presented still different formulations. Burnside (1927), for example, who also made his formulations from motion pictures a decade earlier, described only three stages. These he called crawling, or prone progression with the abdomen resting on the floor; hitching; and creeping, or forward movement on hands and knees or hands and feet.

Bipedal Locomotion

The development of erect walking involves a series of qualitative changes marked by signal points along its course. The reader will recall that Chapter 4 introduced the concept of the maturity indicator, a signal point—a stage—in the sense of a new structural feature or a new pattern of performance, as in the case of the development of a particular function. The development of upright walking, of course, involves the serial appearance of stages.

The sequential character of the development of walking has long been noted and described (McGraw, 1943). It is quite obvious that before a baby can get himself into a sitting position he must first achieve the ability to turn from the prone lying position to the supine position. Likewise, he must be in a standing position before he can take steps. In general, however, the findings have been that, with help from others and with the use of chairs and other pieces of furniture to pull themselves to standing positions, many babies are able to take steps alone before they can arise to their feet from the floor unaided. In other words, because of the help of others, both directly and in their encouragement of the baby's use of environmental objects, a locomotor-developmental sequence that is maturationally fixed and that thus meets the criterion of universality is not to be found.

Students of locomotion, nevertheless, are generally agreed that the development of the walking function is based upon an underlying developmental sequence. McGraw, for example, relates this functional development directly to the development of the neuromuscular system and particularly to the progressive assumption of control by the cerebral cortex of the brain, thus emphasizing the relatively fixed sequential nature of walking development. Ames (1937), Shirley (1931), and others also have stressed the relative stability of the locomotor sequence as evidence for the idea that *capacity* for the achievement of walking is a function of maturation.

A Sequence of Progress Indicators

Recognizing the tremendously variable effects of the environment upon the course of walking achievement, we should look for broad functional stages that are relatively dependent upon structural development for their unaided performance. In that search the lists of stages that have been described by the various investigators of the walking function were examined. The following four broad part functions seemed, in a general way, to meet our criteria:

1. Roll over from supine to prone
2. Independent sit up
3. Independent stand
4. Independent walk (on a level plane)

Babies are commonly observed quite early in infancy to perform the roll-over rather independently of help or encouragement from others. Likewise, even though they are frequently placed by others in a sitting position and are helped in their own efforts to sit up, they do gain the ability to sit up independently and later to arise unaided to their feet and to walk independently.

In order to make a preliminary test of this sequence and to identify any regular developmental phases that might appear in the course of the establishment of these stages, an investigation (unpublished, was conducted by the present author) which involved the participation of more than 100 mothers of young babies. These mothers were asked to keep records of the motor development of their babies on a specially prepared, illustrated record form.

An analysis of the data bearing on the four stages clearly suggested that, as the child achieves and perfects each indicator stage, four rather distinct phases can be noted and described in his behavior. A generalized description of these phases follows:

A. Attempting: The child shows signs of readiness for the particular act (indicator) in behavior which suggests that he is *trying* to accomplish it. (For example, he appears to be trying to turn over from back to stomach.)

B. Nodal phase: This phase is marked by the baby's *first observed success in accomplishing* the feat (for example, arising to stand unaided).

C. Practicing phase: The feat is performed over and over. The pattern gradually takes on organization, but it is not as yet easily accomplished.

D. Integrated phase: The pattern is now smoothly organized and easily performed, apparently without conscious direction. It has become automatized and *integrated to further purpose*. For example, the child sits up now, not as an end in itself, but in order to reach a desired object, or to pull himself to a stand.

The data also permitted the designation of approximate age equivalents (median ages) for each of the four main indicator stages and its four phases. Table 7.1 briefly describes each of these stages and phases and gives its approximate age equivalent in weeks. This tabulation provides a tentative scale for appraising upright locomotor-developmental status of a child and a means of plotting the course of his development in this important function.

Plotting Locomotor Development

Obviously, our progress-indicator scale (Table 7.1) has utility only during the first 2 or 3 years of the child's life. At any point during this early period, however, careful observation of the child when free to play and to pursue his interests, together—perhaps with a discussion of his locomotor behavior with his mother—should provide sufficient data for assessing his status in locomotor ability.

Figure 7.5 is a form designed for the purpose of plotting the development of erect locomotion in an individual child. The different stages and phases (those listed in Table 7.1) are reordered in terms of their tentative age equivalents and are superimposed upon the developmental-age scale of the form. The five points on this scale, which we were able to identify in the

TABLE 7.1   Progress Indicators in the Development of Bipedal Locomotion

Indicator and Phase	Age Expected (months)
I. Roll-over from supine to prone	
A. While on back raises head as if trying to roll over	1.8
B. First success in rolling over	4.8
C. Roll-over not easy, practicing	5.5
D. Roll-over now easy, "automatic," apparently without conscious direction, in order to accomplish further purpose (reach toy, and so on)	5.8
II. Independent sit-up	
A. Pushes self up from stomach, apparently trying to sit up	2.5
B. First success in pushing self from stomach to sitting posiiton	7.6
C. Practices sit-up over and over, not easily accomplished	7.8
D. Sit-up well organized and easily accomplished with attention apparently on some further purpose	8.3
III. Independent stand	
A. Tries to arise to feet by pulling on furniture	8.1
B. First success in independent stand	8.3
C. Apparently enjoys standing up and balancing without support	8.8
D. Stands apparently in order to try taking steps or to reach desired object	9.0
IV. Independent walk	
A. Tries to take independent steps, falls	8.8
B. First success with several independent steps	11.3
C. Persistently practices walking alone	12.5
D. Walks grown-up fashion, apparently without conscious direction *with purpose* of going somewhere or doing something	13.8

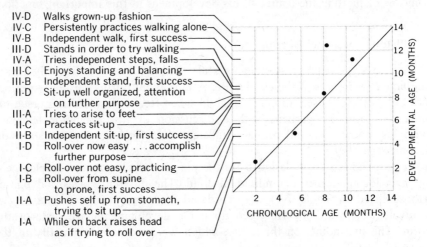

Figure 7.5 Locomotor development of Paul 695 in terms of progress indicators outlined in Table 5.1.

record of Paul 695, are indicated in the figure. From the data at hand, then, locomotor development in this child appears to have been quite regular. He generally reached the various phases in the course of his development near the expected ages (median ages based on the reports of our group of mothers).

Development of Motor Skills

As we saw early in this chapter, the two basic areas of motor development—the two major motor developmental tasks of infancy and early childhood—are prehension and upright locomotion. Although these acts are commonplace and are largely taken for granted as simple accomplishments of babyhood, upon analysis each is seen as an extremely complex and variable skill. As such they represent tremendous developmental accomplishments for children so young.

These elementary patterns are, as we have seen, joint products of maturation and learning. Indigenous motivation to function[2] is strong at each level of maturational readiness, and under ordinary environmental stimulation the various stages in the developmental sequence unfold in regular order, varying from child to child mainly in timing. Much the same overall patterns can be followed in children generally.

[2] Indigenous motivation has been established as an important principle of development.

But these basic patterns constitute only the foundation for subsequent motor-skills development. Objects soon are grasped not just to be grasped but to be "handled," examined, and manipulated. New eye-hand coordinations are built upon the basic prehension pattern. Similarly, many elaborations are built upon, and into, the basic walking pattern.

At this point in development, however, greater variation among children begins to appear in the number and kinds of skills developed. Maturation now plays a less determining role. The child now *learns* to grasp and to manipulate the objects which his particular environment provides for him. He will soon learn to thumb through and "read" books, if they are available to him. He learns to write, to color with crayon or brush, to manipulate toys, to build with blocks, to use the typewriter or not to use it, depending upon what his environment provides and what it denies him. He learns to run, to jump, to climb, again within the limitations set by his environment and by those who care for him. A view of the activities of a nursery school play area reveals the variety of motor skills already acquired as well as wide individual differences already evident among children before elementary school age. And it is difficult to think of a single motor skill that does not bear some direct relation to either the basic prehensile function or locomotion, or both (Wickstrom, 1970).

Motor Skills of the Preschooler

From about eighteen months of age much of motor development consists of the acquisition of skills based upon or related to walking. Gutteridge (1939) made a rather thorough observational study of the development of these skills in children. Her purpose was "to portray the child engaged in his usual activities, under everyday conditions in school or playgrounds, without any attempt at special training or preparation, and without distracting his attention from his own pursuits" (p. 5). Her results were presented in the form of percentages of children at different ages who achieved each skill at particular defined proficiency levels.

Running, perhaps the most common of all activities developing out of walking, in the beginning "is little more than fast walking with uneven steps and a general clumsiness of the entire body that leads to many falls" (Hurlock, 1972, p. 142). Like other newly acquired motor abilities, it is engaged in at first apparently because of the satisfaction the child gains from the act itself. Later it is used primarily as an instrumental activity. The child uses it to achieve some further purpose. By age five or six years children generally can run well with relatively few falls.

Jumping also develops from exaggerated stepping into skill in propelling the body upward and forward, landing in a standing position. Gutteridge found that 42 percent of 3-year-old children jumped well and 81 percent of 5-year-olds were skillful jumpers.

Hopping on one foot is a modification of the jump. Gutteridge found that 33 percent of 4-year-olds were skillful hoppers. At age 5 and a half years 67 percent were rated as proficient, while 80 percent of the 6-year-olds were so rated. Again, with increasing age, hopping skill ranged from a very awkward, irregular series of jumps to a regular and precise performance.

Skipping apparently is a more difficult pattern to acquire than hopping. Only 14 percent of Gutteridge's 4-year-olds were able to skip. At age 6, however, 91 percent could skip.

Many other skills acquired during childhood, of course, involve the elaboration of basic bipedal locomotion. Riding the tricycle today is practically a universal skill among preschoolers. By age 2 years 17 percent can ride well, and by age 4 years 100 percent are successful, according to Gutteridge's findings.

Bayley (1935) developed a scale for the measurement of motor ability in children. This scale consisted of 76 items arranged in order of difficulty, each with its age placement. For our particular purpose we selected only those items from Bayley's scale which refer to certain of the motor skills developed by the child *after* he has achieved walking (see Table 7.2). Figure 7.6 is a form for plotting the development of these skills for an individual child (these data are for Paul 695). Bayley's age equivalents are superimposed upon the developmental-age scale of Figure 7.6.

As might be expected, these motor-progress indicators present a much more irregular pattern than do the more basic locomotor progress indicators of Figure 7.5. Secondary skills are much more closely related to experience and special environmntal opportunity and encouragement than are the

TABLE 7.2   A General Motor Developmental Sequence[a] for Paul 695, Birth to 5 Years[b]

Sequence	Age Expected (months)	Age of Achievement (months)
Pulls self to feet	10	10
Stands momentarily alone	14	——
Walks alone, toddles	15	——
Walks alone well	18	17
Walks up and down stairs alone	24	18
Runs well	24	——
Walks on tiptoes	30	19
Jumps with both feet	30	31
Stands on one foot momentarily	36	19
Rides tricycle	36	——
Walks down stairs, one foot to step	48	——
Throws ball overhand	48	——
Hops on one foot	54	——
Alternate feet descending stairs	60	——

[a] Fourteen of the seventy-six items of Bayley's scale of motor development (Bayley, 1935, p. 3).

[b] Paul's record did not list all of the observable items.

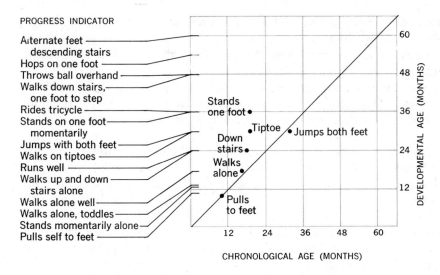

PROGRESS INDICATOR

Alternate feet
    descending stairs
Hops on one foot
Throws ball overhand
Walks down stairs,
    one foot to step
Rides tricycle
Stands on one foot
    momentarily
Jumps with both feet
Walks on tiptoes
Runs well
Walks up and down
    stairs alone
Walks alone well
Walks alone, toddles
Stands momentarily alone
Pulls self to feet

Stands
one foot ●

● Tiptoe   ● Jumps both feet

Down
stairs ●

Walks
alone ●

● Pulls
to feet

DEVELOPMENTAL AGE (MONTHS)

60
48
36
24
12

CHRONOLOGICAL AGE (MONTHS)
12   24   36   48   60

Figure 7.6   Motor development in the preschool period of Paul 695. From Bayley (1935) standards.

sequence of stages involved in upright locomotor development (Kjer, 1971; Cratty, 1969; Cratty and Hutton, 1969).

Skills of the School Years

By the time a child has reached school age he is master of a great variety of skills, both manipulatory and locomotor. Most of the games and activities of these years involve many and various combinations, coordinations, and integrations of skills built upon the basic functions of the two pairs of limbs.

Gross Bodily Activities

The elementary school years are the physically active years. The child is interested in the use of his body and in the exercise of the many specific bodily coordinations and skills that he has already acquired. It is a period when toys and tools are of relatively little importance. Total bodily activities, rather than those requiring the finer muscular coordinations, are preferred. Vigorous activities are more effective in providing release of the child's abounding energy during this period: Running, jumping, climbing, swimming, bicycle riding, and "stunting" of various kinds are typical activities, varying in form and detail, of course, from culture to culture.

The element of daring is a common feature, particularly in prepuberal play activities. Children during this period are concerned with little more than their status among their peers, which they enhance by achieving greater motor skills and by performing stunts and acts that require daring and courage. They challenge one another in such activities as walking high fences, climbing and swinging, performing on the high bar or the trapeze. As yet they are not at all concerned with the general problem of achieving status as an autonomous member of adult society.

There is a steady and rapid development of the more complex gross motor skills, particularly from 9 to 12 years. A great variety of skills involving agility and precise, large-scale muscular coordination are features of play at these ages.

Also characteristic of the play activities of school-age children are the more formal ages involving gross motor skills. Gutteridge (1939) studied the development of the skills involved in such games as baseball. She found that, although children begin practicing throwing at ages 2 or 3, it is not until they have reached 5½ or 6 years of age that the majority (75 to 85 percent) of children can throw a ball well. Throwing a ball, of course, is a complicated act. Gesell, Halverson, Thompson, Ilg, Castner, and Ames (1940) analyzed the process of throwing:

> Throwing involves visual localization, stance, displacement of bodily mass, reaching, release, and restoration of static equilibrium. Skill in throwing a ball requires a fine sense of static and dynamic balance, accurate timing of delivery and release, good eye-hand coordination, and appropriate functioning of the fingers, as well as the arms, trunk, head, and legs, in controlling the trajectory of the ball. [pp. 84–85]

Interdisciplinary cooperation in observation and in helping children in their motor development have proved effective. Such a cooperative effort by an early-education teacher and a physical education specialist revealed wide variation in throwing and catching skill among 4-year-olds (Williston, in Kjer, 1971). In their efforts to help individual children to gain greater competence and feeling of success, they "chose to lessen or increase the challenge of a task as we saw children showing mastery or frustration with the equipment." "The ball is coming toward your hands"; "Try to throw the bean bag softer this time" are examples of the verbal means employed. During a relatively short period of time they observed much skill improvement and many signs of increased satisfaction in motor activity in individual children (Kjer, 1971, pp. 47–49).

It is during the preteen years, however, that throwing skill, along with catching, fielding, batting, and the other fine points of the game of baseball, are perfected. Team games requiring a rather high degree of motor skill constitute an important aspect of life during this period. Girls frequently participate with the boys in certain of these games, often acquiring skills comparable to those of boys. Govatos (1959), for example, found that on the average, at 10 years of age, boys did not differ significantly from girls in such motor skills as the jump and reach, standing broad jump, 25-yard dash, underhand ball throw for distance, and accuracy of ball throw. Only on those tests that involved superior strength in arms and legs (soccer kick for distance and ball throw for distance) were the boys found to be significantly superior to the girls.

It is during these preadolescent years, however, that sex cleavage generally is most pronounced. Blair and Burton (1951) describe this apparent sex antagonism:

> The apparent antagonism between boys and girls at this age is one of the most commonly observed characteristics of childhood. Parents and teachers have long recognized an inordinate amount of teasing between the sexes in the upper elementary grades as well as the almost complete exclusion of the opposite sex from the other's play groups. . . .
>
> Although this teasing and antagonism usually appears about equally reciprocal, there is some indication that it is more pronounced in boys. On the basis of her observation Zachry (1940) notes that girls of this age spend most of their time with girls of their own age. Often, however, they seem to be doing so less of choice than of necessity. If they assert that boys are horrid or nasty, their scorn does not always ring quite true. It is less convincing than the aloofness or teasing with which the young boy meets them; more often than not it is a mode of self defense or retaliation. [pp. 34–35]

Boys, nevertheless, recognize playing skill, and in spite of any tendency they may show generally to reject girls from their company, they often welcome a good girl ballplayer on their team.

Fine Motor Coordination

During these middle years great strides are also made in the development of the more finely coordinated muscular skills. These middle years are the school years. The schoolroom becomes an important segment of the child's environment. It is the business of the school among other things, to see that the child acquires some degree of proficiency in such essential skills as reading, writing, music, and other arts.

The complicated process of learning to see objects and to discriminate fine differences, as we have seen, requires time. Reading from the printed page is a highly complex and difficult psychomotor skill which is acquired in varying degrees of proficiency during elementary school years.

The companion skill of handwriting, likewise, is acquired at many levels of proficiency. Handwriting involves a complicated pattern of learned muscular coordinations. The muscles of the shoulder and wrist develop very rapidly during the early school years, but the muscles of the fingers and hand used in writing develop more slowly. Writing is another finely coordinated skill, in which both maturational readiness and practice are important factors in its achievement. It is but one of a large repertory of finely coordinated psychomotor skills of school-age children.

Influences and Trends in Prepuberal Motor Behavior

As was stated earlier, the range of variation in the achievement of motor skills by children becomes steadily greater with age. The variable influence of the environment plays an increasingly important role in determining both the particular kinds of motor activities in which children engage and the level of proficiency they attain.

Cultural Differences

The often-heard saying that children are alike the world over is true in a general sense, even with respect to the extent and nature of their motor activities. Prepubescent children, regardless of where they may be seen at play, are generally engaged in gross bodily activities—running, jumping, climbing, stunting, and the like. But the particular games they play and the specific motor-behavior patterns and skills involved in their play activities may actually differ greatly from culture to culture. Skillful ice skating and the game of hockey, for example, are very common among children in certain areas of the United States, but the environment of the islands of the South Pacific does not include the essential conditions for the achievement of these specific skills. Many other common patterns of play activity in children are specific to the particular environmental conditions that surround the child's growth.

Family Influences

It is a common observation that children differ widely in their play interests and in the specific skills in which they become proficient, even within the environmental limitations of a particular cultural setting. Family influences, of course, are among the important factors here. To be sure, most children in an ordinary American neighborhood play ball in the vacant lot or playground or in the street, but the degree of interest in baseball and the level of baseball skill a boy develops, in many instances, depend very largely upon the father's interest and the extent of his participation in such activities as playing catch with his young children in the backyard. Skill in instrumental music most frequently develops in musical families, and mechanical skill tends to develop in families where interest and proficiency in things mechanical are aspects of the paternal model.

Sex Differences

There is a tendency toward sex cleavage among preadolescents. During the early elementary school years, however, there is, as yet, little evidence of this antagonism. Sex differences in motor ability, in general, or interest in active muscular skills are relatively insignificant. It will be recalled that

Govatos (1959), in his study of motor-skill development, observed no significant sex differences, at age 10 years, in such skills as the jump and reach, standing broad jump, 25-yard dash, underhand ball throw, and accuracy of ball throw.

However, during these preadolescent years subtle changes are taking place in both boys and girls which gradually become manifest in differences in physical strength and in motivation to excel in feats of strength and skill. In general, boys develop superiority in activities involving large muscles and those requiring strength, bodily speed, and endurance. Govatos' 12-year-old boys were significantly superior to their female counterparts in such activities. Girls, on the other hand, generally excel in the more delicate movements involving eye–hand coordination and in body balance, such as ballet dancing and fancy skating.

Associated with the development of these differences in motor skills is a gradual shift in interests common to girls in the direction of femininity and interpersonal relations. As puberal changes take place, girls tend to lose interest in athletic activities and therefore do not practice them. It would seem to be important, from the standpoint of good health, that girls be encouraged to maintain some interest in gross physical activities. Thoughtfully designed programs in physical education for adolescent girls based upon, or coordinated with, the characteristically feminine interests of that age level should have a place in the school curriculum.

Importance of Motor Skills in Adolescence

Peer relations during adolescence take on new significance in the life of the young person. It is very important to the boy that he be able to participate effectively in the activities of his age group. Without the appropriate motor skills for such participation the youngster may tend to withdraw and become isolated. Again, proper guidance is important. In some instances individualized help and instruction can raise a poor or mediocre performance to a level which allows the youngster to experience success and to attain social acceptance.

During the postpuberal period there is generally a marked increase in speed and accuracy of movement as well as in physical strength. Adolescence is not the "awkward age." When growth is rapid, as during the puberal growth spurt, the child might actually be unfamiliar with his own physical dimensions, and thus he may appear to be awkward as he moves about, occasionally bumping into furniture or knocking things over. Self-consciousness, which is especially characteristic of early adolescence, might also contribute to the youngster's apparent awkwardness.

In general, however, adolescence is a period of great vigor, speed, and fine muscular coordination. Agility, rather than awkwardness, generally characterizes adolescent motor behavior.

Temperament and Motor Activity

As in many other aspects of their development, our subjects Paul and Sally presented an interesting contrast in motor behavior and competence. This contrast relates back to a basic temperamental difference between them noted earlier (and examined in greater detail in Chapter 13). At various points in his developmental record Paul is described as serious, contemplative, stable, deliberative, persistent, shy, and "a bit socially unresponsive," as compared with his vivacious, gay, friendly, charming, graceful, impulsive sister. This contrast in behavior and temperament persisted through the years of their development.

In gross bodily movements, Sally was more rapid and skillful. Paul was superior in fine muscular coordinations. As a preschooler, Paul was interested in music and liked to sing. Block building was his favorite motor activity. He designed elaborate trains and was "extremely careful in placing the blocks, being very sensitive to spacing." However, he showed interest in a wide range of play materials, particularly those that involved skillful manipulation. Although he was not as active as most 6-year-olds, he was described as "flexible" in his work with materials, showing considerable ingenuity and fine muscular control. As a school-age child in the crafts shop he "used the electric saw with confidence and accuracy far above that expected of a child of his age."

Sally, more vigorous and impulsive, delighted in the active, more social kinds of recreational activities. As a teenager she especially liked bowling, horseback riding, and swimming. Although as adolescents the twins often enjoyed some of these recreational activities together, Paul continued to spend relatively more time by himself, often listening to classical music on the family record player.

As to the possible relation between Paul's constitutional nature and his preferences in motor functioning, one can only conjecture. It will be recalled, (Chapter 4), however, that his somatotype, as assessed from posed photographs by an expert, was judged to be such as not to favor Paul in competition with his peers in athletic sports. The one activity for which his particular body type was well suited was swimming. This was Paul's favorite sport.

Physical Fitness and Motor Development

The physical fitness status of the population of the United States in the recent past became a matter of national concern. There appeared to be general agreement that American youth did not "measure up" well on the physical fitness tests, but there was lack of consensus as to how these findings were to be interpreted. McCammon and Sexton (1958) pointed out:

> Fitness at best is a vague concept which can only be defined in terms of the purposes for which the individual desires to be fit. . . . Fitness at the

time of testing may vary markedly, dependent on the standard of measurement used. The response to conditioning programs, such as athletic participation, is a highly individual thing rather than a group or age phenomenon. . . . The expectation is unrealistic that any conditioning program applied to a general population of any age level will produce uniform response. [p. 1440]

The suggestion here is that more research, particularly of a longitudinal nature, is called for regarding the physical fitness status of American youth. According to Govatos (1960):

It becomes evident, then, that an approach which takes cognizance of periodic measurements of a child's motor skill development in relation to size, weight, structure, speed, strength, and overall coordination is needed. . . . Furthermore, additional information in this area permits one to use the "whole child" concept and to apply it to the field of motor skill development. [p. 132]

There is no question about the importance of physical fitness. Nor is there any question that the development of motor skills is still an essential aspect of development, even in a society where the trend is toward effortlessness and gadget living. Questions are raised only as to methods of appraising fitness level and of promoting higher levels of health and physical fitness.

Summary

Adequate motor performance is a tremendously important and pervasive human need. It is a source of profound satisfaction. By contrast, to be unable to *do*, or to be environmentally prevented from functioning according to the situation at hand, normally gives rise to negative emotions and to ego damage. Nothing will more surely and immediately enrage a young infant, for example, than physically hampering his free bodily activity. It is the functioning process, more than the product of the activity, that is the source of human satisfaction.

Throughout the course of development beyond infancy, the child's sense of self-esteem and personal worth is largely a matter of how he views himself in terms of his motor facility and competence. And a sense of functional competence generally makes for ease and confidence in interpersonal and other social relations.

Aside from the child's self-image, his actual status in terms of others' reactions to him is largely determined by his motor competence. As we shall see in Chapter 8, the only available basis for evaluating an infant's intelligence is his motor performance. Later in his development his motor prowess will become even more important in relation to the reactions of others toward him.

Effective motor functioning is completely dependent upon the maturity of the physical structures involved. Motor-behavior patterns obviously cannot appear until the structures involved have developed within the organism. As has already been emphasized, early exercise through stimulation of individual muscles and other involved structures is an important factor, along with biological maturation, in producing the necessary level of maturity (structural readiness). In order, then, to trace the development of the motor abilities we must begin at the point where the muscle and neural tissues involved develop to the point of readiness to function, which may actually be an early period in prenatal development. The fetus becomes "quickened." Its newly formed muscles begin to twitch. It begins to move. It is appropriate for us, therefore, to think of motor behavior as beginning its course of development through exercise months before birth.

By the time of birth two general orders of motor activity are well established: simple, specific reflexes and uncoordinated, nonspecific mass activity. Very soon the reflexes begin to become organized and intercoordinated, and out of the mass activity are developed integrations and coordinations of muscular activity which eventually come under voluntary control.

These coordinated patterns very largely center around the functioning of the two sets of limbs, and these developments become some of the more important distinguishing characteristics of the human species. Hence, it is meaningful to identify two basic functional developmental tasks of infancy: the development of the reaching-grasping-manipulatory function of the upper limbs and the development of erect bipedal locomotion, the basic human function of the lower limbs. From these two basic patterns of motor activity and their intercoordinations are derived the vast majority of motor activities and skills that characterize the normally functioning human being.

CHAPTER 8

The Nature and Development of Intelligence

In the preceding chapter we were concerned primarily with the development of the child's ability to function *overtly* in his external environment. We followed the course of this aspect of developmental change from its prenatal origins through the relative helplessness of infancy to the smooth and efficient performances of later adolescence. Our focus was the manner in which the child acquires the abilities to move about independently, to grasp objects and manipulate them manually, and to investigate and deal directly with objects and features of the material world.

Emergence in the Child of the Cognitive Function

We now concern ourselves with a "higher level" of functioning in relation to the environment in which the central nervous system plays a more prominent role. This higher level of activity is generally referred to as *cognitive* activity—activity in the mind, in contrast to motor activity that is concerned with the activity of the body.

It must be remembered that this motor-mental distinction is artificial. Both categories involve the functioning of physical structures, but are arbitrarily divided by the nature of the manipulative act involved. In the one case material objects are grasped, moved, and manipulated through the use of physical structures of the body. In the other symbols and ideational representations of the concrete world are centrally manipulated with relatively little involvement of gross physical structures. Thus the distinction between motor and mental is largely one of degree of overt neuromuscular activity involved. Motor activity, however, is centrally mediated and controlled by cognition, and some degree of motor activity is usually (if not always) involved in cognitive activity.

As we have seen, the functioning of the neonate appears to be completely neuromuscular, but with time we find that mental (centrally mediated) behavior gradually emerges. Very quickly the baby begins to "know" and to cope with his environment through his motor responses to stimulation. His eyes follow a patch of color or a patterned object. He responds to the sound of another's approaching footsteps. He kicks and thrashes about with his arms in a random, disorganized manner, thus bringing his hands in contact with objects within his reach. These he grasps, mouths, and shakes and bangs and thus experiences them with his senses. There is no evidence, however, that in the very beginning these simple sensorimotor activities involve the *awareness* of the *objects* from which the stimulation comes.

But development is rapid. Soon, with further maturation and experience, the baby learns to differentiate objects and to respond to them *as* objects. His motor behavior now is associated in his experience with the cognitive awareness of things and people. His behavior with them becomes meaningful and purposive. His motor manipulations become more effectively coordinated and more frequently directed toward adjustment to and coping with the environment. From such experiences *concepts* of objects, situations, and relations are gradually formed. These concepts can now be ordered and manipulated implicitly. The child becomes more and more able to foresee the probable outcomes of alternative overt acts. He tries them out mentally before performing them physically.

The basis for differentiating between motor activity and cognitive activity, then, is that the latter involves to a greater degree the functioning of the central nervous system. It consists of a greater degree of manipulation of ideational representations of objects and situations rather than the objects and situations themselves. Implicit behavior of this sort is referred to as mental or cognitive behavior. But the so-called motor behavior of the infant, in a very legitimate sense, is also cognitive behavior. The infant does reveal his mentality in a test by means of his motor performance.

Intelligence—Many-Faceted Concept

The cognitive aspect of the child's functioning continues to expand as he develops. As he interacts with his environment, the effectiveness of his behavior improves as the controlling influences of his emerging cognition become more and more pervasive.

The term *intelligence* is generally applied to this whole area of central functioning together with its guiding and controlling influence upon behavior. "Intelligence" is a word on everyone's lips. It carries a large core of common meaning in ordinary conversation. Everyone "knows" what the speaker means when the term "intelligence" is used, and no one is likely to ask for a definition. But in case someone, a stray psychologist, perhaps, should demand a definition, the difficulty and confusion begins. A search is made for synonyms in common usage. "Knowledge," the "mind," "understanding," "power to comprehend," "good sense," "knowing what it's all about" are among the likely attempts.

The "Common Sense" Meaning of Intelligence

What intelligence really means to people in daily life, however, becomes obvious as one listens to what is said in common conversation about the behavior of specific individuals.

"He handled the job very well."
"That was a stupid thing to do."
"He's such a bright little boy."

People are called "dumb," "clever," "thoughtful," "silly," "bright," "capable," "undiplomatic," and these evaluations and comments always refer to *performance*, to behavior in specific situations. People are often heard to

express satisfaction or dissatisfaction with their own performance in a group
or in some critical situation.

> "I felt so inadequate."
> "I really acted very stupidly."

Thus a person is regarded as "clever," "bright," "intelligent," and so on,
when he functions adequately in terms of the requirements of a particular
situation. He is called "dumb" or "stupid" when he "goofs" a situation.
Intelligence, then, in everyday life means *functional adequacy*, competence,
capability, effectiveness. General intelligence is a pervasive characteristic of
an individual. It is interesting to note that this "common sense" definition of
the term corresponds very closely with the current widely held view of the
nature of intelligence by students of education.

Problem Areas and Theoretical Views

Historically, there have been three main areas of concern from which
theories have been derived and in terms of which definitions of intelligence
have been formulated:

1. The question of the factors which underlie individual differences
2. The question of the nature and structure of intelligence
3. The nature of the process of mental development.

We shall examine each of these highly interrelated questions separately
to try to arrive at a concept of the nature and development of intelligence.

Determining Factors of Individual Differences

In other chapters we have made reference to man's perennial
interest in his own "inner life." Man has always been particularly curious
about his own capacities and abilities and about how he came by them. He
has always observed wide differences in level of ability among individuals,
as has been evident from the variations in their functional effectiveness in
everyday life. Society has been plagued with the problem of what to do with
or how to care for the extremely deficient. The approach to this problem has
ranged from the custom of exposure of defective infants during ancient times
to placing them in Church asylums in the early Christian era, where they
were pitied but not understood. Then society went through a period of strong
Protestant influence when the emphasis was upon the repsonsibility of the
individual himself for his deeds and misdeeds, and the mentally deficient
were punished and tortured. Finally, with the advent of the scientific era of
modern times, efforts have been made to understand the nature of intellectual

deficiency and to improve the lot of the mentally defective through education and training. In dealing with this perennial problem through the ages, the assumption has usually been that these extreme deviates were "born" that way, and that society itself, with its customs and modes of social interaction (the environment), could not in any way be responsible as a causal or complicating factor to the problem.

The scientific study of individual differences in performance began during the latter part of the nineteenth century (Chapter 1). Work in Wundt's laboratory in Leipzig was an important stimulus and suggested techniques for the appraisal of abilities. James McKeen Cattell championed the work in this country. As early as 1890 we find, for the first time, the word "test" in relation to problems of evaluation. In 1894 Cattell began to administer his tests to students of Columbia College. He urged the establishment of measurement norms and the standardization of tests.

Biological Inheritance

Many other individuals have made significant contributions to the development of techniques for the measurement of individual differences. Perhaps the greatest advance, and certainly the strongest reinforcement, of the assumption of the hereditary nature of individual differences came from the work of the great British scientist Sir Francis Galton. In his book *Hereditary Genius,* originally published in 1869, Galton implanted the idea of a biologically inherited intelligence: "I propose to show in this book that a man's natural abilities are derived by intelligence under exactly the same limitations as the form and physical features of the whole organic world."

He also introduced the concept of continuous quantitative variations among individuals and thus began the breakdown of the then commonly accepted idea of the existence of specific types such as "idiots" and "geniuses." Galton's idea was that people differ from each other in ability by measurable amounts and cannot be grouped into separate types. Galton's greatest emphasis was upon biological heredity as the only factor that determines individual differences in intelligence. American psychologists tended generally to accept this view without question as an established fact.

In the prevalent theory of development during this period the concept of *maturation* as a basic biological process was stressed. This emphasis, of course, was in complete harmony with the then-current biological deterministic view. Accordingly, children should not be pressured in any way. Parents and teachers should take care not to interfere with this fundamental process of natural development in children. The children should be protected from the possible undesirable effects of a lively environment rather than to be stimulated by it. Arnold Gesell, one of the early "greats" in the field of child development, stressed the importance of maturation—the biologically controlled "unfoldment"—of an inherent design in individual development.

The idea of inherited general intelligence was the basic assumption from which intelligence tests were devised and in terms of which their results were interpreted. A clear distinction, of course, was drawn between intelligence and knowledge and acquired abilities. It was realized that a child's responses to the items of the test and his solutions to the problems presented to him had been learned from his environment. However, in theory at least, in the test situation the environmental factor as a determiner of individual differences could be controlled experimentally by the nature of the test items themselves. These were presumed to be either so much a part of the daily environment of all children, or so strange and new and apart from common experience, that individual differences in the testees' performance had to be due to differences in the inborn factor of intelligence.

Inherent in the concept of inborn general intelligence is the idea of increase in amount with age. Intelligence was conceived of, and superficially defined as, an inherited *potentiality* for mental development—and it was assumed that growth in amount as the child grows toward adulthood, was always within the limits of the inherited potentiality. Hence there was need in the business of intelligence testing for two measurement indexes—one representing the level of potential itself, which was presumed not to change, and one for the level of development attained within the limits of his potential by the individual at any particular age.

To provide these indexes of intelligence an *average* test performance for each age level was established. In the testing procedure the particular child's performance is compared with these age averages. If his performance score, for example, is at the average level of 6-year-olds, he is said to have a "mental age" of 6, regardless of his own actual age. Mental age thus defined became the index of *attained* mental status. It was regarded as a very significant measure, a measure of the child's attained—but changing—*level of capacity* to learn and acquire new skills. Thus a common textbook definition of intelligence was derived. "Intelligence is the *capacity* to acquire and perfect new modes of adaptation. . . . What makes a person intelligent is *not* what he knows or can do, but his capacity to easily and quickly acquire that knowledge and ability to do" (Daschiell, 1928, p. 306.). The mental age, then, is taken as an index of this "changing capacity to acquire, and the ratio between the child's mental age at any point, and his chronological age at the time— the *intelligence quotient* (IQ)—is regarded as a rough and very inaccurate index of his mental potentiality—his "general intelligence."

Until the early 1930s the assumption of inherited intelligence remained virtually unchallenged. In the early 1920s the Child Welfare Research Station at Iowa University became established and began its program of research about children, their nature, and how they develop. This was at the beginning of an era of the laboratory nursery schools in this country. Among the areas of interest of the Iowa group was the potential effects of nursery school attendance upon the mental development of children.

Comparative studies were made, and in the mid-1930s the results of these studies began to appear in the research monographs of the Station and in the psychological journals (Wellman, 1934, Wellman and Coffey, 1936, 1937, 1938). These studies were also concerned with other environmental influences, particularly the quality of the early home environment upon cognitive development (Skeels and Filmore, 1937; Skeels, Updegraff, Wellman, and Williams 1938; and Skodak, 1939).

As a result of these reports a controversy among authoritative writers and users of intelligence tests developed. The psychological journal literature of that time indicates the extent to which the assumption of biological determinism had become ingrained in psychological thinking. The great resistance on the part of the authorities to a rational consideration of evidence not in accord with that theoretical position is evidence of the bias of that time (Goodenough, 1940).

Environmental Determinism

As research in the various areas of human development and related disciplines continued and expanded throughout the world, other theoretical positions concerning the nature of intelligence and its determining factors were developed. Sociologists and cultural anthropologists generally tend to assume a theoretical position which is strongly environmentalistic and which emphasizes the importance of cultural influences and other aspects of the environment as factors that determine mental as well as other characteristics.

There is currently a tendency, particularly among educational theorists and students of infant development, to emphasize the efficacy of the environmental factor almost to the point of neglecting completely the factor of genetic endowment. Such programs as Head Start reflect an underlying hope that by placing culturally deprived children in a nurturant and intellectually stimulating environment the commonly observed mental deficit found in such children will be overcome. There also appears in the utterances and writings of some leaders in educational theory the idea that functional intelligence is generated from environmental stimulation, that we can "create intelligence" by controlling and manipulating the environment. Generally, these leaders do not mean to deny the basic reality and importance of genetic endowment. Rather, in their enthusiasm for what can be done for the cognitive development of children by a wise structuring and an understanding manipulation of the environment, they tend to ignore the genetic factor (Bruner, 1968; Combs, Avila, and Purkey, 1971)

Interactionism

Intensive studies of basic developmental processes in such fields as biochemistry, genetics, and developmental physiology and psychology have contributed to the formulation of the general point of view referred to as interactionism, which is currently generally accepted in the fields of human development and psychology. According this viewpoint, the factors of biological heredity and environmental stimulation are equally important and essential to life and to all development. All development is a product of these two factors in interaction.

However, when one is concerned with *differences* between *individuals* in level of development of any structure or function, that *difference*, theoretically, *can* be due entirely to either a difference in heredity or a difference in environment. But the question of which of these two factors, heredity or environment, underlies group differences—that is, differences among socioeconomic, cultural, and racial groups, in average cognitive functional level is currently an unresolved issue.

The Nature-Nurture Controversy

Attempts have been made in recent years to revive what was regarded as a dead issue—the question of whether a given human trait, in this case intelligence, can be entirely a result of heredity or of environment. In one article, for example, published in the *Saturday Review* (Boyer and Walch, 1968) the authors seriously raised the question, "Are children born unequal?" In their discussion they confused the two separate issues briefly discussed above, namely, the question of whether certain human traits and characteristics are genetically determined and the quite different question of the causes of individual differences in any particular trait.

In regard to the first of these two issues Boyer and Walch were not careful to keep clear the further distinction between the *trait* as such (as observed and measured in the individual) and his original *potentiality* for the development of that trait. As was stated earlier, the *limits* of individual developmental potentiality *are* genetically set at conception.[1] Even though there may be no *proof* "that individual intellectual capacity is innately unequal," there is at every hand so much evidence that a wide range of congenital inequality exists among *individuals* within cultural, social, and racial groupings of all sorts as to be unexplainable in terms of environmental influences alone. Children are not *born* equally endowed. It is unfortunate but true that no amount of loving nurturance, no amount of pressure or tutoring, nor any amount of environmental enrichment can close the gap between the mentally deficient and the more richly endowed.

However, if by intelligence one is referring to an individual's *attained* level of capacity to adapt, to learn, to "easily and quickly acquire that knowledge and ability to do," then "intelligence" is most certainly not genetically inherited.

---

[1] It must be realized, of course, that one's genetically inherited potentiality and the potentiality with which one is born can be very different. As is shown in other connections (Chapter 3), there are many possibilties for environmental accidents and influences, both prenatally and paranatally, which can reduce developmental potential to varying degrees below that which was set genetically at conception.

An Unresolved Issue

That individuals differ in congenital mental *potential* seems to be beyond serious question. It is also a well-established observation that children from different racial, cultural, and socioeconomic groups differ in *average* tested mental capacity upon entering elementary school. There are also clearly observed group differences in level of capacity to profit immediately from school experience. However, the question as to what extent, if any, these *average group* differences have a basis in genetic mental endowment is one which still lacks real evidence. This is currently an unresolved issue. There is a tendency to not clearly differentiate between social and cultural *group* differences and *individual* differences within the groups. As was pointed out earlier, the current trend in the thinking of educational theorists and others is in the direction of environmental determinism in relation to racial and cultural group differences.

The Structural Nature of Intelligence

Inseparable from the assumption that intelligence is inborn was the idea of a single, but pervasive, *general* intelligence. According to this view, intelligence is unitary: all mental processes and all mentally directed activities—learning, thinking, adjusting to the environment—are functions of this single ability factor. Individual differences in the effectiveness of these various mental activities are attributed to differences in strength or amounts of general intelligence possessed.

During the 35-year period when most of the currently used intelligence tests were developed, this concept of unitary general intelligence was prevalent. William Stern (1914) formulated a definition that was representative of the thinking among psychologists of that period: "Intelligence is a general capacity of an individual consciously to adjust his thinking to new requirements. It is a general mental adaptability to new problems and conditions of life" (p. 3).

Spearman's Two-Factor Theory

Although Charles Spearman developed a theory known as the two-factor theory of intelligence, his work (1904, 1914, 1927) did much to establish the concept of a general-intelligence factor. The first and most important of his factors he called g. He conceived of it as a "general fund of mental energy," identified as general intelligence. In Spearman's thinking, this general factor is involved in every mental function or performance. Each specific mental function, however, also involves a second specific factor— the individual's specific ability for that particular kind of performance.

Spearman's theory stimulated much discussion. In opposition to the idea of a general factor, a rather different view was held by an equally influential psychologist, E. L. Thorndike (1914), who saw intelligence as consisting of many specific abilities not bound together by a common factor. Alfred Binet, the "father of intelligence testing," in his writings seemed also to share this view (Binet and Simon, 1916). Although Binet gave no single unified definition, he did offer a number of descriptions of the processes involved in intelligence. Intelligence, he wrote, is compounded of "judgment, common sense, initiative, the ability to adapt oneself . . . to judge well, reason well—these are essentials of intelligence" (p. 42). It would seem from these descriptions that Binet saw specific abilities in mental functioning. Nevertheless, his original test and all of its subsequent revisions clearly have been constructed on the theory that a "general fund of mental energy"—a general intelligence factor—was to be tapped into and evaluated.

Multiple Mental Abilities

As indicated above, the alternative view of the structure of intelligence was the concept of many specific abilities. Thorndike (1914), an outstanding early proponent of this view, wrote:

> the mind must be regarded not as a functional unit, nor even as a collection of a few general faculties which work irrespective of particular material, but rather as a multitude of functions each of which involves content as well as form, and so is related closely to only a few of its fellows, to the others with greater and greater degrees of remoteness. [p. 366]

It was not until some 20 years later that Thorndike's view of the nature of intelligence received substantial support from statistical research. In that interval considerable research was stimulated by Spearman's findings of the presence of a *g* factor, along with specifics (*s* factors) in mental functioning. In certain of these studies it was found that the intercorrelations between some pairs of mental tests were too high to be accounted for by their relatively low loadings of *g*. In other words, they appeared to involve a *common* factor in addition to *g*. These additional common factors came to be known as *group factors*. Spearman and his co-workers came to recognize a number of group factors, such as verbal ability, numerical ability, mental speed, mechanical ability, attention, and imagination. Concurrently, other analytical (statistical) procedures were designed to bring out group factors in a battery of tests. As a result, some new methods of factor analysis were devised (Hotelling, 1933; Kelley, 1935; Thurstone, 1935), and the research concerning the structure of intelligence was greatly augmented.

In 1938 Thurstone reported a study in which he applied his own technique to the analysis of the relations among 57 tests that had been designed to measure general intelligence. The data for his study were the scores of 240 university students. Before the advent of the electronic computer a factor analysis involving 57 variables was a tremendous task. Thurstone's analysis resulted in 13 factors. In his effort to interpret these factors, the last 4 of the 13 were discarded as having no significant psychological meaning. Thurstone's tentative designations of the 9 meaningful factors were *spatial, perceptual, numerical, verbal relations, memory, word fluency, induction, restriction,* and *deduction.*

In a later study Thurstone and Thurstone (1941) extended the search for "primary" mental abilities downward to younger ages. On the basis of this study the Thurstones concluded that the following six factors met their criteria of primary abilities:

V   verbal comprehension
W   word fluency
S   space
N   number relations
M   memory
I   induction

Thus, "general intelligence" was found to consist of at least six mental abilities. However, in an evaluation of these findings, Stoddard (1943) stated:

> None of these factors is considered as fixed, indivisable, or noncombining; each one is dependent for its validity on the nature of the tests and the population examined. But each primary ability behaves as a functional unit that is strongly present in some tests and almost completely absent in many others. [p. 165]

Guilford's Three-Dimensional Model of Mentality

Among other investigators using the multiple-factor-analysis approach to the problem of discovering and identifying the components of intelligence are Guilford (1954, 1956, 1957, 1958a,b, 1959, 1963, 1964) and R. B. Cattell (1957). Guilford and his co-workers, especially in connection with their "aptitudes" project, have concentrated particularly on the study of cognitive abilities. According to Guilford:

> the most significant outcome [of the project] has been the development of a unified theory of human intellect, which organizes the known, unique or primary intellectual abilities into a single system called the "structure of intellect." [1959, p. 469]

This system (the three-dimensional model, as shown in Figure 8.1) makes room for a large number of factors, each representing a distinct ability. These various ability factors are identified and ordered in terms of three

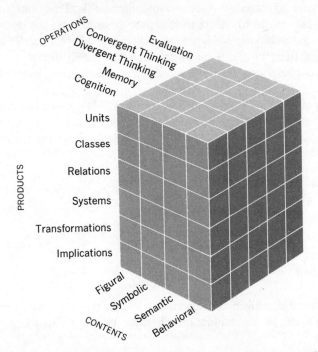

Figure 8.1 Guilford's theoretical model for the complete structure of intellect.

sets of classification categories. One of these bases of classification is a set of categories of *mental operations*. These categories are *cognition, memory, divergent thinking, convergent thinking,* and *evaluation*. In Guilford's conceptualization these categories constitute the basic kinds of mental processes, or *operations*, of the intellect.

The second set of classification categories is concerned with the kinds of *content* involved in the intellectual operations. In terms of an intelligence test, the actual material—the objects, tasks, and problems which compose the test—would be *content*. Mental tests ordinarily contain four kinds of content, as follows: *figural content*—concrete objects actually set before the child; *symbolic content*—letters, digits, and other conventional symbols which are usually organized into systems, such as the alphabet or the number system; *semantic content*—verbal meaning, ideas, and concepts; and *behavioral content*, representing the area of interpersonal relations sometimes called "social intelligence."

The third classification is in terms of the outcomes, or *products*, of the various operations as they are applied to any of the four kinds of content. Again, in terms of the test situation, the products are what the child does with the material with which he is confronted. Guilford's words may be helpful here:

When a certain operation is applied to a certain kind of content, as many as six general kinds of products may be involved. There is enough evidence available to suggest that, regardless of the combinations of operations and content the same six kinds of products are: *units, classes, relations, systems, transformations,* and *implications.* So far as we have determined from factor analysis, these are the only kinds of products that we can know. As such, they may serve as basic classes into which one might fit all kinds of information psychologically. [1959, p. 470]

In the simplest possible sort of test situation, a set of small wooden cubes (figural content) is placed before the baby. He looks at and grasps one of the cubes, thus becoming aware of it (cognitive operation) as a single, unitary object (a unit). Or he may become aware of it as one of a group of similar objects and begin to manipulate others with it in the same way. In this case the product of his cognitive operation in relation to simple figural content would be a *class.* An example at the other end of the complexity continuum in mental functioning in terms of operation, content, and product would be the *evaluation of behavioral implications.*

To summarize Guilford's view, the structure of the adult intellect is represented as a solid, three-dimensional figure (Fig. 8.1), the dimensions of which are the three sets of classification categories—the operations, the content, and the products. This conceptualization makes room for 120 separate factors of intelligence, many of which have already been identified in test behavior and measured. By "slicing" the model, as it were, into vertical layers in terms of the five categories of operations, we have five sets of 24 small cubes each. Each of these five sets, then, would represent a particular category of mental abilities. Thus, there are cognitive abilities, memory abilities, convergent thinking abilities, divergent (creative) thinking abilities, and evaluative, or judgmental, abilities. According to the model, each of the 24 cognitive abilities, for example, is an ability which deals with a particular kind of material, such as symbolic content. The outcome or product of that particular mental operation would then be the cognition of a symbolic unit or class or system, and so forth.

Since the early days of intelligence testing, then, we have seen an interesting shift in the nature of the prevailing notions about the structure of intelligence. As techniques of data analysis have been developed, many researchers have rejected the original view of intelligence as a unitary general ability that accounts for individual differences in any and all sorts of mental functioning in favor of a concept of greater and greater complexity. First, in addition to the *g* factor, certain specific, or group, factors were postulated to account for the observed relations among test variables. More refined analysis, however, soon led to the notion of multiple factors, as *g* became broken down into a relatively small number of primary mental abilities. The advent of the electronic computer, of course, led to a tremendous increase in factor-analytic capacity and efficiency. One currently prevailing concept of mental structure (Guilford's), then, makes room for a great variety of relatively independent mental abilities.

Cattell's Model of the Structure of Intelligence

Raymond B. Cattell is one of this country's most astute students of total personality generally, and more specifically, for our purpose, of the very pervasive and most tested personality variable, intelligence. He, like Guilford, bases his theoretical model of the nature of intelligence upon his own research, which was inspired originally by the approach and findings of Charles Spearman. For both Cattell and Guilford the basic data are individual performance "scores" on a large variety of "ability" tests. Both used the general method of multiple-factor analysis. Cattell, however, did not limit his analysis to the interrelations among the original test scores. He was interested further in the "second-order" factors which result from the analysis of the intercorrelations among the "first-order" factors. This difference in interest and procedure is the basis for the essential difference between these two influential men in their conceptualizations of the structural nature of intelligence.

Cattell found two significant second-order factors. These he called "fluid intelligence" and "crystallized intelligence." In effect, he found not just *one* "general-intelligence" factor, but two, both of which partake of the nature of Spearman's g. His first-order factors from which these were derived were of the same order as the many "abilities" which constitute Guilford's model. These abilities Cattell regards as those which normally develop from growing up in society—from school experience, family living, and so on. One of his second-order factors (crystalized intelligence) proved to be especially heavily loaded with these acquired abilities. Crystalized intelligence, as Cattell defines it, thus appears to be the intelligence referred to by those writers who charge the schools with the responsibility of "creating" intelligence. From this point of view. "Culturally deprived" children are deprived mainly in the sense that their early environments have not provided stimulation for "cognitive growth"—for an adequate level of development of crystallized intelligence.

Fluid intelligence, on the other hand, according to Cattell, "is a general relation-perceiving capacity independent of sensory area, and it is determined by the individual's *endowment* in cortical, neurological connection-count development. . . . The characteristic of fluid intelligence is that it leads to perception of complex relationships in new environments" (Cattell, 1969, p. 339). It appears to be close to what the so-called "I.Q. tests" were theoretically designed to measure indirectly—a mental power, as distinct from knowledge and acquired abilities. The level of one's fluid intelligence is the expression of his genetically determined potential for mental development. "Culture-fair" tests developed by Cattell were designed to be tests of fluid intelligence. These tests have not come into general use.

These two general-ability factors are positively correlated. The level of achievement of crystallized abilities depends not only upon environmental richness but primarily upon the individual's endowment of fluid intelligence.

Both Guilford's and Cattell's conceptualizations of the structural nature of mentality emphasize the complexity—the many-factored nature—of human intelligence. Guilford's model goes into more detail in classifying abilities in a three-dimensional scheme, that is, in terms of the mental operations involved, the content, and the outcome of the mental process in each case. This model theoretically identifies a great variety of separate abilities, each in terms of its three dimensions, but without differentiation in terms of their determinants. Cattell, on the other hand, furnishes a model in which "know-how" sheer acquired abilities to perform ("functional intelligence") are differentiated from the genetically determined potentiality to acquire that know-how and ability to perform. These two aspects of the intellect, Cattell believes, are important enough to be differentiated from both the theoretical and the practical points of view.

The Nature of Developmental Change in Intelligence

As we shall see, the nature of the continuous development that takes place in cognitive functioning between birth and maturity is a complex problem. This problem also is of practical, as well as theoretical, importance. The nature of mental growth is one of the three areas of concern referred to earlier in this chapter. Among the questions which require consideration are:

Does developmental change consist simply of an increase in amount of mental capacity as the child grows older, or is there change in kind?

How is the problem of the structural nature of intelligence involved in this question?

We need to concern ourselves with a number of issues involved in this area of inquiry.

Mental Development Regarded as Quantitative Change

That mentality grows in amount with the age of the child is obvious. The school child has *more* mental capacity than he had as a preschooler. This fact of quantitative change is basic to the early assumption that intelligence is a unitary, general, "inborn" quality. This assumed general factor, it was obvious, grows in amount as the child grows. Intelligence, it was assumed, grows quantitatively.

That this view of mental development was more of an assumption taken for granted than a logically developed conceptualization is suggested by the fact that it is difficult to find definite statements in the writings of psychologists during the early surge of the mental testing era, the first quarter of this century. Its purely quantitative nature was generally assumed with relatively little discussion of the other possible aspects of change.

Intelligence in the sense of mental capacity, of course, *does* grow. This increase, however, presented a problem of measurement. The problem of measuring mental capacity is of a different order of difficulty than that of other types of quantitative measurement such as determining increase in physical dimensions. There was no readily available source of standards for directly appraising mental capacity. It was not possible, therefore, immediately to plot a precise mental-growth curve for an individual child. There were no standard measurement units comparable to those used in the measurement and in the plotting of the physical growth curves shown in Chapter 4.

Investigators of mental development, however, have given this problem of measuring units considerable attention. A number of methods for providing standardized units have been proposed. One of the best-known and most widely used methods is to express the different levels of test performance in terms of *age equivalents*, or mental ages. A mental age, it will be recalled, is a *developmental* age. The mental age of a child at any point in his development is the chronological age of the particular age group of children whose *average* performance on an ability test corresponds to his own performance level on the test. For example, a child whose tested mental age is 10 years has performed on the test at the average level of performance of 10-year-old children. Mental-age units thus are equated to time units.

As we have seen, developmental-age units are very useful in that progress in diverse aspects of development can be rendered comparable. But when the purpose is to study the *actual course* of development in a particular structure, or in a function such as intelligence—in which there are periods of rapid *and* relatively slow change and with gradual leveling off as adulthood is approached—then the need is for equal or absolute units of amount not equated with the passage of time.

There has been much interest in the shape of the mental-growth curve and differences in these curves of individuals with differing mental endowment. Opinions differ as to the ages at which test performance of children with different degrees of endowment reaches its upper limit. As was pointed out by Thurstone (1925), in order to solve such problems, units for the measurement of mental growth must be devised in which *equal increments* of growth are represented equally in all parts of the curve. Thurstone devised a method for determining such measurement units using the statistical determination of an "absolute zero" as a starting point from which theoretically equal scale points are determined. Using this method, Thurstone plotted average mental-growth curves based upon data from various individual tests.

More recently, Bayley (1949, 1955) devised a method for transposing scores from different tests administered at different age levels into comparable units. In the use of this method each individual's scores "at all ages are expressed in terms of the 16-year standard deviations from the mean score at

16 years" (1955, p. 811). This procedure was applied to the test data of the Berkeley Growth Study. The resulting curve is shown in Figure 8.2.

It will be noted that, according to Figure 8.2, mental growth on the average is positively accelerated up to about 9 years of age, at which point it begins a negative acceleration, leveling off somewhat beyond 20 years of age. This generalized curve may be taken tentatively to represent the *average* development of mental capacity ("fluid intelligence," Cattell).

A general curve of mental growth, however, does not tell the whole story. As in every other aspect of development, every individual follows his own pattern, which differs in its details from those of others. Bayley (1949) clearly demonstrates this fact in a longitudinal study of five boys from 1 month to 25 years of age. She derived comparable units of measurement throughout by expressing each test score in terms of standard deviation (SD) units from the 16-year-old mean. Figure 8.3 shows five individual curves of mental growth (Bayley, 1955, p. 814). Note that each of these curves has something of the characteristic of the general curve (compare with Figure 8.2), yet each has its unique features.

Bloom (1964), in studies of longitudinal data, plotted mental-growth curves in terms of increases in correlation between IQ's derived at increasing age levels below the terminal age of 17 years and the IQ's obtained at that terminal age. Bloom's assumption was that increments of growth become smaller as the correlations between IQ's of successive age levels increase as the terminal age is approached.

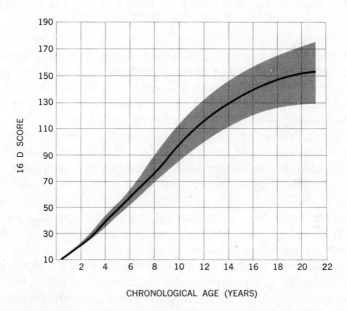

CHRONOLOGICAL AGE (YEARS)

Figure 8.2   Curves of means and SD's of intelligence by 16 D units from birth to age 21 years. From Bayley (1955), p. 811, by permission.

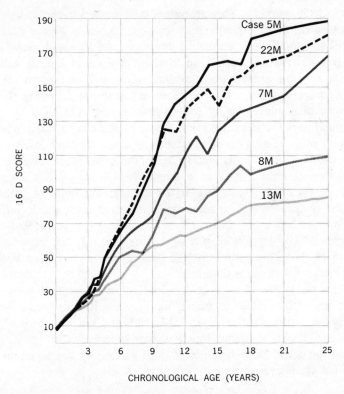

Figure 8.3   **Individual curves of intelligence (16 D units) for five boys, age 1 month to 25 years. From Bayley (1955), p. 815, by permission.**

One outcome of Bloom's work was a suggested general mental-growth curve (1964, p. 68) plotted in terms of percentages of adult status achieved, on the average, by children at various age levels. Figure 8.4 shows Bloom's suggested mental-growth curve. This curve is interesting in that it can be compared directly with the well-known Scammon curves (1930) of the growth of the various types of body tissue. It is interesting to compare Bloom's mental curve with the curve of growth in neural tissue (Scammon) —a direct confrontation of structural and functional development.

To make this comparison we must refer back to Figure 4.2, page 62. Curve B in that figure represents the generalized growth of nervous tissue, including the brain. Note again that this curve (B) very nearly reaches its adult level by age 10 years. Bloom's curve (Figure 8.4) suggests that approximately 86 percent of adult status in mental growth is reached by age 10 years. As has been emphasized throughout this text, the development of function is basically dependent upon development of structure. This presumably can account for the small difference in 10-year growth status in these curves of structure and function.

Thus far we have been concerned primarily with quantitative change in

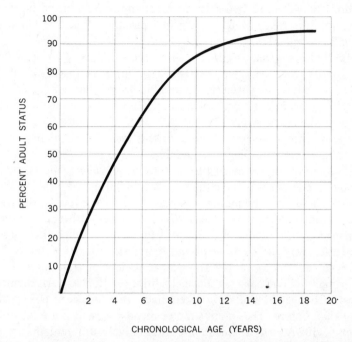

CHRONOLOGICAL AGE (YEARS)

Figure 8.4 A general curve of mental growth as suggested by Bloom (1964) and plotted in terms of percentage of adult status achieved at different ages.

mentality with increasing age. But, as we know, there is more involved in the problem of mental development than simply tracing quantitative growth.

Lack of Predictive Value of Infant Tests

One of the common objectives in mental testing at very early ages is the prediction of cognitive functioning at later ages. Many studies have been made of the relation between scores and ratings of babies on infant intelligence tests and the scores they obtain later as school-age children. Nancy Bayley (1933, 1940a, 1940b, 1955), an outstanding student of this problem, has been involved in the Berkeley Growth Study since its inception in 1928 and has made numerous studies of the mental test data of the project. She has been especially concerned with problems of testing intelligence during infancy and the early preschool periods.

In one of her studies, Bayley (1955) compared scores recorded for 45 infants at ages 6, 9, and 12 months on a test consisting of 31 items selected from her California Five Year Scale, with mental test scores made by these same individuals at ages 16, 17, and 18 years. The 31 test items of the infant test were selected for this purpose because in previous studies they had shown the highest statistical correlation with later test scores. However, Bayley's correlations between the two sets of scores showed the usual lack of significant relationship. They were +.09 for 6 months, +.32 for 9 months, and +.30 for 12 months.

These findings agree essentially with other studies of the problem. They are consistent, for example, with Bloom's findings discussed above. The general conclusion is that it is impossible to predict with any degree of accuracy from an infant's performance on a test what his mental functioning will be when he reaches school age.

There are many possible reasons for this lack of "predictive validity" of infant tests. Actually, findings such as Bayley's are just what is to be expected when thought of in terms of the currently prevalent notion that mental development consists of a continuous accumulation of new abilities, new knowledge, and understanding resulting from a process of transaction between organism and environment. When the interval between tests is short, performance on the second test depends upon interchange that was perhaps actually underway at the time of the first test. When the interval is long, however (6 months to 16 years), a great variety of transations have taken place, bringing about changes that bear little relation to performance on the early tests. Changes in kind have taken place. Intelligence is now qualitatively different than before. The infant's motor responses, which are his only means of dealing with his environment, are qualitatively different than the largely verbal responses of the older individual.

A reliable means of appraising cognitive developmental potential for growth, and thus predicting future mental capacity, would be of considerable practical value, for instance, to adoption agencies and prospective adoptive parents. The lack of such predictive value in the available infant tests clearly brings into question the nature of infant mentality and of developmental change in intelligence with age.

Mental Development as Qualitative Change

As we have noted in other connections, intelligence, according to the currently prevailing view, is a complex accumulation of knowledge, abilities, and skills acquired as the individual meets, copes with, and interacts with his environment. And according to Cattell's model of mentality, this is indeed one "kind" of intelligence—"crystallized" intelligence. This facet of mentality, consisting as it does of continuous acquisitions from the culture, would necessarily change in *quality* (or kind) with age and experience. New qualities, new patterns of adaptation, emerge as the child grows and interacts with his environment.

Although Arnold Gesell strongly emphasized the basic importance in development of the process of biological maturation, which we might think of as underlying the development of *fluid* intelligence, or growing mental capacity, he also strongly expressed in his writings the idea of qualitative change in mental development. He described the mind as a process that is the organizing, integrating, and controlling function of the individual. Mental growth, or growth of the mind, was seen by Gesell as a process of "behavior patterning":

> The child's mind does not grow by a simple linear extension. He has persisting individuality, but his outlook on life and on himself transforms as he matures. He is not simply becoming more intelligent in a narrow sense of this misused term. He *alters* as he grows. [Gesell, Halverson, Thompson, Ilg, Castner, and Ames, 1940, p. 15, italics added]

Gesell identified "mind" with the functioning of the neuromuscular system and other involved physical structures and "mental growth" with the maturation of these structures. In other words, mental development he conceived as the functional aspect of biological maturation—a process that brings about change in kind as well as increase in amount. Gesell further stated that this process, in which environment plays only an "inflecting" and "specifying" rather than an "engendering" role, takes place under the control, and within the limits of, a genetically determined developmental pattern.

Piaget's Epigenetic Theory of Mental Development

Piaget's views regarding mental development were referred to in the discussion of motor development in Chapter 7. He and his associates were the first actually to formulate a theory in which the *nature* of mental-developmental change as such was a primary concern (Piaget, 1952). Certainly there is a strong implication running through his writings that he regards developmental change in mental functioning as qualitative as well as quantitative in nature.

Piaget views intelligence in very dynamic terms. Like Gesell, he defines it as a process—one of organization—"an assimilating activity whose functional laws are laid down as early as organic life, and whose successive structures serving it as organs are elaborated by interaction between itself and the external environment" (1952, p. 359). Three essential elements are contained in his theory. First, he emphasizes the idea that intelligence is a dynamic *process*, an activity. Second, he indicates that the nature of that process is organization and adaptation. The third point is that this process, that is the operation of certain invariant functional laws, assimilation and accommodation, results in many variable structures [schemata or behavior patterns, new acquisitions, abilities, and so on] which in turn become the tools, or means, for further interaction with the environment through assimilation and accommodation.

Piaget's concept of invariant functional laws is central and essential to his theory. The process of organization (*assimilation* and *accommodation*) he sees as fundamental to all aspects of mental development and at all levels. In discussing these principles in their broader application, Piaget wrote:

it can be said that the living being assimilates to himself the whole universe, at the same time that he accommodates himself to it. . . . It is therefore permissible to conceive assimilation in a general sense as being the incorporation of any external reality whatever to one part or another, of the cycle of organization. In other words, everything that answers a need of the organism is material for assimilation, the need even being the expression of assimilatory activity as such. [pp. 407–408]

This, of course, is the process of interchange or interaction with the environment. It was stated in different words in Chapter 5 as the process of augmenting one's "cognitive structure." For example, as a toddler learns to use a new word by associating a sound pattern with its referent, he "assimilates" that bit of his auditory environment to his own cognitive structure. His "intelligence" grows with the acquisition of a new ability.

It is clear that in Piaget's thinking developmental changes in mentality from birth to maturity constitute a fixed sequence of stages, each characterized by its particular organization of structures (schemata). Each stage is qualitatively different from the one from which it emerges. At the same time, there is complete continuity in the course of this development. The same processes are at work from the beginning in the organization of newer schemata on the basis of the older, simpler ones. He states that new schemata "whose appearances mark each stage, are always revealed as developing from those of the preceding stage" (p. 384). Piaget's concept of developmental change, or emergence from one "stage" to another, seems to imply a genetically engendered sequence of stages or *capacity levels*. This process presumably constitutes the development of "fluid intelligence" as Cattell (1971) conceives it. These capacity levels underlie the acquisition, by assimilation and accommodation, of new schemata—that is, patterns of functioning. These patterns of functioning can be compared to Cattell's "crystallized abilities."

Both Piaget and Gesell see mental development as qualitative change, but their thinking is considerably different concerning the basis or explanation of that change. Gesell placed great emphasis upon the importance of the "mechanism of maturation," which brings about these qualitative changes through the natural unfoldment of a predetermined developmental design. Piaget, on the other hand, recognizes the important role of the environment. Mental development for him is not predetermined, is not solely a product of biological maturation, but is rather a result of continuous interaction— accommodation and assimilation—between the individual and his environment.

From Piaget's point of view, the character and variety of environmental stimulation looms as a matter of prime importance. In the very early weeks of life the infant is incapable of direct, voluntary action on his own initiative. He can simply respond to changes and variations in his immediate environment and internal conditions. Therefore, if he is to develop functionally to an optimal degree, his environment must provide changes and variation in conditions for him to cope with. As Hunt (1961) wrote:

The more new things an infant has seen, and the more new things he has heard, the more new things he is interested in seeing and hearing; and the more variation in reality he has coped with, the greater is his capacity for coping. Such relationships derive from the conception that change in circumstances is required during the early sensorimotor stages to force the accommodative modifications in schemata and the assimilations that, in combination, constitute development. [p. 262]

Piaget (1952, 1960) traced the development of intelligence through five major periods, maintaining throughout, of course, that development is continuous and that each stage grows out of, or develops from, the preceding one.

The Sensorimotor Period

Piaget elaborated in considerable detail the earliest period, the sensorimotor period, tracing development through six stages. His description of these early stages was derived mainly from carefully recorded observations of his own three children.

This series of "organizations," which are the products as well as the tools of assimilation and accommodation, begins at birth. But at birth the organizations consist only of congenital sensorimotor schemata and these, as they are further coordinated and elaborated, continue to characterize intelligence throughout the first 18 months or 2 years of the child's life.

The first stage of the sensorimotor period extends roughly through the first month of life. It is characterized by the exercise of the ready-made congenital schemata such as sucking, vocalizing, listening, looking, and so forth. In the very beginning there is simply passive release of these patterns by stimulation. There is, however, during this stage a gradual shift to an active "groping." "The subject does not remain passive but, on the contrary, manifests the behavior pattern emphasized by Jennings: He gropes and abandons himself to a series of 'trials and errors.' That is . . . the origin of intelligence" (Piaget, 1952, p. 396). The reflex thus becomes "consolidated and strengthened by virtue of its own functioning" (p. 32). It is assimilated to the child's needs and functioning. At the same time it becomes adapted (accommodated) to the realities of the situation through the groping trial-and-error process. This trial-and-error, "groping" behavior described by Piaget corresponds very closely to McGraw's (1943) Phase A in her description of the young infant's learning to reach and grasp objects (Chapter 7, p. 150).

The second stage is characterized by the progressive coordination of the ready-made schemata to form motor habits and perceptions. These reflex processes are progressively integrated into cortical activity. Three main developments are recognized during this stage: (1) Variations in schemata appear as a variety of stimuli become associated with them. (2) A reciprocal coordination among schemata takes place, for example, hand movements, to a degree, become coordinated with sucking, and things looked at become something to be reached for and grasped. (3) Although the child is unable developmentally at the time to respond to a "vanished object," repeated stimulation by objects leads to the perceptual recognition of them. This second stage, according to Piaget's observations, extends from about the end of the first month to about age 5 months.

Stage three extends to about 8 or 9 months of age. Here again there is functional continuity between the earlier stage and the increasingly complex structures. As contrasted with the earlier stage when the baby's actions are "centered on themselves"—when he grasps for the sake of grasping—his actions in this third stage become

> centered on a result produced in the external environment, and the sole aim of the action is to maintain this result; furthermore, it is more complex, the means beginning to be differentiated from the ends, at least after the event. [Piaget, 1952, p. 157]

The child now begins to show some anticipation of the consequences of his own acts—the beginning of intentionality.

The fourth stage of the sensorimotor period is characterized by the "coordination of the secondary schemata and their application to new situations." It is during this stage (8 or 9 months to 11 or 12 months of age) that "the first actually intelligent behavior patterns" appear (p. 210). Behavior patterns which heretofore were detached now become coordinated into a single, more complex act with the aim of *attaining an end* which is not immediately attainable or within reach. The infant thus puts to work, *by intention*, series of single schemata now coordinated for a new purpose. In this way the child begins to exhibit behavior in which means are clearly differentiated from ends. In his new relations with his environment the accommodation aspect of his adaptations is especially apparent as he begins to differentiate self from not-self and is able to search, to a limited degree, for the "vanished object." He also shows evidence of an implicit conception of causality, and he appears to foresee events that are independent of his own acts.

This stage four, although it evolves from, and is a further development of the earlier stage, is clearly marked by features that are qualitatively different. However, as Piaget pointed out, the child is still quite limited in the effectiveness of his coping by two related conditions. First, he is limited in his ability to reach his goal through the removal of obstacles or the taking of an essential intermediate step by the fact that, so far, he is able to inter-coordinate and thus to utilize only *familiar* schemata. Second, and because of the first condition, he can see relations between things in his environment only in terms of his own familiar acts in relation to them. Only the coordinations, not the acts themselves, are new, and these "do not lead to the elaboration of objects entirely independent of the actions."

The fifth stage, approximately coincidental in its beginning with the beginning of the second year of life, by contrast, "is primarily the stage of the elaboration of the object." The limitations of the previous stages now are being overcome. The child can now get about on his own power. *New* schemata are established through a sort of experimentation involving an apparent search for new behavioral facilities. These new facilities (schemata) come about, in other words, through efforts directed with more of a purpose to seek novelty for its own sake rather than simply to practice familiar acts which produce desired results by chance, as in the earlier stage.

New relations, new meanings in environmental objects and situations, thus become established through simple experimentation. The child lets an object, which he is holding, fall to the floor, watching intently what happens to it. He shakes objects, knocks them, listens to the sounds they make, throws them, and watches them bounce and roll. He is constantly "experimenting in order to see." In the process of experimentation there is a constant accommodation of patterns (schemata) to the situation and the assimilation of new schemata. This naturally leads to "the discovery of new means" based on the apprehension of new relations.

Piaget refers to this type of mental activity as "inventive intelligence." In his observations one of its earliest manifestations was what he called the "behavior pattern of the support." The pattern, based upon perceiving the relation between an object and whatever is supporting it, consists of grasping the underlying support of the object in order to draw it within reach. For example, the child grasps a cushion and draws it toward him in order to obtain a box placed upon it. A new means of obtaining a desired object is thus discovered and utilized. In the opinion of Piaget, such new means can be discovered only through this experimenting-in-order-to-see activity which is characteristic of stage five.

Much groping, trial-and-error behavior is manifest in the child's experimental attempt to obtain desired objects during this stage. Such behavior leads gradually to an appreciation in him of spacial relations and of causal and temporal sequences. This drive to active exploration and manipulation of objects makes evident the great importance during this stage of an environment rich in appropriate stimulation.

The sixth and last stage of sensorimotor, or "practical," intelligence characterizes generally the latter portion of the child's second year as the deductive or reflective level of intelligence. In discussing this stage Piaget took pains once more to emphasize the fact that the beginning of a new stage "does not abolish in any way the behavior patterns of the preceding stages and that new behavior patterns are simply superimposed on the old ones" (1952, p. 331).

This transitional stage of mental functioning (the sixth stage), in other words, is new not in the sense that the earlier patterns disappear, but rather that "they will henceforth be *completed* by behavior patterns of a new type: invention through deduction or mental combination." There is at this point an emerging awareness of relations, and the child's mental functioning, which formerly was characterized by empirical groping, now is controlled to a greater degree by this new awareness. Awareness of relations allows for simple mental combinations and deductions, and new means may now be "invented." This, of course, implies a rudimentary kind of representation. The child now begins to foresee which acts are likely to succeed or fail without empirically testing them.

An example illustrating this kind of transitional behavior is described by Piaget. This time the "desired object" is inside a partially opened box which is presented to the child. He first resorted to "physical groping." He tried to force open the box but failed. He then reacted in an entirely new way. He stopped using physical force. He now examined more carefully the situation. While doing so he slowly opened and closed his mouth as if in imitation of the desired result—the enlarged opening of the box. This was the moment of *insight*. He suddenly inserted his finger in the narrow opening and thereby succeeded in prying the box wide open. Such a solution to an infantile manipulation problem is the first suggestion of the use of *representation,* that is, "thinking behavior." His own act of opening and closing his mouth "represented" the desired situation, the enlarged opening of the box, (Bruner, 1964). This is the beginning of the transition from the purely sensorimotor approach to the second period in the sequence of mental development, the period of *"concrete operations."* But the child still has a long way to go before he is able to think in terms of "operations" (truly mental representations).

The Preoperational Phase

The child must work through a four- or five-year transitional period of development called the "preoperational" phase. His behavior up to this point has been *prerepresentational.* As stated above, he is now becoming capable of a kind of representation by means of his own acts. This kind of representation Bruner (1964) called "enactive." Piaget sees it as primarily "imitative" behavior, which is symbolic in nature, in that it "signifies" (stands for, represents) something else. He refers to this whole class of representative behavior as the "semiotic function." Piaget and Inhelder (1969) describe this function as follows:

> In the course of the second year (and continuing from stage 6 of infancy), however, certain behavior patterns appear which imply the representative evocation of an object or event not present and which consequently presuppose the formation or use of differential signifiers, since they must be able to refer to elements not perceptible at the time as well as to those which are present. One can distinguish at least five of these behavior patterns whose appearance is almost simultaneous and which we shall list in the order of complexity. [p. 53]

The five patterns to which they refer are *deferred imitation, symbolic play, the drawing of a graphic image, the "mental image,"* and *verbal evocation.* All of these patterns of representation are completely "centered" in the child's own behavior. The child uses his own acts or functions to represent what is not at the moment perceptible.

Deferred Imitation   Children, of course, can imitate what they are seeing quite early in the sensorimotor period. But the preoperational child (2 to 6 or 7) can imitate what he has *previously* perceived but which is not now present. He is now able in that way to "think" of *past* events. The imitative gesture is thus the beginning of a "differentiated signifier."

Symbolic Play   Children often play games of "pretending." This is really a more elaborate form of deferred imitation. They reenact some experience common to them like being bathed and put to bed, using a doll to represent themselves.

Drawing   Drawing as an imitative expression of the not perceptually present appears at age 2 or 2½ years.

The Mental Image   This is an internalized kind of imitation.

Verbal Evocation   During the earlier stages of language development children often use a word or two to signify a past event in their experience, something they have just seen or in which they have recently participated.

As was noted earlier, each of these modes of representation, referred to as the semiotic function, consists in some kind of action, something the child does. The action in each case is expressive of a kind of motor memory. Objects, persons, and events of the recent past are revived, or represented, in terms of "what has already been absorbed on the level of action." Further development of the thinking function must consist of another process called "decentering"—transfering what is now centered at the level of action to a mental (central) level of assimilation.

This difficult process of decentering requires a period of 4 or 5 years (ages 1½ or 2 to 6 or 7). It is more difficult than was the former decentering at the sensorimotor level, from the newborn's centering upon his own congenital patterns of functioning to attention to relations and interactions with objects and persons in the external environment. Now the preschool child is "involved in a much larger and more complex universe with which he must deal cognitively than he was as an infant. The job of "decentering" from the use of his own acts as signifiers (representations) of the not-present, and the achievement of the ability to use instead centrally based *"operations,"* is one that requires much additional maturing and experience with the objective and the social and interpersonal aspects of reality.

The Period of Concrete Operations

The term "operation," as used in Piagetian theory, means "thought" (mental functioning) as opposed to overt "action." It means mental representation of what is not actually present to sense. Thinking in this sense, of course, can take place in the actual presence of an objective situation. Hidden aspects of the situation—features, relations between parts, how these function, and so on, which at the time cannot be directly seen, can, if past experience and understanding permit, be "brought to mind," or imagined. In any event, "thinking" in the sense of *oratory* functioning, involves *central*, as opposed to semiotic, representation of what is not perceptually present.

At the "concrete" level of operations the representation is "decentered" from action (an "imitation" of the object or event). Instead, a *mental* representation is invoked, but one which is tied to, or is a mental representation of, "concrete" perceptual experiences. This level of operation begins at about age 7 and is generally characteristic of the thinking of school-age children.

The fact of having achieved this level of operations—which are not being limited to dealing with the not-present by means of specific acts of imitation—is evidenced by the great generality of the representations involved. This generality permits the child in his thinking to *reverse* the process. His operations consist of "reversible transformations." That is, he can see from his generalized experience, for example, that $-A$ is a reversal of $+A$. Even though its representations are perceptually based, they are not highly differentiated, specific signifiers of specific events, as in the case of imitative, symbolic acts. His operations, his representations, are in the nature of the more generalized "reversible transformations."

This more generalized type of mental functioning also allows for the ability to *"conserve"* the attributes of an object or material which are not

Figure 8.5 The "conservation" experiment.

actually perceived in a transformation in which only the visual dimensions and its form are changed. A typical experiment illustrating *conservation*, or its absence, is as follows: All of the water in a glass container is poured before the child's eyes into another glass which is taller and more slender. A child of 4 or 5 will say there is now "more water" because it is *higher* in the second glass. He fails to "conserve" the attribute of *quantity*. A concrete operational child (7 or 8 or older) will say, "It is the same water." The latter child's mental operation results in the conservation of attributes, in this case, quantity.

Formal Operations

During the age period roughly 12 to 15, the puberal period, often referred to as "preadolescence," some very remarkable developments occur in the youngster's ability to think. It is the period when he indeed frees himself from the concrete. He becomes capable of reasoning correctly about *propositions* or *hypotheses*—"capable of drawing the necessary conclusions from truths that are merely possible" (Piaget and Inhelder, 1969, p. 132).

> The child of twelve to fifteen of course does not establish the relevant laws of logic, nor will he write down the formula for the number of all possible combinations of the colored counters. But it is remarkable that at the level at which he becomes capable of combining elements by an exhaustive and systematic method he is also capable of combining ideas or hypotheses in affirmative or negative statements, and thus to utilize propositional operations hitherto unknown to him. [p. 130]

The child can now try out hypotheses in his mind and discard those that are inappropriate without the need actually to manipulate materials. By contrast, the concrete-operations child does not formulate hypotheses. His accommodations are to objects and events in the real world.

On the other hand the *formal* operations youngster, the adolescent is said to be "like both, and different from each" (Phillips, 1969, p. 101). He also is concerned with reality from which he departs. But his departures are lawful. He sees reality as a "subset within a much larger set of possibilities" (Ibid, p. 101). He can manipulate mentally one variable systematically while holding all others constant. In other words, formal-operations thinking is the thinking which characterizes the scientist.

Phillips (1969) summarizes briefly the sequence of "stages" in the development of intelligence as portrayed by Piaget and his associates as follows:

> The three major periods of development—Sensorimotor, Concrete Operations, and Formal Operations—represent three different fields of cognitive action, and at the beginning of each, there is a relative lack of structural differentiation and functional equilibrium. To the neonate, the world is his

actions upon it; to the Preadolescent child, his *representations* of the world of physical objects are the only ones possible. The adolescent's egocentrism results from the extension of his thinking into realms of the *possible* through the instruments of propositional logic. He fails "to distinguish between the ego's new and unpredicted capacities and the social or cosmic universe to which they are applied." He goes through a phase during which his own cerebrations seem to him omnipotent, and it is at this time that he is likely to annoy his elders with all sorts of idealistic schemes designed to bring reality into line with his own thinking (p. 102).

Summary

Psychologists, for convenience, divide activity into motor activity and cognitive activity. It must be remembered that this distinction is artificial, for all activity involves both motor and cognitive functions. The distinction is one of degree rather than of kind.

Historically there have been three main areas of concern from which theories of intelligence have been derived:

1. What factors underlie individual differences?
2. What is the nature and structure of intelligence?
3. How does mentality develop?

The idea of inherited general intelligence was the basic assumption from which intelligence tests were derived. This factor of general intelligence was conceived of as an inherited potentiality for mental development and was seen to increase with age. The inherited potentiality was thought of as being the genetically determined "upper ceiling" beyond which the individual was unable to pass.

The index of potentiality in intelligence testing is the intelligence quotient (IQ).

Until the 1930s, the assumption of inherited intelligence remained unchallenged. Researchers in various disciplines at that point began to challenge pure inheritance and have now achieved a generally accepted position of "interaction." All development is thought of as a product of heredity and environment in interaction. It was noted that in theory, however, differences between individuals *can* be attributed to a single factor.

Recently the nature-nurture controversy has been reactivated, with many educational proponents espousing programs in response to social pressures, in which the position of pure environmental determinism is a *de facto* assertion. This disregard of genetics may be understood in terms of a national attempt to provide opportunity for the "culturally disadvantaged," but will not stand scientific inquiry or verification.

It was noted in this connection that we must be careful to distinguish between what are thought of as model differences in the average performance of a social group and the individual differences in performance seen when comparing individuals either from the same or differing social groups.

Spearman's theory, known as the two-factor theory of intelligence, did much to establish the concept of a general-intelligence factor, which he called g. All abilities were thought of as possessing an amount of g and a special factor s in some degree.

The advent of multiple-factor analysis gave impetus to the search for "primary mental abilities," from which grew theories of intelligence in which a number of factors were isolated. The work of Cattell and Guilford gave rise to dimensional models of intelligence, rendering mentality as a very complex entity.

It was very early observed that mentality grows in amount as the child grows older. This gave rise to the early view that the development of intelligence was purely a quantitative matter. Research attempted to establish standard increments through which intelligence could be quantitatively compared. Growth curves have resulted from these studies.

It was demonstrated that there is no predictive validity in infant intelligence tests. Such tests are not able to establish future levels of performance.

In more recent years, the original view of quantitative development has given way to the recognition of qualitative development. The theories of Gesell and Piaget have tended to emphasize that the child's intellect passes through changes in kind as well as changes in amount.

Piaget's epigenetic theory of mental development stresses that intelligence is not an entity or factor, but a process. As the organism interacts with the environment, development occurs through universal processes, and each child passes through the same sequence of stages to achieve functional effectiveness.

CHAPTER 9

General Functional Effectiveness and Its Development

In the preceding chapter the essential nature of the gradual and continuous increase in intelligence was discussed. Obviously, as the individual grows from infancy he becomes more intelligent. We must also emphasize again, however, the fact that there are changes in the *nature* of mentality as well as in its amount. New *kinds* of abilities come into being as the child grows. In Chapter 8 the perennial question of the relative importance of the basic factors underlying these two aspects of development was clarified.

We shall turn now to the more practical aspects of mental development. We shall deal in more detail with those factors and influences both within us, and outside us which make us what we become as functioning persons in this modern world of technology and rapid change. We shall also consider those influences which must be realistically accepted and those about which we can do something. Our concern, then, is with the problem of individual achievement of practical (functional) intelligence.

The Concept of Personal Functional Effectiveness

Clearly, the quality and range of "cultural acquisitions"—individual accumulations of abilities to perform, to function effectively—are of great importance to the individual in his everyday life. These acquisitions have an important bearing on his feelings and attitudes toward himself and his adjustments as he interacts with others and copes with life's situations. Furthermore, it is now becoming increasingly clear that this facet of the concept of intelligence (Cattell's crystallized intelligence) is of immense importance in relation to problems of general social welfare. In light of our increased understanding of the effect of living conditions on the growing child—that is, the specific influences of the child's environment that are actually conducive to the development of this type of intelligence—it becomes increasingly obvious that something can be done about the regulation and control of these influences.

In the development of individual mental facility, as is true of all aspects of human development, a great many factors are involved. We shall here resort to the usual dichotomy of "nurture and nature" in our discussion of these factors. Clearly, some of these are intraindividual, having their origin in the inherent biological nature of the individual, and others originate in the culture in which the individual grows up. We may assume that the level of functional effectiveness enjoyed by the individual results from the interaction of these two kinds of influences.

Intraindividual Factors

Perhaps the most basic of all factors in terms of which people differ and which give rise to individual differences in functionability resides in the inherent nature of the individual organism.

Inherent Potentiality for Cognitive Development

In earlier discussions (Chapter 8) the concepts of inherent potentiality and capacity were differentiated and defined. It was noted that potentiality for mental development, like the limits of ultimate physical growth, is genetically set at conception. It does not change with time. Within the bounds of that inherent developmental potential, however, the child's actual *capability* to learn, to acquire new and progressively more effective modes of adaptation, *does* change. It increases as the child develops.

It will be recalled that in intelligence testing and interpretation of findings the mental age (MA) is regarded as an index, however inaccurate it may be, of the current status of the child in this changing *capacity*, while the intelligence quotient (IQ) is taken as a rough index of the level of the child's inherent potentiality for that growth in capacity.

It will also be recalled that both indexes are arrived at indirectly from the way the child performs on the test. And the problem of the *nature* of the factors underlying individual differences in performance is the critical one in mental testing. First, the contents of a test can represent, at best, only a very limited segment of the common culture. It is assumed, furthermore, that the tasks and problems with which the child is confronted in the test are either equally common and available to all individuals or are equally remote from the experience of all, thus "controlling" the environmental factor. Clearly, then, the results of the test—the indexes of inherent potentiality and growing capacity (IQ and MA)—are valid as such only to the degree to which the effects of the purely cultural differences between individuals are nullified by the nature of the test content. The purpose of the various attempts to devise "culture-free" or "culture-fair" tests has been to better provide for this kind of control of the environmental factor.

In testing situations where this control is not adequate, which is generally the case when children from cultural backgrounds different from that of the group on which the test was standardized, the obtained mental age for a child may not be taken as a true index of his current capacity level. A child from a severely disadvantaged environment would surely come out with a tested mental age much below his actual age, when he may actually possess a capacity to acquire which is much beyond that indicated by his level of functioning on the test. He may also function initially very inadequately in the school situation, yet he may have learned a great deal and acquired many abilities which have allowed him to make effective adaptations to the environment in which he lives. He has not been sufficiently exposed, however, to those aspects of modern culture which would have allowed him to acquire the particular skills and attitudes needed to meet the demands imposed upon him as he enters public school. The nature of the cultural acquisitions a child accumulates obviously depends upon the kinds of cultural influences which surround him. Functional intelligence in a child can be fostered and facilitated within the limitations of his inherent potentiality.

Temperamental Nature

Another constitutional factor that can influence the achievement of personal effectiveness is one's basic *temperamental* nature.

Every individual possesses a "constitution" which in the details of its total design is peculiarly his own. His *sensorium* has a unique patterning of relative sensitivities to stimulation; his nervous system has a particular level of plasticity, conductivity, and retentivity. In the same sense a person's total reactor system—his endocrine glands and the smooth muscles of his internal organs under autonomic control—in its structural patterning and its interrelatedness is like that of no other individual. All of these bodily systems, integrated and interrelated, are what we refer to here as the individual's constitutional nature.

This physical structure, the human organism, of course, is distinctly human in its overall design. We as human beings are "all alike" in that we are all human, yet, as we have noted repeatedly throughout this book, we, as organisms, are all different in genetic endowment and in developmental outcome as the biologically given interacts with a unique patterning of environmental influences.

One's temperamental nature, like all else about a living being, undergoes developmental change. As an important intraindividual factor in the achievement of effective functionability we must look at it at the beginning of postnatal life. An infant's temperamental nature immediately makes itself manifest in his peculiar pattern of reactions to extrauterine life. This pattern consists of a combination of behavioral and affective tendencies or "predispositions." Students of infant behavior have identified and described a number of such congenital behavior characteristics which in their strength and patterning differ among neonates.

Kagan (1971), commenting on the "overwhelming variability among infants from the first day," wrote:

> There are quiet and active babies, irritable and contented babies, excitable and placid babies, smiling and dour babies, heavy and light babies, premature and term babies, hypoxic and full-breathing babies. Everyone acknowledges the obviousness of these differences, but only a few believe they play a permanent role in guiding the psychological organization of the older child. [p. 4]

In the early days of child-development research, relatively little attention was given to this important area of behavior and development.

Activity Types

Some of the earlier observations of temperament in children were made by Margaret Fries (Fries and Lewi, 1938; Fries, 1941, 1944; Fries and Woolf, 1953). Fries carefully observed the amount and vigor of bodily activity in infants from birth to 10 days of age under controlled conditions of stimulation and motivation. She differentiated three *activity types* of infants in terms of amount of activity, differences in characteristic muscle tonus, and crying within the "normal" range. She labeled these "types" of babies the *active*, the *moderately active*, and the *quiet*. Extremes beyond either end of the normal range were considered pathological. Fries regarded these variables as biological, that is, constitutional, in nature, but congenital rather than hereditary in that activity tendency is a joint product of the action of genes, intrauterine influences, and birth experiences.

In elaborating on the probable developmental trends and relations with the environment deriving from such congenital predispositions, Fries and Woolf (1953) theorized as follows.

1. Parents with different temperaments differ in their conscious or unconscious preferences for types of children. To the extent to which this is true, the child's activity type may significantly influence the quality of the parent-child relationship and the consequent trend in the child's personal development. The quiet child, for example, in interacting with certain temperamental tendencies in the parent, may predispose toward the establishment of a strongly dependent relationship. With a different parental temperament pattern the outcome might be quite different.

2. Because of cultural mores, a girl of a quiet type and a boy of an active type tend in general to have an easier adjustment, respectively, to their sex roles. Hence, the functional effectiveness of the child in terms of sex-role expectations could be conditioned significantly by his own activity type.

3. The form that the child's reality testing and mastery behavior takes may be, in part at least, a function of his activity type. As was suggested in Fries' (1944) discussion, the highly active child is prone to test reality and to master the situation through his own efforts, whereas the quiet child would be more likely to appeal to and depend upon the adult for help in meeting a situation. The implications for the development of adequacy of functioning are apparent here.

4. To the extent to which these early activity patterns are biological forerunners of later reactions to difficulties, a child's congenital activity type might predispose him to adopt certain defense and escape mechanisms. The quiet type, for example, may be more predisposed to adopt the defenses of withdrawal and fantasy—generally very inadequate modes of functioning as judged externally.

5. The activity type may, to some degree, predispose the child in the direction of a particular neurosis or symptom formation. Fries points out that all types seem to be capable of developing any character trait or neurosis, but individuals also seem to have predispositions to one or another. For example, the two extreme types—the excessively quiet and the excessively active—seem to be more vulnerable to psychological illness. The autistic child described by Kanner (1944) appears to be developmentally related to the pathologically quiet type.

Among the earlier investigators, Cameron and Magaret (1951) also commented on the importance of congenital activity level and tempo, along with other predispositions, as they affect emotional and social interactions between the infant and those about him:

> An active, irritable infant participates in a wider environment than does a quiet, phlegmatic one, and he invites different reactions from those who share the environment with him. The baby who turns, reaches and kicks restlessly in his crib; who cries, smiles, or coos a great deal; or who nurses actively and long, inevitably exposes himself to situations which differ from those which the placid, unreactive child encounters. What these differences in reactivity may mean for the infant's behavior organization is also determined, of course, by the needs and attitudes of his parents and of the others who respond to him. An exuberant, accepting family may welcome noisy activity in its newest member which quieter more restrictive parents would consider irritating, frightening, or bad. [p. 52]

Recent Research

More recently, Thomas, Chess, Birch, Hertzig and Korn (1963) conducted a longitudinal study designed to identify and describe congenital temperamental predispositions. Their data were collected from interviews with parents. They introduced their preliminary report (1963) with the following statement:

> temperamental characteristics of the infant make a fundamental contribution to psychological individuality. It is our view that personality development is the result of the interaction of a baby endowed with definable characteristics of initial reactivity, and an environmental complex including familial and extrafamilial factors. [p. ix]

On the basis of a content analysis of the interview protocols of the first 22 children, the following 9 "categories for the assessment of individuality in behavioral functioning" were adopted:

1. *Activity level:* the extent to which the motor component characterized the baby's functioning.
2. *Rhythmicity:* the degree of regularity of repetitive functions, such as sleeping and waking, eating and appetite, and bowel and bladder functions.
3. *Approach or withdrawal:* a description of the child's characteristic initial reaction to any new stimulus pattern, "be it food, people, places, toys, or procedures."
4. *Adaptability:* "the sequential course of responses that are made to new or altered situations."
5. *Intensity of reaction:* the "energy content of the reaction irrespective of its direction" (negative or positive).

6. *Threshold of responsiveness:* "the intensity level of stimulation that is necessary to evoke a discernible response," the explicit form of the response, in this instance, being irrelevant.
7. *Quality of mood:* "the amount of pleasant, joyful, friendly behavior as contrasted with unpleasant, crying, unfriendly behavior."
8. *Distractibility:* "the effectivness of extraneous environmental stimuli in interfering with, or in altering the direction of, ongoing behavior."
9. *Attention span and persistence:* "this category refers to the definition of a direction of functioning and to the difficulty with which such an established direction of functioning can be altered."

The data relevant to each of these nine behavior characteristics for the 80 children during their first two years of life were analyzed with two objectives in mind: "to determine whether children are discriminably different in the patterning of behavioral reactivity in early infancy; to analyze the degree to which features of behavioral reactivity identifiable in early infancy continue to characterize the child during his first two years" (p. 56).

In brief, the conclusions were as follows (1) "Individual differences among children are demonstrable, particularly for such characteristics as *activity level, intensity of reaction, mood,* and *distractibility*" (p. 57); in terms of the total pattern of reactivity ratings, each baby was unique. (2) Statistical analysis of the data "has contributed evidence that identifiable characteristics of reactivity are persistent features of the child's behavior throughout the first two years of life" (p. 71).

The developmental significance of the child's original temperamental nature seems clear. It is important not only as a predisposing factor, but it can also be a potent influence upon the nature of the infant's initial social environment. Both his emotional and cognitive development may be affected.

Certain other constitutional characteristics of the child may also tend to create for him significant features of his social environment. Parents, usually without intent, react initially in different ways to some of the physical characteristics of their children. An infant's general appearance, size, facial features, expressions, and the like, often evoke emotionally charged reactions from the parents. They constitute differences in the quality of the "welcome" babies receive into the family. A relatively husky, vigorous, and intrusively loud-crying baby boy will inevitably stimulate a different sort of initial reaction and acceptance from devoted parents than will a delicate, fine-featured, and pleasantly appealing infant.

Environment

The term "environment," in its usual sense, encompasses all of the influences upon development which come from outside the individual.

We have discussed the intraindividual factors and have seen evidence of the importance of the interrelation of internal and external influences. The

active-ca   influences of the environment also became obvious. The
child's in   otentiality for development is nothing more than a latent
possibilit   and until the organism is stimulated to action by the
environm   the other hand, as we have seen, certain crucial influences
in the nev   infant's initial environment consist of, or are "created" by,
certain fea   s of his individual pattern of behavioral predispositions, or
by other features of his constitutional make-up. These influences—the effects
of the behavior of others toward him, which behavior is actually stimulated
by his own inherent nature—initiate and to some degree determine the
direction of his further development.

Thus the environment looms large in importance in the development of
individuality, including personal functional effectiveness. Its importance is
more clearly revealed as research brings increasing understanding of the
effects of specific aspects of the various environmental situations. We see
more and more clearly how much can be done to facilitate optimum functional development through the thoughtful regulation, manipulation, and
control of environmental stimulation.

An example of this better understanding from modern research is the
realization of the vital importance of verbal interaction between a mother
and her toddler to his cognitive development (Bernstein, 1960; Deutsch,
1965; R. D. Hess, 1964; Hess and Shipmon, 1965). As was indicated earlier,
if a child is to acquire facility to function in our modern culture, he must
early become involved with it.

Secondary Factors in the Achievement of Functionability

In our discussion of the basic factors underlying the development
of personal effectiveness we have made repeated reference to the interrelatedness of the intraindividual, or organism-based, factors and those from outside
the organism. There are, of course, many variables which are products of the
interaction of these two basic factors which have much to do with the
further development of personal effectiveness in life. We shall now consider
some of these secondary acquired factors.

The Self-Concept

A factor which is of tremendous importance in relation to all
facets of modern living is what is loosely referred to as the self-concept.

The most important single factor affecting behavior is the self-concept.
What people do at every moment of their lives is a product of how they see
themselves and the situations they are in. While situations may change from
moment to moment or place to place, the beliefs that people have about

themselves are always present factors in determining their behavior. The self is the star of every performance, the central figure in every act. [Combs, Avila, and Purkey, 1971, p. 39]

A great deal has been written about "the self," about perceptions of one's self, and about the various attitudes and feelings toward the self. Some of these writings are theoretical, often based upon general observation and generalized clinical experience (Erikson, 1950; Jourard, 1964; Moustakas, 1956; Snygg and Combs, 1949; Sullivan, 1947). Others are reports of research studies that involved measurement or evaluation of the self-concept, usually with the assessment of its developmental aspects (Ames, 1952; Andrews, 1966; Bledsoe, 1964; Coopersmith 1967; Jersild, 1952; Piers and Harris, 1964; Dixon, 1957; Wattenberg and Clifford, 1964).

Attributes of the Self about Which Attitudes and Feelings Arise

There are, of course, a number of aspects of the self about which people, especially adolescents, may have strong and sometimes very disturbing feelings. Among these areas of concern are one's physical body—its size, proportions, and other characteristics—one's capabilities and competencies, and one's sense of personal worth.

Youngsters are often quite unhappy with their bodies. They would like to be taller or not so tall, to be heavier and stronger looking or not so heavy, or to possess facial and other bodily features that conform more nearly to some idealized stereotype. Slow-growing boys who fall behind their age mates at the time of the so-called physical growth spurt often become anxious and fearful about their prospects of attaining adult status.

Some youngsters also have unfounded misgivings about their intellectual capabilities. These feelings are often combined with the tendency to be "shy" and to feel incompetent in and to withdraw from social situations.

Other children, who may or may not have disturbing feelings about their physical selves or their competence, have acquired feelings of unworthiness. Perhaps too frequently the little boy has been told that he is a "naughty" or a "nasty" boy, and he comes to believe that he is. At any rate, some children develop the conviction that they do not deserve the regard and affection others demonstrate toward them. They are inclined to feel that others overvalue them because they themselves give others a dishonest impression of their value and worth; consequently, these children feel guilty and even less worthy.

The Self-Concept in Relation to Living

Jersild (1960) has studied the development of the attitudes toward self in children. One of his approaches was to ask children at different grade levels in school to prepare written descriptions of qualities in themselves that they admired and others that they disliked. The general finding was that "many of the criteria young people use in judging themselves at any level tend to stand out prominently at all levels" (p. 449). The standards used by the children appeared not to be related to age or developmental status. Experiences at school and their attitudes toward school, however, were significantly related to their self-concepts. In an earlier study (Jersild, Goldman, and Lotus, 1941) the results indicated that children "worried" more about school than they did about out-of-school matters. Jersild offered this conclusion:

> Self-acceptance and understanding of self are closely associated. To accept himself, the growing person must be aware of himself. To accept his limitations he must be able to recognize them. Self-acceptance, in other words, requires awareness and perception. But the child's ability to become aware of himself will be influenced by the way he feels about himself, and the way he feels about himself will depend, in part, on the way others feel about him and encourage him in the process of self-discovery. [1960, p. 457]

Clearly, then, an extremely important factor affecting the quality of personal functioning and the development of more adequate patterns has to do with the kinds of things the learner tells himself about himself. There is probably no other factor more potent or pervasive in its possibilities of affecting learning. Evaluative feelings about one's self are "self-fulfilling prophecies." They predispose the child to behave and to function in terms of those evaluations and "images"—images of his physique or his capabilities or his worthiness. If he thinks he is "dumb," he will behave like a "dumb" child. And these feelings and images will resist change. Attention must be given to the conditions of their formation and to the prevention and treatment of debilitating self-concepts in children.

An individual's self-concept obviously is a product of experience, mostly experience which he has had in interaction with the significant others in his life. If a child is to develop positive feelings about himself, he must have the experience of being regarded positively by those who matter most to him.

> How can a person feel liked unless somebody likes him?
> How can a person feel acceptable unless somewhere he is accepted?
> How can a person feel he has dignity unless someone treats him so?
> How can a person feel able unless somewhere he has success? [Avila, Combs, and Purkey, 1971, p. 121]

Such questions, and the answers implied in them, indicate clearly not only the source of self-perceptions and feelings but also what a parent or teacher must do if he is to help a child revamp a negative self-concept.

However, before one can really help another to see himself more positively, one must really *understand* how the other sees and feels about himself. This, of course, requires keen sensitivity. In this connection Combs (1971) draws a distinction between "self report"—what a person is willing, able, or can be tricked into *saying* about himself"—and what he really believes and feels about himself. This "real meaning" must be inferred, which requires sensitivity and insight. It cannot be learned by direct questioning, by "introspection," or from the client's "self report."

Neither can the client be helped much by simply telling him that he is wrong in his self-perceptions and evaluations and that he must think more positively. Rather, he must actually experience being treated with respect and dignity, being accepted and liked unconditionally as he is, and somehow have the real experience of success.

The Self-Concept in Interpersonal Relations

Perhaps in no other area of life are competence and effectiveness more important than in the area of interpersonal relations. The way one sees oneself, and with what level of esteem, largely determine the quality of one's relations with others. Some conclusions of an important research study (Coopersmith, 1967) are relevant here.

> Persons high in their own estimation approach tasks and persons with the expectation that they will be received and successful. They have confidence in their perceptions and judgments and believe that they can bring their efforts to a favorable resolution. . . . They are more likely to be participants than listeners in group discussions, they report less difficulty in forming friendships.
>
> The picture of the individual with less self-esteem that emerges from these results is markedly different. These persons lack trust in themselves and are apprehensive about expressing unpopular or unusual ideas. . . . They are likely to live in the shadow of the social group, listening rather than participating. . . . Among the factors that contribute to the withdrawal of those low in self-esteem are their marked self-consciousness and preoccupation with their problems. . . . The effect is to limit their social intercourse and thus decrease the possibilities of friendly and supportive relationship. [pp. 70–71]

Clearly, a predominantly negative self-concept is a major deterrent to "good" interpersonal relations—an area in which functional effectiveness is especially important to life's satisfactions. If a child is having difficulty "getting along" with others, which, as research has shown, is largely because of his "marked self consciousness and preoccupation with his problems," he can be helped only if someone—a teacher or counselor, perhaps—is sensitive enough correctly to "infer" the nature of his self feelings, and then see to it that he has *experiences* of a sort that will lead to his own reversion of his self feelings.

General Patterns of Adaptation

As the child develops he is constantly forming and refining behavior patterns. At any particular point in his life the level of effectiveness with which he meets and deals with life situations, generally, is clearly dependent upon what he has learned up to that point.

Basic Orientation to the World

One of the most basically important patterns of adaptation is the individual's general orientation to the world in which he lives and to which he must relate—the world of people, social inventions, institutions, and relations. The child gets, or fails to get, this vital orientation very early in life, mainly from the person-to-person, largely verbal, interaction with his mother.

Ongoing research to which we referred earlier (Bernstein, 1961; R. D. Hess, 1964; R. D. Hess and Shipman, 1965) indicates that verbal interchange varies rather widely in "mode"—in quality and degree of elaborateness—among families and particularly among those at different socioeconomic levels. At the one extreme communication is so perfunctory, so restricted, so "status-oriented" as to offer the child a very limited grasp of the world and no basis for an understanding or ability to deal with it. Communication is "restrictive, stereotyped, limited, and condensed, lacking in specificity and exactness needed for precise conceptualization and differentiation" (R. D. Hess, 1964, p. 424).

The other end of the continuum offers much more cognitive stimulation in verbal interchange. The parent is more specific and informative. Of the mother's communication, Hess said it is

individualized and the message is specific to a particular situation, topic, or person. It is more particular, more differentiated, and more precise. It permits expression of a wider and more complex range of thought, tending toward discrimination among cognitive and affective content. [1964, p. 424]

The difference in outcome between these two modes of verbal interaction, along with other associated variables, is presumed to be one of educability. It is a difference in cognitive development, and, since learning is a matter of "subsuming" the new into the already existing cognitive structure (Ausubel, 1965), the difference becomes one of learning acquisition—the acquired level of orientation to the world and the problems of living.

Approach to Tasks and Problems

A product of learning that is also related to competence is one's habitual approach to a task or a problem situation. After an appraisal of the situation, whether one is able to come immediately and vigorously to grips with it or evades and stalls at making a decision often makes the difference between competence and ineffectiveness (Pressey and Robinson, 1944).

Although the approach to tasks and problems is in the nature of an habituated pattern, it is, nevertheless, related to temperamental nature. The individual who is by nature very active and restless is more likely to be unmethodical and haphazard rather than one who plans and is systematic in his approach. The naturally withdrawing child is likely to approach a new problem with tentativeness and a lack of vigor and perhaps without much careful detailed planning. One's characteristic mode of approach in any case, however, is learned; it is a product of the interaction of environmental stimulation and original temperament.

One's habitual emotional patterns may also constitute an important conditioning factor. Emotionality can be either an impeding or a facilitating factor in relation to personal adequacy. One of the lessons from common experience is that thought and rational behavior are incompatible with "emotional upset." On the other hand, the physiological aspect of an emotional episode makes readily available extra amounts of physical energy that can be mobilized for more effective attack upon certain kinds of problem situations.

Skills and Information

Perhaps even more important than an individual's approach to a particular life situation is his fund of readily available information or his repertory of skills—his know-how applicable to a particular situation. The technology that characterizes the world today makes increasingly greater demands upon individuals in terms of training and specialized skills. The place of an unskilled person in the present world economy is practically nonexistent. A disturbing but true fact of economics is that today's useful skill may not long continue to be useful. Flexibility, and a general "learning set" for continued new acquisitions and new adjustments, are great assets to individuals facing the present world, economically, intellectually, and socially.

School Experiences

Earlier in this chapter the relation between the kind of culture surrounding a child and the nature of his "cultural acquisitions"—the kind and level of functional (crystallized) intelligence—that will accrue to him were emphasized. We also noted the importance of the degree to which a child's early preschool experiences relate to and prepare him for the demands of public schooling.

The unspoiled nature of the child is "free, spontaneous, creative." Each child is a unique individual like no other and is wont to behave in relation to his surroundings in his own unique way. Hence, the atmosphere of the school room in which the child finds himself is very important. If it is one of understanding, where his uniqueness is recognized and respected, where he is allowed and given time without pressure to discover and create for himself, he will not so readily lose his inherent creativity. School should be a place where the child is encouraged on his own, but with guidance as needed, to acquire certain skills essential to effective functioning. He must learn how to learn. He must learn to solve problems for himself and to discover and assimilate the world outside his immediate home. He must make critical social adjustments and must learn how to interact effectively and creatively with others. The school is indeed an important aspect of the child's environment. In the school much can be done to foster the development of personal functional effectiveness in the growing generation of children. It is perhaps a sad commentary that many of our schools today have not caught the vision of their vital task and attempt to deny the child his right to individuality. As often as not the child is given an "assembly line" education in which his autonomy is suppressed rather than shaped. Too often the child is forced to accommodate to *normal* or *mediocre* standards or face expulsion from the social setting and the condemnation of his teachers. Often this willful and inexcusable negligence on the part of the school is glossed over by the argument that the child will encounter many kinds of people in his life and therefore he must learn to adjust to them now. Incompetent educators have formulated a rational veneer to justify the continuation of many practices that in hindsight will condemn them for the high crime of twisting, bending, and misshaping children into a blueprint that is inconsistent with what they are.

At the other extreme, perhaps as an overcompensation to the overrigidity of some educational systems, is the open classroom concept. This nuance has some merit, providing that it does not lose sight of the truth that a certain amount of social indoctrination and discipline *must* exist in the school system to foster the development of the self-control that will be needed in later years. On one hand, we must permit children to be individual *children*, but on the other we must insure their eventual personal maturity.

There are, of course, many other factors more or less peculiar to the individual, to his particular pattern of living conditions, to his unique constitutional and temperamental make-up, which cannot be included here because of their very individuality.

People obviously vary widely in pattern of basic personality structure, and these differences appear very early in the child. The particular pattern of behavioral predispositions that largely constitute personality structure in any given child or adult can be an important factor in his overall functional adequacy. One's convictions, attitudes, prejudices, and the like, may also be factors of importance. The extent to which one's emotions either interfere with or facilitate effective functioning is another area of great importance. This topic is dealt with in Chapter 13.

From Helplessness to Functional Adequacy

At this point we shall shift our attention from the various specific aspects of personal functioning and the factors and circumstances that condition their achievement. We shall now trace in brief outline, longitudinally, the overall development of general functional adequacy.

We shall try to see this development in terms of overlapping periods, stages, and accomplishments, from complete initial helplessness to personal competence in meeting and coping with the demands of modern life.

The developmental metamorphosis that takes place in the human being between birth and adulthood continues to be a fascinating phenomenon for analysis. It will be recalled that we have viewed certain facets of human development, in each case, in terms of a series of identifiable "milestones" ("maturity indicators," Chapter 4) or other indicators of progress, periods, and stages (Chapters 7 and 8). These series in varying degrees meet the requirements of a true "developmental sequence." It will also be recalled that among the criteria of such a sequence are that they be fixed in order of appearance and that each be qualitatively distinct from the preceding one in the sequence, yet in their total sequence they portray continuous development. In our longitudinal review of total functionability, however, we shall examine certain broad, overlapping, and interrelated developmental periods and accomplishments, without any implication that they in sequence constitute a true "developmental sequence."

The Predicament of Infancy

Of all living organisms the human infant is perhaps the most profoundly dependent upon the care of other persons for his survival. Other than a few simple reflexes and the physiological processes essential to life, he can do nothing for himself. At the same time, of all living creatures he undoubtedly is endowed with the greatest potential for the development of personal adequacy and effectiveness.

One concomitant of his initial complete helplessness is the baby's relatively strong tendency to react overtly in an all-out fashion to external stimuli. He startles readily and generally shows marked avoidance reactions to strong and noxious stimuli. Even so, babies are observed to differ rather widely in strength of these reactions. This startle-avoidance pattern is particularly in evidence during the earliest weeks of life when the child's extremely immature brain has not yet acquired an inhibitory control over visceral change and upset. Even though infants differ in sensitivity and ease of arousal, as well as in intensity of reaction, this tendency is present to some degree in all children; and as Diamond (1957) suggests, "this normal emotional instability of the infant constitutes a predisposition to anxiety, or generalized fearfulness, which is likely to be established as a lasting disposition if it is given frequent exercise in this period." (p. 106).

Clinicians and keen observers of the plight of infancy and of the typical reactions of the newborn have stressed the significance of this period of instability (Spitz, 1945, 1946, 1949). They have described it in its various aspects, and, in some instances, they undoubtedly have overemphasized the hazards to the neonate's survival as well as to his healthy emotional development when adequate understanding care and nurturance are not provided (Ribble, 1943). The early fear pattern described above is regarded as the organism's natural response to the threatened denial of its basic needs, for example, the need for oxygen during the period immediately following birth when independent respiration must be established. Another vital need during that early period is believed to be the need for the security and comfort of warm, relaxed mothering (Whiting and Child, 1953; Rheingold, 1960).

Harry Stack Sullivan, who wielded a great influence upon modern-day psychiatric thinking, has made much of the predisposition to anxiety in early infancy. It is quite apparent that in his discussions of the early infant-mother relationship Sullivan used the term "anxiety" to refer to the characteristic physiological instability and sensitivity and the startle-fear-withdrawal pattern with which we are here concerned. Sullivan (1953) wrote:

> I cannot tell you what anxiety feels like to the infant, but I can make an inference which I believe has very high probability of accuracy—that there is no difference between anxiety and fear so far as the vague mental state of the infant is concerned. . . . I would like to point out that if an infant is exposed to a sudden loud noise, he is pretty much upset; certain other experiences of that kind which impinge on his zones of connection with the outside world cause the same kind of upset. Almost anybody watching the infant during these upsets would agree that it didn't seem to be fun; the infant didn't enjoy it. . . . I have reason to suppose, then, that a fearlike state can be induced in an infant under two circumstances: one is by the rather violent disturbance of his zones of contact with circumambient reality; and the other is by certain types of emotional disturbance within the mothering one. From the latter grows the whole exceedingly important structure of anxiety, and performances that can be understood only by reference to the concept of anxiety. [p. 9]

Later in his discussion Sullivan is more specific as to the nature of the emotional disturbance within the mothering one which leads to "upset" and the "fearlike state" in the infant:

> *The tension of anxiety, when present in the mothering one, induces anxiety in the infant.* The rationale of this induction—that is, how anxiety in the mother induces anxiety in the infant—is thoroughly obscure. This gap, this failure of our grasp on reality has given rise to some beautifully plausible and perhaps correct explanations of how the anxiety in the mother causes anxiety in the infant. I bridge the gap simply by referring to it as a manifestation of an indefinite—that is, not yet defined—interpersonal process to which I apply the term *empathy*. [p. 41]

As stated earlier, the infant's recurrent organic needs and the physiological disequilibrium resulting from them when not immediately satisfied is also a source of the fear-anxiety state. Thus, the importance of the care of a "mothering one" is obvious. Sullivan describes the significance of this factor in the interpersonal relationship of infant and mother. As the baby's need for food or water or for comfortable body temperature increases, thus disturbing the equilibrium of his being a "tension of needs" mounts in him. This tension is made manifest to the mother in terms of the changed level or character of the baby's activity:

> however manifest the increasing tension of needs in an infant may be . . . the observation of these tensions or of the activity which manifests their presence calls out, in the mothering one, a certain tension which may be described as that of tenderness, which is a potentiality for or an impulsion to activities suited to—or more or less suited to—the relief of the infant's needs. This, in its way, is a definition of tenderness—a very important conception, very different indeed from the miscellaneous, and in general, meaningless term "love." [p. 40]

Sullivan thus stresses the crucial importance of the quality of the mother's emotional reactions to her baby's needs both physical and emotional. The two factors of importance here in determining the general nature of mother-infant interaction are, of course, the baby's temperamental nature and the mother's sensitivity and responsiveness to his basic needs. The nature of the baby's most frequent and prevailing affective experiences in relation to his mother's care can thus range from feelings of anxiety and distress to feelings of security, comfort and "trust" in response to the mother's "tenderness." These prevailing primary feelings in relation to his immediate environment presumably can have much to do with the general nature and quality of the child's cultural acquisitions. His growing repertoire of appropriate and facilitating modes of functioning in society (functional, "crystallized" intelligence) can be hampered, or positively reinforced, depending upon the nature of his affective experiences as he interacts with the significant ones in his life.

In rather close accord with Sullivan's emphasis on the developmental significance of the feeling-interactions between mother and infant is Erikson's (1950) portrayal of the fundamental importance of a "sense of trust," which has its basis in the earliest nurturant care of the neonate by his "warmly dependable"[1] mother. The first of Erikson's stages in his postulated developmental sequence is characterized by the establishment, or the lack of the establishment, of this exceedingly important initial feeling-adjustment of extrauterine life. The mother's "tenderness" behavior in response to the infant's needs, it is presumed, gives rise to feelings of sensuous pleasure

---

[1] The phrase "warmly dependable" in describing an adequate mother comes from I. D. Harris' interesting report (1959).

(love), of comfort and security (freedom from anxiety), and of trust. This basic sense of trust continues to be fundamental in human relations and adjustments throughout life. This sense of trust is particularly important, according to Erikson, during a later stage, which is characterized by the "identity crisis" of youth (1968, p. 105).

Emergence of Social Responsiveness

Without cognitive awareness of his own helplessness, the neonate's first developmental task is the biological one of recovering from the crisis of birth and of adapting to extrauterine conditions of living. But development is exceedingly rapid during infancy. The baby soon begins to react to visual and auditory stimulation. By the middle of his first year he is much aware of objects and events external to himself. He can now differentiate between his mother and other moving objects (people) before him. The presence of his mother has become an essential factor in his life, and in his reactions to her care and ministrations he demonstrates his *affiliative need*—the need to relate affectionately to another.

It is important at this stage, particularly, that the mothering one be warmly dependable. The baby is emerging from the helplessness of infancy into a period in which he can make differential responses to certain stable aspects of his environment. It is the continuation of Erikson's (1950) stage of trust:

> The first demonstration of *social* trust in the baby is the ease of his feeding, the depth of his sleep, the relaxation of his bowels. The experience of a mutual regulation of his increasingly receptive capacities with the maternal techniques of provision gradually helps him to balance the discomfort caused by the immaturity of homeostasis with which he was born. In his gradually increasing waking hours he finds that more and more adventures of the senses arouse a feeling of familiarity, of having coincided with a feeling of inner goodness. [p. 219]

As this trusting affiliativeness develops, the baby also learns something in the way of control techniques. He readily learns that his crying will bring immediate relief from discomfort and immediate gratification of his needs. This, then, is also the period of the *sense of omnipotence* and *volitional independence* (Ausubel, 1958). His trust is reinforced by the fact that what he "wills" happens.

The strength of this tendency to relate with trust to others, as expressed particularly in the infant's attachment to his mother, apparently continues to increase during the latter half of the first year of life. Its early development appears to be dependent upon the constancy and the quality of maternal care the baby receives. "But let it be said here," wrote Erikson (1950), "that the amount of trust derived from earliest infantile experiences does not seem to depend on absolute quantities of food or demonstrations of love, but rather on the quality of the maternal relationship" (p. 221).

This early capacity for trustful affiliation and its nurturance—or lack of nurturance—are presumed to be the basis of individual differences in the adult ability to interact with others in affectionate and love relationships and to respond generally to social stimuli. To the extent to which this is true, this variable of temperament constitutes an important conditioning factor to personal effectiveness in the area of interpersonal and social relations.

Actually, there is relatively little research evidence as to the relation between the kind of mothering young infants receive and their social development (Yarrow, 1961, 1964). Preliminary findings in a longitudinal study of mother-infant interaction indicate, however, that 1-year-old infants who had been cared for by their own mothers only were more active, more emotionally dependent on their mothers, and more emotional in their interactions with their mothers than were infants of the same age who had experienced "polymatric" care (Caldwell, Hursher, Lipton, Richmond, Stern, Eddy, Drochman, and Rothman, 1963). These differences, which were statistically significant, supported the hypothesis that infants reared in monomatric families become more affiliative and more emotionally responsive than those who do not experience single-mother nurturance.

In a later study, however, Caldwell and her coworkers obtained somewhat different results. In their comparison of home-reared babies and those who experienced day care in their especially designed center, they found no significant differences in relation to any of the child–mother relations (Caldwell, Wright, Honio, and Tannbaum, 1970).

Beginnings of Functional Independence

As the child's manipulative and locomotor capacities develop, his drive to explore and perceive more and more of his environment becomes a dominant factor in his behavioral and emotional development. As he moves about among the objects of his environment, grasping and manipulating them in space, he makes real gains in self-identification and in his awareness of the relation of his own acts to the objects about him (Chapters 7 and 8).

At about the same time in the infant's life those significant persons in his environment begin to relate to him in a new way. With his achievement of a measure of independence and competence the dependable ones about him are no longer completely subservient to his demands. They begin now to be more restrictive and even punitive. He may not now be permitted to grasp and to experiment with many of the attractive objects about him.

A further complication of the child's life is the pressure being put upon him to learn to control his eliminative functions (among the vital functions discussed in Chapter 6) as he moves about the house. This concern of others and their interference with his freedom makes him more aware of these functions and the frustrations and gratifications associated with them. He thus becomes more preoccupied with them in relation to his growing sense of autonomy. In Erikson's (1950) words,

> anal-muscular maturation sets the stage for experimentation with two simultaneous sets of social modalities: holding on and letting go. . . . basic conflicts [between these two modalities] can lead in the end to either hostile or benign expectations and attitudes [p. 222]

The child is now in the midst of the "anal" stage of his personal development, the stage that Erikson characterizes as "autonomy vs. shame and doubt." The outcome in terms of personal functioning depends largely upon the wisdom of parental care and handling. According to Erikson (1950):

> Outer control at this stage, therefore, must be firmly reassuring. The infant must come to feel that the basic faith in existence which is the lasting treasure saved from the rages of the oral stage, will not be jeopardized by this about-face of his, this sudden violent wish to have a choice, to appropriate demandingly, and to eliminate stubbornly. Firmness must protect him against the potential anarchy of his as yet untrained sense of discrimination, his inability to hold on and to let go with discretion. [p. 223]

The inner conflicting tendencies interacting with parental efforts at outer control render this period of growing autonomy a crucial one in relation to further development of self-realization and functional adequacy. Perhaps partly in reaction to the restrictive socializing efforts of others, but also because the child's own pattern of interests and drives is changing, he begins now to be even more aggressive and resistant to outer control.

The Period of Aggressivity

The negativistic period of infant aggressivity is a time in the life of the young child when he is presumed to be meeting a developmental crisis: He is more keenly experiencing the loss of the sense of status that he enjoyed during the dependency of earlier babyhood. He seems to be reacting to that vague sense of loss with resistance and with efforts to dominate others. He now says "no" or "I won't" in response to efforts of others to direct or control his behavior. The age at which this period occurs is 2 to 3 years.

Initiative and Guilt

The young child not only resists the control of others but he now tries to exercise control over and manipulate others. It is a period of "initiative and guilt" (Erikson, 1950). According to Freudian theory, the Oedipus complex becomes an important factor. The child becomes strongly and erotically attached to his mother, and consequently the rival of his father for the sexual possession of the mother. This is presumed to be an extremely stressful period for the child. His sense of frustration and guilt are finally relieved through the mechanism of repression and by the formation of a strong identification with the father. Erikson (1950) has noted:

> The danger of this stage is a sense of guilt over the goals contemplated and the acts initiated in ones exuberant enjoyment of new locomotor and mental power: acts of aggressive manipulation and coercion which go far beyond the executive capacity of organism and mind and therefore call for an energetic halt on one's contemplated initiative. [p. 224]

This presumably is a stressful period not only for the child but also for the parent. It is also a significant period in the development of the child's self-concept. Its successful resolution can also provide a basis for later, more mature affectional and other interpersonal relations.

The Period of Motor Skills Acquisition

By the end of the preschool period the child normally has met and coped with the crisis of his loss of infant status. Although he does not yet possess the "executive" competence necessary for functioning as an independent member of society, he, nevertheless, is now free to enjoy a sense of secondary status in a satellite relationship with his parents (Ausubel, 1958).

With the beginning of school attendance, of course, the child's horizons greatly broaden. He forms constructive relations with teachers and other adults. His peer relations now become especially important too. It is in association with his peers and in friendly competition with them that he learns many skills. He learns to handle with skill his play and recreational equipment. He learns to work with tools and to carry a production task through to completion.

Of course, here, as in all activities and at all levels, wide individual differences are apparent. The individual hazard during this period of acquisition is that of developing a sense of inadequacy and inferiority because of the inability to measure up to or to compete successfully with peers.

In anticipation of later developmental problems, the stage of motor-skills acquisition becomes especially important. Through the achievement of these many skills the youngster makes measurable progress toward that level of competence necessary for autonomous functioning and the sense of status.

Transition

At a particular time and stage of individual development, and through some genetically controlled mechanisms within the organism not yet well understood, a tiny organ—the pituitary gland—is geared into greater activity. The stimulating influences of the increased secretions of that gland activate the beginning of a complex series of change processes which we refer to as the onset of puberty. The immature reproductive system is stimulated to develop and to begin to secrete its hormone (androgen in the male and estrogen in the female). The sex hormone, in turn, initiates the development of those body characteristics which differentiate the sexes. Other glands also act in coordination with the pituitary to perform an appropriately balanced function. The whole organism is stimulated to begin its growth spurt, and rapid growth and change, physically and physiologically, result.

Structural changes must bring changes in functioning. Such profound body changes as those beginning at puberty have important psychological accompaniments. The child's rapidly growing body is likely to seem a bit strange to him, and he may misjudge its unfamiliar dimensions. His changing physiology gives rise to feelings and interests that are new and strange to him. Being keenly aware of the outward changes in his body and experiencing the effects of the physiological revolution going on within him, the child may wonder how he is being seen by others. The regard of others is likely to become very important to him because he is unsure as to how to regard and evaluate himself. He is "concerned with the question of how to connect the roles and skills cultivated earlier with the occupational prototypes of the day" (Erikson, 1950, p. 228). In the confusion and uncertainty of change he is "searching for a new sense of continuity and sameness." A developmental task of importance to him is the achievement of a sense of ego identity—"the accrued confidence that the inner sameness and continuity are matched by the sameness and continuity of one's meaning for others" (p. 228). This period of transition from childhood to young adulthood is a crucial stage in the development of dominant feelings and attitudes toward self.

One's attitudes and feelings toward one's self and others, attitudes and approaches to life and to the challenges it presents and the tasks it imposes, all may have some foundation in one's temperamental nature. For the most part, attitudes and feelings are acquired through contacts and associations with others. A fuller discussion of this period of transition is given in Chapter 16.

Adulthood

Growth in competence, of course, need not, and normally does not, cease as one reaches biological maturity. One may go right on acquiring new abilities, new personal and social skills, more knowledge, and better judgment *at his adult level* of capacity to acquire. One's ultimate capability to profit from experience, to achieve new modes of adaptation ("fluid intelligence"), as we know, reaches its leveling-off point at adulthood, but his "crystallized intelligence" (his functionability) may continue to grow indefinitely (Bayley, 1955; Cattell, 1969).

Personal functional competence, then, is "intelligence" in the "common sense," layman's usage of the term. It is also the particular facet of the concept of intelligence which is the concern of some outstanding educational thinkers (Bruner, 1964; Combs, 1961, 1962, 1971; Hunt, 1961, 1944;

Rodgers, 1969) as well practical educators. Functionability, furthermore, in its development and in its pervasiveness involves the whole person. Thus it is an important and essential aspect of personality; this is the topic of Chapter 14.

Summary

It is very clear that the quality and range of experience, or cultural acquisitions, that one obtains from the environment is a factor of immense significance to the individual's functional effectiveness.

Functional intelligence, an outgrowth of interaction with the environment, is broken down into *primary factors* resulting from nature-nurture interaction and *secondary factors* arising from interaction of primary factors.

The capacity of the child to grow in ability to learn, within the bounds of his potentiality, is a tremendously important matter. The achievement of individual functional effectiveness in a particular cultural milieu *can* be fostered and facilitated.

Each child has a temperamental nature that may be defined as the functional aspect of his constitutional nature, and consisting of the peculiar combination of behavioral and affective predispositions mediated by his structural make-up.

Research has indicated that infants may be "typed" in terms of degrees of activity and other predispositions that appear to be present at birth. These predispositions may be of immense importance as determinants of the infant's early experience and development. His early experience, on the other hand, can serve to accentuate tendencies which may result in the retardation or the facilitation of his gradual growth of functional adequacy as well as o fhis total personal development.

Among the secondary factors—secondary only in the sense that the individual acquires them as he interacts with his environment—is the self-concept. The "image" a child has of himself is critical to functional effectiveness. Instilled in him by nurturant others in his life, it may virtually shape his behavior. It is a potent factor affecting learning, and it is especially critical in determining the nature of the individual's interactions with others.

Of all living organisms the human infant is most profoundly dependent upon the care of others for his survival. He comes into this life with but a few reflexes and physiological processes essential to the maintenance of life. From this state of utter helplessness he passes through stages of development in which various milestones, or tasks, are achieved. The child's capability to make these cultural acquisitions increases as he grows from birth to adulthood. In other words, one's "fluid" intelligence reaches its full developmental potential at adulthood. One's *functionability*, however, *can* continue to increase indefinitely as one continues to acquire new abilities, knowledge, skills, and so on, at his particular attained level of capability to acquire.

CHAPTER 10

Language
Development

Communication in its broad aspects is obviously not limited to mankind. Subhuman species commonly interact with one another and influence one another's behavior with sounds, gestures, and other motor patterns. But what about the central or "mental" concomitants of this behavior? Does the bird issue his cry *in order* to warn others of his kind? Does the enraged beast make his ferocious roar with *intent* to frighten or discourage his adversary? Is there really any intentionality in subhuman signals, in the frightening screech of rage or alarm, or the strutting and gentle cooing of birds at mating time, or the clucking of the hen as she conducts her brood about the yard? Or are these various behaviors, effective as they are in eliciting appropriate responses in others, simply "built-in" instinctive or reflexive patterns elicited by external and internal stimuli? The bulk of the evidence suggests the latter interpretation. Although subhuman species do influence one another with their sounds and their gestures and can bring about community of action in the group as well as appropriate individual behavior, it is quite likely that communication *with purpose and deliberate intent* is limited to man.

Communication and Learning

Our present purpose is to trace the development in the individual human being of the ability—voluntarily and with intent—to transmit and receive meaning and information in verbal interaction with others. This is a learning achievement of fantastic proportions, taking place during the early years of childhood, one which clearly sets mankind apart from all other living forms.

This learned ability to transmit and receive information with specialized meaning, furthermore, is a tremendously important factor in the further acquisition of learning generally. A language, in the usual sense, is an elaborate system of specialized verbal symbols generally accepted and used in the transmission of meaning. Clearly, it is through the medium of language that the individual acquires the great bulk of "reception" learning. Mowrer (1954) emphasizes the great importance of language in the transmission of culture:

> language makes it possible for its users to have *vicarious experience*, to learn through and from the learning of others—and this, as I see it, is the essence of education. Culture, in both its technological and social, regulatory aspects, is what our forebears have been taught and have confirmed or modified on the basis of their own experience, which they then pass on to us and which we in turn transmit to our children and students. While the power of example, as opposed to precept, is not to be underrated, yet there seems to be no serious dissent from the assumption that this continuous never ending flow of knowledge and belief which we call culture occurs

mainly through the medium of language and that without it, the cultural stream would quickly shrink to the veriest trickle. [p. 684]

In this connection it will be recalled that in Chapter 5 Bruner (1964) was quoted as emphasizing the great importance of language in the development of the human species. Language he referred to as a "cultural technique" upon which the phylogenetic, as well as the ontogenetic, development of human "intelligence" depends.

Speech and Its Acquisition

Language, in a broad sense, of course, is any means whatsoever of communicating meaning and feeling among individuals. The language of speech, however, is communication through the use of a highly evolved system of articulate vocal and related sounds. Since communication is a two-way process of interaction, speech, in a sense, is a double function: one of comprehending the meanings being expressed by another and one of transmitting meanings to another through the use of commonly understood symbols.

Verbal behavior and its modification is an important area of interest of research psychologists. Verbal communication is the behavioral manifestation and expression of mental functioning of a rather high order. It can, therefore, be viewed in both its behavioristic and its cognitive aspects.

Students of operant conditioning have become quite active experimentally in the area of verbal functioning. From their point of view verbal behavior is defined as "behavior which is reinforced through the mediation of another organism" (Skinner, 1957, p. 20). This, of course, is a statement in neobehavioristic terms of the fact that verbal language is a learned mode of psychological interaction among persons. Operant conditioning studies have shown that in speech learning social reinforcement normally follows verbal responses and that social reinforcement tends to increase the frequency of the responses. Thus, when verbal functioning is viewed in its purely behavioral aspects, its acquisition through learning—like the learning of any other observable and measurable form of behavior—can be studied by use of operant-conditioning methods. And, like other kinds of acquisitions, verbal learning can also be investigated and analyzed in its cognitive aspects.

The living organism, as we emphasized earlier, is a perpetually active organism. Its parts and various organ systems must be active and must function each in ways determined by its particular structure and organization. Earlier chapters were concerned with the functioning of certain of these systems and how they come to be interrelated and coordinated to result in integrated organismic functioning. The sound-making appartus, of course, is an organ system that is vitally important in this respect.

As with other systems, the peculiar structural nature of the organs of speech determines their functional possibilities. At first thought this organ system is a relatively simple structure, yet, from the point of view of its marvelously wide range of functional adjustments and possibilities, it becomes a very complex and intricate system.

Analysis of Speech

In simple outline the physical structures involved in speech are the lungs, the windpipe—at the top of which are the vocal folds and the glottis—the cavities of the throat, nose, and mouth with their intricate systems of muscles, the hard and soft palates, the gums, the teeth, and the lips. The marvel of speech, of course, lies in the regulation and coordination of these various parts as they operate to produce the great variety of speech sounds.

The analysis of speech into its component sound elements is a function of the discipline of linguistics. The first great task in this process was to make an inventory of all the sound elements used in the various languages of the world. Irwin (1949) described the preliminary steps necessary in the analysis of speech:

> For the scientific investigation of speech, the first need is a set of accurate symbols for the basic speech sounds, just as in physics and chemistry scientific progress depended upon the invention of the periodic table with precisely defined symbols for the elements. The English alphabet is not a precise scientific instrument, for one of its symbols may stand for several different sounds, and contrariwise, different combinations of letters may represent the same sound. For example, in the words father, sergeant, and hearth the symbols, a, e, and ea, respectively, all are sounded in the same way, like a in ah.
>
> In the International Phonetic Alphabet, invented about 40 years ago, the speech investigator has a precise tool that makes scientific work possible. This alphabet, unlike conventional ones, has one, and only one, symbol for each elemental sound. [p. 22]

The sound inventory of the International Phonetic Alphabet, with its system of symbols, presumably includes every sound category that the human speech organ system is capable of making.

Researchers have been attempting to designate the particular anatomical parts of the speech apparatus and the particular pattern of coordinated adjustments involved in the production of each of the sound categories.

Infant Speech

The human infant is born structurally equipped to produce the full complement of possible sound categories (phones). This function, like all others, however, develops through exercise (learning). The sounds a newborn infant makes are uttered in his undifferentiated crying. His first post-natal act is the production of a vocal sound—a monosyllabic cry. This sound, in terms of phonetic categories, is usually the *a* sound as in "fat." This particular sound constitutes about 90 percent of the baby's total vocal sounds during the first few days of his life.

A number of studies have been made of infant crying (Aldrich, Sung, and Knop, 1945a, 1945b; Aldrich, Norval, Knop, and Venegas, 1946; Lynip, 1951; McCarthy, 1954). During early infancy there is usually very frequent crying, much of which is "emergency respiration." Crying is, of course, the baby's main defense and only means of making known his discomfort. Brown (1958) emphasized that the crying mode of communication is a very imperfect one: "It has been reported that the infant's cries of distress have the same quality whatever the nature of the distress. If this be so, it would seem to follow that . . . children are often fed when they need to be watered, and bounced when they need to sleep" (p. 196). After a few months, however, the baby has learned to use crying in a more efficient way as means of getting attention apart from any bodily need or discomfort.

The infant's complete sound repertoire during this early period usually consists of about eight distinguishable sounds—five vowels and three consonants. These sounds represent about one fifth of those commonly used by adults (Irwin, 1949).

The baby's early vocal sounds are crying sounds. Soon, however, as an aspect of his general undifferentiated activity, the infant begins to make noncrying sounds as he gradually gains more control over the parts of his mouth cavity for a greater range of vocalizing. He begins to make the "soft cooings and utterances that delight parents" (Irwin, 1949, p. 22). Vocalizing at this level has no directed purpose or meaning. It is nothing more than a reflex air emission through the vocal folds, which are taut and can vibrate. "The infant's vocalizations," wrote Lynip (1951), "have no more relation to an adult's words than his leg kickings have to a grown-up's genuflections."

Soon a new phase in sound making called babbling begins. During this period the baby seems to enjoy exercising his vocal abilities, and he actually practices at random many of the phonetic elements of the International Phonetic Alphabet. Regardless of race or nationality, all babies' babbling sounds are identical. The child seems to be trying new vowels and new consonant sounds, such as bilabials *p, b, and m.* He repeats such sounds "over and over again on varying pitches, with varying intensities and cadences. He mouths them, gets the kinesthetic feel of them with lips, tongue and cheeks, and unconsciously and endlessly practices them" (Irwin, 1949, p. 23). He obviously enjoys his spontaneous vocal activity. It is self-initiated when the infant is comfortable, content, dry, warm, and fed and with reduced external stimuli. The babbling stage is a significant period in speech development.

After about six months of babbling some approximations of word sounds begin to appear in the baby's utterances, probably meaning that the cultural factor is becoming more important. The baby, in connection with his random practice of speech sounds (phones), now is beginning to utter and to practice the *phonemes* of the language of his community.

Practicing phonemes simply means that the child is being influenced in his spontaneous vocalizations by what he hears. When he chances to make a sound that approximates a word, that particular sound has no more meaning to him than his purely random babbling has had. This sort of practice, however, marks a significant stage in speech development, the stage called "echolalia"; babbling now becomes "lalling"—repetition of heard sounds and sound combinations. Successful imitation of his own sounds and those of others seems also to be highly satisfying to him. His imitations improve with practice. In the process of random sound making, he often chances to utter and to repeat a syllable which to his mother, or some other adult in the situation, *seems* to have meaning. He may say "da da," for example. If the father is present, he feels his baby is beginning to talk and that he is calling directly to him. Daddy then is likely to respond immediately by presenting himself to the baby while repeating the baby's "da da." If the father is not present, the mother is likely to think the baby must be asking, perhaps, for the doll or the toy dog and she presents him with the object for which he seems to be asking. She is likewise quite sure her baby is beginning to talk. It is fortunate for the baby's learning that she does so believe, because what she is likely to do each time in reaction to that particular utterance is to place it in association, in the baby's experience, with the person or object to which she believes it refers. Her smiling face while repeating the baby's "ma ma," and gesturing in relation to herself, not only reinforces his tendency to repeat the utterance but also tends to invest the sound with meaning for him. He is taught in that way to use words with meaning.

Learning To Talk

The complex process by which the child actually learns to talk has long been a main concern of research psychologists. In recent years the specialty of *psycholinguistics* has developed, and the central problem of this newer approach is that of unraveling this process, and of identifying the specific tasks of individual speech learning in infancy and early childhood.

Much information, however, has accumulated in the past concerning the quantitative aspects of language acquisition. As we have noted, the various stages in the general development of language have been described.

The Growing Vocabulary

One indication of speech learning that has long been used is increase in the number of words used. During the first two months of life babies use, on the average, between seven and eight sounds. By age 2½ years the average number of sounds has increased to 27. These sounds are among the approximately three dozen English phonemes. This means, of course, that at age 2½ years the child is using two thirds of the speech sounds he will be using later on.

During the early stage of speech learning the child's comprehension vocabulary is much larger than his speech vocabulary. Very early he learns to respond to such commands as "no-no," "lie down," "come here." These words are combined with gestures and with physical guidance and demonstrations, which help to establish a rather large "passive" vocabulary.

The active, or speech, vocabulary is gradually developed through a complicated learning process. It is not until about age 10 months that the baby is likely to have the use of a single word. At age 1 year he may have three words at his command. These first words are useful to him in making known his wants. They are nouns and usually monosyllables pronounced singly, or doubled, such as "ba(ll)," "da(dog)," "ma ma," "da da." With nouns at his command, the child, in his need, begins to learn action words to combine with nouns; verbs such as "go," "come," and "give" are usually among the first to come into use. By the time the baby reaches age 18 months he is likely to have an active vocabulary of 20 words, including a few adjectives and adverbs. "Good," "nice," "naughty," and "hot" are usually among his first adjectives. Other parts of speech come even later. At age 2½ years the child usually has command of some 250 words. As his concepts broaden or become more precise and specific, his word meanings grow in number.

The process of verbal interaction with a "tutor" is an important aspect of the process of word learning (Brown, 1958). The baby's own repeated utterances one by one become equivalent, in his experience, to the words he hears others speak. Through face-to-face rehearsals with his mother the baby perfects his own approximations of these words. Through a process of identifying equivalents in speech sounds he categorizes speech elements.

Concurrently, these utterances gain *referents*. For example, in interaction with his mother, she (her smiling face, the sounds she makes, and the many comforts and gratifications she stands for) becomes the "referent category" associated with his own utterance of "mama" and its variations and with the "mommy" and the "mother" he hears in the speech of others.

In the beginning the referent category is likely to be broad and inclusive. In other words, the child's utterance of a word becomes overgeneralized in its meaning for him. He may be heard to say "da da" when his father and other individuals are near. His father is naturally pleased with the idea that his baby is calling him, and the usual tutoring interaction takes place. The baby at first, however, learns a generalized referent for his utterance, "da da." That is, he may say "da da" at the sight of anyone or any number of people. But with added experience he soon learns to recognize the "invariance" of the speech symbol, and at the same time the referent for his word becomes more specific and invariant. Brown (1958) has called this language-learning process the "original word game." The infant, or other learner of a language, is "the player," and the parent or teacher is the "tutor":

> Because speech has a systematic structure it is easier to learn to recognize invariance in speech than to recognize it in other behavior. For the player of the Original Word Game a speech invariance is a signal to form some hypothesis about the corresponding invariance of referent. . . . Whether or not his hypothesis about the referent is correct the player speaks the name where his hypothesis indicates that it should be spoken. The tutor approves, or corrects this performance according as it fits or does not fit the referent category. In learning referents and names the player of the Original Word Game prepares himself to receive the science, the rules of thumb, the prejudices, the total expectancies of his society. [pp. 227–228]

Thus the baby learns words and their meaning. At first his use of words with meaning constitutes a very small proportion of his vocalizations. But such use becomes rapidly more frequent. By the end of his second year meaningful words have become very prominent in his speech-sound repertory. Not only is there an increase in the number of words used but the accuracy with which the constituent sounds in the words are produced improves with practice. "Ma ma ma" becomes a distinct "mommy," while "da da da" becomes "daddy," and "mi mi" first becomes "mik mik" and finally "milk." In operant-conditioning terms the child's vocal responses become shaped through the reinforcement of his successive approximations.

The learning situation in which sound symbols come to have meaning, that is, gain referents, involves far more than the mere strengthening-of-a-response tendency (reinforcement). Repeated past experiences of the appearance of the mother, for example, have come to mean comfort to the baby. The sight of her, the sounds she makes, the objects she carries, the tastes, the smells, and the cutaneous and kinesthetic experiences she consistently brings to him all are a part of the formation of his rapidly developing cognitive structure. The new cognitive experience of a word sound he makes and which he hears his mother make becomes another aspect of the total repeated experience of "mother." The vocal-sound combination "ma ma" gains much the same quality of meaning as the other experiences he enjoys with her.

Another aspect of word learning has to do with the elementary units of meaningful sound and the patterns of their combination and arrangement in speech. These elementary units are called *morphemes*. A morpheme may be a complete word, or it may be a part of a word, an addition to, or modification of a word that attaches an additional unit of meaning to a word. For example, the word "dog" is a single morpheme referring to an individual member of an animal category. By adding the sound "z" (s) additional meaning is attached to the word. "Dogs" has the added meaning of plurality. It consists of two elements of meaning, two morphemes. Obviously the child in his word learning assimilates these many modifications of, and additions to words and their meanings without the least concern for the rules of linguistics.

The Rules of Speech

As we have seen, during a child's first two years his language acquisition consists largely of learning to say single words and connecting these word symbols with their referents. But as Bruner (1964) stated, the "puzzle begins when the child first achieves the use of productive grammar" (p. 3). A profound change occurs in the child's speech behavior at about the end of his second year when he begins apparently to recognize speech invariants and to learn the "rules" of language construction. Recent research in speech learning has been concerned for the most part with the problem of how speech acquisition takes place.

The child somehow must learn the rules of speech from the generalized model presented to him in the natural language of the adults around him. He learns gradually and implicitly to follow the rules, probably without any deliberate intent or effort to formulate them as rules. He "may begin as a parrot imitating what others say, but he will end as a poet able to say things that have not been said before but which will be grammatical and meaningful in his community. This is the terminal achievement which a theory of language achievement must explain" (Brown and Berko, 1960, p. 1).

Students of speech learning in children view these problems of language composition at two levels: the rules of *grammar* and the rules of *syntax*. Grammar, in this rather narrow, technical sense, is concerned with the classes into which morphemes naturally fall. These classes are usually divided into two groups: the lexical classes, or *contentives*, and the functional classes, or *functors* (Brown and Bellugi, 1964; Miller and Erwin, 1964). The English contentives include the nouns, verbs, and adjectives, which are the words with semantic content. They make reference and give information. Each of these three classes of contentives can also be divided into subclasses. Thus, there are three sorts of English nouns: the mass nouns, the count nouns, and the proper nouns. Verbs are transitive or intransitive. The functors include the other parts of speech: the prepositions, conjunctions, interrogatives, noun determiners, and auxiliaries. These last classes are called functors because their grammatical functions are more obvious than their semantic content.

The rules governing the meaningful arrangements of morphemes are important concerns of grammar. Parts of speech derive their technical definitions largely in terms of these rules. Nouns, for example, are "a class of words having similar 'privileges of occurrence.' " They "can follow articles and can occur in subject and object positions and, in this respect, are distinct from such other classes of words as the verb, adjective, and adverb" (Brown and Berko, 1960, p. 2).

The Infant's Grammar

These classifications of words, the rules of their placement in sentences, their "privileges of occurrence" are, of course, the concern of adult grammar. Slobin (1971) has referred to it as "prescribed grammar." These rules govern adult speech, and for the child ultimately to come to abide by them in his speech is regarded as a mark of his achievement in language learning. But recent observations indicate that the child's earliest learnings of language are in terms of a grammar of his own. In discussing this newer view point, Slobin (1971) points out that,

> the important question is not what part of speech a word is in the adult language, but what role it plays in the child's language system. It seems clear to us now that children form a variety of word categories of their own—based on the functions of words in their own language systems—and so words must be looked at in the light of the child's total system, rather than in terms of the adult system, which he has not yet mastered. [p. 14]

From this point of view the child is seen as gradually developing his own grammar. At this early stage he apparently is not trying to understand the intricacies of adult grammar.

The study of this phase of development begins when the child starts putting two words together. This happens typically at about 18 months of age. Analysis shows that at this stage, two classes of words are used most frequently—a small class of high-frequency words, and a much larger, open class. The words of the first class are stable and rather fixed. They have been referred to as "pivot" words—words that are used over and over, and each is used in conjunction with any of the larger group of words. These latter, mostly nouns at first, express a need, or an observation on the part of the child. Quoting again from Slobin (1971):

> The two-word period is rich with charming examples of such childish utterances (Blaine, 1963): "allgone sticky" (after washing hands), "allgone outside" (said when door was shut, apparently meaning, "the outside is all gone"), "more page" (meaning, "don't stop reading"), "more wet," "more car" (meaning "drive around some more") "more high" (meaning, "there's more up there"), "there high" (meaning, "it's up there"), "other fix" (meaning, "fix the other one"), "this do" (meaning, "do this"). [p. 43]

The analysis of the "pivot" construction of two-word sentences is concerned only with the form of children's utterances. What is perhaps more important is their meaning aspect. Other two-word sentences than the "pivot" type are frequent in children's efforts at talking, and all are used by the child to show various sorts of underlying semantic relationships. Such utterances, however, cannot be unequivocally interpreted as to their meaning apart from the context in which they are made. Hence the importance of the development of longer utterances in individual speech. As in other kinds of learning, much practice is engaged in.

Practice

Rules about privileges of occurrence for individual words and phrases apparently are implicitly observed by the child. As recent evidence indicates, he playfully but deliberately practices these syntactic arrangements. Ruth Weir (1962) recorded the spontaneous utterances of her 2-year-old son while he was alone in his crib before going to sleep. Her recordings were made over a period of 18 evenings. These recordings particularly reveal the fact that although children may not explicitly formulate rules of syntax, they do concern themselves with word order in speech and with relations among words. Young Anthony Weir must have observed the "privileges of occurrence" of different word classes and of the different positions they may occupy in sentences. He quite clearly had assimilated implicitly certain rules of word sequences in speech, and in his solitary soliloquies he practiced word placements and sequences in terms of these rules. Thus, in his little sentences he tried out replacing one noun with another noun or a noun phrase or a pronoun. He interchanged adjectives, trying them out with different proper nouns. He practiced interchanging verbs. He discriminated between word classes and tried out the rules of their appropriate occurrence in speech. Excerpts from the Weir recordings will illustrate:

> Not a yellow blanket—The white—White. . . . What color—What color blanket—What color mop—What color glass. . . . Put on a blanket—White blanket—And yellow blanket—Where's yellow blanket. . . . There's a hat —There's another—There's hat—There's another hat—That's a hat. . . . There is the light—Where is the light—Here is the light. [Weir, 1962 pp. 107-112]

Thus a child learns to identify and to use properly the parts of speech. He comes to identify the class to which a new word belongs by its placement in the utterance and thus to discern something of its utility in speech. This is "one of the ways in which the lawful flexibility of speech is developed" (Brown and Berko, 1960, p. 2). With the new words that he has thus "classified" the child can now create something new in his speech.

The Acquisition of Syntax

It is clear from what we have already noted that as the child learns the different word classes and the rules of their occurrence in speech, he is learning some of the fundamentals of sentence construction. We have seen that by the time he reaches age 18 months he is beginning to use two-word sentences. By age 36 months the child can produce every variety of simple

English sentence. The processes through which the child achieves this remarkable development have recently been the subject of intensive study (Brown and Bellugi, 1964; Brown and Fraser, 1964). As the study by Weir (1962) has clearly indicated, children will experiment with speech and its parts and engage in much practice during their periods of solitude. It is equally clear that the basic learning upon which this solitary experimentation and practice is based takes place as mother and child interact verbally day by day. A longitudinal study reported by Brown and Bellugi (1964) is based on recordings of such mother-child interactions.

Two children, a boy (Adam) age 27 months and a girl (Eve) age 18 months, were selected for intensive study. Each child was visited every second week. At the beginning of the study the average length of Adam's utterances was 1.84 morphemes and of Eve's, 1.40 morphemes. At the end of the period of observation the averages, respectively, were 3.55 and 3.27 morphemes.

The development of the sentence-constructing capacity was the focus of the study. What is the nature of the learning involved as the child progresses from the one-word sentence to utterances grammatically correct of 10 or more words? To what extent is it a matter of imitation of adult speech of which he hears so much and with which he interacts in dialogues with his mother?

One immediate observation of these investigators was that there was frequent imitation on the part of both mother and child. As an example of mother's "imitation," Adam, in one brief interchange, said, "There go one" (truck), and the mother responded with, "Yes, there *goes* one." Examples of the child's imitations were the following utterances taken from the record (Brown and Bellugi, 1964, p. 136):

Mother's Utterance	Child's Imitation
Wait a minute	Wait a minute
Daddy's brief case	Daddy brief case
Fraser will be unhappy	Fraser unhappy
He's going out	He go out
That's an old-time train	Old time train

A second significant observation was that in such interchanges the mother's sentences were short and similar in structure to the child's, but they were perfectly grammatical in structure with no words missing. The child's sentences, on the other hand, although generally correct in word order, were usually reduced by the elimination of certain classes of words. The child's speech, even in his direct imitations, tended to be "telegraphic" in form, not only in the sense that the number of words was reduced but also in the classes of words that were left out. In composing telegraphic messages the adult retains the contentives, the words that carry the meaning, while eliminating many of the functors, which do not carry meaning. Interestingly, the child reduces his sentences in the same manner. An important problem is to explain the significance of this tendency and how the child acquires it.

> Why should young children omit functors and retain contentives? There is more than one plausible answer. Nouns, verbs and adjectives are words that make reference. One can conceive of teaching the meanings of these words by speaking them, one at a time, and pointing at things or actions or qualities. And of course parents do exactly that. These are the kinds of words that children have been encouraged to practice speaking one at a time. The child arrives at the age of sentence construction with a stock of well-practiced nouns, verbs and adjectives. Is it not likely then that this prior practice causes him to retain the contentives from model sentences too long to be reproduced in full, that the child imitates those forms in the speech he hears which are already well developed in him as individual habits? There is probably some truth in this explanation but it is not the only determinant since children will often select for retention contentives that are relatively unfamiliar to them. [Brown and Bellugi, 1964, p. 138]

Another feature of mother-child conversation, which does not support the explanation of children's telegraphic speech contained in the previous quotation, is the tendency on the part of mother to *expand* her imitations of the child's speech. The child, for example, said "Baby highchair." The mother expanded his utterance with "Baby *is in the* highchair." Other examples were "Mommy eggnog" to "Mommy *had her* eggnog," "Throw Daddy" to "Throw *it to* Daddy," and "Pick glove" to "Pick *the* glove *up*." Mother-child conversation is largely a cycle of reductions and expansions.

The mother's expansions, to be sure, add meaning, but they are not made in accordance with any specific grammatical rule. They are made with reference to the specific circumstances giving rise to the child's utterance as well as in direct response to the child's utterance. Generally these additions are functors, but such corrections and the learning that accrues from them apparently affects minimally, if at all, the child's tendency to neglect them in his utterances.

Brown and Bellugi concluded that the child's many and varied attempts at verbal expression—in conversation with mother or in solitude—in general represent a continuing effort on his part to assimilate the regularities of English syntax. His speech development is not merely a matter of learning to say word by word and sentence by sentence what others about him say. This study and other important recent research in this area of development clearly indicate that verbal responses as such are not *all* that is learned. Speech acquisition is, rather, a matter of gradually inducing the rules and principles of language structuring that make it possible for the child to *generate sentences*. He thus "processes the speech to which he is exposed so as to induce from it a latent structure" (Brown and Bellugi, 1964, p. 144). Brown and Fraser (1964) were more explicit in their summary statement:

> For the present, then, we are working with the hypothesis that child speech is a systematic reduction of adult speech largely accomplished by omitting

function words that carry little information. From this corpus of reduced sentences we suggest that the child induces general rules which govern the construction of new utterances. As a child becomes capable (through maturation and the consolidation of frequently occurring sequences) of registering more of the detail of adult speech, his original rules will have to be revised and supplemented. As the generative grammar grows more complicated and more like the adult grammar, the child's speech will become capable of expressing a greater variety of meaning. [p. 79]

Such a complicated process of acquisition is not wholly accounted for in terms of current learning theory. Undoubtedly, there are along the way many specific learnings that are facilitated by reinforcement. In the verbal interchanges between mother and child, for example, the latter receives rich reward for his speech achievements from the attention and approval centered upon him. His pronunciations in the course of interchange are shaped toward perfection by the process of successive approximations with their self-produced reinforcements.

As the studies of speech learning in children suggest, there is something about the overall acquisition of speech facility that is not touched by mechanistic theory. Here cognitive theory seems to offer an explanation. Bruner (1964), it will be recalled (Chapter 5), suggested that cognitive growth is the epitome of the interaction between the individual child and his culture. Also:

> Growth depends upon the mastery of techniques and cannot be understood without reference to such mastery. These techniques are not, in the main, inventions of the individuals who are "growing up"; they are, rather, skills transmitted with varying efficiency and success by the culture—language being a prime example. Cognitive growth, then, is in a major way from the outside in, as well as from the inside out. [p. 1]

Language, then, may be regarded as a "technique" provided by and made available to the child by the culture in which he grows. Language is so pervasive in his experience and in his life that he is constantly interacting with it. Modifications and additions to his cognitive structure are very largely the results of the progressive mastery of this cultural technique, which makes it possible for him not only to *represent* his experiences but also to *transform* them and thereby to generate in himself new understandings (Bruner, 1964).

Factors Affecting Speech Development

One of the striking facts about acquisition of speech in children is the wide range of individual variations in rate of achievement. Since speech development is a very complicated and involved learning process, any of the factors that, in various ways, affect learning in general may be crucial in an individual child's learning to talk.

There is much evidence, for example, that the rate of progress in mental development is a basic factor in speech facility. Studies of early speech sounds in children have led to the suggestion that the types of consonant sounds and the consonant-vowel frequency ratios in babies' babbling may prove to be the best predictors of later intelligence (Catalano and McCarthy, 1954). Children who are precocious in mental development have repeatedly shown marked linguistic superiority. Studies have also shown that the lower the intellect rating, the poorer the speech (Cruickshank and Johnson, 1958).

As with any other learned function, the various aspects of the environment in which the child develops become crucial factors in language development. In other connections we have emphasized the importance of adequate and appropriate stimulation for optimal development. Homes that provide books and other forms of appropriate literature and stimulating materials that invite constructive play, along with free access to them for the child, constitute a basically favorable environment. The number of adults with whom the child daily interacts, the extent to which he is talked with, told stories to, and read to, and the number of playmates he has have been found to be important home-environmental factors affecting speech development (McCarthy, 1960).

Social Class and Language Acquisition

Research evidence clearly indicates a significant relation between a family's social class and language development in its children (Bernstein, 1961; Deutsch, 1963, 1965; Deutsch and Brown, 1964). The social-class differences in language, however, are not limited to the purely quantitative aspects of language facility, such as size of vocabulary. According to Bernstein's (1960) study of this problem, the "differences in language facility result from entirely different *modes* of speech found within the middle-class and the lower working-class" (p. 271). Because of the difference in social organization between rather widely differing social classes, quite different emphases are placed upon language as a potential to be developed in children. "Once this emphasis or stress is placed," wrote Bernstein, "then the resulting forms of language use progressively orient the speakers to distinct and different types of relationships to objects and persons, irrespective of the level of measured intelligence" (1960, p. 271). Thus, the very nature of the child's orientations to his social and material world, as well as the form and the quality of his speech, may be significantly affected by social-class-imposed "emphases," or attitudes toward the speech function.

Bernstein compared samples of teenage boys from middle-class and lower working-class families of England as to their performances on two types of intelligence tests: a vocabulary (verbal) test and a nonverbal test. His findings were quite revealing. Fifty-eight of the 61 working-class boys had language-test IQ's within the average range (90–110). The other three boys scored below IQ 90. On the nonverbal test, however, more than half of the boys (36 of the 61) obtained IQ's of 110 or above.

The middle-class boys, on the other hand, presented quite a different picture of the relation between the two types of performances. On both the language and the nonlanguage tests all of the 45 subjects scored IQ's of 100 or above, with very similar distributions throughout.

A comparison of the mean raw scores of the two groups highlighted the same basic facts. The mean scores on the nonverbal test for the middle-class and the working-class groups were 51.4 and 41.36, respectively. On the language test the corresponding differences were 60.2 and 41.9. This difference of 18.3 is highly significant.

The results of this study quite clearly indicate that the "relational operations" required by the nonverbal test "are available to members of the working-class, whereas the concepts and principles required for the upper ranges of the verbal test are not" (1960, p. 273). For these children, language does not become an effective technique for cognitive development. It fails to become an adequate internalized program for ordering experience. Bruner (1964) suggested that the internalization of language, so that it can function effectively as a technique of cognitive development, "depends upon interaction with others, upon the need to develop corresponding categories and transformations for communal action. It is the need for cognitive coin that can be exchanged with those on whom we depend" (p. 14). The paucity of verbal interchange within the lower-class family does not provide enough "cognitive coin" of the higher denominations.

Deutsch's (1965) study of social class and language development led to essentially the same conclusions as Bernstein's. The tendency of parents of lower-class families is to answer the child's request with a perfunctory single word, "yes" or "no" or "go away," rather than with a complete sentence or an explanation:

> as compared with the middle-class homes, there is a paucity of organized family activities in a large number of lower-class homes. As a result, there is less conversation, for example, at meals, as meals are less likely to be regularly scheduled family affairs. . . .
>
> In general, we have found that lower-class children, Negro and white, compared with middle-class children, are subject to what we've labeled a "cumulative deficit phenomenon" which takes place between the first and the fifth grade years. [p. 80]

Deutsch's findings indicate that language in the lower-class family tends to be used in a restrictive fashion, rather than in a fashion that would broaden the child's perspective. As Deutsch (1963) pointed out, the preschool child in the crowded lower-class apartment typically is subjected to much noise, but noise that is generally not meaningful to him. With the paucity of instructional conversation directed toward him, he is in an ideal situation to learn *in*attention. He "does not get practice in auditory discrimination, or feedback from adults correcting his enunciation, pronunciation and grammar" (p. 171).

In general, as Bernstein (1960) stated, in the lower-class family the emphasis is not placed upon language as a potential to be developed. Language is not valued as a technique to be used by the child in his cognitive, and his total personal, development. Consequently, no effort is made by the parent to present a good linguistic model for the child or in any other way to encourage correct and adequate speech development. Children take into themselves the attitudes and the values as well as the behavioral and speech patterns of the specific culture in which they grow up.

Minority-Group Membership

In many instances the factor of race and ethnic-group membership of a family is associated with its social class. The child of a black family in a lower-class slum area, for example, is doubly disadvantaged in the area of language development. The black community during the hundred years since slavery has occupied, for the most part, a marginal position on the economic scale. Because of this chronic economic instability, the black male, particularly at the lower-class levels, has suffered continuous discouragement and feelings of inadequacy. This, of course, has contributed to family instability. The status of the father as the family head is affected adversely by his inability to provide the material needs of the family. Broken homes due to absence of the father are most frequent in this group. Hence, the lack in the family of an adequate father figure, and in many instances the complete absence of a male model of any kind in the child's home experience, would in general limit still further the adult sources of cognitive stimulation for the child and the possibilities of his learning through verbal interchange. "One can postulate on considerable evidence that language is one of the areas which is most sensitive to the impact of the multiplicity of problems associated with the stimulus deprivation found in the marginal circumstances of lower-class life" (Deutsch, 1963, p. 173).

Bilingualism

Another minority-group situation that creates language-learning difficulty is that of the "child of immigrant parents who at home continue to speak the native tongue and maintain most of the native customs, beliefs and value patterns" (Soffietti, 1955, pp. 224–225). In this situation bilingualism develops. But the child of an immigrant family faces more than a matter of dealing with two distinct linguistic habits. He is clearly involved with two distinct cultures. During his preschool years the language of the parents has precedence, and only after entrance into the school system will the child find it essential to learn English.

Bilingualism has long been a school problem in the United States. Children do not easily lose the effects of the parental language and culture upon their own English speech. According to the findings of Smith and Kasdon (1961), during a period of 20 years (between 1938 and 1958) the Filipino and Japanese parents of Hawaii had practically ceased using their native tongues, and the language ratings of their homes indicated the Anglicizing of their speech. The children, furthermore, no longer were regarded as bilingual. Yet Smith and Kasdon found that

> Although there has been a gain in children's command of English since 1938, the task of teaching standard English is still a major one for the kindergarten teachers inasmuch as the children in the two racial groups studied are retarded slightly more than a year in their use of oral English in terms of the measures used in this study. [p. 138]

Interpersonal relations very early in the child's linguistic development are extremely important. For the infant to have regular intimate and nurturant contacts with a "mothering one" is especially important in this connection, because these contacts naturally involve a kind of vocal interaction from the beginning. The baby cries and the mother soothes with words and appropriate actions. When comfortable and contented, the baby gurgles and coos and the mother responds vocally to his utterances. The mother is alert to her baby's vocal sounds and soon begins to respond to them in ways that invest them with meaning for the child.

Obviously, there are many ways of encouraging speech learning. In the ordinary family situation, especially where other children are present, the baby naturally gets much stimulation and encouragement. Parents can further promote speech learning by deliberately encouraging family conversation at levels at which the younger members can participate.

Speech directed specifically toward a young child stimulates and encourages vocal response. This was demonstrated in an experimental study of 3-month-old infants by Rheingold, Gewirtz, and Ross (1959). They found that by responding each time to the baby's vocalization with a "complex of social acts," including a vocal sound and a smile, the frequency of the baby's vocalizing increased significantly. Vocal speech is the natural mode of social interaction, for it can develop only through social interaction.

The Assessment of Speech Development

In view of the complexities of the process of learning to talk, the usual language achievement of the child during his early years is truly remarkable. To parents, that progress sometimes seems slow. Indeed, it is not smooth and steady. Like other aspects of development, there are discernible cyclic variations in rate of progress, periods during which the child may be consolidating his gains and periods in which other aspects of his total development presumably have preeminence (Jersild, 1946). Characteristically during these periods of relatively rapid progress, which are separated by "plateaus," certain specific levels of performance, or stages, in speech development are achieved. These stages have been established, together with the age at which they most frequently appear, by students of speech development. Such stages may be regarded as indicators of progress, and, when listed in their sequential order and with their respective age equivalents, they constitute a rough developmental sequence. An individual child's status in speech learning can be roughly appraised by referring his level of performance to such a scale.

Table 10.1 lists stages in speech development. The age equivalents for

TABLE 10.1   Progress Indicators of Speech Development

Indicators	Age Expected (Months)
I. *Pre-speech Vocalizations*	
Crying—explosive sounds, grunts, sneezes, sighs, coughs, guttural sounds	0–2
Vowel sounds—"a" as in "fat," "i" as in "fit," "e" as in "set," "u" as in "up," and "u" as in "food"	4
Babbling stage—sounds "uttered for the mere delight of uttering them"	8
Lalling period (echolalia)—phoneme practice, imitation of heard sounds, "ma ma," "da da," "ba ba"	11
II. *Speech*	
Understands assortment of action words—"drink," "go," "come," "give," "bye bye"	12
Generalized meaning of nouns—"da da" may refer to any man	12
Single-word sentences—"give," "ball," "dog"	12
Early sentence stage—nouns, verbs, and some adverbs and adjectives, "good," "nice," "hot." No prepositions or pronouns	17
Understands simple sentences—"Where is the ball?" "Give mother the spoon." "Want to go bye bye?" Active vocabulary about twenty words	18
Short sentence stage—two-word sentences, excess of nouns, lack of articles, prepositions	24
Comprehends simple requests and is able to carry them out—"Give me the kitty." "Put the spoon in the cup." Stanford-Binet Test	24
Identifies objects by use	30
Question-asking stage—questions asked mainly for pleasure of asking	36
Complete sentence stage—five-word sentences, virtually all parts of speech present	48
Counts three objects (Stanford-Binet)	60
Knows meaning of numbers	72
Knows meaning of "morning," "afternoon," "night," "summer," "winter" (Stanford-Binet)	78

the various levels of performance are based upon the observations of a number of different investigators (Carroll, 1960; Irwin, 1949; Lewis, 1951; Lynip, 1951; McCarthy, 1960; Nice, 1925, 1932; Simon, 1957; Terman, and Merrill, 1937).

The items in Tables 10.2 and 10.3 were abstracted from the developmental records of Paul and Sally 695, respectively. Some of these items were taken from their actual performance records, developmental and intelligence tests, and written analyses of the test results. The others were found in observational reports and in summaries by staff and student observers. These speech items, in each case, were arranged in chronological order, then listed with the age of the child at the time of the report. An attempt, only partially successful, was then made to identify each item with an item in the scale of speech development (Table 10.1) and thus to arrive at an approximate age equivalent for it.

Paul's and Sally's progress in speech development, as appraised in this manner, are shown graphically in Figure 10.1. These plottings reflect what is quite evident in the comments in the records. Both of these children were consistently described as being "advanced," "very advanced," and "superior" in their language performance in the test situation. Recorded examples of

TABLE 10.2   **Speech Development of Paul 695 as Appraised from Examples in his Developmental Record and from Test Results and Comments**

Speech Item	Age Observed (months)	Age Expected (months)
"A great deal of babbling"	6.5	8
Consonants beginning to appear in his speech	6.5	
Seems to respond to his own name	6.5	
Said "bow wow" and "meow" in response to pictures	13	18
"Baa baa" in response to picture of sheep	15	18
Complete-sentence stage (five- to eight-word sentences) "Paul, Daddy, Mama, going downtown on bus." "Going to Aunt Mary's school." "Going to play with ball."	24	48
Eleven distinct words recognized by tester, two of which referred to body parts "hair" and "neck"	18	
Responded correctly to all four directions with ball	18	24
Named eight objects on picture cards, including "smoke" coming from chimney	18	30
Mother noted over 200 sounds "with definite associations—not all made complete words"	18	24
Tester noted he "has command of virtually every form of sentence structure: 'I want to go to the car store to buy a big coal truck, and then I can get into it and drive it away.' "	31	72
Defines words in terms of use: "Dresses to put on ladies and little dresses to put on little girls"	38	70

TABLE 10.3   Speech Development of Sally 695 as Appraised from Examples in her Developmental Record and from Test Results and Comments

Speech Item	Age Observed (months)	Age Expected (months)
One-word sentences "da da" and "ma ma"	8	15
Chattered about the "bow wow" and "meow" as she looked at pictures	13	18
"Baa baa," pointing at picture of black sheep on wall	15	18
Uses many approximations to common words, "bu bu" (button), "na na" (down), "co co" (cold, when her hands are against window pane), "woo" (shoe), "ya ya" (sock)	15	18
Carried out two verbal directions with ball on test	18	——
Named three test objects	18	——
Named five items on picture cards	18	——
Said "ball ball" when handed ball	18	——
Gives use of ball: "ball rolls"	18	30
Repeats practically everything she hears	23	——
Correcting many pronunciations as "down" in place of "na"	23	——
Long sentences, expresses original ideas	24	48
Some use of pronouns	24	——
Picture vocabulary of sixteen words	24	——
Uses nouns, verbs, adjectives, and adverbs	31	——
Many sentences of seven and eight words	41	——

their sentences consistently used in play also portrayed high levels of speech performance.

Learning To Read

Very closely related to the process of learning to talk is that of learning to read. In fact, in the experience of many children these are two phases of a continuous process—the process of associating symbols with their referents. In speech acquisition the symbol in each case is a vocal sound; in reading the symbol is visual in nature. Both symbols have the same referent. The vocal sound "dog," for example, through repeated association comes to stand for (mean) a class of objects: the noisy animal outside, the little wiggly animal inside, the toy animal with which the child plays. The common characteristics of this variety of objects are abstracted and together become the referent for which the vocal sound "dog" becomes established in the child's cognitive structure as the invariant sign.

Subsequently, or in some cases concurrently, children become intensely interested in their books containing pictures of dogs, each labeled with the printed and written symbol "dog." These visual symbols also readily become

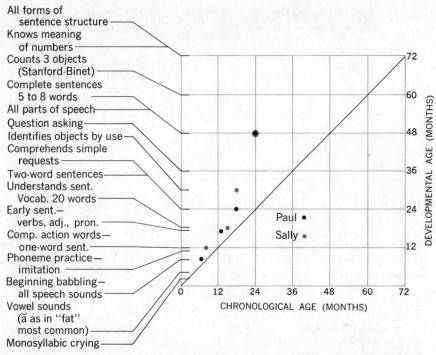

Figure 10.1 Speech development of Paul and Sally 695 in terms of approximate age equivalents.

associated in the child's experience with the animal category "dog" and with the vocal sound "dog" which he hears and which he himself makes. Thus, the sight of the dog outside, along with the sound of his bark and the picture of the dog in his book, along with the associated printed word, become adequate stimuli, alone or jointly, for his utterance "dog." When he is able to say "dog" in response to the printed word the latter has become a sign with meaning—much the same meaning as have the actually perceived animals, the pictures of the animals, and the word "dog" as heard. These all may be regarded, then, as "equivalent stimuli" (G. W. Allport, 1960) for the "meaning disposition" (Brown, 1958, p. 103)—the concept dog. The child's cognitive organization, to that extent, has been altered and amplified. To the child, the symbol "dog" has acquired "representational properties" such that "it evokes an image, or other ideational content in the reacting subject (the child) that is cognitively equivalent to that evoked by the designated object itself" (Anderson and Ausubel, 1965, p. 64). The child has learned to read the word "dog."

Reading Readiness

As with other sorts of functional facility, we assume that acquisition always must await structural readiness. A child, it is assumed, cannot establish connections between objects or his experiences with these objects and their representational equivalents (printed symbols) until the maturation of his organism has progressed to the point where such connections are organically possible. The question as to *when* that point of readiness in children is reached is one which has received much attention in recent decades. Tests of reading readiness have been developed, and scores on these tests have replaced the older readiness criteria of chronological age and mental age for determining at what point in the child's school experience he should be launched on the task of learning to read. In terms of readiness-test scores, some children are started in reading at age 5 years, others are not deemed ready for such learning until age 7 or later.

Clearly, reading readiness involves the capacity to perceive. The child must first become repeatedly aware of objects, persons, and relations *as* objects, persons, or relations. This perceiving function itself develops during the first months of the child's life through further maturation and the exercise of his sensory equipment. Then, through the many and varied perceptual experiences with objects and classes of objects, experiential backgrounds (cognitive structure) become established. Into this structure can then be assimilated the associated sounds (heard names) and the visually apprehended configurations (printed names). These latter can then become symbols for the perceived objects with which they have been associated. Symbols thus "become meaningful when they are able to evoke images that are reasonable facsimiles of the perceptions evoked by the objects they signify" (Ausubel, 1963, p. 67). Development sufficient for this level of functioning obviously is a prerequisite for learning to read.

A Complex Process

As was suggested earlier, reading in a sense, is an extension of talking. The child first learns that certain vocal sounds and combinations of sounds are symbols representing objects, persons, acts, and relations. The next step is for him to learn that certain graphic, visually apprehended symbols customarily are made to represent the sound symbols which he already comprehends and can use. As this learning task is accomplished, the printed word comes to represent the sound which stands for the object. The child is learning to read.

In a simple statement of this process there is little to suggest the real difficulties involved in the developmental task with which the child is confronted when he enters the first grade and is expected to learn to read. Gates (1957) clearly portrayed the situation:

> Reading is probably the most difficult and subtle of all the scholastic abilities and skills to teach, and the critical period comes at the very beginning of school life when the children are least experienced and most readily bewildered. It is very difficult to show a child, for example, all the tricks of

working out the recognition and pronunciation of the weirdly artificial little hieroglyphics which printed words are. To be successful a child must catch on to good techniques. What is good for one word is often poor for another. To learn to recognize sound, and blend the sounds of the letters may suffice for *hat* or *bag* but be utterly confounding for *haughty* or *hippopotamus*, the former because of phonetic inconsistency and the latter because the number of letters exceeds the child's immediate memory span. [p. 531]

As Gates further pointed out, in many instances learning to read turns out to be one of the most difficult and critical learning tasks of one's lifetime. There are, of course, many possible factors which may, in various combinations and variations, contribute toward making the experience a zestful and generally happy one or one full of confusion, frustration, and anxiety. As we have already pointed out, maturational and experiential readiness are perhaps the most basic factors. With a lack of sufficient maturity and experiential background, a child's own expectations, as well as the expectations of others, may be very slow and difficult or even impossible of realization. "If he learns to read well, all is well; if he does poorly or fails, the respect of his parents and acquaintances and his own self esteem are threatened" (Gates, 1957, p. 528).

The vital importance of adequate environmental stimulation must once more be emphasized in connection with this developmental task of learning to read. Because of the close connection between talking and reading, anything that encourages the use and comprehension of speech will also facilitate reading learning. The richness of the preschool child's experience with things, places, and people, and enjoyable language activities in connection with them, is a tremendously important factor. In stores, museums, libraries, and in his books and play materials he will see and hear things in association with their names. In a great many ways a child may be led pleasantly and naturally to learn much that is basic to meaningful reading.

The Concept of Readiness

In recent years much interest has developed in the periods of infancy and early childhood. New approaches to the evaluation of early cognitive ability are being devised which are leading to certain revisions of the concept of functional readiness. Suggestions, with some supporting evidence, of infant learning capacity of an order formerly unimagined are beginning to appear in the literature. By the use of carefully designed techniques and with adequate and appropriate stimulation very young children are being trained to discriminate and to respond differentially to visual and auditory cues. Children as young as 2 years have been taught to read (Fowler, 1962a, 1962b, 1964).

In view of such findings, the older concept of readiness to learn requires reexamination. Is reading readiness, for example, really a condition, a stage, of structural development which comes about through the process of biological maturation, a process whose pattern and tempo in each case are genetically determined? To what extent is it valid to assert that development cannot be "forced," that we must await the signs of readiness in the child without any effort to hurry the process; that when a child is ready to achieve sphincter control, to learn to walk, or to talk or to read, he will begin to take on those functions, and that attempts to teach or to train before the signs of readiness appear should be avoided? Do recent research findings indicate that the process of biological maturation in each instance can be modified in pattern and speeded up in tempo through environmental stimulation and manipulation, thus making it possible, for example, to produce reading readiness in children at considerably earlier ages than would be the case without such stimulation or environmental manipulation?

An alternative view of the matter, which is more in line with the current conceptions of the nature of human development, regards learning readiness as something more than a result of biological maturation alone. The experiential aspect of readiness must also be regarded as of prime importance. In the past the young child's accumulating background of casual learning—his developing cognitive structure—has been generally neglected in the concept of readiness. Research is currently demonstrating the importance of the predominant nature of the verbal interchange between the very young child and his mother in relation to his cognitive development (Bernstein, 1961; Hess and Shipman, 1965). In terms of these findings, different degrees of experiential readiness in children to acquire the early stages of vocal language are probably a function of the extent of the mothers' use of a rich, elaborative mode of communicating with them from the beginning. Likewise, the readiness with which a child acquires implicitly the use of the rules of grammar and syntax in his speech may well be a result of this type of prior cognitive structure building. Again, learning to read, which is essentially a process of relating visual cues with associated auditory sounds and their meanings, is possible of accomplishment by a child only to the extent to which he is experientially ready in terms of a background of relevant learning which has accrued from the ubiquitous experience of language sounds gradually becoming meaningful to him almost from the time of birth.

This experiential-readiness concept does not preclude the importance of the maturation process. Maturation must provide the capacity, in terms of level of structural development, for relevant learning all along the way. Two children, for example, exposed from birth to the same quality of experience and amount of environmental stimulation may be quite far apart in their ability to read because of a difference in level of *maturational readiness*. On the other hand, a child whose mother talks to him in terms of verbal cues that "relate events to one another and the present to the future" (an elaborative mode of verbal communication) presumably would acquire an experiential readiness for language learning earlier than another child at the same level of capacity (maturation) but whose background of verbal interchange is limited, restricted, stereotyped, "lacking in specificity and exactness needed for precise conceptualization and differentiation" (Hess and Shipman, 1965, p. 871).

Summary

The story of speech acquisition by young children is a fascinating one, certain features of which are still not completely understood.

The weight of the evidence suggests that man is the only living creature that can vocally communicate meaningfully, and with purpose and intent, by means of verbal symbols. The acquisition of this ability by the individual child in such a relatively short period of time is, to say the least, a prodigious accomplishment. It is a complex learning task involving important cognitive accomplishments as well as an intricate pattern of fine motor coordinations.

Speech learning, like other complicated learning tasks, goes through a series of developmental periods. The neonate immediately begins to make known his discomfort with vocal sounds. He is congenitally equipped physically to utter all the sounds (phones) of all the human languages, and he proceeds immediately to make them. At the very beginning his sound repertory is limited pretty much to crying sounds, but very soon he begins not only to express his discomfort but to make a great variety of utterances apparently with satisfaction. The sounds he makes, particularly his cries, communicate meaning to his mother and others, but apparently without any conscious intent so to communicate. During his waking and comfortable hours his vocalizations are continuous. He is in the "babbling stage."

The second recognizable "stage" is called the period of "echolalia," when the baby begins to utter more and more frequently the vocal sounds he hears from those about him. The sounds he makes are now being influenced by the "culture" in which he lives. These sounds, which are involved in the speech he hears, are called "phonemes," but as far as the baby is concerned they still have no meaning.

But as the infant "imitates" sounds he hears, an important process of interaction between himself and others occasionally takes place—a process in which he begins to attach meaning to his own utterances and the sounds he hears. He begins to attach "referents" to speech sounds. They now begin to become morphemes—*meaningful* units of speech. His "da da" comes to mean "Daddy," through the teaching of those about him. He learns words.

The intriguing problem for students of speech has been that of discovering how the child learns how to *use* the rules of grammar, syntax, and sentence construction without ever learning the rules themselves. He apparently learns implicitly the nature and function of the different classes of words, or parts of speech, and by practice learns their proper places of occurrence in speech.

The facility with which this learning takes place depends upon a number of factors in addition to the child's inherent learning potential: the amount and quality of the speech he hears, the number of persons with whom he interacts, his playmates, and especially the amount and quality of the verbal communication he has with his mother or the person who cares for him. Membership in a minority group and bilingualism are also factors.

Learning to read is often closely related to learning to talk.

CHAPTER 11

Thinking

As we move from one topic to another in our study of development, the essential unity and relatedness of the processes described become increasingly clear. We noted that the basic functions that are vital to life have a part in and are affected by the "higher" cognitive and emotional functions. We also noted that the varieties of "mental" activity which reveal one's "intelligence" are not separable from overt motor activity, and indeed can be appraised in the earlier years of development only in terms of the motor behavior of the whole organism. It was also noted that learning is but one aspect of the total unitary process of continuous change in the individual which we call development. Learning in this broad sense, of course, is functional (behavioral) change, that aspect of development with which developmental psychology is most generally concerned. Thus it follows that the development of personal functional effectiveness, which in one meaning of the term is "intelligence," is an outcome of the unitary developmental process. In Chapter 10 we saw meaningful speech, so common in our experience as to be largely taken for granted, as perhaps the most prodigious of the developmental achievements of early childhood. Now we shall view the learned vocal-sound combinations which become meaningful in verbal interaction as constituting the implicit symbols which represent objects, acts, and situations of daily experience not immediately present to the senses. These representations constitute much of the content of thinking. This "higher" cognitive process is the concern of the present chapter.

Thinking, of course, is one of the most distinctive human categories of functioning. It is the implicit cognitive process by which further knowledge is apprehended, organized, and transformed. As a broad functional category, thinking includes the mental activities commonly referred to as reasoning, imagination, remembering, reverie, fantasy, and the like.

Thinking activity differs from motor functioning or perceptual apprehension, particularly, in that it is free of the limitations of time and space. We can think of absent objects and of perceptually inaccessible situations. We can also regard the world in novel ways by transforming and manipulating our representations of previous learning.

The common element in all such processes is some kind of representation, some substitute in consciousness for previous direct cognitive (perceptual) experience.

Modes of Representation

Much of our mental representation is, of course, in the form of speech-sound symbols. Hence, as mentioned earlier, there is a close relation between talking and thinking. Talking can be "thinking out loud," and thinking very often is implicit speech. The range and richness of one's verbal competence largely defines the limits of one's symbolic thinking. In terms of this kind of representation we can indulge in "flights of imagination," solve problems, or creatively expand our concepts about the world. In this discussion of thinking activity, therefore, we shall be dealing mainly with the "stream of thought," with reasoning and problem-solving, with creativity and with the expansion of our conceptualizations.

But even though implicit speech is a predominate means of dealing with things not present to sense, there are, of course, other kinds of mental representations of past experience. Bruner (1965) postulates a developmental sequence of three modes of representation in the cognitive development of children. The child first deals with past experience *"enactively,"* that is, through direct motor action. A child reenacts his perceptual experience of a horse by galloping like a horse or experiences a social event by going through the motions of pouring and serving refreshments. With more experience the child recreates experiences *"iconically,"* by means of sensory images, and finally by the use of verbal or other *symbols.*

Memory

The reliving in memory of past experiences is one of the most common of human representational activities. The term "memory" in its broad sense refers to any manifestation or evidence of remaining traces of previous learning—any kind of revival, reinstatement, or manipulation of past experience or behavior. Traditionally, three quite different kinds of facts or processes, all referred to as memory, have been differentiated. These are *retention, recall,* and *recognition.*

Retention

The fact that the effects of functioning remain with us is referred to as memory. In Chapter 5 we examined in detail the various phenomena of learning—the changes in functional facility that take place in the individual due to the actual exercise of function. Retention refers to the latent aspect of learning changes that are made manifest in the act of recall.

Recall

Recall, or remembering, then, is the active aspect of memory, the proof that change, or learning, has taken place and is retained. There are three kinds of recall activity according to the nature of the learned content: (1) the reenactment of learned overt behavior patterns completely or in part or in various arrangements and combinations of parts according to present needs and circumstances (as in typewriting); (2) the reinstatement of previously perceived reality through sensory imagery; and (3) the "shorthand" mental (or overt) representation and manipulation of past experience and learning by the use of symbols. These three modes of remembering, it will be noted, correspond to Bruner's three modes of representation (enactive, iconic, and symbolic).

The recall function plays a crucial role in continuing cognitive development. Bruner (1964) emphasized this point:

> If we are to benefit from contact with recurrent regularities in the environment, we must represent them in some manner. To dismiss this problem as "mere memory" is to misunderstand it. For the most important thing about memory is not storage of past experience, but rather the retrieval of what is relevant in some usable form. This depends upon how past experience is coded and processed so that it may indeed be relevant and usable in the present when needed. The end product of such a system of coding and processing is what we may speak of as a representation. [p. 2]

The second mode of recall—the reinstatement in consciousness in some degree of completeness and vividness of a previously experienced event, object, person, or situation which is not, at the time, present to sense—has been a difficult phenomenon to explain. The image is obviously mentalistic in nature, yet it has been "explained" in stimulus-response terms. Since an image comes to mind in response to some stimulus, external or internal, that stimulus must have had some associative connection with the specific stimulus or situation which gave rise to the original experience of which the image is a representation. The stimulus, whatever it may be that now elicits the image, can be thought of, therefore, as a conditioned response (Mowrer, 1960a; Skinner, 1953). The young child looking for the "vanished object" (Piaget, 1952), it would seem, experiences an image of the previously perceived object.

The reality of images in experience as a result of sensory conditioning has been admitted by Skinner (1953). In his words, "a man may see or hear 'stimuli which are not present' on the pattern of conditioned reflexes: he may see X, not only when X is present, but when any stimulus which has frequently accompanied X is present. The dinner bell not only makes our mouth water, it makes us see food" (p. 266).

The symbolic mode of representation is by far the most frequently used and most effective thinking facility, particularly in the more productive levels of thinking that are discussed later in this chapter. The elaborate system of sound symbols used in speech are internalized in the sense that they and their referents are readily represented in consciousness. These representations, as we shall see, are very important tools of thought.

Development of Representational Capacity

It is clear, then, that the essential element in thinking activity is representation. This means that a child is not capable of thinking until he has developed the capacity to represent, in consciousness, objects, situations, and relations that are not, at the time, present for direct sensory experience.

Piaget (1952) referred to the first 18–24 months of the child's life as the sensorimotor period (see Chapter 8). Observations of children's behavior during these early months indicate that they literally live in the "here and now," that their behavior is completely dominated by immediate sensory stimulation. Their capacity for mental representation has not yet emerged.

This early period, however, is an important one in the development of representational ability. It is a period of perceptual learning. The child learns to see and to react to objects as such. In his manipulation of things he coordinates and assimilates the various sensory impressions he gets from them. He experiments with objects "in order to see."

Prevision

It is in the later stages of this sensorimotor period that the child also begins to recognize signs of immediately following events. He has experienced these sequences many times. These perceptions of movements and sequences, which Piaget calls mobile schemata, involve characteristic sounds of various kinds. A particular sound thus becomes a sign "which permits the child to *foresee*, not only an event connected with his action but also an event conceived as being independent and connected with the object" (Piaget, 1952, p. 248—italics added). Thus the child acquires a kind of "prevision." He anticipates the usual sequel from the sign.

> Thus the signs consisting of creaks of the table or of chairs, of the person rising, etc., were acquired, like most of the others, as a function of the schemata of the meal. They are henceforth utilized in any circumstance whatever. . . .
>
> Finally let us remark . . . that the term prevision which we have used must not create an illusion or evoke more than concrete expectation. Deduction does not yet exist, because there is doubtless still no "representation." When Jacqueline expects to see a person where a door is opening, or fruit juice in a spoon coming out of a certain receptacle, it is not necessary, in order that there be understanding of these signs and consequently prevision, that she picture these objects to herself in their absence. It is enough that the signs set in motion a certain attitude of expectation and a certain schema of recognition of person or of food. [Piaget, 1952, p. 252]

Thus Piaget distinguished between perceptual (concrete) prevision (an "attitude of expectation and a certain schema of recognition") and representation in consciousness of objects or events not present to sense and of which the child is, as yet, incapable.

Elaboration of the Object

As we have seen, the child during these early stages of intellectual development acquires the ability to see objects as objects. His deliberate reaching-prehensile ability becomes well established with fairly precise eye-hand coordination (Chapter 7). He manipulates objects and experiments with them "in order to see." He also acquires the ability to differentiate means from ends in his experimentation. But, as Piaget (1952) pointed out, not until about the beginning of the second year of life (the onset of the fifth stage) does the child begin "a new putting into relationship of objects among themselves" (p. 263). Up to that point in his development the child has not established relations among objects independent of his actions with respect to them. He begins now, however, to see objects in a different relation with himself. In Piaget's words,

this kind of accommodation to things, combined with the coordination of schemata already acquired during the preceding stage, results in definitely detaching the "object" from the activity itself while inserting it in coherent spatial groups in the same way as in the causal and temporal series which are independent of self. [p. 265]

In the child's efforts to assimilate new objects into his already acquired behavior patterns he discovers that some objects resist. He is unable to manipulate them as he wishes. He discovers that such objects have properties which cannot be reduced to the level of his available schemata. Thus, as he encounters difficulty in his efforts to assimilate things to his own purposes, he becomes curious about the unforeseen properties of the objects which underlie their resistance. He then seeks to *accommodate* to them. Accommodation becomes an end in itself. Henceforth, "accommodation exists before every assimilation" (Piaget, 1952, p. 277). The child gradually realizes the independent nature of objects as he finally becomes able to assimilate them to his purposes.

These efforts to discover constitute a kind of "empirical groping" behavior, but different from earlier groping. Now "the groping is oriented as a function of the goal itself, that is to say, of the problem presented . . . instead of taking place simply 'in order to see' " (Piaget, 1952, p. 288). The "problem presented" is the discovery of "centers of force," the discovery of the nature of objects. This discovery is the process of "the elaboration of the object," a prerequisite to mental representation.

The child's mental functioning, however, is still in the realm of the concrete. It is in a more advanced stage of development, but "the subject's experience remains immediate and consequently a victim of the most naive phenomenalism" (p. 326). Further cognitive developments with respect to knowing the concrete world are necessary as a prerequisite to mental representation.

In this connection Piaget (1952) pointed out more specifically that there are two interrelated conditions prerequisite to the higher level of mental function: (1) "Permanent" objects must be constituted in a system of spatial and causal relations, which can occur only from intimate experience with the objective environment. (2) "One must place oneself among these objects and, in order thus to come out of one's own perspective, one must elaborate a system of spatial, causal and objective relations" (p. 327). The small child necessarily sees objects from his own limited perspective. In order really to know objects in their varied relations he must experience his environment from *many* perspectives by mingling and interacting with the objects of which his environment is composed, just as a toddler is wont to do with his newly developed locomotor and prehensile abilities. This mingling of self with things is also essential in the development of self-perception. The "most difficult obstacle to perceive in everything is oneself" (p. 327).

This is the stage of "discovery of new means through active experimentation." Moreover, "this more advanced adaptation of intelligence to the real is accompanied by a structurization of the external environment into permanent objects and coherent spatial relations as well as by a correlative objectification and specialization of causality and time" (p. 330).

Invention and Representation

On the basis of the foregoing developments there is a gradual change in the direction of greater awareness of relations. Clearer foresight and an ability of "invention operating by simple mental combination" gradually develop. Now when confronted by a novel situation the child's reactions, rather than being of the nature of empirical groping, are more likely to result from sudden invention. In other words, the solution is arrived at by *a priori* mental combination, by foreseeing which maneuvers will fail and which will succeed, rather than by a process of overt trial and error. To quote again from Piaget:

> Henceforth there exists invention and no longer only discovery; there is, moreover, representation and no longer only sensorimotor groping. These two aspects of systematic intelligence are interdependent. To invent is to combine mental, that is to say, representative, schemata and, in order to become mental, the sensorimotor schemata must be capable of intercombining in every way, that is to say, of being able to give rise to true inventions. [1952, p. 341]

This stage of mental development is ordinarily reached during the latter half of the second year of life. The emergence of the ability to represent in consciousness the possible outcomes of behavior means the emergence of the ability to think. The abstractions the child has learned and the categories he has thus formed in direct contact with objective reality he can now begin to manipulate, organize, and transform as mental representations of reality.

The Development of Concepts

The child's ability to think, then, grows directly out of his varied direct contacts and sensory experiences with his world outside. He develops the ability to represent mentally these experiences in the absence of the actual objects of sensory experience and to manipulate, reorganize, and transform them. His cognitive structure is augmented. He can now *conceptualize*.

The Nature of Concepts

It is important at this point that we distinguish clearly between the processes of perception and conceptualization. Perception is the direct and immediate awareness (knowing) of an objectively present object or situation. Perception is the "clear awareness of the properties of objects and situations" that are present to sense. It is the individual, concrete object that is perceived (Chapters 7 and 8).

By contrast, conceptualization is an abstracting, generalizing, and categorizing process based upon sense perception. It is a process of perceptual learning. On the basis of repeated perceptual cognition of individual members of a class of objects, say oranges—experiences involving the various sense modalities—certain common properties or attributes are experienced in association with the orange. Its characteristic color, spherical shape, odor, and taste, each by itself comes to mean "orange." Thus when any one of these attributes is sensed the experience is immediately categorized and the verbal label "orange" comes to mind. "It is an orange." The concept "orange" has been formed. A concept, then, is the result of abstracting from many individual perceptual experiences the common properties of an object category.

The Study of Concept Formation in Children

There is, of course, no disagreement among students of thinking as to the essential role of learning in concept formation. There are, however, different research approaches to the problem in which the specific role of learning is seen differently and receives varying degrees of emphasis.

The Objectivistic Approach

The behavioristically inclined investigator, for example, sees the process primarily as the establishment of common responses to particular classes of stimuli, and his research approach is the experimental-learning approach. The child subjects are placed in various controlled situations in which they learn new modes of categorizing. The factors involved in the learning process are thus studied.

To take a specific example, many different pairs of words, such as "dog" and "tree," "robin" and "truck," and "cow" and "cloud" were presented to a child. In each instance in which the child chose the animal in the pair of stimuli to respond to, he was rewarded; thus the animal response was reinforced. The child therefore learned consistently to make a common response to a *class* of stimuli. The child ultimately learned to discriminate animals in entirely new stimulus pairs belonging to that class and to respond to them correctly. Obviously this is an example of learning in a perceptual situation, one in which a concept is established. Presumably some sort of generalized representation of animal-ness arises in the subject which leads to the appropriate response to any new stimulus of that class (Palermo and Lipsitt, 1963).

Interestingly enough, one special problem in concept formation with which objectivistic research has become concerned is the problem of mediation, or conscious representation. More specifically, the concern is with the problem of establishing definite criteria for the existence of implicit mediating responses and the accompanying response-produced stimuli and with demonstrating the role of these in discrimination learning and categorization (Kelleher, 1956; H. H. Kendler and D'Amato, 1955; T. S. Kendler, 1963; T. S. Kendler and H. H. Kendler, 1959; T. S. Kendler, H. H. Kendler, and Leonard, 1962; T. S. Kendler, H. H. Kendler, and Wells, 1960; Spiker, 1963).

Findings from this line of research indicate that mediating responses do not appear regularly in the cognitive behavior of children before age 8 years, but that when the use of response-produced cues becomes established the phenomenon of "inference" becomes possible.

The Cognitive View

Investigators with the more "cognitive" point of view see the problem of concept development much more in terms of internal states of the organism—what is the developmental status of the organism, what is its background of learning at the time of the new learning, and so forth. Thus, while they recognize the fact that an individual's cognitive structure reflects his history of learning, they are not so much concerned with the *particular* antecedents of new learning. Ausubel (1963), for example, wrote that "existing cognitive structure—is the major factor influencing the learning and retention of meaningful new material" (p. 26). Bruner expressed this same emphasis in a summary statement: "In any case, we know that, when people associate things with each other, they most often do it by the extension or combination of groupings previously formed" (Bruner and Olver, 1963, p. 127).

Bruner and Olver's (1963) study was concerned with the rules and strategies (procedures) people use in the associative grouping of stimuli. They described a number of strategies "that have nothing to do with the content used in the grouping." Rather, these strategies were related to what the subject "was up to" at the time. In other words, the strategy that is used depends upon the child's mental status and his previous grouping experience (cognitive structure). Such experience, of course, is related to the age and the intelligence level of the child. An interesting finding in this research was that change in classifying strategy with development proceeded, in a sense, from the complex to the simple. The words of the investigators will be helpful here:

> The development of intelligence, given intervening opportunity for problem solving in the life of the growing organism, moves in the direction of reducing the strain of information processing by the growth of strategies of grouping that encode information in a manner (a) that chunks information in *simpler* form, (b) that gains *connectedness* with rules of grouping already formed, and (c) that is designed to *maximize the possibility of combinatorial operations* such that groupings already formed can be combined and detached from other forms of grouping. In a word then, what distinguishes the young child from the older child is the fact that the younger one is more complicated than the older one, not the reverse. [Bruner and Olver, 1963, pp. 133–134]

With the growth of ability, then, perceived objects and events are classified and categorized *more* in terms of how they relate to prior groupings and progressively *less* in terms of the actual content of the things being grouped. Stated in terms of concepts, the child's representations of his perceived world become progressively more comprehensive, more flexible, and interrelatable, and they therefore constitute a more versatile and efficient facility for thinking activity.

Styles of Categorization

In recent years a number of research workers have been studying the strategies children adopt in their grouping and categorizing behavior. These investigators recognize immediately that concepts vary in degree of generality, from the broad and inclusive to the specific, with very limiting boundaries. Different specific-object categories, however, share common attributes. When an assortment of objects, all different in most respects, are presented to a child with the request that he pick out those that are alike, he can usually quite readily group them in terms of what he perceives as common attributes or in terms of some other relation he sees among them. However, the specific bases for grouping the same set of objects by different children have been found to vary with the child's past perceptual experiences and with other personal qualities (Kagan, Rosman, Day, Albert, and Phillips, 1964; Sigel, 1961). The particular strategy a child characteristically adopts in his grouping behavior is called his cognitive style.

The styles of categorization used by children have been classified and described by Sigel (1965). One of these bases for categorization is the *descriptive part-whole* abstraction. Objects are grouped and labeled as belonging together because of observed "similarity in one or more elements within the stimulus complex." For example, pictures of a policeman and a soldier are chosen as alike because "they both have shoes" or "they both have uniforms" (p. 1).

Another style for grouping is based on the *relational-contextual* abstraction. An *"interdependence* among two or more stimuli" is seen by the child as the basis for grouping. For example, a man and a woman are selected as belonging together "because the woman helps the man." A hammer and a nail are selected "because you use the hammer to bang in a nail" (p. 1).

A third basis for grouping, according to research findings, is the *categorical-inferential* quality. In these cases the label itself "reflects an inference about stimuli grouped together." Every item grouped together by this criterion is an "instance" of the label. For example, "they are professional people," "animals," and so on. Two subclasses of this mode of grouping were also noted. One of these is the *categorical-functional*, where inference is made regarding a common function, and the second is *class-naming*, where the label itself directly reflects the inference (Sigel, 1965, pp. 1–2).

Labeling and Daily Living

Life would indeed be chaotic were it not for the human tendency to discern common features among objects and situations, to categorize them according to their common features, and to interact with the world in terms of concepts. To deal separately and individually with every stimulus that impinges upon our senses would be overwhelmingly impossible. "For us, as adults, diversity is neither distressing nor chaotic, for we have created order out of the seeming disorder" (Sigel, 1964, p. 209).

Not only do we deal with the objectively present "world" in terms of categories, but, as has already been noted, concepts become freed from the necessity for direct external stimulation. In other words, already-formed categories of objects, situations, and relations can be represented in consciousness. As our concepts become more and more highly abstracted and can be represented with greater facility by symbols, the more important they become in our thinking function.

Some Common Concepts

The realities of life—the objects, the situations, the relations with which human beings must constantly deal in the course of living—are so numerous and so involved as to make for utter confusion and futility were it not for the human capacity to group, categorize, or conceptualize. With this mental facility we are able to achieve a "reduction in load" (Bruner and Olver, 1963). "Concepts function as an adaptive mechanism through which we cope with reality" (Sigel, 1964, p. 209). But concepts and their utilization in thinking, as we have seen, are joint products of maturation and learning. Among the most important developmental tasks of childhood, therefore, is the acquisition of the generalized ability to categorize, and hence to deal conceptually and relatedly with categories of experience. Early concepts are relatively simple. They usually represent concrete objects and simple situations. With development, the level of conceptualization becomes more complex and abstract.

Object Concepts

Quite naturally, object concepts are the first to develop. Concrete objects are directly and immediately experienced. The child's object categories are at first broad and loosely bounded. With added experience they become delimited and with more specific referents. The child soon begins also to learn words in association with the objects he is experiencing. Specific words become "attached" to specific categories of experience. At the same time broader category concepts also develop. The dog, the kitten, and perhaps the bear in one picture book are now "animals."

Attribute Concepts

Concepts of *attributes* of objects are more difficult to formulate, for greater demands are made upon the abilities of abstraction. According to research findings (Sigel, 1953, 1954, 1961), abstracting size attributes is a more difficult process than abstracting such attributes as color or form because the size of an object is apprehended only when it is compared with another object. Children at 3–5 years of age begin to acquire this ability to compare and thus to abstract and conceptualize the size attribute of objects.

Interesting research has been conducted in regard to children's concepts of the object attributes of *amount, weight,* and *volume* (Smedslund, 1961a, 1961b). As we noted in another connection, young children have difficulty keeping their concepts of weight, for example, distinct and independent from the shape of the object. In one sort of experiment one of two identical balls of clay is changed in shape before the child's eyes. When questioned about the change the child is likely to say that the ball that is changed in shape also becomes heavier. Children, according to such research findings, acquire the concept of the "conservation" of quantity at an average age of 7 or 8 years, of weight by age 9 or 10 years, and of volume not until age 11 or 12 years.

Relation Concepts

Dealing mentally with information concerning relations between objects, people, and situations involves another sort of concept. The idea of space, for example, usually implies objects in relation. When we think of space it is usually space between or among things. Even the concept of "outer space" is rather incomprehensible except as it relates to something or someone.

Concepts of space and space relations have received considerable research attention as well as theoretical consideration. As in other areas of conceptual development, Piaget's work here has contributed much and has stimulated others to do research in the development of space concepts.

According to Piaget's theorizing, the child grows through a series of developmental stages which eventuate in his ability to think in terms of concepts of spatial relations. These stages all relate to the child's sensory experiences and his prehension-manipulation of objects within his reach. In the beginning, before prehension has developed, the child "is in the center of a sort of moving and colored sphere whose images imprison him without his having any hold on them other than by making them reappear by movements of head and eyes" (Piaget, 1954, p. 145).

As prehensile ability develops, the child begins to grasp the objects within his reach. The process of the "elaboration of the object" is essential at this stage of development. The child searches for an object that has just become hidden by a screening object. The desired object is identified as behind and beyond the screen. Thus, perceptions of relative distance in terms of perspective are developed. As the child pulls objects toward himself and throws them away from himself and as he stacks them one on top of another or puts them in and takes them out of containers, he experiences relative distances in space and he sees the space within the container in relation to object size. He comes to see objects together with or separate from each other as he handles them and moves them about. By age 4 years the child also sees himself as an object among objects and in spatial relations with other objects (Meyer, 1940).

Another sort of relation concept is the concept of *causality*. It is vital to our understanding of events, and of objects and people in relation to events, that we view them in terms of causal sequences. The ability to conceptualize cause-and-effects relations, as with other representational abilities, is based upon earlier direct observations of the objective world. We acquire concepts of causality by directly observing causal sequences in nature. Underlying this acquisition from experience, of course, is the assumed factor of biological, or functional, maturation.

Again, the thinking and the observations of Piaget (1929, 1930) set the stage for a great deal of research regarding the child's development of concepts of causality. Piaget's own observations led him to postulate a sequence of developmental stages, again taking the child through his perceptual development in relation to things in his environment. Piaget noted that very young children differ in their basic orientation to reality. He noted three sorts of orientation, each based upon the child's initial inability to differentiate between self and not self, between his own thoughts and feelings and the aspects of physical reality which give rise to those subjective experiences.

One of the orientations giving evidence of this basic "undifferentiation" is the tendency of children to react to their own thoughts and desires as physical entities. This tendency develops into what Piaget called realism. The second orientation postulated by Piaget is the reverse of the first—the tendency to clothe these undifferentiated physical realities with such subjective qualities as consciousness and purpose, which he called animism. The third orientation is to come implicitly to "see" the physical aspects of experience as products of human creation. Thus, every object and event in the objective world is assumed to have been made by people, hence artificialism. These three tendencies, according to the results of Piaget's experiments, precede the formation of causal concepts. The period is referred to as the precausal period.

A great deal of research was stimulated by Piaget's published material. The findings in many of the other studies failed to substantiate Piaget's conclusions. There is considerable disagreement, for example, as to the frequency with which animism is to be found in children (Deutsche, 1937; Huang, 1943; Jahoda, 1958; Russell, 1940). Sigel (1964), at the end of his brief review of research on concepts of causality, wrote:

> We can conclude that children do provide different kinds of explanations for physical and psychical phenomena, that there is a crude correspondence with age but not a one-to-one relationship, and that the existence of stages of causal explanations is still a tenable hypothesis. The invariance of these stages needs more precise and rigorous testing, assessing the role of experience and knowledge in the onset of particular stages. [pp. 235–236]

Concepts of cause and effect, along with the other relational concepts, are importantly involved in the processes of thinking.

Varieties of Thinking

There are a number of motivational situations that give rise to different varieties and levels of representational functioning. We shall consider now one conceptualization of the major varieties of controlled thinking activity.

Guilford's conceptual model of intelligence was briefly discussed earlier (see Chapter 8). The three dimensions of that model were concerned with the *operations* or functions of the intellect, the *content* with which those operations deal, and the *products* or outcomes of those functions. In other words, intelligence, from Guilford's point of view, is mental activity. Since the term "thinking" is in its broad sense mental activity, the functioning of the intellect, and since thinking, as we have noted, always involves content (we think about something), and since the activity eventuates in some sort of product, the Guilford model can be used as a framework for a discussion of thinking (the functioning of the intellect) (Guilford and Merrifield, 1960).

The five operations that constitute the first dimension of the model really designate five main types of thinking: *"cognitive" thinking, memorative thinking,* two types of *productive thinking,* and *evaluative thinking* (Merrifield, 1966).

"Cognitive" Thinking

Cognition involves thinking in the sense of knowing, being aware of, "having in mind," or comprehending. In this sense we "think about," or are cognizant of, what is objectively before us. Even though the object of thought, the situation, is being perceived and comprehended directly, usually also mental representation and manipulation are involved in the process of "knowing." Cognition of a totally new situation, such as that faced by a child when he first enters school, involves more than the mere awareness of individual objects and people. It would also involve some sort of discrimination and classification. The process of placing objects in classes or categories has been identified as concept formation, which is one important aspect of cognitive thinking (Bruner and Olver, 1963).

Memorative Thinking

The second category of mental operation is memory. This, of course, is thinking in which there is direct recall of past learning and experience. All types of mental reinstatement and representation may be involved in memorative thinking.

A rather large proportion of this type of functioning consists of the free flow of consciousness, or autistic thinking, the kind of representational activity that just takes place with no particular outcome or objective to be reached. It is thinking for the enjoyment of the activity itself. Much of the thinking of persons in their later years, for example, is likely to consist largely of memories of experiences and activities of their earlier, more active years, recalled in an unsystematic sequence and for no immediate purpose other than the satisfaction derived from the reliving of those experiences. Reveries of this sort, however, are likely to become embellished and exaggerated in varying degrees with repetition.

Young people are also often disposed to think autistically. However, they are more likely to live in the future, to imagine themselves in situations or activities that they have experienced only vicariously. This type of autistic thinking does not involve "true" memories. It is, however, a kind of memorative activity, involving the recall and manipulation of what has been learned through contacts with people and the various mass media.

Productive Thinking

When one thinks productively one generates or discovers what was not evident before. He educes, makes anew, and thinks differently from the general.

There are two types of productive thinking: *divergent production* and *convergent production*. Divergent production is original, creative in the sense that it is flexible, unlimited, free, imaginative. "Creative thinking is invention, for one thing, and invention is a form of production" (Guilford and Merrifield, 1960, p. 11).

Convergent production, on the other hand, is thinking of a more contained and controlled nature. It is thinking in the direction of *the* solution or, at most, a limited number of "correct" solutions to a structured problem. The criteria for an acceptable solution are well defined. Convergent thinking is generally called problem-solving. In contrast to the autistic type of conscious activity, it is mental activity with a specific purpose other than the sheer enjoyment of the activity itself. Objects, situations, relations, and implications are manipulated symbolically in trial-and-error fashion but oriented toward the solution of a problem or the resolution of a conflict situation.

Practical problems involving physically present objects or difficult environmental situations being objectively faced may be solved through the use of images or symbolic representations of one sort or another. Images of possible modifications or rearrangements of objects or of relations among objects may be conjured up and tried out in imagination. In such instances, the objective problem situation is being faced directly, and, as thinking continues, is being perceptually surveyed. Thus, perception and mental representation are involved simultaneously. "Learning sets" previously established in the person's cognitive structure are utilized, and, in terms of "shorthand," ideational trial and error, the problem may be solved as if by sudden insight (Harlow and Harlow, 1949). Problem-solving itself is a more controlled and directed kind of cognitive thinking than that which was described earlier.

In certain instances the problem to be solved may be a purely theoretical one in which no objective environmental situation is being immediately faced. The symbols are likely to be other than direct sensory images. Highly abstract symbols representing conceived scientific entities or relations are mentally manipulated, combined, and recombined in various ways in search of a solution. Verbal symbols, mathematical symbols, and chemical and physical notations are utilized in scientific thinking. This is the process of *reasoning*.

Even though divergent thinking is more closely identified with creativity, in the general sense of the term convergent thinking can be equally creative. As noted above, Guilford and Merrifield (1960) stated that creativity implies invention. "There is a connotation that in invention we get away from the conventional answers, hence conclusions are not uniquely determined. All this points clearly toward the category of divergent production" (p. 11). These authors go on to say, however, that they have come to realize

> that the redefinition of abilities, which are in the convergent-production category . . . are also of much importance in creative thinking. They represent transformations of thought, reinterpretations, and freedom from functional fixedness in the derivation of unique solutions. It may be that the transformations category rather generally makes contributions to creative thinking. [p. 11]

Evaluative Thinking

The fourth kind of thinking, as a type of operation of the intellect, is *evaluation*. "To judge, to compare correctly elements with reference to a given standard, to assign consistent values to elements in a group, to rate in terms of consensus, to leap over uncertainty and to land 'on target' " (Merrifield, 1966, p. 24) is a brief but apt description of this type of thinking. Binet saw this level of mental activity as the essence of intelligence when he wrote his frequently quoted statement: "to judge well, understand well, reason well—these are the essentials of intelligence" (Binet and Simon, 1916, p. 42).

Learning and Thinking

Thinking is a function of the intellect. Consequently, one's potentiality for the development of thinking ability, like all original developmental potentialities, is genetically determined (Chapter 8). This potentiality varies widely among individuals. A person's many and varied abilities to function have developed within the limits of his inherent potential and are largely matters of learning. Hence, whatever thinking abilities one may possess have been acquired through learning, through the exercise of one's thinking (representational) apparatus.

It is also clear that the sort of environment in which the child grows up has much to do with the extent to which he exercises and thus learns each of the various types of thinking activity. The school and the quality of teaching the child receives is an important aspect of his general developmental environment. Bruner (1957, 1959) stressed the importance of what he termed generic learning, particularly in the schoolroom, in relation to the development of productive thinking. Generic learning is not merely the gaining and storing of information in the form in which it is given. Rather, it is learning that leads to the recoding of information and, hence, to the education of general principles, or concepts, that allow the child to "cross the barrier into thinking." Thinking that results directly from generic learning, then, is thinking that "goes beyond the information given." Through insightful teaching children can be helped to learn generically, thus enabling them to use their learning creatively (Bruner, 1959).

Cognitive Structure and Learning To Think

The concept of cognitive structure was introduced in the discussion of learning in Chapter 5. One's cognitive structure is conceived of as one's fund of knowledge, which is organized in terms of hierarchical relations and conceptual systems. It presumably results largely from generic learning. Learning in these terms involves the process of relating new material to this structure. New items of information, new knowledge, are assimilated into already organized systems in meaningful ways. In the words of Ausubel:

> as new material enters the cognitive field, it interacts with and is appropriately subsumed under a relevant and more inclusive conceptual system. The very fact that it is subsumable (relatable to stable elements in cognitive structure) accounts for its meaningfulness and makes possible the perception of insightful *relationships*. If it were not subsumable, it would constitute rote material and form discrete and isolated traces.
> [Anderson and Ausubel, 1965, pp. 105–106]

Learning Sets

All new learnings that are functionally useful are achieved only in terms of what has been previously acquired and organized into the cognitive structure. General approaches to learning problems and learning skills are learned in this way. Acquired skills in learning are called learning sets. Thus, one learns *how* to learn. One learns generalized *techniques* of thinking through problems. These learning sets become incorporated into the cognitive structure as systems under which related new learnings are subsumed. In summarizing their experimental findings concerning the operation of learning sets, Harlow and Harlow (1949) wrote:

> Thus the individual learns to cope with more and more difficult problems. At the highest stage in this progression, the intelligent human adult selects from innumerable, previously acquired learning sets the raw material for thinking. . . . Thinking does not develop spontaneously as an expression of innate abilities; it is the end result of a long learning process. . . . The brain is essential to thought, but the untutored brain is not enough, no matter how good a brain it may be. An untrained brain is sufficient for trial-and-error, fumbling-through behavior, but only training enables an individual to think in terms of ideas and concepts. [pp. 38–39]

Children can learn to think, and they can be helped and facilitated in their acquisition of thinking approaches and skills. They can be helped to learn generically by being given practice in the manipulation of materials and ideas related to those materials, and they can learn in problem situations that encourage the development of learning sets in both divergent and convergent thinking.

Summary

Thinking is the "higher" cognitive process by which one comes to know about one's world and oneself. It differs from perception in that it is free of the limitations of time and space. The ability to think, perhaps more than any other attribute, separates mankind from all other living forms. *Representation* in consciousness of objects, persons, situations, and relations not at the time perceptually present is the distinguishing attribute of the process of thinking.

Mental representation is usually involved in the class of phenomena we call *memory*. The term "memory," as commonly used, refers either to *retention* (the fact that the effects of a particular experience upon one's "cognitive structure" persist and ordinarily can be recalled or otherwise reinstated) or to the actual process of *recall*. Learned motor behavior patterns can usually be performed (reinstated) at will. Learned verbal patterns can usually be repeated. Perceptual experiences can usually be recalled in terms of sensory images. Thus there are various modes of mental representation.

As modes of representation have been observed in developing children, three general categories have been identified. These are (1) the *enactive* mode—the child represents, or thinks about, objects or activities by means of his own overt performance; (2) the *iconic* mode—the child represents objects or activities by means of sensory images; and (3) the mode by which the child represents objects or activities by *symbols*—words, numerals, and so on.

Much research has been done concerning the nature of *concepts* and the process of conceptualization. Concepts are built up out of perceptual experiences of objects and situations as these are sorted, labeled, and categorized. This human tendency to "label" and categorize experiences, to conceptualize, makes it possible for us to deal with, and to function in, an extremely complex world.

In terms of underlying motivation there are two general classes of thinking behavior: *autistic* (reverie and "daydreaming," thinking with no specific objective or goal other than the enjoyment of the activity itself) and *productive* (reasoning, problem-solving, creative imagination). We think in the midst of and in relation to perceptual situations. We also think by means of memory images of past experiences, and we think evaluatively with a final decision or judgment as the outcome. Human consciousness is largely thinking behavior.

CHAPTER 12

Emotional
Development

It is interesting to try to conceive of what human existence would be like without feelings and emotions. To live without ever experiencing pleasure or displeasure, delight or distress, elation or depression, love or anger, joy or sorrow is difficult to imagine. Our emotions give us motive power to live, to move, to strive. The baby nurses at his mother's breast not *just* to have a full stomach. He continues to nurse because the process as such is pleasant and gratifying to him. It is not the child's well-nourished body or his newly won ability to walk upright or the nature of his self-image *as such* that move him to further activity. It is, rather, the *feeling* of well-being, the joy of freedom of activity, and the gratification that comes from exploration and manipulation that activate him, make him "open to the world," and keep him striving to experience more and more of the world about him.

The Nature of Emotions

Emotionality as an area of functioning is complex and difficult to investigate. Important as it is in our lives, when viewed objectively it is a behavioral area which man has in common with subhuman species. Furthermore, although man's cognitive processes are importantly involved, his affective experiences and his emotional behavior are largely mediated by lower centers of the brain. These centers and the other bodily structures involved in emotional functioning are intact and in a state of readiness at birth. The human being is born well equipped for experiencing feelings of pleasure and displeasure and for displaying emotional behavior. In that particular respect man is more like the subhuman species. In that particular respect also maturational changes between birth and adulthood are relatively minor. Hence, even though emotionality is complex and multi-faceted, involving as it does the whole organism, it is the most "primitive" major area of human functioning.

Aspects of Emotionality

Emotionality has been defined in various ways and has been seen from different theoretical points of view by students of human behavior. One of these approaches, objective in nature, is to define an emotion in terms of the external situation—the perceptual field that gives rise to it. Thus, those emotional reactions which result from situations that are judged objectively to be dangerous would be labeled fear or terror. Likewise, reactions to confining or frustrating situations would be anger or rage, and so on. This was the approach used by early investigators of emotions in infants and children. Watson (1924), for example, in his efforts to account for all infant emotions, defined the three emotions fear, anger, and love in terms of the relatively few stimuli to which he found infants responsive. The infants' response to a sudden loud noise or a sudden loss of support he labeled fear, their reactions to restraint he labeled anger, and responses to being rocked, to stroking, fondling, and the like, were love.

A second objective approach to the study of emotions, closely related to the first, is in terms of the observable reactions, or measurable bodily changes, that constitute emotional behavior. Emotional behavior from this viewpoint is both external and internal. External behavior, of course, is quite readily observed. When the behavior is destructive or assaultive in nature it is labeled anger or rage. When it appears as less violent it is affection or love or lust or even elation. When behavior appears as retreat or flight it is fear. Quite obviously, the mere observation of external behavior without more information, including a knowledge of the eliciting stimuli, is not a sufficient basis for an adequate classification of emotion.

The internal responses involved in emotion are very complex and, of course, cannot be observed directly. Their effects, however, can be measured by the use of instruments. The study of the internal, or visceral, changes involved in emotion has contributed much to our understanding. Complicated sequences and patterns of change involving the vascular system, the endocrine system, and the involuntary muscular system are extremely important aspects of the complex we call emotion. These physiological reactions are controlled and regulated by the autonomic division of the nervous system. In a very general way the "approach" and "avoidance" aspects of behavior are mediated by the parasympathetic and the sympathetic segments of the autonomic division, respectively. The internal aspects of emotional behavior, however, are always widespread and diffuse, and so far only very rough correlations with specific nervous structures have been established.

A third approach to the problem of the emotions is to regard emotion as a conscious experience. In spite of efforts on the part of some students of human behavior to avoid a consideration of the conscious aspect of emotions, no "normal" human being—including the objective psychologist himself—can doubt the reality of the consciously experienced emotion. When we *act* angry in response to an anger-provoking stimulus we also *feel* angry.

A Response of the Total Person

In view of these three approaches to the study of emotional behavior, an important fact stands out: Emotionality is an extremely complex area of human functioning which involves the whole organism. The stimulus aspect cannot be neglected. Cognition is always involved. There is no emotion without either the actual perception of the provoking situation or the anticipation of it in terms of images. Normally, a situation does not provoke genuine fear or anger or jealousy or joy or elation unless it is first perceived or thought of as something about which one must be fearful or angry or jealous or joyful or elated. Even in the case of irrational anxiety or worry, images or other symbols representing past cognitive experiences or imagined ones are being centrally manipulated.

The external behavioral aspects, the so-called expressive movements of emotion, are equally essential to the total complex. In full-fledged anger, for example, although actual destructive aggression may be held in check, there are, nevertheless, implicit if not overt patterns of muscular contractions and gross bodily movements that express hostility and tendency to aggression. The kinesthetic stimuli produced by these expressive behaviors give rise to sensory experiences that are important ingredients in the total experiential aspect of the complex.

Simultaneously with overt behavior come the internal responses, which are mediated by the autonomic division of the nervous system in response to cognitive awareness of the situation. The whole pattern of changes is "designed" to prepare the organism *physically* for biologically appropriate activity. In the case of fear or anger, the joint action of the autonomic nervous system and the endocrine glandular system supplies the blood with additional energy-giving blood sugar and produces changes in the pattern of blood-vessel tension so as to shunt that energy-laden blood into the skeletal muscles for greater strength in meeting the "emergency." Internal organs, like skeletal muscles, are equipped with sense receptors that are stimulated by the internal activity, thus giving rise to patterns of sensations, which add to the "unanalyzed mass" that constitutes the emotional experience.

A realization of the importance of these sensory components arising from response-produced stimuli was what led William James, in 1890, to make his famous paradoxical statement that "we do not tremble because we are afraid, but we are afraid because we tremble." According to his theory, which was also stated independently by the Danish physiologist Carl G. Lange, an emotion *is the way the body feels* when in a disturbed internal state and while making various overt expressive movements. The massive, unanalyzed experience arising from the bodily processes and the expressive movements *is* the emotion, according to James.

The important point here is that an adequate consideration of an area of human behavior as complex as the emotions must deal with overt behavioral, as well as psychological, aspects. We would agree essentially with Ausubel (1958):

> Emotion may be defined as a heightened state of *subjective experience* accompanied by skeletal-motor and autonomic-humoral responses, and by a selectively generalized state of lowered response thresholds. . . .
>
> The following sequential steps are involved in the instigation of an emotional response: (a) *interpretive* phase—perception or anticipation of an event that is interpreted as threatening or enhancing an ego-involved need, goal, value, or attribute of self; (b) *preparatory reactive* phase consisting of a selectively generalized lowering of the particular response

thresholds implicated in a given emotion; (c) *consumatory reactive* phase with subjective, autonomic-humoral, and skeletal-motor components; and (d) *a reflective reactive* phase involving subjective awareness of the drive state and of visceral and skeletal responses. [p. 317]

Positive and Negative Emotions

As is obvious and common in everyone's experience, there are two general directional types, or categories, of emotional behavior and experience. These types are so different qualitatively that they seem, subjectively, and appear objectively, to have nothing in common. "Pleasant," "positive," and "approach" apply to the one directional type, while "unpleasant," "negative," "escape," "injure," and "destroy" apply to the other. Not only are they logical and subjective opposites but the two types of experiences also involve mutually antagonistic autonomic functioning, thus mediating overall patterns of visceral change that are quite different. Yet the common term "emotion" applies equally well and without conflict to both categories of experience. Both types are heightened states of subjective experience. Both are extreme deviations from the comfortable, normal internal state of affairs, both being, in a sense, "emergency" reactions.

As we shall see in other connections later, the relative dominance of one or the other of these two emotional types has important implications in the child's personal development. Chapter 5 showed how readily new stimuli and new situations can become effective in eliciting emotional behavior. The prevailing nature of the young child's environment will have much to do with determining whether the social aspects of his life become attached to the positive or the negative categories of emotion.

The Study of Emotional Development

Emotional experiences and outward emotional behavior are matters of universal, firsthand acquaintance. Daily we all experience a variety of emotions in ourselves, and we are constantly meeting the problem of dealing with them in others. Underdeveloped emotional capacity, uncontrolled emotional behavior, and pathological expressions of emotion are major areas of concern among those who must deal with human problems at any level, whether individual, group, national, or international; hence the need for greater understanding of the nature and development of emotionality.

Controlled research in this area is extremely difficult. Behavior under emotion-arousing conditions in natural settings can be observed directly and descriptions of that behavior can be recorded. But affectivity itself—what the individual is actually experiencing under those conditions—obviously cannot be observed objectively. Affectivity must be inferred in terms of the situation and the observed external behavior associated with the situation. We include in the behavior that can be observed the individual's subjective *report* of his feelings.

Our greatest insights into the nature of emotionality have come from the clinical approach. In the clinical setting, real emotional problems of individuals with widely varying backgrounds and experiences are studied. The clinician must, in each case, understand and deal with a total, unique emotional situation. Clinical studies have brought to focus the facts of individuality in human behavior and the great diversity of environmental influences that affect individual emotional development. They clearly portray, for example, the fact that each child has his own inner strivings and frustrations, his own "self image," his attitude toward himself in relation to others. The evidence suggests that nothing gives the child more help and support in resolving his personal problems, and thus facilitating his emotional growth, than the feeling that he is really understood, that someone important to him really knows how he feels.

In our longitudinal studies of individual children our aim·is to approximate as nearly as possible a "clinical" understanding of the particular emotional behavior patterns that characterize each child. The aim is to arrive at an estimate of his level of emotional development at specific points in time and thus to trace that development through time.

Congenital Affectivity

The first breath of the newborn infant appears to be an outward expression of an emotional disturbance—a "protest" against intolerable conditions. The newborn apparently keeps on breathing because breathing promotes a satisfying state of affairs. It eliminates discomfort.

During the neonatal period the baby normally shows signs of emotional excitement only when conditions, external and internal, are such as to cause him bodily discomfort or sensuous pleasure. When he feels pain from some physical disorder or external condition, when he is hungry, or when he is wet or cold or otherwise uncomfortable, he "reports" immediately with signs of distress. No condition outside his own body which does not impinge directly upon his sense organs is of his slightest concern. He is completely egocentric in that sense; he cannot be otherwise. When he senses discomfort he reacts immediately. He "demands" immediate relief from discomfort and immediate gratification of his needs with loud and insistent crying. He does not have to learn these patterns; they are built-in.

Babies, of course, are not all alike. They vary widely with respect to a number of temperamental tendencies. Some are by nature highly active, others are unusually quiet; some of them almost from the beginning seem to be relatively undisturbed and calm in their new conditions of existence, others appear to be displeased and uncomfortable. Babies also vary widely in their reactivity to strong stimuli. The "excitement" pattern (reactions of startle, shock, and withdrawal), with its wide individual variation, is common in infants, particularly during the first month of life before the development of the inhibiting function of the brain.

Rather marked congenital differences in temperament were observed in our subjects Paul and Sally. Paul was relatively quiet, with an observant and "thoughtful" appearance, while Sally, from the beginning, was an active child, inclined toward "unevenness of disposition." She was more reactive to restrictions, with ready tears when her movements were hampered. Both babies were alert when awake and quite reactive to stimulation.

Congenital temperamental differences presumably constitute the beginnings of individual differences in later emotionality.

The Role of Learning in Early Emotional Development

Emotional learning, however, gets underway very soon. The baby's emotional expressions begin to vary with the situation, the particular source or locus of discomfort, and he begins to show differentiated expressive signs of pleasure from gratification as well as distress from pain or discomfort. As development continues with experience, he becomes responsive emotionally to a wider and wider range of stimuli. Thus the direction of the child's emotional development and the characteristic quality of his emotional expressions are influenced by his environment, and particularly by the kind of care and handling he receives. Once again, development is a product of organism-environment interaction.

The baby's responsiveness to other human beings soon becomes pronounced, and, although evidence is not always clear, the consensus is that the quality of the attention and care he receives during this early period has much to do with the development of his later capacity to accept love and affection *from* others or to feel love *for* others. The evidence for this facet of emotional development comes largely from clinical observations. The development of the capacity for love is discussed in greater detail in a later section of this chapter.

Developmental Sequences

For an accurate assessment of developmental status in emotionality, however, just as in other functional areas, some sort of scale or sequence of stages is necessary. As is true with other generalized qualities of behavior, no completely satisfactory series of indicators has been established, although several formulations have been proposed. Probably the best known of these is the series of stages postulated by Freud.

The Freudian Stages

The series of stages in the psychosexual development of the individual adopted by many psychologists as the basic framework of personality development are the *oral*, the *anal*, the *phallic*, the *latency*, and the *genital* periods.

Certain of these stages were briefly described in the discussion of the vital functions (see Chapter 6). We shall sketch this series of stages again specifically as an example of a sequence in the development of emotionality.

The *oral* period covers early infancy, when taking food through nursing at the breast and being made comfortable by this process are the totality of life. Much of the baby's experiences of release from tension and gratification come from or are associated with the oral activity of food taking. When gratification through nursing is not forthcoming, when tension has mounted, feelings of frustration are experienced; anxiety and the sense of insecurity arise. With gratification come pleasure and a sense of security. This period, during which emotional experience—either pleasurable or otherwise—centers around infant oral activity, lasts to about the end of the first year, thus corresponding to the period of greatest dependency.

The generalized pleasure aspect of infant oral activity, quite apart from the mere relief from hunger, is emphasized by the psychoanalytically oriented students of child behavior.

Throughout this early period the child is rapidly learning to do things for himself. He begins now to explore more widely as he masters the ability to move about on his own power. His abilities to manipulate with his hands the objects about him appear now to be replacing the pleasure he has been deriving from *sucking* his fingers. Furthermore, as he becomes more and more able to "get into things," restrictions are placed upon him. He begins to experience new demands and pressures. The attitudes of those around him regarding order and cleanliness begin to be felt. The job of toilet training begins in earnest. Since the eliminative functions pertain to and directly involve his own body and its sensitivities, they are "closer" to him than are any other activities. They involve tension, release from tension, frustrations, and gratification. The child's preoccupation is thus shifted from oral activity to the anal region. According to the Freudian account, the child has now reached the *anal* stage.

Certainly, this period in the child's life is extremely important from the standpoint of determining developmental trends, and it can be a very difficult period for both the child and his parents.

By the time the child has reached the age of 3 years oral pleasures, as a rule, are no longer predominant in his life. He is also well along in achieving bowel and bladder control. Concentration upon anal activities has also lessened as his manipulative and locomotor abilities and his interests in things outside himself gain precedence. His curiosity about and interest in people also are expanding. He begins to observe people, particularly their behavior toward one another. In the typical family situation, although he takes it for granted, he is aware of and enjoys the special kind of intimacy and the love his parents show for him and for each other; in this close relationship his love for his parents deepens. He identifies with his parents. The little boy wants to be like Daddy.

According to Freudian theory, however, a change begins to take place in the child's feelings toward his mother. He becomes especially strongly attached to her, and his attachment is erotic in nature. He is now entering the *phallic* phase of psychosexual development. Very strong "object cathexis" develops toward his mother. In his desire to have her to himself his father becomes his great obstacle. Despite his great love for his father he wishes his elimination. He is in the midst of the *Oedipus complex*.

This naturally becomes a very conflictful situation. He experiences "bad" wishes. He desires incest with his mother and the elimination, even death, of his father. According to theory, he may also experience deep *anxiety*. His father is powerful. As his rival, his father, he fears, might retaliate and rob him of his phallus. *Castration anxiety* may thus develop.

In his need to escape from the stressful predicament certain "mechanisms" may come to the child's aid. *Repression* of his shameful, guilt-arousing wishes, along with the childish associations and memories connected with them, takes place. At the same time, he may gain some degree of satisfaction of his need for his mother by strongly *identifying* with his father, the one who possesses her.

Freud (1938) describes the period of infancy and early childhood as characterized by "infantile sexuality," which reaches its height during this third, or phallic, stage. He held that the apparent later loss of memory of experiences of the latency period was not "a real forgetting of infantile impressions but rather amnesia similar to that observed in neurotics of their later experiences, the nature of which consists of the memories being kept away from consciousness [repression]" (p. 582). He further maintained that "the influx of this [infantile] sexuality does not stop, even in this latency period, but its energy is deflected either wholly or partially from sexual utilization and conducted to other aims . . . a process which merits the name *sublimation*." [p. 584]

At any rate, according to Freudian theory, the resolution of conflict and the relief from stress through repression and amnesia mark the beginning of the *latency* period, the fourth period in emotional (psychosexual) development. This period covers approximately the ages 5 or 6 to 10 or 11 years. In certain respects development does seem to be latent during this period. Anatomically, the reproductive system shows no appreciable growth (see Figure 3.4). Although the body as a whole grows steadily in size, there is little change in bodily contours and features. Relatively little sex differentiation takes place.

Functional development both motor and cognitive, however, makes marked progress. A large number of locomotor and manual skills are acquired and the child's interests and his range of information expand greatly. As a person there is steady development. During the five or six years of so-called latency a rather remarkable behavioral metamorphosis frequently takes place. The child is likely to change from a rather agreeable, compliant, talkative, and generally delightful individual to a loud, intrusive, and rather impudent preadolescent.

With the onset of puberal changes, the child experiences a period of physiological instability. During this fifth, or *puberal* period, there is much preoccupation with the body and its changes. A step-up in interest in the opposite sex and many other changes in feelings and attitudes make this period an extremely important one developmentally. In terms of Freudian theory, pubescence sets off a reawakening, a resurgence, of sexuality that for a time has been latent.

These five periods may be taken in broad outline to represent emotional development. Theoretically, at least, they are directly related to specific stages in the maturation of the organism. The oral period is one of infant helplessness. The anal period begins as the child, through the maturation of body structures, begins to overcome his helplessness, to operate with some degree of independence, and thus to have shifted to himself some measure of responsibility for his independent acts. He must begin now to conform to the cleanliness requirements of society by gaining control of his hitherto involuntary eliminative processes. The demands of society force upon him a preoccuption with anal functions during the period when maturation is in the process of bringing the body and those neural structures involved to a stage of development in which voluntary control is possible. The maturational basis for the early phallic period, however, is not so clear. Perhaps general maturation of the child's organ systems, particularly of the brain cortex and the neuromuscular systems, makes possible a shift from conscious efforts to control the eliminative processes, and a preoccupation with them, to an increased interest in his parents and their relationships with each other and with him. Hence, the development of the Oedipus situation, with its tensions and conflicts.

The latency period begins with the gradual cessation of the stressful genital period. Controls have been achieved, the pressure is off, and considerable independence has been gained. The child's tensions and gratifications are no longer so largely determined by the functions of the alimentary canal and his intense relations with his parents. They come now largely from a physically active life in an interesting world of things and people outside his home and family situation. The developmental changes that characterize the puberal period are quite dramatic. They furnish an obvious basis for the many changes in interests and activities which take place during this period. Implications of puberal changes for emotional development and adjustment are profound.

A Development Sequence Based on Infant Observation

The Freudian sequence of phases in psychosexual development, as we have noted, has mainly to do with change in sources of gratification and objects of affectional attachment. For many students of personality, and particularly for those engaged in clinical diagnosis and treatment, this conceptual sequence has been found useful and meaningful, and has been widely accepted.

For many of the more objectively oriented students of emotional development, however, there is a need for more specific behavioral indicators of the onset and development of the various emotional behavior patterns and affective experiences of daily life.

Perhaps the nearest approach to a useful series of developmental stages for the first two years of life comes from an investigation by Bridges (1932). In this study, based on observations of the emotional behavior from birth of 62 children, a careful record was made in each case of a response and the environmental conditions that preceded it. One outcome of the study was a generalized description of emotional development in terms of four kinds of change, as follows:

1. Intense emotional responses become less frequent.
2. The reaction to any given stimulus becomes more specific.
3. Emotional responses are transferred from one situation to another which did not originally evoke them.
4. Emotional responses gradually become more differentiated.

In relation to the fourth aspect of change, that is, differentiation, Bridges described, with approximate timing, the sequence that takes place from birth to 2 years of age (Fig. 12.1). From the beginning certain kinds of stimulation give rise to a generalized, overall *excitement*, which Bridges regarded as the original emotion. Infants who are thus excited are described in terms of

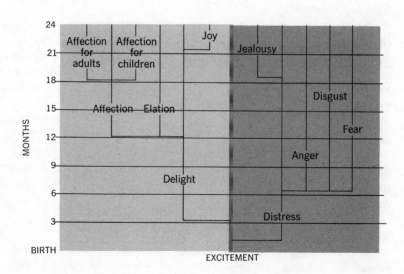

Figure 12.1   The early development of emotions. Adapted from Bridges (1932), p. 340, by permission.

suddenly tensed muscles, quickened breath, jerky, kicking leg movements, and wide-open eyes gazing into the distance. This pattern was found to persist throughout the first 2 years of life.

At about 3 weeks of age the first step in differentiation takes place. *Distress*, or unpleasurable excitement, as distinct from generalized excitement, appears. In distress there is greater muscle tension, more interference with breathing, louder and more irregular crying at a higher pitch. Tears may flow, the face becomes flushed, the mouth distorted, and the fists clenched.

Not until the age of about 3 months does the distinctly pleasurable sort of excitement, *delight*, become differentiated. This pattern involves kicking, faster breathing, opening of the mouth, crooning sounds, and smiling. In contrast with the distress pattern, the movements in delight are free rather than restrained, the eyes are opened rather than closed, there are smiles rather than frowns, and approach movements rather than withdrawal.

The next differentiations in the sequence are on the unpleasurable side. According to Bridges, at about 5 months of age the baby shows unmistakable signs of *anger*, as differentiated from the more generalized distress. The clearest sign of anger is a wail, as if in protest, without the closing of the eyes. Closely following anger comes *disgust*, characterized by coughing, sputtering, and frowning while the baby is being fed. The third differentiation from distress, according to this study, is *fear*, observable at about 7 months of age. The presence of a stranger is the most frequent stimulus to fear. The behavior pattern includes general inhibition of movement, tears, and steady crying, with eyes tightly closed and head bent. The body remains rigid and inactive.

At about the same time (7 months) a pleasurable emotional pattern, elation, becomes distinguishable from generalized delight. The baby smiles, takes a deep breath, and appears to express satisfaction in a sort of grunt.

By the eleventh month there are clear signs of *affection for adults*. The baby at this time will put his arms around the adult's neck and stroke or pat the face with obvious delight. Sometimes he will approximate a kiss by bringing his lips close to the adult's face. By age 15 months he makes an *affectionate response* to *other children* as well as to adults.

Very shortly after affection manifests itself, *jealousy* appears as a further differentiation of distress. It is characterized by tears, bent head, and by standing stiff and motionless. In some instances anger and aggression are part of the picture.

Finally, at about 20 to 21 months, the pattern described as *joy* makes its appearance.

This sequence of differentiations described by Bridges perhaps comes nearest to meeting the requirements of a series of progress indicators in emotional development. However, as we have noted, it covers only the first two years of life. The different behavior patterns are extremely difficult to recognize and distinguish in a baby's behavior. A given child's status in emotional development, we must therefore conclude, must be estimated mainly in terms of a general understanding of emotionality and of the changes that take place with age, rather than in terms of a definite scale of progress indicators.

Maturation and Learning in Emotional Development

As was suggested in our discussion of the Freudian sequence, maturation as well as learning is involved in the development of emotions. Freud's psychosexual stages relate directly to bodily structures and their maturation.

Emotionality in general, however, since it is so pervasive, involving as it does the functioning, more or less, of the total organism, is not so closely bound in its changes with time to the maturation of a specific bodily structure as is the case, for example, with the development of mentality. The great diversity of emotional patterns and modes of emotional adjustment to be found among otherwise mature people must be accounted for very largely in terms of learning in environmental diversity. This, of course, is not to discount the fact that individual differences in constitutional nature have much to do with determining idiosyncrasies in reactions to given environmental situations. It appears to be true, then, that beyond the early period of affective differentiation, as described by Bridges, the role of the maturational factor in the direction and extent of emotional change is of relatively minor importance.

Planned and Incidental Learning

That significant changes in the quality and patterning of emotions do take place, particularly during childhood, there is no doubt. Earlier in this chapter the two opposing categories of emotional experience were mentioned, and in that connection we emphasized the importance of the prevailing quality—positive or negative—of the child's home environment in determining the general nature of his emotional and social attitudes and behavior. More specifically, evidence suggests that the prevailing quality of the experience the child has with his mother during early childhood is of paramount importance.

I. D. Harris (1959), in an intensive study of a group of children and their mothers, concluded that a mother's loving care—her warm dependability and her understanding of her child's individual needs for expression —was "crucially" related to later desirable emotional and social adjustment and that the lack of such warmness and understanding was a factor in later maladjustment. In the words of Harris:

> The mother can be a source of nutriment and pleasure for an infant as he feeds, but she can also be a source of pain, tension and frustration. If she

is a source of pleasure, then the growing child will look upon others, and later humans as gratifiers; if she is a source of pain and tension, the growing child will react to others and to later humans as frustrating. [p. 25]

During the toddler period, when the "socialization" of the child is underway in earnest (see Chapter 13), progress in learning takes place at a rapid rate. Two general types of learning influences can be identified during this period particularly. First, the child, of course, learns those patterns of behavior —personal and social habits and ways of speaking and thinking—which the parents set out to teach him in order to make of him an acceptable member of society. But while this deliberate inculcation of the culture is taking place the child also learns things that were not deliberately planned or consciously taught by the parents. There is likely to be much *incidental emotional* learning taking place. For example, the child is likely to learn, by association, a joyful response or an indifferent one or one of dread and resentment at the appearance of his father. He may learn to react to his parents generally with positive, approaching affection, or he may learn to associate them with frustration, anger, or fear.

The sort of emotional learning that does take place, in any case, depends upon the quality of the emotional interaction that prevails between the child and his parents. And the quality of that prevailing interaction is dependent upon two sets of factors: (1) the particular personal make-up of each parent (predominant traits, attitudes, expectations, frustrations); and (2) the child's unique pattern of temperamental tendencies such as those discussed in Chapter 9 (another example of organism-environment interaction).

Imprinting versus Healthy Emotional Learning

There is another line of evidence from recent research, mainly animal research regarding the imprinting phenomenon,[1] however, which suggests a somewhat different interpretation of the relation between learned emotional patterns and environmental stimulation (Scott, 1962). The suggestion coming out of these studies is that perhaps it is not so much the pleasant quality of the emotional interaction between parent and young child that makes for positive emotional attachment as it is that there be *strong* emotional content

---

[1] The observations of ethologists have established the fact that the newborn of the various animal species possess certain simple unlearned, and biologically adapted, response patterns appropriate to their particular modes of existence, such, for example, as the "following" behavior of newly hatched chicks and ducklings, and certain herd animals, and the "clinging" response of the jungle monkey. These patterns are normally emitted by their biological mothers, but they are also readily elicited by, and can become attached (imprinted) to the first object to present itself, be it the mother, another animal, or a human being (Scott, 1963; Lorenz, 1935; E. H. Hess, 1959; Harlow, 1958). This imprinting process is a primitive form of learning.

of *some* sort in the interaction during the early critical period. In Scott's words:

> It should not be surprising that *many kinds* of emotional reactions contribute to a social relationship. The surprising thing is that emotions which we normally consider aversive should produce the *same* effect as those which appear to be rewarding. . . . [This fact] provides an explanation for certain well-known clinical observations such as the development by neglected children of strong affection for cruel and abusive parents.   [p. 954]

In view of apparent conflict in the evidence cited by such investigators as Scott (1962), I. D. Harris (1959), and Diamond (1957), it is clear that a distinction must be drawn between an early emotional bond due to the "imprinting process" and healthy emotional adjustment and development in children. E. H. Hess's (1960) ducklings did become the more strongly imprinted to follow the mechanical model duck the greater the effort and the *pain* they encountered in following it. Harlow's (1958) infant monkeys did crawl desperately toward their rejecting, punishing mothers, who, in their own infancy, had been reared on terrycloth dummy "mothers" instead of interactive monkey mothers. Children have been known to become emotionally attached to cruel, unloving parents. But Harlow's dummy-reared monkey mothers had not developed the normal monkey *interactive* behavior patterns in their association with and close attachment to their dummy mothers. Furthermore, in the vast majority of instances, human individuals who have been reared by neglecting and cruel parents must overcome great handicaps in acquiring the capacity to interact warmly and affectionately with others. Scott (1962) summarized the evidence as follows:

> There are demonstrable *positive mechanisms*, varying from species to species, *which bring young animals close to other members of their kind*: the clinging response of young rhesus monkeys; the following response of chicks, ducklings, and lambs, and other herd animals; social investigation, tail wagging, and playful fighting of puppies; and the visual investigation and smiling of the human infant. These are, of course accompanied by *interacting responses* from adults and immature members of the species: holding and clasping by primate mothers, brooding of mother hens and other birds, calling by mother sheep, investigation and play on the part of other young puppies, and the various supporting and nurturing activities of human mothers. [p. 951, italics added]

These interacting responses, on the part of others, normally involve pleasurable and satisfying emotional content and make the difference between simple imprinting of an emotional bond and the establishment of the foundation for healthy interpersonal relations and emotional adjustment. The capacity to interact warmly and creatively with other human beings is generally the product of early emotional learning in interaction with a warmly dependable and understandingly nurturant "mothering one." This kind of emotional learning is qualitatively different from, and more than, the simple imprinting of an emotional bond.

Love: A Process of Interaction

Throughout our discussion of emotionality, the active aspect of emotion—that is, the idea that an emotion is a function of the organism and that when one is emotional a complex *process* is underway—has repeatedly come to the fore. We were also reminded of the two-directional nature of emotionality. There are emotions in which the direction of activity is away from or in opposition to the object of the emotion. These are the negative emotions. The action is individualistic, separating, alienating. One becomes angry at, fearful of, and withdraws from another.

Approach behavior characterizes the positive type of emotion. One draws near to and acts in relation with another. Love is the prototype of positive emotion. Love is uniting, integrating, need satisfying. The action is *interaction*. Each of the two persons involved is both actor and object of the action, giver and receiver. The relation is reciprocal. The mother, for example, holds her baby close, thus gratifying their mutual need for closeness. Her acts of love stimulate in her child reciprocal love responses. The interaction is uniting and mutually gratifying. It tends to be what Erich Fromm (1956) called "interpersonal fusion."

Emotional Deprivation

The term "emotional deprivation" refers to a lack, in the child's experience, of a positive reciprocal relationship with another person. It refers either to the rather precipitous loss of an accustomed relationship with a nurturing person in which his need for warm, loving care has been regularly gratified or to the absence from the beginning of conditions that permit the formation of such a relationship. Available evidence suggests that both of these types of deprivation can have profound effects upon the development of the capacity to function in the reciprocal love relationship.

We have already noted the importance of adequate and appropriate stimulation for optimal development during infancy. Stimulus deprivation is perhaps the more appropriate term to apply to the situation of an infant lying by itself in an "institution" crib during the first few months of its life. At first, other persons, *as persons*, are of no significance to a baby regardless of where he may be. He spends much of his time sleeping. But when he is awake he is very responsive to *stimuli* both external and internal. He cries immediately at any bodily discomfort and is just as immediately comforted by being cuddled in warm and close contact with another person. He may respond with excitement to the sights and sounds of persons moving about him and particularly to being "talked to" and to the other noises people make to babies.

In the usual family situation, the baby does not want for stimulation. The baby is likely to get much patting, stroking, and fondling, particularly if there are other children in the home, and this attention along with the frequent feeding and bodily care he receives often leaves little waking time for him to be "bored." This kind of stimulation, of course, is what was lacking in the traditional "institution" as described by Goldfarb (1945), Spitz (1945, 1946), and others. Furthermore, the indications are that it is the lack of general stimulation, rather than the lack of a specific "mothering one," that is responsible for the retarding effects of institution care during the early months of the baby's life. It is likely also that this retarding effect is the result of the lack of opportunity to learn rather than an actual maturational retardation (Dennis and Najarian, 1957). In this connection Yarrow (1964), after a careful survey of the relevant literature, summarized the situation as follows:

> The institution is not simply an environment lacking in a mother-figure with whom the child has developed an attachment; institutional environments tend to be deviant in many other respects, such as in the amount, the quality, and the variety of sensory and social stimulation, and in the kinds of learning conditions provided (Goldfarb, 1955; Rheingold, 1960, 1961; Provence and Lipton, 1962; David and Appell, 1962). The low care-taker-infant ratio is associated with significant deprivation in the sheer amount of maternal care. This quantitative deprivation in maternal care, in turn is associated with inadequate kinesthetic, tactile, social and affective stimulation. [p. 99]

Although studies from a variety of sources indicate that environmental deprivation may have serious effects even on very young infants, there are very few data on the important questions of how early in infancy *separation* from a mother figure begins to have an impact. Schaffer's (1958) research is one of the few studies with data directly relevant to this issue. On the basis of findings that overt protest reactions to maternal separation, such as excessive crying, fear of strangers, clinging to the mother, are not evident before 7 months of age, Schaffer concluded that separation reactions appear "relatively suddenly and at full force around 7 months of age" (p. 98). By definition, true separation reactions cannot appear until after a focused relationship with the mother has developed.

The baby soon begins to show signs of an emerging ability to perceive— to react differentially to objects as objects and to people as people. He begins to respond differently to different people. His affiliative interest increases, and he begins to relate to persons as individuals and to interact emotionally with them. The pleasures of gratification and of relief from pain and discomfort soon become associated in his experience with a particular person, usually his mother. A strong affectional bond thus becomes established between mother and baby. Thereafter, no amount of casual or impersonal stimulation can take the place of that person-to-person emotional relationship. From that point on, to have that relationship disrupted, and for the child to be denied dependable, intimate contact with the "mothering one," would be more than stimulus deprivation. The term "emotional deprivation" would, under those circumstances, more accurately describe the child's situation.

Research Concerning Emotional Deprivation

Most of the early studies of maternal deprivation in institutions involved children who were separated from their mothers and placed in the institutions at ages over 1 year (Robertson and Bowlby, 1952; Roudinesco, David, and Nicolas, 1952; Spitz and Wolf, 1946). The reports of these investigations were practically unanimous in regard to the emotional damage these children suffered. The general pattern of immediate reactions to separation were crying and strong protest, followed by progressive withdrawal from relations with people. After the immediate protest and crying came signs of despair and resignation and apathetic behavior. As a rule, these children formed no emotional attachments to any of the institution personnel and even showed very little feeling toward the parents when they visited them later on. They acted as if "neither mothering nor any contact with humans has much significance for them" (Robertson and Bowlby, 1952, p. 133).

However, there is relatively little direct research evidence regarding the long-term effects of maternal separation. Certain follow-up studies have produced suggestive evidence. Bowlby (1944), for example, in a clinical study of a group of young thieves, characterized certain of them as "affectionless characters." An analysis of the backgrounds of these individuals indicated that they had been separated from their mothers in infancy. In general, however, results of these follow-up studies have been quite varied. Different children have different experiences in relation to separation, and, due to the diversity of temperamental nature among the children, these experiences have different meanings for different children. In a summary statement Yarrow (1964) wrote:

> The research data can be integrated with regard to their implications in terms of the following major variables: the developmental stage of the child at the time of separation; the character of the relationship with the mother prior to separation; the character of maternal care during a temporary separation or following permanent separation; subsequent experiences, that is, experiences which are reinforcing or ameliorating of separation trauma; and individual differences in vulnerability to separation.
> [p. 121]

The mere fact of being reared by the biological mother in the family home, of course, does not preclude the possibility of emotional deprivation.

The quantity as well as the quality of mothering that babies actually experience from their mothers obviously varies through a wide range.

Emotional Problems of Childhood

Individual Differences

In Chapter 9 certain ways in which infants vary one from another by congenital temperamental nature were discussed. One of these variables is the ease of emotional arousal and upset. Some infants, it was pointed out, are generally highly reactive to intense stimulation. These infants startle easily and rather violently and are likely, therefore, to be more inclined toward the fear-withdrawal pattern than babies who are less strongly reactive to noise and other intense stimuli.

Some babies also seem, by congenital nature, to react with a sort of characteristic displeasure. They seem to be expressing a perpetual dissatisfaction and irritation with extrauterine life. At the other extreme are babies who, from the beginning, seem generally to be pleased with and contented in the world in which they find themselves. Some children also can withstand frustrating and anger-provoking situations with much greater equanimity than others. In other words, aside from the characteristic reaction of pleasure or displeasure with life in general, babies, as well as older people, differ in frustration tolerance.

Such observations indicate that an individual's characteristic moods have some basis in the sort of temperamental balance with which he is born. But these congenital emotional predispositions are only predispositions. The pattern of moods and emotional dispositions that soon come to characterize a person is largely a matter of learning, and *what* is learned depends very largely upon the nature of environment and particularly upon the interpersonal atmosphere that predominates in one's daily life.

Thus, growing out of organism-environment interaction is a wide variety of emotional problems that beset children and often continue to plague them throughout life.

Anxiety

Anxiety may develop very early in infancy in relation to the nursing situation. The tenseness and anxiety of the young mother is transmitted to her infant. "Thus anxiety is called out by emotional disturbances of certain types in the significant person—that is, the person with whom the infant is doing something" (Sullivan, 1953, p. 9). Anxiety, of course, is one of the common immediate effects of separation from mother during infancy. The theory is that from these early anxiety experiences "grows the whole exceedingly important structure of anxiety, and performances that can be understood only by reference to the conception of anxiety" (p. 9).

Later in childhood the attitudes and the behavior of parents continue to be the prime causes of anxiety. Regarding parental punishment and its effects, Sullivan wrote:

> The punishments are commonly the inflicting of pain, the refusal of contact or of attention, and of course, the inducing of anxiety—a very special punishment. I know of no reason why punishment should be undesirable as an educative influence excepting it be anxiety-ladened.
>
> [p. 155, by permission]

Sullivan suggests, further, that anxiety at any age is an important complicating factor in learning as well as in coping effectively with the environment. "The effect of severe anxiety reminds one in some ways of a blow on the head in that it simply wipes out what is immediately proximal to its occurrence" (p. 152). It produces useless confusion and loss of effectiveness in performance. As Sigel (1964) pointed out, anxiety is an inhibiting factor in children's conceptual learning: "Children who are highly anxious tend to employ concepts dealing with the emotional aspects of the situation more than do those who are not" (p. 239).

Less severe anxiety, on the other hand, may facilitate learning. In the process of becoming "socialized," certain degrees of anxiety may help the child to distinguish anxiety-provoked situations and actions and thus to alter his activities accordingly.

Anxiety, like other human attributes and functions, is universal. Everyone experiences anxiety, but there are, of course, wide individual differences in vulnerability. It is also clear that parental care and the relations thus established between parents and children are vital factors in the development of anxieties in children. Kagan noted that the lack of a masculine father figure with which to identify was found to interfere with sex-role identity and thus to be a cause of anxiety. [Hoffman and Hoffman, 1964, p. 148]

Childhood Fears

A useful distinction between fear and anxiety is in terms of the emotion-provoking situation. The term "anxiety" is usually applied to a fearlike state induced by anticipated or imagined threats to one's physical or psychological well-being. The danger or threat is not immediately and objectively present to sense. Fear, on the other hand, is the emotional reaction to an objectively present situation which is perceived as threatening to one's well-being.

In our discussion of the developmental sequences in emotionality, the concept of an undifferentiated beginning stage was presented. Emotionality in the neonate, accordingly, consists of undifferentiated excitement without distinction between even the pleasant and the unpleasant. Only after some 6 months of age, according to Bridges (1932), is it possible to identify the emotion of fear as distinct from other forms of distress. At that level, of course, there are only a very few originally adequate, or unconditioned, stimuli to fear. The presence or the approach of a stranger, for example, may call forth the frightened distress pattern. Loud noise and sudden lowering of his body also appear to be among the relatively few originally adequate fear stimuli. The baby is thus protected during his early months of life from a great deal of distressing fear.

The baby's cognitive abilities, however, are rapidly developing, which means that he is gaining in his ability to recognize danger and to perceive more objects and situations as threatening. Through the process of conditioning, stimuli not inherently frightening become, for the particular child, fear-provoking.

Thus, developmental changes take place in relation to children's fears. Up to the age of 23 months, according to the findings of Jersild and Holmes (1935), noise, objects that make noise, and strange objects, persons, and situations most frequently are the causes accounting for about one fourth of all fear experiences. During the next two years, these two classes of stimuli account for a smaller and smaller percentage of fear episodes (10 percent at age 4 years). By contrast, imaginary creatures, darkness, being alone, dreams, and the like, increase dramatically in frequency as fear stimuli during the same two-year period, from only about 5 percent to nearly 30 percent. Our subject Paul at age 4½ years over a period of some months had considerable trouble going to sleep at night and asked for his door to be left open. He apparently was resisting sleep because of "those animals" that came into his room. These findings of Jersild and Holmes are presented in Figure 12.2.

Changes continue to take place in the character of the threatening situations as the child gets older. During the elementary school period imaginary, fanciful, supernatural, and remote dangers are relatively frequent fear evokers. Children are also inclined to fear the elements, such as lightning and storms. They worry about such matters as death or injury and the recall of "scary" stories, movies, and television dramas. Some of the fears from these latter classes of stimuli are more of the nature of anxieties (Angelino, Dollins, and Mech, 1956).

Children at these ages were also found to worry frequently about matters related to self, for example, their own adequacy and status. They worry about possible failure, about being different or being ridiculed.

Only one study of children's fears has been published during the past 15 years. Croake (1969) interviewed 53 pupils from the third, the sixth, and the ninth grades. His sample consisted of approximately equal numbers of children from the "upper" and the "lower" socioeconomic levels. They came also from both small-town and large-city school systems.

In certain respects Croake's findings were not greatly different from

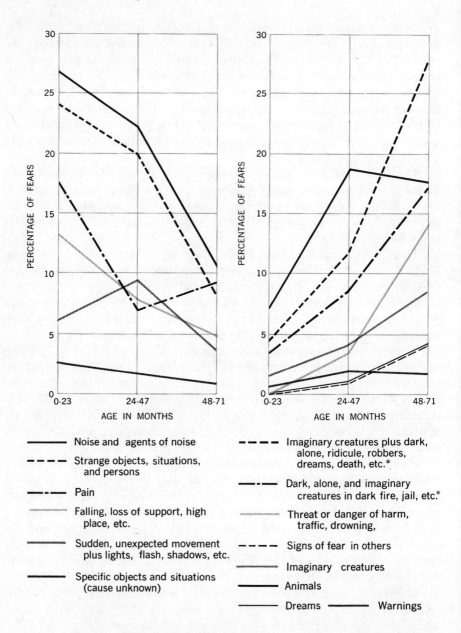

Figure 12.2 Relative frequency of fears in response to various situations reported by children or observed in children by parents or teachers. The data include 146 records of observation of children for periods of 21 days (31, 91, and 24 at the respective biyearly levels), combined with occasional records of 117 additional children (26, 27, and 23 at the respective levels). Starred items represent the cumulative tally of two or more categories that also are depicted separately. Adapted from Jersild (1960), p. 261, by permission.

those of the earlier studies reviewed above. He found that girls generally had more fears than boys, and children of the lower socioeconomic group reported more fears than those of the higher socioeconomic group.

One interesting difference was that in the earlier studies "supernatural" and "animal" fears were reported most frequently, while in this study "political" and "natural phenomena" fears were found to be most common. This difference was attributed to improved mass communication and to the Vietnam war.

Coping with Children's Fears

Dealing with excessive fears in children is difficult and sometimes distressful for parents. Fear of the dark and fear of harmless objects and animals are among the irrational fears that most frequently concern parents. The immediate reaction of the adult to a childish fear is to try to explain it away or, as in the case of fear of the dark bedroom, simply not to "give in" to the child (turn off the light or close the door) on the theory that the child will "find out" that there is really nothing to be afraid of and thereby overcome his fear. Such methods generally are of no avail. Rational explanations to young children have no real effect upon the emotion of fear, regardless of how irrational the basis of the fear may be. Forcing a child to remain in a dark room with his fear is more likely to reinforce the fear reaction itself than to help him to overcome it.

Studies of children's fears and of methods of dealing with them have demonstrated a number of procedures that are in varying degrees effective (Jersild and Holmes, 1935; M. C. Jones, 1924a, b). Among the methods tested: (1) setting up counterresources and skills that are helpful in meeting the fearful situation when it occurs; (2) promoting familiarity with the feared object by providing situations in which there is opportunity, but not coercion, to become acquainted with it; (3) arranging for the child to observe others who show no fear in the feared situation; and (4) direct reconditioning.

These methods, of course, vary in their usefulness with different types of fear situations. The acquiring of new skills, for example, might be quite a helpful approach to overcoming the fear of deep water. For the child to acquire competence as a swimmer in the relative safety of shallow water might release him from his fear of deeper water. When one knows what to do in a feared situation and how to do it, to the point of having confidence in one's ability to do it, one is not likely to continue to be terrified by it.

When a child is given the opportunity, without any pressure or coercion, to become better acquainted with a feared object or situation, his fear often subsides. In one of M. C. Jones' (1924b) experiments, a child who was afraid of rabbits lost his fear after a rabbit had been in his vicinity where he could observe it for some time. He simply became better acquainted with the rabbit, its appearance, and its activities.

The method of social imitation is in certain respects similar to the method of acquaintance. Here the child observes the behavior of his friends as they react fearlessly to the object he fears:

> Bobby was playing in the pen with Mary and Laurel. The rabbit was introduced in a basket. Bobby cried, "no, no," and motioned for the experimenter to remove it. The two girls, however, ran up readily enough, looked in at the rabbit, and talked excitedly. Bobby became promptly interested, said "What? Me see," and ran forward, his curiosity and assertiveness in the situation overmastering other impulses. [M. C. Jones, 1924b, p. 387]

Perhaps the most generally effective method of helping children overcome their fears is the method of reconditioning. In another case reported by M. C. Jones (1924a), the child had acquired an extreme fear of furry animals. The method of social imitation had been tried with him, but it had relatively little success. The procedure of reconditioning, as used with him, was described as follows:

> At lunch time the child was seated at a low table in a room about forty feet long. Just as he began to eat his lunch, the rabbit was displayed in a wire cage at a distance just far enough away not to disturb his eating. This was a very important point, for were the strong conditioned stimulus allowed to work too actively, it is quite to be expected that the positive reactions to the food would change. That is, the food might in turn become a conditioned stimulus for the fear response. To prevent accidents in this admittedly ticklish matter, the rabbit was kept in his cage during the early phases of the work. Each day the position of the cage was marked. The next day the cage and rabbit were brought somewhat closer. Eventually the rabbit could be placed on the table and even in Peter's lap. In the final stage of the experiment he ate with one hand as he stroked the rabbit with the other. We may assume from this that Peter's inner emotional response had been re-conditioned even as his outward behavior toward the rabbit had been re-directed. [pp. 308–316]

It is clear in this account that reconditioning can be quite effective. It is also clear that it must be used with caution and by one who understands well the principles of learning involved.

In a great many instances children, as they grow older and gain better understanding, "naturally" outgrow many of their burdensome fears.

Anger

Anger and fear, in certain respects, are rather closely related. In the first place, they are both "emergency" responses of the unpleasant variety and consequently involve very similar patterns of change in physiological processes, changes designed to prepare the organism for immediate, strenuous, overt activity. In part, at least, because of this close correspondence in the physiological component, the two emotions are sometimes aroused simultaneously and by the same stimulus. Sometimes, also, the child vacillates between the two affective experiences. However, because ordinarily there are more anger-provoking than fear-arousing occasions in the protected life of the child in our culture, anger is a more frequent response than fear in children.

It will be recalled, however, that Bridges observed that anger, as a differentiated emotional pattern of behavior and experience, does not exist at birth. Furthermore, as the specific anger pattern emerges, there are relatively few originally adequate stimuli for its arousal. In general, the situations that do give rise to anger in early infancy are those involving pain or discomfort or bodily restraint.

The number and variety of restraining factors and situations rapidly grow. Very soon there are a great many ways in which others, even as they care for the child, interfere with his free bodily movements. His own in-abilities quickly become sources of frustration. His activities are frequently interfered with or blocked. Thus the over-all situation with respect to anger rapidly changes. As Jersild (1954) put it, "The occasions that elicit anger parallel the course of development. A child's susceptibility to anger at any given maturity level is influenced by the limitations and by the urges, strivings, and activity tendencies that are characteristic of that level" (p. 883).

Overt Aspects of the Anger Response

The character of the overt expression of anger also changes with the age and experience of the child. Infant anger can be described generally in terms of four characteristics (Morgan, 1934). (1) The young infant may be said to be completely *egocentric*. As was mentioned in connection with the Freudian stages of emotional development, he becomes concerned only when conditions within and outside his own body cause him pain, discomfort, or frustration. He is completely self-centered in that sense. (2) Along with his egocentricity is his complete *intolerance* of bodily discomfort or restraint. When he is hungry or wet or otherwise in pain or discomfort, for example, he makes the fact known in no uncertain terms. He cries, kicks with abandon, arches his back, struggles, and twists. (3) The young infant is exceedingly demanding. In his intolerance of discomfort he demands *immediate relief*. He cannot defer satisfaction of his needs. (4) Finally, the baby is very *explosive* and violent in his anger expression.

These attributes of infant expressions of anger are not limited to early infancy. As Morgan pointed out, when such attributes are observed in the older child or the adult they are signs of so-called emotional immaturity. Violent outbursts of rage are common in young children. The preschool child is likely to express anger in much the same manner as the infant.

In the expressions of anger, as in other kinds of behavior, however, there is much diversity among children. We have already mentioned the wide variation in frustration tolerance; some children can withstand anger-provoking situations with much greater equanimity than can others. The variation is undoubtedly related to original temperamental nature as well as to factors in the child's environment and the experiences he has undergone.

The family environment and the kind of training the child has had are important factors in determining the frequency as well as the explosiveness of anger expression. Socialization of the child means, among other things, bringing his aggressions under control. But the very nature of the training creates frustrations that are likely to result in angry aggressive behavior on the part of the child. "The socializer thereby becomes an instigator to the very action she is trying to change" (Levin and Turgeon, 1957, p. 304). In spite of this situation, however, mothers generally do succeed in this aspect of socialization.

The more authoritarian the parents' attitudes and approaches to discipline in their efforts to make the child's behavior conform to their conceptions of what is socially desirable, the more frequent are likely to be angry outbursts of the child (Levin and Sears, 1956). Since authoritarian procedures are more prevalent in homes of the lower socioeconomic class, children from these homes experience more thwarting and consequently display more intense and more frequent anger than do children from homes of higher socioeconomic levels.

Jealousy

As Jersild (1954 pointed out, rivalry between siblings can be a source of much thwarting, hostility, anxiety, and grief. Jealousy appears to be a combination of emotions, rather than a single, primary one. Descartes' definition of jealousy was "a kind of fear related to the desire we have for keeping some possession."

> Components of jealousy, as described by Ribot, include a pleasurable element related to something desired or possessed, an element of depressing vexation arising through the idea of dispossession or privation and destructive tendencies such as hatred and anger directed toward the real or imagined cause of this dispossession or privation. [Jersild, 1954, p. 899]

Jealousy in children usually arises from a competitive situation between siblings. Children often compete for the attention and the demonstrations of affection of parents or other significant adults in their lives. Jealousy often originates with the birth of a sibling when the child is from 2 to 5 years old, and particularly when he is the first born. He is disturbed by being displaced as the center of attention in the family. He resents the time and attention now given to the new baby, and, not receiving the amount of attention he is accustomed to, he feels neglected. He may experience anger, self-pity, grief, dejection, fear, and anxiety.

The jealous child may express his feelings in overt hostile behavior, such as a sly pinch or shove or some substitute form of attack. This anger and hostility may also be directed against the person whose affection or attention is desired. The latter may also be the recipient of reproachful remarks or appeals for sympathy.

Because of the differences in temperament, appearance, age, and other personal attributes in their children, parents may actually show a disproportionate share of interest in, and give more attention to, one child than to another, without realizing that they are showing favoritism. Fathers often are more lenient and affectionate with their daughters than with their sons, whereas mothers appear to favor their sons.

Children are usually quite sensitive to these forms of differential treatment, and jealousy and resentment sometimes develop, even among older children. At these older ages, jealous responses are more varied and more indirect, often taking the form of teasing or bullying. The older child may resort to "babyish" behavior or become clinging and overdemanding of the parent. He may become sulky, surly, and disagreeable or even destructive. Many instances of undesirable behavior in children, not easily understood as to origin, actually have arisen as expressions of jealousy.

Emotional Development in Our Twin Subjects

As was mentioned earlier, our twins Paul and Sally differed in temperamental nature from the beginning. Their mother quite naturally was very aware of these differences. On a questionnaire only a few months after the babies' birth she stated that Paul resembled his father in "his quiet thoughtfulness and sense of humor and that Sally was much more like her mother in her unevenness of disposition and a tendency to tears."

At age 5 months both babies gave clear evidence of their ability to differentiate between people. It will be recalled that Bridges observed fear in her infants, on the average, at about age 7 months. Paul and Sally gave clear evidence of fear when at 5 months of age they were undressed, weighed, and measured by an examiner strange to them.

At age 7 months, the twins were subjected to their first "developmental" examination. Even though Paul was awakened for the test he accepted the strange examiner without concern and showed marked interest in the test materials. Sally "in contrast to her brother showed a very keen interest in people, paying somewhat less attention to things." There was also evidence that she was a little fearful of the strange examiner.

Throughout their development, however, Paul was more inclined to be reserved in his reactions to people. Sally was more outgoing and spontaneous in her relationships. For example, on their visit to the infant laboratory for their tests and measurements at age 13 months, it was observed that "while Sally made immediate overtures toward the examiner who came to greet them in the waiting room, Paul hung back and clung close to his mother." Paul at this visit was quite resistant to the whole procedure. Only after a period of time did he accept the tester.

Perhaps the most significant indicator of emotional difficulty in Paul was his tendency to wakefulness and some sleep disturbance which began at about 8 months of age and continued with considerable variation for some additional years. Since the children were together much of the time, this erratic sleep pattern, to a lesser degree, was also followed by Sally. In Paul, particularly, this difficulty was accompanied by thumb sucking and bed wetting. When he was about 2½, his mother stated that his uneasiness about going to sleep seemed to be related to a fear that she might leave him. About this time he complained about his mother's frequent absence from the home. He also began to have "night fears."

There were, however, indications that he was working through his difficulties. For example, on one occasion while he was being undressed for bed, he went to the window and raised the shade, saying that he wanted to see things, that he wasn't afraid anymore. His need for his blanket, which he held to his lips while he sucked his thumb, was also lessening.

Throughout the preschool period Sally was becoming increasingly outgoing. She frequently brought her girl friends home to play with her. On these occasions, and also at nursery school, the girls began to ostracize Paul from their play. This proved to be a bit difficult for him to "take." He began objecting mildly to going to nursery school. This was of relatively short duration.

Clearly, Paul, like most children, had his adjustment difficulties, but when an overall view is taken of his emotional development, it becomes apparent that he "jumped his hurdles as he came to them" and made healthy progress in his affective development. Sally developed into a charming vivacious and outgoing young lady.

It will be noted in the foregoing account of affective behavior in our twins that most of the items had perhaps more to do with social behavior than with emotionality. The items of information in the developmental file made very little reference to the items in Bridges' developmental sequence (Fig. 12.1).

Summary

This chapter has looked particularly at the "activity" aspect of emotionality. From this point of view emotion involves certain physiological changes, but in a more general way it involves the total person. At the same time, the experiential aspect of emotional functioning is of vital importance in human living and interpersonal relations. The negative and the positive behaviors give meaning to human existence.

Emotion, since it is a kind of total functioning, involves bodily structures, and these structures obviously are the result of biological growth and maturation. The structures involved in emotionality, however, are already well advanced in their development, and are, for the most part, ready for functioning at the time of birth. Postnatal emotional development, therefore, with certain conspicuous exceptions, is very largely the product of learning from environmental influences.

Individual developmental progress can best be traced in terms of an established developmental sequence of stages. However, relatively little success, thus far, has been achieved in the identification of universal and invariable developmental stages which are adequate to the task of tracing emotional development. The Freudian stages of psychosexual development and Bridges' infant stages of affectivity are perhaps the nearest approaches to such sequences.

Since environmental influences are so important as determiners of the extent, direction, and quality of developmental change in emotionality, adequate and appropriate stimulation, particularly during infancy and early childhood, is essential. We suggest that the kind of stimulation a baby normally and naturally receives from the constant care and handling by his mother is perhaps the most adequate and appropriate stimulation for normal emotional development. Development resulting from this kind of care and stimulation is of quite a different order from what has been referred to as "imprinting" in animal experimentation.

Emotional "problems" in children also arise most often from environmental influences, and they can be controlled or alleviated only by the wise manipulation of the environment or by protecting the child from being subjected to undesirable environmental influences.

CHAPTER 13

Personality Development

The Concept of Personality

In common usage the term "personality" refers to a vaguely conceived human quality which everyone recognizes as of special importance in interpersonal relations. It is a term frequently used in conversation, particularly when the topic involves social interaction. Individuals are spoken of as having "difficult" personalities, "charming" personalities, "pleasing" personalities, "ugly" personalities. People are also charged with having "no personality" or are said to be "full of" or "radiating" personality. We all know, in a general way, what is meant by such expressions. They convey a common meaning that is readily understood. In common conversation, then, personality is what one has or lacks as a person, what one is or is not, what one can, or cannot give out with. And interestingly enough, such varied characterizations apparently cause no perplexity.

The Problem of Definition

There is, however, much diversity to be found among textbook definitions of personality. It is difficult to give precise technical meaning to such a commonly used word. Usually each writer or investigator formulates his own definition, emphasizing the particular facet of the concept that suits his own disciplinary bias or that is consistent with the material he has to present.

Theories of Personality

A variety of theories of personality have been developed. People trained in a particular scientific discipline or in a particular professional field tend to have similar disciplinary biases and thus tend to make the same, or similar, assumptions and to formulate similar theoretical frames of reference in terms of which to interpret their observations of human behavior. For example, the sociologist or the cultural anthropologist "sees" human behavior with his particular bias and from his particular level of observation. He is likely, therefore, to observe first the behavior patterns and traits that are common to a particular cultural or ethnic group and thus to regard individual personality as largely a product or a mere "reflection" of the culture.

Most sociological definitions, however, merely put special emphasis upon the cultural factor in the development of personality. Although some of these writers go so far as to contend that personality is nothing more than the individual counterpart or expression of the culture, a fairly common contemporary point of view among students of society is expressed in the following statement by Parsons (1963):

> My view will be that, while the main content of the structure of the personality is derived from social systems and culture through socialization, the personality becomes an independent system through its relations to its own organism and through the uniqueness of its own life experiences; it is not a mere epiphenomenon of the structure of the society. There is, however, not merely interdependence between the two, but what I call interpenetration. [p. 35]

Biologically trained observers, on the other hand, with quite different frames of reference, find the explanations of behavior and of the characteristic traits of individuals in their physiology and constitutional make-up. Thus, the biological emphasis in personality theory has developed. One outstanding proponent of this emphasis is W. H. Sheldon (1940, 1942, 1949; Sheldon, Dupertuis, and McDermott, 1954). We have reviewed certain aspects of his work in earlier discussions. He has stated his theoretical position as follows:

> It has been growing increasingly plain that the situation calls for a biologically oriented psychology, or one taking for its operational frame of reference a scientifically defensible description of the *structure* (together with the behavior) of the human organism itself. This is perhaps tantamount to saying that psychology requires a physical anthropology for its immediate foundation support. More than that, it requires a physical anthropology couched in terms of components, or variables, which can be measured and quantified at both the structural and behavioral ends—the anthropological and psychological ends—of the structure-behavior continuum which is human personality. [1949, p. xv]

Longitudinal studies of child development generally have stressed the biological factor in the personal adjustments and development of children (M. C. Jones and Bayley, 1951; M. C. Jones and Mussen, 1958; Mussen and Jones, 1957: Sontag, Baker, and Nelson, 1958).

Within the limits of a particular scientific discipline or professional group there are also differing points of view. Thus, from the general field of psychology have come many contrasting theories as to the structure and the origin and development of personality. Books have been written from these various points of view. Comparative explications of the major theories and groupings of theories also have been published and are available to the student (G. W. Allport, 1960; Hall and Lindsey, 1957; Hunt, 1944). It is not our present purpose, therefore, to attempt a comparative discussion of these theoretical positions. Even to attempt to classify them and then adequately characterize the major groupings is not feasible here. We shall therefore, only point briefly to certain major issues raised in the theoretical writings of students of the psychology of personality and to some of the contrasting positions held regarding those issues.

The Problem of Motivation

One of the major issues about which theories of personality differ is the nature and the sources of motivation. Obviously the motives, drives, wishes, needs, and purposes that activate people are of central importance to the understanding of how personalities develop. As to the importance of this problem, there is no disagreement among theorists. As to the source, the locus and origin of the "mainspring" of human conduct, there is currently rather basic disagreement. In order that we may see clearly the setting and the development of this issue we shall first turn briefly once more to some of the thinking of Sigmund Freud.

Psychoanalytic Theory

Freud is given credit for formulating the first comprehensive theory of personality. This complex theoretical framework, as it evolved in Freud's thinking, was many years in the making, undergoing changes, additions, and deletions up to the time of his death in 1939. His "discoveries" and his thinking have wielded a tremendous influence upon the fields of psychology and psychotherapy. His many followers are still busy expanding and, in varying degrees, modifying his formulations.

Freud's concept of the *unconscious* is basic to his theory of motivation. He conceptualized the mental activity of an individual as being very much more elaborate and complicated than that of which the individual is consciously aware. The analogy which Freud used to point up this comparison was that of an iceberg. The great mass of the floating iceberg is under the surface of the water with a relatively small proportion of it in view above the water. The visible and the submerged portions of the iceberg were analogous, in Freud's thinking, to the conscious and the unconscious portions, respectively, of human mental activity. He pictured the content of the unconscious as a great accumulation of unseen but vital forces (urges, feelings, passions, and so on) which exercise control over much of the conscious life of man. In other words, motivation, from the Freudian point of view, is very largely *unconscious*.

Not only are these mainsprings of our conduct hidden from consciousness but they continue as mainsprings throughout life. We are either born with them as "instincts" or they originate from the experiences of infancy and early childhood. Hence, Freud's *structural* and *genetic* approaches to the problem of motivation were developed.

Structurally, Freud saw the mind as consisting of three main divisions, the *id*, the *ego*, and the *superego*. The id we are born with. It consists of biologically determined impulses largely sexual in nature. It is the source of drive energy which is somatic in origin. This energy arises from internal or external stimulation that upsets the homeostatic balance in the organism and thus creates tension. The id cannot tolerate tension. It counteracts increases in tension by invoking processes (primary process). The individual is driven to do something to relieve the tension, thus restoring equilibrium. This relief from tension is pleasurable. All of this id activity is completely unconscious. It is the original (genetic) source of a drive, which, as such, continues throughout life.

As the infant develops, out of its experience a differentiation, a change, takes place in the original id situation. Experience teaches that the processes of the id (reflexes and images, the primary processes) are not adequate to meet the needs of the organism for relief from tension (hunger, erogenous-zone tension, and so on). To meet these needs in a real sense, transactions with the outside world are necessary. This function of relating to reality is the province of the *ego*, which is a differentiated portion of the id. The ego, according to Freud, has no motivating drive as such. It is only the mediator of drive gratification from the outside world.

With further experience in relating to reality, the child learns what is permitted in terms of gratification and what is prohibited. The prohibitions and the exhortations of the culture (the parents) become internalized. This is seen as a further differentiation from the original, unconscious id. This function is called the *superego*. The superego is sometimes portrayed as consisting of two divisions: the *conscience*, the internalized prohibitions; and the *ego ideal*, which represents the strivings toward what the parents praise (toward perfection). Freud became struck with the fact that the conscience can be as compelling and irrational in its demands as the id itself.

This structural conception of the operation of the mind, then, is the motivational system of psychoanalytic theory. Freud's conceptualization of the development of these three functions of the mind also constitutes his genetic approach to the understanding of mental life. Motivation thus is infantile in origin. According to Freudian theory, then, the id, the primitive reservoir of instinctual energy, is the original and lifelong source of motivation. It remains the mainspring of conduct, and the aim of the conduct continues to be the reduction of tension and restoration of homeostatic balance.

There are, then, two aspects to this motivational issue posed by Freudian theory that have developmental implications in relation to personality. These are (1) unconscious versus conscious motivation and (2) the question of tension reduction as the sole aim of motivated activity.

It is undoubtedly true that the neonate is activated entirely by tensions set up by internal organic conditions and by external stimuli impinging directly upon him and entirely without his conscious awareness of those stimulating conditions. It is also true, of course, that throughout life a great deal of one's motor activity is carried on without conscious direction, that one does many things "without thinking." Due very largely to Freudian influence, many psychologists have assumed that the "real" reasons that people do what they do most often are hidden reasons and that the consciously stated reasons are likely to be nothing more than rationalizations. This assumption has given rise to the development of many so-called projective devices and their wide use in psychological measurement.

The Importance of Conscious, Ego-mediated Motives

G. W. Allport (1960), who decries the prevalence of the assumption of hidden reasons for people's actions, has described the general trend of psychological thinking since Freud:

> This prevailing atmosphere of theory has engendered a kind of contempt for the "psychic surface" of life. The individual's conscious report is rejected as untrustworthy, and the contemporary thrust of his motives is disregarded in favor of a backward tracing of his conduct to earlier formative stages. The individual loses his right to be believed. And while he is busy leading his life in the present with a forward thrust into the future, most psychologists have become busy tracing it backward into the past.
> [p. 96, by permission]

Allport obviously believed in the efficacy of present desires and interests which are conscious and reportable for the understanding of the healthy personality.

"Holistic" theorists such as Angyal (1941), Goldstein (1939), and Maslow (1954) also find relatively little use for the concept of unconscious motivation and are little concerned with other than contemporary drives. For this group of students of personality, the pervasive, all-inclusive human motive is self-actualization, and the various consciously experienced "drives," such as those toward the satisfaction of hunger, sex, and the need to achieve, are merely manifestations of the master motive of self-realization.

Work with the war neuroses since World War II has contributed to the development of the various self, or ego, psychologies, reviving interest in and appreciation of contemporary and conscious, ego-mediated drives and motives. Carl Rogers' self-theory is an example of this contemporary orientation. His related client-centered therapy involves the mutual acceptance by client and therapist of the client's present drives, emotions, and attitudes and his facing up to them realistically (Rogers, 1942, 1951). From several points of view, then, relatively little importance is assigned to the past as a determinant of present behavior. The "here and now" is sufficient unto itself. Motivation "may be—and in healthy people usually is—autonomous of its origins" (G. W. Allport, 1960, p. 29).

The Question of Aim in Human Functioning

The Freudian concept of tension reduction as the prime source of gratification and pleasure, and as continuing to be the *only* aim of the organism, receives little support from present-day theorists. As was suggested earlier, the newborn infant is probably disturbed and activated only by tension-producing internal conditions and noxious stimuli, and there is no question that gratification and pleasure continue throughout life to result from relief from the basic "drive" conditions (hunger, pain, sex deprivation, and so on). But this is not to say that tension reduction remains the *only* motivational aim in life. It is a common observation that young children very early begin to seek *more* stimulation rather than simply to return to a tensionless state (Schachtel, 1959). Holistic theory holds strongly that the goal of normal, healthy people is not simply to discharge tension. On the contrary, the goal is to utilize energy, to bring it into balance, to mobilize it to the end of the greatest possible realization of individual potentiality (Hall and Lindzey, 1957, p. 303).

Other Theoretical Emphases

Theories also differ as to the role that learning plays in personality formation. Here again it is largely a matter of emphasis. All theories would agree that learning is importantly involved. Some theories, however, are concerned mainly with the *development* of personality, and with this emphasis personality theory in some instances becomes primarily learning theory. Other theories are concerned with the stable, persistent aspects of personality and with their modification or their resistance to modification with time rather than with the processes of development.

There are, of course, many other special emphases regarding the nature and development of the complex and pervasive human quality we call personality. It is necessary here only to point to this diversity and to suggest a few of the broader areas of difference in thinking among students of personality.

Research Approaches to the Study of Personality

There are two general research approaches to the understanding of personality which are of significance in relation to our present interest: the generalistic, or statistical and the individualistic, or idiographic (G. W. Allport, 1937, 1942, 1960).

The great bulk of personality research has been concerned with the identification and description of *common* traits—the qualities, characteristics, and behavior traits that are presumed to exist to *some* degree in people in general —and with the development of techniques and devices for the assessment of those traits. Many variations of this general approach have been used. In recent years, however, the most effective means of identifying and describing common personality traits has come to be the method of factor analysis (R. B. Cattell, 1957; Eysenck, 1947). Statistically determined "factors" are interpreted as traits of personality, and tests and "inventories" are devised for the quantitative appraisal of those traits.

From certain theoretical points of view, however, the essence of individual personality is entirely missed by such generalized approaches. The "self" psychologists, such as Rogers (1951), Maslow (1954), and others, and those who are "personalistic" in their thinking, such as Murry (1938), are among those who are not satisfied with the general statistical approach. Since each person is unique, he must be regarded as qualitatively different from others, not just different in the amounts of the various common traits he possesses. G. W. Allport has long advocated a greater use of the idiographic approach.

But methods for individual personality study that are scientifically acceptable are relatively few in number and, perhaps because they are difficult to apply, have not been widely used. One of the most promising methods of individual personality analysis is the Q-methodology of Stephenson (1953). In this procedure a reliably large, balanced sample of statements of feelings, attitudes, or personal inclinations is sorted by the subject into categories, each statement according to its relevance to *himself* and the degree to which it expresses his own self-evaluation. The results of the sorting are then analyzed and ordered, presenting one view, at least, of that person's unique personal organization.

Baldwin (1942, 1946) has also described two procedures for analyzing statistically the contents of personal documents and other material which relate to the adjustments and development of the single individual.

What We Shall Mean by "Personality"

As we shall use the term, "personality" refers to the quality or the fact of being a person. A person is an individual human being, unique and different from every other individual. In the words of William Stern (1938), "The person is a living whole, individual, unique, striving toward goals, self-contained and yet open to the world around him; he is capable of having experience" (p. 70).

One's personality, then, is that total quality or that complex combination of qualities that makes one unique and gives one his individual identity. Personality, this quality of individuality, is that to which we respond in our daily contacts and interactions with others. It is true, of course, that in our immediate reactions to others we tend to categorize each person in terms of a system of classification. We "type" him in terms of some outstanding quality. We assign him to a place among the dynamic or the quiet or the extroverts or the pleasing, and so on. But if we know him well, we never confuse him with anyone else. When we relate to him or interact with him, we are relating to *his individuality*. In all interpersonal relations we interact, in each case, with *a person*, not with a type or a category of persons.

Personality study, from this point of view, is the study of personal uniqueness. It involves in each case an analysis of the combination (pattern) of qualities and attributes that characterize the individual person.

It is a fact that babies at birth are persons, each by virtue of his individual identity and uniqueness. The processes of biological heredity, except in the case of monozygotic twins, provide for no other alternative than individual uniqueness in hereditary pattern (see Chapter 4). It is, of course, the *overall pattern* of attributes and traits that makes one baby different from every other baby. Millions of babies at birth may have exactly the same length as measured in inches. They are exactly alike in one attribute: length. Relatively few of these same babies would weigh exactly the same, and, as feature after feature is added to the pattern of attributes being considered, the number of like individuals would become smaller and smaller. Finally, no two of these millions of babies could be found to be exactly alike in every respect. They are alike only in that they all have the common quality of uniqueness.

Uniqueness in each case, then, results from an *individual combination* of attributes, qualities, and behavior patterns. Since one's personality *is* his uniqueness, in order to understand or appraise it we must know something of its underlying variables and the dynamics of their organization and change.

Determinants of Individuality

Some of the variables that constitute individual uniqueness are structural in nature, that is, they are features and attributes of the physical organism. Others are behavioral, or functional, in nature. Individual differences in certain of them are largely genetic in basis; others are more clearly due to environmental variation.

It is obviously not possible to catalog completely all of these variables. Our present purpose, rather, is to suggest some of the important categories of variables that in their countless combinations and relationships constitute personality in its individual manifestations. It is possible to trace the development of a personality only in very general terms. And to do this some analysis is necessary. We must resort to the piecemeal procedure of "looking at" particular aspects of the total, one at a time, noting briefly some of the modes of thinking and inquiry that have developed with regard to each.

Conceiving of a personality, then, as a particular patterning of structural and functional variables which constitute individuality, these variables may be roughly categorized as follows: (1) morphological and physical qualities and features, (2) capabilities and other acquired qualities and facilities that make for general functional adequacy and effectiveness in life, and (3), learned patterns of attitudes and behavioral skills that affect the quality of one's relations with others. Then finally, a category at a more profound level of behavioral organization which overrides, and includes, many of the functional variables just mentioned: (4) *behavior dispositions*. These "down-deep" and pervasive dispositions to behave largely determine what one actually and characteristically does in life situations, and particularly in relation to, and in interaction with, others (Allport, 1960; R. B. Cattell, 1957, 1971; Guilford, 1958).

Some of the more important variables included in the first three categories have been considered in other connections (Chapters 5, 8, 9, and 12).

Physical and Morphological Characteristics

As we have already noted, each individual is born with a unique constitutional make-up. He possesses at birth a combination of physical features all his own which constitute one important aspect of his individuality. As a physical being he is different and will continue to be different from every other individual throughout his life.

But what is more important is the possible influence his particular pattern of physical and morphological traits may have upon the development of other aspects of his uniqueness. It may, for example, have much to do with his parents' immediate reaction to him and the kind of reception they give him as a newcomer in the family. A lusty, robust baby with a loud, demanding voice may inspire in his parents quite different feelings and ways of regarding and handling him than would be the case were the baby frail, delicate, and finely featured. Congenital physical attributes in their unique combination may thus be important determinants of parent-baby interaction (Blauvelt and McKenna, 1961; Levy and Hess, 1952). As we shall see, the degree and type of interaction begins immediately to operate as a factor influencing the direction of developmental change in personality.

It is clear also that physical features may continue to be important factors determining one's self-concept and the quality of one's interactions with others throughout life. Preschool children's physical endowments, attractive or otherwise, strongly influence the behavior and the attitudes, expressed or implicit, toward them of the nursery school teacher and other adults who are important in their lives. Children soon begin to "see" themselves as others seem to see them. They design their self-concepts in terms of their interpretations of others' attitudes and feelings toward them.

For a boy of adolescent age to be too small or too fat or lacking the usual signs of sexual maturity may be very disturbing to him, particularly because of the behavior or the remarks of his peers; this disturbance might even give rise to unfortunate social behavior patterns and attitudes. Physical features are not only important factors contributing to uniqueness in and of themselves, but they also play *crucial* roles in the development of other attitudinal and behavioral attributes of individuality.

Physique-Temperament Relations

The importance of the various attributes that constitute physique in relation to personal adjustment and development has long been recognized. Theories concerning this relationship antedate the birth of academic psychology by several centuries. Psychologists generally, however, with certain notable exceptions, have not found evidence of relations between types of physique and patterns of temperament or personality, although probably no student of human behavior would deny the obvious fact that to the individual adolescent, for example, his body has great significance. Most psychologists, therefore, are likely to hold that morphological features have individual and idiosyncratic, rather than common or universal, significance. Investigators, nevertheless, continue to search for more general relations.

Chapter 4 considered the physical and morphological features of the human individual and how they develop. In that connection Sheldon's method of studying the components of physique in particular was presented and illustrated.

Sheldon was especially interested in the problems of the physique-temperament relation. In an elaborate program of research Sheldon (1942) made a correlational analysis of a long list of emotional and behavioral traits as observed in young adults. The analysis resulted finally in three sets, or "clusters," of highly interrelated traits. Each of these clusters, which he regarded as components of temperament, Sheldon associated, in terms of its apparent meaning, with one of the three components of physique. Thus he labeled them, respectively, *viscerotonia*, *somatotonia*, and *cerebrotonia*.

In his detailed somatotype study of 200 men Sheldon (1940) obtained surprisingly high correlations between the physique components and the associated components of temperament, as follows:

Endomorphy—viscerotonia   + .79
Mesomorphy—somatotonia   + .82
Ectomorphy—cerebrotonia   + .83

As a general rule, American psychologists have ignored Sheldon's findings. Certain writers (Diamond, 1957; Hall and Lindzey, 1957), however, regard them as significant and worthy of careful consideration. Such correlations do furnish evidence in support of the commonly held assumption that physique and temperament are related in a general sense.

Walker (1962, 1963) studied 125 nursery school children with the purpose of assessing the relation between body build and behavior. The children were rated on a specially prepared behavior-rating scale by their nursery school teachers. Nine "cluster scores" were developed from the intercorrelations among the items of the rating scale. Following the procedures prescribed by Sheldon, somatotyping photographs (front, side, and rear views) were obtained for each child. Three judges independently rated the photographs for each of the three physique components on Sheldon's 7-point scale.

A number of significant relations between physique components and specific behavior items were found. Some interesting relations also appeared for the total cluster scores. Endomorphy, for example, showed least relation with behavior. Only aggressive, assertive behavior in boys and cooperative, conforming behavior in girls tended slightly to be related to endomorphy. Mesomorphy, on the other hand, correlated significantly in boys with eight of the nine cluster scores. According to these correlations, boys in whom mesomorphy was a strong component tended to be aggressive and assertive, energetic, active, alert and curious, social and friendly, excitable and unstable, and cheerful and expressive and tended not to be fearful and anxious or cooperative and conforming. Mesomorphic girls also tended to be energetic and active and aggressive and assertive, but tended not to be fearful and anxious. By contrast, ectomorphy in boys was positively associated with the tendencies to be cooperative and conforming and not to be aggressive and assertive; in girls ectomorphy was associated with the tendencies not to be social and friendly. Walker (1962) summarized the findings of his study as follows:

> In this group of preschool children important associations do exist between individuals' physiques and particular behavior characteristics. Further, these associations show considerable similarity to those described by Sheldon for college-age men, though the strength of the association is not as strong as he reports. It is suggested that the relations are multiply deter- mined, arising from primary bodily conditions (e.g., strength, energy, sensory thresholds), from direct learnings concerning the efficacy of modes of behavior and adjustment techniques, and from less direct learn- ings regarding expectations and evaluations accorded to different physiques by others. [p. 79]

Physique in Relation to Other Personal Attributes

A number of research studies have verified the importance of physique and its components in relation to other personal characteristics. It has been found, for example, that children with "muscular solidarity" (mesomorphic tendency) also tend to be shorter and heavier and to grow at a faster rate and thus to reach the peak of their puberal growth spurt earlier than children with more linear and delicately built bodies (Dupertuis and Michael, 1953). Sheldon's morphological types have been found to differ significantly in average physical strength (H. E. Jones, 1949). In one of the best-known studies of juvenile delinquency it was found that the sturdier body build was more characteristic of delinquents than of nondelinquents (Glueck and Glueck, 1956).

Such research evidence, of course, supports Sheldon's basic assumption that the components of one's body structure, in combination, constitute the foundation of one's inherent organismic nature and must, therefore, bear an important relation with temperament, which is an expression or function of organismic nature.

Although the accumulating evidence indicates that certain morphological attributes do have a general significance in relation to behavior and temperament, it nevertheless seems quite clear that the most important relations between the physical and the psychological aspects are individual and personal in nature. There is no doubt that bodily attributes in their combinations and patterning can be important factors making for uniqueness, both in an immediate, direct sense and as they influence behavior.

Level of Effectiveness in Personal Functioning

The "intelligence" of an individual, which most definitely is an important component of his personality, can be roughly appraised in terms of the observed general level of effectiveness with which he meets and copes with life situations (Chapters 8 and 9). It is a factor in which individuals vary widely (1) with respect to inherent *potentiality* for its development, (2) with respect to the child's growing *capacity* to function ever more adequately as he grows toward adulthood, and (3) with respect to the variety and the quality level of acquired specific abilities to function. Chapters 8 and 9 are devoted to a more detailed consideration of this factor.

Learned Patterns of Behaving and Thinking

As we have seen, every individual is unique in total pattern of morphological and physical characteristics and in general level of inherent potentiality for intellectual development. He is also born with his own individual pattern of behavioral inclinations and predispositions. As this unique organization of congenital qualities comes in contact with a constantly changing personal environment, "coping" reactions begin and behavioral development through learning is underway. The range of things a person characteristically does—the total patterning of his behavior—perhaps more than anything else, portrays his individuality.

Habits

One's many patterned ways of doing things often reflect clearly the culture into which one is born and the specific conditions of living that surround him. Children are taught to dress themselves in certain routine ways. They are taught to behave at the family dinner table in ways that are acceptable. They learn to be polite, or not to be polite, to their elders. As they grow older, these patterns, or habits, change according to circumstances and in relation to changes in their general milieu. When they go away to college or into the army or into some other field of activity they usually discard many of their early habits and take on many new ones. But, even though the patterns of specific habits do change from time to time, certain generalized ways of doing things tend to resist change and to become characteristic of the individual. Each person at any particular time is characterized by his particular pattern of habits, his idiosyncrasies of personal and social behavior.

Attitudes

One's habitual ways of regarding and thinking about people, about manners, institutions, and life in general, develop from one's experiences, life circumstances, and the people around him. And, like other habits, specific attitudes can change with time and circumstances.

Many, perhaps most, of our attitudes are in each case the immediate result of prejudgment, the distinctly human process of generalization (that is, "labeling" and fitting objects of the external world into categories, Chapter 12). The conditions of human existence are too complex to be dealt with always item by item. Objects and people and situations must be classified, labeled, and categorized. The fundamental mental process of cognition appears to be largely one of naming and categorizing. One area of research in cognition in young children is concerned with the styles and "modes of perceptual organization and conceptual categorization of the external environment" (Sigel *et al.*, 1963, p. 4). "The human mind must think with the aid of categories. Once formed, categories are the basis for normal prejudgment. We cannot possibly avoid the process. Orderly living depends upon it" (G. W. Allport, 1954, p. 20). "Normal" prejudgment, then, is not to be decried. It is an extremely important process in the economy of living. Allport pointed out that our adjustments to the constant flow of daily problems are largely made in terms of performed categories. Furthermore, research concerning "styles" of categorization used by young children, and developmental changes in style produced by age, promise to underline the basic importance of the processes of prejudgment and categorization in human existence and to throw new and important light upon certain qualitative aspects of intellectual development (Sigel, 1963).

Throughout life, from early childhood, people, objects, situations, and circumstances of living are thus classified, labeled, and put into categories. In this process our attitudes are born. They develop and, most often, are modified through relabeling and perhaps more refined categorizing. The 8-month-old child, in his immature way, is likely to put a strange face in the category of objects to be feared. With more maturity and experience the same face might have become shifted to quite a different category. At age 2½ years the child might now greet that face with an attitude of joyous acceptance. Attitudes do change with experience. Prejudgment is a continuous process upon which orderly living depends.

Prejudice, likewise, is prejudgment. It is the *nondeliberate* labeling and assignment of a person or a group or an event to a previously established category. The labeling process, in the case of prejudice, however, is not only nondeliberate but it is also emotionally charged, and the category of assignment is one high in affective value. Thus, there are "love-prejudices" as well as "hate-prejudices" (G. W. Allport, 1954), and in either case a vital personal "value" is involved in the labeling. In the absence of a personal value (a love prejudice) there could be no hate prejudice. G. W. Allport, in discussing the "normality of prejudgment," wrote:

> Now there is good reason to believe that this love-prejudice is far more basic to human life than is its opposite, hate-prejudice (which Spinoza says "consists in feeling about anyone through hate less than is right"). One must first overestimate the things one loves before one can underestimate their contraries. Fences are built primarily for the protection of what we cherish.
>
> Positive attachments are essential to life. The young child could not exist without his dependent relationship on a nurturant person. He must love and identify himself with someone or something before he can learn what to hate. [1954, p. 25.]

The process of prejudgment is psychological. It is obvious that the *values* involved in the formation of categories used in everyday adjustments, and from which attitudes and prejudices arise, are personal in nature. Like any other aspect of human development, however, attitudes and prejudices develop through individual-environment interaction. In his social and emotional interchange with his parents, his larger family, and his community, the child "takes on" as his own many ready-made values. He gradually comes to share with the members of his "in-groups" many readily available classification categories and, thus, many attitudes and prejudices. As the child identifies with parents and others, their modes of labeling (prejudices) become his.

Research findings indicate that group prejudices thus adopted by the individual continue to be his as long as he remains a member of the group. Group pressures upon individual members are strong. In regard to this aspect of the problem of prejudice, G. W. Allport (1954) wrote:

> A strong argument in favor of this view is the relative ineffectiveness of attempts to change attitudes through influencing individuals. Suppose a child attends a lesson in intercultural education in the classroom. The chances are this lesson will be smothered by the embracing norms of his family, gang, or neighborhood. To change the child's attitudes it would be necessary to alter the cultural equilibrium of these, to him, more important groups. It would be necessary for the family, the gang, or the neighborhood to sanction tolerance before he as an individual could practice it. [p. 40]

The acquisition of prejudices is thus largely a matter of incidental learning. The category labels applied to persons, groups, or institutions by parents and other significant ones in the child's life will readily and inevitably become his own labels and prejudices.

Behavior Dispositions

We have yet to discuss what are probably the most pervasive of all the determinants of individuality, namely, what have been described as "source traits" of personality (R. B. Cattell, 1957). They are presumed to be the "substantial and enduring *dispositions* of which personality is composed" (G. W. Allport, 1960, p. 8).

These "major dispositions of character" lie deep in the individual's behavioral nature. A behavior disposition may be further described as a highly generalized and pervasive personal quality which is made manifest in a variety of different behavior patterns (equivalent responses) made in a variety of different situations (equivalent stimulations).

One example of a common behavior disposition has to do with the quality of one's interactions with others. People vary widely in this trait, from a strong, assertive, and dominating tendency to one of being overly agreeable, conforming, and submissive. This disposition is pervasive in that it appears in all kinds of situations and is expressed in a variety of ways. The assertive person will "have his mind made up" on most questions and issues and will express them in interaction with almost anyone and in any situation in which the issue arises. The submissive person, by contrast, may actually have quite definite ideas and opinions of his own but will "go along" with the more dominant person rather than get involved in any kind of disagreement.

Individual differences in this "source trait," as in many others, become established early in life. As early as age 4 differences are pronounced. The particular situations which give rise to dominant or submissive behavior, of course, might be quite different from time to time and at different age levels, and although they may be different, they are "equivalent" in that they are expressive of the same "psychophysical system" (disposition), and they (the overt action patterns) take place in response to a variety of different yet "equivalent" stimuli. A behavior disposition, then, is not just a patterned way of performing in a given situation. Rather, it is a deep-lying tendency which gives rise to many specific behavior patterns. It is a component of the individual's basic personality structure which endures throughout life.

Temperamental Predispositions.   Behavior dispositions, like all other personal qualities and attributes, develop through organism-environment interaction. As we have already noted (Chapter 9), the individual is born with certain tendencies and predispositions to react in characteristic ways to stimulation. A number of these constitutionally based predispositions have been identified and described as congenital, temperamental variables. "Temperament," in the sense in which it is used here, refers only to those original, constitutionally based tendencies to react affectively to internal and external stimulating conditions (Fries, 1941, 1944; A. Thomas *et al.*, 1960, 1961, 1962). Among these original reaction tendencies are activity level, approach or withdrawal, adaptability, threshold of responsiveness, intensity of reaction, quality of mood, distractability, and attention span and persistence. They were described somewhat more fully in Chapter 9 as variables that can influence the development of general functional effectiveness. Our hypothesis here is that the individual patterning and the relative strength of these congenital reaction tendencies which characterize an infant constitute the *origin* from which his basic "personality structure" develops. The other essential factor in development, of course, is the unique environmental situation into which the child is born.

The Environmental Factor in the Development of Behavior Dispositions

A substantial body of evidence indicates that the most crucial single factor in personality development is the interaction, largely emotional in nature, between the child, with his pattern of temperamental predispositions, and the more intimate, human aspects of his environment (other individuals, his parents, who care for him and exercise control over him).

Much of this interchange, generally, is gratifying and pleasant to both parent and child, but sometimes it is fraught with anxiety, frustration, and rage. The *prevailing* nature and quality of this emotional interchange is important, and in the beginning its nature and quality obviously depend upon how the inborn temperamental nature of the infant relates to the personal make-up and adjustments of his mother.

In this primary mother-infant situation there are, of course, two complex individualities in interaction, the baby with his congenital nature and the mother with her own pattern of attitudes and feelings about parenthood, about children, and particularly about her present situation of having a little stranger to care for. Her own unique pattern of dominant dispositions to react, to behave toward people and to life generally—her personality—is an important determining factor in the situation.

The "Same" Mother-Family Environment Is Different for Each Child

For a different infant entering this same family situation, the nature of the interaction that would develop with the mother might be very different. Some babies are by congenital nature "difficult," some are relatively "easy" to care for and relate to. And sometimes, in spite of sincere devotion and "wise" care, a child develops behavior dispositions not in line with parental expectation and desire.

The Changing Interpersonal Situation

The nature of the interpersonal environment for any given child also changes as the child grows and changes. During early infancy, the period of complete dependency, the "mothering one" and the quality of her nurturant care is the all-important factor. Later, however, as a toddler and preschooler the control aspect of the larger environment becomes relatively more important. Much of the child's learning related to his personal development is identificatory or imitative in nature (Bandura, 1962). The child normally adopts as his or her model the same-sex parent. *Whatever* that parent does is good in the child's eyes, and is something to be imitated.

Basic "Personality Structure" Becomes Established Early

In any event, the evidence supports the view that by the time the child reaches school age his basic pattern of behavior dispositions (primary personality traits) is already pretty well established. A great deal of "socialization" has already taken place. Much parental effort ordinarily has gone into direct teaching—the inculcation of socially desirable behavior patterns. But much "incidental" learning has also taken place. And it is largely through incidental learning, that is, learning not deliberately sought by the parents, that the basic behavior dispositions become established. As stated earlier, the *nature* of these tendencies depends largely upon the overall, predominating quality of the emotional interaction that takes place between the child and his parents.

Ascendance-Submissiveness in Two Children

The account of the contrasting development in two young children of the behavior disposition, ascendance-submissiveness, will serve to illustrate some of the varying behavioral content and the determining factors involved (Stott, 1957).

The behavioral records of these children consisted of checked items on a standardized checklist which were judged in each case by the nursery school teachers, and later by recreational club leaders, as characterizing the children's social behavior. The particular patterns of checked items which stood out in these two cases were those which portrayed the disposition to be dominating or to be submissive.

The first chart in the following report shows the characteristic pattern of behavior and its tendency to persist in child A. J.'s record. A cross (X) under a particular item in the chart indicates that at least during the age

Case: A. J.

Column items (in table order, by checklist number):

- 4 — Submits to a leader only after a struggle to dominate.
- 8 — Directs all activity about him.
- 15 — Definitely schemes to get others to carry out his plans.
- 16 — Gives commands with an air of finality.
- 26 — Fights for his place as leader.
- 27 — Opposition spurs him on to greater activity.
- 28 — Insists that other children do as he wishes.
- 3 — Dominates children more mature than himself.
- 5 — Usually leads a small group.
- 6 — Decides who shall participate in the group activities.
- 7 — Is a leader in any group.
- 11 — Dominates other children through his ability to talk effectively.
- 22 — Usually takes the initiative.
- 10 — Other children make many appeals to him for information.
- 12 — Other children appeal to him to make decisions for the group.
- 13 — Dominates other children through their love or admiration for him.
- 14 — Dominates other children through his wealth of ideas.
- 30 — Gets willing cooperation easily.
- 9 — Neither leads nor follows; plays alone.
- 21 — Can take the initiative if it is absolutely necessary.
- 25 — Stands aside to let others participate.
- 18 — Hesitates to initiate activity.
- 19 — Hesitates to make suggestions to other children.
- 23 — Seeks the approval of the leader before he acts.
- 24 — Does not push the issue in case of opposition.
- 1 — Submits to any child who takes the initiative.
- 2 — Even submits to younger children.
- 17 — Helpless unless someone organizes activity for him.
- 20 — Usually follows the ideas of others for activity.
- 29 — Does not defend his own rights with other children.

Age in Years and Months	Domination (Bossiness)							Ascendance (Undifferentiated)						Natural Leadership					Individualistic Tendency			Polite, Timid, Conforming				Dependent Submissiveness				
	4	8	15	16	26	27	28	3	5	6	7	11	22	10	12	13	14	30	9	21	25	18	19	23	24	1	2	17	20	29
2–7	X						X	X					X						X											X
3–1			X	X	X			X				X	X						X	X										
3–7	X	X			X	X	X	X	X	X	X	X	X	X	X	X	X	X	X	X	X									
4–1			X	X	X	X	X	X	X				X	X	X	X	X	X	X					X						
4–7		X		X	X	X	X	X	X	X	X	X	X	X		X	X	X	X											
5–1			X	X	X	X	X	X	X		X	X	X						X											
6–1																														
7–1	X			X	X	X				X	X		X						X	X										
8–1																														
9–1	X			X	X	X							X						X	X										
10–1																														
11–1																														
12–1	X	X		X	X					X	X	X	X							X	X									

Figure 13.1   Ascendance-Submission checklist pattern (Case A.J.).

range indicated at the left, that statement was judged to characterize this child's behavior.

The Case of A. J.

It will be noted that during a period of more than 10 years (ages 2½ to 13 years) this child's general pattern of behavior changed very little. He was observed to exhibit certain qualities of constructive leadership, especially during the nursery school period (to age 5). Some of the most consistently checked items indicate that he was usually able to take the initiative and tended to dominate but that he was able, when he wished, to effect this dominance through his wealth of ideas and his ability to talk effectively.

However, along with these more admirable leadership qualities, and perhaps more consistently characteristic of him, A. J. was strongly inclined to be forcefully domineering. He was likely to try to direct all activity about him and he would submit to another leader only "after a struggle to dominate" being always ready to "fight for his place as a leader." Opposition to his efforts to dominate in a situation "spurs him on to greater activity" and he would scheme "to get others to carry out his plans."

The pattern suggests also that perhaps as a reaction to the refusal of others to submit to his domineering behavior, he would isolate himself. The item "neither leads nor follows; plays alone" was one of the most frequently checked items.

In addition to the formal recording of behavior tendencies on the check lists, there are many comments and more individualized descriptions of the child and his behavior in the files. Many of these comments are interesting in connection with the more rigid check list pattern. They indicate that from the very beginning of his nursery school experience A. gave evidence of his tendency not only to force his will on others but also to vent considerable hostility in acts of aggression upon them. "A. is very rough with the other children, slaps them hard. He is also a very determined child" was one of the first comments regarding him by his nursery school teacher. A month later (age 2 years 7 months) he continued "to slap the children and he has twice been removed from the playground because of this." During this early period other comments were: "A. has really very little respect for adults, particularly the students, but as soon as he understands you mean business he is most cooperative." "A. is an outcast from the group. He interferes quite often with the play of the other children." He was reported to push children off their tricycles, grab their caps off, tear down their 'houses'. It is quite clear that during this period before he reached the age of 3 he was expressing in his behavior something more than a healthy urge to lead or to be constructively dominant in interesting group activities.

During A.'s second year in Nursery School (age 3-6 to 4-3) there was only one mention by the staff of overly hostile behavior: "when A. becomes very angry with the other children in order to have his own way he sometimes bites." There was repeated reference to his tendency to play alone, and to his close association with one other boy. There was evidence that A. was the dominant one in this duo.

During his third nursery school year, however, A.'s tendencies toward hostility and aggression in his attempts to dominate were even more strongly evident. This is indicated in the following entries in the record:

A.'s ego is getting the better of him. Wants to always do just the opposite to what the other children are doing. Attacks the other children in a vicious manner if they are not doing what he would have them do. One day recently J. had marks on his face from an attack by A.

A. is very tense and definitely unstable. When he does something which he knows ought not to be done he accuses another child of the wrong doing. Seems to definitely try to be annoying.

A. is scratching the other children if they interfere with his way of thinking. Let another child try to assert himself against A.'s will and he is sure to be scratched.

There were, however, in the record of this period references to many desirable qualities in A. He was obviously a very bright child. He was described as alert, with very quick comprehension and an excellent memory for past events. He was "very quick to sense any uncertainty in an adult's dealing with a situation." He characteristically contributed many suggestions as to how to do things or what to do for group activity. He was very adept at organizing group play and was "always the center of attention in things he organized himself." Thus it is evident that A. possessed the qualities and personal resources which make for what we have called "natural leadership." However, the predominant note throughout the record of A.'s last nursery school year is "domineering bossiness" expressing itself in a forceful and hostile manner.

There are, however, evidences in the record of fluctuations or temporary breaks in the pattern which seem to be characteristic of the tense, insecure child. One comment was as follows: "A. is much improved since spring vacation. He now makes an effort to please. His manner and speech are much improved." But at the end of that same month the comments were concerned with hostile "scratching" of other children indicating a complete return to his former aggressive pattern.

During A.'s five years in the Recreational Clubs much the same pattern persisted. During the first club year, however, there was generally less aggressive behavior of a hostile or teasing nature and he tended somewhat more strongly to pursue his own individual interests and activities. He continued to show lively interest in activities of his own choosing.

When A. was between 8½ and 9 years of age and during his third year in the club's program, staff comments concerning his interactive behavior with peers became more frequent. These comments ran as follows:

A. came in feeling very mean and threw his coat up on top of the rack. I told him he was crushing C.'s hat. He said, 'Well, that's my sister's hat anyway so what do I care.' While I went after him to see that he hung his coat up another boy left his on the radiator. I asked A. whose coat it was and he said, 'What do I care, that isn't my business. I'd like to sock that guy anyway.' Then he rushed towards some little fat fellow with glasses and began to strike him.

We had a problem this evening with A. He was very uncooperative and a poor sport at the games. We continually had to reprove him until finally he became sulky.

A. jumps on the other children. He is rough and often hurts them. Students cannot manage him. He is quiet for a little while, then he will suddenly jump up and go wild. He is not accepted by the group. He is not able to play the organized games. He prefers . . . individual pastimes. Students observed that the uncooperative things he does are to attract attention. He hates to be criticized and will get mad and leave the game. He starts fights with smaller boys and girls.

During his tenth year of life, A. continued to present much the same pattern of behavior in relation to his peers that was characteristic of him as a preschool child. A written staff summary of the child's behavior through the years of the School's contact with him states that "all past records show that A. was determined and resistant. They indicate that his behavior was not a 'passing phase' that will be easily outgrown. He has always shown that only the firmest authority could manage him." However, he often accepted and used correction constructively. He was also responsive to approval.

In the Brownies (Club) he was creative, original, more so than almost any other child. If he could be kept busy and could talk to an appreciative and interested adult, he was good. Otherwise he became destructive, wild, uncontrollable.

One cannot get away from the fact that A. is of a definite constitutional type, highly excitable, seemingly overactive, never being able to delay action, nor to act if it does not suit him. He is emotionally unstable with a tendency to be dishonest.

A.'s Environment

By the time A. was 2½ he had developed "negativism" to a point where his mother sought help from the Merrill-Palmer staff regarding it. The child "absolutely refuses to do as directed and this is occurring very often of late." In the interviews with the mother at this time certain inconsistencies in parental handling became apparent. "Mr. J. is apparently somewhat of a martinet in his ideas of discipline and does not wish to wait long for the obedient response of the child." Mr. J. was said to adore the baby sister who was described as "a lovely doll-like little creature," and he was always on the alert lest A. hurt the baby. He, therefore, was constantly cautioning A., telling what he must and must not do in relation to the baby. It was also reported that except for disciplinary measures, the baby was receiving all the attention at home. Mrs. J. realized that A. was beginning to play for attention at home.

At this time the J.'s were living with Mrs. J.'s parents. Sometimes the grandmother would call for A. at the end of the Nursery School day. On one such occasion the grandmother said, "I've been telling A. that if he did not stop sucking his thumb he would have to have his teeth pulled like I had mine." Mrs. J. reported that both grandparents were "after him every minute in regard to his thumb sucking. They expected 'immediate response to discipline' and they are constantly saying 'don't do this—don't do that'."

The grandmother was said to have been "very nervous and fussy about her things and utterly unable to cope with such a lively child as A." Neither the parents nor the grandparents had ever been around little boys before and "they apparently in many instances are setting standards of behavior which are utterly beyond possibility. Mrs. J. seems to realize this fact to a certain extent but she has not enough knowledge to cope with it successfully." The grandmother would take it upon herself to punish the child against her daughter's wishes, criticizing her for being "too easy going." The J.'s apparently realized that the situation was not good for the children but under the economic situation that existed at the time they were unable to maintain a home of their own.

When A. was 6 years 10 months of age the mother in an interview reported that A. was quite irresponsible in the neighborhood and that he could not be depended upon not to destroy other people's property. As a result he had been excluded from many of the homes of the neighborhood. This naturally was a matter of much concern to the parents.

In interviews, Mrs. J. referred several times to tension between herself and her husband, saying that they often argued at the table seriously enough so that their voices were raised in anger. They had stopped arguing about the children and how to handle them in their presence but they "constantly argued about other things." There were indications during the conversation that an active antagonism existed between mother and father.

On the whole, A. was said to obey his father who was quite severe in his discipline. It was not uncommon for him to spank A. three or four times in the course of a Sunday afternoon for various kinds of misdemeanors.

In A., then, we have a case in which the interchange between a highly excitable, overactive, emotionally unstable constitutional temperament, and a restrictive, somewhat punitive and inconsistent environment resulted in a particular pattern of interactive behavior—one aspect of his "personality structure"—which was highly resistant to change. According to this interpretation "home influences" were extremely important in the child's development, but the effects of those influences were probably specific to the child's inherent "constitutional type."

The Case of B. R.

The checked behavior pattern of B. R. stands in contrast to that of A. J. With only a few scattered exceptions, all of his checks are on the submissive side of the pattern sheet (Figure 13.2). This pattern, however, is similar to that of A. and consistent with the large majority of the 109 patterns in that it did not change significantly during the nine years of observation. The picture of B. is predominantly one of polite, timid conformity. He commonly "stood aside to let others participate" in activities where "taking turns" was the rule. He "hesitated" to initiate group activity or to make suggestions to others and willingly submitted to any child who would take the initiative. He would even submit to children younger than himself. He would not "defend his own rights with other children" and would rarely "push the issue in case of opposition." He was also dependently submissive in the sense of being "helpless unless someone organizes activity for him" and in being inclined to "follow the ideas of others for activity." Rather consistent with this picture of timid submissiveness was his tendency to play by himself.

A suggestion that this rather extreme shyness and submissiveness probably was not due to any lack of innate ability or potential for leadership is found in the fact that five of the six other items checked for B. were in, or consistent with, the "natural leadership" category. He was checked twice as being able to get "willing cooperation easily" and once each as "dominating other children through his wealth of ideas" and for the fact that "other children make appeals to him for information."

The comments and observational reports of staff and students generally support the view of B. presented in the check list pattern of Figure 13.2. At age 18 months the Merrill-Palmer Test of Mental Ability was administered to him. The results of this test were not too satisfactory due to "very poor cooperation," probably a result of his timidity. "B. insisted that both parents sit very close to him" during the test.

At age 2 years, at the beginning of his nursery school experience B. was described as quite dependent and strongly attached to his mother. However, he accepted the routine procedures of the Nursery School as a matter of course, accepted authority and was responsive to requests made of him. He played almost entirely by himself but he watched the other children a great deal. He showed, even that early, an inclination to keep in the background. He habitually sucked his thumb but he would remove his thumb from his mouth willingly when such a suggestion was made.

Four months later B. was referred to as "a passive, rather timid child inclined to withdraw from other children." However, he was judged to be "a stable child with good self control. He showed no signs of over-stimulation." He was deliberate in his movements, slow in manner of walking. He ate his lunch in the same manner—"slowly matter of fact and deliberate." One comment was that he likes "slyly to take toys from others but if there is resistance he gives up immediately."

At 2½ he was "quite babyish" when his father visited the Nursery School. He pretended he could not climb the slide. He was very timid and attached himself to his father. He continued to suck his thumb but would cooperate by removing his thumb when reminded to do so. He was described as "cooperative but not self-reliant in routine."

The comments continued to describe this general pattern of shyness, self-consciousness, and compliance throughout the whole nursery school period. At age 3½ B. underwent an appendectomy after which he showed even more shyness and also a tendency to react negatively to the attention of others. At around 4 years of age, however, a somewhat new pattern was reported. He was said at this time to be very independent and self-reliant—"he does not want to be helped in any way." He also began playing more with bigger boys, entering into the activities and even "holding his own" with the others. But this promise of a new trend in development toward more self assertiveness seems not to have materialized.

When he was approaching five, one staff comment was that the School had been trying to help him overcome his introvertive, withdrawing tendencies by putting him in situations that would force him to participate in group activity. However, these efforts apparently had little lasting effect. At age 11 years when a Stanford-Binet test was administered he "submitted to the test willingly" and was "very attentive to instructions." Again at 12½

Case: B. R.

Legend (item descriptions):

Domination (Bossiness):
- 4. Submits to a leader only after a struggle to dominate.
- 8. Directs all activity about him.
- 15. Definitely schemes to get others to carry out his plans.
- 16. Gives commands with an air of finality.
- 26. Fights for his place as leader.
- 27. Opposition spurs him on to greater activity.
- 28. Insists that other children do as he wishes.

Ascendance (Undifferentiated):
- 3. Dominates children more mature than himself.
- 5. Usually leads a small group.
- 6. Decides who shall participate in the group activities.
- 7. Is a leader in any group.
- 11. Dominates other children through his ability to talk effectively.
- 22. Usually takes the initiative.

Natural Leadership:
- 10. Other children make many appeals to him for information.
- 12. Other children appeal to him to make decisions for the group.
- 13. Dominates other children through their love or admiration for him.
- 14. Dominates other children through his wealth of ideas.
- 30. Gets willing cooperation easily.

Individualistic Tendency:
- 9. Neither leads nor follows; plays alone.
- 21. Can take the initiative if it is absolutely necessary.
- 25. Stands aside to let others participate.

Polite, Timid, Conforming:
- 18. Hesitates to initiate activity.
- 19. Hesitates to make suggestions to other children.
- 23. Seeks the approval of the leader before he acts.
- 24. Does not push the issue in case of opposition.

Dependent Submissiveness:
- 1. Submits to any child who takes the initiative.
- 2. Even submits to younger children.
- 17. Helpless unless someone organizes activity for him.
- 20. Usually follows the ideas of others for activity.
- 29. Does not defend his own rights with other children.

Age in Years and Months	Domination (Bossiness)							Ascendance (Undifferentiated)						Natural Leadership					Individualistic Tendency			Polite, Timid, Conforming				Dependent Submissiveness				
	4	8	15	16	26	27	28	3	5	6	7	11	22	10	12	13	14	30	9	21	25	18	19	23	24	1	2	17	20	29
2–7													X						X	X	X	X	X		X	X	X		X	X
3–1																														
3–7																				X	X	X		X	X	X			X	X
4–1																			X	X	X	X	X	X	X	X	X	X	X	X
4–7																			X										X	X
5–1																	X	X	X	X	X	X	X	X	X	X	X	X	X	X
6–1				X									X						X	X	X	X	X			X	X	X		X
7–1													X						X	X		X	X	X	X				X	
8–1																														
9–1																			X	X	X	X	X			X	X	X	X	X
10–1																			X	X	X	X				X		X		

Figure 13.2 Ascendance-Submission checklist pattern (Case B.R.).

he was described as "very serious and business like" in his approach to the test. Always the impression was that he did what he did because it was expected of him—to be compliant with the wishes of someone else.

Even with B.'s apparent lack of drive to assert himself and his slow and deliberate manner of approach he did well on intelligence tests. At 4½ his Binet I.Q. was 127. At 6 years 3 months it was 115, and at 11 years 4 months it was 140. As his check list profile suggested he possessed the necessary intellectual potential for real leadership.

B.'s Original Constitutional Nature

In the records of B.'s early infancy there is very little information regarding his original temperamental nature. As we have seen during his attendance in the School services his behavior was repeatedly described as slow, deliberate, careful and compliant. This suggests a rather "low activity type" of constitution, with low sensitivity to the environment. On the other hand his shyness and social apprehensiveness suggests a basically keen sensitivity to other persons, and that his response system early became one of apprehension and withdrawal rather than one of pell-mell approach activity. The probability that B.'s low activity-shyness-withdrawing pattern was not, as such, identical with his original constitutional nature, but rather was of psychogenic origin—a result of early interchange between his original nature and his effective environment—is suggested by comments of Mrs. R. in a staff interview when B. was almost 2 years old. In describing B.'s "disposition" as a baby the mother said he was "happy, very determined." She said she had had "quite a hard time getting him *not* to do the things he wanted to do." For a time he had temper tantrums "but he doesn't try that now." She also described him as "very active." She stated that "recently B. has been biting his finger nails when at all excited." Thus it would seem probable that by original constitutional nature B. was highly sensitive to his environment and even of a fairly high "activity type." His high sensitivity rendered him readily susceptible to early conditioning.

Home Influences

Mrs. R. was well above the average in educational status, having obtained an M.A. degree. She had taught in an institution of higher learning. During the early years of B.'s life, however, she was judged as being "not as stable as she should be." She was inclined to feel "pushed by the pressure of work." Her high standards of housekeeping she found difficult to maintain.

She habitually "bit her nails" until she was 20 years of age. Her responses to the Bernreuter Personality Inventory, when B. was about 4, gave her a percentile score of 68 in "neuroticism" and 69 in "introversion." She said the main thing she worried about was "sin" and that she feared being alone, mice, snakes, and deep water.

Mrs. R. felt that her relationship with her husband was "good," that they have similar interests and that disagreements between them were rare. She characterized her husband as kind, nervous, a plodder, a procrastinator, worrisome, gentle, self reliant and dependable.

Mr. R. was described by a staff member as having a "good disposition," even tempered and "easy going." He was judged to have more patience with B. than did Mrs. R. He felt that his wife tended to "expect too much" of the child.

It would seem that on the whole the R. family situation, judged by ordinary standards, would have been rated as "favorable" as an environment for children. It is quite possible, however, that B.'s persistent pattern of shy, submissive, compliant interaction with others had its basis established at a very early age through the interchange between a very sensitive, responsive and rather active temperamental nature, and the most effective aspect of his environment, viz., a rather repressive, somewhat harassed mother with, perhaps, a "pressure-y", somewhat punitive, rather than a completely accepting, attitude toward her young child. This interpretation is in line with the view of Karen Horney regarding the nature and origin of extreme submissiveness which she refers to as a form of masochism. This quality of interaction, she says, arises from "certain conflicts in interpersonal relations" in "the attempt to gain safety and satisfaction in life through inconspicuousness and dependency." (p. 113)

Discussion

The cases of A. and B. are merely illustrative of the large majority of case records under study in which the quality of social interaction which the child displayed in the beginning of his nursery school experience continued to be characteristic of him, in many instances, in spite of considerable effort on the part of the service staff to bring about the desired change. Each case, of course, is unique. The pattern of behavior varied widely as did the individuality of the child and the environmental situation. Furthermore, many aspects of each child's personality did change in the sense of becoming more mature, and marked changes in overall social behavior occurred. But even with these changes in capacity to function and modifications of patterns of functioning, the fundamental qualities of his person and of his functioning remained to give him uniqueness and individuality among his play peers.

Cases A. and B. by themselves prove nothing. But they, along with many others in our group, at least strongly suggest that these pervasive, persisting qualities of personality with which we are dealing are not inherited, as such, in the biological sense, nor are they traits that parents and teachers deliberately set about to inculcate in the young. Rather, they are psychogenic in origin. . . . [Reprinted by permission, *The Merrill-Palmer Quarterly*, Spring 1957.]

The Personality Profile

The concept of "source traits" (behavior dispositions) assumes the existence of many such variables in the human personality. The further assumption is that each constitutes a continuum on which individuals vary from zero amount of the trait to a maximum, or from the extreme negative end of the continuum to the extreme positive end. Cattell (1957, 1971), for example, has identified 16 traits and has devised means of appraising them quantitatively. The complete list of these traits is given in Appendix A.

In our own work in analyzing children's behavior data we have tentatively identified 13 variables comparable to those on Cattell's list. Figure 13.3 contains the "behavior profiles" of our twin subjects in terms of these 13 variables. Some of these at least appear to represent behavior dispositions in Allport's (1960) meaning of the term (source traits in Cattell's terminology). These profiles serve to illustrate individual differences in early personality pattern.

In certain of the variables these children were rated to be much alike. In traits I, IV, VI, and XI for example, both were rated near the middle of the scale. Neither was outstanding in either direction. In the tendencies to be "assertive and self-assured" (II), "independent and resourceful" (III), "relaxed and spontaneous" (VI), "ascendant" in the sense of showing "natural leadership" (VIII), and "self-reliant" they were also much alike. These similarities presumably are largely due to the kind of family environment these children enjoyed as toddlers and preschoolers. However, in four of the traits interesting differences are shown in the figure. Paul was more strongly inclined to be "individualistic" and "self-sufficient" and more inclined to play alone and to be "controlled, stable, and systematic" than was Sally, who was very much in the middle of these scales. Sally, on the other hand, was inclined to be more "socially adaptable and flexible" and more "at ease, unaffected, and natural" than was Paul, who in these traits occupied middle positions. These differences seem to relate to differences in congenital temperamental nature—differences that were apparent from the beginning.

These diverse patterns in a pair of twins illustrate the point of view that "individuality" is expressed in the "total pattern" of an individual's expressions of commonly shared traits. These profile patterns, of course, are different for each individual.

The Complexity of the Behavioral Aspects of Personality

It should be emphasized here that a profile such as shown in Figure 13.3 represents only a very limited aspect of personality. Our discussions of personality have implied an extremely complex combination of attributes and qualities which are indeed myriad. In any assessment of personality it would, of course, be impossible to account for more than a meager sampling of the relevant variables. Other analyses of child behavior using other sources of data have portrayed somewhat different constellations of traits (Becker and Krug, 1964; R. B. Cattell and Coan, 1957).

The behavioral aspects of individuality are perhaps more meaningful and more vitally important in human living than are the other areas of uniqueness. They are also more fluid, more subject to change, and therefore

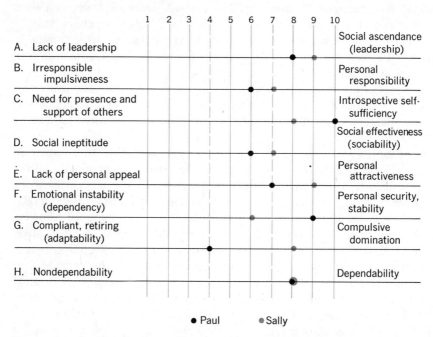

Figure 13.3   **Social behavior profiles of Paul and Sally 695 based upon checklist ratings at age 4.**

more dynamic in relation to effective personal and social adjustments. At the same time these attributes of the person are most elusive and difficult to measure. One of the difficulties often made much of is that every life situation involves a different set of behavior patterns. Although a given person may have acquired an "organization" of fundamental behavior dispositions which, in general, characterize his functioning in all of life's situations, in terms of specific behaviors he may perform quite differently in the different areas of his life. These studied diverse behavior patterns have given rise to the concept of multiple "selves." "A man," said William James (1910), "has as many selves as there are distinct groups of persons about whose opinion he cares" (p. 179). Role theory also emphasizes the diversity of behavior from situation to situation. From this point of view one can scarcely conceive of a behavior profile such as Figure 13.1, based as it is upon only 13 traits, as adequately portraying the behavior aspects of one's personality.

On the other hand, the concept of "behavior dispositions" implies more than is seen in purely situational behavior. In other words, even though Sally in many respects may have been a "different child" at home than she was in nursery school, in association with her peers in the home play yard she probably would have shown the same general dispositions to be "ascendant" and also to be characteristically "self-reliant" rather than to be dependent upon the support of others in her play (Allport, 1960).

Stability and Change in Personality

An important question regarding human personality to which developmental psychologists have given considerable attention is that of the relative persistence or change in specific aspects and traits of personality. The fascinating study of Kagan and Moss (1962), which is based upon the data of the longitudinal investigation of child development of the Fels Research Institute[1] is an outstanding example.

In this study considerable evidence is presented for some degree of continuity of basis behavior tendencies, particularly between the later period of childhood (10 to 14 years of age) and adulthood. In general the results of the study "offer strong support to the popular notion that aspects of adult personality begin to take form during early childhood" (p. 266).

The three variables for which both sexes showed most stability were *concern about achievement, sex-typed activities*, and *spontaneity*. These correlations were all significant in magnitude.

"However, the degree of continuity of these response classes was intimately dependent upon its congruence with traditional standards of sex-role characteristics" (p. 268). For example, *passivity* as a reaction to frustration in girls in middle childhood was found to be a highly significant precursor of the *tendency to withdraw* from failure situations in adulthood (.67). This relationship, however, did not hold for males. This finding was interpreted as due to greater conflict on the part of the male over withdrawal behavior. Another interesting sex difference was that in the relation between early dependency and adult dependence upon family. The relationship was practically zero for males but was quite significant for females (over .40).

Child Behavior Precursors of Adult Behavior Dispositions

Among the many variables in terms of which people vary, and which constitute the complex we call personality, we have suggested that certain of these variables appear to be especially basic and dependable as indicators of individuality. They are conceived of as constituting the "basic personality structure," as deep-lying, pervasive dispositions to react and to behave in characteristic ways in daily life. The implication is also that they are "psychogenic" in origin, having developed during early childhood, largely through the emotional interaction between the child and his parents.

The 13 childhood behavior variables described above were tentatively regarded as behavior dispositions. There was, however, no solid evidence to support this assumption. The stability, the persisting quality of these behavior

---

[1] One of the most fruitful long term research programs has been that of the Fels Research Institute in Yellow Springs, Ohio, under the leadership of Dr. L. W. Sontag.

trends, had not been established. Preliminary studies indicated that certain of them continued to characterize individual children throughout the period of childhood (Stott, 1957), but the extent to which they would relate to adult personality structure was not known.

With the purpose of gaining some evidence on this interesting question, a follow-up study was attempted. It was possible to contact 29 individuals for whom scores on the 13 childhood variables described earlier were available. At that time these people were near 40 years of age. Thus the time interval between the collection of the childhood data and the follow-up study was some 35 years.

Included in the data of the follow-up were "self ratings" of each of the 29 individuals on the "Sixteen Personality Factor Questionnaire" (Cattell, 1957). The 16 "factors" are purported to represent source traits that are stable. Scores on these traits were derived and the correlations between these and the childhood behavior variables are being computed. So far only preliminary studies have been made.

Certain rather significant correlations, however, have been calculated. For example, those of our group who as children were inclined to "behave in self-gratifying ways, selecting only certain children with whom they would play, and contriving to get others to do what they wanted them to do"—who showed a rather strong *need for belonging* (childhood variable V)—tended to become the "surgent" ones as adults. They tended to score high on adult factor F (*enthusiastic, talkative,* versus *glum, silent*). High scorers on this trait were described by Cattell as *cheerful, responsive, energetic, impulsively kind.* They tended to be initially chosen as leaders, showing "popularity and success" in an immediate group but with "lower performance in long-term, serious undertakings." This correlation was +.60.

Another childhood factor which appeared in our results to relate with some significance to this "happy-go-lucky" adult trait (Cattell, F) was variable XIII. This means that those of our group who as children scored *low* in this factor, thus showing a *lack of concentration,* being *easily distracted* and *"giving up" easily,* and who had to be *urged constantly* in carrying out routine duties tended to become the *cheerful, sociable, humorous* (surgent) ones. The correlations was −.40. Thus it appears that the child behavior patterns which were expressive of those two early dispositions (V and XIII) were precursors of adult "surgency."

Another interesting correlation which has appeared thus far (+.50) showed that those who as children were rated as *socially ascendant, resourceful, original, forceful,* and as *naturally a leader* (factor VIII) tended as adults to rate themselves as *persevering, responsible, conscientious, attentive to people* (adult factor G).

These few relations suggest that it is possible in early childhood to identify behavior dispositions—deep-lying, pervasive tendencies that as such tend to persist and to influence behavior throughout life.

Opposition to Group Approaches in Personality Study

As was indicated earlier, students of personality with different theoretical points of view are often not happy with the group-statistical approach nor with the idea of common traits. The contention is that if every person is really unique, to describe a given person in terms of common traits —traits that are really composites, or distillates from the pooled behavior of many individuals—is *not* to portray his individuality.

The contrast between the two approaches becomes apparent at the very beginning of the study of personality, the point of data compilation. In the case of the common-traits approach, even though the checklist or inventory is filled in with specific reference in each case to a particular child, the items, or the behavior descriptions, in terms of which that child is checked are descriptions of behaviors that have been observed in many children, behaviors common to the population of which that child is a member. They are not specific descriptions of *him*, and with him and only him in mind. Hence, even though many of the items may "fit" him very well and in combination present a profile that is unique, it may well be that the very qualities that are peculiarly his are not at all registered on his checklist. Even though certain significant behavior dispositions in their relative strengths may be expressed quantitatively on the individual's common-traits profile, it probably often happens that other unique behavior dispositions may not appear on the profile. Thus, certain qualitative differences between him and others—the differences that really constitute individuality—may be entirely missed in the common-traits approach.

Idiographic Evaluation

Since our primary interest is in the individual and his development, we attempted to portray our two young personalities idiographically. The procedure described by A. L. Baldwin (1942) was adapted to our situation and to the kinds of data that are available in the developmental records of our twin subjects. Using this procedure the mass of material in each of our two subjects was analyzed in terms of categories and tabulated chronologically.

Personality Portrayals

In terms of the regularly occurring patterns of behavior, feelings, and relations thus revealed in the table of frequencies, the following personality portrayal of Paul emerged:

1. The quality of deliberateness runs consistently through all of Paul's record. At age 20 months the unusually careful and deliberate way in which

he aligned his blocks and placed them in patterns was noted. At age 20 months, also, his speech was described as "slow and deliberate." This speech characteristic was frequently noted throughout the nursery school period. At age 30 months the tester noted that Paul worked "deliberately and persistently" on the tasks presented to him. "He gets so involved in an activity that he can hardly be distracted from his work." His slow and deliberate approach to activities was again noted at age 5 years. When Paul was in the twelfth grade, as a part of our testing program he was asked to sort a set of statements about "self" in a Q-sort test (Chapter 2). At the end of more than an hour. when twice the allotted time had elapsed, he had not finished the task. He was deliberately and critically analyzing each statement from the standpoint of its grammar, ambiguity, and other criteria.

2. The next most requently noted quality in Paul's functioning, particularly during his preschool period, was his need for stability in his relations with his environment. This quality, at times, appeared as rather strong negativism. He rather consistently resisted the morning inspection procedure at nursery school. He tended to resist arbitrary directions from adults which required too sudden (for him) change in activity. He was bothered by the continually changing student personnel in the nursery school. At the beginning of his nursery school experience he resisted "violently" the toileting procedure.

Another indication of this need for stability, or for the feeling of being in control, was his need, even beyond age 4, to have with him constantly his blue blanket from his bed. This had more of the appearance of insecurity than of negativism. Paul was also much disturbed when during the summer, as he was approaching age 4, the backyard of his family home was used as a nursery play yard for (to him) strange children. He resented the children's presence in *his* yard and refused to participate to any extent in their play. Another disturbing factor which upset his need to keep things under control occurred when Paul and his sister were about 4½. Sally and her girl friends excluded him from their play for several months. Paul during this time frequently wanted to stay home to avoid facing the situation. It was stated in the record that Paul during this disturbed period showed more of a "sense of importance" at nursery school on days when Sally was absent with a cold.

3. A third outstanding quality in Paul was his independence and self-sufficiency. Even at age 3 years he was described as having definite ideas of his own for play. At age 4 he chose his own books at the children's section of the library. In nursery school his interests were more in relation to things and materials, and he showed unusual ingenuity in working with materials. He would go ahead with his own ideas, and as other children followed his lead he often became the center of activity. His relations with the other children were good, but he rarely became involved in group play except as

others joined in activities which he initiated. As a club member he often incorporated much dramatic play in the activities in which the others joined and participated.

In most respects the portrayal of Sally obtained from the analysis of her behavioral record contrasted markedly from that of her brother. In certain other areas, however, there was considerable similarity. In terms of the relatedness of the behavioral categories, five clusters appeared.

1. Sally was most frequently described as vivacious, lively, excitable, jestful, and very expressive of pleasure, particularly in relating to and interacting with other children and adults.

2. In her relations with her peers she characteristically took the initiative and usually was the leader, although she could readily join a group-play situation and participate immediately in cooperative play. Sally was usually ready to help a younger playmate in need. She was inclined, however, to be selective as to whom she would play with, and she was quite adept in manipulating the play group, or an individual playmate, toward gaining her own ends.

3. As an individual Sally was realistically competent and independent. She was able relatively efficiently to care for herself in the toilet and washroom. She was spontaneous in her selection of play materials, with a tendency to use a wide variety from day to day. She also exhibited considerable creativity in her use of these materials. She was able to relax effectively during rest periods, and she realistically accepted the morning inspection routine of the nursery school.

4. Sally was oriented toward and interested in people more than material things. She generally was very cordial and talkative with adults, and she enjoyed especially the social aspects of mealtime. She readily developed special affectional attachments to certain of the nursery school teachers, and she was inclined to "play" for their attention and approval.

5. Sally not only showed some dependence upon the attention and approval of the teachers but also some tendency to be jealous of the attention or affection they gave to others, and particularly to her brother. She expressed some hostility toward Paul by delighting in destroying his creative products. She also deliberately excluded Paul from her play with her girl friends.

Clearly, the two sets of characterizations—the common behavior-factor profiles and the individual, qualitative portrayals—are in no way inconsistent or contradictory, and in certain respects they agree quite closely. The idiographic accounts, however, do bring out in each case certain aspects of individuality that the checklist approach could not capture. Idiosyncrasies, such as Paul's need for his blanket or Sally's jealousy of and related hostile feelings toward her brother, add bits of uniqueness to the total picture.

Summary

This chapter has outlined a very broad conception of personality. Personality is simply the "quality or fact" of being a unique person. But the attributes, the traits, the variables which, in unique combination and patterning, give one uniqueness and individuality are myriad. We arbitrarily grouped these variables under four headings: (1) morphological and physical features; (2) abilities that determine the level of effectiveness in personal functioning; (3) incidentally learned patterns of personal and social behavior, including attitudes, beliefs, and prejudices; and (4) generalized behavior dispositions.

These groupings of variables differ widely as to origin, as to their susceptibility to change, and as to the conditions of their development. The environment plays a much greater role in determining individual differences in some characteristics than in others. Differences in external environment, for example, as a rule, have little to do with making some individuals very tall and some very short.

Every individual is also born with a particular temperamental nature. Developmental changes in the expression of that temperament, unlike changes in height, may be greatly influenced by the environment. A basic tendency to be active, to be constantly doing something, for example, is mostly likely to continue to characterize an individual throughout his life, regardless of whether he becomes an evangelist, a business tycoon, or a gangster. Thus the same pattern of original predispositions, in interaction with one sort of socializing environment, might give rise to quite different traits of personality (behavior dispositions) than might have developed had the socializing environment been of a different sort.

One's individuality thus persists throughout life, but its modes of expression may, nevertheless, undergo radical change. The outward manifestations of one's affective tendencies and the specific behavior patterns representing one's broadly generalized behavioral dispositions continue to adapt to changing circumstances and social expectations as one moves through the various levels of physical and personal development. With all the changes in a person's "surface" behavior, which manifestly are changes in personality, he remains basically the same person. He maintains his individuality.

CHAPTER 14

From Dependency toward Autonomy

The objective of this chapter, and the two to follow, is to pull together the various facets of human development and to follow them longitudinally through the complete individual life cycle. Thus far these various aspects of organismic and functional change have been treated separately, and although considerable care has been taken to show their relatedness and interdependence, an integrated review of the course of overall individual development is in order.

This account of developmental change obviously must be in terms of generalities. As we have repeatedly emphasized, every human being is a unique individual in his own right. He is born with his individuality, and that individuality persists throughout his life even though he changes tremendously and in myriads of ways. He is unique in his total pattern of measured degrees and stages achieved at any age level. His "developmental front" is not an even front. As a young child he might be ahead of most other children of his age in walking, for example, and behind in learning to talk or in "cutting" his teeth. The unevenness of his developmental profile is like that of no other child. We are concerned with the development of individuality. First we shall review briefly the determining factors of individuality.

The Origins of Individuality

Old issues in development, for years now dead and abandoned, involved such questions as "Which is more important, heredity or environment?" "Is walking a product of maturation or is it learned?" "Is personality inherited or is it merely an individual expression of the culture?" Such "either-or" questions now seldom occur to students of human development.

There are, nevertheless, strong disciplinary biases in the current literature dealing with personality and human development concerning the *relative* importance of biological and cultural factors. Progress, however, is being made on both fronts, and the mysteries of biological heredity are gradually being unlocked. As we saw in Chapter 2, with modern equipment for technical research the sciences of genetics and biochemistry are making steady progress toward an understanding of the intracellular mechanisms of hereditary control and development. In light of present knowledge, on the other hand, no one would question the essential role of the environment in all aspects and phases of development.

The generally accepted viewpoint, then, is that all development, whether physical or psychological, is the result of the interaction between the organism and its environment.

From the moment of conception there is implicit in the individual a developmental potential and a particular design in terms of which the vital interaction of organism and environment will take place. The nature of this potential and design is determined by the particular combination of hereditary determinants present. The genetic factor determines the nature of and potentiality for organic response to and interaction with the environment. Heredity lays down the overall pattern of development and the individual limits of developmental achievement beyond which the individual cannot pass.

Of equally vital importance is the quality and adequacy of the environment. Obviously, if the environment does not provide the essential stimulation—the necessary nourishment and nurture—for optimum response and interchange, the process of development cannot proceed to the level of greatest potential. The interaction of the individual with his environment are treated in depth in the chapters dealing with functional development.

The Mechanism of Hereditary Endowment

Individuality has its beginnings in the union of the ovum, or egg, and the spermatozoon, or sperm. Each of these original cells, microscopic in size, is made of a material called cytoplasm and a nucleus, or central body. The tiny nucleus of each cell contains 23 minute, active, threadlike structures called chromosomes. Careful study of chromosomes, under the most powerful magnification, has revealed that they differ considerably from each other, each being identifiable in terms of shape and size and each consisting of a great many gelatinous, beadlike structures called "genes" strung closely together. It is estimated that the chromosomes, with their constituent genes, packed within the fantastically small nucleus of the sperm of the father and the ovum of the mother, comprise all the hereditary material from which the individual generates. As the sperm enters the egg the two cells fuse and become a single fertilized ovum with a single nucleus containing 23 matched pairs of chromosomes, or 46 in all. Thus, with the union of the two germ cells two separate lines of heredity come together with a total of some 80,000–120,000 genes, each with its determining potential. The process of the development of a new individual is underway.

> The parent cells have a twofold function in reproduction. Together they initiate the most remarkable and dynamic event in nature: the assembly of a living body out of single molecules of proteins, carbohydrates, and other biochemicals. In addition, the parent cells control the specific design of the body. It is a design that will follow a pattern passed along a chain of inheritance, going back to the biological roots of this family. In a sense each new life actually has no definite beginning. Its existence is inherent in the existence of the parent cells and these, in turn, have arisen from the preceding parent cells. When any two parent cells unite they bring together a blend of the attributes of all ancestors before them. Thus, since all people are descended from a small number of early human beings they are linked by a common heritage [Flanagan, 1962, p. 19].

This subject is treated in detail in Chapter 3.

Environment

The term "environment" is generally used rather loosely to refer to conditions under which human beings live and develop. Recently "the environment" has become a matter of common conversation and popular concern as people generally have been made aware of the growing problems of air, water, and land pollution. They have become generally more concerned about the abandon with which the world's natural resources are being exploited and wasted and the shrinking areas of wilderness are being defaced and littered.

In our present discussion, however, "environment" is given a more limited and precise meaning. It refers more specifically to those conditions, both in the external world and within the organism itself, which are sources of stimulation and motivation and which collectively are regarded as a determining or influencing "factor" in human development. Actually, in this connection the term is used in two rather distinct senses. First, there is the more general reference to the complex of conditions and influences common to a population, or to a particular segment of a population such as a certain age group or a group presumed to be going through a certain phase of development. Environment in such instances refers to the totality of living conditions external to the organism and objectively regarded. Thus we speak of *the* home environment, *the* "impoverished" environment of a particular geographic area, the prenatal environment, the "enriched" environment of a certain nursery school. The reference is to conditions, sources of stimulation common to many.

We also use the term "environment" in a more individualized sense to refer to the particular constellation of conditions and stimuli, internal as well as external, that are actually affecting the development or influencing the behavior of a particular individual at a given time. This is one's *effective* environment. The adequacy, in both the qualitative and the quantitative senses, of the child's food intake or the health care tendered him are important items in his effective environment. Attempts are often made to modify or to enhance a child's learning environment by providing demonstrations or interesting materials for him to manipulate or challenging situations with which he must cope. The lack of adequate and appropriate stimulation of particular "institution" babies that have been studied, when matched with family-reared babies, appears to have been the chief deterrent to their developmental progress. They suffered "stimulus deprivation." Their individual effective environments were inadequate for optimum development. In general, the socialization of a child is a matter of regulating and manipulating his effective environment to bring about desired change.

Interaction

The essential "facts of life" and development have been stated earlier in a number of connections. They, of course, are (1) that every individual begins life as a single cell containing a blueprint of developmental potentialities and a controlling and guiding mechanism essential for their realization, and (2) that from the moment of that beginning in order for life and development to continue there must be a protecting, catalyzing, and nurturant environment. That the processes of development must somehow consist of the "interaction" between these two essential factors is generally assumed. But this interaction process—that is, development—cannot be observed directly, and it is generally not well understood. The explication of its basic nature is a task of biochemistry toward which progress is being made.

But development begins immediately. The minute organism grows and becomes more complex. This means, of course, that the interaction, almost from the beginning, is actually between the *organism* as is and the environment (the organism at any point in time being a product of earlier interaction).

At a more macroscopic level there has been considerable theorizing concerning the nature of the process of interaction between organism and environment. From the strictly stimulus response (S→R) point of view, of course, the role of the organism in the process is hardly a matter of consideration. The response, and the consequent learning, or development, is regarded as the direct result of the stimulus. But as Hebb (1958) and others have insisted, the precise pattern of activity which follows stimulation is not a function of the stimulus alone, but also of what is going on in the constantly changing brain—the "mediating processes." In other words, the input, the stimulus, is modified in its effects by the mediating processes, and the mediating processes are modified by the stimulus. The resulting development, new acquisitions, takes place as it becomes related to or "subsumed" into the already organized but changing "structure." This is roughly what Piaget (1952) means by his term "assimilation."

Piaget has given much consideration to the processes of organism-environment interaction. First, he distinguishes between what he calls "functions," the *processes* of interaction (development), which never change, and "structures" (schemata, patterns, or organizations of behavior), which continually change through the processes of development. He discusses two related processes of interaction (functions): *assimilation* and *accommodation*. Assimilation is the process by which "reality data are treated or modified in such a way as to become incorporated into the structure of the subject" (Piaget and Inhelder, 1969, p. 5). Whenever the organism uses something from the environment and incorporates it, the process of assimilation is in operation. The ingestion of food as it is changed by the organism and is incorporated into the organism is assimilation at the gross physical level. The organism is thus changed. Likewise, stimulus input is modified by the mediating processes underway, and its meaning is assimilated into the cognitive structure, thereby bringing about a change (development).

In *assimilation*, then, the interaction consists of, or results in, a modification of the input and its incorporation into the structure—the physical body, or the "cognitive structure." *Accommodation,* on the other hand, comes about in a situation in which the input, the stimulating object, or problem situation, resists action or manipulation by means of previously established patterns of manipulation, thus making necessary an adaptive change in approach. For example, the infant sitting in his highchair has previously learned, that is, has assimilated the fact, that his rubber ball bounces and rolls when he drops it to the floor. He has enjoyed seeing it bounce and roll many times. He now has before him not his ball but his dish of cereal. He drops it, first presumably with the expectation that it will behave like his ball, but it does something quite different. It "refuses" to fit in with his present cognitive structure. He is likely then to experiment with dishes of cereal—push them off from different places on his table, dropping them from different positions, throwing them with force; but they refuse to behave like his ball. He thus learns the differences in the *properties of objects*. His cognitive structure becomes enhanced through accommodation (adjustment) to the properties of a bowl of cereal. In Piaget's words:

> the child then tries to make all new objects enter into the schemata already acquired and this constant effort to assimilate leads him to discover the resistance of certain objects and the existence of certain properties irreducible to these schemata. It is then that *accommodation* assumes an interest in itself and that it becomes differentiated from assimilation, subsequently the two become more and more complementary.
>
> [Piaget, 1952, p. 276]

As Piaget insists, the processes of interaction—assimilation and accommodation—are "invariant." The processes are the same through the various periods of the life cycle while the "structure," physical and psychological, as we have already seen, changes greatly, continuously, and in many ways. Development is change.

Infancy

The so-called crisis of birth consists of the sudden radical change in total environment to which the neonate must adapt. His living medium has suddenly become radically different. He is no longer enveloped and cradled in relative quiet and darkness in a fluid medium of constant temperature. William James described the probable immediate situation of the newborn infant as one of being caught up in a "big buzzing, blooming confusion" of air currents, pain, pressures, light, and noise. But what is important to his survival is the fact that he reacts in special ways to certain specific stimuli within that confusion, thereby initiating certain physiological functions essential to postnatal existence. He responds, for example, to a slap on the buttocks or to a chilling air current with an inhalation and a gasp, thus initiating independent breathing. In his interactions with this new environment there is both accommodation and assimilation. The human neonate is the most helpless and dependent of all creatures, but he is also possessed with the greatest potentiality and capacity for adjustment and developmental change. The long process of development toward the realization of that potentiality soon gets underway as he thus interacts with his environment.

Early Experience

During the past decade or two much research on the nature of infancy and infant development has been done with both animal and human infants. This has led to a much greater general appreciation of the importance of the infant's environment. Much emphasis is now being placed upon the effects of early experience and stimulation. For example, the work with primates at the University of Wisconsin has demonstrated that infant monkeys, under conditions of social isolation and with a deficiency of sensory stimulation, show a lack of the tendency to explore or to examine objects in the immediate surroundings—behavior which is characteristic of normal monkeys. These deprived animals showed marked ineptness later on as adults in social interaction, particularly in their sexual and parental behavior (Harlow and Harlow, 1969; Suskett, 1965). In general, the evidence from animal research indicates that when an infant does not experience normal contacts and association with his kind it fails to acquire some of the patterns of interaction that are "universal" and characteristic of his kind. In other words, what has been regarded as instinctive and "natural" to a particular species, in certain instances, might better be regarded as "developmental tasks" which must be achieved by the individual at the appropriate times (critical periods) in interaction with others of the species (J. P. Scott, 1962, 1963).

Studies of human infant development generally indicate the crucial importance of early environmental stimulation, particularly with respect to emotional and social development. The early studies of "maternal deprivation" of infants reared in institutions showed that when compared with infants reared by their mothers in the normal family situation there was a marked developmental deficit in the institution children (Goldfarb, 1944, 1945, 1955, Spitz and Wolf, 1946). Bowlby (1951), in his review of these studies, revealed clearly the dire consequences of the lack of interpersonal stimulation that the home-reared baby normally experiences.

Psychoanalytic theory has placed great emphasis upon the importance of the gratification the baby normally experiences as he nurses at his mother's breast. According to theory, emotional ties between mother and child thus become established. It has been further assumed that in this early experience is formed the basis of the capacity to receive and to give love. The research evidence in general, however, indicates that affectional ties are not dependent upon the gratification at the breast of hunger needs. Other kinds of sensory experiences, particularly those from the tactile stimulation of close bodily contact and other tactile and kinesthetic stimulation incidental to normal infant care and handling, are believed to be important in this respect.

So intimately related to this basic "love" interaction between mother and baby as to be another aspect of the same unitary experience is what Erik Erikson (1968) calls a "sense of trust." He regards this experience, engendered as it is in the feeding relationship between mother and baby, as "the cornerstone of a vital personality."

> For the most fundamental prerequisite of mental vitality, I have already nominated *a sense of trust* which is a pervasive attitude toward oneself and the world derived from the experiences of the first year of life. By "trust" I mean an essential trustfulness of others as well as a fundamental sense of one's own trustworthiness. [1968, p. 96]

This "sense" arises from the fact that the neonate's "inborn and more or less coordinated ability to take in by mouth meets the mother's more or less coordinated ability and intention to feed him and to welcome him." The infant must learn to coordinate his getting with his mother's way of giving, "as she develops and coordinates her means of giving." To the extent to which this coordination takes place, along with the affective quality of the interaction, the baby's sense of trust is established.

The level and the quality of the mother's ability to fulfill her part in this vital interaction is dependent upon a number of factors, such as her personal development, her experiences during pregnancy and delivery, her feelings generally about babies, and her attitudes toward nursing and caring. The baby's congenital temperamental nature, as we have seen, can also be an important factor here.

At any rate, the establishment of this sense of trust is regarded as of far-reaching importance.

> But in thus getting what is given, and in learning to get somebody to do for him what he wishes to have done, the baby also develops the necessary groundwork "to get to be" the giver—that is, to identify with her and eventually to become a giving person. [Erikson, 1968, p. 90]

> It must be said, however, that the amount of trust derived from earliest infantile experience does not seem to depend on absolute quantities of food or demonstrations of love, but rather on the quality of the maternal relationship. Mothers create a sense of trust in their children by that kind of administration which in quality combines sensitive care of the baby's individual needs and a firm sense of personal trustworthiness within the trusted framework of their community's life style.
> [Erikson, 1968, p. 103]

Other writers also have emphasized the importance of the quality of infant care—of the mother being "warmly dependable" and understanding in the care and nurturance of her baby (I. D. Harris, 1959). When such quality is lacking in infantile experience a basic sense of distrust can be engendered. This may be expressed in individual personality as a tendency to withdraw from social contacts and to be insecure, suspicious, and generally unhappy.

Studies also show that general "mothering" and the physical and emotional nurturance thus received results in more marked social responsiveness than is demonstrated by babies who are deprived of such special mothering (Rheingold, 1956). It has been shown in Russian studies of infant care that the behaviors of the adult caretaker *incidental* to the process of alleviating the baby's hunger are the crucial factors in stimulating positive responses. Such behaviors as talking, smiling, and facial expressions, rather than the actual alleviation of hunger, stimulate smiling and positive emotional responses in the infant (Kistyakovskaya, 1965).

Infant Capabilities

Social change—changes in vital problem areas of national and overall social concern in recent years—has had a marked influence upon trends and areas of research in developmental psychology. Demands for social and racial "equality," for example, have stimulated much reexamination of long-standing theories about the nature of mental ability and the factors which underlie differences in children of different social and racial groups in their readiness to meet and cope with school demands and expectations. Such group differences have long been observed. The unresolved question as to the origin and source of these differences has been a factor in the shift in research interest to the study of infancy. There is general agreement among researchers in infant development that young infants possess considerably more competence than was formerly believed.

Congenital Equipment

Challenged by the current need to know the origin and source of group differences in cognitive ability, psychologists became interested more than ever before in what the human infant is like at birth. With what "standard equipment" does he come? And especially, what is the functional level of this congenital equipment and how does it change with time?

The traditional view, of course, was that during early infancy, the period of complete helplessness, the child was too immature even to learn. His functional development was thought to be entirely dependent upon biological maturation. And even though he was equipped at birth with sense organs, they were completely nonfunctional at first. The tiny organism must first become "ready" through the process of biological maturation before he can learn to use his senses.

Perceptual Development

The fact that learning, the effect of exercise, is a continuous aspect of development from the very beginning has already been emphasized. Infancy is a time of rapid learning. But recent and ongoing infant research has shown that infants are much more competent in the use of their sensory equipment than was formerly thought. Researchers are now interpreting their results to mean that perception does not develop through a "process of construction," that is, that the infant does not gradually build an ordered perceptual world through repeated and varied sensory experience, but rather that "infants can in fact register most of the information an adult can register" immediately (Bower, 1966). Visual discrimination interpreted as perceptual ability was found in very young infants in the fact that they exhibited a "preference" for (fixated their eyes for longer periods of time upon) certain visual stimulus patterns (Fantz, 1958, 1963). It was further found that an infant "at any age" can discriminate visually between solid and nonsolid objects, and that by the second week of life "an infant expects a seen object to have tactile consequences" as it is made to approch his face (Bower, 1971). From the results of many ingenious experiments Bower reached the conclusion that "in man there is a primitive unity of the senses with visual variables specifying tactile consequences, and that this primitive unity is built into the structure of the human nervous system" (1971, p. 32). This is to say, of course, that the awareness of the properties and attributes of "solid" objects, including their "tactile consequences," does not have to be acquired (learned) through experience, but is a congenital ability—that such awareness is immediate and unlearned.

This, of course, is contrary to much of the earlier accumulated evidence concerning this basic cognitive process which we call perception. Ausubel (1958) quite clearly states the more widely accepted point of view:

> Since all perceptual and cognitive phenomena deal by definition with the *contents of processes of awareness*, they cannot always be inferred from overt behavior. Behavior, for example, frequently reflects the organism's capacity for experiencing differentially the differential properties of stimuli. Nevertheless, since all differential psychological experience preceding or accompanying behavior does *not* necessarily involve a content or process of awareness, we cannot always consider it perceptual or cognitive in nature. Several examples may help to elucidate this distinction.
>
> We have previously shown that a young infant will follow a patch of color across a multicolored background. Will cease crying when he hears his mother's footsteps, and will respond differentially to various verbal commands. Conditioning experiments during infancy also show that the child is able to "differentiate" between different sizes, colors and shapes of objects and between pitches of sound. Does this constitute evidence of genuine perception . . .?
>
> . . . it is reasonable to suppose that much of the sensory experience impinging on the infant is too diffuse, disorganized and uninterpretable to constitute the raw material of perception and cognition despite evidence of differential response to stimulation. Clear and meaningful contents of awareness presupposes some minimal interpretation of incoming sensory data in the light of an existing ideational framework. In the first few

months of life not only is the experiential basis for this framework lacking, but the necessary neuroanatomic and neurophysiologic substrate for cortical functioning is also absent. [pp. 544–545]

It is quite clear from the foregoing that this difference in viewpoint is very largely one of semantics and interpretation. The currently active researchers in the field of infant behavior and capabilities have contributed and are contributing much to the general understanding of early human development. Because of their findings the whole concept of "readiness" to learn, for example, has undergone drastic revision. However, the question of whether young infants have the unlearned ability to perceive depends upon what one means by the term "perception." In the traditional and universally accepted definition of the term, perception is a cognitive (a *knowing*) process involving the conscious awareness of the properties and attributes of an object or a situation, which can only have been gained from previous experience. Such an act, or process, of "knowing" is not congenital.

If, on the other hand, the term "perception" is construed to mean simply sensory discrimination, then in *that sense* infants may be said to perceive almost from the time of birth. Even Bower's finding, interesting as it is, that a baby will make protective responses to the rapid approach toward his face of a "solid object" does not necessarily involve a conscious process of awareness (an actual apprehension of danger) of the "tactile consequences" of the approaching object. It can mean nothing more than a protective, inborn reflex to a sensory stimulus.

In any event, the neonate *does* react to sensory stimulation, and the fact that he does something means that whatever he does brings about developmental change. The structural unit involved in what he does, simple as it may be, is exercised. Change (learning) takes place. As Piaget observed, during the first weeks of life the baby exercises his various congenital sensorimotor schemata. Their functioning becomes stronger and more precise. Through exercise his seeing mechanism functions with ever-increasing clearness, and things touched and grasped become things seen. He thus begins to experience the *properties* of objects. His experience of his noisy, brightly colored rattle in his mouth is different from his experience of his fist or his thumb in his mouth. Through such experience he is "coming to know" about things and their properties as different from himself. The basis of his ability to discriminate cognitively between what is a part of himself and what is not himself, the beginning of self-awareness, presumably is thus gained early in his experience. Thus development is an integrated process. The baby's cognitive development (coming to know) is not something separate and apart. It is dependent upon, and indeed is an aspect of, the development of the reaching-prehensile-manipulation pattern. The affective experiences resulting from failure and frustration, or from success in grasping and handling result in changes in attitudes and emotional patterns. Thus the infant develops cognitively, behaviorally, and emotionally from his simple sensory experiences and his own overt responses to them. Early infancy is exceedingly important in overall personal and social development.

Development in all its aspects proceeds at a rapid pace during infancy. Even as early as 2½ months the baby is especially responsive to the human face. He shows an increasing need for association, to be with others. By age 4 or 5 months his "affiliative" need is obvious. He distinguishes between familiar and unfamiliar people. He definitely recognizes his mother and is likely to demand more and more of her attention.

Achievement

During the earlier period of his complete dependency, as we have seen, the baby has enjoyed what has been referred to as "volitional independence" (Ausubel, 1958). What he "demanded" he usually got. He displayed what looks like a "sense of omnipotence." But as he gains more and more ability to interact with his environment and to do for himself there is a concomitant change in the character of his relations with those about him. There is a growing degree of interaction, behavioral and affiliative, and a lessening of demand on his part, and subservience on the part of others.

By the middle of his first year the baby has gained considerable command over his body. He can roll over from back to stomach and can sit up momentarily. By this time also he is likely to have learned to crawl.

Recent work on the perceptual and learning capabilities of infants suggest that by the end of the first six months an interesting aspect of visual perception is clearly evident. In one experiment it was found that 6-month-old babies could not be prevailed upon to crawl across an area covered with heavy glass arranged so as to give the illusion of a drop-off to a dangerous depth. The infants apparently perceived the drop-off or "cliff" effect, which meant danger to them (Gibson and Walk, 1960).

The second half of the baby's first year is a period of signal behavioral achievements. There is a great deal of handling and manipulation of objects within his reach. He seems now to grasp things, not just for the sake of grasping. His actions are more "centered on a result produced in the environment . . . the means are beginning to be differentiated from the ends" (Piaget, 1952, p. 152). He begins now to show some anticipation of the consequences of his acts—the beginning of "intentionality." He can also use his hands more expertly, both at the same time.

By his eighth month the baby is able to respond to more than one person at the same time. He likes to be "bounced" and handled, but may easily become overexcited. He vocalizes happily to himself, imitates sounds, and is beginning to respond to his name and to some other words such as "no."

By the time he is a year old, simple patterns of manipulation have become coordinated into more complex acts performed with the definite aim of attaining a specific end. He thus puts to work *by intention* a series of single schemata now coordinated for a new purpose. The "accommodation" aspect of his adaptations is especially apparent as he definitely begins to differentiate self from not self and is able to search, to a limited degree, for a "vanished object." He also shows evidence of an implicit conception of causality. He appears to foresee events that are independent of his own acts.

In his social responsiveness the baby can now play "peek-a-boo" and "patty cake." He may be saying "ma ma" and "da da" with definite reference to his parents. He notices differences in his mother's tone of voice when she approves or disapproves of his behavior.

By this time also he may be beginning to toddle about. He is now in a transition phase of development. He is moving on from his babyhood.

Infantile Individuality

During this transition phase the integratedness of development and the interdependence of some of its signal aspects become especially evident. For example, both locomotion and speech learning are major developmental tasks of this time. Both are especially important to the child's general cognitive and social development. In many cases it appears that two tasks of such prodigious proportions cannot, in the child's economy, be given full attention at the same time. One of them for a period gains preeminence and spurts ahead while the other lags behind. The child may seem to be concentrating on learning to walk while his speech learning is neglected (Jersild, 1946).

We should at this point be reminded again that every infant even at birth is a person in his own right. Regardless of whether our focus is upon the relatively profound dependency and helplessness of the human infant or whether it is upon his remarkable level of capability which is only currently being fully recognized, we realize that babies are not all alike. Each is by genetic endowment unique, and with his individual pattern of congenital potentialities and temperamental inclinations he is born into a family situation which is like no other. His original individuality, moreover, is likely to become enhanced as it interacts with his effective environment. We have noted how the child's realization of his potential for cognitive development is dependent largely upon the quality and adequacy of the stimulation he receives, and how his achievement of a basic sense of trust, together with a basic experience of a reciprocal love relationship, for example, is dependent upon the manner and the readiness with which his need and ability to take nourishment at his mother's breast is met by his mother's ability and dependability in giving him that nourishment and satisfaction. Human individuality begins at the very beginning.

Toddlerhood

With the achievement of independent locomotion the child's effective environment becomes greatly expanded. As he moves about he is confronted moment by moment with a new array of objects which to him are exciting and attractive—things to be reached for, grasped, and manipulated. Without experience he has no basis for judgment as to what may be grasped, mouthed and manipulated, thrown down, and what may not be touched. This he must learn. It is one of the earliest learning problems in his socialization. He learns these and many other lessons of conduct through interaction with the human aspect of his environment, particularly his parents.

The effective environment of the toddler, thus, has rather precipitously become much more complex. It is two-sided. There is the world of things, which holds much promise of the gratification of an intrinsic tendency within him to seek stimulation, to "take in" his world. The other aspect of his environment, the human side, has suddenly become repressive, limiting, frustrating. In his interactions with this two-sided environment, the child learns something of the nature of reality and his own relation to it. His ego develops.

A Shift in Bodily Locus of Gratification

During the dependency of early infancy, as we have seen, the baby's psychological life presumably consists largely of the experiences and satisfactions associated with food taking, the cutaneous and kinesthetic experiences of being handled and cuddled, the relief from hunger, and the primary pleasure of sucking. This is the "oral stage" described by Freud, a time when life is centered in oral satisfaction and related experiences.

With the achievement of locomotor freedom and his expanded perceptual-motor capacity the child's sources of gratification also become broadened. By this time the child ordinarily has been weaned from the breast or bottle with the consequent loss of much of the oral satisfaction he formerly experienced. At the same time his mother's increasing concern for cleanliness in relation to his eliminative functions, with her bathing, diapering, and other "caring" procedures connected with them, tends to center the child's attention upon those activities and the sensory pleasures derived from such stimulation of the anal region. The eliminative processes themselves and the relief they give are primary sources of pleasure. These various factors in the child's experience conspire during this period of toddlerhood to give the anal region precedence over the mouth as the main bodily locus of gratification. This period, in terms of the Freudian stages of development, is the anal stage.

The Drive To Explore

Perhaps what most characterizes the toddler child is his drive to explore his environment. His concentration in this reaching-grasping and manipulating activity is most intense. His approach to objects within his reach is one of "irresponsible impulsiveness." In this need to explore and manipulate he demands freedom to do just that—freedom to exercise his developing "executive independence," the ability to do for himself. With seeming abandon he moves from place to place grasping and manipulating objects, sensing their properties. He now sees things from new perspectives. He gains new sensory experiences of them. Some things yield readily to his grasp, allowing him to smell and taste them and more fully to "come to know" (assimilate) them. Other things resist his pull upon them. He must adapt his behavior differently toward these objects (accommodation). Thus in such varied experiences an important aspect of perceptual development, which Piaget calls "the elaboration of the object," is rapidly taking place.

The child's demand for free access to his surroundings, however, often leads to conflict. At his level of maturity the child is not ready for such free and complete access. In our Western culture his surroundings must somehow be protected from his impulsivity. Restraint of some kind is usually resorted to. His freedom is curtailed and his "socialization" gets underway.

Emotional and Social Development

As those about him become restrictive, frustrating, even pain-inflicting, the child learns new lessons about relations and interactions with others. He must also revise his sense of self. In a sense he is in a crisis situation. His former "sense of omnipotence" is being frustrated. Some children react with the commonly observed "negativism" of toddlerhood. He too says "no no," and anger tantrums are not uncommon.

During this conflictful period of transition from babyhood, the child is also likely to fluctuate from time to time between a strong bid for independence and a clinging dependency. At times he may need the security of being "loved" and cuddled like a baby. It is important that his earlier acquired sense of trust in his environment not be impaired here. Dependability and consistency of treatment, with love and with respect for his individuality on the part of parents, is important during this period of socialization.

Toilet Training

In Chapter 6 the eliminative functions were discussed in some detail. The gaining and exercise of control of elimination is generally one of the most difficult developmental tasks of the early preschool period. Children differ widely in the ease of its achievement and the time required. This is frequently a problem of great concern for parents.

The toddler in his preoccupation with things outside himself is developmentally unready to show any concern or to assume the least responsibility in relation to the time or place for the exercise of his eliminative functions. For him these functions operate automatically, as they have done from the beginning, under the control of the autonomic division of the nervous system. The child is completely oblivious of the concern of his parents for the maintenance of standards of cleanliness and order in the home. And, of course, parents usually take this for granted. Accordingly, suitable provisions are made in the way of diapering and clothing.

But soon the problem of elimination training becomes an uppermost concern of the mother. There is no set time when such training should begin. Knowing when the child is ready physically and psychologically is most difficult. To begin training procedures too early is likely only to prolong the process. One can only be alert to the signs of readiness which are not easy to recognize. Physical readiness is a matter of being able to exercise sufficient muscular control to stop natural release. When the child is able to communicate by signal—by word or sound or look—that there is need to eliminate, and when he begins to show his ability to understand and accept the suggestions of adults, he may then be regarded as psychologically ready to learn voluntarily to control and to regulate these functions.

The very erratic course of progress made by our subject, Sally, in gaining night-time control is shown in Figure 6.1. This child was reared according to the *"self*-regulation" regime. The regulation of her eliminative processes as well as her feeding schedule were largely self-initiated rather than imposed upon her from without. According to the record, no "training" of any sort had been initiated at age 18 months. At age 27 months, although she still wet her bed nightly, Sally had gained good daytime control. Although she was "taken" periodically and was encouraged to indicate her need, no pressure was ever used and the only reward she received for her successful self-regulation were the words "good girl." Sally's record illustrates dramatically the wide individual variation that must be expected in the achievement of voluntary sphincter control; ultimately, when success is achieved, it may occur rapidly.

Feeding

As we earlier noted (Chapter 6), the feeding of the young preschooler is often a "problem area" for parents. It is an activity in which the child shows strongly his need to be independent. Because of the usual "mess" the child makes in his efforts to do for himself, and also because of the parent's need to insure the proper amount of food intake, the parent too often "takes over." Thus the child is denied the fun of self-feeding. He is likely to lose interest in the whole feeding procedure.

Feeding problems are usually created. Feeding time is another situation in which the interaction between the child and his parents can range from a happy and positive experience to one fraught with emotional conflict and frustration for both. The importance of the quality of toddler-mother interaction was emphasized in the preceding chapter.

The Preschool Child

There is no definite age or point of development separating toddlerhood from the following three years, which we call the "preschool period." Nevertheless, there are certain distinctive developments, certain changes in the prevailing interests and activities and in the nature and quality of child-parent relations, and related problems through which the child works, which particularly characterize the later years before he enters school. It is a time of great importance in the child's social and emotional development.

Physical Growth

The preschool period should not be regarded as a "stage." It is, rather, a span of time, covering roughly the third, fourth, and fifth years of life, during which rapid developmental progress continues to take place. Physically, the rate of growth—increase in overall body size, as measured by units of size gained per unit of time, although rapid, is gradually decelerating (see Figure 4.3). In terms of actual measurements, at the end of his second year the child is most likely to measure 37 or 38 inches in height and to weigh about 33 pounds. Three years later the averages are around 46 inches in height and 45 to 46 pounds in weight.

Motor Development

In terms of overt motor behavior there is generally a vast difference between the 3-year-old and the 6-year-old. At the end of his first year of upright locomotion the child's walking is still not a "thing of ease and vigor." However, he is on the verge of a period of great achievement in skills involving both pairs of limbs. Soon he apparently comes no longer to need to consciously direct and control his walking as such. He can forget that he is doing the walking. He now walks to *get* someplace or to *do* something.

His eye-hand coordination becomes more precise, and a great many skills, both manual and locomotor, are developed.

Cognitive Development

Inseparable from the achievement of the skills for the control of the body and its parts in relation to the things and the conditions of the environment quite obviously is the acquisition of knowledge (cognition) about those things and conditions. Especially during the periods of development with which we are concerned in this chapter, the development of motor skills and cognitive development are, in a real sense, "one of a piece." A motor skill is the ability to manage effectively the body and its parts in relation to the environment. This ability involves the awareness of the body and its limitations, as well as a *knowledge* of the nature of the environment —the objects and conditions with which the skill is concerned. Knowing an object comes through its sensing and manipulation, and as that knowledge grows, more and more proficiency in bodily management develops for its further examination and manipulation. Thus the child's coming to know about the world about him (cognitive development) and the development of the motor abilities and skills in dealing with it are actually one and the same process. As we study separately one by one the various facets of development we tend to lose sight of the unity, the integrated nature of human development. Even at age 3 the child is usually well along in what Piaget calls the "period of concrete operations." He is rapidly learning words and their use in speech. He can manipulate word symbols that represent the environment about him and thus communicate with others. His cognitive processes are still "preoperational," however. He is incapable of conceptual thought. During the latter portion of his preschool years the child's thinking is *intuitive* in nature in the sense that it is still lacking in logical analysis. It is based upon immediate, unanalyzed impressions of the objective situation. It is dominated by subjective perceptual judgments. For example, when confronted with two like glasses filled to the same level with water he will correctly observe that each contains the same amount of water. But after he has observed one of the glasses being emptied into a taller, slenderer glass, he will now say that the tall, slender glass contains more water than the other. His judgment is not a logical one based upon observed relations and related events. It is a prelogical schematization of perceptual data, an incomplete intellectual construction. The child at this level is not aware of his own mental processes. He does not think about his own thoughts. He "acts *only* with a view toward achieving the goal; he does not ask himself why he succeeds" (Inhelder and Piaget, 1958, p. 6). Development through this intuitive period, however, leads to the threshold of operational functioning.

Social and Emotional Adjustments

The preschooler becomes more and more observant of the activities of those about him. He notes differences and makes comparisons between individuals of different ages and between the sexes. He tries to comprehend the various roles people play in life and in imagination "anticipates" his own roles and areas of future functioning. The little boy becomes clearly aware that he is a boy and will become a man, and the girl is equally conscious of her role and her destiny as a female.

The child at this age is likely to become more or less preoccupied with that area of behavior. He may become especially curious and imaginative. He may also experience special genital excitability. But as Erikson points out:

This "genitality" is, of course, rudimentary, a mere promise of things to come; often it is not particularly noticeable. If not specifically provoked into precocious manifestation by especially seductive practices or by pointed prohibitions and threats of "cutting it off" or special customs such as sex play in groups of children, it is apt to lead to no more than a series of peculiarly fascinating experiences which soon become frightening and pointless enough to be repressed. [1968, p. 16]

By the time the child is 3 years old, however, in addition to what he has experienced in the process of socialization, much human behavior, personal, interpersonal, and emotional, has transpired before his eyes and in his hearing. He has "incidentally" observed a variety of emotional interaction between his parents and other family members. And the things he experiences and observes in his home are what family living and its relationships *mean* and will continue to mean to him. Normally the child has become strongly "attached" to both his parents. By this time the little boy is beginning to identify with his father, the little girl with her mother. Whatever the child has observed in the behavior of his model tends to have positive meaning for him and he tends to emulate it. He wants to "be like Daddy."

But his love for his mother is said to begin to undergo a change in quality during this period. In terms of psychoanalytic theory, as was noted particularly in Chapter 12, the child at this time is entering the phallic stage in his psychosexual development. He is becoming enmeshed in the so-called "Oedipal situation" in which he is said to become a rival of his father for the erotic love of his mother. His father, the only obstacle to his complete possession of his mother, is very large and powerful, hence the child wishes his father's death. Such unworthy wishes bring feelings of guilt and fear. "Castration anxiety" may now beset him—a fear of retaliation by his powerful rival. The resolution of this intolerable situation comes about through repression and a strong identification with his father—becoming like father means gaining "fatherly privileges."

The Role of Conscience

Presumably the preschool child would already have developed conscience (Erikson 1968, p. 119). The socialization process has been, to varying degrees, effective. The child would probably keenly realize that the feelings and the wishes he is experiencing during the Oedipal crisis are contrary to his parents' teachings about "right and wrong," what is "evil" and what is "good," and he may become frightened by his own thoughts and feelings. Erikson (1968) regards conscience as the "great governor of initiative" ("initiative" is his descriptive term for the phallic phase):

The child, we said, not only feels afraid of being found out, but he also fears the "inner voice" of self-observation, self-guidance, and self-punishment, which divides him radically within himself; a new and powerful estrangement. This is the ontogenetic corner stone of morality.

For the conscience of the child can be primitive, cruel, and uncompromising, as may be observed in instances where children learn to constrict themselves to the point of overall inhibition; where they develop an obedience more literal than the one the parent wishes to exact; or where they develop deep regressions and lasting resentments because the parents themselves do not seem to live up to the conscience which they have fostered in the child. One of the deepest conflicts in life is caused by hate for a parent who served initially as the model and the executor of the conscience, but who was later found trying to "get away with" the very transgressions which the child no longer tolerates in himself. [p. 119]

Individuality among Preschool Children

Earlier in this chapter the obvious fact was emphasized that even though human beings possess many traits and characteristics in common, children at birth vary widely in the strength and intrusiveness with which these common features manifest themselves. Hence in his total patterning and combination, each infant at birth is unique. He is an *individual,* a person in his own right, different from every other. There was also the reminder that each and every infant, with his congenital uniqueness and with a great potential for development, enters a parental situation, an overall effective environment, which is also unique, and that through the interaction of these two uniquely patterned factors development in all its aspects immediately gets underway.

What happens as the various behavioral features and predispositions with which the baby is born develop depends in each instance upon such factors as its relative strength, kinds and degrees of environmental nurturance or neglect, and pressure or discouragement it receives, particularly during the period of infancy and early childhood. The child continues to be a unique person, but the eventual patterning of his individuality appears to be a matter of development. A child with a congenital predisposition to be highly active physically and with good potentiality for mental development, for example, could be ready to enter school at age 5 or 6 as a very capable beginner, with self-confidence, spontaneity, and full readiness to meet the expectations and cope with the demands of the school situation. However, with a different kind of care and handling, perhaps with many restrictions upon his freedom, vigor, and spontaneity of expression, this same child could have been entering school with limited ability to act on his own initiative or to be readily disposed to hostility and aggression when frustrated or when things do not go according to his expectations and therefore not well fitted for the new experiences of school.

The determining factor in many aspects of personal, social, and emotional development during this early period, then, appears to be the general, predominant quality of the emotional interaction between parent and child. Whatever the direction of development any of the child's congenital predispositions may take, the evidence suggests that by the end of the preschool period his basic personality structure—his individuality—is pretty well modeled and established.

The Period of Elementary School Attendance

The descriptive term "latency" is often used to designate the period of elementary school attendance, a span of about eight years. In most areas of development, however, a great deal of change takes place. As is true of all the segments into which we arbitrarily divide the years from birth to adulthood, this is a time of marked and steady development. Generally speaking, it is in no sense a stage of latent or arrested development.

Physical Development

The only suggestion of latency during these years is, of course, in the physical growth of the reproduction system. As was noted in Chapter 4, there is much diversity and change in the nature and rate of growth in the various tissues and organ systems of the body (Fig. 4.2). In overall body growth, however, this period, roughly ages 5–12 years, is one of steady progress with relatively little change in rate and with no significant difference between boys and girls in either height or weight. Height as a rough average, with much individual variation, at 5 years is about 43 inches. At age 12 the average is in the neighborhood of 59 inches—an average gain of roughly 6 inches. In weight the average at age 5 is near 42 pounds. At age 12 the average is about 87 pounds, more than double the weight at the beginning of the period. At age 12 the girls are beginning to take the lead in physical growth.

Motor Skills of the School Years

The elementary school years are the *physically active* years. The child is interested in the use of his body and in the exercise of the many specific bodily coordinations and skills that he has already acquired. It is a period when toys and tools are of relatively little importance. Total bodily activities, rather than those requiring the finer muscular coordinations, are preferred. Vigorous activities are more effective in providing release of the child's abounding energy during this period: running, jumping, climbing, swimming, bicycle riding, and "stunting" of various kinds are typical activities, varying in form and detail, of course, from culture to culture.

The element of daring is a common feature, particularly in prepuberal play activities. Children during this period are concerned with little more than their status among their peers, which they enhance by achieving greater motor skills and by performing stunts and acts that require daring and courage. They challenge one another in such activities as walking high fences, climbing and swinging, performing on the high bar or the trapeze. As yet they are not at all concerned with the general problem of achieving status as an autonomous member of adult society.

There is a steady and rapid development of the more complex gross motor skills, particularly from age 9 years to 12 years. A great variety of skills involving agility and precise, large-scale muscular coordination are features of play at these ages.

Also characteristic of the play activities of school-age children are the more formal games involving gross motor skills. Gutteridge (1939) studied the development of the skills involved in such games as baseball. She found that although children begin practicing throwing at age 2 or 3, it is not until they have reached 5½ or 6 years of age that the majority (75–85 percent) of children can throw a ball well. Throwing a ball, of course, is a complicated act. Gesell *et al.* (1940) analyzed the process of throwing:

> Throwing involves visual localization, stance, displacement of bodily mass, reaching, release, and restoration of static equilibrium. Skill in throwing a ball requires a fine sense of static and dynamic balance, accurate timing of delivery and release, good eye-hand coordination, and appropriate functioning of the fingers, as well as the arms, trunk, head, and legs, in controlling the trajectory of the ball. [pp. 84–85]

It is during the preteen years, however, that throwing skill, along with catching, fielding, batting, and the other fine points of the game of baseball, are perfected. Team games requiring a rather high degree of motor skill constitute an important aspect of life during this period. Girls frequently participate with the boys in certain of these games, often acquiring skills comparable to those of boys. Govatos (1959), for example, found that on the average, at 10 years of age, boys did not differ significantly from girls in such motor skills as the jump and reach, standing broad jump, 25-yard dash, underhand ball throw for distance, and accuracy of ball throw. Only on such tests as involved superior strength in arms and legs, such as soccer kick for distance and ball throw for distance, were the boys found to be significantly superior to the girls.

It is during these preadolescent years, however, that sex cleavage generally is most pronounced. Blair and Burton (1951) describe this apparent sex antagonism:

> The apparent antagonism between boys and girls at this age is one of the most commonly observed characteristics of childhood. Parents and teachers have long recognized an inordinate amount of teasing between the sexes in the upper elementary grades as well as the almost complete exclusion of the opposite sex from the other's play groups. . . .
>
> Although this teasing and antagonism usually appears about equally reciprocal, there is some indication that it is more pronounced in boys. On the basis of her observation Zachry (1940) notes that girls of this age spend

most of their time with girls of their own age. Often, however, they seem to be doing so less of choice than of necessity. If they assert that boys are horrid or nasty, their scorn does not always ring quite true. It is less convincing than the aloofness or teasing with which the young boy meets them; more often than not it is a mode of self defense or retaliation.

[pp. 34–35]

Boys, nevertheless, recognize playing skill, and in spite of any tendency they may show generally to reject girls from their company, they often welcome a good girl ballplayer on their team.

Fine Motor Coordinations

During these middle years, great strides are also made in the development of the more finely coordinated muscular skills. The schoolroom becomes an important segment of the child's environment. It is the business of the school, among other things, to see that the child acquires some degree of proficiency in such essential skills as reading, writing, music, and other arts.

The complicated process of learning to see objects and to discriminate fine differences, as we have seen, requires time. Reading from the printed page is a highly complex and difficult psychomotor skill which is acquired in varying degrees of proficiency during elementary school years.

The companion skill of handwriting, likewise, is acquired at many levels of proficiency. Handwriting involves a complicated pattern of learned muscular coordinations. The muscles of the shoulder and wrist develop very rapidly during the early school years, but those of the fingers and hand used in writing develop more slowly. Writing is one of the skills in which both bodily maturation and practice are important factors in its achievement. It is but one of the many finely coordinated psychomotor skills achieved during this period.

Cognitive Functioning

During this seven- or eight-year period the cognitive aspect of this total functional development, when focused upon specifically, is prodigious. By virtue of this total development the child continues to function cognitively at progressively higher levels of effectiveness. As we have already noted, he reaches school age (5 or 6 years) with a well-established ability to use symbols to represent familiar objects and situations.

A symbol is something which, in a particular culture, has come to stand for something else. The former "something," the signifier, may be a word heard or spoken, or in visual form a written or printed word, letter, number notation, and so on. The "something" for which the symbol stands, the significate, may be a familiar object or class of objects, situations, or relations. Symbols, then, are names or labels for concepts. They become invested with representational value by repeated association, in each case, with whatever they come to stand for in perceptual experience.

It will be recalled from our earlier discussion of the different "modes of representation" in thinking (Chapter 11) that the preverbal child often uses his own concrete acts to represent objects and their functions. His first signifiers are not words. They are his private symbols. "Shaking his legs represents the bassinet fringe; laying down his head, grasping the blanket, and sucking the thumb represent going to sleep; opening and closing his mouth represents opening and closing a match box" (J. L. Phillips, Jr., 1969, p. 57).

But now at age 5 years many of the child's representations have become internalized. Sensory images can represent absent objects and past activities, and word symbols are used with facility as signifiers. This ability to manipulate word symbols is a feature of the school-age period (Piaget's period of concrete operations) which distinguishes it from the earlier preverbal period. The 5-year-old can now think with much greater facility.

But the 5-year-old thinks in concrete rather than in abstract terms. He is as yet incapable of analyzing and synthesizing, of rationally solving problems mentally. His thinking is in terms of representations of actual events and activities as he actually perceives them and participates in them.

> 1. The child is perceptually oriented; he makes judgments in terms of how things look to him. Piaget has shown that perceptual judgment enters into a child's thinking about space, time, number, and causality. It is only as the child goes beyond his perceptions to perform displacements upon the data in his mind that conservation appears.
>
> 2. The child centers on one variable only, and usually the variable that stands out visually; he lacks the ability to coordinate variables.
>
> 3. The child has difficulty in realizing that an object can possess more than one property, and that multiplicative classifications are possible. The operation of combining elements to form a whole and then seeing a part in relation to the whole has not yet developed, and so hierarchical relationships cannot be mastered. [Stendler, 1965, p. 332]

This concreteness, this rigid adherence in his thinking to perceived sequences of events in experience, does not permit the 5-year-old to *reverse* the sequence. He cannot as yet "return to the point of origin" in his thinking. For example, if he is asked whether he has a brother he might answer "yes, his name is Jimmy." Then if asked whether Jimmy has a brother, he is likely to answer "no." His thinking progresses in an irreversible direction just as the events in his experience do. This is "preoperational thought."

As his cognitive development proceeds, however, he soon overcomes such rigid irreversibility, as well as a relative lack of "conservation" in his thinking. Even as a 7-year-old the child can "retrace" to some degree occurrences in the reverse direction in his thinking. He can, for example, judge the *quantity* of liquid to be unchanged when he sees that although the level of the liquid rises when poured into a thinner glass container, the width of the column decreases. His thinking is still concrete but more "operational" in Piaget's terms; he can manipulate representations—images and word symbols—of "concrete" objects and events in his thinking.

The child continues to live and function mentally largely in terms of actual objects, events, and activities throughout this period of "middle childhood," but with ever-increasing facility. These "concrete operations" establish a foundation for logical thinking, for "formal operations" as he approaches adolescence. But as a prepubescent he is not yet ready to be concerned with problems that require conceptual thinking.

Emotional and Social Adjustments

By the time a child is old enough to enter school his parents ordinarily have already done a fairly thorough job of "socializing" him, for better or for worse. As we have noted, his basic behavior dispositions have become largely shaped. His individuality has thus become established. And even though he may have developed certain unpleasant or difficult emotional patterns and behavioral tendencies, as a general rule the 5- or 6-year-old is a relatively comfortable individual to live with.

It was noted above that with respect to one aspect of the child's physical maturation—the development of his reproductive system—the term "latency" is applicable. In other areas of development, both physical and psychological, progress is steady and substantial. However, there appears to be less surgency in his sex interests during this period as compared with either the earlier period or the puberal period to follow.

The later preschool years were described in the previous section as a time in which emotions are high pitched and the attachments to the parent of the opposite sex are often intense and presumed to be erotic in quality. According to theory, the whole situation, the Oedipal crisis, becomes quite intolerable, and relief from it comes through the mechanism of *repression*.

The child thus enters the school-age period relatively free from emotional conflict. He generally is quite content to conform to the behavioral standards set by his parents. His own level of competence as a person outside the home provides little basis for a feeling of importance. He feels warmly attached to his parents, his primary source of security. His sense of importance and of status is based upon his conceptions of and feeling toward his parents. As Ausubel (1954) put it, the child "revolves" about his parents. He adopts the role of a satellite to them.

> By doing this he acquires a *derived* status which he enjoys vicariously by the mere fact of their [the parents'] accepting and valuing him for himself, regardless of his competence or performance ability [p. 171].

Such "satellization" apparently satisfies a real need at that stage of development, and the degree to which that need is satisfied depends very largely upon the general family situation and the attitudes and activities of the parents.

In any event, the release of the child into the world outside as he enters school brings changes in the general family routines and arrangements. The child is no longer completely under the control and care of his mother. The teacher now assumes part of that responsibility. With this change the parent often feels a sense of relief. Parents are likely also to begin to see their child as less in need of their care and direction. The tendency often is to relinquish much of their former control over his activities, and the closeness of their relations with him is likely to decrease. The child spends more and more of his time with his age peers, both in school and out. Consequently, one of his major concerns gradually comes to be his ability to compete satisfactorily with his peers. This, of course, results in his acquisition of the many skills to which we earlier made reference. The child's sense of personal adequacy thus develops, and his need for the "satellizing" relationship with his parents diminishes. The whole trend is for the parents to pay less and less attention to their school child's activities, and hence to know him less intimately, and for the child to identify less closely with the parents and to be less interested in the parents' daily activities. Family interaction thus tends to diminish or to cease. The later "alienation of youth"—"the generation gap"—could have its basis during this period of middle childhood.

In the meantime certain other behavioral and attitudinal changes are taking place in the youngster. Because of the usual lack of closeness between parent and child, these changes can come almost imperceptibly to the parent. Many important and desirable interests and competencies, of course, are likely to develop, but there is also likelihood of less socially desirable developmental trends. The prevalence of peer associations and peer-group activities results in "clubs," gang organizations, "secret societies," and the like, some of which may have constructive purposes and results, while others may result in different forms of juvenile delinquency.

The behavioral development of the individual child, of course, depends upon the interaction of many factors. The general trend, however, is for the child to begin his period of school attendance as a pleasant, compliant, and "satellizing" little person, but to end up as a rather brusque, intrusive, impudent 10–12-year-old, a pattern of "surface traits" which is the common stereotype of the preadolescent.

Summary

In this chapter we reviewed briefly the developmental changes that take place in the individual human being from birth to the onset of puberty. These are the years that are ordinarily thought of as the period of childhood. In the preceding chapters development was traced in some detail as it becomes manifest in the various aspects of change and areas of functioning. The effort in this chapter has been to view development as a single unitary process with many facets and aspects, to see it more as continuous, overall change in the "typical" individual child. We have seen him at birth as the most helpless and dependent of all living creatures, and we have followed him in his gradual achievement of relative independence and autonomy of behavior.

But at this point, the onset of puberty and the beginning of the dramatic period of adolescence, the child still has far to go developmentally; he has much to achieve toward the realization of his inherent potentialities.

CHAPTER 15

Moving into Adulthood— Adolescence

Introduction

The title of this chapter suggests the view we shall take of this arbitrary segment of the lifespan of the human individual which we call adolescence. It is really not a "stage," and it is a "period" only in the sense of having arbitrarily divided a continuity into manageable segments for purposes of study. This period of development, as indeed are all human developmental periods, is a time of transition, of moving along a continuum from one signal point to the next.

On the other hand, even though each "period" is a continuation—a growing out of the preceding one—each has its distinctive features, its identifying attributes which make it unique and qualitatively different from all the others.

The dynamic, moving aspect of adolescence is further emphasized in the fact that the child, while maintaining his individuality throughout, is quite a different total person in many respects at the end of these 10 or so years than he was at the beginning. So, in our study of adolescent development we resort to the same procedure that is used in studying progress in any aspect of development. We examine and appraise developmental status at arbitrarily selected points in the course of change, just as the play-back of a motion picture of a football game can be stopped momentarily for a careful examination of a particularly critical instant in the sequence. We study these status points, comparing what we see, and then make inferences about the nature of the intervening developmental process. Thus we note what the child is like at the onset of puberty, which usually occurs between ages 10 and 13, and again during middle adolescence (ages 12–14 or 15), and finally we view him as he is about to move into adulthood (late adolescence, ages 16 to 20).

As was suggested earlier, even though the period of adolescence is continuous with both the preceding and the following developmental periods, it has its unique features which make it qualitatively distinct as a total period. Each of the three phases of adolescent development mentioned above, furthermore, has its distinctive features. This is particularly true of the pubescent phase.

Bodily Changes

The exact timing of the onset of the various changes collectively called pubescence in each case seems to be genetically determined. Some large-scale studies have been made of onset using various criteria such as the presence of pubic hair, voice change in boys, or breast development in girls. The range of variation is quite wide, the modal age for boys being about 13 years and for girls about a year younger.

Role of the Endocrine Glands

During childhood prior to puberty the secretions of certain of the endocrine glands are normally held in a nice balance of minimal functioning. The pituitary gland with its secretions is in control. Its anterior portion secretes three different hormones. One of these, its *corticotropic* hormone, is secreted only to a minimal degree, stimulating the cortex of the *adrenal* gland, whose function is to put balanced amounts of the two sex hormones, androgen and estrogen, into the blood stream of both boys and girls. This balanced secretion, however, is somewhat different in the two sexes. The proportion of androgen is greater in the male, but the difference is normally insufficient to bring about appreciable sex differentiation. These adrenally produced sex hormones apparently are not qualitatively different from the *gonadal* sex hormones of the postpuberal phase. There is no evidence that the gonads are functionally active before puberty.

At the genetically determined time, however, the pituitary pattern of control is radically changed. The floodgates of its three hormones are opened, but still in controlled balance. Its *gonadotropic* hormone begins to act upon the gonads, causing them to begin their primary function, the production of functionally mature reproductive cells (spermatozoa in the male and ova in the female). At the same time, the gonads are also stimulated to begin their endocrine glandular function of secreting the sex hormones, androgen and estrogen. The secretion of the *corticotropic* hormone by the anterior pituitary is increased, thus bringing about an increase in secretion by the adrenal cortex. These two last-mentioned hormones together are responsible for a group of third-level changes, the development of the *primary* sex characteristics—enlargement of the genitalia—and the *secondary* sex characteristics—voice changes, breast development, growth of pubic hair, and so on. Along with all these changes come the effects of the third hormone, the *growth hormone* from the anterior pituitary gland—the puberal "growth spurt."

This complicated but interrelated and coordinated functioning of the endocrine glandular system, in a relatively short period of time, results quite dramatically in a whole complex of physical changes, both physiological and anatomical.

Body Growth and Maturation

Growth of the body as a whole and its various parts is a main topic in Chapter 4. The underlying structural framework of the body, of course, is the skeleton. The child's height increases as the long bones of his skeleton grow in length. The story of bone development in its details is a fascinating one, but beyond the scope of this book. A brief description of this process however, is also given in Chapter 4. The relatively close relation between this aspect of development and the maturation of the reproductive system was described. As we have just seen, the role of the endocrine system, particularly the fact that the anterior pituitary gland simultaneously releases its gonadotropic, and its body-growth hormones makes clear the basis for this developmental relation.

A comparative study of the course of body growth in boys and girls reveals basically the same sequence of phases in rate of development. The timing of these phases throughout the growth period, however, constitutes an important sex difference. Figure 15.1 portrays some of these similarities and differences. The solid lines of the graph were plotted directly from the growth data (height in inches) of the twins Paul and Sally 695. The broken lines are comparable curves plotted from *average* heights of boys and girls at succeeding age levels (from the Iowa Growth Studies, Jackson and Kelly, 1945). The individual measurements of our subjects, however, are so near the average values as to make it impossible to show them clearly on the figure for years prior to about puberty.

It will be noted that the pubertal growth spurt is most clearly shown in Sally's graph. This phase began at about age 10, followed by a decelerating phase which was already underway by age 12. By her fourteenth birthday Sally was very near her terminal height. Paul's growth spurt was more gradual and of longer duration, beginning at about the same age as Sally's (10 years), but continuing to age 13 years and 9 months. His leveling-off phase began at that point, but he did not reach his terminal adult height until somewhat beyond age 16, more than two full years later than Sally.

It will also be noted that Sally was a bit taller than Paul beginning in early middle childhood and continuing to about age 13. At this point Sally's height was already decelerating and Paul's pubertal acceleration was well underway. Paul quickly gained in height, exceeding his sister by nearly 10 inches by age 16.

The *average* growth curves in general show the same characteristics as the individual curves but much less dramatically. The boys, on the average, were somewhat shorter than the girls until about 11 years of age. This average age was some two years less than the age at which Paul's height began to exceed that of Sally. The average curves also show a relatively small sex difference for a period of four years. The average terminal sex difference of 7 or 8 inches is gradually attained only during later adolescence (15–18 or 20 years).

These contrasts between a pair of normal individual growth curves and curves based upon averages point up the need for caution in judging individual growth levels in terms of averages, especially during these years of dramatic change which we call the adolescent years. The lack of an indication of growth acceleration, the growth spurt, in the average curves is undoubtedly due to the averaging of wide individual differences in abruptness and magnitude and particularly in timing of changes in growth rate. Individual differences in these attributes tend to cancel each other when

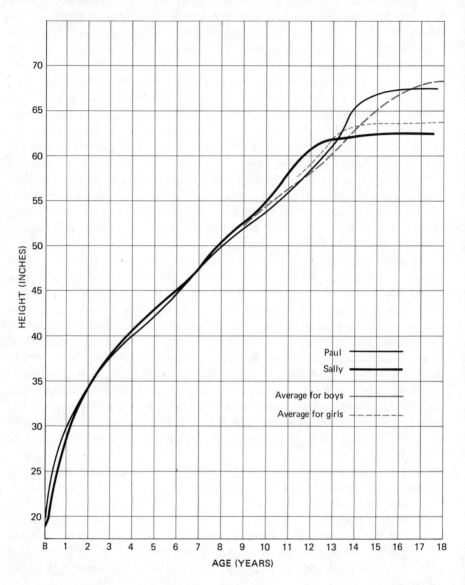

Figure 15.1   Growth curves in height of Paul and Sally showing sex similarities and differences. Average values from the Iowa growth data for boys and girls are also plotted in for the periods of the growth spurt and leveling off at terminal height.

averaged. Figure 15.2, showing individual growth curves of five boys in the Berkeley Growth Study at the University of California, viewed in comparison with the average curves of Figure 15.1, clearly shows how the true character of individual growth is lost in an average growth curve.

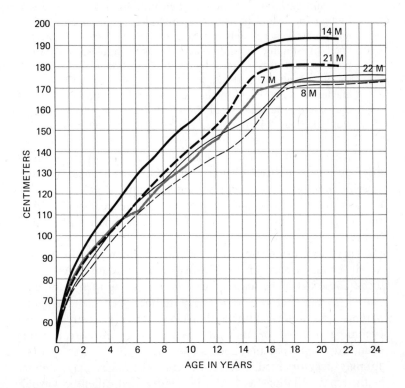

Figure 15.2   Growth curves in height of five boys in the Berkeley Growth Study (Bayley, 1956, p. 62).

Psychological Accompaniments of Growth Changes

As the young person approaches adulthood certain factors in his experience conspire to make him more consciously concerned about himself as a person. He becomes self-conscious in a way that he never was before. The glandular changes described above initiate feelings and emotional qualities that are new and strange to him. The physical changes that are rapidly taking place in body dimensions, in physiognomy, in genital organs, the beginning of the boy's beard growth and voice change and the swelling of the girl's breasts, all contribute to feelings of strangeness. And when the child almost suddenly, as it seems to him, finds that his reach is longer, his feet bump into things like they never did before, that things about him more than ever before get in his way and get knocked over, he begins to feel as if he is dealing with a different person than his former self which he was able to manage so expertly.

The early part of the adolescent period has sometimes been called the "awkward age." Many adolescents are self-conscious concerning their posture and gait. Some show a certain inhibition or hesitancy of movement as though they were holding their muscles in check and did not feel free to let themselves go. Self-consciousness with respect to height may express itself by sloping shoulders, and the short adolescent boy may try to compensate for his shortness by an upward tilt of his head, squaring of his shoulders, and a tendency to let his weight rest more on his toes than on his heels. Sometimes, in his bearing and by the character of his physical movement, the adolescent calls attention to physical features which he would actually like to conceal. [Jersild, 1957, p. 60]

If there is such a thing as an awkward age, it is during this relatively brief period of puberal change. All of this strangeness, confusion, and lack of self-management contributes greatly to what is called the identity crisis. It is the problem of reconciling present experiences, perplexities, and embarrassments with ones past and of orienting oneself toward a meaningful future.

There are, of course, wide individual differences in the seriousness and the disturbing aspects of this identity problem. Many young people appear not to be bothered in the least. They continue to be their outgoing selves, maintaining their usual easy relations with their peers, older persons, and with parents and family. Others, however, tend to "retreat into themselves," becoming affected or difficult to live with or critical, antagonistic, and alienated from parents and adults generally. These youngsters become strongly peer oriented, but at the same time they may experience difficulty in their peer relations as well. Such individual differences would be difficult to trace to their origin. Differences in congenital temperamental predispositions (Chapter 9) undoubtedly are often important factors. And, as Erikson (1968) suggests, experiences in early parent-child interaction which contribute or do not contribute to a sense of trust in the environment, such as the care of a mothering person during early infancy who is "warmly dependable," may also be at the basis of a difficult identity crisis. This identity problem is discussed more fully in a later section of this chapter.

Adolescent Sensitivity to Deviations in Physical Traits

As was noted in Chapter 4, young people, although they may want to be different to a degree—to express their individuality—also have a strong need not to deviate too much physically from the currently popular stereotype. Girls entering adolescence, as a rule, particularly if their inherent body type tends to be in the direction of endomorphism, react quite negatively to a condition of overweight. Neither do they want to be too tall. Boys, on the other hand, are likely to be disturbed by an unusually short stature. They are especially sensitive to and disturbed by signs of sexual immaturity due to the late onset of pubescence.

This latter problem was noted particularly in a pair of brothers, ages

12 and 14, whose development was followed longitudinally. The older of the two entered the pubescent phase somewhat later than average, while his younger brother tended to be an early developer. As the older boy approached his fourteenth birthday he still maintained all the characteristics of a pre-puberal child—a relatively short stature, a high-pitched voice, and no obvious signs of genital organ growth. At the same time his 12-year-old brother was rapidly exhibiting all the signs of puberty. For a period of several months this contrast in maturational status was a source of considerable anguish on the part of the older sibling. In an interview he expressed much concern as to whether he was "ever going to grow up." This disturbance was reflected in his relations with his family, particularly with his brother, and his age peers as well.

H. E. Jones (1949) in his studies of adolescence has pointed out that the effects of early or late maturing often affects boys and girls differently. Girls who mature earlier than average often experience it as a disadvantage in their relations with peers of both sexes. An early-maturing adolescent girl is much ahead of boys of her own age in size and in intellectual and social development. Normally adolescent boys and girls, even when they are of the same age, differ as much as a year or more in these areas of development. Such sex differences are often sources of some difficulty on the part of school personnel in dealing with mixed-sex groups of same-age youngsters.

In contrast with the early-maturing girl, the boy on an early-maturing schedule may experience some advantages. He will be larger and stronger than many of his age peers. Jones and Bayley (1950) found that early-maturing boys were more attractive physically, less affected, and more relaxed when their behavior was judged in comparison with nonearly maturers.

Young people in early adolescence often are particularly sensitive to and concerned about relatively trivial deviations from the usual, or what they regard as desirable, in physical make-up. Such things as too slender or too plump legs, breasts that are underdeveloped or too large and pendulous in girls, and in boys what they regard as poor muscle development can be matters of keen personal dissatisfaction. Bow legs and calves that are not sufficiently round are sometimes causes of anguish in either sex, especially during times when clothing styles call special attention to such irregularities.

Menstruation and Its Psychological Impact

The *menarche*—the beginning of the menstrual cycle of a young girl—is the most reliable indication that she has reached puberty and is now capable of conceiving and bearing children. There is no strictly comparable criterion of sexual maturity in boys.

Menstruation is a natural phenomenon, a normal phase in the cyclic production and discharge of mature ova. This process is explained in detail in Chapter 3. In the past there have been many misconceptions and super-stitions about this very important normal function. It has been referred to as a "monthly sickness" with which women are afflicted. Such views are not now widely accepted.

However, the fact that menstruation, which involves rather complicated bodily changes largely physiological in nature, begins at the onset of pubes-cence can have an important psychological impact, according to several studies. It is true that the process is frequently accompanied by unpleasant physical symptoms such as abdominal cramps, headache, backache, nausea, and fatigue. The attention of the pubescent girl is naturally drawn to this cyclical event in its association with puberty, and she may under certain circumstances regard it with resentment as a penalty for being a female. It is also true that even now in our culture menstruation is sometimes associ-ated with considerable shame, embarrassment, secrecy, and dread. It is, how-ever, accepted unemotionally and even eagerly by the majority of girls.

As was noted earlier, the attainment of sexual maturity, or the ability to reproduce, in boys has no single indicator criterion which compares with the menarche in girls for reliability. The full growth of genitalia and ejacula-tion of semen are perhaps the most definite indicators. These and other changes and events marking the developmental phase also have their potent psychological impacts. Voice change, clearly a result of structural maturation (a qualitative change in the vocal organs) is perhaps most embarrassing to the boy. The unpredictable "breaking" of the voice in social conversa-tion is very disconcerting to some boys while to others it is nothing more than a slight annoyance.

Motor Functioning

We have just been concerned with the widespread and dramatic physical and morphological changes which characterize the approximately 10-year period which we call adolescence. As we now center our attention more specifically upon the functional aspects of that development we shall note many equally interesting changes—changes in strength, speed, and smoothness of performance, as well as in the importance of motor abilities and skills in the adjustments of individual youngsters. We shall particularly note some important sex differences in the nature and direction of change in interests as well as actual abilities in areas of physical activity. Wide individual differences among both boys and girls in interest and ability to perform are seen in relation to school programs in physical education.

Changes in Motor Performance

The rapid growth of the body during the puberal phase, and the great amount of physical activity that continues to characterize adolescence, result in marked increases in physical strength. The youngster normally very soon becomes accustomed to his new and changing physical dimensions. Precision and smoothness in motor performance, as a rule, are soon developed. The adolescent's senses are keen and his reaction time is relatively short. Consequently, his speed of performance is generally high. Unfortunately, however, due to his lack of experience, his judgment and discretion often do not match the level of his behavioral pace. He, of course, carries over his preadolescent interest in sports, and with his added size, strength, and speed of reaction his athletic skills generally are perfected. Thus we see a marked change from the so-called awkwardness of early pubescence.

These enhanced athletic abilities often play a significant role in social relations, particularly among boys. Comparable developments in girls, however, may play an equally important but more subtle role in the social development of adolescent girls. Clearly, nothing lends more to a boy's sense of importance and status during his high school years than recognized competence in athletics. As everyone knows, the football star is the envy of his male age peers and is often the idol of the female crowd.

Cognitive Development

From an earlier discussion (Chapter 8) it will be recalled that the course and progress of brain growth from birth to adulthood closely parallels that of intellectual development (Figure 8-6). It is only logical to assume that in the general speed up of body development, the puberal growth spurt described earlier, the brain would be involved. Students of cognitive development are in general agreement that a significant rise in quality of mental functioning also occurs during approximately the same period of time as the physical growth acceleration.

The Influence of Piaget

In Chapter 8 we reviewed briefly Piaget's account of the development of mentality, or cognitive functioning. Cognitive development, as we have seen, begins with what is probably a complete lack of mental functioning at the time of birth and culminates in adult capacity to function with understanding, effectiveness, and facility in relation to the external environment. To reason, to solve problems through the study and manipulation of things, events, and relations not perceptually present is perhaps the most complicated and involved aspect of human development. It is an area in which much research has been done and is now underway.

Perhaps no other person has stimulated as much research or has directly contributed as much to the present level of understanding in this area as the Swiss psychologist Jean Piaget. His meticulous observations of child behavior and his many "experiments" have led to the formulation of a complete and integrated theoretical account of cognitive development. Many other highly competent psychologists have made important contributions. Many of them have raised questions about Piaget's findings and theoretical statements, and many disagree with him at points. Piaget's account, nevertheless, continues, in its general outline, to be widely accepted. We shall now briefly review the steps in the development of intellect during the period of adolescence as traced by Piaget and his co-workers.

The Emergence of the Adult Level of Cognitive Functioning

According to Piagetian thinking, at about 11 or 12 years the youngster normally begins "freeing himself from the concrete" and orienting himself toward the nonpresent and the future (Piaget and Inhelder, 1969). At this level, however, he still thinks in terms of "concrete operations." Concrete operations provide a transition between schemata of action—the semiotic function—and the general *logical* structures, the "formal operations" of the mature intellect.

The child at this concrete operations level thinks in terms of *mental* representations. He is no longer limited to representing by "imitating" an object or even in the form of an overt act. The representation is "decentered" from action. His operations, that is, his thinking, are concrete, however, in the sense that they are tied to actual perceptual experience. He cannot yet deal mentally with propositions, with hypothetical situations not directly experienced perceptually. This level of thinking is exemplified in the simple "conservation" experiment in which all of the water in a glass container is poured, before the child's eyes, into another glass which is taller and more slender. If the child is at the concrete operations level, he will say that "it is the same water," "it is the same amount." He can represent mentally the attribute of a constant amount because he has perceived the dimensional changes in the water mass.

The transition from this stage to that of formal operations comes about gradually.

Formal Operations

The advance the young person makes in the quality level of his thinking as he frees himself from the "concrete"—from representations of *things* and of their perceived qualities and relations which he sees as true—and begins to reason correctly "about propositions he does not believe, or at least not yet; that is, propositions that he considers pure hypotheses" (Piaget and Inhelder, p. 132), is indeed remarkable. And, as was noted earlier, this step forward is quite contemporaneous with the general pubescent acceleration of organic development.

The final "decentering" process in which one frees oneself for "propositional" thinking, for the consideration of all possible ways of solving a problem, requires time. It is not until about age 14 or 15, on the average, that the full level of formal operations is attained. The individual by that time can isolate the various elements of a problem and systematically explore a variety of approaches to its solution. The formal operations level of thinking thus makes possible the adoption of a generalized orientation to problem-solving. This may involve the controlled, critical evaluation of hypotheses, with final selection and testing—the thinking of the scientist.

Emotional Adjustments of Adolescence

According to Piagetian theory, this continuous yet sequential development of the cognitive functions is paralleled by an equally important emotional growth and increased capacity for social functioning. Along with the repeated process of "decentering" from earlier modes of behavior toward more "mature" levels of cognitive functioning, this increase in capacity for higher level emotional and social functioning, can also be seen. For example, there is a gradual growth from complete egocentricity through varying degrees of capacity for sensitivity and empathy with respect to the feelings and welfare of others. There might also be growth in the capacity to defer gratification and to control and regulate the nature of one's emotional expressions with due regard to the situation and the presence of others.

Special note was made earlier of the psychological impact of growth and maturational changes of the puberal period. The changing pattern of endocrine glandular secretions, bringing about changes in the chemical content of the blood, result in new patterns of physiological functioning. These changes naturally affect directly the emotional experiences of the young individual. They give rise to the so-called sex drive and the whole related area of interest in and feelings toward members of the opposite sex.

Sex Differences—Changes with Development

During middle childhood there is usually little evidence of interest on the part of either boys or girls in the opposite sex. On the contrary, a kind of sex antagonism, real or pseudo, often builds up. Boys play with boys and organize their "no-girls-allowed" play clubs. Girls likewise prefer girls as companions. However, the situation begins to change in late preadolescence. Boys' interest in girls begins to develop. There are wide differences among boys as to the extent to which they manifest this interest, depending very largely upon their experiential backgrounds in family, school, and social groups. Some boys strongly deny and try to hide any interest they might have in girls. Other boys feel no need to hide their interest and they begin to enjoy friendships and association with girls. Prepuberal girls are more likely to frankly show their interest, especially in boys' activities. They more frequently participate, when allowed, in the rough-and-tumble games and stunts of the boys.

With puberal change, as already noted, come changes in emotionality in general, with a strong surge in interest in and need to associate with the opposite sex. At first this interest is likely to be quite general and nonspecific. There is simply pleasure in associating, talking together, bragging, "showing off," trying to impress one another. It is in such group associations, however, that the more intense mutual pair attachments develop. Pairing off and "going steady" tends to begin. However, by this time girls are one to two years ahead of boys in physical development. This results in a general age differential between boys and girls as they begin these more intimate relationships. Girls, who are also ahead of boys in social development, see the boys of their own age as crude and childish, and they turn their interest to older boys who are more nearly on their level developmentally. The "rejected" boys, the age peers of these girls, do not feel rejected. They are usually rather disdainful of the "put-on" airs of their former girl associates. A year or two later these boys begin to relate to girls somewhat younger than themselves.

The Nature of Adolescent Sex Adjustment Problems

It is, of course, at the point when boys and girls begin to pair off and to establish the more intimate, one-to-one relationships that problems are likely to begin.

Depending on one's individual make-up and background of experience, any of a number of problems might arise when person-to-person intimacy begins. At first there may be simply the problem of just what does one do, how does one behave when alone with one of the other sex. Relationships established early, of course, are not all of the same nature. In some situations a rather serious problem of intelligently dealing with one's urgent "need" for sexual gratification develops. How this problem is dealt with, together with whether any inner conflict develops between what one does and one's internalized standards, depends upon factors in one's background.

As was suggested earlier, in the beginning of mixed-sex group associations the person-to-person relationships are generally of a very nonspecific nature. That is, the pleasure of associating together is largely based upon "differing social roles and complementary psychological natures." Boys and girls enjoy being together because they are of different sex and thus complement one another in the group situation. According to some students of adolescent behavior, this same kind of interaction is sometimes carried over into the later, more intimate pair relationships (Staton, 1963). The couple find that they share many common interests and a mutual respect, and a closeness develops between them.

There are, of course, the more highly emotionally charged pair relationships. According to some observers (Grant, 1957; McKinney, 1960), these are of two general sorts, differing mainly in the quality of the predominant pattern of their emotional interactions and motives—the "amorous" or love attachment and the more specifically erotic or "genital" kind.

According to this view, heterosexual attraction may be based upon motives other than the specific desire for sexual intimacy. The amorous type of relationship presumably is one in which there is genuine and complete devotion of boy and girl to each other. There is sensitivity to each other's feelings, desires, and aspirations, and effort is made to facilitate each other in his or her personal fulfillment. There are mutual feelings of closeness and spontaneity in expressions of love and affection.

Not everybody, according to recent research, is capable of this kind of love experience. The findings suggest that such a temperament, that is, the capacity to give and to receive love, has its basis in sensory and affective experiences of early infancy. The work of a number of investigators (Harlow, 1966; Marquis, 1941; Rheingold, 1956) indicates that the adequate meeting of the infant's need for appropriate stimulation and maternal care is the foundation for the development of affectional capacity.

The "genital" type of relationship, by contrast, is one in which the primary bond is the realization, or the promise, of mutual gratification of erotic love. There would be other expressions of regard for each other and other kinds of intimacy, but erotic gratification is the primary motive.

Sex Differences in Sexuality

So far, our discussions of adolescent adjustment problems have proceeded with the implicit assumption that there is much similarity and mutuality between the sexes in manner and mode of coping with common problems. And indeed there is. But there are, nevertheless, certain problems and difficulties that are peculiar to the boy or the girl. Some of these, of course, are associated with a commonly shared area of difficulty; others are quite distinct and specific to either boys or girls.

With respect to the "sex drive," as such, for example, there are some rather significant sex differences. The main difference here seems to be not so much in the overall strength of the drive as in its immediacy and readiness of arousal. At any time and under almost any set of circumstances erotic feelings and interests may arise immediately in the boy's consciousness in response to visual, auditory, or other sensory stimuli. This aspect of the drive in boys is "imperious and biologically specific." The boy also seems subject in some degree to direct hormonal stimulation. Feelings thus aroused give rise to erotically charged thoughts and imagination. "He must confront [such arousal] directly, consciously, find within himself the means of obtaining discharge without excessive guilt, and means of control without crippling inhibitions" (Douvan and Adelson, 1966, p. 110).

In girls, on the other hand, the early "sex drive" is not specifically erotic in nature. The girl is likely to experience, instead, rather "disturbing longings, unknown stirring of feelings, feelings of tenderness and soft affection, a desire to love someone . . ." (Staton, 1963, p. 351). Whereas boys readily become strongly aroused sexually through nothing more than thinking or conversation about girls or viewing female nude pictures, girls usually require much more direct stimulation of the erotogenic zones (lips, breasts, genitalia). "Their sexual feelings, too, are enjoyable for their own sake, constitute a pleasurable state of feeling to be maintained," rather than, as in boys, a feeling which immediately becomes erotic, a state of high tension which tends to mount, propels toward climax after which it rapidly subsides (Stone and Church, 1968; Grant, 1948; Mohr and Despers, 1958).

Individual Differences

There is, of course, wide individual variation in both boys and girls in the nature and strength of sexual motivation and expression. The evidence suggests, however, that the range of individual differences in this area is greater for girls than for boys. Boys more frequently and more closely follow the "typical" male pattern. Girls, on the other hand, show a wider spread of variation. A greater proportion of girls, at the older adolescent ages, in both "readiness" to function and in mode of sexual response tend to approach the pattern that is more characteristic of the male.

> Sometimes from the dawning of physical signs of adolescence, and occasionally even before, a boy or girl will display unmistakable signs of erotic sexual desire and make physical approaches, seductive in the case of girls and aggressive in the case of boys, aimed at sexual activity.
>
> [Staton, 1963, p. 352]

Cultural Influences

Not only is the young person beset by compelling new physiologically based drives from within but he also finds himself on the threshold of a complex, inconsistent, and confusing adult world on the outside—a world with which he has had little involvement or concern heretofore. In his earlier, relatively carefree years of middle childhood he was not immediately faced with the problem of relating himself to and becoming a member of adult society. He was not yet concerned very seriously with his probable future status or his realm of functioning in it. His primary concern very largely had been his relations with his peers and his performance status among them. Because of this preoccupation with things that were of concern for him as a child, along with the fact that he received relatively little attention from adults, he finds himself on that threshold knowing little about the real day-to-day activities of adults, their concerns, their thinking. In most instances he has probably seen more of the sordid and the frivolous aspects of adult life, the recreational, pleasure-seeking activities. He is also likely to have observed and otherwise been made more aware of the competitiveness, the deceitfulness, and the lack of trustworthiness in society than of the truly social concerns, the honesty and integrity, that characterize most adults. In short, he is not prepared for the adjustment problems he faces.

The Self-identity Problem

Youth has always been a problem which has concerned adult society. This concern, however, has been not so much with the inner perplexities and difficulties young persons themselves experience as with how to manage them, how to get them integrated with a minimum of disruption.

Of course, the young adolescent has his own problems. He almost suddenly finds himself with the bodily dimensions of the adults around him, and with his adultlike mental capacity he senses what the expectations of society with respect to him will be. Yet at the same time his parents and others from whom he might expect to get most help probably continue to talk to him and generally to treat him as a child. Before he can do anything else he must understand these and many other contradictions. He begins a serious examination and reevaluation of himself, his present feelings, desires, and competencies in relation to those close to him and to society in general as he sees it. He begins the primary "developmental task" of adolescence.

> This task is self-definition. Adolescence is the period during which a young person learns who he is, and what he really feels. It is the time during which he differentiates himself from his culture, though on the culture's terms. It is the age at which, by becoming a person in his own right, he becomes capable of deeply felt relationships to other individuals perceived clearly as such. [Friedenberg, 1969, pp. 9–10]
>
> Thus in the later school years young people, beset with physiological revolution of their genital maturation and the uncertainty of the adult roles ahead, seem much concerned with faddish attempts at establishing an adolescent subculture with what looks like a final rather than a transitory or, in fact, initial identity formation. They are sometimes morbidly, often curiously, preoccupied with what they appear to be in the eyes of others as compared with what they feel they are, and with the question of how to connect the roles and tasks cultivated earlier with the ideal prototype of the day. In their search for a new sense of continuity and sameness, which must now include sexual maturity, some adolescents have to come to grips again with crises of earlier years before they can install lasting idols and ideals as guardians of a final identity. [Erikson, 1968, p. 128]

Erikson thus sees the achievement of a sense of identity not so much as the meeting of a sudden, full-blown "crisis" related only to the period of adolescence but rather as a long-term developmental process having its beginning in the earliest experiences of infancy, with "stages" in its epigenesis along the way. This crucial adolescent stage in the process normally results in a rather thorough revision of the self-concept.

As Erikson points out, an important factor determining the "satisfactory" working through of this problem is the adequacy with which one has been allowed to pass through each of the earlier critical periods of childhood and to achieve the related developmental tasks. It should be realized, too, that this universal problem, and responsibility of discovering one's true self and of working toward the fulfillment of one's potentials, really continues throughout life. However, a crucial step must be taken during the critical, transitional period of adolescence, but the process of self-discovery is generally not completed "once and for all" at adolescence.

An important facet of adolescent change, certain aspects of which we have already noted, is an upsurge in the so-called sex drive. One facet of normal erotic expression is the experience of "tenderness"—of loving and cherishing another individual as a person. As was noted earlier, this quality of tenderness seems to be more characteristic of girls than of boys. It will be recalled also that much emphasis has been placed upon the importance of early infancy as a time when the foundation is laid for the capacity to give as well as to receive affection and love. A wide range of differences is evident in individual level of this capacity. However, along with the adolescent advance in mental capacity, and associated with the simultaneous upsurge in erotic functional capacity, is growth in the capacity to love. The adolescent, then, must deal with this new urge to erotic love as an attribute of himself in his task of coming to know himself.

Difficulties

Reference to *the* ego-identity problem suggests a single common crisis of adolescence. The problem is, of course, a common one, in the sense that certain of its broad aspects are essentially the same for all. But since every person at the beginning of adolescence, or at any other level of development, is an *individual*, different from every other, the particular identity "crisis" *he* faces is in many respects a highly personal one. It differs as a problem in its total pattern and in its details as seen by the young person himself. It is personal in the nature and the degree of inner conflict and travail it involves, and it is individual in the pattern of its resolution—in changes which may ensue, in the direction of behavior, overt, emotional, social.

Indeed, a goal toward which adolescent self-examination is implicitly or explicitly striving is the discovery and the expression of individuality. The young person, with his newly acquired ability to think critically about his own thinking—his feelings, desires, aspirations—strives to discover the various facets of himself and then to *be* himself through self-expression, all this in relation to the world of people to which he must relate and harmonize himself.

It is, of course, at this point of relating to society that youth encounters his greatest difficulty. He is by nature inclined to be idealistic. He wants love and trust in his relations with others. He looks for truly loving and valuing behavior in the mature models about him. He looks for honesty, trustworthiness, genuineness, integrity, but too often and in too many places he sees quite the opposite in human interaction—in business, politics, government, education, and organized religion.

These discrepancies between his ideals and what he finds in society sometimes lead a youth to become critical and contentious. The erroneous assumption of a general "conflict of generations" at the time of adolescence has developed.

It is true, of course, that adolescent contentiousness sometimes takes the form of a rebellion against parental restrictions or an open conflict of ideas between the youngster and his parents. The parents, their ideas and motivational systems, sometimes become equated with those of adult society in general, and the conflict may lead to the youngster's complete rejection of the adult world. He turns to his peers for support, and like-minded peer groups attempt to establish subcultures of their own.

Young people with different temperamental natures and experiential backgrounds, however, react differently to essentially similar situations. Some may lead out in open protest as, for example, in "activist" movements among students. Others are inclined to react with hostility and destructiveness. This type of "conflict," of course, is one which has stirred society to action. The rise of "juvenile delinquency" and crime has led not only to corrective and punitive measures against the young offenders but also to efforts to determine some of the causes of delinquency and to institute preventive measures such as providing better facilities for the constructive use of leisure time. Psychological research has thrown much light upon the various expressions of adolescent ego disturbance and the many factors underlying them.

Nature of the "Adolescent Crisis"

Our concern in this chapter thus far has been primarily with the developmental aspects of the period we call adolescence. We have noted at points certain essential relations between these various aspects of change—the relation between physical structure and physiological functioning, for example, and the "psychological accompaniments" of physical and physiological change. All of these changes, taking place as an integrated process in a relatively short period of time, constitute a complex and often difficult problem—perhaps more aptly, a set of difficult problems—for the child and for those about him. There are, of course, the problems of psychological adjustment which beset the young person himself, problems of parents and others who relate to him, trying to understand more clearly his specific needs, and the broader societal problems—problems of education, problems of environmentally providing for healthy adjustment and preventing maladjustments.

The degree to which such problems can be intelligently coped with obviously depends upon the clarity with which the real nature of the "adolescent crisis," with its complex dynamics and its many variations, is comprehended.

The Traditional Conception

Many studies of adolescence, psychological, sociological, and anthropological, have been made through the years. Adolescence has been studied as a period of development, as a crisis period in the child's life and in his interpersonal and social relations, and also as a social problem confronted by each succeeding adult generation. Consequently, an overall "traditional" conception of the nature of adolescence has become quite thoroughly established. The following statement is an attempt to characterize that traditional conception.

As a result of physical growth changes, and changes in physiological functioning the child experiences a complex of psychological accompaniments—feelings, emotional stirrings, motivating "drives"—that are completely new and strange to him. He even feels strange to himself as a physical being. He is disturbed by the new quality of his emotions. He experiences an upsurge of erotic desires along with the resurgence of the old so-called Oedipus complex—his earlier erotic attachment to his mother and rivalry feelings toward his father. These feelings he finds inconsistent with the ideals and standards of right and wrong which he had previously internalized, and so there is conflict (id vs. superego). Anxieties, feelings of guilt, apprehension, resentment arise. He finds himself in a state of bewilderment, a state of "storm and stress."

His sense of growing up also makes him realize that he is approaching adulthood, and therefore he must soon assume that role and meet the expectations associated with it. He consequently becomes more concerned with the nature of the adult world, and with how he will be able to relate to it and function in it. But with his idealism he is likely to see little about the world to be pleased with. He is likely to become disenchanted with the adult generation (the "generation gap"). He begins to feel pressure to detach himself from his family physically and emotionally. He must discover "a means of escaping his dependent status in the family, and even more urgently the dimly recognized drives and feelings toward his parents. This is the psychological irritation which pushes the child from home, leading him to negotiate or battle with the parents for greater freedom." (Douvan and Adelson, 1966, p. 351)

All of these new psychological experiences combine to lead the youngster to a serious self-examination. He must try to make some sense of it all. He is faced with ego identity crisis—the problem of relating past to present, to future.

In facing this problem he sees no source of help and support except his age peers—others who presumably also are dealing with their identity problems. Hence the peer group takes on its crucial importance to him. The peer group and culture supplant the family as an anchor. It "provides a haven in which the delicate task of self-exploration and self-definition can be accomplished" (Douvan and Adelson, 1966, p. 352).

The reports of social workers and clinicians who daily work with individual problems of disturbed youngsters and their families, of course, differ in details, but in general terms they correspond rather closely to the above picture of the adolescent in crisis. Theoretical writers, generally drawing on clinical studies for their data, also describe the adolescent predicament, with certain individual and cultural variations, in the same general terms (Erikson, 1962, 1968; Blos, 1962; Stone and Church, 1968; Eisenstadt, 1956).

The general implication in the literature about adolescence is that this growing-up crisis is universal and not to be escaped—that all youth actually experience the "storm and stress" syndrome, disenchantment with the "establishment" and the need for detachment from family in their drive for autonomy. Although most writers suggest that the problem of the female adolescent may be different in detail from that of the male, the description generally is spelled out in terms of the male youth. What seems to be indicated here is the need for more "normative" data based upon samples of youth which more fairly and adequately represent the general adolescent segment of the population. Clinical studies, without doubt, most accurately portray the nature of the problem or problems with which the clinician works, but clinicians do not work with individuals who are not embroiled in problems of maladjustment serious enough to require therapy. They deal with pathology, and their descriptions and generalizations may not apply at all to the nonpathological majority. The need is for more careful studies that are not subject to the "pathologist's error."

The Study of "Normal" Youth

Unfortunately, not many extensive normative studies have been made of the psychological development and adjustments of young people during adolescence. The major longitudinal projects of the past half century, of course, have made important contributions, particularly in their portrayal of individual psychological development in relation to family and other cultural influences (Kagan and Moss, 1962; Jones and Bayley, 1950). But these studies of relatively small and rather highly "selected" groups may not be fairly applicable to any general population. Moreover, they often furnish relatively little data which are directly comparable from case to case concerned specifically with the problems and development of adolescence. Consequently the definitive generalizations of these studies, valuable and enlightening as they are, may not aptly portray adolescence generally.

Some rather extensive surveys of the attitudes and adjustments of adolescent boys and girls have been conducted by the Survey Research Center of the University of Michigan (Douvan and Adelson, 1966). The data for these studies were obtained by interview involving some 1045 boys and 2005 girls from school grades 6 through 12. Careful sampling techniques were used in the selection of the subjects. The individual interviews were from one to four hours in duration, conducted at the schools. This means, of course, that the study was limited to students in school, which rather definitely "underrepresents 'problem' children in the population at large" (Preface, p. ix).

The findings of this research, then, have reference specifically to ordinary nonpathological, school-attending youth of the late 1950's. The following paragraphs present a brief summary of the results and the conclusions based upon them.

The Forward Thrust of Adolescence

The tendency in ordinary American youth, according to these studies, generally was *not* to turn their backs upon the prospect of a life in the world of adults—to become "alienated" and without a goal in relation to society as it exists. On the contrary, the adolescent "is both pushed and pulled toward a future" by forces within him. He does experience the organically aroused "psychic conflicts" associated with puberal change. The "regressive dangers" sensed in connection with these conflicts "assemble the power of the past to urge the child to leave family and childhood" (Douvan and Adelson, 1966, p. 341). There was, in other words, the urge toward the independence of adulthood. It was, however, a pull in the positive, forward direction rather than a denial, a rejection of something regarded as inherently evil to be repudiated. To the American adolescent, then, the future was by no means a remote or irrelevant prospect.

> . . . It is crucial as it is absorbed, integrated and expressed in current activities and attitudes. In one form or another the future orientation appears again and again as a distinguishing feature of the youngsters who are making adequate adolescent adjustments. [Douvan and Adelson, 1966, p. 341]

Sex Differences

This forward thrust was found to be common to both boys and girls, but its style and focus differ markedly between the sexes. Boys were concerned with quite different kinds of future activity than were girls. Boys' choices were concrete and reality oriented. They thought in terms of preparation for specific work roles in relation to their own interests, tastes, and capabilities. Their choices, as a rule, were not colored by "dreams of glory." They thought in terms of work not much above the level of their own fathers' occupations. The findings also suggested a relation between the clarity of vocational goals, along with realistic notions of what it takes to achieve those goals, and patterns of personal adjustment in their current lives.

Girls, on the other hand, according to this study were not strongly oriented toward jobs and vocational activities. Their focus was upon the interpersonal and social aspects of future life. Marriage was the common goal, with special concern in their thinking with the roles of wife and mother. However, they did have ideas about "instrumental acts" appropriately leading to the primary goals. Thus their choices of vocations were those which express their feminine interests and which were likely to place them in settings which will bring them in contact with prospective husbands. Again, the results indicated a relation between clarity of goal aspiration and personal adjustment.

> A clear concept of her adult femininity, of feminine goals and interpersonal skills, functions for the girl like the vocational concept for the boy. It bridges the worlds of adolescence and adulthood, brings the future concretely into current life, and allows the future to contribute meaning and organization to adolescent activities and interests. Girls who have relatively clear notions about the goals in adult femininity show a high degree of personal integration. Those girls who specifically reject a feminine future are troubled adolescents. [Douvan and Adelson, 1966, p. 343]

Presumably the implication here is that these girls are "disturbed" in the sense of a realization of, and rebellious concern about, the inequities in the currently prevailing sex roles in society.

The authors see the expression of these sex differences in their characteristic mobility aspirations. Those of boys typically were very realistically oriented. They were seen as "the concrete expression of a boy's faith in himself. The goal he chooses is realistic in light of his talent and opportunities, but is not overblown. And is cast in the phrasing of reality—what is the job like?" (p. 343). The girl's mobility aspirations were less tied to reality. Since their future mobility up or down depends upon the husband they get they "may as well dream big" (p. 343).

Another difference which showed up between the sexes was in relation to the felt need to detach oneself from the family and to develop a measure of independence. In the first place, the researchers saw in general a less dramatic, and less conflictful process "than tradition and theory hold." They also noted a significant sex difference. The urge to be free and "to be one's own master is almost exclusively a masculine stirring" (p. 343). The girls of the study, up to the age of 18, showed no significant drive for independence.

Closely associated with the urge for independence was the issue of the importance of the peer group. A conclusion of this study was that in theory the importance of the peer group to the ordinary adolescent has been much exaggerated. There was also an interesting sex difference in allegiance to the group. The boys more frequently saw "the gang" as a loyal group who could give support to its members. Girls, they concluded, may use their peer relations in quite a different way. Two-person friendships were more common. The girl more frequently needed and sought the loyalty and support of a best friend. This person-to-person shared intimacy transcended the importance of the group in meeting needs of girls.

The Identity Problem

With respect to the search for personal identity Douvan and Adelson (1966), from the results of their studies, characterized this problem also largely in terms of differences they noted between boys and girls. They conclude that "there is not one adolescent crisis, but two major and clearly distinct ones—the masculine and the feminine" (p. 350).

> The identity problem is also phased differently for boys and girls in our culture, and the distinction again revolves around their different requirements for object love and for autonomy. We have noted that feminine identity forms more closely about capacity and practice in the personal arts, and we have seen in our findings evidence that the girl's ego integration co-varies with her interpersonal development. Masculine identity, in contrast, focuses about the capacity to handle and master nonsocial reality, to design and win for oneself an independent area of work which fits one's individual talents and tastes and permits achievement of at least some central personal goals. The boy's ego development at adolescence already bears the mark of this formulation and reflects his progress in mastering it. Identity is for the boy a matter of individuating internal basis for action and defending these against domination of others. For the girl it is a process of finding and defining the internal and individual through attachments to others. [p. 148]

The overall view of the *common* adolescent crisis presented by Douvan and Adelson, as they found it among ordinary school-attending American adolescents in the late 1950s, clearly differs in significant ways from the "traditional" view. In the latter view the youngster is described as becoming intensely concerned with ethical values, religious beliefs, and political ideologies. His need to detach himself from his family comes about largely because of a value crisis—a conflict between his idealism and the views of his elders, the "establishment." The interview material of these investigators supports the view that "American adolescents are, on the whole, *not* deeply involved in ideology, nor are they prepared to do much individual thinking on value issues of any generality" (p. 353), probably because to do so would endanger their relations in the community and complicate their personal problems of ego synthesis. These defenses, they concluded, tend to curtail experience and actually to hamper growth and self-differentiation. The traditional pattern of conflict and detachment "can be found in adolescence, but it is found in a bold, sometimes stubborn, and often unhappy minority" (p. 353). These bold ones are the ones who, according to Friedenberg (1969), constitute the diminishing group of young people in our society who succeed in actually "identifying" and defining their true selves. They are Friedenberg's "vanishing adolescents."

Social Change and Adolescent Adjustment

Nearly 20 years have elapsed since the Michigan survey of adolescence was made. During this period of rapid social change much has happened. Times have changed. The general social environment in many respects is quite different now and is constantly changing. It is reasonable to expect, therefore, that in general the attitudes, aspirations, and common behavior patterns of young people are also quite different from what they were 20 years ago.

In this connection it is important to return briefly to a general viewpoint which has been maintained throughout this text, namely, (1) that developmental change results from the joint influence of biological nature and the currently effective environment, and (2) that the relative weight of the environment in its influence upon change varies with the nature of the particular variable under consideration.

As to the adjustments and development characteristics of the adolescent period, investigators and authoritative writers have taken different positions on the question of biology versus environment in terms largely of their disciplinary biases. Cultural anthropologists and sociologists generally, for example, have been inclined to give much weight to the cultural factor in relation to the crisis—the "storm and stress" of adolescence assumed to be common in Western society. Margaret Mead (1928), for example, found little evidence of difficulty or conflict in the lives of adolescent girls in the relatively simple and conflict-free Samoan society. There was no implication, of course, that these girls did not undergo the biological changes of puberty, and experience the natural "psychological accompaniments" of these changes. For Samoan children, however, there was no mystery about physical sex differences. Boys and girls grew up in close association. Sex interest and experimentation was taken for granted.

Although Samoan society was monogamous, both marriage and separation were easy and common. For the wife and mother, at the time of a mutually agreed-upon separation it was simply a matter of changing residence from one extended family or village to another.

Life in Samoa involved few social and occupational role choices, especially for girls. The adolescent girl soon became a wife and mother and lived securely in a large family. With so few alternatives and variations in life, the "identity problem" was simple and constituted no problem. Hence the cultural factor is indeed important. It can have much to do with the ease or difficulty with which the biological aspects of growing up are coped with.

In contrast with Samoan society of half a century ago, present-day Western society presents a kaleidoscope of constantly changing patterns of social and occupational alternatives which greatly complicate decision making for the adolescent. It is also understandable that such complications create strain and conflict within such long-established customs and institutions as marriage. Attitudes toward traditionally sanctioned relations between the sexes have changed and are changing, and a variety of alternatives to traditional marriage is currently being tried.

Such apparent breakup of the institution of marriage and family living without doubt is having its effect upon the personal adjustments of adolescents. Their patterns of thinking and their levels of sophistication are undoubtedly different than was the case 20 years ago. Their attitudes generally regarding relations between the sexes have been influenced.

It is interesting to note, however, that in spite of these changes and their influence upon attitudes and behavior in general the most recent evidence indicates that there is still a basic interest in, and need among young people for some form of stable marriage which is widespread and as strong as ever. In a summary statement D. H. Olson (1972) wrote:

> . . . marriage still continues to be the most popular voluntary institution in our society with only three to four percent of the population never marrying at least once. And national statistics on marriage indicate that an increasing number of eligible individuals are getting married, rather than remaining single (*Vital Statistics*, 1970). For the third consecutive year, in 1970 there were over two million marriages in the country. The rate of marriage has also continued to increase so that the 1970 rate of 10.7 marriages per 1000 individuals was the highest annual rate since 1950. There has also been very little change in the median age of first marriage between 1950 and 1970, 22.8 to 23.2 years for males, and 20.3 to 20.8 years for females respectively (Population census, 1971). [page 383]

As another indication of the effects of general attitudinal change, along with the increase in marriage rate, the rate of divorce has also changed.

To our knowledge, no one has determined unambiguously the origin and development in the human being of this apparent need for the marriage relationship. It is evidently deep-seated and quite resistant to environmental change. In view of all the evidence it is probable that the reality oriented aspirations of adolescents of the 1970s are not greatly different than they were in 1950, in spite of radical social change in general.

Summary

Adolescence spans a relatively long period of transition from childhood to adulthood. For purposes of discussion it is useful to divide this period of some 10 years into three phases: pubescence, middle adolescence, and later adolescence, recognizing all along that all the changes involved are continuous and that there are no real lines of separation between the phases.

There are, however, certain features which especially characterize each phase.

Puberty (pubescence) is especially marked by dramatic developmental change, physical and psychological. The underlying factor is largely physiological—a complex change in the functioning of the endocrine glandular system. This apparently is genetically initiated. As a result, a marked step-up takes place in overall body growth and in development of the primacy and secondary sex characteristics, and there are changes in general affectivity, especially in feelings toward and interest in members of the opposite sex. This complex of rather precipitous changes tends to give the youngster a feeling of strangeness toward his own body and a temporary awkwardness.

During the second (middle) phase particularly motor abilities, both gross and fine muscular, are developed. Strength, agility, and speed characterize behavior generally during this period.

One of the most remarkable developmental accomplishments during adolescence is in the cognitive area. At the beginning of the period the child's mental representations of nonpresent objects and events are still "concrete." He can think only in terms of his actual perceptual experiences. He cannot hypothesize. At about age 11 or 12, however, is the inception in him of the ability to think in terms of propositions, or possible situations and events which are not tied to his perceptions. He develops the ability to hypothesize, to think "scientifically." This is the stage of "formal operations." It is especially during the later years of adolescence that he gains this ability to think like an adult. This development appears to be directly correlated with the "spurt" in physical development.

The problem of "self-identity" is also brought to a focus for the youngster as he sees himself approaching adulthood with its responsibilities. He must "take stock," do some self-evaluation, harmonize past with present. The difficulty, or ease, with which this problem is dealt with depends upon a number of factors—developmental history, family background, nature of present relations with parents and family, and so on. Erikson (1968) suggests that the "epigenesis of identity" is co-extensive with the sequence of stages in the life cycle from birth through adolescence. He emphasizes particularly the importance, in relation to later coping with the identity crisis, of the basic "sense of trust" in the environment which is engendered, or fails to be engendered, in the quality of the care received during the helplessness of early infancy.

Evidence from a direct survey of adolescent attitudes and aspirations some 20 years ago indicated a common "forward-thrust" orientation, but with some significant sex differences. The males of the study were primarily concerned with future occupational roles and the problem of making a living, while the girls' aspirations more frequently involved marriage and social relations. There is at present no strong evidence, even in view of radical social change, and particularly in view of the current general disenchantment with traditional marriage, that the basic orientation and aspirations of adolescents of the 1970s are greatly different.

CHAPTER 16

Maturity and Intergenerational Influences

In Chapter 2 the term "development" as applied to the human individual was defined in its broadest meaning to encompass any and all changes in the body and in its functioning which take place as time passes throughout the complete life span. There is a tendency, of course, for us to think of human development as taking place during the so-called developmental period, that is, from birth, or conception, to adulthood. It is obvious, however, that significant changes occur throughout life and that many of these changes, particularly changes in functioning and in functional capacity, which occur after adult status is reached are of particular interest and importance in developmental psychology. Adulthood, which for convenience of discussion we divide into a number of subperiods or phases, is our main interest and concern in this chapter.

As was noted in relation to the preadult periods of development, the lines dividing a particular postadolescent period or phase from the one before or the one following are very "fluid" and indefinite, especially as they are experienced by the individual himself. One tends to experience adult life especially as continuous and generally without demarking change points. As the course of development is studied, however, there are noted certain gradually developing differences in people, in physical appearance, in ready energy and vigor, in tenor and speed of performance, in social interests and behavior patterns, in predominant concerns and values, and in general circumstances of living, to name a few, which characterize, in a very general way, the various phases of adult development.

We should be reminded also that with increasing age individual differences within a particular age group or developmental period become greater and qualitatively more diversified. People, as we have seen, differ widely in general developmental pace and in overall pattern. Hence any description of a phase or level of development can apply only in a very general sense— to people in general and on the average.

The postadolescent, or adult, period of life, viewed as a whole and in general, covers most of the span of individual life—some 50–60 years. It is the time to which youth looks forward, often with some impatience, and the time to which the aging are wont to cling. It is also the time when *inter-stimulation* and the *reciprocal influence* of two generations, parents and offspring, are of exceedingly great importance in human development.

For our purpose we shall arbitrarily regard the period of adulthood as consisting of four subperiods: *young adulthood, maturity—the peak years, middle age,* and the period of *retirement and aging.*

Problems and Developmental Tasks

This long period of adulthood obviously is not different from the preadult periods with respect to encountering and coping with problems of living and progressing through the various levels of development. Even with the great diversity of adult individuality and the tremendous range of changing circumstances and conditions of living there are certain common problems and crises to be met, certain developmental tasks more or less common to each general level or phase of adulthood. There is also a wide range of effectiveness and of degree of success with which these crises are met and these "tasks" are accomplished. Birren (1964) observed that

> it is rather difficult to avoid giving attention to the problems and crises of various periods of life. Thus the life span may appear, from technical descriptions, to be filled with a collection of unpleasant hurdles, resulting in a stumbling, bruising journey for the individual. This is obviously not a balanced picture, since there are many problems that are successfully met and solved and satisfactions gained that are not readily apparent. In a sense, the rewards of adult life take care of themselves; it is only the problems that demand attention. Because of rising standards, family life is often thought to have degenerated from a more blissful, earlier period of history; evidence suggests rather that the individual and the family have advanced not only economically, but also psychologically, mentally, and socially. [p. 3]

Young Adulthood

Typically the person at 20 is at his height in physical vigor. Intellectually he is likewise at his full capacity. For the several years preceding, he has been functioning at this full level of capacity "to acquire new modes of adjustment"—to profit from experience, to learn. With that level of cognitive facility he has become a very "knowledgeable person." He has established himself as an individual with his own thought patterns, attitudes, and feelings about people and society. By now he sees himself rather clearly in relation to the world and his functional role in it.

The young woman has had time to realistically assess her abilities and interests, and she is likely to have resolved for herself the marriage–career problem. She is likely already to have married or to have marriage as an immediate prospect. She sees herself either as combining marriage with career or as devoting her energies completely to one or the other and performing the social roles related to it. To the young man, however, it is most frequently not a question of "either/or." He must launch himself into an occupation or profession with the objective of supporting a developing family. He typically marries soon out of college and begins immediately an occupational career and the establishment of his family. This is the middle-class mode and ideal.

At this level of adult development, however, as we have already noted, there is extremely wide variation. There is much deviation from the usual or typical. Many college graduates who are professionally oriented are not yet ready to function in their chosen life's work. They must enter graduate or professional school for more years of study and preparation. These individuals often marry, and with the cooperation of their mates begin a rather difficult but relatively brief period of "subsistence living."

But of course a great many youth sense no need or desire for college education. Many drop out without completing high school. These individuals tend to marry early and often find themselves with the responsibility of marriage and parenthood unprepared personally as well as economically. On the other hand, many of these young people, although they assume the functions and responsibilities of adulthood earlier than the social norm, make good adjustments and become constructive and desirable citizens in their communities.

Marriage and Family Establishment—the Social Expectation for Young Adulthood

Even though some individuals by choice or for other reasons remain single and childless, marriage and parenthood is the norm for adult living in our society. This means that the greatest and most important function of adulthood is producing and rearing the next generation. Adulthood, then, is the time when two generations of human beings normally, and by necessity, live together and interact in close relationships. Family living is *the "effective,"* the all-important, aspect of the "environment" as a factor in human development. It is in these intimate relationships that the influences upon each other of the adult and the new generation are of crucial importance. And since the continuing quality of these influences and these relations depends very largely upon their beginnings, the great responsibility of young adulthood, when parenthood usually begins, becomes clear and obvious. It is then that the human developmental environment is established and its quality determined.

When a pair of young adults, a man and a woman, have established a love relationship with each other they are generally ready developmentally and psychologically to assume this responsibility. Erikson (1964) characterizes this level of development in the following words:

> It must be an important evolutionary fact that man, over and above sexuality, develops a selectivity of love: I think it is the *mutuality of mates and partners in a shared identity*, for the mutual verification through an experience of finding oneself, as one loses oneself, in another. [p. 128]

It is out of this shared experience of a chosen active love of mates—this "mutuality of devotion forever subduing the antagonisms inherent in divided function"—that the capacity and the readiness to *care* in the most complete sense for the helpless new life comes to them as a product of their mutual devotion.

A Time of Mutual Need Satisfaction

The plight of the newborn infant, and the concurrent "emergency" nature of the parents' situation when a baby comes into their lives, have been reviewed in earlier chapters. Our primary purpose at this point is to emphasize the importance of a peculiar relationship of interdependence and mutual influence that exists between parents and their newborn baby.

We have already noted the state of "incompleteness," the profound immaturity and helplessness, of the neonate. We have also reviewed the radical changes in his physiological functioning which "nature" brings about at the time of birth for his survival. We have noted the tremendous impact of new living conditions with the great increase in external stimulation which he undergoes at birth. His "desperate" need for the comforting protection and the warm and nurturant care of a mother is obvious.

The biological, particularly the neurological, state of development of the infant at birth precludes any *conscious awareness* on his part of his plight or of his need (Spitz, 1965). The evidence from much skilled technical observation however, strongly suggests that the newborn baby does "sense" deep disturbance or comfort and quiescence, depending upon the degree to which these fundamental needs are neglected or are met in the infant's care.

Margaret Ribble (1944), an early observer of infant adjustment, was more specific than other writers concerning the importance of maternal care of the neonate. She related "mothering" to three kinds of sensory stimulation—tactile, kinesthetic, and auditory, all of which are adequately supplied normally by the mother as she takes the baby up, cuddles and fondles him, feeds him, and "talks" to him.

Most of the literature concerning early infant care, which has been well reviewed by Yarrow (1961), was concerned particularly with "maternal deprivation" and with special reference to satisfying the infant's nutritional needs. The more recent studies, however, tend to bear out the earlier observations of Ribble that sensory stimulation is perhaps of even greater importance to certain aspects of the child's development. Psychoanalytic theory, as we have seen, stresses the importance of sucking and the gratification of hunger in the establishment of an emotional attachment between the infant and his mother. Research findings, however, do not support the assumption of the all-importance of the feeding relationship. Heinstein (1963), for example, in a study of different modes of infant feeding found no support for the psychoanalytic emphasis upon the feeding relationship. There was no evidence of the superiority of breast feeding over bottle feeding in the formation of a mother-infant attachment.

Another study in this same area by Reingold (1956) resulted in similar conclusions. She studied a group of institution babies which she "mothered," in the sense of providing much nurturant stimulation, in comparison with a control group who were given ordinary institution care. Her nurtured group showed significantly greater "social responsiveness" than did the control group.

The work of Harlow and his associates, although they did not work directly with human infants, has, nevertheless, contributed greatly to the theory of infant care in relation to development. In studies published in

1949 Harlow presented convincing evidence of the great importance of tactile and kinesthetic stimulation in the early development of his primate subjects. His results gave special emphasis to the importance of tactile stimulation, and one of his conclusions was that the emotional attachment between mother and child has little to do with the actual feeding process.

One important implication of these studies is that perhaps the most crucial aspects of nurturant care are not dependent upon the specifically maternal function of suckling the baby, that they can be equally adequately supplied by a *fathering* person. In other words, while in no way depreciating the importance of the care of the mother, the emphasis should be upon *parental care*. Perhaps our cultural stereotype of the male, and particularly of the father, as one without capabilities and therefore relatively free from responsibilities in relation to the care of his babies, needs revision. There is evidence that, from the standpoint of their *mutual development*, the relationship between a father and his children cannot be started too early in the children's lives.

Father's Role

The literature on child care indicates that our society in general is definitely mother-centered. This was the general finding in a survey of research literature by Nash (1965). One of his conclusions was that

> psychologists have adopted this cultural philosophy of child care [that in an industrial society the child caring function must be largely delegated to mothers], perhaps uncritically, and many appear to have assumed that it is both the only and the most desirable pattern of child care. In consequence, the majority of psychologists have not perceived the father as important in child-rearing, and this is reflected in their writings. Some psychologists have adopted the cultural assumption so thoroughly as to ignore the father entirely or even to deny him a position of significance.
>
> This culturally determined concept of child care has further removed the father by enhancing the assumption that the rearing of children is a specifically feminine duty. [p. 292]

Sociologists, however, have more frequently noted and decried this culturally determined philosophy (Gorer, 1948; Elkin, 1946; Rohrer and Edmondson, 1960).

Although the writings of psychologists generally fit very well Nash's summary quoted above (Sears, Maccoby, and Levin, 1957; Carmichael, 1954; Bowlby, 1951), at least one significant study has been published in which fathers' own feelings and conceptions of their roles in their families were investigated. The indication was that fathers tend not to see their roles as they have been portrayed by psychologists.

A study by Tasch (1952), although 20 years have elapsed since its publication, is especially significant in that she got her data directly from fathers, a fairly representative sample of urban American fathers living in the greater New York area. She interviewed 85 fathers of 160 children, 80 boys and 80 girls. The interviews were characterized as "flexible," which "allows for the emergence of a 'pattern of spontaneity and not a dutiful response' " (p. 320).

The results of this study showed that these 85 fathers felt quite differently and saw their role in their families as of greater importance than has usually been described by theoretical writers. These fathers did not see themselves as merely "vestigial" but rather as active participants serving a function in the care of the children which they felt was in no way secondary to that of the mothers. As a group they felt that their role was not limited to "supporting" the family. The results generally indicated also that companionship with the children was highly valued by these fathers. The relatively small proportion of them who expressed dissatisfaction with their role usually gave lack of companionship with children as the main cause.

This is but one study of one small segment of our society. Obviously, the need is for more investigations of the father's role in the home in which other segments of the population are sampled. We need more reliable information from fathers themselves regarding the satisfactions they experience and the personal values they see in their relationships with their children.

Evidence of a recent trend toward more attention given by researchers to the role of the father and his importance in child rearing is suggested in a study by Eron, Banta, Walder, and Laulight (1961). Their study was primarily concerned with parental child-rearing practices in relation to aggression in children. The study involved ratings by fathers and mothers of their children's behavior in relation to their own interactions with the children. An interesting conclusion was that the fathers' ratings were more significantly related than were those of the mothers. They concluded: "Only recently studies emphasizing the importance of the father in socialization of the child have begun to appear. These results are further evidence of his importance both as the new method and the new dimension in childbearing research" (p. 472).

Caring as a Factor in Personal Development

"Care" has been described as the "virtue" and the need which characterizes the young adult stage of development (Erikson, 1964). This is a time when babies are born, when the role and function of parenthood begins, and when the *caring* attitude is vitally important to the development and welfare of the new life. The exercise of this caring function is no less important to the personal development of parents, both father and mother. As Erikson puts it: "Once we have grasped this interlocking of the human life stages, we understand that adult man is so constituted as to *need to be needed* lest he suffer the mental deformation of self-absorption in which he becomes his own infant and pet" (p. 130; italics in the original).

The stereotype of the incompetent and uninterested young father in relation to the care of his infant was referred to above as a cultural creation perpetuated in the authoritative literature. We also reviewed some evidence that fathers generally do not see themselves as they have been described. It is undoubtedly true, nevertheless, and even though the "need to be needed" is equally strong in fathers as in mothers, that many young fathers have tacitly accepted the stereotype. They recognize the constitutional fitness of the mother and the priority of her relationship in the suckling and comforting of the infant, and with a sense of inadequacy and without encouragement they miss the opportunity and relinquish the privilege of early coming to know their baby through actually participating in its care. The young father sometimes does feel left out and even rejected by his wife in her preoccupation with her baby, and so he tends to become "his own infant and pet" in his own "self-absorption."

Harry Stack Sullivan (1953) stresses the great importance of the interpersonal interaction between parent and infant. He describes the "tension of need" in the hungry or otherwise distressed infant, the expression of which, in crying, induces tension in the parent. In his words:

> The tension called out in the mothering one by the manifest needs of the infant we call *tenderness*, and a generic group of tensions in the infant, the relief of which requires cooperation by the person who acts in the mothering role, can be called *need for tenderness.* . . . [p. 40]

Although Sullivan makes no specific mention of the father's role in this vital parent-infant interaction, the implication is clear that the father can function in many instances of "tension of need" in his baby by taking the role of the "mothering one." In such a relationship he can experience the "tension of tenderness." It is in this kind of parent-infant interaction that one finds and exercises his capacity to be completely other-centered, to give without demanding or expecting anything in return—a capacity that comes only with maturity.

Maturity, the Peak Years

People generally, by age 30, have passed through a period of settling down, and of becoming well launched and established in occupational and social roles which are likely to characterize them throughout life. Although men, particularly those who enter the professions, often marry after age 30, the mode is by then to be well into the period of family expansion with two to four children. Women generally marry at ages from two to five years younger than men.

Intellectually there has been development during the first 10 years of adulthood. By age 30, men and women have been functioning for some 15 years at the highest level of cognitive capacity (Piaget, 1952; see Chapter

8). They have learned much and have profited greatly from experience. They have acquired many skills, mental, social, and occupational, and have grown greatly in wisdom. Their "crystallized intelligence" (Cattell, 1969) has grown.

A Period of Achievement

For the majority of people this 15–20-year period of "maturity" is marked by serious and consistent striving for accomplishment. Occupational skills and effectiveness increase under conditions of business and occupational competition. Earning power increases, keeping pace generally with increasing financial demands of the family. As the family grows in number the need for better and more adequate housing becomes acute. As the children grow their educational and cultural needs increase. In general this period of family development is a lively and challenging time of life. And it is a time when intergenerational living and interaction are at their peak.

Family Roles and Role-Relationships

As these changes in personal competencies, challenges, and conditions of living come about with family development there are, of course, accompanying changes in the complexity of family role patterns and relationships. The range of ages of family members generally widens considerably during this period of parental "maturity" as the parents grow older and as new babies join the family group. Thus role relationships increase in number and the potentialities for intergenerational influences multiply. In order to highlight some of these potentialities for personal development we shall examine in somewhat greater detail some of the typical family role patterns in Western society.

Adult Family Role Patterns

The man of the family finds himself functioning in a number of discrete roles as his family develops. The primary male role pattern would include functioning as an *individual person*, as a *husband*, as a *home provider* and "breadwinner," as a *father*, and as the male *head of the family*. The woman likewise assumes a parallel and complementary pattern of roles: as a *person* in her own right, as a *wife*, as a *home maker*, as a *mother*, and as the female *family head*.

In actual family interaction, of course, roles and role relationships are much more varied in form and in affective quality than is suggested in these brief listings. It should be emphasized, too, that an individual functions in a particular role always *in relation to* someone else—another family member—and that the quality, the meaningfulness, the effectiveness of role functioning and interaction vary greatly in different person-to-person combinations and from time to time and in different situations.

All of these separate family roles and the relationships involved are important, encompassing as they do very largely the functions and the activities that constitute family life. However, since our main concern in this chapter is with relationships and interactions between the older and the younger generations of family members, the discussions that follow will deal mainly with those family roles which in a special way involve generational interactions with high potentials for stimulating personal growth, particularly the roles of *being a person* and the *parental* roles.

The Person

Functioning simply as an individual person may not immediately be thought of as a family role, but with careful consideration it may appear to be perhaps the most basically important area of functioning in family life. The degree of consistency and the level of autonomy with which the man of the family functions, for example, with his personal uniqueness and his pattern of idiosyncrasies is potentially of greatest influence upon the overall quality of family interaction and thus upon the adjustments and development of the younger family members. Individual uniqueness is always a factor in interpersonal relations. And as we have seen, the way a person "sees" himself and feels about himself largely characterizes him as a person. In a very real sense, one's "self-concept," his self-evaluations, his sense of personal worth and competence, are the easily read labels he pins upon himself, and these self-written labels are to a large degree accepted by others, even by members of his own family. They largely determine the expectations of others with respect to him.

In another way a parent's sense of personal security is important. His or her ability, for example, to adjust with equanimity to such realities of life as growing older or approaching middle age—accepting without alarm or attempts to hide the loss of physical or athletic prowess or sexual potency or, in the case of the woman, the gradual loss of the bloom of youth or the onset of the menopause—is an important personal attribute affecting the quality of interaction with the younger generation.

Another exceedingly important factor in intergenerational relationships is a parent's ability as a person to *listen*—to value, to respect, to take into consideration, to integrate into his own thinking and expressions the views and opinions of those about him that may be at variance with his own (H. H. Anderson, 1939a, b). Nothing contributes more to a young person's sense of personal security and self-esteem than to have his ideas and points of view recognized and treated with respect.

Carl Rogers (1961) in his discussion of the characteristics of a "helping relationship" emphasizes the importance of making the person whom one wishes to help feel valued and accepted:

> Can I meet this other individual as a person who is in the process of *becoming*, or will I be bound by his past and my past? If, in my encounter

with him, I am dealing with him as an immature child, an ignorant student, a neurotic personality, or a psychopath, each of these concepts of mine limits what he can be in the relationship. Martin Buber, the existentialist philosopher of the University of Jerusalem, has a phrase, "Confirming the other," which has had meaning for me. He says "confirming means . . . accepting the whole personality of the other. . . . I can recognize in him, know in him, the person he has been . . . *created* to become . . . I confirm him in myself, and then in him, in relation to this potentiality that . . . can now be developed, can evolve." If I accept the other person as something fixed, already diagnosed and classified, already shaped by his part, then I am doing my part to confirm this limited hypothesis. If I accept him as a process of becoming, then I am doing what I can to confirm or make real his potentialities. [p. 57]

In the eyes of little children, of course, anything that Daddy does is good and to be emulated. But later, as adolescents, they often are embarrassed and annoyed by the personal and social habits and traits of their parents. To young persons in their quest for a sense of identity, the social and occupational status of their parents can be a matter of some importance. It is important to them to be proud and not be ashamed of their parents (Stott, 1940).

The way ones sees himself and feels about himself can set the tone and quality of family life. The personal role one plays is significant also because of the basic relation between personality and one's functioning in the more specifically family roles.

The Role of Father

As we have already noted, the rather generally accepted stereotype of the father of the family pictures his role as one of little consequence, particularly during the early periods of family establishment and child bearing. Little research has been published which concerns itself with how the father actually functions or with his attitudes and feelings concerning his participation in family activities and child care.

The usual view of the father's role in the family during the more "mature" period of his occupational achievement and of family expansion (roughly ages 30 to 50) is one of even less family involvement. One often gets the picture of the suburban family matriarchy in which the father's participation in family management is limited to an occasional meting out of punishment for wrongdoing which the mother delegates to him. He leaves for work early in the morning and often returns late. Sometimes he is present for the family dinner but often not.

This description of parental functioning as children grow up applies particularly to the so-called affluent, middle-class American situation. However, according to the report of one of the committees of the recent White House Conference on Children (Report to the President, 1970), the pressures of living in our society which mitigate against adequate paternal functioning are no less strong for other segments of society (Bronfenbrenner, 1971). The situation is indeed grim

> for the family of poverty where the capacity for human response is crippled by hunger, cold, filth, sickness and despair. No parent who spends his days in search of menial work, and his nights in keeping the rats from the crib can be expected to find time—let alone the heart—to engage in constructive activities with his children or to serve as a stable source of love and discipline. [p. 7]

The whole tenor of the committee report was that the "pressures" of the social order, not the lack of parental concern, are to be blamed for the lack of constructive interaction between father and children.

The fact that fathers have to such an extent moved out of the lives of children, according to evidence, has led to a greater dependence on the part of children upon their age peers. This tendency has been shown in cross-cultural research (Devereux, Bronfenbrenner, and Suci, 1962; Devereux, Bronfenbrenner, and Rodgers, 1969; Bronfenbrenner, 1970). Recently a comparative study was made of the strength of the influence of parents and of the peer group upon the activities in which teenagers engage (Condry and Simon, 1968). The results indicate that peer-group influence was significantly stronger, and this was particularly true of "antisocial activities."

The implications are clear. The roots of alienation, drug abuse, and youthful delinquency generally largely reside in inadequate parental functioning, and especially the lack of father-child interaction in the home. Without parental influence and support the youngsters turn to their age peers. This weakness of parental influence appears not to be because fathers generally are not interested and do not desire to play a more adequate parental role, but rather because the pressures and conditions of modern living make it difficult, if not impossible, for them thus to function.

The Role of Mother

Our emphasis upon the importance of the father's participation in family activities and the constructive influence he can wield upon the development of his children, is in no way to depreciate the basically important and essential role of mother. We have already noted earlier in this chapter and in other previous discussions how completely dependent the young infant is upon the nurturant care which his mother by inherent nature ordinarily is best equipped to tender him (Ribble, 1944; Spitz, 1965). Division of labor between the sexes, based as it is primarily upon biological sex differences, especially in our present highly individualized society, has made the care of infants and children a special domain and responsibility of the female. And even though, as pointed out earlier, the human male is also capable of warmth and tenderness and of giving nurturant care to an infant, it is never-theless true that these functions are inherent in and more natural to the role of mother. It is most frequently the privilege of the mother to participate with the infant in the mutual granting of the fulfillment of a basic need. As described by Montague (1966),

> The nursing couple, mother and infant, confer basic benefits upon one another—for when a baby is born a mother is or should be born. In the reciprocal relationship in which mother and child are involved it becomes increasingly evident that the gift they make to each other is their own selves—selves that are striving for fulfillment and development. The gift unaccompanied by the committal of the giver is arid, a mere thing unen-riched by the human meaning to the recipient of the giver. . . .
>
> The self grows by the interactive involvement with others. Whether the self develops as an affectionate one or as more or less defective in that quality, it will depend largely, if not entirely, upon whether its experience of such qualities from others, especially the mother, has been of a loving kind. [p. 94]

There is no doubt that the quality of mother's care and "interactive involvement" is an all-important factor in the child's personal development. As suggested, the role of mother and child rearer can be an exceedingly fulfilling one for a woman. Even in this age of independence for women and their freedom to take part in all aspects of modern living, of all the possible roles and activities open to them probably no other can be more satisfying and fulfilling than that of motherhood.

This is by no means to suggest that a mother should confine herself, and devote her life full time to the rearing and care of her children. This would not be good for either the child or the mother. Wise and adequate motherhood means "listening" to the individual child—being sensitive to his needs—and ordering the nature, the amount and intensity of his care in terms of his changing developmental needs. And this kind of mothering can best come from a mother who is enjoying the fulfillment of her own personal needs through participation in her chosen variety of interests, activities, and rela-tionships outside as well as within the family. Work or other activity outside the home, under wisely ordered circumstances, can enhance the mother-child relationship. A child needs to be proud of his parents as they function in the world outside the home.

However, as the children grow older and as the family expands during the period of maturity, the problems of child care and rearing obviously become much more complicated and the responsibilities often devolving upon the mother as the principal child rearer greatly increase. Typically, she finds herself living a rather hectic life, managing the household and striving to meet the multifarious needs and demands of her children, often ranging in age from infancy into adolescence.

Social Influences and Parental Roles

But the child-rearing and training function has not always been, to the currently prevalent degree, the responsibility of the mother. The social orders of the past in relation to family management and child training and control have frequently been more patriarchal than matriarchal in nature. As we have seen, philosophies regarding child nature and development have varied within wide extremes. Children have been regarded as inherently bad, who must be purged of their evil tendencies through forced adherence to rigid rules and cruel punishment. At other times the philosophical viewpoint held that they were inherently good and that the environment— the parents—must protect and encourage rather than coerce and punish. During the brief history of child development as a field of scientific study parents have received help and advice based upon research reports from child-care specialists and parent educators.

In a review of these recommendations through the years, however (Wolfenstein, 1953), one is struck with the wide swings in emphasis from one extreme position to another and the sweeping changes that have taken place in the nature of the advice and guidance offered. The need for parental guidance was keenly sensed, and as a consequence, advice was sometimes formulated from too little or incomplete evidence or evidence from separate facets rather than from a completely comprehensive view of an urgent problem or issue. Thus a number of different points of view and child-care regimes have successively waxed and waned in influence during the past half century.

For example, at about the turn of the century the medical profession became especially concerned about the high infant mortality rate. Work in microbiology seemed clearly to indicate that unsanitary infant feeding was a main cause of this high mortality rate. As a corrective measure pediatricians in their guidance to parents instituted an infant-feeding regime emphasizing the importance of sterile conditions. It involved feeding from sterilized bottles and nipples rather than by breast. Specifically prescribed amounts of "formula" were to be fed to the baby according to a strict clock-dictated schedule. This regime soon became the vogue, particularly among the upper socioeconomic and educational levels of society.

The infant mortality rate was drastically reduced,[1] but many of the leading students of infancy and infant care were unhappy with the regime because they felt that certain of the baby's important psychological needs were being ignored. Through their influence a reaction to the strictly controlled regime began to develop. Certain influential child psychiatrists, pediatricians, and others (Aldrich, 1944; Trainham and Montgomery, 1946) began to recommend infant-care procedures that were a radical departure

---

[1] During the first two decades of the present century the infant mortality rate was 82.8 per 1000 birth. By 1941 the rate had been reduced to 45.3 per 1000 births.

from the prevailing ones. Breast feeding, regulated in timing only by the demands of the infant, was strongly advised. Similar permissiveness was recommended in regard to training in elimination control. This new infant-care regime was accepted by many young mothers, but many others found it distasteful or difficult for various reasons. Furthermore, there appeared to be considerable ambivalence among the child-care professions generally concerning the claims of superiority of one infant-feeding procedure over another (Sewell, 1952; Orlansky, 1949; Culdwell, 1964).

In recent decades a more moderate point of view has developed as research findings have accumulated. It has been shown, and it is becoming more generally realized, that the *feeling* relationship between mother and infant—the quality of their interaction—rather than the specific procedures and feeding techniques, as such, are the important considerations (I. D. Harris, 1959).

As we have noted in other connections, the currently prevailing view concerning the determining factors of development, research, particularly at the infancy level, has been a major factor in bringing about this change in emphasis, with the recognition of the crucial importance of the role of mother in individual development. Since the mother in our highly technical industrial society is very often left with the complete responsibility of child rearing, the role of mother is one of awesome import.

To be sure, the mother's role changes with the growth of the child. The burdens of physical care obviously lessen as the child acquires "executive independence" (Ausubel, 1958). But there should be no change in the amount and quality—the genuineness—of love for the child as he traverses his course toward adulthood: from complete dependency and helplessness as a neonate to the status and autonomy of the 20-year-old, from the lovable and compliant 3-year-old to the loud and intrusive 11-year-old, from the "satellizing" and home-loving 6-year-old to the moody, rejecting adolescent. At all levels of development, particularly at times of stress or disequilibrium, when he may appear least to deserve it, the child needs especially the feeling that he is truly "understood" and loved.

Child-rearing Practices

The question as to how mothers actually perform their function of child rearing is one for which there is no single general answer. There are, of course, many factors of influence here. Every parent, obviously, has grown up in some kind of family situation and therefore is, herself or himself, a product of some kind of parental care and control. And there is observable in people generally a strong tendency in their own lives and in their relations with their own children to follow the family patterns of which they themselves are products.

Within our own society there are wide differences in ethnic background, and within each ethnic and cultural group there are subcultural and individual variations in childhood background experience. One factor which research has shown to be important in relation to child-rearing practices is the social class of the family.

Duvall (1962) described the social-class situation with respect to its self-perpetuating influences upon children:

> A child at birth is placed within society according to the social status of his parents. He may live out his life within the family status into which he was born. Or he may move up or down the social ladder as he "betters himself," or "is no credit to his family." . . .
>
> A family generally is aware of its status within the community. Others are seen as "our kind of folks," or "better than we are," or "not the kind of people we want to associate with," as families identify with those of similar status, those of higher and those of lower status respectively. Families who have social access to each other are generally considered to be of the same general social class. [p. 70]

People who thus feel akin to one another tend to think alike and to share common attitudes and patterns of living. Their somewhat common attitudes and beliefs about children and how they should be "brought up" tend to resist the influences for change from outside their social realm. Thus today, even though the popular magazines and other mass media make readily available to all levels of society the popularized versions of the most up-to-date research findings, as well as the current points of view of the "authorities" in the fields of child psychology, child care, and family relations, still rather wide social-class differences remain in degree of sophistication, in attitudes about children, and in patterns of child rearing.

As an environmental influence upon the development and adjustments of children, Rodman (1965) clearly portrayed the factor of social class:

> A person's social class background has a pervasive influence upon his life. The lower the class background the likelier they are to have tuberculosis, to die early, to receive poor justice in the courts, to bear illegitimate children, to have unstable marital relationships, to have "less" motivation and "lower" aspirations. An exceedingly wide variety of injustices and deprivations can be documented for members of the lower class of society— physical, social, occupational, legal, economic, and political. Even in affluent society like the United States, the poor are plentiful, and the injustices and deprivations they face are facts of life. [p. 213]

It is interesting to note how the relation between social class and child-rearing practices changes as social change generally takes place.

Martha C. Ericson, in her 1946 study of child rearing in relation to social status, found some interesting differences between the middle- and the lower-class parents in their attitudes and expectations concerning their children:

> Middle-class families were generally found to be more exacting in their expectations. Training was generally begun earlier in middle-class than in

lower-class families. In the middle-class families there was more emphasis on early responsibility, closer supervision of children's activities, and greater emphasis on individual achievement. [p. 191]

A more recent study by Sears, Maccoby, and Levin (1957) compared middle-class and working-class mothers as to their child-training practices. They found that the working-class mothers were significantly more severe in toilet training, more inclined to punish, scold, or shame the child for "accidents" than were the middle-class mothers. Although the working-class mothers did not begin this training earlier, they achieved results sooner. The difference in degree of severity and punitiveness was found in all areas of child guidance and training. The working-class parents tended to have less patience in relation to their children's dependency needs and to be less permissive with respect to such matters as sex play and expressions of aggression. Their method of control and training in these areas also tended to be more severe. In general, according to the findings of this study, the educational level of parents was the differentiating factor:

> The middle-class mothers, and those with higher education, seemed to impose fewer restrictions and demands upon their five-year-olds than did the working-class mothers of lesser education. Messiness at the table was somewhat less often permitted for children in the lower groups, and those children were subject to more stringent requirements about such things as hanging up their clothes, keeping their feet off the furniture and being quiet around the house. [Sears, Maccoby, and Levin, 1957, p. 429]

In comparing the results of these two studies, M. C. Ericson's in 1946 and Sears *et al.* in 1957, some interesting changes seem to have taken place during that 11-year period. In the earlier study middle-class families were the "more exacting in their expectations" and seemed generally to be more inclined to pressure their children; they began toilet training earlier, and there was "greater emphasis on individual achievement." By comparison, the middle-class mothers in the later study seemed to be more relaxed and less severe and punitive than the working-class mothers.

The extent to which these apparent differences in middle-class attitudes and practices represent a real secular change in so short a period of time, of course, is not known. The group of Chicago mothers designated as middle class in 1946 may or may not correspond in terms of socioeconomic status or cultural and educational level to a group of mothers from "two suburbs of a large metropolitan area of New England" 11 years later, also designated as middle class. The probabilities are great, in fact, that the two middle-class groups represented quite different positions in the social-class hierarchy with respect to the lower-class mothers and the working-class mothers with whom they were respectively compared. On the other hand, social change in general, including the great increase in amount of educational literature in the popular magazines during the 11-year period, might well have brought about real attitudinal changes. Perhaps as middle-class mothers, as a group, became better educated and gained a fuller understanding of child nature, they lost some of their tendencies to pressure their children. Perhaps they did become more relaxed and permissive. It is likewise possible that parents at the lower socioeconomic levels, with generally improved economic conditions and more leisure, became more upward striving and thus more inclined to subject their children to "more stringent requirements" and to impose upon them more restrictions and demands in their efforts to obtain the "better things of life" for their families. At any rate, all comparative studies of social classes have found rather striking differences in attitudes of parents toward children and in child-rearing and training practices.

The Home Environment

The crucial importance of the general home environment in the lives and the development of children has been noted in earlier discussions in this book. Undoubtedly, the influence of the female head of the family is by far the most important factor determining the character and quality of the home environment as she performs her roles as a person, as a wife, and particularly as a mother and child rearer. In Chapter 8, for example, research findings were reviewed which showed the rather wide variation in the amount and quality of verbal interaction between mothers and their toddler-age children. This was found to be an exceedingly important home-environmental factor in the child's cognitive development. Hess and Shipman (1965), referring to the *restrictive* sort of mother-child interaction, a mode which is generally devoid of individualized communication "specific to a particular situation, topic or person," made this brief summary statement:

> This environment produces a child who relates to authority, rather than to rationale, who although often compliant, is not reflective in his behavior, and for whom the consequences of an act are largely considered in terms of immediate punishment or reward rather than future effects and long-range goals. [p. 885]

Parent behavior in relation to the development of children has been studied for many years. Champney (1939), at the Fels Research Institute, developed a set of rating scales for appraising parent behavior. Continued work with these scales, using factor-analytic methods, resulted in a suggested set of parent behavior "syndromes" or clusters. From his analysis Roff (1949) interpreted and labeled these parent attitude-behavior variables as follows:

I   Concern for child
II   Democratic guidance
III Permissiveness
IV   Parent-child harmony

    V   Sociability adjustment of parents
    VI Activeness of the home
    VII Nonreadiness of suggestion

Some Family-Life Patterns

In an earlier study the reactions of teenage children to questions regarding their home situations were analyzed. Four quite distinct common patterns of family life were revealed (Stott, 1939). This study involved groups of youngsters, over 1800 in all, representing three different home settings: the urban setting, the small Midwestern town, and the farm in the open country. The questionnaire to which the youngsters responded included questions about the amount of recreation the family enjoyed both outside and in the home, expressions of affection in their relationships with their parents, the extent to which they confided in their parents, their feelings about the personal characteristics and habits—personal and social—of their parents, the health, both physical and emotional, of their parents, and the recency of parental punishment.

The responses of the three residence groups were analyzed separately by means of factor analysis. The outcome of the analysis, in each case, was a number of clusters of questionnaire items (factors), which were interpreted as family-life patterns, each distinct and different from the others. Each factor could also be interpreted as representing a particular type of family environment.

These common factors were (1) a pattern of intrafamilial relationships which is characterized by "confidence, affection and companionability"; (2) a somewhat related, but less inclusive family-behavior pattern of "congeniality"; (3) a factor involving family discord—frequent punishment of the child and misconduct—which predisposes the adolescent child to offer criticism of his parents' behavior; and (4) a "nervous tension" factor, "nervousness," or something which the child interprets as nervousness on the part of the parents, and usually such other items as illness of parents and infrequent demonstrations of affection.

This investigation also showed significant relationships between family pattern and the personality adjustments of the children. For example, "self-reliance" in the sense of being independent in working through personal difficulties and problems was associated to a significant degree with the family pattern of "confidence, affection, and companionability" in all three residence groups. A measure of "personal adjustment" bore a similarly significant relation with that same family-life factor.

More recently E. S. Schaefer (1959, 1961) used factor analysis in his study particularly of maternal attitude and behavior material. The outcome of his analysis was the suggestion that the many variables of maternal behavior can be brought into the framework of two main factors. These factors, again, are regarded as dimensions, or continua. They were interpreted as love-hostility and control-autonomy. Figure 16.1 is based on a model developed by Schaefer, which summarized his findings.

Emotional Behavior Dispositions in Parents

The two main axes in Schaefer's "circumplex" (love-hostility and control-autonomy) seem fairly well to fit Allport's (1960) concept of the "behavior disposition" (see Chapter 14). As we noted, people do differ in their capacity to love, and if a random sample were rated on the continuum represented by Schaefer's love-hostility axis they might conceivably occupy positions ranging from the complete lack of love (hostility) to full capacity and disposition to love. Likewise, people by disposition vary in their relations with others from the need to control and dominate to the tendency to allow freedom and autonomy to others. Such dispositions in parents have much to do with the quality of the environment in which their children develop. In many studies and discussions of parent-child relationships through the years these two variables have been central.

Parental Love

Authoritative writers of the past 50 years have not always been in agreement concerning the matter of parental love. Perhaps in no other area in the study of child nature and parent-child relationships has professional thinking differed more sharply or changed more radically. Freud, in his

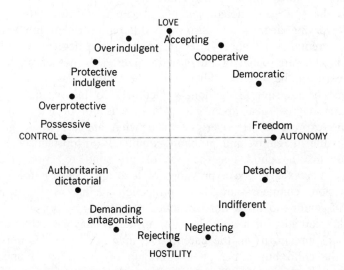

Figure 16.1   E. S. Schaefer's (1959) circumplex model for maternal behavior.

earlier writings (1913), contended that too much "parental tenderness" "spoils" the child and causes difficulty for him in later life when he must be satisfied with lesser amounts of love. A few years later the American behaviorist-psychologist J. B. Watson much more strongly expressed the same point of view. In his book (1928), written specifically for parents, he devoted a full chapter to the dangers of too much mother love. Among his pronouncements were the following:

> All too soon the child gets shot through with too many of these love reactions. In addition, the child gets honeycombed with love responses for the nurse, for the father, and for any other constant attendant who fondles it. Love reactions soon dominate the child. . . . In conclusion won't you then remember when you are tempted to pet your child that mother love is a dangerous instrument? An instrument which may inflict a never healing wound which may make infancy unhappy, adolescence a nightmare, an instrument which may wreck your adult son or daughter's vocational future and their chances for marital happiness. [p. 87]

During the decade or two following Watson's manual, the pendulum of expert opinion swung to the other extreme in relation to infant care. A number of writers have been equally forceful in stressing the child's need for parental love and its crucial importance in the emotional development of young children (Ribble, 1943; Spitz, 1945, 1946).

Margaret Ribble, one of the most ardent believers in the importance of a close mother-infant relationship, stated that "invariably the child who is deprived of individual mothering shows disordered behavior, with a compensatory retardation in general alertness" (1943, p. 82).

As we have already noted, parents "accept" and love their children in widely varying degrees and also with different sorts of motivation. To rephrase, parental acceptance varies not only in the degree to which it is manifest in outward behavior but also in quality. A mother might exhibit great concern for the welfare of her child. She might "fuss" over him, insist on extreme or unusual precautionary measures to insure his safety. She might worry a great deal about him when he is out of her sight and in other ways express in her overt behavior what appears to be great love for him, while in reality, and probably completely unconsciously, her basic feeling toward the child may be one of profound rejection. Her over-acceptance, her exaggerated expressions of love and concern for him, may be unconscious compensation for or protection against her basic rejection and lack of genuine love for him (Symonds, 1939).

Pseudoacceptance of a child in some instances may be exploitative due to emotional immaturity in the parent. The manifest "love" is not genuine love for the child but rather an exploitation of the child in unconscious self-seeking efforts on the parents' part to obtain gratification of unmet emotional needs (I. D. Harris, 1959). The overt behavior of parents in relation to their children, in most instances, however, probably truly expresses, in varying degrees, genuine acceptance and feelings of love on the one hand or frank rejection on the other.

Individuals, as they become parents, do differ rather widely in the capacity and disposition to love and accept their children (Porter, 1955; Sloman, 1948; von Maring, 1955). Evidence also indicates that this capacity is determined to a large extent by the quality of the parents' own family experiences as children.

Parental Domination

The other personality variable in parents, which perhaps has much to do with the quality of parent-child interaction, is the tendency, or need, to dominate. When this tendency is strong, it is rooted in the individual's own early childhood experiences and is likely to remain throughout life as a fundamental personality characteristic. In a person thus strongly disposed to be the dominant one, to be "boss," and always to be right are, to him, vital sources of inner security. To be domineering is not to be understanding of the other's feelings or opinions. As a parent, the dominating personality is likely not to be sensitive to his child's individual needs or to have much sympathetic understanding of childish idiosyncrasies, Parents vary widely with respect to this variable also, from complete domination and strict and rigid control to overpermissiveness and even complete relinquishment of control.

Figure 16.2 is a hypothetical representation of these two dimensions of

Figure 16.2 **Possible combinations of, and relationships between, the domination-permissiveness and the love-rejection dimensions of parental attitude, with suggested outcomes in terms of treatment of the child.**

parental disposition in relation to each other.[2] The area in each quadrant of this figure may be taken to represent the various possible combinations and degrees of that particular relationship. For example, oversolicitousness may be combined with domination. In the upper-left quadrant can be plotted any degree of each of these tendencies in relation to the other. Or oversolicitousness might be combined with overpermissiveness in various combinations of degrees as represented by the upper-right quadrant. The area in the figure which might be enclosed by a circle at the center represents the most desirable positions on both continua, the positions that would be occupied by the "warmly dependable" and "understanding" mother as described by I. D. Harris (1959). These mothers would give their children abundantly adequate wholesome love, and they would neither rigidly dominate and control them nor be overpermissive, but would be understanding of the children's individual needs, giving them freedom within carefully defined limits and positive guidance as they come to need it.

As is indicated in Figure 16.2, too much domination combined with oversolicitousness might be expressed in overprotective behavior toward the child, but when strong domination is combined with rejection the most likely result is cruel treatment. On the other hand, overpermissiveness and the relinquishment of control combined with oversolicitousness would mean overindulgence, while the combination of no control with frank rejection would mean complete indifference and neglect.

There are many other ways in which these dispositions toward feeling and behavior might combine in the make-up of individual parents. A hovering, "smothering" mother for example, who compulsively overwhelms her child with "love," conceivably might be neither domineering nor overpermissive. It is likewise quite possible that a parent who cares not at all for her child and frankly shows her lack of feeling for him in her behavior might also occupy a middle ground on the domination versus overpermissiveness continuum.

These descriptions of the parent-child situation, of course, are oversimplifications. Normally there are two parents, each with a different pattern of attitudes and behavior dispositions in relation to others. They are not likely, therefore, to react to their children with the same quality and intensity of feeling. Both father and mother might love the child, but the *quality* of that love and its expression might be quite different. (One might be inclined to dominate while the other might be on the side of permissiveness.) The number and variety of interaction patterns that might develop within the triad—father, mother, and child—are indeed many. For a child to be overindulged or neglected, overprotected or treated cruelly by a mother or a father, may be deeply disturbing to him. But in each case the effect

---

[2] P. M. Simonds in an early study (1939) described these two parental attitude variables and represented them as continua in a figure after which Figure 16.2 is drawn. Simonds also described their various combinations and some of the probable outcomes in terms of child adjustment and behavior.

might be softened and partially compensated for by more healthy and constructive relationships with the other parent or with other significant persons in his life.

Middle Age

During the extremely busy period of life which we have labeled "maturity" time passes very rapidly. As one pauses to note that his older children are approaching adulthood, one almost suddenly realizes that he is getting along in years. He may find himself quite unprepared when he is confronted as if by a stranger instead of his little boy or girl. He is forced to realize that his family is beginning a new phase in its development and that he is not as young as he once was.

This period of middle age is generally a time of crisis. It is often a time of personal disturbance for parents, for example, as they face the fact that they are now among those who are called middle-aged. It is often hard for them to admit that they have already taken on the "middle-aged spread" with its associated limitations; that she must now accept herself as she is with the quieter charm of her age, and he must accept the fact that he is "slowing down," that he no longer can be the model of strength and dexterity for his son, who now can "run circles around him." Reuben Hill (1951) describes some of the difficulties of middle age:

> Both husband and wife face similar problems in the middle years because ours is a youth-oriented society. As a young country, America has rewarded youth and depreciated middle age and later maturity. Our schools and families have failed to prepare us systematically for the roles that may be played in middle age, and consequently we approach the period with great hesitancy and conflicting emotions. This is true whether we are burdened with the task of launching our children into jobs and marriage or are facing the complications of a childless old age. For it is in the middle years . . . that men must face their diminishing bargaining power in the market place, their decreasing vitality and powers of attraction for women, and their limited stature as persons in a society geared to poor-boy-makes-good stories. It is in the middle years that the wife-and-mother discovers that raising one or two children and caring for a husband turns out not to be a permanently full-time job. [p. 30]

Evelyn Duvall (1957) presents another view of the problems of the modern middle-aged wife:

> Being middle aged today is a far more powerful business than it used to be in the days of Whistler's mother. Then, a woman in her forties was physically and psychologically ready to retire to her knitting. Today's middle-aged woman, thanks to better nutrition, medical services, lightened burdens at home, and shifting feminine roles, still has a "head of steam up" both

physiologically and emotionally. She is apt to be vigorous, often feeling better than she has in her whole life. Even menopause, the dread of women in earlier eras, now can be taken in stride. The woman with nearly grown children has found her strengths and weaknesses. She has tasted the sweetness of affection and learned to enjoy creative companionship with her husband and children.

Now, suddenly, before she is quite prepared herself for it, her children are no longer children, they are taking their confidences and their loves outside. Her husband is engrossed in the peak of his business or career. Her house is in order. And she—where does she go from here? What love can take the place of those so suddenly torn away? What tasks can absorb the energies and the skills that cry for channeling? If she clings to her children she is a "Mom." If her interests in her husband's work becomes too absorbing, she is a "meddler." If she spends her time in a dizzy round of matinees, bridge parties, and beauty parlors, she is a "parasite." If she devotes herself to a quest for her soul through devious cults and sundry religions, she is suspect. [p. 376]

Perhaps with the changes in interests and values which seem to characterize youth generally today, women will enter the later stages of maturity having been less intensely involved in their motherhood role and be better prepared personally for the changes in role relations as the children mature. By the time the grown-up stage in family development is reached, however, family interaction patterns most certainly have changed in character and in the kind of meaning they have for the persons involved. In certain of these relationships the changes may constitute real crises in individual lives. In any event, interpersonal and intergenerational relationships generally continue to be of great personal significance.

The Middle-aged Husband–Wife Relationship

Even though the intimate relationship between husband and wife, as such, does not involve direct interaction between generations, it is none the less the most basically important of all family relationships. It has greatest potential for affecting the development, the welfare and lives of all family members. This is an especially important consideration at this point because a number of factors and conditions, both intraindividual and interpersonal, typically take place which characterize this period of personal and family development.

We have already referred to the disturbing effects in both men and women of facing the facts of middle-aged life. There is research evidence indicating that many couples fail to find happiness together in their relationship during these middle and later years (Bossard and Boll, 1955). As we have seen, there are a number of factors which contribute to this unhappy situation. For the wife, there is the fact that her function as a mother has markedly changed. It may seem as though she is jobless. Her children no longer need her mothering. Now, when she especially needs her husband's attention and closeness to fill the gap, she often becomes unhappy with the inadequacy of her middle-aged husband as a sexual partner. Then there is the problem of the menopause.

Husbands, most frequently in their fifties, according to this research (Bossard and Boll, 1955), are also often unhappy in their marriages but for different reasons. The data (information furnished by their brothers) identified two rather different groups of husbands:

> One consists of men who have attained some degree of prominence and success in their chosen field, only to find that their wives have not kept pace with them in their upward climb. Such men often make a determined effort to remain loyal to their mates. Some of them are reported as succeeding; others fail and are aware of it; and still others appear to their siblings as failing in spite of outward evidence of success.
>
> A second group of men, identified by their siblings, are in their fifties and have failed, absolutely or relatively, in their occupational efforts. Such failures lead them to rationalizations: they never had a chance to succeed, they say. Their wives were no help to them. If it were not for the handicaps which their wives imposed, they would have succeeded, as did other men. Such wives become scapegoats for the failure of their husbands. [p. 14]

The Menopause

The end of the reproductive period in women, the menopause, or climacteric, usually comes during the fifth decade of a woman's life. The average age is 49 years. Physiologically it is brought about by a decrease in the hormones secreted by the ovaries.

As was noted in the discussion of the onset of puberty in Chapter 15, the endocrine glands constitute a complex, interrelated, and marvelously timed and regulated system of chemical control in the organism. The cessation of the ovarian function, which ends the possibility of bearing children, is the result of a complex glandular operation. The pituitary gland, the master regulator of chemical balance, along with the thyroid and adrenal glands, is involved.

The cessation of menstruation, of course, is only one of the phenomena which occur at the climacteric. There is a complex interrelation between the glandular system and the nervous system, particularly the autonomic division. Not only are changes in glandular functions initiated by the nervous system, but it is in turn affected, with varying degrees of influence, by glandular secretions. The autonomic system is the nervous network which controls the vital life processes of the organism. Since these processes have much to do with the emotions and with the sense of physical well-being—arising from respiratory and heartbeat rates, digestion, and other physiological processes —a train of subjective effects occur which can render the person uncomfortable and disturbed.

Investigations during the past few decades, however, suggest that in the past the menopause has been used as a popular excuse for personal inadequacies in many instances. It has been estimated that only about 20 percent of women actually experience any serious menopause problems and that these difficulties are of short duration. It appears that the menopause, the dread of women in former times, is now "taken in stride" by modern women (Duvall, 1957).

Relations between Generations

As we have already seen, the middle-years period generally is a time of emotional crisis and many factors and circumstances seem to conspire thus to characterize it. In many instances not only is there strain and tension in parents due to their personal problems, but it is also a time of serious inter-generational conflict. Sometimes the emotional upset of the menopause in mother coincides with the adolescent's quest for independence and his search for personal identity. In such instances each is so involved and preoccupied with his or her own subjective concerns as to be unable to respond in any constructive way to the emotional needs of the other. In reaction the adolescent's tendency to alienation and rejection may be reinforced.

A recent research team has concluded that if a father is really to assist his boy through the problems and conflicts of adolescence he must himself achieve resolution of his own life problems peculiar to middle age and the declining years. This developmental task of maturity Erikson (1968) has called the crisis of "integrity." Integrity is the eighth and last of his "stages" in the life cycle of man, that is, in his development of personality.

> In the aging person who has taken care of things and people and has adapted himself to the triumphs and disappointments of being, by neces-sity, the originator of others and the generator of things and ideas—only in him the fruit of the seven stages gradually ripens. I know of no better word for it than *integrity*. Lacking a clear definition, I shall point to a few attributes of this stage of mind. It is the ego's accrued assurance of its proclivity for order and meaning—an emotional integration faithful to the image bearers of the past and ready to take, and eventually to renounce, leadership in the present. It is the acceptance of one's one and only life cycle and of the people who have become significant to it as something that had to be and that, by necessity, permitted of no substitutions. It thus means a new and different love of one's parents, free of the wish that they should have been different, and an acceptance of the fact that one's life is one's own responsibility. It is a sense of comradeship with men and women of distant times and of different pursuits who have created orders and objects and savings conveying human dignity and love. Although aware of the relativity of all the various life styles which have given meaning to human striving, the possessor of integrity is ready to defend the dignity of his own life style against all physical and economic threats. For he knows

that an individual life is the accidental coincidence of but one life style with but one segment of history, and that for him all human integrity stands and falls with the one style of integrity of which he partakes.

[pp. 139–140]

The alternative—the opposite—to this sense of integrity is "despair." This integrity crisis involves the increasing awareness of declining powers, loss of self-esteem and the like, with loss of motivation and the tendency to give up. With this attitude of despair on the father's part, according to the study referred to above, a distorted relationship with his adolescent son develops which leads to irrational conflict ("annihilating fights") in which the father defines the son as "an incorrigible criminal" instead of discussing specifically what he does and its rational implications.

By contrast the father who has successfully resolved his personal problems—who has achieved "integrity"—"gives his son an example of commitment to values and meanings" and even though the son may strongly disagree with those values and meanings their differences are dealt with in what the authors call a "loving fight." The son can then identify with his father's sense of commitment and react to him generally as one who is trustworthy (Goodall, 1972).

Clearly, the middle years of family development are crucial years in the lives of both the older and the younger generations. This, of course, is the period of the much-discussed "generation gap." It is a time when a sense of implicit trust in the integrity of his parents is of crucial importance to the young person. Such a trust, as we noted earlier (Chapter 15), has its origin during the months of early infancy and is developed throughout childhood in the interactions between the child and parents who are truthworthy. With a background of early experience of always feeling that he was listened to and understood in trying moments and emotional upsets, now as an adolescent he is likely to express freely his impatience and intolerance with things as they are, his need to change the world, or to get away from it, knowing that he will be listened to with respect and understanding rather than with ridicule and condemnation. With such a realization he is much more disposed to listen to his parents and to recognize their more mature judgment.

The Period of Retirement and Aging

During these later stages of human development people tend normally to continue to do what they have become accustomed to do. Subjectively, as an aging person, one's self-image tends not to change. Normally one's declining vigor and decreasing capacity for accomplishment come upon one in imperceptible degrees. Time alone, as viewed in relation to accomplishment, seems to pass with ever-increasing velocity. In this gradual process of maturing, as one brings together and orders one's life values, as one succeeds in achieving personal integrity (Erikson), or because of personality difficulties, when the crises of life have been so devastating that the person experiences only varying degrees of discouragement and despair—these processes of development also continue throughout the middle and declining years.

Actually, it is only as signal or crisis events take place in one's life—as a physical disability or a debilitating illness strikes, or as one suddenly realizes that his daily activity routine is about to be interrupted by "retirement"—that one accepts the fact that he has reached a critical point and is entering a new epoch in his life.

Decline in Sensory Acuity

During these years of maturing, however, development generally is of the nature of gradual decrement, rather than increment in functional facility. "Generally with advancing age there is a reduction in sensory acuity as a consequence of injury, disease, and changes in the structures and functions of neural tissues that are probably due to primary aging" (Birren, 1964, p. 82). Some of reduced acuity can be tolerated without an obvious effect upon behavior. Nature has provided a wide margin of safety in that there ordinarily is more sensory input than is necessary for the adequate detection of signals. However, with wide individual variation, there is, on the average, a gradual impairment of both visual and auditory acuity well underway by age 40. The frequencies of defects and impairment in these two vital sense modalities rise in positively accelerating curves. By age 60 the frequency of serious visual defects has reached approximately 70 in 1000 population.

Changes in the functioning of the interoceptors, or sense receptors in the internal organs, proprioceptors, or muscle sense receptors, and the vestibular receptors in the inner ear are usually not so apparent and are more likely to take place without any conscious awareness. But these sources of information are very important to appropriate movement in and orientation with respect to space. Without proprioceptive information, for example, one would have to guide his gross motor activities entirely by vision. Without these senses and without vestibular sensitivity one would be without the sense of balance. Gradual loss of acuity in these sense modalities generally comes with advancing age. Our knowledge of the extent and the rate of impairment of the various senses in relation to aging has been considerably expanded by recent research sponsored by the U.S. Department of Health, Education and Welfare. This information is reported in summary by J. E. Birren (1964). The extent to which these sensory losses become seriously disturbing factors in the life of the aging person obviously largely depend upon the nature of one's life's work and the kinds of activities in which he likes to engage. Serious impairment of vision, of course, is always debilitating. The loss of hearing especially has damaging effects upon one's ability to interact socially and intellectually with others and thus can seriously interfere with one's need to function in the ongoing life of the family.

Retirement

One of the inevitable consequences of aging is the necessity eventually to withdraw from one's major occupation or field of activity. The idea of retirement has widely differing connotations for individuals in the various occupations and vocations. Some persons, particularly those engaged in physically taxing kinds of work, as in industry, tend to anticipate with eagerness the time of retirement. They look forward to a time for rest and freedom from the tyranny of the time clock. For persons in the more sedentary types of work, like positions in the academic field, retirement is generally something to be delayed as long as possible and an event for which they are often unprepared when it comes. For the self-employed—the independent craftsman or the business or professional person—retirement is not something imposed upon him when he reaches some mandatory retirement age. The time of his partial or complete withdrawal from active participation is usually self-determined, and is, therefore, an event toward which he can gradually work and prepare for at his own discretion.

In many instances, however, retirement is the most abrupt and radical change experienced by an active individual, and it often involves rather serious adjustment problems. These difficulties may be largely family problems of adjusting to reduced financial income. They may be primarily personal in nature.

In any event retirement for the person himself should not mean cessation of activity, a time with nothing to do. On the contrary, he should "retire" into a new and planned program of activity, a program designed by and for himself personally and for which he has thoughtfully prepared himself. Nothing can facilitate the aging process more or can contribute more to physical and psychological decline in a person who has always been active than to withdraw completely from active life.

Personality and Retirement

Growing old, and particularly withdrawing from the stimulation and pressures of the work-a-day world, like any other significant change in one's environment and one's pattern of daily activity, can bring about noticeable change in one's personality. As was noted particularly in Chapter 13, the concept of "personality" is many faceted. The "core" of one's personality, one's "individuality," resists change. One continues to be the same person, uniquely himself throughout life. But just as truly, one is never a completely "finished product" as long as one is alive and interacting with the world about him. Changes in outlook, in attitudes, ways of reacting to life situations do take place as one's effective environment changes.

As Birren (1968) suggests, "a working definition" of personality with reference to aging is that it is "the characteristic way in which an individual responds to the events of adult life" (p. 223). There is no doubt that an individual's response to life's events as he sees them from the perspective of retirement and the other accompaniments of aging are often different in certain respects than they were before as a more active participant in those events.

Research evidence indicates also that an individual's responses to the events associated with retirement and to the changes brought about in his daily routine depend very largely upon his basic personality structure, his unique pattern of basic dispositions to respond to life's events generally. A general conclusion of one extensive investigation of the adjustments to retirement of men at different ages was that those who were better equipped personally to stand up under stress generally adjusted most successfully to retirement (Reichard, Livson, and Peterson, 1962).[3] These were the ones who found satisfaction in their activities and were able to accept change with greater equanimity. They were also those who tended to seek rather than to avoid social contacts.

These investigators, in the statistical analysis of their data, were able to describe three groups of men of roughly similar patterns of behavior dispositions who adjusted "successfully" to retirement. These groups were the "mature" ones described as having a more constructive approach to life, the "rocking chair type" who were inclined to be dependent upon others, and the "armored" type who maintained well-developed sets of psychological defenses against anxiety.

Thus it may be concluded that not only does one undergo some change in personality in the broad sense as a result of retirement, but the *manner* in which one adjusts to the associated events and the changes depends upon one's "individuality"—one's pattern of basic dispositions to respond to life in general.

Women who have worked for years also have their problems of adjusting to retirement, adjustments which in most instances are probably not greatly different from those of men. Since it has been only in relatively recent years that great numbers of women have taken permanent jobs and have entered the professions, published research is lacking regarding their particular retirement problems.

Developmental Tasks of the Aging

The meaning of the fact of growing old, to the individual, and the manner in which he responds and adjusts to it, as we have seen, is largely a matter of basic personality—of the individual's pattern of emotional behavior dispositions.

> Some older men and women become petulant, demanding and difficult to please. Life becomes a burden for them, and for those who care for them. They resent the "insults of aging" as they gradually lose their physical attractiveness and powers, their jobs and status, their loved ones, and their former sources of satisfaction and fulfillment.

[3] The earlier study of Terman and Oden (1959) of the factors contributing to successful adaptation to aging is also pertinent here.

Other aging men and women find the "golden years" of life the most fruitful of all, as they gather the harvest of a lifetime and keep on vigorously growing to the very last. Oliver Wendell Holmes observed in his later years that being seventy years young is far better than being forty years old.

[Duvall, 1957, p. 436]

However, even though one's basic personality structure may have become pretty well organized quite early in life (Chapter 13) and may, therefore, continue to play a dominant role in determining the nature of one's responses to his world of events, the many years of unique experience prior to the period of aging undoubtedly also have had much to do with his capacity to adjust "successfully" to the processes of aging and the events associated with them.

Modern society, of course, is concerned about the problems of retirement and aging and has provided facilities to help the individual prepare ahead of time for a comfortable and constructive old age. The elderly, it is assumed, can also be helped to realize that the period of aging is a period of development with its particular "developmental tasks" which can be worked at and achieved.

As has already been implied, perhaps the most basic general developmental task of the elderly person—one upon which much else depends—is that of finding life meaningful for himself. And it is in the areas of interpersonal, particularly intergenerational, relationships that the most meaningful and rewarding experiences lie. A number of specific developmental tasks for enhancing family interaction in the later stages of family development have been proposed (Duvall, 1958). Older persons can often find ways of making life more meaningful and more personally satisfying in the following ways:

> Making more close, warm, and creative one's relations and interaction patterns with one's mate.
>
> Keeping in touch with the "children," and without being overintrusive or exploitive cultivate close and meaningful adult-adult relationships with them.
>
> Developing the role of grandparent and making one's self warmly available to the growing grandchildren. Perhaps nothing will be remembered and more cherished in the life of a child than knowing and doing things with a grandparent.

Life in later years can indeed be full and meaningful.

Summary

The emphasis in this final chapter has been upon the importance of the relations between generations in the family setting during the periods of family establishment, maturity, and aging.

In young adulthood marriage normally takes place, and very shortly children are born. That, of course, is the beginning of intergenerational relationships. It is emphasized that from the very beginning parent-child interaction—father-infant as well as mother-infant—is an exceedingly important factor in the personal development of both parent and child. Since the father's role in the family has been rather generally neglected, its significance and its potentiality for healthy personal development in both father and baby are discussed.

Likewise, the importance of adequate mothering, especially during infancy and early childhood, was stressed, both from the standpoint of the infant's needs and as a satisfying and personally fulfilling role for women.

In general, the years of family expansion and achievement are hectic years. They are crucial years because it is then that patterns of family interaction are established. The quality of these patterns determines family atmosphere and has much to do with the psychological development of the younger generation.

Common problems of middle age stem largely from the realization of the processes of physical change, including changes in physiological functioning, such as the menopause in women, and the accompanying loss of the idealized characteristics of the younger years. Associated with these personal concerns often come disturbances of husband-wife and parent-adolescent relationships. The degree of integrity attained by parents is a crucial factor in meeting and resolving these emotional crises of middle age.

The time of retirement from one's major life's occupation is looked forward to, or dreaded, in varying degrees. In any event, personal adjustment to such a radical change must be made. Aging generally also involves gradual loss in sensory acuity, muscular strength, and general motor dexterity. The cultivation and enjoyment of relationships and positive patterns of interaction with children and grandchildren can bring much satisfaction to the aging person and can be an important factor in the development of the younger ones.

APPENDIX A

Standards and Techniques for Assessing and Tracing Individual Development

The Iowa Growth Norms

It is obvious that raw quantitative measurements of the dimensions of a child's body, accurate as they may be, *by themselves* are of no value in appraising his growth status. Some standard of reference with which to compare a particular measurement is necessary to give it meaning.

The following tables contain average heights and weights of boys and of girls, together with measures of variation, based upon the growth data collected at the Iowa Child Welfare Research Station (Jackson and Kelly, 1945). Weights and measurements of some 1500 boys and 1500 girls of the Iowa population were used. Even though these were children living in a particular locality during a particular period of time, it is believed that they are sufficiently representative of American children generally for our purpose here. The student will find them useful as standards of reference for interpreting individual measurement values.

Forms for Plotting Growth Progress

A set of forms prepared by the staff of the Iowa Child Welfare Research Station facilitates the plotting of growth curves of stature and weight (Jackson and Kelly, 1945). These forms contain growth curves based upon the Iowa growth data referred to earlier. There are, in all, six forms— three for boys and three for girls. These six sheets thus present, in graphic form, the complete set of norms derived from 13,500 height observations

TABLE A.1   Median Weights (with 16th and 84th Percentiles) and Mean Heights (with Standard Deviations) for the Iowa Samples of Boys[a]

Age	Weight			Height	
Years–Months	Pounds	16th Percentile	84th Percentile	Inches	SD
Birth	7.5	6.6	8.3	20.0	0.7
0–1	9.8	8.7	9.3	21.6	0.7
0–2	12.3	11.0	13.8	23.0	0.8
0–3	14.3	12.8	15.8	24.2	0.8
0–6	18.3	16.3	20.3	26.8	0.9
0–9	21.2	18.8	23.4	28.5	1.0
1–0	22.8	20.8	25.6	30.0	1.0
1–6	25.0	23.6	29.0	32.6	1.0
2–0	28.5	25.9	31.8	34.6	1.1
2–6	31.0	27.6	34.4	36.3	1.4
3–0	33.3	29.4	37.0	37.8	1.5
4–0	37.7	32.9	42.0	40.7	1.5
5–0	42.0	37.5	46.5	43.2	1.6
6–0	46.0	40.7	51.0	45.7	1.6
6–6	48.0	43.5	54.0	46.8	1.8
7–0	50.8	45.5	57.5	48.0	2.0
7–6	53.5	47.5	61.0	49.2	2.0
8–0	56.8	50.0	65.0	50.2	2.2
8–6	60.0	52.0	69.0	51.5	2.3
9–0	63.0	54.7	72.7	52.5	2.4
9–6	65.9	57.0	76.8	53.5	2.4
10–0	69.6	60.0	81.0	54.5	2.4
10–6	73.0	62.7	85.2	55.4	2.5
11–0	76.0	65.2	89.8	56.4	2.5
11–6	79.8	68.0	94.0	57.2	2.5
12–0	83.5	71.0	99.0	58.2	2.7
12–6	87.5	74.0	104.0	59.3	2.7
13–0	92.7	78.0	110.5	60.5	3.1
14–0	105.5	87.0	125.0	62.9	3.5
15–0	119.9	98.0	139.0	65.0	3.5
16–0	130.2	110.0	147.0	67.0	3.0
17–0	137.5	119.0	152.0	68.0	2.4
18–0	142.7	125.0	156.0	68.5	2.5

[a] These values were derived from the Iowa normative growth curves (Figures A.1 through A.3 are examples.), based on measurements made at the Iowa Child Welfare Station by Jackson and Kelly (1945).

and 11,000 weight observations made upon some 3,000 boys and girls from birth to age 18 years.

The three forms for boys are shown in Figures A.1 through A.3.[1] They represent average growth in boys (1) during the first year of life, (2) from birth to age 6 years, and (3) from 5 to 18 years, respectively. The upper

[1] These forms may be obtained from the Iowa Child Welfare Research Station, Iowa University, Iowa City, Iowa.

TABLE A.2   Median Weights (with 16th and 84th Percentiles) and Mean Heights (with Standard Deviations) for the Iowa Samples of Girls[a]

Age	Weight			Height	
Years–Months	Pounds	16th Percentile	84th Percentile	Inches	SD
Birth	7.5	6.5	8.5	19.7	0.7
0–1	8.7	7.7	9.8	21.2	0.8
0–2	11.0	9.5	12.2	22.5	0.8
0–3	13.0	11.0	14.3	23.6	0.8
0–6	17.0	14.8	18.7	26.2	0.9
0–9	19.4	17.2	21.6	27.8	0.9
1–0	21.3	19.0	24.2	29.3	1.0
1–6	24.6	22.4	27.4	32.0	1.0
2–0	27.3	25.0	30.1	34.3	1.2
2–6	30.0	27.0	32.8	36.0	1.4
3–0	32.4	29.4	35.5	37.5	1.4
4–0	37.0	33.6	41.5	40.3	1.4
5–0	41.1	36.7	46.0	42.9	1.5
6–0	45.2	39.8	49.5	45.3	1.6
6–6	47.2	42.0	53.0	46.5	1.7
7–0	50.0	44.0	56.3	47.6	1.8
7–6	52.5	46.0	59.8	48.8	1.9
8–0	55.5	48.2	63.2	49.8	2.0
8–6	58.0	50.5	67.0	51.0	2.1
9–0	61.4	53.0	71.5	52.0	2.3
9–6	64.3	56.0	76.0	53.0	2.5
10–0	68.0	58.4	81.5	54.1	2.5
10–6	71.7	61.9	89.0	55.3	2.5
11–0	76.0	65.0	93.5	56.5	2.5
11–6	81.0	68.8	100.0	57.9	2.6
12–0	87.0	73.0	106.0	59.0	3.0
12–6	92.0	78.0	112.0	60.3	2.8
13–0	99.0	83.7	117.7	61.4	2.8
14–0	107.5	93.2	127.5	62.9	2.1
15–0	113.3	100.0	133.0	63.4	2.0
16–0	116.0	103.0	135.5	63.5	2.3
17–0	117.5	105.5	136.0	63.5	2.3
18–0	118.0	107.0	135.0	63.5	2.4

[a] These values were derived from the Iowa normative growth curves for girls, based on measurements made at the Iowa Child Welfare Station by Jackson and Kelly (1945).

half of the sheet, in each case, shows the curve of increase in weight in terms of average (median) weights at each successive age level. Curves based upon measures of variation about the average (16th and 84th percentiles) are plotted. The curves in the lower portion of the sheet, in each case, similarly represent the norms for height. Note, however, that the average-height curves are drawn from *mean* values, and the deviation curves represent −1 and +1 standard deviation units from the mean.

In using these sheets for portraying growth progress, we plot the indi-

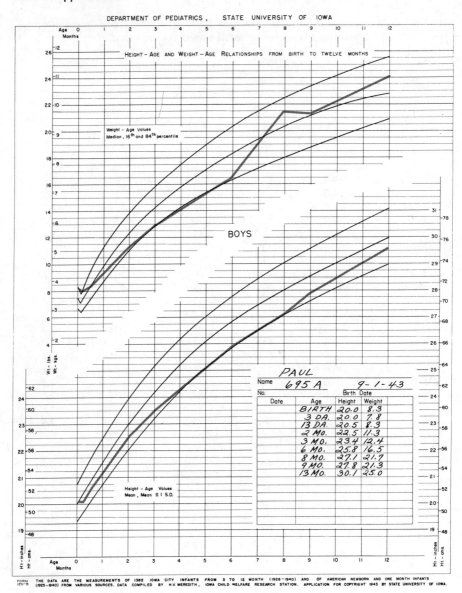

DEPARTMENT OF PEDIATRICS ,   STATE UNIVERSITY OF IOWA

HEIGHT – AGE AND WEIGHT – AGE RELATIONSHIPS FROM BIRTH TO TWELVE MONTHS

Weight – Age Values
Median , 16th and 84th percentile

BOYS

Wt – lbs.
Wt – kgs.

Height – Age Values
Mean , Mean ± I S.D.

Name		PAUL	
No.	695 A	Birth Date	9- 1- 43
Date	Age	Height	Weight
	BIRTH	20.0	8.3
	3 DA.	20.0	7.8
	13 DA.	20.5	8.3
	2 MO.	22.5	11.3
	3 MO.	23.4	12.4
	6 MO.	25.8	16.5
	8 MO.	27.1	21.7
	9 MO.	27.8	21.3
	13 MO.	30.1	25.0

Ht – inches
Ht – cms.

Age
Months

FORM
120-B   THE DATA ARE THE MEASUREMENTS OF 1382 IOWA CITY INFANTS FROM 3 TO 12 MONTH (1926–1940) AND OF AMERICAN NEWBORN AND ONE MONTH INFANTS
(1925–1940) FROM VARIOUS SOURCES. DATA COMPILED BY H.V. MEREDITH, IOWA CHILD WELFARE RESEARCH STATION. APPLICATION FOR COPYRIGHT 1943 BY STATE UNIVERSITY OF IOWA.

Figure A.1   Iowa form for plotting length of infant through the first year of life.

vidual child's measurements against the corresponding chronological ages on the form, using the scales provided. We can then directly compare the individual curves with the existing normative curves.

As the authors of these devices point out, much information can be read from the plotted growth curves (Jackson and Kelly, 1945). The graphic picture shows the individual's course of growth in height and in weight separately and the average or expected path of growth in height and in

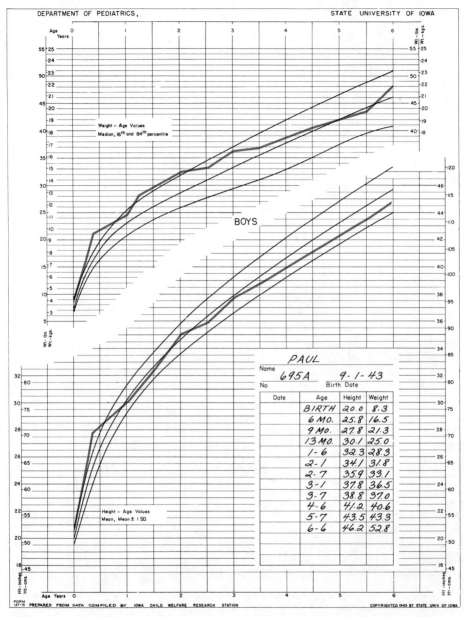

Figure A.2   Iowa form for plotting height of a child through the first six years of life.

weight, and comparisons can be easily made. Then, by examining the level of the height-age curve in relation to the weight-age curve at corresponding points, a clear appraisal of body build as well as relative size can be made.

On Figures A.1 through A.3, for example, are plotted the growth progress of our subject Paul from birth to age 17 years 8 months. From these curves

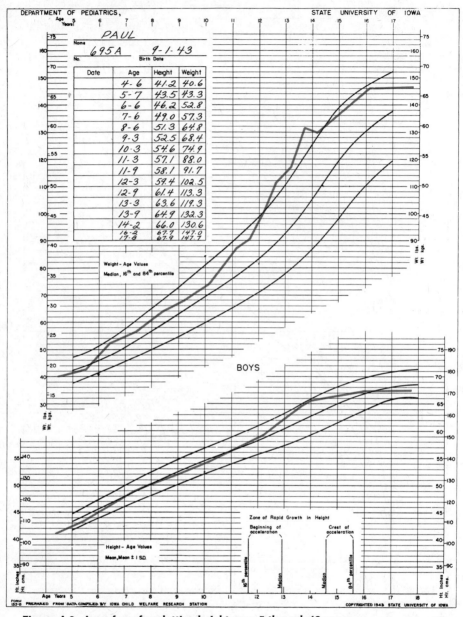

Figure A.3 Iowa form for plotting height ages 5 through 18 years.

alone we can gain a fairly accurate impression of the relative size and body build of this boy at any point in his development. Changes in body build and relative size from time to time are also readily seen.

The fact that growth in height remains more stable than weight may be seen in these graphs. Weight is more readily influenced by environmental factors and by variations in nutritional status and health than is height. Note the clarity of this variation in the curves covering the first 12 months. Although Paul was a somewhat smaller-than-average baby during his first 6 months (and he continued to be shorter than average), at 8 months he was considerably heavier than average. From that point on, with some fluctuations in weight status, he tended to be heavy for his height.

The puberal growth spurt is particularly evident in Paul's growth curves. At 12 years of age he was close to the Iowa mean in height, but considerably above the median in weight. At that point he began to gain status in height as well as in weight until age 14 he would have been among the taller 17 percent of the Iowa boys and approximately among the heaviest 10 percent. Thus during his puberal period he fit the pattern of the "fast grower," and, like fast growers generally, he leveled off rather abruptly toward his terminal height and weight. He showed relatively little increase in height after age 16.

A disadvantage of this simple-growth-curve method of plotting in terms of raw measurements is that different aspects of growth cannot be plotted together for direct comparison. Weight must be plotted separately from height because their scale units are qualitatively different and in no sense equivalent. The two curves, of course, are drawn in close proximity, as in these examples, thus facilitating comparisons in terms of their respective group norms, but basically the two curves are of two different orders and are not directly comparable.

The Grid Technique for Appraising Growth[2]

In 1941 Norman C. Wetzel developed a device for depicting graphically the longitudinal growth of individual children in terms of changes in body size and shape. This device, known as the Wetzel grid (Fig. A.4), is a chart of growth that can be read directly from the age period between 2 and 18 years. It consists of two distinct but related divisions, each with a different purpose and function. The left portion consists essentially of two logarithmic scales. One of these, the vertical axis, is the weight scale; the other, the horizontal, is the height scale. Running diagonally across the form from the lower left is a set of parallel lines that demarcate seven principal "physique channels." These channels, "taken crosswise, cover a range of physique (body build) from the obese to the extremely slender type, and channel-wise, a range of development from infancy to maturity" (Wetzel, 1941, p. 1195).

[2] Much of the present explanation of the structure of the grid forms and the method of interpreting the growth of an individual child when it has been plotted on these forms has been extracted from Wetzel's original articles (1941 and 1946). The reader is referred to these articles for Wetzel's complete explanation of the meaningfulness of the technique and for his own illustrations of growth curves of individual children, which of necessity have been omitted from this explanation.

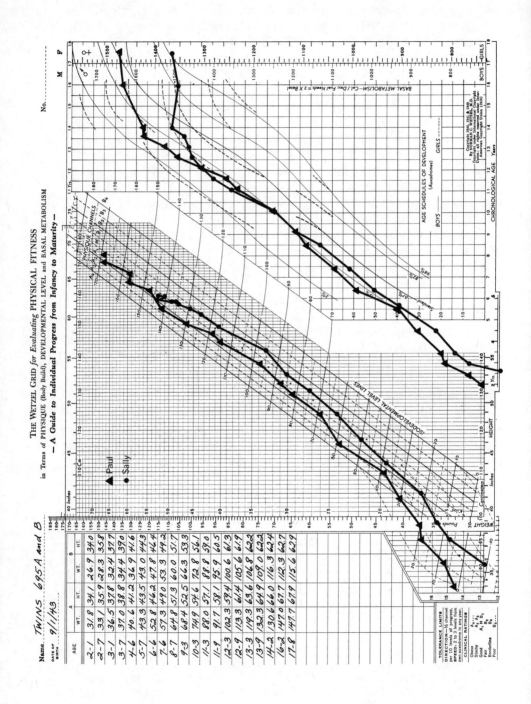

The Wetzel Grid for Evaluating PHYSICAL FITNESS
in Terms of PHYSIQUE (Body Build), DEVELOPMENTAL LEVEL and BASAL METABOLISM
— A Guide to Individual Progress from Infancy to Maturity —

The Physique-Channel System

The assumption underlying the channel construction of the Wetzel grid is that in normal, healthy growth height and weight tend to keep pace with each other throughout the growth period. To the extent to which this stable relation holds for a given child, his growth progress when plotted on the grid's channel system (the left-hand portion of the form) will follow consistently the particular physique channel that is "natural" for him. Wetzel states the significance of up-channel progress as follows:

> Healthy developmental progress continues in an established channel as though this were a preferred path; channel width accounts for accidental variation which does not exceed one-half channel per 10 units of advancement. Channel-wise progress indicates development with preservation of given physique; cross-channel progress is accompanied by change in physique. The latter type, sufficiently continued, culminates in a pathological state. An upward trend greater than that of the channel slope indicates that obesity is in the making; a downward trend less than that of the channel system suggests that "malnutrition" is not far removed. [1941, p. 1195]

The channel system of the grid, then, portrays the child's body build and reveals the consistency with which he maintains it throughout the growth period. The child's progress up-channel can also be seen and measured from one date to another in terms of *isodevelopmental* levels. These levels are marked off by solid and broken lines that cut across the channels. The distance from one solid line to the next (10 levels) represents the growth in size that children on the average make in a period of about 10 months. Thus we can learn from the channel graph something about the child's size and his growth in size as well as his body build.

The Auxodromes

The isodevelopmental-level lines are continued across to the right portion of the grid and thus establish the vertical-level scale for overall body size. This scale, along with the chronological-age scale on the corresponding horizontal axis, forms the boundary of the *auxodrome field* for plotting body size against chronological age.

A set of normative growth curves are drawn in this right-hand panel. The curves are called auxodromes, or schedules of growth. They

> display advanced, normal and retarded patterns of developmental progress and may, accordingly, be taken to show how physical development proceeds with respect to age during its channel course on the grid. These curves are, in a very real sense schedules of progress which indicate how far the ad-

Figure A.4   (Left) The Wetzel Grid with data plotted for Paul (A) and Sally (B) 695.

vanced, regular and retarded child may be expected to have developed at a given age. . . .

The percentage figure at the lower end of each curve indicates the relative number of children who are on, or ahead of the respective schedule. Thus, only 2 per cent will have advanced in their development at successive ages to the comparatively high levels which the uppermost curve calls for; 67 per cent will have reached the levels given by the center auxodrome on or before the corresponding ages to which it refers; finally, 98 per cent of children will at least have reached the lowest curve, so that 2 per cent may be expected to remain behind this in their development. The 67 per cent curve is taken as the standard of reference by which physical advancement or retardation in a given child may be measured.

Distinction is made between boys and girls. During the earlier stages from 5 to 9 years, to which Stratz referred as "neutral childhood," boys and girls follow a common course to the lower point of bifurcation. Thenceforward girls [broken curves in Figure A.4] tend quite characteristically to proceed ahead of boys [solid curves] toward their own upper boundaries and with earlier cessation of development. [Wetzel, 1941, p. 1191]

The grid also provides a satisfactory means of estimating the basal metabolic rate of children, and, from that, their required daily caloric intake at the time measurements are taken. Basal heat production is estimated directly from developmental level (body size). To take proper account of sex differences, the basal heat production scales for boys and girls are separately aligned with the developmental level on the right-hand edge of the grid. Furthermore,

To obtain the maximum daily caloric intake for either sex at any developmental level one has merely to multiply the corresponding basal heat value by 2. Average values, such as those given in the White House Conference Reports [1932] are, of course, somewhat lower, the factor being 1.9 for boys and 1.8 for girls. The 10, 20, 30 and 50 per cent above basal values used in calculating reducing diets are likewise easily computed. [Wetzel, 1941, p. 1193]

The Baby Grid

Later, in 1946, Wetzel published his baby grid, which is an application of the grid technique to the period from birth to age 3 years.

An Abstract of a Developmental Record

The Source: A Program of Study and Service

The longitudinal studies program was begun in the early days of the Merrill Palmer School in order to provide a facility for the firsthand observation and study of children and families. Mothers with their newborn infants, and prospective mothers, were enrolled on a long-term basis and services were set up to suit the changing needs of both the children and their parents as the family developed.

In this program the three primary purposes of the school were facilitated:

1. *Education.* This was in the areas of child development and family relations. A "laboratory" was provided in which students could observe children and their behavior, along with the associated circumstances and influences, and record what they saw.

2. *Research.* Behavioral and developmental records were kept of observed behavior and personal characteristics of anthropometric measurements and of tests administered and ratings made by the faculty of the school.

3. *Service.* An infant service, a nursery school, and a recreational club program were set up to serve the social and other needs of the children as they developed, and a consultation service was provided for the benefit of the parents. These "services," of course, also provided the settings for the school's educational and research functions.

The Record Abstract

Judy 730 and her mother were enrolled in the school's program before she was born. The following material was abstracted from her rather voluminous record that accumulated through the years of her contact with the school.

Judy's Parents and their Background

Both of the parents of Mr. 730 came from Russia and were of Jewish heritage. The father was a smallish man, 5 feet 4 inches and 150 pounds. He had completed two years of college work in Russia. He was a grocer by occupation. The mother finished high school in Russia. She had no occupation other than that of wife and mother.

Mr. 730 was born in Minneapolis, Minnesota. At the early age of 19 he became manager of a market, and later he was advertising manager of a manufacturing firm. It was at this time that he met and married his life partner.

About a year after marriage Mr. 730 entered the United States Army and began training to be a pilot.

Mrs. 730's father was a Polish immigrant who graduated with honors in mechanical engineering from an American college. Her mother ended her

TABLE A.3   Physical Growth Data of Judy 730

Age (Years–Months)	Weight (Pounds)	Height (Inches)
Birth	6.5	18.7
0–2	10.1	21.3
0–4	13.7	23.7
0–6	17.0	25.0
0–8	19.2	26.5
0–10	21.5	27.4
1–2	23.2	29.5
1–4	23.5	30.5
1–6	24.2	31.2
1–8	25.9	32.2
1–10	26.2	32.8
2–3	28.7	34.3
2–8	30.7	36.4
3–4	34.1	38.5
3–8	36.3	39.5
4–4	38.8	41.4
4–10	42.1	42.1
5–7	45.3	44.6
6–6	52.5	47.0
7–6	66.9	49.3
9–3	96.5	53.8
9–9	95.3	54.9
10–3	103.8	55.9
10–9	109.5	56.7
11–3	109.8	57.8
11–9	117.7	59.3
12–6	121.8	60.8
13–8	132.0	62.6
14–9	134.6	63.1
16–7	138.6	63.4

formal education with high school graduation. Her parents were inclined to be strict and not to demonstrate affection.

Mrs. 730 graduated from college with a bachelor of science degree in education. She also did some work toward an advanced degree. At the time of her marriage she was teaching health education. During her husband's aviation training she did some additional graduate work in vocational education.

At maturity, Mrs. 730 was just under 5 feet tall and weighed 125 pounds.

Judy arived at the end of a full-term, normal pregnancy. Her father, who had been serving overseas, was on a 30-day leave at the time of her birth.

The period following Judy's birth undoubtedly was a rather trying time for Mrs. 730. Having to care for and manage her first baby without the presence and support of her husband, she found her situation rather difficult. She was living in the home of her parents, who gave her no support or encouragement in her desire to try "new" methods of child rearing about which she had been reading.

When Judy was about 4 months old, Mr. 730 was released from the service to return to his family. For some time the young family continued to live with Mrs. 730's parents while the couple looked for a place of their own.

Immediately, Mr. 730 began sharing in Judy's physical care. This young couple felt that it was important that their baby should be helped to be acquainted and to feel equally "at home" with both parents.

TABLE A.4   Skeletal Maturation Data of Judy 730

Age (Years–Months)	Skeletal Age
0–4	0–4
0–6	0–6
0–9	0–9
1–3	1–2
1–6	1–6
2–3	2–3
2–6	2–6
3–6	3–6
4–3	4–2
4–6	4–6
4–10	4–11
5–6	5–7
5–9	5–9
6–6	6–7
7–6	7–8
8–6	8–8
9–3	9–6
9–9	10–2
10–3	10–8
10–9	10–11

TABLE A.5   Mental Test Data of Judy 730

Age (Years–Months)	Test	DA or MA	DQ or IQ
0–6.5	Gesell Developmental	0–8	123[a]
1–3	Gesell Developmental	1–6	120[a]
2–3	Gesell Developmental	3–0	134[a]
2–10	Stanford-Binet	3–8	129
3–7	Stanford-Binet	4–6	126
9–3	WISC	—	109

[a] Estimated average values.

TABLE A.6   Developmental Chronology of Judy 730

Age	Environmental Events and Circumstances	Development (Physical, Behavioral, Cognitive, Social)
Birth	Full term; labor 27 hours, spontaneous delivery	"Good" condition at birth Birth weight 6 pounds 5 ounces, length 18.7 inches
0–2	Breast milk gave out, baby put on formula; now on self-demand, four feeding schedule Father away, but two uncles very fond of Judy	Plays with hands; has rolled from supine Responds with smiles to adult advances Pushes self up from stomach
0–4	Father now at home; "rough house" with father or uncles Family still living with mother's parents	Can roll from supine to prone; crawls backward; reaches with right hand for object "Squeals, gurgles, bubbles, coos"
0–6	Now in home of their own Mother a happy, relaxed kind of person—keen interest in children	Now starting to creep; raises self to hands and knees; pulls to sitting position "A friendly, happy baby"
0–8	Many visitors on Sundays	Picked up block—pincer grasp; creeps all over house Says "da da," "ma ma," imitates barking dog Some shyness
0–9	Parents play with Judy in bed	
1–3	Gesell Developmental Test Mr. 730 showed some concern about Judy's terrific destructiveness Had been left one week with maid	"Very advanced" in gross motor coordination; walks and runs easily; squats in play; "high average" fine-motor coordinations "High average" in language and adaptive behavior Advanced in personal–social area
1–6	Gesell Developmental Test Overstimulation at times at home; visitors—uncles and grandparents; mother concerned about Judy's wakefulness at night	*Advanced* in gross motor; walks up and down stairs without assistance High average in fine-motor coordinations, adaptive behavior, and language; mother reports vocabulary of more than 20 words; uses 3- and 4-word sentences

TABLE A.6 (continued)   Developmental Chronology of Judy 730

Age	Environmental Events and Circumstances	Development (Physical, Behavioral, Cognitive, Social)
		Very advanced in personal-social development: Feeds self completely
1–8	Practically no toilet training up to now	Beginning of voluntary urinary control on Judy's part
1–10	No pressure or much effort made to train Judy in elimination control	Now "very reliable" in using nursery seat for urination; seems also to be "taking over" bowel control
2–0	Family temporarily at home of grandparents; have acquired a dog Judy accepted for nursery school Parents left for two weeks	
2–3	Family back to own home Mother upset by a friend, a "lay analyst," visiting in home who said Judy seemed to be bothered by "some deep-seated frustration"—cause of her temper tantrums Gesell Developmental Test	Judy able to "act for herself" on her own decision Both affectionate and aggressive toward other children; much "emotional energy," healthy, energetic, curious At times wanted what other child had, at other times much affection shown for other children Skilled motor coordinations, advanced language; advanced in all areas, particularly personal-social
2–4	Entered nursery school; new glasses bothered Judy Stanford-Binet test attempted, not completed Mother concerned about Judy's sleep pattern Parents now allow her to remain with them when she comes to their bed Neighborhood playmate with blond hair is much admired by adults to Judy's neglect; she also hears adults remark that "it's a crime" that Judy must soon wear glasses; mother tries to make wearing of glasses a more attractive prospect	Goes to parents' bed many times during night; apparent "insecurity feeling" about mother; protests mother leaving her at nursery school Judy in nursery school was observed to pull the light, curly hair of two children
2–7	Many interesting activities at home—ice skating with father, finger painting A recent period of illness Mother pregnant—hopes to get Judy into a good sleep routine before new baby arrives	Has trouble with new glasses at nursery school Has given up diapers at night; wet only one night in recent weeks; bladder "accidents" rare during daytime Poor appetite since illness "Whimpered a few tears" when mother left her at nursery school

TABLE A.6 (continued)   Developmental Chronology of Judy 730

Age	Environmental Events and Circumstances	Development (Physical, Behavioral, Cognitive, Social)
2–9	Baby brother born	
2–10	New baby in the home	Judy delights in helping care for baby
	Broken glasses—appears to have difficulty seeing any distance	
	Mother concerned about Judy's "adjustment" at nursery school; thinks child is emotionally disturbed, suggests getting help from a psychiatrist	
	"Often looks ragged and neglected, underwear sometimes dirty, seems unbathed" (staff report)	Very active at play when at nursery school, enjoys other children
	Stanford-Binet Test, child handicapped without glasses	Attention span brief; some irritable refusals in test, MA = 3–8, IQ = 129; results of test somewhat indecisive because of refusals
	Judy's total situation at this time appears to be one of stress	
3–3	Beginning new nursery school year	Engages in more cooperative play at nursery school than formerly
	Now has breakfast with family	Becoming more ambivalent toward little brother; some regressive behavior —sucked on a bottle for two days, said, "I wanted to be a baby"
	Mother pregnant again	
	Father absent on business trip	
	House hunting	
	Comments about coming of new baby	
3–5	Having play therapy interviews	Seems to be overcoming some of her emotional difficulties
3–7	Stanford-Binet test; neglect at home? (looks uncared for, clothes seem to be "thrown together," hair not well cut or combed)	Judy gives impression of toughness both physically and psychologically; she whined and complained about tasks of the test—MA = 4–6, IQ = 126
3–9	New baby in the home	In nursery school Judy is now more absorbed in social contacts with children, less clinging to teachers; often shows qualities of leadership; generally "more relaxed, smiling, and prettier than we have ever seen her" (staff report)
	Family now living in a more adequate home	
4–3	Beginning of new nursery school term	
	Mother reported that parents had tried to make past summer "especially for Judy"; many pleasant home activities—trips, getting wood for fireplace, making jack-o-lanterns	
4–7	Certain "leaders" in nursery school, and those she regards	Plays almost exclusively with children she admires; sometimes engages with

TABLE A.6 (continued)   Developmental Chronology of Judy 730

Age	Enviromental Events and Circumstances	Development (Physical, Behavioral, Cognitive, Social)
	as important, wield much influence upon Judy	them in nonconforming activities
		Expresses definite likes and dislikes for her peers; very expressive in her feelings—cries when hurt, laughs when happy, frowns when irritated, refuses to participate when not interested.
		Occasionally irritable and "out of sorts," expresses this in hitting or asking another child to do the hitting for her; "nothing seems to satisfy her"
		Has planned her own sleeping schedule at home
		Objected to wearing her glasses—"look ugly"
5–0	Joined a special, older group for her final nursery school period; this was an especially important change for Judy	Judy gives impression of being "stocky" —somewhat shorter and heavier than other children, but is now extremely skillful in handling her body
	Now makes the noon meal a social occasion	Is always busy and must be involved in every activity
	Was accepted as the fourth member of a little subgroup with whom Judy is especially congenial	More independent; no longer irritable. seems completely freed for happy activity
5–8	Baby sister born	Judy enters vigorously into hostile activities against club leader (locking her in closet)
	Now a member of recreational club; club leaders see Judy as one who needs help and support in art work and other activities	
6–0	At home, children are free to express their feelings	Mother feels that Judy has "regressed" since birth of sister
	Grandmother living in the home, often does not approve	In competing for leadership among neighborhood children Judy is at times inclined to use bribery
6–6	Occupies a middle position in club as to age	Personality was not particularly pleasing in comparison with others in club; not as pretty
	Leader tries to give Judy extra attention	Demands considerable attention; becomes impatient, irritable if not given immediate attention
		More of a follower than a leader
		Did not relate strongly to any one member of group
7–6		Judy's personality described as "not very attractive, but refreshing"; tends to be aggressive, outspoken,

TABLE A.6 (continued)   Developmental Chronology of Judy 730

Age	Environmental Events and Circumstances	Development (Physical, Behavioral, Cognitive, Social)
		demanding, and impatient; "frustration threshold" low
		Appears to be leader of group by making plans, but gives directions in an autocratic manner; children resist this (report of a club leader)
8–0		Judy is pretty well balanced though she has her problems
		Stands up for her rights, not shy
		Will also defend the rights of others; inclined to assert herself
		Independent and self-reliant most of the time
9–3	WISC administered Interviewed on food likes and dislikes	Described as "short heavy girl"; talks in a loud voice, says things emphatically
		Made loud protestations that test items were too hard
		Responded well to reassurance and praise; full scale IQ = 109
		Concerned about her weight and size, and so on

APPENDIX **C**

An Approach to the Study of the Social Behavior of an Individual Child

Development of the Rating Procedures

In Chapter 14 reference was made to a long-term study of personality development. It included the analysis of social behavior data collected many years ago on a group of nursery children. The instrument used in collecting these data was a set of behavior checklists containing some 220 items. In order to provide for students a practical procedure patterned after the earlier study for the firsthand study and portrayal of the typical social behavior and personality trends of a particular child, the following materials were developed:

> A revised and abbreviated version of the checklists used in the earlier study (Roberts and Ball, 1938; Stott, 1962), consisting of 166 selected items, was drawn up. During the early 1960s, through the cooperation of the directors and teachers of nursery schools in the Detroit area, rating of 310 children were obtained by use of this checklist. As before, the raters were asked to consider carefully the child's overall behavior over a period of time and to check for him only those items which most truly characterized him.

Children's Behavior Checklist

Name _____ School or Agency _____

Age _____ Grade _____ Sex _____ Time of Day _____

Directions: Check only those statements which you feel are *really true* of the child. Do not guess if you are not reasonably sure.

    1. ☐ Vigorous and energetic in his attack on a project

2. ☐ Overcautious, not venturesome, afraid to attempt the untried
3. ☐ Nearly always accomplishes task in spite of difficulties
4. ☐ Voice animated, alive
5. ☐ Does not become fatigued easily
6. ☐ Poor in concentration
7. ☐ Merely copies other children's reactions, not original
8. ☐ Concentrates well at his task
9. ☐ Original and inventive reactions
10. ☐ Curious and questioning
11. ☐ Expresses himself well for his age
12. ☐ Resourceful in dealing with difficult situations
13. ☐ Poor use of language for his age
14. ☐ Patient
15. ☐ Absorbed; self-sufficient in his activity
16. ☐ Restless; a certain dissatisfaction with his own activity
17. ☐ Retiring; wishes to be in the background
18. ☐ Even-tempered
19. ☐ Frequently disturbed; easily upset by the disagreeable or exciting
20. ☐ Seldom disturbed; sudden changes in mood infrequent
21. ☐ Slow to adjust to a novel experience
22. ☐ Original in play
23. ☐ Is easily distracted from task at hand
24. ☐ Gives up easily, lacks persistence
25. ☐ Submits to any child who takes the initiative
26. ☐ Dominates children of his own age (either sex)
27. ☐ Will submit to a specific child only
28. ☐ Submits to a leader only after a struggle to dominate
29. ☐ Is a follower in one specific group only
30. ☐ Occasionally dominates a group
31. ☐ Usually leads a small group
32. ☐ Decides who shall participate in the group activities
33. ☐ Can organize the activities of a group to carry out a definite purpose
34. ☐ Leads or follows as the occasion demands
35. ☐ Neither leads nor follows; plays alone
36. ☐ Dominates other children through his ability to talk effectively
37. ☐ Dominates other children through their love or admiration for him
38. ☐ Dominates other children through his wealth of ideas
39. ☐ Definitely schemes to get others to carry out his plans
40. ☐ Gives commands with an air of finality
41. ☐ Helpless unless someone organizes activity for him
42. ☐ Hesitates to initiate activity
43. ☐ Usually follows the ideas of others for activity
44. ☐ Usually has his own ideas for activity
45. ☐ Usually takes the initiative
46. ☐ Does not push the issue in case of opposition
47. ☐ Fights for his place as leader
48. ☐ Insists that other children do as he wishes
49. ☐ Does not defend his own rights with other children
50. ☐ Easily led into mischief by others

51. ☐ Fails to secure cooperation when he tries to direct activities
52. ☐ Gets willing cooperation easily
53. ☐ Almost never laughs or smiles
54. ☐ Has an unusually good sense of humor
55. ☐ Has a way of making an appeal with his eyes
56. ☐ Has a pleasing manner of speech
57. ☐ Thoughtful of others
58. ☐ Moderately selfish
59. ☐ Sympathetic nature
60. ☐ Inconsiderate of others
61. ☐ Polite
62. ☐ Mischievous
63. ☐ Brave when hurt
64. ☐ Truthful
65. ☐ Seldom cries
66. ☐ A good sport
67. ☐ Rough and ready
68. ☐ Forgiving nature
69. ☐ Wanders around aimlessly
70. ☐ Self-conscious
71. ☐ Intelligently cooperative
72. ☐ Often shows off or acts silly
73. ☐ Makes pleasant conversation with adults
74. ☐ Unaffected, spontaneous, natural
75. ☐ Imaginative
76. ☐ Lacks imagination
77. ☐ Eager to try new things
78. ☐ Seems to have a plan for every minute
79. ☐ Brimming over with ideas for activity
80. ☐ Plays or works vigorously
81. ☐ Haphazard methods of work or play
82. ☐ Lacks self-confidence
83. ☐ Adjusts immediately to the daily routine
84. ☐ Always goes through the daily procedure willingly
85. ☐ Has to be constantly urged to carry out routine activities
86. ☐ Takes a long time to adjust to the daily routine
87. ☐ Responds readily to direction in the day's routine
88. ☐ Proceeds as usual with routine in the presence of visitors
89. ☐ Is businesslike and systematic in endeavoring to carry out routine activities
90. ☐ Dawdles over routine activities
91. ☐ Always cooperates in trying to keep the schoolrooms neat and clean
92. ☐ Perfectly natural in the presence of adults
93. ☐ Matter of fact in his relations with adults
94. ☐ Independent of adult in overcoming difficulties
95. ☐ Dependent upon adult to solve difficulties
96. ☐ Independent of adult in having ideas about or planning work or play activities
97. ☐ Resents aid from adults

98. ☐ Pays no attention to visitors
99. ☐ Bids for attention from adults
100. ☐ Craves affection from adults but is afraid to show it
101. ☐ Beautiful features
102. ☐ Usually pleasant facial expression
103. ☐ Expressive eyes
104. ☐ Stands erect
105. ☐ Walks with ease and grace
106. ☐ Does not take possessions of other children without permission
107. ☐ Takes good care of school property while using it
108. ☐ Wants to keep a particular piece of equipment even if not using it himself
109. ☐ Gives up equipment to other children as soon as finished with it
110. ☐ Extreme sense of property rights and keen desire to see this enforced
111. ☐ Shows extreme consideration for school property
112. ☐ Shows extreme consideration for possessions of others
113. ☐ Takes good care of his own possessions
114. ☐ Takes good care of the possessions of other children
115. ☐ Adds cooperatively to suggestions
116. ☐ Lags in following suggestion
117. ☐ Responds without undue delay to authority
118. ☐ So absorbed in his own thoughts that does not comprehend
119. ☐ Cooperative and responsible
120. ☐ Makes friends with other children easily
121. ☐ Finds it difficult to approach other children and make friends
122. ☐ Makes friends with any child who happens to be around him
123. ☐ Resents interest shown by other children; wants to be left alone
124. ☐ Does not respond to friendly advances
125. ☐ Tries to make entry into group of children but fails
126. ☐ Unhappy if he is not playing with other children
127. ☐ So absorbed in his own ideas that he pays no attention to other children
128. ☐ Contributes to the ideas of the group though not a leader (cooperative companion)
129. ☐ Hesitant in making suggestions to other children
130. ☐ Assumes a protective attitude toward other children
131. ☐ Usually pleasant with other children
132. ☐ Often abrupt and surly with other children
133. ☐ Has a pleasant manner of securing cooperation from other children
134. ☐ Has strong likes and dislikes for other children
135. ☐ Rather placid attitude toward other children; neither likes or dislikes them to any degree
136. ☐ Quarrels with other children, often over trivial things
137. ☐ Seldom quarrels with other children over trivial matters
138. ☐ Rough and mean with other children
139. ☐ Hurts other children often due to carelessness
140. ☐ Impatient with other children
141. ☐ Very critical of other children
142. ☐ Is a good sport when he loses to some other child
143. ☐ Is sympathetic toward other children

144. ☐ Affectionate toward other children
145. ☐ Tries to help the smaller children
146. ☐ Resents aid from other children
147. ☐ Forgiving of other children who have hurt him, taken his belongings
148. ☐ Tries to get even with a child with whom he is angry
149. ☐ Talks to other children a great deal
150. ☐ Seldom talks to other children
151. ☐ Cries easily in playing with other children
152. ☐ Generous in letting other children share activities and possessions
153. ☐ Attention from other children leads him to "show off" or act silly
154. ☐ Not jealous if other children play with his particular friends
155. ☐ Faces the issue squarely
156. ☐ Concentrates his energy to accomplish a difficult task
157. ☐ Meets situations in a quiet matter-of-fact manner
158. ☐ Dawdles to avoid a difficult task
159. ☐ Accepts necessary facts as a matter of course
160. ☐ Does the best he can with what he has
161. ☐ Recognizes and accepts the superiority of another child
162. ☐ Accepts just criticism willingly
163. ☐ Finds it difficult to accept just blame for his faults
164. ☐ Regresses to babyish behavior in the face of difficulty
165. ☐ Quietly accepts success
166. ☐ Knows when he has done a task well

Statistical Procedures

In general, the same statistical procedures were used in processing these data as were used in the earlier study. Intercorrelations among the 166 items, as checked by the teachers, were computed. In terms of these correlation coefficients the items were grouped into 40 "clusters." Cluster scores for each child were then derived and correlations among these 40 item-clusters were computed. The resulting matrix of coefficients was then factor analyzed. The outcome was eight factors.

All this, of course, means that the 166 specific behavior descriptions had finally become segregated and grouped, in terms of mutual affinity and meaning, into eight groups (factors). Each factor was interpreted in terms of the generalized meaning of its constituent items, and an identifying label was attached. As before, these factors are tentatively regarded as representing common and pervasive childhood "behavior dispositions." Each has its positive and its negative aspects. Children differ over a wide range in strength of each tendency from strong positive (high score) to strong negative (low score). The height "dispositions" are listed as follows:

Factor A. Social ascendance—lack of leadership
Factor B. Personal responsibility—irresponsible impulsiveness
Factor C. Introvertive self-sufficiency—need for the presence and support of others
Factor D. Social effectiveness (sociability)—social ineptitude

Factor E. Personal attractiveness—lack of personal appeal
Factor F. Personal security; stability—emotional instability (dependency)
Factor G. Compulsive domination—compliant, retiring (adaptability)
Factor H. Dependability—nondependability

These names, of course, were arbitrarily attached to the factors in an effort to convey as clearly as possible the interpreted meaning in each case. As the names suggest, there are some rather close relations among them. For example, factor A, "social ascendance," would seem to be similar in meaning to factor D, "social effectiveness." As a matter of fact they proved to be statistically correlated to the extent of +.65. However, even though some factors do have meaning in common, when their constituent items are examined side by side each is seen to have quite a different aura. There is justification for regarding them as two rather distinct behavior dispositions.

Nature of the Behavior Variables

The distinctive quality of each disposition, and the relations among them, may be sensed in an examination of the listings that follow. The tentative name of each factor appears, along with its complement of item clusters. Following each cluster label is its factor loading in that particular factor.

TABLE A.7   Some Child Behavior Variables with Item Clusters

Factor A   Social Ascendance versus Lack of Leadership

Positive Clusters (Social Ascendance)	Negative Clusters (Lack of Leadership)
Leadership behavior .76	Ineffectiveness − .54
Managerial tendency .74	Fatigability − .51
Vigor .71	Cautious, withdrawing behavior − .51
Originality .70	
Dominance in groups .68	
Zest .66	
Self-reliant behavior .54	
Talkativeness .54	

Factor B   Personal Responsibility versus Irresponsible Impulsiveness

Positive Clusters (Responsibility)	Negative Clusters (Irresponsible Impulsiveness)
Cooperative behavior .69	Impulsive behavior (easily led, mischievious) − .60
Ability to concentrate .64	
Tendency to conform .64	
Empathic tendency .57	
Unselfishness .57	
Responsible behavior .57	
Reality oriented .51	

Factor C   Introvertive Self-sufficiency versus Need for the Presence and Support of Others

Item Clusters (All Positively Loaded)

Self-containedness .37
Self-reliance .37
Resourcefulness .33

Factor D   Social Effectiveness

Item Clusters (All Positively Loaded)

Social ease .65
Friendly behavior .62
Social sensitivity .62

Factor E   Personal Attractiveness

Item Clusters (All Positively Loaded)

Effective personal bearing .70
Pleasant voice .65
Positive physical endowment .51

Factor F   Sense of Personal Security, Stability

Item Clusters (All Positively Loaded)

Independent of adults .65
Emotional maturity .63
Unself-consciousness .56
Affective stability .34

Factor G   Compulsive Domination versus Compliant Adaptability (Retiring)

Positive Clusters *(Compulsive Domination)*	*Negative Clusters* *(Compliant, Retiring)*
Bossiness .44	Submissive behavior −.70
	Affective stability −.42
	Cautious withdrawal −.41

Factor H   Personal Warmness

Positive Clusters *(Warmness)*	*Negative Clusters* *(Lack of Warmness)*
Decisiveness .76	Evasive behavior −.37
Affectionateness .34	
Responsibility .33	

Procedures for Rating an Individual Child

The student may use this checklist method to obtain a view of the social-behavior aspect of the personality of any child with whom he is well acquainted and whose play behavior in relation to others he has observed over a period of time.

A copy of the checklist must first be carefully checked through according to instructions with that particular child in mind. Then, by use of the scoring key, a numerical score on each of the eight traits may be derived.

Scoring Instructions

The letters A–H on the scoring key designate the factor, or factors, for which each item is scored. The x or its absence, in the case of each item, is the key to its scoring. Items on a given child's checklist are counted for the factors indicated when they are checked or not checked, according to this key. The total factor score in each case is the simple count of the items designated for that factor that agree with the key. These raw scores must then be converted into modified standard scores in order to make them comparable and meaningful.

TABLE A.8   Scoring Keys

1. ⊠ A	28. ⊠ G	55. ⊠ DE	82. □ D
2. □ ADG	29. ⊠ A	56. ⊠ D	83. ⊠ B
3. ⊠ A	30. □ A	57. ⊠ B	84. ⊠ B
4. ⊠ D	31. ⊠ A		85. □ B
5. ⊠ A	32. ⊠ G	59. ⊠ B	86. □ B
6. □ B	33. ⊠ A	60. □ B	87. ⊠ B
7. □ A	34. ⊠ D	61. ⊠ B	88. ⊠ F
8. ⊠ AB	35. ⊠ C	62. □ B	89. ⊠ B
9. ⊠ A	36. ⊠ A	63. ⊠ C	
10. ⊠ D	37. ⊠ A	64. ⊠ B	91. ⊠ B
11. ⊠ D	38. ⊠ A	65. ⊠ F □ G	92. ⊠ F
12. ⊠ C	39. ⊠ A	66. ⊠ B	93. ⊠ F
13. □ D	40. ⊠ G	67. □ D ⊠ G	94. ⊠ AC
14. ⊠ B	41. □ A	68. ⊠ B	95. □ AC
15. ⊠ B	42. □ G	69. □ A	96. ⊠ AC
16. □ B	43. □ G	70. □ F	
17. □ ADG	44. ⊠ A	71. ⊠ D	98. ⊠ F
18. ⊠ F □ G	45. ⊠ A	72. □ B	99. □ F
19. □ F ⊠ G	46. □ G	73. ⊠ D	100. □ F
20. ⊠ F ⊠ G	47. ⊠ G	74. ⊠ D	101. ⊠ DE
21. □ A	48. ⊠ G	75. ⊠ A	102. ⊠ D
22. ⊠ A	49. □ AG	76. □ A	103. ⊠ DE
23. □ B	50. □ B	77. ⊠ A	104. ⊠ E
24. □ A	51. ⊠ G	78. ⊠ A	105. ⊠ E
25. □ G	52. ⊠ A	79. ⊠ A	106. ⊠ B
26. ⊠ G	53. □ D		107. ⊠ B
27. ⊠ G	54. ⊠ E	81. □ C	108. □ B

TABLE A.8 (Continued)   Scoring Keys

109. ☒ B	124. ☒ C	139. ☐ B	154. ☒ F
110. ☒ BH	125. ☐ D	140. ☒ G	155. ☒ H
111. ☒ B	126. ☐ C	141. ☐ D	156. ☒ H
112. ☒ B	127. ☒ C	142. ☒ B	157. ☒ B
113. ☒ BH	128. ☒ D	143. ☒ D	158. ☐ C
114. ☒ BH	129. ☐ D	144. ☒ D	159. ☒ B
115. ☒ A	130. ☒ DH	145. ☒ DH	160. ☒ B
116. ☐ H	131. ☒ DH	146. ☐ D	161. ☒ B
117. ☒ B	132. ☐ F ☒ G	147. ☒ DH	162. ☒ F
118. ☒ C	133. ☒ D	148. ☐ DH	163. ☐ F
119. ☒ B	134. ☒ H	149. ☒ AD	164. ☐ H
120. ☒ D	135. ☐ H	150. ☐ AD	165. ☒ B
121. ☐ D	136. ☐ F ☒ G	151. ☐ F ☒ G	166. ☒ B
122. ☒ D	137. ☒ F ☐ G	152. ☒ F	
123. ☐ D	138. ☐ D	153. ☐ B	

Derivation of Standard Scores

Table A.9 has been prepared for converting raw numerical scores into modified standard scores.

TABLE. A.9   For Converting Raw Scores into Modified Standard Scores

Modified Standard Score Equivalent	Raw Factor–Score Range							
	A(1)	B(2)	C(3)	D(4)	E(5)	F(6)	G(7)	H(8)
1	0–1	0	—	0–7	—	0	0	0
2	2	1	0	8	—	1	1	1
3	3–6	2–5	1	9–11	—	2–3	2–3	2
4	7–9	6–10	2	12–15	0	4–6	4–6	3
5	10–13	11–16	3	16–19	1	7–8	7–9	4–5
6	14–17	17–21	4	20–23	2	9–11	10–11	6
7	18–21	22–26	5	24–26	3	12–13	12–14	7
8	22–25	27–32	6	27–30	4	14–15	15–17	8–9
9	26–29	33–37	7	31–34	5	16–18	18–19	10
10	above 29	above 37	above 7	above 34	above 5	above 18	above 19	above 10

The Behavior Profile

The eight derived modified standard scores may then be plotted together on a profile form (Fig. A.5). Standard scores with possible range of 1–10 may be indicated with a dot on the appropriate vertical line.

Name _____   Age _____   Rater _____

Standard Score

	1	2	3	4	5	6	7	8	9	10	
A. Lack of leadership											Social ascendance (leadership)
B. Irresponsible impulsiveness											Personal responsibility
C. Need for presence and support of others											Introspective self-sufficiency
D. Social ineptitude											Social effectiveness (sociability)
E. Lack of personal appeal											Personal attractiveness
F. Emotional instability (dependency)											Personal security, stability
G. Compliant, retiring (adaptability)											Compulsive domination
H. Nondependability											Personal warmness

FIGURE A.5 Social Behavior Profile form. The area between the heavy rules marks the average range of scores.

References

Ackerman, N. W. (ed.). *Family Process.* New York: Basic Books, 1970.

Adamson, J. W. *The educational writings of John Locke.* London: Cambridge University Press, 1922.

Adelman, H. S. Reinforcement effects of adult non-reaction on expectancy of underachieving boys. *Child Develpm.,* 1969, 40: 111–122.

Ainsworth,, M. D. S., S. M. Bell, and D. J. Slaton. Individual differences in the development of some attachment behaviors. *Merrill-Palmer Quart.,* 1972, 18: 123–143.

Aldrich, C. A. The significance of a complete preventive medical program for children. *Am. J. Diseases Child.,* 1955, 86: 186–171.

Aldrich, C. A., M. A. Norval, Catherine Knop, and F. Venegas. The crying of newborn babies IV, a follow-up study after additional nursing care had been provided. *J. Pediat.,* 1946, 28: 665–670.

Aldrich, C. A., C. Sung, and Catherine Knop. The crying of newly born babies. *J. Pediat.,* 1945b, 27: 313–326.

Aldrich, C. A., C. Sung, and Catherine Knop. The crying of newly born babies II. *J. Pediat.,* 1945a, 27: 89–96.

Allport, G. W. *Personality and social encounter.* Boston: Beacon Press, 1960.

Allport, G. W. *Becoming: basic considerations for a psychology of personality.* New Haven: Yale University Press, 1955.

Allport, G. W. *The nature of prejudice.* Reading, Mass.: Addison-Wesley, 1954.

Allport, G. W. *Pattern and growth in personality.* New York: Holt, Rinehart and Winston, 1961.

Allport, G. W. *The use of personal documents in psychological science.* New York: Social Science Research Council, 1942.

Allport, G. W. *Personality: a psychological interpretation.* New York: Holt, 1937.

Ames, Louise B. The sense of self of nursery school children as manifested by their verbal behavior. *J. genet. Psychol.,* 1952, 81: 193–232.

Ames, Louise B. The sequential patterning of prone progression in the human infant. *Genet. Psychol. Monogr.,* 1937, 19: 409–460.

Anderson, H. H. An experimental study of dominative behavior and integrative behavior in children of preschool age. *J. soc. Psychol.,* 1937a, 8: 335–345.

Anderson, H. H. Domination and integration in the social behavior of young children in an experimental play situation. *Genet. Psychol. Monogr.,* 1973b, 79: 341–408.

Anderson, J. E. Child development: an historical perspective. *Child Develpm.,* 1956, 27: 181–196.

Anderson, J. E. The limitations of infant and preschool tests in the measurement of intelligence. *J. Psychol.,* 1939, 8: 351–379.

Anderson, R. C., and D. P. Ausubel (eds.). *Readings in the psychology of cognition.* New York: Holt, Rinehart and Winston, 1965.

Andrews, R. J. The self-concept in pupils with learning difficulties. *Child,* 1966, 13: 47–54.

Angelino, H., J. Dollins, and E. V. Mech. Trends in the "fears and worries" of school children as related to socioeconomic status and age. *J. genet. Psychol.,* 1956, 89: 263–276.

Angyal, A. *Foundations for a science of personality.* New York: Commonwealth Fund, 1941.

Aries, P. *Centuries of childhood.* Trans. by R. Baldick. New York: Knopf, 1962.

Ashton, R. The state-variable in neonatal research. *Merrill-Palmer Quart.*, 1973, 19: 3–20.

Asimov, I. *The human brain: its capacities and functions.* New York: Houghton Mifflin, 1964.

Ausubel, D. P. Cognitive structure and the facilitation of meaningful verbal learning. *J. teacher Educ.*, 1963, 14: 217–221.

Ausubel, D. P. Introduction. In R. C. Anderson and D. P. Ausubel (eds.), *Readings in the psychology of cognition.* New York: Holt, Rinehart and Winston, 1965, 3–17.

Ausubel, D. P. *Theory and problems of child development.* New York: Grune & Stratton, 1958.

Ausubel, D. P. *Theories and problems of adolescent development.* New York: Grune & Stratton, 1954.

Avila, D. L., A. W. Combs, and W. W. Purkey (eds.). *The helping relationship sourcebook.* Boston: Allyn and Bacon, 1971.

Baer, D. M. A technique of social reinforcement for the study of child behavior: behavior avoiding reinforcement withdrawal. *Child Develpm.*, 1962b, 33: 847–858.

Baer, D. M. Laboratory control of thumbsucking by withdrawal and representation of reinforcement. *J. exp. anal. Behav.*, 1962a, 5; 525–528.

Baer, M. J. *Growth and maturation—an introduction to physical development.* Cambridge, Mass.: Howard A. Doyle, 1973.

Baldwin, A. L. The study of the individual personality by means of the intra-individual correlation. *J. Pers.*, 1946, 14: 151–168.

Baldwin, A. L. Personal structure analysis: a statistical method for investigating the single personality. *J. abnorm. soc. Psychol.*, 1942, 37: 163–183.

Baldwin, A. L., J. Kalborn, and F. Breeze. Patterns of parental behavior. *Psychol. Monogr.*, 1945, 58: 1–73.

Baldwin, B. J. Physical growth of children from birth to maturity. *Univ. of Iowa Studies in Child Welfare*, 1921, I, No. 1.

Baller, W. R. (ed.). *Readings in the psychology of human growth and development.* New York: Holt, Rinehart and Winston, 1962.

Baller, W. R., and D. C. Charles. *The psychology of human growth and development.* New York: Holt, Rinehart and Winston, 1962.

Bandura, A. Social learning through imitation, In M. R. Jones (ed.), *Nebraska symposium on motivation.* Lincoln, Neb.: University of Nebraska Press, 1962.

Bandura, A., Dorothea Ross, and Sheila Ross. A comparative test of the status envy, social powers and the secondary reinforcement theories of identification learning. *J. abnorm. soc. Psychol.*, 1963, 67: 527–554.

Bandura, A., Dorothea Ross, and Sheila Ross. Transmission of aggression through imitation of aggressive models. *J. abnorm. soc. Psychol.*, 1961, 63: 575–582.

Bandura, A., and R. H. Walters. *Social learning and personality development.* New York: Holt, Rinehart and Winston, 1963.

Bayley, Nancy. Individual patterns of development. *Child Develpm.*, 1956, 27: 45–74.

Bayley, Nancy. On the growth of intelligence. *Amer. Psychologist*, 1955, 10: 805–818.

Bayley, Nancy. Consistency and variability in the growth of intelligence from birth to eighteen years. *J. genet. Psychol.*, 1949, 75: 165–196.

Bayley, Nancy. Size and body build of adolescents in relation to rate of skeletal maturing. *Child Develpm.*, 1943, 14: 51–90.

Bayley, Nancy. Mental growth in young children. *39th Yearbook of the National Society for the Study of Education*, Part II, 1940a, 11–47.

Bayley, Nancy. Factors influencing growth in intelligence. *39th Yearbook of the National Society for the Study of Education*, Part II, 1940b, 49–79.

Bayley, Nancy. The development of motor abilities during the first three years. *Monogr. Soc. Res. Child Develpm.*, 1935, 1: 1–26.

Bayley, Nancy. *The California first year mental scale.* Berkeley, Calif.: University of California Press, 1933.

Becker, W. C. Consequences of different kinds of parental discipline. In M. L. Hoffman and Lois W. Hoffman (eds.), *Review of child development research* I. New York: Russell Sage Foundation, 1964, 169–208.

Becker, W. C., and R. S. Krug. A circumplex model for social behavior in children. *Child Develpm.*, 1964, 35: 371–396.

Becker, W. C., D. R. Peterson, L. A. Helmer, D. J. Shoemaker, and H. C. Quay. Factors in parental behavior and personality as related to problem behavior in children. *J. consult. Psychol.*, 1959, 23: 107–118.

Beckwith, Leila, Relationships between infants' social behavior and their mothers' behavior. *Child Develpm.*, 1972, 43 (No 2): 397–411.

Bee, Helen L. Parent-child interaction and distractibility in 9-year-old children. *Merrill-Palmer Quart.*, 1967, 13: 175–190.

Bellugi, U. The acquisition of negation. Unpublished doctoral dissertation, Howard University, 1967.

Bellugi, Ursula, and R. Brown (eds.). The acquisition of language. *Monogr. Soc. Res. Child Develpm.*, 1964, 29 (No. 1).

Berko, Jean, and R. Brown. Prelinguistic research methods. In P. H. Mussen (ed.), *Handbook of research methods in child development.* New York: Wiley, 1960.

Berlyne, D. E. The influence of albeds and complexity of stimuli on visual fixation in the human infant. *Brit. J. Psychol.*, 1958, 48: 315–318.

Berlyne, D. E. Recent developments in Piaget's work. *Brit. J. educ. Psychol.*, 1957, 27: 1–12.

Bernstein, B. Language and social class. *Brit. J. Psychol.*, 1960, 11: 271–276.

Bernstein, B. Social class and linguistic development: a theory of social learning. In A. H. Halsey, Jean Floud, and C. A. Anderson (eds.), *Education, economy and society.* New York: Free Press, 1961.

Berrill, N. J. *The person in the womb.* New York: Dodd & Mead, 1968.

Bigge, M. L. *Learning theories for teachers.* New York: Harper & Row, 1964.

Bijou, S. W. Patterns of reinforcement and resistance to extinction in young children, *Child Develpm.*, 1957, 28: 47–55.

Bijou, S. W., and D. M. Baer. *Child Development* (Vols. 1 and 2). New York: Appleton, 1964.

Bijou, S. W., and D. M. Baer. Some methodological contributions from a functional analysis of child development. In L. P. Lipsitt and C. C. Spiker (eds.), *Advances in child development and behavior.* New York: Academic Press, 1963.

Bijou, S. W., and R. Orlando. Rapid development of multiple-schedule performances with retarded children. *J. exp. anal. Behav.*, 1961, 4: 7–18.

Biller, H. B. A note on father absent and masculine development in lower-class negro and white boys. *Child Develpm.*, 1968, 39: 1003–1006.

Binet, A., and T. Simon. *The development of intelligence in children.* Trans. by Elizabeth S. Kite. Baltimore: Williams & Wilkins, 1916.

Bing, Elizabeth. Child rearing practices in the development of cognition. *Child Develpm.*, 1963, 34: 631–648.

Birren, J. E. *The psychology of aging.* Englewood Cliffs, N.J.: Prentice-Hall, 1964.

Blair, A. W., and W. H. Burton. *Growth and development of the preadolescent.* New York: Appleton, 1951.

Blauvelt, Helen, and J. McKenna. Mother-neonate interaction. In B. M. Foss (ed.), *Determinants of infant behavior.* London: Methuen, 1961.

Bledsoe, J. C. Self concepts of children and their intelligence, achievement, interests and anxiety. *J. indiv. Psychol.*, 1964, 20: 35–38.

Bloom, B. S. *Stability and change in human characteristics.* New York: Wiley, 1964.

Blos, P. *On adolescence: a psychoanalytic interpretation.* New York: Free Press, 1962.

Bossard, J. H. S., and Eleanor S. Boll. Marital unhappiness in the life cycle. *Marriage and Family Living,* 1955, 17: 10–14.

Bower, T. G. R., J. M. Broughton, and N. K. Moore. Infant responses to approaching objects: an indication of response to distal variables. *Percept. and Psychophys.*, 1971, 9: 193–196.

Bower, T. G. R. Development of the object concept. In J. Mehler (ed.), *Handbook of cognitive psychology.* Englewood Cliffs, N.J.: Prentice-Hall, 1970.

Bower, T. G. R. The visual world of infants. *Sci. Amer.*, 1966, 215; 80–92.

Bower, T. G. R. Discrimination of depth in premotor infants. *Psychon. Sci.*, 1965, 3: 323–324.

Bowlby, J. Attachment and love, Vol. I, *Attachment.* New York: Basic Books, 1969.

Bowlby, J. The nature of a child's tie to his mother. *Int. J. Psychoanal.*, 1958, 39: 350–373.

Bowlby, J. *Maternal care and mental health.* Geneva: WHO, Monogr. Ser. No. 2, 1951.

Bowlby, J. Forty-four juvenile thieves. *Int. J. Psychoanal.*, 1944, 25: 1–57.

Bowlby, J. The influence of early environment. *Int. J. Psychoanal.*, 1940, 21: 154–178.

Boyers, W. H., and P. Welch. Are children born unequal? *Saturday Review,* 1968, 51 (Oct 19): 61–63, 77–79.

Brackbill, Yvonne. *Behavior in infancy and early childhood.* New York: Free Press, 1967.

Brackbill, Yvonne. Extinction of the smiling response in infants as a function of reinforcement schedule. *Child Develpm.*, 1958, 29: 115–124.

Breckenridge, Marion E., and Margaret N. Murphy. *Growth and development of the young child,* 7th ed. Philadelphia: Saunders, 1963.

Breckenridge, Marion E., and E. Lee Vincent. *Child Development,* 6th ed. Philadelphia: Saunders, 1968.

Breckenridge, Marion E., and E. Lee Vincent. *Child Development,* 5th ed. Philadelphia: Saunders, 1965.

Brenner, A., and L. H. Stott. *School readiness factor analyzed.* Detroit, Mich.: The Merrill-Palmer Institute, 1972.

Bridges, K. M. B. Emotional development in early infancy. *Child Develpm.,* 1932, 3: 324–341.

Brim, O. G. *Education for child rearing.* New York: Russell Sage Foundation: 1959.

Brodbeck, A. J., and O. C. Irwin. The speech behavior of infants without families. *Child Develpm.,* 1946, 17: 145–156.

Brody, S. *Patterns of mothering.* New York: International Universities, 1956.

Bronfenbrenner, U. (ed.) *Influences on human development.* New York: Dryden Press, 1972.

Bronfenbrenner, U. *On making human beings human* (an address). Detroit: The Merrill-Palmer Institute, 1971.

Bronfenbrenner, U. *Two worlds of childhood.* New York: Russell Sage, 1970.

Bronfenbrenner, U. The changing American child. *J. soc. Issues,* 1961a, XVII (No. 1): 9.

Bronfenbrenner, U. Toward a theoretical model for the analysis of parent-child relationships in a social context. In J. C. Glidewell (éd.), *Parental attitudes and child behavior.* Springfield, Ill.: Charles C Thomas, 1961b.

Brown, R. *Psycholinguistics.* New York: Free Press, 1970.

Brown, R. *Words and things.* New York: Free Press, 1958.

Brown, R., and Jean Berko. Word association and the acquisition of grammar. *Child Develpm.,* 1960, 31: 1–14.

Brown, R., C. B. Cazden, and U. Bellugi. The child's grammar from I to III. In J. P. Hill (ed.), *Minnesota Symposium on child psychology,* vol. 2. Minneapolis: University of Minnesota Press, 1969.

Brown, R., and U. Bellugi. Three processes in the child's acquisition of syntax. *Harvard educ. Rev.,* 1964a, 34: 133–151.

Brown, R., and U. Bellugi. The acquisition of language. *Monogr. Soc. Res. Child Develpm.,* 1964b, 29 (No. 1): 43–79.

Brown, R., and C. Fraser. The acquisition of syntax. In Ursula Bellugi and R. Brown (eds.), The acquisition of language. *Monogr. Soc. Res. Child Development,* 1964, 29, (o. 1): 43–79.

Brown, R., and C. Fraser. The acquisition of syntax. In C. N. Cofer, and Barbara Musgrave (eds.), *Verbal behavior and learning.* New York: McGraw-Hill, 1963.

Bruner, J. S. Organization of early skilled action. *Child Develpm.,* 1973, 44: 1–11.

Bruner, J. S. *The relevance of education.* New York: Norton, 1971.

Bruner, J. S. *Processes of cognitive growth: Infancy,* vol. III, Heinz Werner lecture series. Worcester, Mass.: Clark University Press, 1968.

Bruner, J. S. The course of cognitive growth. *Amer. Psychologist,* 1964, 19: 1–15.

Bruner, J. S. Learning and thinking. *Harvard educ. Rev.,* 1959, 29: 184–192.

Bruner, J. S. Going beyond the information given. In H. E. Gruber, K. R. Hammond, and R. Jessor (Cognition Symposium Committee), *Contemporary approaches to cognition.* Cambridge, Mass.: Harvard University Press, 1957.

Bruner, J. S., J. Goodman, and G. Austin. *A study of thinking.* New York: Wiley, 1966.

Bruner, J. S., and Rose Olver. Development of equivalence transformation in children. *Monogr. Soc. Res. Child Develpm.,* 1963, 28 (No. 2): 125–141.

Bruner, J. S., Rose Olver, and R. Greenfield. *Studies in cognitive growth.* New York: Wiley, 1966.

Burgess, E. W., and H. J. Locke. *The family.* New York: American Book, 1945.

Burnside, L. H. Coordination in the locomotion of infants. *Genet. Psychol. Monogr.*, 1927, 2: 284–372.

Caldwell, Bettye M. The rationale for early intervention. *Early Childhood Education Conference of the Council for Exceptional Children,* 1969.

Caldwell, Bettye M., L. Hursher, E. L. Lipton, J. B. Richmond, G. A. Stern, Evelyn Eddy, R. Drachman, and A. Rothman. Mother-infant interaction in monomatric and polymatric families. *Amer. J. Orthopsychiat.*, 1963, 33: 653–664.

Caldwell, Bettye M., C. M. Wright, A. S. Honig, and J. Tannbaum. Infant day care and attachment. *Amer. J. Orthopsychiat.*, 1970, 40: 397–412.

Cameron, N. A., and Ann Margaret. *Behavior pathology.* Boston: Houghton Mifflin, 1951.

Candill, W., and H. Weinstein. Maternal care and infant behavior in Japan and America. *Psychiatry*, 1969, 32: 12–43.

Carmichael, L. The onset and early development of behavior. In L. Carmichael (ed.), *Manual of Child Psychology*, 2nd ed. New York: Wiley, 1954.

Carroll, J. B. Words, meaning and concepts. *Harvard educ. Rev.*, 1964, 34: 178–202.

Carroll, J. B. Language development. In *Encyclopedia of educational research,* 3rd ed.; New York: Macmillan, 1960.

Casler, L. Maternal deprivation: a critical review of the literature. *Monogr. Soc. Res. Child Develpm.*, 1961, 26 (No. 2).

Catalano, F. L., and Dorothea McCarthy. Infant speech as a possible predictor of later intelligence. *J. Psychol.*, 1954, 38: 203–209.

Cattell, Psyche. *The measurement of intelligence of infants and young children.* New York: The Psychological Corporation, 1940.

Cattell, R. B. *Abilities, their structure, growth, and action.* Boston: Houghton Mifflin, 1971.

Cattell, R. B. Are I.Q. tests intelligent? In *Readings in psychology today.* Del Mar, Calif.: CRM, 1969, 336–342.

Cattell, R. B. Theory of fluid and chrystallized intelligence: A critical experiment. *J. educ. Psychol.*, 1963, 54: 1–22.

Cattell, R. B. *Personality and motivation, structure and measurement.* New York: Harcourt, 1957.

Cattell, R. B. *The IPAT test of G: culture free, scale I.* Champaign, Ill.: Institute of Personality and Ability Testing, 1950.

Cattell, R. B., and R. W. Coan. Personality factors in middle childhood as revealed in parents ratings. *Child Developm.*, 1957, 28: 439–459.

Cavan, Ruth S., E. W. Burgess, R. J. Havighurst, and H. Goldhammer. *Personal adjustments in old age.* Chicago: Science Research, 1949.

Champney, H. C. The variables of parent behavior. *J. abnorm. soc. Psychol.*, 1941, 36: 525–542.

Charlesworth, W. R. Cognition in infancy: where do we stand in the midsixties? *Merrill-Palmer Quart.*, 1968, 14: 25–46.

Charlesworth, W. R. Persistence of orienting and attending behavior in infancy as a function of stimulus-locus uncertainty. *Child Develpm.*, 1966, 37: 473–491.

Chess, S., A. Thomas, and H. Birch *Your child is a person.* New York: Viking Press, 1965.

Chess, S., A. Thomas, and H. Birch. Characteristics of the individual child's behavior responses to the environment. *Amer. J. Orthopsychiat.*, 1950, 27: 791–802.

Church, J. *Language and the discovery of reality.* New York: Random House, 1961.

Clarizio, H. F., R. C. Craig, and W. A. Mehrens (eds.). *Contemporary issues in educational psychology.* Boston: Allyn and Bacon, 1970.

Cole, M., and Shiela Cole. Russian nursery schools. *Psychol. Today,* 1968, 2 (No. 5): 22–28.

Collard, R. R. Social and play responses of first born and later born infants in an unfamiliar situation. *Child Develpm.,* 1968, 39: 225–234.

Combs, A. W., Chairman ASCD 1962 Year Book Committee, *Perceiving, behaving, becoming.* Washington, D.C.: National Education Association, 1962.

Combs, A. W., D. L. Avila, and W. W. Purkey. *Helping relationships.* Boston: Allyn and Bacon, 1971a.

Combs, A. W. Some concepts of perceptual psychology. In D. L. Avila, A. W. Combs, and W. W. Purkey. *Helping relationships source-book.* Boston: Allyn and Bacon, 1971b.

Conel, J. L. *The postnatal development of the human cerebral cortex,* vol. VI: *The cortex of the twenty-four month infant.* Cambridge, Mass.: Harvard University Press, 1959.

Conel, J. L. *The postnatal development of the human cerebral cortex,* vol. V: *The cortex of the fifteen-month infant.* Cambridge, Mass.: Harvard University Press, 1955.

Conel, J. L. *The postnatal development of the human cerebral cortex,* vol. IV: *The cortex of the six-month infant.* Cambridge, Mass.: Harvard University Press, 1951.

Conel, J. L. *The postnatal development of the human cerebral cortex,* vol. III: *The cortex of the three-month infant.* Cambridge, Mass.: Harvard University Press, 1947.

Conel, J. L. *The postnatal development of the human cerebral cortex,* vol. II: *The cortex of the one-month infant.* Cambridge, Mass.: Harvard University Press, 1941.

Conel, J. L. *The postnatal development of the human cerebral cortex,* vol. I: *The cortex of the newborn.* Cambridge, Mass.: Harvard University Press, 1939.

Coopersmith, S. *The antecedents of self-esteem.* San Francisco: Freeman, 1967.

Cratty, B. J. *Motor activity and the education of retardates.* Philadelphia: Lea and Febiger, 1969.

Cratty, B. J., and R. S. Hurton. *Experiments in movement behavior and motor learning.* Philadelphia: Lea and Febiger, 1969.

Croake, J. W. Fears of children. *Human Develpm.,* 1969, 12: 239–247.

Cruickshank, W. M., and G. O. Johnson. *Education of exceptional children and youth.* Englewood Cliffs, N.J.: Prentice-Hall, 1958.

Dashiell, J. F. *Fundamentals of objective psychology.* Boston: Houghton Mifflin, 1928.

David, M., and G. Appell. Etude des facteurs de carence effective dans une pouponniere. *Psychiat. Enfant.,* 1962, 4.

Dennis, W. *Readings in child psychology*, 2nd ed. Englewood Cliffs, N.J.: Prentice-Hall, 1963.

Dennis, W. Causes of retardation among institutional children: Iran. *J. genet. Psychol.*, 1960, 96: 47–59.

Dennis, W. Infant development under conditions of restricted practice and of minimum social stimulation: a summary report. *J. genet. Psychol.*, 1938, 53: 149–158.

Dennis, W. A description and clarification of the responses of the newborn infant. *Psychol. Bull.*, 1934, 31: 5–22.

Dennis, W. The role of mass activity in the development of infant behavior. *Psychol. Rev.*, 1932, 39: 593–595.

Dennis, W., and P. Najarian. Infant development under environmental handicap. *Psychol. Monogr.*, 1957, 71: 1–15.

Deutsch, J. A. *The structural basis of behavior*. Chicago: University of Chicago Press, 1960.

Deutsch, J. A., and D. Deutsch. *Physiological psychology*. New York: Dorsey, 1966.

Deutsch, M. P. The role of social class in language development and cognition. *Amer. J. Orthopsychiat.*, 1965, 35: 78–88.

Deutsch, M. P. The disadvantaged child and the learning process: some social psychological, and developmental considerations. In A. H. Passow (ed.), *Education in depressed areas*. New York: Teachers College, 1963.

Deutsch, M. P., and B. Brown. Social influences in Negro-white intelligence differences. *J. soc. Issues*, 1964, 20: 24–35.

Deutsche, J. M. The development of children's concepts of causal relations. *University of Minnesota Institute of Child Welfare Monogr.*, 1937, 13.

Devereux, E. C. Jr., U. Bronfenbrenner, and R. R. Rodgers. Child rearing in England and the United States: a cross-national comparison. *J. Marriage and the Family*, 1969, 31: 257–270.

Devereux, E. C., U. Bronfenbrenner, and G. Suci, Patterns of parent behavior in the United States of America and the Federal Republic of Germany: A cross-national comparison. *Internat. Soc. Sci. Journal*, 1962, 14: 488–506.

Diamond, S. *Personality and temperament*. New York: Harper & Row, 1957.

Dixon, J. C. Development of self-recognition. *J. genet. Psychol.*, 1957, 91: 251–256.

Douvan, Elizabeth, and J. Adelson. *The adolescent experience*. New York: Wiley, 1966.

Dubos, Rene. *So human an animal*. New York: Scribner, 1968.

Dupertuis, C. W., and N. B. Michael. Comparison of growth in height and weight between ectomorphic and mesomorphic boys. *Child Develpm.*, 1953, 24: 203–214.

Duvall, Evelyn M. *Family development*, 2nd ed.; Philadelphia: Lippincott, 1962.

Duvall, Evelyn M. *Family development*. Philadelphia: Lippincott, 1957.

Eisenstadt, S. N. Patterns of leadership and social homogeneity in Israel. *Int. soc. Sci. Bull.*, 1956, 8: 36–54.

Elkin, H. Aggressive and erotic tendencies in army life. *Amer. J. Sociol.*, 1946, 15: 408–413.

Elkind, D. Conservation and concept formation. In D. Elkind, and J. Flavell (eds.), *Studies in cognitive development*. New York: Oxford University Press, 1969, 171–190.

Elkind, D. Cognitive development in adolescence. In J. F. Adams (ed.), *Understanding adolescents*. Boston: Allyn and Bacon, 1968, 128–158.

Elkind, D., and Jo Ann Deblinger. Perceptual training and reading achievement in disadvantaged children. *Child Develpm.,* 1969, 40: 11–19.

Elkind, D., and J. Flavell (eds.). *Studies in cognitive development*. New York: Oxford University Press, 1969.

Ellingson, R. J. Study of brain electrical activity in infants. In L. P. Lipsitt and C. C. Spiker (eds.), *Advances in child development and behavior*. New York: Academic Press, 1967, 53–98.

Ellis, N. R., C. D. Barnett, and M. W. Pryer. Operant behavior in mental defectives: exploratory studies. *J. exp. soc. Psychol.,* 1960, 1: 63–69.

Emmerich, W. Personality development and concepts of structure. *Child Develpm.,* 1968, 39: 671–690.

Endler, N. S., L. R. Boulter, and H. Ossler. *Contemporary issues in developmental psychology*. New York: Holt, Rinehart and Winston, 1968.

Engel, L. *The new genetics*. Garden City, N.Y.: Doubleday, 1967.

Engel, M., and W. J. Paine. A method for the measurement of the self-concepts of children in the third grade. *J. genet. Psychol.,* 1963, 102: 125–137.

English, H. B., and Ava C. English. *A comprehensive dictionary of psychological and psychoanalytical terms*. New York: McKay, 1958.

Ericson, Martha C. Child rearing and social status. *Amer. J. Sociol.,* 1946, 52: 190–192.

Erikson, E. H. *Identity–youth and crisis*. New York: Norton, 1968.

Erikson, E. H. *Insight and responsibility*, New York: Norton, 1964.

Erikson, E. H. Youth, fidelity and diversity. *Daedalus,* 1962, 91: 5–27.

Erikson, E. H. *Childhood and society*. New York: Norton, 1956.

Eron, L. D., L. O. Walder, R. Toigo, and M. M. Lefkowitz. Social class, parental punishment for aggression and child aggression. *Child Develpm.,* 1963, 34: 849–867.

Eron, L. D., T. J. Banta, L. O. Walder, and J. H. Laulight. Comparison of data obtained from mothers and fathers on childrearing practices and their relation to child aggression. *Child Develpm.,* 1961, 32: 457–472.

Ervin, S. M. Imitation and structural change in children's language. In E. H. Lennenberg (ed.), *New directions in the study of language*. Cambridge, Mass.: M.I.T. Press, 1964, 163–189.

Escalona, Sibylle. Basic modes of social interaction: their emergence and patterning during the first two years of life. *Merrill-Palmer Quart.,* 1973, 19 (No. 3); 205–232.

Escalona, Sibylle. Emotional development in the first year of life. In M. J. E. Senn (ed.), *Problems of infancy and childhood*. New York: Josiah Macy, Jr. Foundation, 1953.

Escalona, Sibylle, and H. Corman. The impact of mother's presence upon behavior: the first year. *Human Develpm.,* 1971, 14: 2–16.

Escalona, Sibylle, and Grace M. Heider. *Prediction and control: a study in child development*. New York: Basic Books, 1959.

Escalona, Sibylle, and A. Moriarty. Prediction of school-age intelligence from infant tests. *Child Develpm.,* 1961, 32: 597–605.

Espenshade, Anne, and Helen M. Eckert. *Motor development*. Philadelphia: Saunders, 1966.

Eysenck, H. J. *Dimensions of personality*. London: Routledge, 1947.

Falkner, F. *Human development*. Philadelphia: Saunders, 1966.

Fantz, R. L. Pattern discrimination and selective attention as determinants of perceptual development from birth. In A. H. Kidd, and J. J. Rivoire (eds.), *Perceptual development in children*. New York: International Universities Press, 1966.

Fantz, R. L. Pattern vision in newborn infants. *Science*, 1963, 149: 296–297.

Fantz, R. L. Pattern vision in young infants. *Psychol. Rev.*, 1958, 8: 43–47.

Fantz, R. L. Visual perception from birth as shown by pattern selectivity. *Ann. N.Y. Acad. Sci.*, 1965, 118: 793–814.

Fantz, R. L. Visual experience in infants: decreased attention to familiar patterns relative to novel ones. *Science*, 1964, 146: 668–670.

Fantz, R. L., J. M. Ardy, and M. S. Udelf. Maturation of pattern vision in infants during the first six months. *J. comp. physiol. Psychol.*, 1962, 55: 907–917.

Fantz, R. L., and S. Nevis. Pattern preferences in perceptual cognitive development in early infancy. *Merrill-Palmer Quart.*, 1967, 13: 77–108.

Feld, S. C. Longitudinal study of the origins of achievement strivings. *J. Personality and soc. Psychol.*, 1967, 7: 408–414.

Ferster, C. B., and B. F. Skinner. *Schedules of reinforcement*. New York: Appleton, 1957.

Fischer, L. K. Psychological appraisal of the "unattached preschool child." *Amer. J. Orthpsychiat.*, 1953, 23; 803–814.

Flanagan, Geraldine L. *The first nine months of life*. New York: Simon & Schuster, 1962.

Flavell, J. H. *Developmental psychology of Jean Piaget*. Princeton, N.J.: Van Nostrand, 1963.

Fowler, W. Structural dimensions of the learning process in early reading. *Child Develpm.*, 1964, 35: 1093–1104.

Fowler, W. Cognitive learning in infancy and early childhood. *Psychol. Bull.*, 1962a, 116–152.

Fowler, W. Teaching a two-year-old to read: an experiment in early learning. *Genet. Psychol. Monogr.*, 1962b, 66: 181–283.

Frailberg, Selma H. *The magic years*. New York: Scribner, 1959.

Frank, L. K. Tactile communication. *Genet. Psychol. Mongr.*, 1957, 56: 209–243.

Frank, L. K. *Human development—by 29 authors*. Philadelphia: Saunders, 1966.

Freud, S. *Totem and taboo*. London: Hogarth, 1955.

Freud, S. *An outline of psychoanalysis*. New York: Norton, 1949.

Freud, S. Three contributions to the theory of sex. In *Basic writings of Sigmund Freud*. New York: Random House, 1938.

Freud, S. *Totem and taboo*. Leipzig and Vienna: Haller, 1913.

Freud, S. *Fragments of an analysis of a case of hysteria*, Standard Edition 7: 1905.

Friedenberg, E. *The vanishing adolescent*. Boston: Beacon Press, 1959.

Fries, Margaret E. Psychosomatic relationships between mother and infant. *Psychom. Med.*, 1944, 6: 159–162.

Fries Margaret E. National and international difficulties. *Amer. J. Orthopsychiat.*, 1941, 11: 562–573.

Fries, Margaret E., and B. Lewi. Interrelated factors in development. *Amer. J. Orthopsychiat.*, 1938, 8: 726–752.

Fries, Margaret E., and P. J. Woolf. Some hypotheses on the role of the congenital activity type in personality development. In *Psychoanalytic study of children,* vol. VIII, New York: International Universities, 1953, 48–62.

Fromm, E. *The art of loving.* New York: Harper & Row, 1956.

Fuller, J. L., and W. R. Thomson. *Behavior genetics.* New York: Wiley, 1960.

Gagné, R. M. *Conditions of learning.* New York: Holt, Rinehart and Winston, 1965.

Galton, F. *Hereditary genius.* (Reprint). New York: Appleton, 1880.

Gardner, D. B., G. R. Hawkes, and L. C. Burchinal. Development after non-continuous mothering. *Child Develpm.*, 1961, 32: 225–234.

Gardner, E. *Fundamentals of neurology,* 4th ed. Philadelphia: Saunders, 1963.

Gardner, R. W., and Alice Moriarty. *Personality at preadolescence.* Seattle, Wash.: University of Washington Press, 1968.

Gates, A. I. What we know and can do about the poor readers. *Education*, 1957, 77: 528–533.

Gesell, A. *The mental growth of the preschool child.* New York: Macmillan, 1925.

Gesell, A., and Catherine S. Amatruda. *The embryology of behavior.* New York: Harper & Row, 1945.

Gesell, A., and Catherine S. Amatruda. *Developmental diagnosis.* New York: Hoeber, 1941.

Gesell, A., H. M. Halverson, Helen Thompson, Frances L. Ilg, B. M. Castner, and Louise B. Ames. *The first four years of life.* New York: Harper & Row, 1940.

Gesell, A., Frances L. Ilg, and Glenna E. Bullis. *Vision: its development in infant and child.* New York: Hoeber, 1949.

Gibson, Eleanor J. Perceptual development. *Yearbook of the National Society for the Study of Education, Part I*, 1963, 62: 144–195.

Gibson, Eleanor J., and R. R. Walk. The "visual cliff." *Scientif. Amer.*, 1960, 202: 64–71.

Gilmer, B. V. H. An analysis of spontaneous responses of the newborn infant. *J. genet. Psychol.*, 1933, 42: 392–405.

Ginott, H. G. *Between parent and child.* New York: Macmillan, 1966.

Glidewell, J. C. (ed.). *Parental attitudes and child behavior.* Springfield, Ill.: Charles C Thomas, 1961.

Glueck, S., and Eleanor Glueck. *Physique and delinquency.* New York: Harper & Row, 1956.

Goethals, G. W., and D. S. Klos. *Experiencing youth: first person accounts.* Boston: Little, Brown, 1970.

Gold, M., and Elizabeth Douvan (eds.). *Adolescent development—readings in research and theory.* Boston: Allyn and Bacon, 1970.

Goldfarb, W. Emotional and intellectual consequences of psychologic deprivation in infancy: a re-evaluation. In P. Hoch and J. Zubin (eds.), *Psychopathology of childhood.* New York: Grune & Stratton, 1955.

Goldfarb, W. Variations in adolescent adjustment of institutionally reared children. *Amer. J. Orthopsychiat.*, 1947, 17: 449–457.

Goldfarb, W. Psychological privation in infancy and subsequent adjustment. *Amer. J. Orthopsychiat.*, 1945, 15: 247–255.

Goldfarb, W. Infant rearing as a factor in foster home replacement. *Amer. J. Orthopsychiat.*, 1944, 14: 162–166.

Goldfarb, W. The effects of early institutional care on adolescent personality. *J. exp. Educ.*, 1943, 12: 106–129.

Goldstein, K. *The organism.* New York: American Book, 1939.

Goodenough, Florence L. New evidence on environmental influence on intelligence *39th Yearbook of the National Society for the Study of Education, Part I*, 1940.

Gordon, E. W. Characteristics of socially disadvantaged children. *Rev. Educ. Res.* 1965, 35: 377–388.

Gorman, J. J., D. G. Cogan, and S. S. Gellis. An apparatus for grading the visual acuity of infants on the basis of optokinetic nystagmus. *Pediatrics*, 1957, 19: 1088–1092.

Govatos, L. A. A proposal for a more realistic approach in studying children's motor skill development. Inter-institutional Seminar in Child Development. *Collected Papers*, 1960, 132–137.

Govatos, L. A. Relationships and age differences in growth measures and motor skills. *Child Develpm.*, 1959, 30: 333–340.

Grant, V. M. *The psychology of sexual emotions: the basis of selective attraction.* New York: Longmans, Green & Co., 1957.

Greenberg, D. J., and W. J. O'Donnell. Infancy and the optimal level of stimulation. *Child Develpm.*, 1972, 48 (No. 2); 639–646.

Greene, J. S. *Learning to talk.* New York: Macmillan, 1946.

Greulich, W. W., and S. Idell Pyle. *Radiographic atlas of skeletal development of the hand and wrist*, 2nd ed.; Stanford, Calif.: Stanford University Press, 1959.

Guilford, J. P. *The nature of human intelligence.* New York: McGraw-Hill, 1967.

Guilford, J. P. Zero correlations among tests of intellectual abilities. *Psychol. Bull.*, 1964, 61: 401–404.

Guilford, J. P. Preparation of scores for the correlation betwen persons in a Q factor analysis. *Educ. Psychol. Meas.*, 1963, 23: 1322.

Guilford, J. P. Three faces of intellect. *Amer. Psychologist*, 1959, 14: 469–479.

Guilford, J. P. A system of psychomotor abilities. *Amer. J. Psychol.*, 1958a, 71: 164–174.

Guilford, J. P. A system of primary traits of temperament. *Indian J. Psychol.*, 1958b, 135–150.

Guilford, J. P. A revised structure. *Reports from the Psychological Laboratory.* Los Angeles, Calif.: University of Southern California Press, 1957 (No. 9).

Guilford, J. P. Some recent findings on thinking abilities and their implications. *J. Commun.*, 1953, 3: 49–58.

Guilford J. P. The structure of intellect. *Psychol. Bull.*, 1956, 53: 267–293.

Guilford, J. P., and P. R. Merrifield. The structure of intellect model: its uses and implications. *Reports from the Psychlogical Laboratory.* Los Angeles, Calif.: University of Southern California Press, 1960 (No. 24).

Guthrie, E. R. *The psychology of learning.* Revised ed. New York: Harper & Row, 1952.

Guthrie, E. R. Conditioning: a theory of learning in terms of stimulus, response and association. *40th Yearbook of the National Society for the Study of Education, Part II*, 1942, 17–60.

Gutteridge, Mary V. A study of motor achievements of young children. *Arch. Psychol.*, 1939 (No. 244): 178.

Haimowitz, M. L., and Natalie R. Haimowitz (eds.). *Human development: selected readings.* New York: Crowell, 1960.

Haith, M. M. Visual scanning in infants. Paper read at regional meeting of Society for Research in Child Development, Worcester, Mass., March, 1968.

Haith, M. M. Response of the human newborn to visual movement. *J. exp. child Psychol.*, 1966, 3: 238–243.

Hall, B. F. The trial of William Freeman. *Amer. J. Insanity*, 1848, 5: 34–60.

Hall, C. S., and G. Lindzey. *Theories of personality.* New York: Wiley, 1957.

Hall, G. Stanley. *Adolescence—its psychology and education.* vol. I. New York: Appleton, 1905.

Hallgren, B. *Enuresis: a clinical and genetic study.* Copenhagen: Ejnar, Munksgaard, 1957.

Halverson, Lolas E. Development of motor patterns in young children. *Quest VI*, 1966, 44–53.

Halverson, H. M. A further study of grasping. *J. genet. Psychol.*, 1932, 7: 34–64.

Halverson, H. M. An experimental study of prehension in infants by means of systematic cinema records. *Genet. Psychol. Monogr.*, 1931, 10: 107–286.

Hardy, J. B. Rubella and its aftermath. *Children*, 1969, 16: 91–96.

Harlow, H. F. The nature of love. *Amer. Psychologist*, 1958, 13: 673–684.

Harlow, H. F. The formation of learning sets. *Psychol. Rev.*, 1947, 56: 51–65.

Harlow, H. F., and Margaret Harlow. *Effects of various mother-infant relationships on rhesus monkey behavior*, IV. London: Methuen, 1969.

Harlow, H. F., and Margaret K. Harlow. Learning to love. *Amer. Scientist*, 1966, 54 (No. 3): 244–272.

Harlow, H. F., and Margaret K. Harlow. Learning to think. *Scientif. Amer.*, 1949, 181: 36–39.

Harlow, H. F., and R. R. Zimmerman. Affectional responses in the infant monkey. *Science*, 1959, 730: 421–432.

Harlow, H. F., and R. R. Zimmerman. Affectional responses in infant monkeys. *Proc. Amer. Phil. Soc.*, 1958, 192: 501–509.

Harris, D. B. (ed.). *The concept of development.* Minneapolis: University of Minnesota Press, 1957.

Harris, I. D. *Normal children and mothers.* New York: Free Press, 1959.

Harris, J. A., C. M. Jackson, D. G. Paterson and R. F. Scammon. *The measurement of man.* Minneapolis: University of Minnesota Press, 1930.

Havighurst, R. J., and Hilda Taba. *Adolescent character and personality.* New York: Wiley, 1949.

Hebb, D. O. *A textbook of psychology.* Philadelphia: Saunders, 1958.

Heinstein, M. I. Behavioral correlates of breast-bottle regimes under varying parent-infant relationships. *Monogr. Soc. Res. Child Develpm.*, 1963, 28 (No. 88).

Henle, Mary. Some effects of motivational processes on cognition. *Psychol. Rev.*, 1955, 62: 423–452.

Hess, E. H. Effects of drugs on imprinting behavior. In L. Uhr, and J. G. Miller (eds.), *Drugs and behavior.* New York: Wiley, 1960.

Hess, E. H. Imprinting. *Science*, 1959, 130: 133–141.

Hess, R. D. Educability and rehabilitation: the future of the welfare class. *J. Marriage and Family Living*, 1964, 26: 422–429.

Hess, R. D., and Virginia C. Shipman. Early experiences and the socialization of cognitive modes in children. *Child Develpm.* 1965, 36: 869–886.

Hilgard, E. R. *Theories of learning*. New York: Appleton, 1956.

Hill, R. Revision of W. Waller, *The family: a dynamic interpretation*. New York: Dryden Press, 1951.

Hoerr, N. S., S. Idell Pyle, and C. C. Frances. *Radiographic atlas of skeletal development of the foot and ankle: a standard of reference*. Springfield, Ill.: Charles C Thomas, 1962.

Hoffman, M. L. Parent discipline and the child's consideration for others. *Child Develpm.*, 1963, 34; 573–588.

Hoffman, M. L. Power assertion by the parent and its impact on the child. *Child Develpm.*, 1960, 31: 129–143.

Hoffman, M. L. An interview method for obtaining descriptions of parent-child interaction. *Merrill-Palmer Quart.*, 1957 3 (No. 2): 76–83.

Hoffman, M. L., and Lois W. Hoffman (eds.). *Review of child development research*, vol. I. New York: Russell Sage Foundation, 1964a.

Hoffman, M. L., and Lois W. Hoffman. *Review of child development research*, vol. II. New York: Russell Sage Foundation, 1964b.

Hoffman, M. L., and H. D. Saltzstein. Parent discipline and the child's moral development. *J. Pers. soc. Psychol.*, 1967, 5: 45–57.

Holden, R. H., E. B. Mann, and W. P. Jones. Maternal hypothyroidism and developmental consequences during the first year of life. Paper presented at the meeting of the Society for Research in Child Development, Santa Monica, Calif., 1969.

Hollenberg, E., and M. Perry. Some antecedents of aggression and effects of frustration in doll play. *Personality*, 1951, 1: 32–43.

Hooker, D. *The prenatal origin of behavior*. Lawrence: University of Kansas Press, 1952.

Horowitz, Frances D. Infant learning: retrospect and prospect. *Merrill-Palmer Quart.*, 1968, 14; 101–120.

Hotelling, H. Analysis of a complex of statistical variables into principal components. *J. educ. Psychol.*, 1933, 24: 417–520.

Huang, I. Children's conceptions of physical causality: a critical summary. *J. genet. Psychol.*, 1943, 63: 71–121.

Hull, C. L. *Principles of behavior*. New York: Appleton, 1943.

Humphrey, T. Photographs. *Alabama J. Medical Science*, 1968, 5: 126–157.

Hunt, J. McV. *Intelligence and experience*. New York: Ronald, 1961.

Hunt, J. McV. (ed.). *Personality and the behavior disorders*. New York: Ronald, 1944.

Hunt, J. McV., and I. C. Uzgiris. Cathexis from recognitive familiarity: an exploratory. Paper presented at the 1964 Convention of the American Psychological Association, Los Angeles, California 1964.

Hurlock, Elizabeth B. *Child Development*, 5th ed. New York: McGraw-Hill, 1972.

Inhelder, B., and J. Piaget. *The growth of logical thinking from childhood to adolescence*. New York: Basic Books, 1958.

Irwin, O. C. Infant speech. *Scientif. Amer.*, 1949, 181: 22–24.

Irwin, O. C. The amount and nature of activities of newborn infants under constant external stimulating conditions during the first ten days of life. *Genet. Psychol. Monogr.*, 1930, 8: 1–92.

Jackson, R. L., and H. G. Kelly. Growth charts for use in pediatric practice, *J. Pediat.*, 1945, 27: 213–229.

Jahoda, G. Child animism, I: a critical review of cross-cultural research. *J. soc. Psychol.*, 1958, 47: 213–222.

James, W. *Principles of psychology.* New York: Holt, 1890.

James, W. *Psychology, briefer course.* New York: Holt, 1910.

James, W., and C. G. Lange. *The emotions.* Baltimore: Williams & Wilkins, 1922.

Jersild, A. T. *Child psychology*, 5th ed. Englewood Cliffs, N.J.: Prentice-Hall, 1960.

Jersild, A. T. *The psychology of adolescence*, New York: Macmillan, 1957.

Jersild, A. T. Emotional development. In L. Carmichael (ed.), *Manual of child psychology.* New York: Wiley, 1954.

Jersild, A. T. *In search of self.* New York: Teachers College, 1952.

Jersild, A. T. *Child development and the curriculum.* New York: Teachers College, 1946.

Jersild A. T., B. Goldman, and J. Loftus. A comparative study of worries of children in two school situations. *J. exp. Educ.*, 1941, 9: 323–326.

Jersild, A. T., and F. B. Holmes. *Children's fears.* New York: Teachers College, 1935.

Joffe, J. M. *Prenatal determinants of behavior.* New York: Pergamon Press, 1969.

John, E. R. *Mechanisms of memory.* New York: Academic Press, 1967.

John, E. R., P. Chessler, F. Bartlett, and I. Victor. Observation learning in cats. *Science*, 1968, 159: 1489–1491.

Johnson, Beth, and L. F. Beck. The development of space perception I: Stereoscopic vision in preschool children. *J. genet. Psychol.*, 1941, 58: 247–254.

Johnson, P. E. *Learning: theory and practice.* New York: Crowell, 1971.

Jones, H. E. *Motor performance and growth; a developmental study of static dynamometric strength.* Berkeley, Calif.: University of California Press, 1949.

Jones, H. E. Physical ability as a factor in social adjustment of adolescence. *J. educ. Res.*, 1946, 40: 287–301.

Jones, H. E. Development of physical abilities. *Yearbook of the National Society for the Study of Education*, Part I, 1944, 43: 100–122.

Jones, H. E. *Development in adolescence: approaches to the study of the individual.* New York: Appleton, 1943.

Jones, Mary C. The later careers of boys who were early- or late-maturing. *Child Develpm.*, 1957, 28: 113–128.

Jones, Mary C. A laboratory study of fear: the case of Peter. *Ped. Sem.*, 1924a, 31: 308–316.

Jones, Mary C. The elimination of children's fear. *J. exp. Psychol.*, 1924b, 7: 382–390.

Jones, Mary C., and Nancy Bayley. Physical maturing among boys as related to behavior. *J. educ. Psychol.*, 1950, 41: 129–148.

Jones, Mary C., and P. H. Mussen. Self-conceptions, motivations and interpersonal attitudes of early- and late-maturing girls. *Child Devlpm.*, 1958, 29: 491–501.

Josslyn, Irene M. Cultural forces: motherliness and fatherliness. *J. Orthopsychiat.*, 1956, 26: 264–271.

Jourard, S. M. *The transparent self.* Princeton, N.J.: Van Nostrand, 1964.

Kagan, J. *Change and continuity in infancy.* New York: Wiley, 1971.

Kagan, J. Reflection-impulsivity: the generality and dynamics of conceptual tempo. *J. abnorm. Psychol.*, 1966, 71: 17–24.

Kagan, J., and H. A. Moss. *Birth to maturity—a study in psychological development.* New York: Wiley, 1962.

Kagan, J., H. A. Moss, and E. Sigel. Psychological significance of styles of conceptualization. *Monogr. Soc. Res. Child Develpm.*, 1963, 28: 73–112.

Kagan, J., Bernice L. Rosman, Debora Day, J. Albert, and W. Phillips. Information processing in the child: significance of analytical and reflective attitudes. *Psychol. Monogr.*, 1964, 78.

Kanner, L. Early infantile autism. *J. Pediat.*, 1944, 25: 211–217.

Katz, Judith. Reflection-impulsivity. *Child Develpm.*, 1971, 42: 745.

Kelleher, R. T. Discrimination learning as a function of reversal and non-reversal shifts. *J. exp. Psychol.*, 1956, 51: 379–384.

Kelley, T. L. *Essential traits of mental life.* Cambridge: Harvard University Press, 1935.

Kendler, H. H., and M. F. D'Amato. A comparison of reversal shifts and non-reversal shifts in human concept formation behavior. *J. exp. Psychol.*, 1955, 49: 165–174.

Kendler, T. S. Development of mediating responses in children. *Monogr. Soc. Res. Child Develpm.*, 1963, 28: 33–48.

Kendler, T. S., and H. H. Kendler. Reversal and non-reversal shifts in kindergarten children. *J. exp. Psychol.*, 1959, 58: 56–60.

Kendler, T. S., H. H. Kendler, and B. Leonard. Mediated responses to size and brightness as a function of age. *Amer. J. Psychol.*, 1962, 75: 571–586.

Kendler, T. S., H. H. Kendler, and D. Wells. Reversal and non-reversal shifts in nursery school children. *J. comp. physiol. Psychol.*, 1960, 53: 83–87.

Kessen, W. Stage and structure in the study of children. In W. Kessen and C. Kuhlman (eds.), Thought in the young child. *Monogr. Soc. Res. Child Develpm.*, 1962, 27: 65–68.

Kessen, W. *The Child.* New York: Wiley, 1965.

Kessen, W., and A. W. Lentzendorff. The effects of non-nutritive sucking on movement in the newborn. *J. comp. physiol. Psychol.*, 1963, 56: 69–72.

Kesseler, Jane W. *Psychopathology of childhood.* Englewood Cliffs, N.J.: Prentice-Hall, 1966.

Kistyakovskaya, M. Yu. Stimuli that elicit positive emotions in infants. *Voprosy Psikhologii*, 1965, 2: 129–140.

Kjer, Dell C. (chairman). The significance of the young child's motor devlopment. *Proceedings of a Conference, National Association for the Education of Young Children.* Washington, D.C.: 1971.

Kluckholm, C. *Mirror for Man.* New York: McGraw-Hill, 1949.

Kneller, G. F. *The art and science of creativity.* New York: Holt, Rinehart and Winston, 1965.

Koffka, K. *The growth of the mind: an introduction to child psychology.* New York: Harcourt, 1924.

Kohlberg, L., Judy Yaeger, and Else Hjerthorn. Private speech: four studies and a review of theories. *Child Develpm.*, 1968, 39: 691–736.

Kohler, W. *The mentality of apes*. New York: Harcourt, 1925.

Kretschmer, E. *Physique and character*. New York: Harcourt, 1925.

Krogman, W. M. The physical growth of the child, In M. Fishbein,, and R. J. R. Kennedy (eds.), *Modern marriage and family living*. New York: Oxford, 1957.

Krogman, W. M. The physical growth of children: an appraisal of studies, 1950-1955. *Monogr. Soc. Res. Child Develpm.*, 1956, 20 (No. 1).

Krogman, W. M. The physical growth of the child. In M. Fishbein and E. W. Burgess (eds.), *Successful Marriage*. New York: Doubleday, 1955.

Krogman, W. M. A handbook of measurement and interpretation of heights and weight in the growing child. *Monogr. Soc. Res. Child Develpm.*, 1948, 13 (No. 3).

Kuhlman F. A revision of the Binet-Simon system for measuring the intelligence of children. *J. Psychol. Asthen.*, 1912.

Lakin, M. Personality factors in mothers of excessively crying (colicky) infants. *Monogr. Soc. Res. Child Develpm.*, 1957, 20 (No. 1).

Lansing, A. I. (ed.). *Problems of aging*, 3rd ed. Baltimore: Williams & Wilkins, 1952.

Lecky, P. *Self-consistency: a theory of personality*. New York: Island Press, 1951.

Leuba, C. Images as conditioned sensations. *J. exp. Psychol.*, 1940, 26: 345–351.

Levin, H., and R. R. Sears. Identification with parents as a determinant of doll-play aggression. *Child Develpm.*, 1956, 27: 135–153.

Levin, H., and V. F. Turgeon. The influence of the mother's presence on children's doll-play aggression. *J. abnorm. soc. Psychol.*, 1957, 55: 304–308.

Levine, S. Maternal and environmental influences on the adrenocortical response to stress in weanling rats. *Science*, 1967, 156: 258–260.

Levine, S. The psychophysiological effects of infantile stimulation. In E. S. Bliss (ed.), *Roots of behavior*. New York: Hoeber, 1962.

Levine, S. Stimulation in infancy. *Scientif. Amer.*, 1960, 436: 81–86.

Levine S. Infantile experience and resistance to physiological stress. *Science*, 1957, 126–405.

Levine, S. A further study of infantile handling and adult avoidance learning. *J. Pers.*, 1956, 25: 70–80.

Levine, B., and R. Levine. Nyansongo, A Gusu community in Kenya. In B. Whiting (ed.), *Six cultures: studies of child rearing*. New York: Wiley, 1963, 15–202.

Levy, D. M. *Maternal overprotection*. New York: Columbia University Press, 1943.

Levy, D. M., and Audrey Hess. Problems in determining attitudes toward new-born infants. *Psychiatry*, 1952, 15: 273–286.

Lewin K. *Field theory in social science*. New York: Harper & Row, 1951.

Lewin, K., R. Lippitt, and R. K. White. Patterns of aggressive behavior in experimentally created "social climates." *J. soc. Psychol.*, 1939, 10: 271–299.

Lewis, M. M. *Infant speech: a study of the beginnings of language*. New York: Humanities Press, 1951.

Lewis, M., and H. McGurk. Evaluation of infant intelligence: Infant intelligence scores—true or false? *Science*, 1972, 178: 1174–1177.

Lipsitt, L. P. Learning processes of human newborns. *Merrill-Palmer Quart.*, 1966, 46–71.

Locke, John. Some thoughts concerning education (1693). In J. W. Adamson, (ed.), *The educational writings of John Locke*. London: The Cambridge University Press, 1922.

Loring, A. B., and W. E. McClure. The influence of color-blindness on intelligence and achievement of college men. *J. appl. Psychol.*, 1935, 19: 320–330.

Lyle, J. S. Reading retardation and reversal tendency. *Child Develpm.*, 1969, 40: 833–843.

Lynip, A. W. The use of magnetic devices in the collection and analysis of preverbal utterances of an infant. *Genet. Psychol. Monogr.*, 1951, 44: 221–262.

Lytton, H. Observation studies of parent-child interaction: A methodological review. *Child Develpm.*, 1971, 42: 651–684.

MacFarlane, Jean W. Studies in child guidance, I: methodology of data collection and organization, *Monogr. Soc. Res. Child Develpm.*, 1938, 3 (No. 6).

Madsen, C., Jr. Nurturance and modeling in preschoolers. *Child Develpm.*, 1968, 39: 221–236.

Malmivarra, K., and P. Kolho. The personality of 5 to 7 year-old enuretics in the light of Sceno and Rorschach tests. *Ann. Pediat.*, Fenniae, 1964, 8: 160–172.

Mann, I. *The development of the human eye*. New York: Grune & Stratton, 1950.

Mann, L. Differences between reflective and impulsive children in tempo and quality of decision-making *Child Develpm.*, 1973, 44 (No. 2): 274–279.

Marquis, Dorothy P. Learning in the neonate—the modification of behavior under three feeding schedules. *J. exp. Psychol.*, 1941, 29: 263–282.

Maslow, A. H. *Motivation and personality*. New York: Harper & Row, 1954.

Maslow, A. H., and R. Diaz-Guerrero. Delinquency as a value disturbance. In J. C. Peatman and E. L. Hartley (eds.), *Festschrift for Gardener Murphy*. New York: Harper & Row, 1960, 228–240.

McCammon, R. W., and A. W. Sexton. Implications of longitudinal research in fitness programs. *J. Amer. Med. Assn.*, 1958, 168: 1440–1445.

McCarthy, Dorothea. Language development. *Monogr. Soc. Res. Child Develpm.*, 1960, 25 (No. 3): 5–14.

McCarthy, Dorothea. Language development in children. In L. Carmichael (ed.), *Manual of child psychology*, 2nd ed. New York: Wiley, 1954.

McGraw, Myrtle B. *The neuromuscular maturation of the human infant*. New York: Columbia University Press, 1943.

McGraw, Myrtle B. Neural maturation as exemplified in the reaching-prehensile behavior of the human infant. *J. Psychol.*, 1941, 11: 127–141.

McGraw, Myrtle B. *Growth: a study of Johnny and Jimmie*. New York: Appleton, 1935.

McKinney, F. *Psychology of personal adjustment*. New York: Wiley, 1960.

McNeill, D. The development of language. In P. H. Mussen (ed.), *Carmichael's manual of child psychology*, 3rd ed., vol. 1, New York: Wiley & Son, 1970, 1061–1161.

Mead, Margaret. *Coming of Age in Samoa*. New York: Morrow, 1928.

Meichenbaum, D., and J. Goodman. Reflection-impulsivity and verbal control. *Child Develpm.*, 1969, 40: 785–797.

Meredith, H. V. Body size in infancy and childhood: a comparative study of data from Okinawa, France, South Africa, and North America. *Child Develpm.*, 1948, 19: 179–195.

Meredith, H. V. The rhythm of physical growth. *University of Iowa Studies in Child Welfare*, 1935, 11 (No. 3).

Merrifield, P. R. An analysis of concepts from the point of view of the structure of intellect. In H. J. Klausmeir and C. W. Harris (eds.), *Analyses of conceptual learning.* New York: Academic Press, 1966.

Merry, Frieda K., and R. V. Merry. *The first two decades of life.* New York: Harper & Row, 1950.

Meyer, E. Comprehension of spacial relations in preschool children. *J. genet. Psychol.*, 1940, 57: 119–151.

Millard, C. V. A comparison of organismic concordance-discordance rating with projective appraisals of personal adjustment. *Merrill-Palmer Quart.*, 1957, 3: 198–210.

Miller, N. E. Learning of visceral and glandular responses. *Science*, 1969, 163: 434–445.

Miller, N. E., and J. Dollard. *Social learning and imitation.* New Haven, Conn.: Yale University Press, 1941.

Miller W., and Susan Erwin. The development of grammar in children. *Monogr. Soc. Res. Child Develpm.*, 1964, 29 (No. 1): 9–34.

Mohr, G. J., and Marian Despers. *A stormy decade: adolescence.* New York: Random House, 1958.

Montagu, A. *Human heredity*, 2nd ed. Cleveland: World Publishing, 1963.

Montagu, A. *Prenatal influences.* Springfield, Illinois: Charles C Thomas, 1962.

Montagu, A. The sensory influences of the skin. *Texas reports on biology and medicine, II*, 1953.

More, D. M. Developmental concordance and discordance during puberty and early adolescence. *Monogr. Soc. Res. Child Develpm.*, 1953, 18 (No. 1).

Morgan, J. J. B. *Keeping a sound mind.* New York: Macmillan, 1934.

Moss, H. A. Sex, age and state as determinants of mother-infant interaction. *Merrill-Palmer Quart.*, 1967, 13: 19–36.

Moustakas, C. (ed.). *The self: explorations in personal growth.* New York: Harper & Row, 1956.

Mowrer, O. H. *Learning theory and behavior.* New York: Wiley, 1960a.

Mowrer, O. H. *Learning theory and the symbolic processes.* New York: Wiley, 1960b.

Mowrer, O. H. The psychologist looks at language. *Amer. Psychologist*, 1954, 9: 660–694.

Munn, N. L. *The evolution and growth of human behavior.* Boston: Houghton Mifflin, 1955.

Munroe, Ruth L. *Schools of psychoanalytic thought.* New York: Holt, Rinehart and Winston, 1955.

Murphy, G. *Human potentialities.* New York: Basic Books, 1958.

Murphy, Lois B. *The widening world of childhood—paths toward mastery.* New York: Basic Books, 1962.

Murry, H. A. (and collaborators). *Explorations in personality.* New York: Oxford, 1938.

Mussen, P. H., and Mary C. Jones. Self-conceptions, motivations and interpersonal attitudes of late- and early-maturing boys. *Child Develpm.*, 1957, 28: 243–256.

Nash, J. *Developmental psychology: a psycho-biological approach.* Englewood Cliffs, N.J.: Prentice-Hall, 1970.

Nash, J. The father in contemporary culture and current psychological literature. *Child Develpm.*, 1965, 36: 262–297.

Nelson, Katherine. Some evidence for the cognitive primacy of categorization and its functional basis. *Merrill-Palmer Quart.*, 1973, 19: 21–39.

Nelson, W. E. (ed.). *Textbook in pediatrics*, Philadelphia: Saunders, 1954.

Neugarten, Bernice L. Social class and friendship among school children. *Amer. J. Sociol.*, 1946, 51: 305–311.

Nice, M. M. An analysis of the conversations of children and adults. *Child Develpm.*, 1932, 3: 240–246.

Nice, M. M. Length of sentence as a criterion of a child's progress in speech. *J. educ. Psychol.*, 1925, 16: 370–379.

Olson, D. H. Marriage of the future: revolutionary or evolutionary change? *The Family Coordinator,* 1972, 21: (No. 4), 383–393.

Olson, W. C. Seeking self-selection and pacing in the use of books by children. *The Packet* (University of Michigan), 1952, 7: 3–10.

Olson, W. C. The development of healthy personality in children and youth. *Amer. Council on Educational Studies,* 1951, 53: 61–76.

Olson, W. C. Pupil development and curriculum. Bureau of Reference and Research. Ann Arbor: University of Michigan Press, 1937.

Olson, W. C., and B. O. Hughes. The concept of organismic age. *J. educ. Res.,* 1942, 36: 525–527.

Olson, W. C., and B. O. Hughes. *Tables for the translation of physical measurements into age units.* Ann Arbor, Mich.: Child Development Laboratories, University of Michigan Elementary School, 1938.

Orlando, R., and S. W. Bijou. Single and multiple schedules of reinforcement in developmentally retarded children. *J. exp. anal. Behav.* 1960, 3: 339, 343.

Orlansky, H. Infant care and personality. *Psychol. Bull.*, 1949, 46: 1–48.

Osgood, C. E. A behavioristic analysis of perception and language as cognitive phenomena (Symposium). *Contemporary approaches to cognition.* Cambridge, Mass.: Harvard University Press, 1957, 75–118.

Palermo, D. S., and L. P. Lipsitt (eds.). *Research readings in child psychology.* New York: Holt, Rinehart and Winston, 1963.

Parsons, T. Social structure and the development of personality. Freud's contribution to the integration of psychology and sociology. In N. J. Smelser and W. J. Smelser (ed.), *Personality and social systems.* New York: Wiley, 1963.

Parsons, T., and E. A. Shils. *Toward a general theory of action.* Cambridge, Mass.: Harvard University Press, 1951.

Pasamanick, B., and H. Knoblock. Retrospective studies on the epidemiology of reproductive causality: old and new. *Merrill-Palmer Quart.*, 1966, 12: 7–26.

Pavlov, I. P. *Conditioned reflexes.* London: Oxford, 1927.

Pease, Damris, and D. B. Gardner. Research on the effects of non-continuous mothering. *Child Develpm.*, 1958, 29: 141–148.

Penrose, L. S. (ed.). *Recent advances in human genetics.* Boston: Little, Brown, 1960.

Phillips, J. L. *The origins of intellect: Piaget's theory.* San Francisco: Freeman, 1969.

Piaget, J. *The mechanism of perception.* Trans. by G. N. Seagrum. New York: Basic Books, 1969.

Piaget, J. *The psychology of intelligence.* Paterson, N.J.: Littlefield, Adams, 1960.

Piaget, J. *The construction of reality in the child.* New York: Basic Books, 1954.

Piaget, J. *The origins of intelligence.* Trans. by Margaret Cook. New York: International Universities, 1952.

Piaget, J. *The child's conception of physical causality.* New York: Harcourt, 1930.

Piaget, J. *The child's conception of the world.* New York: Harcourt, 1929.

Piaget, J., and Barbel Inhelder. *The psychology of the child.* Trans. by Helen Weaver. New York: Basic Books, 1969.

Pierce, C. M., R. M. Whitman, J. W. Maas, and M. L. Gay. Enuresis and dreaming. *Amer. Arch. gen. Psychiat.,* 1961, 4: 166–170.

Piers, E. V., and D. B. Harris. Age and other correlates of self-concepts in children. *J. educ. Psychol.,* 1969, 55: 91–95.

Pinneau, S. R. The infantile disorders of hospitalism and anaclitic depression. *Psychol. Bull.,* 1955, 52: 429–452.

Pitts, C. E. *Introduction to educational psychology—an operant conditioning approach.* New York: Crowell, 1971a.

Pitts, C. E. (ed.). *Operant conditioning in the classroom—introductory readings in educational psychology.* New York: Crowell, 1971b.

Porter, B. M. The relationship between marital adjustment and parental acceptance of children. *J. home Econ.,* 1955, 47: 157–164.

Prentice, W. C. H. Some cognitive aspects of motivation. *Amer. Psychologist,* 1961, 16: 503–511.

Pressy, S. L., and F. P. Robinson. *Psychology and the new education.* New York: Harper & Row, 1944.

Provence, S., and R. Lipton. *Infants in institutions.* New York: International Universities, 1962.

Pyle, S. Idell, and N. L. Hoerr. *Radiographic atlas of skeletal development of the knee: a standard of reference.* Springfield, Ill.: Charles C Thomas, 1955.

Rand, Winifred, Mary E. Sweeny, and E. Lee Vincent (revised by M. E. Breckenridge and M. N. Murphy). *Growth and development of the young child,* 5th ed.; Philadelphia: Saunders, 1953.

Reichard, Suzanne, Florine Livson and P. G. Peterson. *Aging and personality.* New York: Wiley, 1962.

Rheingold, Harriet L. The effect of a strange environment on the behavior of infants. In B. M. Tobe (ed.), *Determinants of infant behavior,* vol. 4. London: Methuen, 1969, 137–166.

Rheingold, Harriet L. The effects of environmental stimulation upon social and exploratory behavior in the human infant. In B. M. Foss (ed.), *Determinants of infant behavior.* New York: Wiley, 1961.

Rheingold, Harriet L. The measurement of maternal care, *Child Develpm.,* 1960, 31: 565–573.

Rheingold, H. L. The modification of social responsiveness in institutional babies. *Monogr. Soc. Res. Child Develpm.,* 1956, 21, No. 2.

Rheingold, Harriet L., and C. O. Eckerman. Departures from mother. In H. R. Schaffer (ed.), *The origin of social relations.* London: Academic Press 1971, 3–82.

Rheingold, Harriet L., J. L. Gewirtz, and Helen W. Ross. Social conditioning of verbalization in infants. *J. comp. physiol. Psychol.,* 1959, 52: 68–73.

Ribble, Margaret A. Infantile experience in relation to personality development. In J. McV. Hunt (ed.), *Personality and the behavior disorders*, vol. II. New York: Ronald, 1944, 611–651.

Ribble, Margaret. *The rights of infants*. New York: Columbia University Press, 1943.

Ripin, R. A comparative study of the development of infants in an institution with those in homes of low socio-economic status. *Psychol. Bull.*, 1933, 30: 680–681.

Roberts, Katherine E., and Rachel S. Ball. A study of personality in young children by means of a series of rating scales. *J. genet. Psychol.*, 1938, 52: 79–140.

Robertson, J., and J. Bowlby. Responses of young children to separation from their mothers. *Courr. Cent. int. d' Enfance*, 1952, 2: 131–142.

Rodman, H. (ed.). *Marriage, family and society: a reader*. New York: Random House, 1965.

Roff, M. A factorial study of the Fels Parent Behavior Scales. *Child Develpm.*, 1949, 20: 29–45.

Rogers, C. R. *Freedom to learn*. Columbus, Ohio: Merrill, 1969.

Rogers, C. R. Learning to be free. In S. M. Farber, and R. H. L. Wilson, *Conflict and creativity: control of the mind*. New York: McGraw-Hill, 1963.

Rogers, C. R. *On becoming a person*. Boston: Houghton Mifflin, 1961.

Rogers, C. R. *Client-centered therapy: its current implications and theory*. Boston: Houghton Mifflin, 1951.

Rogers, C. R. *Counseling and psychotherapy: newer concepts in practice*. Boston: Houghton Mifflin, 1942.

Rohrer, J. H., and M. S. Edmondson. *The eighth generation*. New York: Harper & Row, 1960.

Rosenthal, R., and Lenore Jacobson. *Pygmalion in the classroom—teacher expectation and pupil individual development*. New York: Holt, Rinehart and Winston, 1968.

Rostan, L. *Cours élémentaire d'hygiene*, 2nd ed. Paris: Bechet, Jeune, 1824.

Roudinesco, J., M. David, and J. Nicolas. Responses of young children to separation from their mothers, I: observation of children, ages 12 to 17 months recently separated from their families and living in an institution. *Courr. Cent. int. d'Enfance*, 1952, 2: 66–78.

Rousseau, Jean Jacques. *Emile: or, concerning education*, 1762. Extracts. (Translated by Eleanor Worthington). Chicago: D. S. Heath, 1883.

Rowland, G. T., and J. T. McQuire, *The mind of man—some views and a theory of cognitive development*. Englewood Cliffs, N.J.: Prentice-Hall, 1971.

Rugh, R., and L. B. Shettles. *From conception to birth*. New York: Harper & Row, 1971.

Russell, R. W. Studies in animism II: the development of animism. *J. genet. Psychol.*, 1940, 56: 353–366.

Rutherford, E., and Mussen, P. Generosity in nursery school boys. *Child Develpm.*, 1968, 39: 735–765.

Salapatek, P., and W. Kessen. Visual scanning of triangles by the human newborn. *J. exp. Child Psychol.*, 1966, 3: 113–122.

Salzinger, Suzanne, K. Salzinger, Stephanie Portnoy, Judith Eckman, Pauline M. Bacon, M. Deutsch, and J. Gubin. Operant conditioning of continuous speech in young children. *Child Develpm.*, 1962, 33: 683–695.

Sarbin, T. R. A preface to a psychological analysis of the self. *Psychol. Rev.*, 1959, 59: 11–22.

Scammon, R. E. The measurement of the body in childhood. In J. A. Harris, *The measurement of man.* Minneapolis: University of Minnesota Press, 1930.

Scarr, Sandra. Social introversion—extraversion as a heritable response. *Child Develpm.*, 1969, 40: 823–832.

Schachtel, E. G. *Metamorphosis.* New York: Basic Books, 1959.

Schaefer, E. S. Converging conceptual models for maternal behavior and for child behavior. In J. S. Glidewell (ed.), *Parental attitudes and child behavior.* Springfield, Ill.: Charles C Thomas, 1961.

Schaefer, E. S. A circumplex model for maternal behavior. *J. abnorm. soc. Psychol.*, 1959, 59: 226–235.

Schaffer, H. R. Objective observation of personality development in early infancy: *Brit. J. med. Psychol.*, 1958, 31: 174–183.

Schaffer, H. R., and P. E. Emerson. Patterns of response in early human development. *J. child Psychol. and Psychiat.*, 1964, 5: 1–13.

Scheinfeld, A. *Your heredity and environment.* New York: Lippincott, 1965.

Schour, I., and M. Massler. The development of human dentition. *J. Amer. dent. Ass.*, 1941, 28: 1153–1160.

Scott, J. P. Critical periods in behavioral development. *Science*, 1962, 138 (No. 3544): 949–958.

Sears, R. R., Eleanor E. Maccoby, and H. Levin. *Patterns of child rearing.* New York: Harper & Row, 1957.

Sears, R. R., J. W. M. Whiting, V. Nowlis, and Pauline S. Sears. Some child-rearing antecedents of aggression and dependency in young children. *Genet. Psychol. Monogr.*, 1953, 47: 135–234.

Sewell, W. N. Infant training and the personality of the child. *Amer. J. Sociol.*, 1952, 58: 150–159.

Sheldon, W. H. *The varieties of temperament.* New York: Harper & Row, 1942.

Sheldon, W. H. (with collaboration of S. S. Stevens and W. B. Tucker). *The varieties of human physique: an introduction to constitutional psychology.* New York: Harper & Row, 1940.

Sheldon, W. H. (with collaboration of E. M. Hartl and E. McDermott). *Varieties of delinquent youth: an introduction to constitutional psychology.* New York: Harper & Row, 1949.

Sheldon, W. H., C. W. Dupertuis, and E. McDermott. *Atlas of men: a guide for somatotyping the adult male at all ages.* New York: Harper & Row, 1954.

Shirley, Mary. *The first two years: postural and locomotor development.* Minneapolis: University of Minnesota Press, 1931.

Sigel, I. E. The attainment of concepts. In M. L. Hoffman and Lois W. Hoffman (eds.) *Review of child development research.* New York: Russell Sage Foundation, 1964.

Sigel, I. E. Sex and personality correlates of styles of categorization among young children. *Amer. Psychologist*, 1963, 18: 350.

Sigel, I. E. *Cognitive style and personality dynamics.* Interim progress report for National Institute of Mental Health, 1961.

Sigel, I. E. The dominance of meaning. *J. genet. Psychol.*, 1954, 85: 201–207.

Sigel, I. E. The developmental trends in abstraction ability of young elementary school children. *Child Develpm.*, 1953, 24: 131–144.

Sigel, I. E. Styles of categorization in elementary school children: the role of sex differences and anxiety level. Paper read at Biennial Meeting, Society for Research in Child Development, 1951.

Simmons, Mae W., and L. P. Lipsitt. An operant-discrimination apparatus for infants. *J. exp. anal. Behav.*, 1961, 4: 233–235.

Simon, C. T. The development of speech. In L. E. Travis (ed.), *Handbook of speech pathology*. New York: Appleton, 1957.

Skeels, H. M., and E. A. Filmore. Mental development of children from under-privileged homes. *J. genet. Psychol.*, 1937, 50: 427–439.

Skeels, H. M., R. Updegraff, Ruth Wellman, and H. M. Williams. A study of environmental stimulation: an orphanage preschool project. *University of Iowa Studies in Child Welfare*, 1938, 15 (No. 4).

Skinner, B.F . *Beyond freedom and dignity*. New York: Knopf, 1971.

Skinner, B. F. *Cumulative record*. New York: Appleton, 1959a.

Skinner, B. F. Teaching machines. *Science*, 1959b, 128: 969–977.

Skinner, B. F. *Verbal behavior*. New York: Appleton, 1957.

Skinner, B. F. *Science in human nature*. New York: Macmillan, 1953.

Skinner, B. F. *The behavior of organisms*. New York: Appleton, 1938.

Skodak, Marie. Children in foster homes: a study of mental development. *University of Iowa Studies in Child Welfare*, 1939, 16 (No. 1).

Slobin, D. I. *Psycholinguistics*. Glenview, Ill.: Scott, Foresman, 1971.

Sloman, Sophie S. Emotional problems in "planned-for" children. *Amer. J. Orthpsychiat.*, 1948, 18: 523–528.

Smedslund, J. The acquisition of conservation of substance and weight in children, I: introduction. *Scandinav. J. Psychol.*, 1961a, 2: 11–20.

Smedslund, J. The acquisition of conservation of substance and weight in children, II: external reinforcement of conservation of weight and of the operations of addition and subtraction. *Scandinav. J. Psychol.*, 1961b, 2: 71–84.

Smith, G. M. *A simplified guide to statistics for psychology and education*, 3rd ed. Holt, Rinehart and Winston, 1962.

Smith, Madorah E., and L. M. Kasdon. Progress in the use of English after twenty years by children of Filipino and Japanese ancestry in Hawaii. *J. genet. Psychol.*, 1961, 99: 129–138.

Snow, C. E. Mother's speech in children's learning language. *Child Develpm.*, 1972, 43: 549–565.

Snygg, D., and A. W. Combs. *Individual behavior: a new frame of reference for psychology*. New York: Harper & Row, 1949.

Soffietti, J. P. Bilingualism and biculturalism. *J. educ. Psychol.*, 1955, 46: 222–227.

Sontag, L. W. The significance of fetal environmental differences. *Amer. J. Obstet. Gynec.*, 1941, 42: 996–1003.

Sontag, L. W., C. T. Baker, and Virginia L. Nelson. Mental growth and personality development: a longitudinal study. *Monogr. Soc. Res. Child Develpm.*, 1958, 25 (No. 2).

Sontag, L. W., and E. L. Reynolds. The Fels composite sheet, I: a practical method for analyzing growth processes. *J. Pediat.*, 1945, 26: 327–335.

Spearman, C. The theory of two factors. *Psychol. Rev.*, 1914, 21: 101–115.

Spearman, C. *The abilities of man*. New York: Macmillan, 1927.

Spearman, C. General intelligence objectively determined and measured. *Amer. J. Psychol.*, 1904, 15: 201–293.

Spence, K. W. *Behavior theory and learning.* Englewood Cliffs, N.J.: Prentice-Hall, 1960.

Spiker, C. C. Verbal factors in the discrimination learning of children. *Monogr. Soc. Res. Child Develpm.*, 1963, 28: 53–69.

Spitz, R. A. *The first year of life.* New York: International Universities, 1965.

Spitz, R. A. Motherless infants. *Child Develpm.*, 1949, 20: 145–155.

Spitz, R. A. Hospitalism: a follow-up report. In A. Freud *et al.* (eds.), *Psychoanalytical studies of the child, II.* New York: International Universities, 1946, 113–117.

Spitz, R. A. Hospitalism, an inquiry into the genesis of psychiatric conditions, in early childhood. In A. Freud *et al.* (eds.), *Psychoanalytical studies of the child, I.* New York: International Universities, 1945, 53–74.

Spitz, R. A., and K. M. Wolf. Analytic depression: an inquiry into the genesis of psychiatric conditions in early childhood, II. In A. Freud *et al.* (eds.), *The psychoanalytical study of the child.* New York: International Universities, 1946, 313–342.

Staats, A. W. *Human Learning.* New York: Holt, Rinehart and Winston, 1964.

Staats,, A. W. Verbal habit families: concepts and operant conditioning of word classes. *Psychol. Rev.*, 1961, 68: 190–204.

Staats, A. W. Verbal and instrumental response hierarchies and their relationship to human problem solving. *Amer. J. Psychol.*, 1957, 70: 442–446.

Staats, A. W., and Carolyn B. Staats. *Complex human behavior: a systematic extension of learning principles.* New York: Holt, Rinehart and Winston, 1963.

Staats, A. W., and Carolyn B. Staats. A comparison of the development of speech and reading behavior with implications for research. *Child Develpm.*, 1962, 33: 831–846.

Staats, A. W. and Carolyn B. Staats. Meaning and M: correlated but separate. *Psychol. Rev.*, 1959, 66: 136–144.

Staton, T. F. *Dynamics of adolescent adjustment.* New York: Macmillan, 1963.

Sten, Aletha H. The influence of social reinforcement in the achievement behavior of fourth-grade boys and girls. *Child Develpm.*, 1969, 40: 707–736.

Stendler, Celia B. Aspects of Piaget's theory that have implications for teacher education. *J. Teach. Ed.*, 1965, 16: 329–335.

Stephens, J. M. *The psychology of classroom learning.* New York: Holt, Rinehart and Winston, 1965.

Stephenson, W. *The study of behavior: Q-technique and its methodology.* Chicago: University of Chicago Press, 1953.

Stern, W. *General psychology from the personalistic standpoint.* Trans. by H. D. Spoerl. New York: Macmillan, 1938.

Stern, C. *Principles of human genetics.* 2nd ed. San Francisco: Freeman, 1960.

Stern, W. I. *The psychological methods of testing intelligence.* (Trans. by G. M. Whipple) New York: Warwick and York, 1914.

Stoddard, G. D. *The meaning of intelligence.* New York: Macmillan, 1943.

Stogdill, R. M. Experiments in the measurement of attitudes toward children: 1899–1936. *Child Develpm.*, 1936, 7: 31–36.

Stolz, H. R., and Lois M. Stolz. *Somatic development of adolescent boys.* New York: Macmillan, 1951.

Stone, L. J., and J. Church. *A psychology of the growing person,* 2nd ed. New York: Random House, 1968.

Stone, L. J., and J. Church. *Childhood and adolescence.* New York: Random House, 1957.

Stott, L. H. Personality at age four. *Child Develpm.*, 1962, 33: 287–311.

Stott, L. H. Identification of four childhood personality traits as expressed in the social behavior of preschool children. *Merrill-Palmer Quart.*, 1959, 5: 163–175.

Stott, L. H. The nature and development of social behavior types in children. *Merrill-Palmer Quart.*, 1958, 4: 62–73.

Stott, L. H. Persisting effects of early family experiences upon personality development. *Merrill-Palmer Quart.*, 1957, 3: 145–159.

Stott, L. H. *The longitudinal study of individual development.* Detroit: The Merrill-Palmer School, 1955.

Stott, Leland H. Training children for self-reliance. *Nebr. agricult. Expe. Sta. Bull.*, 1960, 66.

Stott, L. H. Some family life patterns and their relation to personality development in children. *J. exp. Educ.*, 1939, 8: 148–160.

Stott, L. H., and Rachel S. Ball. Consistency and change in ascendence and submission in the social interactions of children. *Child Develpm.*, 1957, 28: 259–271.

Stott, L. H., and Rachel S. Ball. Infant and preschool mental tests: review and evaluation. *Monogr. Soc. Res. Child Develpm.*, 1965, 30 (No. 3).

Strauss, A. A., and N. C. Kephart. *Psychopathology and education of the brain injured child,* vol. II: *Progress in theory and clinic.* New York: Grune & Stratton, 1955.

Stuart, H. C., and D. G. Prugh (eds.). *The healthy child: his physical, psychological, and social development.* Cambridge, Mass.: Harvard University Press, 1960.

Stutsman, Rachel. *Mental measurement of preschool children.* New York: Harcourt, 1931.

Sullivan, H. S. *The interpersonal theory of psychiatry.* New York: Norton (London: Tavistock), 1953.

Sullivan, H. S. *Conceptions of modern psychiatry.* Washington, D.C.: William Alanson White Psychiatric Foundation, 1947.

Suntrock, J. W. Relation of type and onset of father absence to cognitive development. *Child Develpm.*, 1972, 43: 455–470.

Symonds, P. M. *The psychology of parent-child relationships.* New York: Appleton, 1939.

Tanner, J. M. *Education and physical growth: implications of the study of children's growth for educational theory and practice.* London: University of London Press, 1961.

Tapia, F., J. Jekel, and H. R. Domke. Enuresis: an emotional syndrome? *J. nerv. ment. Dis.*, 1960, 130: 61–66.

Tasch, Ruth J. Interpersonal perceptions of fathers and mothers. *J. genet. Psychol.*, 1955, 87: 59–65.

Tasch, Ruth J. The role of the father in the family. *J. exper. Educ.*, 1952, 20: 319–361.

Terman, L. M. *The measurement of intelligence.* Boston: Houghton Mifflin, 1937.

Terman, L. M., and M. A. Merrill. *Measuring intelligence.* Boston: Houghton Mifflin, 1937.

Terman, L. M., and M. Oden. Status of the California gifted group at the end of sixteen years. *Yearbook nat. Soc. Stud. Educ.*, 1940, 39, Part I: 67–89.

Thomas, A., H. G. Birch, Stella Chess, and L. C. Robins. Individuality in responses of children to similar environmental situations. *Amer. J. Psychiat.*, 1961, 117: 798–803.

Thomas, A., and Stella Chess. An approach to the study of sources of individual differences in child behavior. *Quart. Rev. Psychiat. Neurol.*, 1957, 18: 347–357.

Thomas, A., Stella Chess, and G. B. Birch. *Temperament and behavior disorders in children.* New York: New York University Press, 1968.

Thomas A., Stella Chess, H. G. Birch, Margaret E. Hertzig, and S. Korn. *Behavioral individuality in early childhood.* New York: New York University Press, 1963.

Thomas, A., Stella Chess, H. G. Birch, and Margaret E. Hertzig. A longitudinal study of primary reaction patterns in children. *Comprehen. Psychiat.*, 1940, 103–112.

Thomas H., and B. Blevin. Life before birth. In W. R. Baller (ed.), *Readings in the psychology of human growth and development.* New York: Holt, Rinehart and Winston, 1962.

Thorndike, E. L. *Educational psychology*, vol. 3. New York: Columbia University Press, 1914.

Thorndike, E. L. *Educational psychology*, vol. 1. New York: Columbia University Press, 1913.

Thorndike, E. L. *Education.* New York: Macmillan, 1912.

Thurstone, L. L. Primary mental abilities. *Psychometr. Monogr.*, 1938, No. 1.

Thurstone, L. L. *The vectors of the mind.* Chicago: University of Chicago Press, 1935.

Thurstone, L. L. A method of scaling psychological and educational tests. *J. educ. Psychol.*, 1925, 16: 433–451.

Thurstone, L. L., and L. Ackerson. The mental growth curve for the Binet tests. *J. educ. Psychol.*, 1929, 20: 569–583.

Thurstone, L. L., and Thelma G. Thurstone. Factorial studies of intelligence. *Psychometr. Monogr.*, 1941, (No. 2.)

Tizard, Barbara, O. Copperman, Anne Joseph, and T. Tizard. Environmental effects on language development: a study of young children in long-stay residential nurseries. *Child Develpm.*, 1972, 43: 337–358.

Todd, T. W. *Atlas of skeletal maturation.* St. Louis: Mosby, 1937.

Torgoff, I. *Synergistic parental role components: application to expectancies and behavior—consequences for child's curiosity.* Paper presented at the 1960 convention of the American Psychological Association. Mimeographed.

Torgoff, I., and A. S. Dreyer. *Achievement-inducing and independence granting-synergistic parental role components: relation to daughter's "parental" role orientation.* Paper presented at the American Psychological Association Meeting, 1961.

Torrance, E. P. *Constructive behavior: stress, personality, and mental health.* Belmont, Calif.: Wadsworth, 1965.

Trainham, Genevieve, and J. C. Montgomery. Developmental factor in learning bowel and bladder control. *Amer. J. Nurs.*, 1946, 46: 841–844.

Trainham, Genevieve, and J. C. Montgomery. Self-demand feeding for babies. *Amer. J. Nurs.* 1946, 46: 767–770.

Trainham, Genevieve, J. Grace Pilafian, and Ruth M. Kraft. A case history of twins breast-fed on a self-demand regime. *J. Pediat.*, 1945, 27: 97–108.

Tulkin, S. R. Social class differences in attachment behavior of ten-month old infants (females). *Child Develpm.*, 1973, 44: 71–74.

Tulkin, S. R., and J. C. Cohler. Childrearing attitudes and mother-child interaction in the first year of life. *Merrill-Palmer Quart.*, 1973, 19 (No. 2): 95–106.

Tulkin, S. R., and J. Kagan. Mother-child interaction in the first year of life. *Child Develpm.*, 1972, 43: 31–42.

Turnure, J. E., and J. E. Rynders. Effectiveness of manual guidance, modeling, and trial and error learning procedures on the acquisition of new behaviors. *Merrill-Palmer Quart.*, 1973, 19: 49–65.

Viola, G. *Le legge de correlazone morfolagia dei tippi individuali*. Pedova, Italy: Prosperini, 1909.

von Maring, F. H. Professional and non-professional women as mothers. *J. soc. Psychol.*, 1955, 42: 21–34.

Waldrop, M. F. and R. Q. Bell. Effects of family size and density on newborn characteristics. *Amer. J. Orthopsychiat.*, 1966, 36: 544–550.

Walker, R. N. Body build and behavior in young children, II: body build and parents' ratings. *Child Develpm.*, 1963, 34: 1–23.

Walker, R. N. Body build and behavior in young children, I: body build and teachers' ratings. *Monogr. Soc. Res. Child Develpm.*, 1962, 27 (No. 3).

Walsh, F. B. *Clinical neuro-ophthalmology*, 2nd ed.; Baltimore: Williams & Wilkins, 1957.

Ward, W. C. Creativity in young children. *Child Develpm.*, 1968, 39: 736–754.

Warner, W. L., Marchia Meeker, and K. Eells. *Social class in America*, 2nd ed. New York: Harper & Row, 1960.

Washburn, S. L., and F. C. Howell. Human evolution and culture. In S. Tax (ed.), *The evolution of man*, vol. 2. Chicago: University of Chicago Press, 1960.

Watson, J. B. *Psychology from the standpoint of the behaviorist*. Philadelphia: Lippincott, 1924.

Watson, J. B. *The ways of behaviorism*. New York: Harper & Row, 1928.

Watson, J. S. Memory and contingency awareness in infant learning. *Merrill-Palmer Quart.*, 1967, 13: 55–76.

Watson, J. S. Perception of object orientation in infants. *Merrill-Palmer Quart.*, 1966a, 12: 73–74.

Watson, J. S. The development and generalization of contingency awareness in early infancy: some hypotheses. *Merrill-Palmer Quart.*, 1966b, 12: 123–135.

Wattenberg, W. W., and C. Clifford. Relation of self-concept to beginning achievement in reading. *Child Develpm.*, 1964, 35: 461–467.

Weir, Ruth H. *Language of the crib*. New York: Humanities Press, 1962.

Wellman, Beth L. The intelligence of preschool children as measured by the Merrill-Palmer performance tests. *University of Iowa Studies in Child Welfare*, 1938, 15 (No. 3.).

Wellman, Beth L. Mental growth from preschool to college. *J. exp. Educ.*, 1937, 6: 127–138.

Wellman, Beth L. Growth of intelligence under different school environments. *J. exp. Educ.*, 1934, 3: 59–83.

Wellman, Beth L., and H. S. Coffey. The role of cultural status in intelligence changes for preschool children. *J. exp. Educ.*, 1936, 5: 191–202.

Werner, H., and Edith Kaplan. The acquisition of word meanings: a developmental study. *Monogr. Soc. Res. Child Develpm.*, 1950, 15 (No. 1).

Wetzel, N. C. The baby grid: an application of the grid technique to growth and development in infants. *J. Pediat.*, 1946, 29: 329–454.

Wetzel, N. C. Assessing physical fitness in children, I: case demonstration of failing growth and the determination of "par" by the grid method *J. Pediat.*, 1943a, 22: 32–110.

Wetzel, N. C. Assessing physical fitness in children, II: simple malnutrition: a problem of failing growth and development. *J. Pediat.*, 1943b, 22: 208–225.

Wetzel, N. C. Assessing physical fitness in children, III: the components of physical status and physical progress and their evaluation. *J. Pediat.*, 1943c, 22: 329–361.

Wetzel, N. C. Physical fitness in terms of physique: development and basal metabolism. *J. Amer. Med. Assn.*, 1941, 116: 1187–1195.

Wheeler, R. J., and J. B. Dusek. The effects of attentional and cognitive factors on children's incidental learning. *Child Develpm.*, 1973, 44 (No. 2), 253–258.

White, B. An analysis of excellent early educational practices. In A. Effrat (ed.), *Interchange.* Toronto: Ontario Institute for Studies in Education, 1972.

White, B. L., P. Castle, and R. Held. Observations on the development of visually directed reaching. *Child Develpm.*, 1964, 35: 349–364.

Whiting, H. T. A. *Acquiring ball skills.* London: Bell and Sons, 1969.

Whiting, J. W., and I. L. Child. Child training and personality: a cross-cultural study. New Haven: Yale University Press, 1953.

Wickstrom, R. *Fundamental motor patterns.* Philadelphia: Lea & Febiger, 1970.

Willerman, L. Activity level and hyperactivity in twins. *Child Develpm.*, 1973, 44: (No. 2): 288–293.

Williams, J. H. Whittier scale for grading home conditions. *J. Delinq.*, 1916, 1: 271–286.

Williston, Judy. The young child . . . the child moves. In D. C. Kjer, chairman, *Proceeding of a Conference, National Association for the Education of Young Children.* Washington, D.C., 1971, 47–55.

Winchester, A. M. *Heredity and your life.* New York: Vintage, 1958.

Witkin, H. A., H. B. Lewis, M. Hertzman, P. B. Meissner, and S. Wapner. *Personality through perception.* New York: Harper & Row, 1954.

Wolfenstein, Martha. Trends in infant care. *Amer. J. Orthopsychiat.* 1953, 23: 120–130.

Wolff,, P. H. Observations on newborn infants. *Psychosom. Med.*, 1959, 21.

Wyatt, G. L. *Speech and interpersonal relations.* New York: Free Press, 1959.

Wylie, Ruth C. *The self-concept: a critical survey of pertinent research literature.* Lincoln: University of Nebraska Press, 1961.

Yando, Regina M., and J. Kagan. The effects of teacher tempo on the child. *Child Develpm.*, 1968, 39: 27–34.

Yarrow, L. J. Separation from parents during early childhood. In M. L. Hoffman, and Lois W. Hoffman (eds.), *Review of child development research*, vol. I, New York: Russell Sage Foundation, 1962.

Yarrow, L. J. Maternal deprivation: toward an empirical and conceptual re-evaluation. *Psychol. Bull.*, 1961, 58: 469–490.

Yarrow, L. J., and Marion R. Yarrow. Leadership and interpersonal change. *J. soc. Issues*, 1958, 14: 47–50.

Yarrow, Radke M., J. D. Campbell, and R. V. Burton. Recollections of childhood. *Monogr. Soc. Res. Child Develpm.*, 1970, 35 (No. 5), 1–83.

Yearbook Committee, 1962, Association for Supervision and Curriculum Development. *Perceiving, behaving, becoming: a new focus for education.* Washington, D.C.: National Education Association, 1962.

Zachry, Caroline, B., and M. Lighty. *Emotion and conduct of the preadolescent.* New York: Appleton, 1940.

Zogler, E., and E. C. Butterfield. Emotional aspects of change in I.Q. test performance of culturally deprived nursery school children. *Child Develpm.*, 1968, 39: 1–14.

Name Index

Subject Index